CLASSICAL COOKING
The Modern Way

Recipes

CLASSICAL COOKING
The Modern Way

Recipes

THIRD EDITION

Translated by
Arno Schmidt

Edited by
Margaret Schmidt

Translation Consultant
Hannelore Dawson-Holt

Photography
J. Gerard Smith

Food Styling
Arno Schmidt

JOHN WILEY & SONS, INC.
New York • Chichester • Weinheim • Brisbane • Singapore • Toronto

This publication is designed to provide accurate and authoritative information in regard to the subject matter covered. It is sold with the understanding that the publisher is not engaged in rendering professional services. If professional advice or other expert assistance is required, the services of a competent professional person should be sought.

Library of Congress Cataloging-in-Publication Data:

Pauli, Philip.
    [Lehrbuch der Küche. English]
    Classical cooking the modern way / Philip Pauli; translator, Arno Schmidt; edited by Margaret Schmidt; translation consultant, Hannelore Dawson-Holt.—3rd ed.
        p. cm.
    Includes index
    Contents: [v.2] Recipes.
    ISBN 0-471-28670-2 (v.2)
    1. Cookery. 2. Food service. I. Schmidt, Arno, 1937-
II. Dawson-Holt, Hannelore. III. Schmidt, Margaret. IV. Title.
TX652.P3513 1996
641.5'7—dc20   96-18125

Printed in the United States of America

10 9 8 7 6 5 4 3 2

Contents

When I was asked by Van Nostrand Reinhold to translate Pauli's *Rezeptbuch der Küche*, I was deeply honored.

I have been familiar with this book since May 1954, when I traveled to Bern, Switzerland as a member of the Austrian National team to compete in HOSPES, the international cooking competition.

While in Bern, the Austrian team worked next to the Swiss Team, and I heard the name Pauli for the first time. He was probably there, but I did not meet him. I did, however, meet Adelrich Furrer, the best garde manger of his time, a contemporary of Pauli, and I am sure they knew each other well.

In the following years, when I worked in Switzerland and in Swiss kitchen brigades in many parts of the world, the name Pauli came up whenever a cooking technique was discussed or a recipe researched.

As this translation took shape, I mentioned the book to many of my colleagues. An unsolicited endorsement came from Anthony Wall, Executive Chef at the Grand Hyatt Hotel in New York, who said, "If you want to learn to do it right, read Pauli."

I thank Hanne Dawson-Holt for valuable technical research in translating some Swiss ingredients. Hanne recently worked in Switzerland and was up-to-date with the names of some Swiss menu components.

Special thanks go to the editor, my wife Margaret. She is a stickler about the proper use of English, and about details. I translated the book in the spirit in which it was written—in short, using kitchen lingo. She smoothed over the language, so the book reads well, uses English properly, and can be understood by people who have not spent a lifetime in professional kitchens. She also checked, and double-checked, all measurements.

The book would not be complete without Jim Smith, the photographer. He moved into our house for days at a time to photograph the pictures in this book. The assignment was challenging because we tried to convey the image that the food is Swiss, as served in Swiss grand hotels and country inns. And the rewards were delicious. All food prepared for the photographs followed the recipes, and we enjoyed delectable luncheons and dinners every day!

Arno Schmidt

Editor's Foreword

I have great respect for the English language as well as gastronomy, and this project presented an interesting and special challenge for me.

"Pauli," as the book is familiarly referred to in the trade, was written by a team of Swiss chefs, not by one person. Commercial kitchen terminology was used to explain certain cooking methods. In addition, the translator assumed that all readers would understand the kitchen lingo. I wanted to make this classic book more accessible to the general public.

Fortunately, I have a long association with the culinary trade. I am a long-time member of the International Wine & Food Society and La Confrerie de la Chaine des Rotisseurs; I have an extensive cookbook collection; and I am married to the translator who is the well-known chef Arno Schmidt. There was an added benefit in having the German- and English-speaking cookbook author Hanne Dawson-Holt review my edit.

Aside from the standard job of editor, such as checking for grammatical correctness, I weighed every phrase with respect to general understanding and clarity. It took a while, and my husband Arno, by his own admission, got weary from explaining things that many professionals take for granted. But perseverance carried the day, and I hope this book is finally user-friendly to a broad audience.

Thank you, my dear Arno. Thank you, Hanne, for attending to all of my questions. Thank you, Melissa Rosati, our publisher, for your patience. And thank you, Joan Petrokofsky, project development editor, for the laughs we shared when we got "punchy" with details.

Margaret Schmidt

The recipe book was written to supplement *Pauli's Lehrbuch der Küche*, the official text book for chef's training in Switzerland. Detailed information about cooking methods and recipe theory are provided therein.

About the Translation

The book is written for professional cooks, and a basic knowledge of cooking methods and procedures are needed to execute many recipes. However, the translator, an experienced chef, has taken into consideration various levels of expertise as well as regional differences, and made no assumptions that readers will understand all cooking terms that are familiar to Swiss chefs.

All recipes are listed alphabetically in German as in the original book. The recipe titles are in English, German, and French. The English translation of titles was a challenge. Translating titles literally in some cases would not have made sense because the customers outside Switzerland would not be familiar with them. The translator used his years of experience writing menus to create titles which communicate, and also sell the dishes.

The recipes are organized into categories and are numbered. The original numbering system has been retained as a reference link between the two language editions. You can find all the recipe titles, whether in English, German, or French, in alphabetical order in the index.

The translation is faithful to the original text, but labor-saving steps are mentioned when practical. The book was written as a textbook for use in classroom kitchens, there fore the translator has added comments which the instructor would add in the classroom setting. These comments also address sanitary issues and in some cases adjustments of temperatures.

Most recipes are organized into *Mise en Place*—the French expression for pre-preparation—and *Method*. In some cases, *Presentation* is added as a separate section. The Swiss text contained additional *Notes*, which were translated and are contained herein for your reference.

When recipes call for ingredients indigenous to Switzerland, or are difficult to obtain, acceptable substitutes are suggested.

All weights and liquid measurements are given in both U.S. and metric weights, and temperatures are given in both Fahrenheit and Celsius.

In order to give precise conversions and maintain the integrity of the original recipe, the U.S. equivalents often appear as awkward fractions. The experienced chef will round off as he or she sees fit.

Translator's Notes

In most cases, the recipes are for ten servings to give con-sistency to the book. Originally, the recipes were created for commercial operations, and therefore were for much larger quantities. The experienced chef will understand that it is difficult, if not impossible, to process some ingre-dients in the amounts given.

In many cases, French terms common in Switzerland, but not universally used elsewhere, are given in parentheses. When equipment is mentioned, the translator has refered equipment that is most commonly found in commercial kitchens internationally.

Ingredients

Water is considered an ingredients when the exact amount is crucial, such as in stocks, doughs, and batters.

Eggs are listed by weight of shelled eggs for the recipes for doughs, batters, and creams. In all other cases, eggs are listed by unshelled quantities.

Vegetables and fruits are listed fresh, by weight, before cleaning and trimming. The amount of waste and trimmings vary greatly depending on the specification of the products, time of year, and skill of user. The experienced chef will be able to adjust the recipes accordingly.

Fabricated ingredients, whether purchased, in forms such as canned or frozen, or made in house, such as vegetable bun-dles and flavoring vegetables, are assumed to be ready to use.

Spice quantities are mentioned only in selected recipes. In most cases, the quantity is left to the user, and written as "season to taste." This reflects established industry practice.

Portion sizes vary, and in some cases, the recipes seem awk-ward by U.S. standards. Again, the chef can adjust the recipes according to regional expectations.

CLASSICAL COOKING
The Modern Way
Recipes

Basic Preparations

Basic Preparations

1

Shrimp Butter

Danieli-Butter
Beurre Danieli

YIELD: 2 LB 3 OZ (1 KG)

Shallots	2 1/3 oz	65 g
Butter	1 lb 7 oz	650 g
Shrimp, cooked and peeled	41/2 oz	130 g
Red peppers	5 1/3 oz	150 g
Anchovy fillets, drained	1/2 oz	15 g
Egg yolk[a]	2 1/3 oz	65 g
Cognac	1/3 oz	10 ml
Lemon juice	1/3 oz	10 ml
Seasoning (salt and pepper)	1x	1x

MISE EN PLACE
Peel and chop shallots; sauté in 1 oz (30 g) butter, and let cool.

Cut shrimp into small dice.

Split red peppers, remove seeds, wash, and cut into very small dice. Sauté peppers with 1 tbsp butter, and let cool.

Chop anchovy fillets.

METHOD
Cream egg yolk[a] with softened remaining butter.

Add in all other ingredients and blend.

Season with salt and pepper.

NOTE: Shrimp butter is served with grilled crustaceans and mussels.

2

Mushroom Stuffing for Vegetables

Duxelles für Gemüsefüllungen
Duxelles pour légumes farcis

YIELD: 2 LB 3 OZ (1 KG)

White bread	5 1/3 oz	150 g
Tomato purée	1 2/3 oz	50 g
Butter	1 oz	30 g
Dry duxelles (mushroom filling) (Recipe 20)	1 lb 12 oz	800 g
Dry white wine	1 pt 1 oz	500 ml
Glace de viande[a]	1 2/3 oz	50 g
Seasoning (salt and pepper)	1x	1x

METHOD
Remove crusts from white bread and make bread crumbs.

Sauté tomato purée in butter to reduce acidity.

Add dry duxelles.

Add white wine and *glace de viande.*[a]

Add bread crumbs, mix well, and cook to desired consistency.

Season to taste.

3

Mushroom Stuffing for Tartlets

Duxelles für Törtchenfüllungen
Duxelles pour tartelettes farcies

YIELD: 2 LB 3 OZ (1 KG)

Ham, boiled	1 lb 2 oz	500 g
Dry duxelles (mushroom filling) (Recipe 20)	1 lb 2 oz	500 g

MISE EN PLACE
Cut ham into very small dice (*brunoise*).

METHOD
Combine ham with dry duxelles.

NOTE: Depending on use, the duxelles can be mixed with a Mousseline Farce (Recipe 17) instead of ham.

[a] Raw egg yolks can cause salmonella food poisoning. Pasturized egg yolks are suggested.

[a] *Glace de viande*, literally translated "meat glaze," is made by reducing meat stock to a syrupy consistency.

4

*F*ish Aspic
Fischsulze
Gelée de poisson

YIELD: 5 QT 9 OZ (5 L)

Merlan[a] (whiting) fillets, skin on	1 lb 5 oz	600 g
Pike fillet, skin on	1 lb 5 oz	600 g
Matignon (Recipe 13)	3 1/2 oz	100 g
Egg white	1 2/3 oz	50 g
Sachet bag	1	1
Leaf gelatin	4 1/3 oz	125 g
Fish fumet (Recipe 25)	6 qts 28 oz	6.5 L
Dry white wine	8 1/2 oz	250 ml
Fresh mushroom trimmings	1 2/3 oz	50 g
Salt	2/3 oz	20 g
Dry vermouth[b]	1 2/3 oz	50 ml

MISE EN PLACE
Remove bones and skin from merlan and pike fillets. Grind fish through medium-size plate of meat grinder.

Blend fish with matignon, egg white, and a small amount of ice water; refrigerate for at least 2 hours. This will become the clarification.

Make sachet bag consisting of peppercorns, bay leaves, and dill.

Soak gelatin in cold water.

METHOD
Blend clarification with fish fumet and white wine.

Add mushroom trimmings; bring mixture to simmer.

Skim frequently; add salt and sachet bag.

Simmer for 30 minutes.

Strain carefully through double layer of cheesecloth.

Squeeze all water from soaked gelatin leaf and add to hot fish stock.

Remove all fat with absorbent paper. Add dry vermouth.

NOTES: Fish aspic should be clear and colorless.

The amount of gelatin needed varies according to the gelatin content of the fish used. Before aspic is cold, check the consistency by dripping a small amount on a chilled plate. If not thick enough, add more gelatin.

---

[a] If whiting is not available, any other low-fat white fish fillets can be used.

[b] The recipe specifies Noilly Prat, but any brand of dry vermouth can be used. Vermouth comes in dry and sweet varieties; use only dry in this recipe.

5

*M*eat Aspic
Fleischsulze
Gelée de viande

YIELD: 5 QT 9 OZ (5 L)

Lean beef[a]	1 lb 12 oz	800 g
Matignon (Recipe 14)	7 oz	200g
Egg whites	3	90 g
Veal bones	11 lb	5 kg
Calves' feet	6 lb 10 oz	3 kg
Pork rind (from fresh fatback)	1 lb 2 oz	500 g
Sachet bag	1	1
White veal stock (Recipe 28)	2 gal 2 1/2 qt	10.0 L
Salt	1 oz	30 g
White bouquet garni (Recipe 8)	1 lb 5 oz	600 g
Seasoning (salt)	1x	1x

MISE EN PLACE
Grind clarification meat (lean beef) through coarse plate of meat grinder. Mix ground meat with matignon, egg whites, and some ice cubes. Refrigerate for at least 2 hours.

Chop veal bones and blanch together with calves' feet and pork rind.

Make sachet bag consisting of marjoram, thyme, peppercorns, bay leaves, and cloves.

METHOD
Combine blanched bones, calves' feet, and pork rind with cold veal stock. Bring slowly to boiling point. Skim and add salt.

Simmer carefully for 4 to 5 hours. Skim as needed.

Add sachet bag and white *bouquet garni* after about 4 hours. Simmer 1 hour longer.

Strain stock through double layer of cheesecloth. Let cool. Remove fat.

Add beef clarification mixture and bring to a boil, stirring occasionally and carefully with paddle.

Simmer, without further stirring, for about 1 1/2 hours.

Strain through double layer of cheesecloth, adjust seasoning, and remove any remaining fat.

NOTE: The amount of gelatin needed varies according to the gelatin content in the meat bones. Before aspic is cold, check the consistency by dripping a small amount on a chilled plate. If not thick enough, add more gelatin.

---

[a] The meat should be as lean as possible. Meat from beef shank is good to use because it is very lean and has a high gelatin content.

6

𝒫oultry Aspic

Geflügelsulze
Gelée de volaille

YIELD: 5 QT 9 OZ (5 L)

Poultry clarification meat[a]	1 lb 12 oz	800 g
Matignon (Recipe 14)	7 oz	200 g
Egg whites	3	90 g
Veal bones	2 lb 3 oz	1 kg
Poultry necks and backs	8 3/4 lb	4 kg
Calves' feet	6 lb 10 oz	3 kg
Pork rind, skin (from fresh fatback)	1 lb 2 oz	500 g
Sachet bag	1	1
Chicken stock (Recipe 26)	2 gal 2 1/2 qt	10.0 L
Salt	1 oz	30 g
White bouquet garni (Recipe 8)	1 lb 5 oz	600 g
Seasoning	1x	1x

MISE EN PLACE
Grind clarification meat through coarse plate of grinder. Add *matignon*, egg whites, and some ice cubes. Refrigerate for at least 2 hours.

Chop veal bones, and blanch together with poultry bones, calves' feet, and pork rind.

Make sachet bag consisting of marjoram, thyme, peppercorns, and bay leaves.

METHOD
Combine blanched bones, calves' feet, and pork rind with cold chicken stock; bring slowly to boiling point. Skim. Add salt.

Simmer carefully for 3 to 4 hours. Skim as needed.

Add sachet bag and *bouquet garni* after about 3 hours. Simmer for 1 hour longer.

Strain stock through double layer of cheesecloth. Let cool. Remove fat.

Add clarification meat and bring to boil, stirring occasionally and carefully with paddle. Simmer, without further stirring, for about 1 1/2 hours.

Strain through double layer of cheesecloth, adjust seasoning, and remove any remaining fat.

NOTES: Before stock is chilled, check the consistency by dripping a small amount on a chilled plate. If not thick enough, add more gelatin.

Poultry aspic should have a pale yellow color.

7

𝒱egetable Bundle for Clear Beef Stock

Gemüsebündel für Bouillon
Bouquet garni pour bouillon

YIELD: 2 LB 3 OZ (1 KG)

Onions	10 1/2 oz	300 g
Leeks	10 1/2 oz	300 g
Carrots	10 1/2 oz	300 g
Knob celery (celeriac)	10 1/2 oz	300 g
Parsley stems, fresh	2/3 oz	20 g
Bay leaves	2	2
Cloves	2	2
White peppercorns	10	10

METHOD
Cut onions in half horizontally, and brown the surfaces.[a]

Wash and trim leeks; be sure sand is cleaned from layers. Cut into quarters.

Wash and clean carrots and knob celery, and cut into quarters.

Tie vegetables, parsley, bay leaves, cloves, and peppercorns into bundles.

Notes: The spices can be wrapped in leek leaves or in cheesecloth to make them easier to remove.

If desired, white cabbage can be added.

The composition and amounts of ingredients can vary according to taste and use; vegetable trimmings can be added.

---

[a] The most economical clarification meat to use is turkey legs.

[a] This is accomplished by placing the onion, cut side down, on a hot stove. The heat will caramelize the sugar in the onion, which in turn will color the stock.

8

$\mathcal{V}$egetable Bundle for White Stocks

Gemüsebündel für weisse Fonds
Bouquet garnie pour fonds blancs

YIELD: 2 LB 3 OZ (1 KG)

Leeks (white leaves only)	1 lb 2 oz	500 g
Onions	1 lb 2 oz	500 g
Knob celery (celeriac)	8 3/4 oz	250 g
Parsley stems, fresh	2/3 oz	20 g
Bay leaves	2	2
Cloves	2	2
White peppercorns	10	10

METHOD

Wash and trim leeks; be sure sand is cleaned from layers.

Trim onions.

Wash and trim knob celery.

Cut vegetables into quarters.

Wash parsley.

Tie vegetables, parsley, bay leaves, cloves, and peppercorns into bundles.

NOTES: The spices can be wrapped in leek leaves or in cheesecloth to make them easier to remove.

The composition and amounts of ingredients can vary according to taste and use.

9

$\mathcal{S}$easoning Salt for Meat

Gewürzsalzmischung für Fleisch
Sel epicé pour viande de boucherie

YIELD: 3 1/2 OZ (100 G)

Salt	2 oz	60 g
White pepper, ground	2/3 oz	20 g
Paprika, mild	1/2 oz	15 g
Thyme, ground	1/6 oz	5 g

METHOD

Combine ingredients and store in closed container.

NOTE: The composition and amounts of ingredients can vary according to taste and use.

10

$\mathcal{S}$easoning Salt for Poultry

Gewürzsalzmischung für Geflügel
Sel epicé pour volaille

YIELD: 3 1/2 OZ (100 G)

Salt	2 oz	60 g
White pepper, ground	2/3 oz	20 g
Paprika, mild	1/3 oz	10 g
Rosemary, ground	1/6 oz	5 g
Sage, ground	1/6 oz	5 g

METHOD

Combine ingredients and store in closed container.

NOTE: The composition and amounts of ingredients can vary according to taste and use.

11

ℒobster Butter

Hummerbutter
Beurre de homard

YIELD: 2 LB 3 OZ (1 KG)

Lobster shells[a] for stock/butter	1 lb 12 oz	800 g
Lobster trimmings	7 oz	200 g
Thyme twig, fresh	1	1
Dill, fresh	2/3 oz	20 g
Butter	2 lb 10 oz	1.2 kg
Matignon (Recipe 13)	5 1/3 oz	150 g
Tomato purée	1 2/3 oz	50 g
Cognac (or any brandy)	2/3 oz	20 ml
Dry white wine	6 3/4 oz	200 ml
Fish fumet (Recipe 25)	10 oz	300 ml
Seasoning	1x	1x

MISE EN PLACE
Crush lobster shells and trimmings, using food processor or Buffalo chopper.

Wash thyme and dill.

METHOD
Sauté lobster shells and trimmings slowly in butter. Add herbs and *matignon*, and continue cooking.

Add tomato purée, and continue cooking.

Add Cognac, and ignite.

Add wine, and boil down until almost evaporated.

Add fish fumet and seasoning, and simmer for 30 minutes.

Strain and press through fine mesh china cap.

Strain resulting stock through double layer of cheesecloth and refrigerate.

Lift solidified lobster butter from top.

Clarify this butter by warming it in a steam table and straining once more through a double layer of cheesecloth.

NOTE: The remaining stock can be used to make a fumet of crustaceans or a bisque (soup).

---

[a] Cooked or raw lobster shells and carcasses can be used.

12

ℳarinade for Meat and Game

Marinade für Schlachtfleisch und Wildbret
Marinade pour viande de boucherie et pour gibier

YIELD: 5 QT 9 OZ (5 L)

Onions	14 oz	400 g
Carrots	7 oz	200 g
Knob celery (celeriac)	5 1/3 oz	150 g
Garlic, crushed	2/3 oz	20 g
Clove	1 clove	1
White peppercorns	20	20
Bay leaves	2	2
Thyme twig, fresh	1	1
Rosemary twig, fresh	1	1
Red cooking wine	4 qt 24 oz	4.5 L
Red wine vinegar	1 pt 1 oz	500 ml

METHOD
Clean onions, carrots, and knob celery and cut into *mirepoix* size (coarse cubes).

Combine cubed vegetables with garlic, spices, herbs, wine, and vinegar.

Pour mixture over meat to be marinated.

Place weight on top to keep meat submerged.

Marinate meat for a few days in refrigerator.

NOTES: To shorten marinating time, bring mixture to boil, let cool, and use as above.

When marinade is intended for white meat, the cooking wine and wine vinegar should be white.

The spices can vary according to taste and use: for example, juniper berries are used with game.

13

*F*lavoring Vegetables for Fish Stock
Matignon für Fischfond
Matignon pour fond de poisson

YIELD: 2 LB 3 OZ (1 KG)

Leeks, white leaves only	1 lb 2 oz	500 g
Onions	1 lb 2 oz	500 g
Knob celery (celeriac)	8 3/4 oz	250 g
Parsley stems, fresh	2/3 oz	20 g
Bay leaves	2	2
Cloves	2	2

METHOD
Wash and trim leeks; be sure sand is cleaned from layers; cut into small dice.

Clean onions and knob celery and cut into small dice.

Add herbs and spices.

NOTES: The composition and amount of ingredients can vary according to taste and use.

If desired, mushroom trimmings, dill or fennel leaves can be added.

14

*F*lavoring Vegetables for Meat
Matignon für Fleischgerichte
Matignon pour mets de viande

YIELD: 2 LB 3 OZ (1 KG)

Carrots	14 oz	400 g
Onions	14 oz	400 g
Knob celery (celeriac)	10 1/2 oz	300 g
Bacon rinds (skins)	3 1/2 oz	100 g
Garlic	1/3 oz	10 g
Thyme twig, fresh	1	1

METHOD
Clean carrots, onions, and knob celery, and cut into small dice.

Cut bacon rinds into small dice.

Peel garlic. Wash thyme twig.

NOTES: The components and amount of ingredients can vary according to taste and use.

If desired for a particular recipe, leeks can be added after the vegetables have been browned.

If a less smokey taste is desired, fatback skins can be used in place of bacon.

The shorter the cooking time, the smaller the vegetables should be cut.

15

*M*irepoix for Brown Stock
Mirepoix für braune Fonds
Mirepoix pour fonds bruns

YIELD: 2 LB 3 OZ (1 KG)

Onions	1 lb 2 oz	500 g
Carrots	1 lb 2 oz	500 g
Knob celery (celeriac)	8 3/4 oz	250 g
Parsley stems, fresh	1 oz	30 g
Bay leaf	1	1
Cloves	1	1
White peppercorns	10	10
Thyme twig, fresh	1	1
Marjoram, fresh	1/6 oz	5 g

METHOD
Peel onions.

Wash and trim carrots and knob celery.

Cut vegetables into coarse cubes.[a]

Wash parsley.

Combine all ingredients.

NOTES: The components and amount of ingredients can vary according to taste and use.

If desired for a particular recipe, chopped leeks and crushed garlic can be added after the vegetables have been browned.

[a] *Mirepoix* for brown stock is cut into coarser cubes than *mirepoix* for white stock, because it is cooked for a longer time. When chefs use the term "*mirepoix* size," it refers to this coarser cut.

16

Mirepoix for White Stock

Mirepoix für weisse Fonds
Mirepoix pour fonds blancs

YIELD: 2 LB 3 OZ (1 KG)

Leeks, white part only	1 lb 2 oz	500 g
Onions	1 lb 2 oz	500 g
Knob celery (celeriac)	8 3/4 oz	250 g
Parsley stems, fresh	2/3 oz	20 g
Bay leaves	2	2
Cloves	2	2
White peppercorns	10	10

METHOD

Wash and trim leeks; be sure sand is cleaned from layers.

Peel onions.

Wash and trim knob celery.

Cut vegetables into small dice.[a]

Wash parsley.

Combine all ingredients.

NOTE: The components and amount of ingredients can vary according to taste and use.

17

Mousseline Farce (raw)

Rohe Mousseline-Farce
Farce mousseline

YIELD: 2 LB 3 OZ (1 KG)

Veal shoulder, boneless	1 lb 14 oz	850 g
Salt	1/4 oz	7 g
Ice cubes	3 1/2 oz	100 g
Heavy cream (36%)	15 oz	450 ml
Seasoning (white pepper)	1x	1x
Nutmeg (pinch)	1x	1x

MISE EN PLACE

Remove sinew and fat from veal, cut into small cubes, and refrigerate.

METHOD

Grind veal through medium-size plate of meat grinder.

Add salt and ice, and grind into a smooth mixture in food processor or Buffalo chopper.

Pass through fine wire mesh sieve[a] and put in a stainless steel bowl.

Place bowl on ice and add heavy cream in small amounts, stirring with paddle.

Season with white pepper and nutmeg. Add additional salt if necessary.

18

Mousseline Farce for Fish (raw)

Rohe Mousseline-Farce für Fischgerichte
Farce mousseline de poisson

YIELD: 2 LB 3 OZ (1 KG)

Pike fillets	1 lb 5 oz	600 g
Whiting fillets[b]	10 1/2 oz	300 g
Heavy cream (36%)	12 oz	350 ml
Egg whites	1 2/3 oz	50 g
Seasoning (salt, cayenne pepper)	1x	1x
Seasoning (white pepper)	1x	1x
Dry vermouth[c]	1 2/3 oz	50 ml

MISE EN PLACE

Trim, skin, and remove bones from fish fillets; cut into small dice. Refrigerate.

METHOD

Grind fish into fine purée in food processor or Buffalo chopper, with salt and a small amount of cream.

Pass through fine wire mesh sieve,[d] put in a stainless steel bowl, and refrigerate.

Lightly beat egg whites.

---

[a] *Mirepoix* for white stock is cut into smaller cubes than *mirepoix* for brown stock, because it is cooked for a shorter time. When chefs use the term "*mirepoix* size," it refers to the coarser (brown stock) size cut.

[a] If a commercial food processor is used, this step can be eliminated.

[b] Halibut or sole can be substituted for the whiting. The fish should be fresh, not frozen. Sea scallops also make excellent mousse, but have a strong flavor.

[c] The recipe specifies Noilly Prat, but any brand of dry vermouth can be used. Vermouth comes in dry and sweet varieties; use only dry in this recipe.

[d] If a commercial food processor is used, this step can be eliminated.

Place bowl with fish on ice and add remaining cream in small amounts, stirring with paddle. Carefully fold in beaten egg whites.

Season with salt, cayenne, white pepper, and dry vermouth.

Notes: At least one-third of fish should be pike because the flesh binds well.

The amount of cream used depends on the fish variety and the desired consistency.

All ingredients should be combined as cold as possible.

Always test a small sample before poaching.

19

Red Wine Butter

Rotweinbutter
Beurre au vin rouge

YIELD: 2 LB 3 OZ (1 KG)

Shallots	7 oz	200 g
Butter	1 lb 9 oz	700 g
Red wine[a]	1 pt 9 oz	750 ml
Parsley, Italian, fresh	1 2/3 oz	50 g
Seasoning (salt and pepper)	1x	1x

MISE EN PLACE
Peel and chop shallots. Sauté in a small amount of butter.

Add red wine and reduce to about 3 1/3 oz (100 ml). Let cool.

Wash parsley, remove stems, and chop fine.

METHOD
Cream remaining butter.

Add wine reduction and chopped parsley.

Season with salt and pepper.

NOTES: Use full-bodied red wine for this recipe.

Red wine butter is especially good with grilled beef.

---

[a] A standard bottle of wine contains 750 ml.

20

Dry Duxelles (mushroom filling)

Trockene Duxelles
Duxelles sèche

YIELD: 2 LB 3 OZ (1 KG)

Shallots	6 oz	170 g
Parsley, Italian, fresh	1 2/3 oz	50 g
Mushrooms, fresh	2 lb 14 oz	1.3 kg
Butter	3 1/2 oz	100 g
Lemon juice	1/2 oz	15 ml
Seasoning (salt and pepper)	1x	1x

MISE EN PLACE
Peel and chop shallots.

Wash parsley, remove stems, and chop fine.

Clean and wash mushrooms and chop fine.

METHOD
Sauté shallots briefly in butter, without getting color. Add chopped mushrooms.

Add lemon juice. Season with salt and pepper.

Cook, uncovered (without lid), until all liquid has evaporated.

Add chopped parsley.

21

*G*ame Farce
Wildfarce
Farce de gibier

YIELD: 2 LB 3 OZ (1 KG)

Venison shoulder, boned and trimmed[a]	1 lb 2 oz	500 g
Pork neck, trimmed and boneless	5 1/3 oz	150 g
Fatback, unsalted	5 1/3 oz	150 g
Shallots	2 oz	55 g
Apples[b]	3 1/2 oz	100 g
Chicken livers, raw	5 1/3 oz	150 g
Butter	2/3 oz	20 g
Cognac (or any brandy)	1 1/3 oz	40 ml
Madeira wine	1 1/3 oz	40 ml
Heavy cream (36%)	3 1/3 oz	100 ml
Salt	1/4 oz	7 g
Seasoning	1x	1x

MISE EN PLACE

Remove sinews from venison. Cut venison and pork into cubes.

Cut fatback into cubes.

Peel and chop shallots.

Peel and core apple; cut into thin slices.

METHOD

Sauté shallots, apples, and chicken livers quickly in butter.

Flame with Cognac, add Madeira wine, and cool mixture.

Grind fatback separately through coarse plate of meat grinder.

Grind game and pork meat through coarse plate of meat grinder. Chop meat quickly, in food processor or Buffalo chopper, into a smooth paste.

Gradually add ground fatback into meat, along with the shallots, apple, and liver mixture; and continue to purée.

Pass/strain through fine wire mesh sieve.[a]

Put in stainless steel bowl and refrigerate. Place bowl on ice and add cream in small amounts, stirring with paddle.

Season with salt and pepper.

NOTE: All ingredients should be kept chilled during the preparation, or the mixture might curdle.

---

[a]The game meat most commonly used in Switzerland is roebuck.

[b]A suitable apple variety is Granny Smith.

[a]If a commercial food processor is used, this step can be eliminated.

Basic Stocks

22

ℬouillon/Plain Beef Stock[a]

Bouillon
Bouillon d'os

YIELD: 2 GAL 2 1/2 QT (10 L)

Beef bones	17 lb 10 oz	8.0 kg
Water	4 gal	15.0 L
Bouquet garni (Recipe 7)	1 lb 2 oz	500 g
Sachet bag	1	1
Salt	1 2/3 oz, or to taste[b]	50 g

MISE EN PLACE
Chop and blanch beef bones.

Rinse bones first with hot water, then with cold water.

Make *bouquet garni*.

Make sachet bag consisting of bay leaves, cloves, peppercorns, and thyme.

METHOD
Cover blanched bones with cold water and bring to boil.

Add salt; skim occasionally.

Simmer for 3 to 4 hours.

After 2 hours, add *bouquet garni* and sachet bag.

Strain carefully through double layer of cheesecloth.

NOTE: If bones are very fresh, blanching is not necessary.

23

ℬrown Veal Stock

Brauner Kalbsfond
Fond de veau brun

YIELD: 2 GAL 2 1/2 QT (10 L)

Veal bones	13 lb 4 oz	6.0 kg
Calves' feet	4 lb 7 oz	2.0 kg
Sachet bag	1	1
Peanut oil	5 oz	150 ml
Mirepoix (Recipe 15)	2 lb 3 oz	1.0 kg
Tomato paste	3 1/2 oz	100 g
Dry white wine	1 qt 2 oz	1.0 L
Water	4 gal	15.0 L
Salt	1 2/3 oz, or to taste[a]	50 g

MISE EN PLACE
Chop veal bones as small as possible.

Chop calves' feet.

Make sachet bag consisting of peppercorns, cloves, thyme, bay leaves, and rosemary.

METHOD
Roast veal bones and calves' feet slowly in oil. Use tilting frying pan, convection oven, or roasting oven.

Add *mirepoix* and continue roasting.

Pour off all excess fat.

Add tomato paste and continue roasting.

Add a small amount of water two or three times and reduce each time until almost evaporated.

Transfer bones and pan drippings to suitable kettle. Add wine and water. Bring to a boil, add salt, and skim. Simmer for 3 to 4 hours.

After 2 hours, add sachet bag.

Strain through double layer of cheesecloth.

NOTE: If bones are roasted at low temperature in a convection oven, no oil is needed.

---

[a] When other recipes call for bouillon as an ingredient, this is the stock to use, unless Vegetable Bouillon (Recipe 27) is specified. If a finished bouillon to be served on its own is desired, use the finished soup (Recipe 127).

[b] Since bouillon is used as an ingredient in other recipes, use salt sparingly and correct to taste in the final recipe.

---

[a] Since veal stock is used as an ingredient in other recipes, use salt sparingly and correct to taste in the final recipe.

24

*F*ish Stock

Fischfond
Fond de poisson

YIELD: 2 GAL 2 1/2 QT (10 L)

Fish bones and trimmings from saltwater fish	13 lb 4 oz	6.0 kg
Sachet bag	1	1
Cold water	2 gal 2 1/2 qt	10.0 L
Dry white wine	1 qt 2 oz	1.0 L
Matignon (Recipe 13)	1 lb 5 oz	600 g
Mushroom trimmings, fresh	3 1/2 oz	100 g
Salt	1 oz, or to taste[a]	25 g

MISE EN PLACE

Remove heads and bloody parts, if any, from fish bones.

Cut bones and trimmings. Soak in cold water.

Make sachet bag consisting of peppercorns, bay leaves, cloves, parsley stems, and dill.

METHOD

Cover fish bones with cold water.

Bring to a slow boil and skim.

Add sachet bag, dry white wine, *matignon*, mushroom trimmings, and salt.

Simmer for 30 minutes.

Strain carefully through double layer of cheesecloth.

---

[a] Since fish stock is used as an ingredient in other recipes, use salt sparingly and correct to taste in the final recipe.

25

*F*ish Fumet

Fischfumet
Fumet de poisson

YIELD: 2 GAL 2 1/2 QT (10 L)

Fish bones and trimmings from saltwater fish	13 lb 4 oz	6.0 kg
Shallots	1 2/3 oz	50 g
Butter	1 2/3 oz	50 g
Matignon[a], (Recipe 13)	1 lb	450 g
Mushroom trimmings, fresh	3 1/2 oz	100 g
Dry white wine	1 qt 2 oz	1.0 L
Fish stock (Recipe 24)	2 gal 2 1/2 qt	10.0 L
Salt	2/3 oz, or to taste[b]	20 g

MISE EN PLACE

Remove heads and bloody parts, if any, from fish bones.

Cut bones and trimmings into small pieces. Soak in cold water.

Peel shallots and slice fine.

METHOD

Sauté shallots in butter.

Add *matignon* and mushrooms and continue cooking.

Add fish bones and trimmings and continue cooking.

Add wine and fish stock, bring to boil, and skim.

Add salt. Simmer for 30 minutes, skimming frequently.

Strain carefully through double layer of cheesecloth.

---

[a] The *matignon* indicated in this recipe is in *addition* to the *matignon* already included in the fish stock.

[b] Since fish fumet is used as an ingredient in other recipes, use salt sparingly and correct to taste in the final recipe.

26

Chicken Stock

Geflügelfond
Fond de volaille

YIELD: 2 GAL 2 1/2 QT (10 L)

Chicken necks and backs and carcasses	11 lb	5.0 kg
Boiling fowl[a]	2 lb 3 oz	1.0 kg
Sachet bag	1	1
Water	3 gal 22 oz	12.0 L
Salt[b]	1 2/3 oz, or to taste	50 g
Bouquet garni (Recipe 8)	1 lb 7 oz	650 g

MISE EN PLACE

Blanch chicken bones and fowl.

Make sachet bag consisting of bay leaves, cloves, peppercorns, and thyme.

METHOD

Add water to bones and fowl and bring to a slow boil.

Add salt and skim frequently.

Simmer for 1 to 2 hours.

Add sachet bag and *bouquet garni* after 1 hour.

Strain carefully through double layer of cheesecloth.

NOTE: If bones are fresh, blanching is not needed.

[a] A whole boiling fowl weighs about 4 to 5 lb (1.8 to 2.25 kg).

[b] Since chicken stock is used as an ingredient in other recipes, you may want to use salt sparingly and correct to taste in the final recipe.

27

Vegetable Bouillon

Gemüsebouillon
Bouillon de légumes

YIELD: 2 GAL 2 1/2 QT (10 L)

Leeks, green leaves	1 lb 5 oz	600 g
Onions	10 1/2 oz	300 g
Garlic	1/3 oz	10 g
Carrots	1 lb 5 oz	600 g
Cabbage	10 1/2 oz	300 g
Fennel bulb (anise)[a]	7 oz	200 g
Stalk celery[b]	10 1/2 oz	300 g
Tomatoes	7 oz	200 g
Sachet bag	1	1
Margarine	3 1/2 oz	100 g
Water	3 gal 22 oz	12.0 L
Salt	1 2/3 oz, or to taste[c]	50 g

MISE EN PLACE

Wash and trim leeks; be sure sand is cleaned from layers.

Clean and trim onions, garlic, carrots, cabbage, fennel bulb, and celery.

Cut vegetables into medium dice.

Cut tomatoes into cubes.

Make sachet bag consisting of peppercorns, cloves, bay leaves, parsley stems, and thyme.

METHOD

Sauté leeks, onions, and garlic in margarine.

Add remaining vegetables and continue to cook.

Add water, bring to a boil, and skim.

Add sachet bag and salt.

Simmer for 30 minutes to 1 hour.

Strain carefully through double layer of cheesecloth.

[a] Fennel is sometimes referred to as anise.

[b] The stalk celery specified is known as "English celery" in Europe, and is called *Stangensellerie* in German. In the United States, it is the standard celery and is referred to simply as celery.

[c] Since bouillon is used as an ingredient in other recipes, use salt sparingly and correct to taste in the final recipe.

28

White Veal Stock
Weisser Kalbsfond
Fond de veau blanc

YIELD: 2 GAL 2 1/2 QT (10 L)

Veal bones	13 lb 4 oz	6.0 kg
Sachet bag	1	1
Water	3 gal 3 qt	14.0 L
Salt	1 2/3 oz, or to taste[a]	50 g
Bouquet garni (Recipe 8)	1 lb 12 oz	800 g

MISE EN PLACE

Chop veal bones and blanch.

Rinse bones first with hot water, then with cold water.

Make sachet bag consisting of bay leaves, cloves, peppercorns, and thyme.

METHOD

Add water to bones and bring to a slow boil.

Add salt and skim frequently.

Simmer for 2 to 3 hours.

Add sachet bag and *bouquet garni* after 2 hours.

Strain carefully through double layer of cheesecloth.

---

[a] Since veal stock is used as an ingredient in other recipes, use salt sparingly and correct to taste in the final recipe.

29

Game Stock
Wildfond
Fond de gibier

YIELD: 2 GAL 2 1/2 QT (10 L)

Game bones	11 lb	5.0 kg
Sachet bag	1	1
Game trimmings	2 lb 3 oz	1.0 kg
Peanut oil	5 oz	150 ml
Mirepoix (Recipe 15)	2 lb 3 oz	1.0 kg
Tomato paste	3 oz	80 g
Water	3 gal 3 qt	14.0 L
Dry red wine	2 qt 4 oz	2.0 L
Salt	1 2/3 oz, or to taste[a]	50 g

MISE EN PLACE

Chop game bones as small as possible.

Make sachet bag consisting of peppercorns, juniper berries, bay leaves, cloves, and thyme.

METHOD

Roast bones and trimmings slowly in peanut oil (use a tilting frying pan, or roast in oven).

Add *mirepoix* and continue roasting.

Pour off excess fat.

Add tomato paste and carefully continue roasting.

Add a small amount of water two or three times and boil down each time, until almost evaporated.

If bones are roasted in oven, transfer bones and pan drippings to a suitable pot or kettle.

Add remaining water and wine.

Bring to a boil, add salt, and skim.

Simmer for 3 to 4 hours.

Add sachet bag for final hour.

Carefully strain through double layer of cheesecloth.

NOTE: Depending on final use, red wine can be replaced with white wine.

---

[a] Since game stock is used as an ingredient in other recipes, use salt sparingly and correct to taste in the final recipe.

Sauces

Aïoli Sauce

Ailloli-Sauce
Sauce ailloli

YIELD: 1 QT 2 OZ (1 L)

Potatoes	8 3/4 oz	250 g
Garlic	4 1/4 oz	120 g
Salt	1/3 oz	10 g
Egg yolks	3	3
Olive oil	1 pt 4 oz	600 ml
Lemon	1	1
Seasoning (salt, cayenne)	1x	1x

MISE EN PLACE

Peel potatoes. Boil or steam. Purée potatoes and let cool.

Peel garlic. Crush with salt until puréed[a].

Allow egg yolks and oil to reach room temperature[b].

METHOD

Blend potatoes, egg yolks[b], and garlic into a smooth paste.

Add olive oil in a thin stream, mixing vigorously (as in making mayonnaise).

Season with lemon juice, salt, and cayenne.

APPLICATIONS

This is the universal sauce for garlic lovers.

It is the classic accompaniment to bouillabaisse.

Chicken Cream Sauce with Red Pepper Coulis

Albufera-Sauce
Sauce Albuféra

YIELD: 1 QT 2 OZ (1 L)

Chicken cream sauce (Recipe 56)	1 pt 13 oz	850 ml
Glace de viande[a]	3 1/2 oz	100 g
Red pepper coulis (Recipe 79)	1 2/3 oz	50 ml
Seasoning	1x	1x

METHOD

Bring chicken cream sauce to a boil.

Melt *glace de viande*.

Add melted *glace de viande* and red pepper coulis to hot cream sauce.

Boil briefly.

Season to taste.

APPLICATION

Serve with poultry dishes.

---

[a] A food processor can be used to purée the garlic.

[b] Raw egg yolks may contain salmonella bacteria. It is advisable to use pasteurized egg yolks.

---

[a] *Glace de viande*, literally translated "meat glaze," is made by reducing meat stock to a syrupy consistency.

32

*A*pple Sauce

Apfelsauce
Apple sauce

YIELD: 1 QT 2 OZ (1 L)

Apples	6 lb 10 oz	3.0 kg
Lemon juice	2 lemons	2
Dry white wine	10 oz	300 ml
Cinnamon stick	1/2 stick	1/2
Seasoning (sugar, salt)	1x	1x

METHOD

Peel and core apples; cut into slices.

Blend apple slices with lemon juice and wine.

Add cinnamon stick, cover, and cook slowly in oven until apples are soft. Remove cinnamon stick.

Strain apples through fine mesh china cap.

If necessary, reduce sauce until no longer runny.

Season with small amount of sugar and salt.

APPLICATION

Serve with roast goose, duckling, or pork.

33

*B*earnaise Sauce

Bearner Sauce
Sauce béarnaise

YIELD: 1 QT 2 OZ (1 L)

Chervil, fresh	1/3 oz	10 g
Tarragon, fresh	2/3 oz	20 g
Tarragon vinegar	1 2/3 oz	50 ml
Dry white wine	1 oz	30 ml
Hollandaise sauce (Recipe 60)	1 qt 2 oz	1.0 L
Seasoning	1x	1x

MISE EN PLACE

Wash chervil and tarragon and chop leaves.

METHOD

Combine tarragon, tarragon vinegar, and wine.

Reduce until almost evaporated.

Blend reduction with Hollandaise sauce.

Add chopped chervil.

Season to taste.

APPLICATIONS

Serve with sautéed, roasted, or grilled beef dishes, or with grilled fish.

Use to fill artichoke bottoms or tomatoes.

34

*B*echamel Sauce (with milk)[a]

Bechamel-Sauce
Sauce Béchamel

YIELD: 1 QT 2 OZ (1 L)

Onion	1 1/3 oz	40 g
Butter	1 2/3 oz	50 g
White flour	2 oz	60 g
Milk	1 qt 8 oz	1.2 L
Seasoning (salt and cayenne)	1x	1x

METHOD

Slice onion into thin slices and smother in butter.

Add flour and cook briefly.

Cool resulting roux.

Bring milk to a boil and add to roux.

Bring to a boil, stirring continuously. Simmer for about 30 minutes.

Strain through fine mesh china cap.

Season to taste.

APPLICATIONS

Use as a component in various preparations.

Use as a binding ingredient for vegetable or mushroom fillings or for croquettes. To use as a binding ingredient, the amount of roux must be increased by at least 40%.

[a]See also Recipe 40, Cream sauce (with cream).

35

ℬeurre Blanc (for fish)

Beurre-blanc-Sauce
Beurre blanc

YIELD: 1 QT 2 OZ (1 L)

Shallots	8 3/4 oz	250 g
Dry white wine	8 3/4 oz	250 g
White wine vinegar	5 oz	150 ml
Fish fumet (Recipe 25)	1 qt 2 oz	1.0 L
Butter, cold	1 lb 9 oz	700 g
Seasoning (salt and pepper)	1x	1x

METHOD

Peel shallots and chop fine.

Combine shallots with dry white wine and reduce.

Add white wine vinegar and reduce again.

Add fish fumet and reduce to about 10 oz (300 ml).

Remove from heat and add the cold butter in small amounts, whipping vigorously.

Whip sauce once more with a hand-held electric mixer (if available).

Season with salt and freshly ground white pepper.

Be sure sauce does not return to a boil.

APPLICATIONS

Serve with grilled ocean fish and crustaceans.

Serve with warm fish terrines.

Serve with poached fish.

36

ℬordelaise Sauce

Bordeleser Sauce
Sauce bordelaise

YIELD: 1 QT 2 OZ (1 L)

Marrow bones, cut into slices	1 lb 12 oz	800 g
Black peppercorns	10	10
Shallots	3 oz	80 g
Dry red wine	1 pt 1 oz	500 ml
Bay leaf	1/2 leaf	1/2
Thyme twig	1 twig	1
Demi-glace (Recipe 44)	1 pt 14 oz	900 ml
Seasoning (salt and pepper)	1x	1x
Butter, cold	1 oz	30 g

MISE EN PLACE

Soak marrow bones and carefully remove marrow. Cut marrow into small dice or slices.

Crush peppercorns.

Chop shallots.

METHOD

Combine red wine, peppercorns, shallots, bay leaf, and thyme. Heat and reduce until liquid is almost evaporated.

Add *demi-glace* and simmer for about 5 minutes.

Strain through fine mesh china cap.

Adjust seasoning.

Add cold butter in small nuggets.

Warm marrow in hot water; add to the sauce at the last moment.

APPLICATIONS

Serve with grilled or sautéed beef.

Serve with braised vegetables such as lettuce, celery, or fennel.

37

ℳushroom Cream Sauce

Champignonrahmsauce
Sauce aux champignons

YIELD: 1 QT 2 OZ (1 L)

Shallots	1 oz	30 g
Mushrooms, fresh	14 oz	400 g
Butter	1 2/3 oz	50 g
Dry white wine	3 1/3 oz	100 ml
Cream sauce (Recipe 40)	1 pt 13 oz	850 ml
Seasoning	1x	1x

MISE EN PLACE
Chop shallots.

Clean, wash, and slice mushrooms.

METHOD
Smother shallots in butter.

Add mushrooms and continue cooking.

Add dry white wine and bring to a boil again.

Drain off mushrooms; save stock.

Reduce mushroom stock to a glaze consistency.

Heat cream sauce.

Add mushroom glaze and mushrooms to cream sauce.

Bring sauce to a boil; reduce for a few minutes.

Season to taste.

APPLICATIONS
Serve as second sauce, along with natural *jus*, with roasted or braised main dishes.

Serve with sautéed light luncheon platters.

Serve with vegetable or pasta dishes.

38

𝒞horon Sauce

Choron-Sauce
Sauce Choron

YIELD: 1 QT 2 OZ (1 L)

Dry white wine	1 oz	30 ml
Tarragon vinegar	1 2/3 oz	50 ml
Tomato puree	2 oz	60 g
Hollandaise sauce (Recipe 60)	1 pt 14 oz	900 ml
Seasoning	1x	1x

METHOD
Combine dry white wine and tarragon vinegar and reduce almost completely.

Add tomato puree and heat.

Blend with Hollandaise sauce.

Season to taste.

APPLICATION
Serve with sautéed, roasted, or grilled beef.

39

𝒞ocktail Sauce

Cocktailsauce
Sauce cocktail

YIELD: 1 QT 2 OZ (1 L)

Horseradish, fresh	1 oz	30 g
Mayonnaise (Recipe 71)	1 lb 5 oz	600 g
Tomato ketchup	8 1/2 oz	250 ml
Diet cottage cheese[a]	3 1/2 oz	100 g
Cognac (or any brandy)	1 oz	30 ml
Seasoning (Tabasco sauce)	1x	1x
Seasoning (lemon juice)	1x	1x

MISE EN PLACE
Peel and grate horseradish.

METHOD
Combine all ingredients.

Season with Tabasco sauce and lemon juice.

Add spices according to taste to give the sauce a tangy flavor.

[a] The original recipe calls for *Quark*, a generic German word for cottage cheese. The cottage cheese for this recipe should be fine curd and strained. Skim-milk ricotta cheese makes a good substitute.

40

$\mathcal{C}$ream Sauce (with cream)[a]

Cremesauce
Sauce à la crème

YIELD: 1 QT 2 OZ (1 L)

Onions	1 1/3 oz	40 g
Butter	1 2/3 oz	50 g
White wheat flour	2 oz	60 g
Milk	1 qt 8 oz	1.2 L
Heavy cream (36%)	8 1/2 oz	250 ml
Seasoning (salt, cayenne)	1x	1x

METHOD

Slice onions into thin slices and smother in butter.

Add flour and cook briefly.

Cool resulting roux.

Bring milk to boiling point and add to roux.

Return to a boil, stirring continuously.

Simmer for about 30 minutes.

Strain through fine mesh china cap.

Add cream and bring to a boil again. Strain again, and season to taste.

APPLICATIONS

Use as a component in various preparations.

Use as a binding ingredient for vegetable or mushroom fillings or for croquettes. To use as a binding ingredient, the amount of roux must be increased by at least 40%.

Use as a finished sauce with vegetables, mushrooms, or pasta.

41

$\mathcal{C}$umberland Sauce

Cumberland-Sauce
Sauce Cumberland

YIELD: 1 QT 2 OZ (1 L)

Oranges	2	2
Lemons	2	2
Dry red wine	3 1/3 oz	100 ml
Horseradish, fresh	1 oz	30 g
Ginger, fresh	1/3 oz	10 g
Red currant jelly	1 lb 2 oz	500 g
Mustard powder	1/4 oz	6 g
Red Port wine	6 3/4 oz	200 ml
Seasoning	1x	1x

MISE EN PLACE

Wash oranges and lemons in hot water; dry with a towel. Peel outer skin (zest) and cut into very fine *julienne*. Blanch zest and boil in red wine until soft. Squeeze juice from oranges and lemons.

Peel horseradish and ginger and grate fine.

METHOD

Melt red currant jelly.

Add orange juice and lemon juice to red currant jelly.

Add red wine/zest mixture.

Mix mustard powder with Port wine; add to fruit juice/jelly mixture.

Add horseradish and ginger.

Mix well, season to taste, and chill.

APPLICATIONS

Serve with cold poultry or game dishes.

Serve with meat patés and terrines.

---

[a] Also see Recipe 34, Bechamel Sauce (with milk).

42

Curry Sauce

Currysauce
Sauce curry

YIELD: 1 QT 2 OZ (1 L)

Onions	5 1/3 oz	150 g
Garlic cloves, peeled	2 cloves	2
Apple, Granny Smith	3 1/2 oz	100 g
Tomatoes	2 oz	60 g
Butter	1 2/3 oz	50 g
Madras curry powder	1 oz	30 g
Coconut flakes, dried, unsweetened[a]	1 1/3 oz	40 g
Chicken stock (Recipe 26)	1 pt 14 oz	900 ml
Chili sauce	2/3 oz	20 ml
Mango chutney, chopped	1 1/3 oz	40 g
Heavy cream (36%)	6 3/4 oz	200 ml
Cornstarch	2/3 oz	20 g
Seasoning	1x	1x

MISE EN PLACE
Slice onions and garlic.

Core apple and cut into thin slices.

Remove seeds from tomatoes and cut into large dice.

METHOD
Smother onions and garlic in butter.

Add apples and continue cooking.

Dust with curry powder and continue cooking.

Add tomatoes, coconut flakes, and chicken stock.

Simmer for 20 minutes.

Add chili sauce and chutney.

Purée[b] and strain through fine china cap.

Bring to a boil and add cream.

Mix cornstarch with small amount of cold chicken stock and add to boiling sauce to thicken.

Adjust seasoning.

APPLICATIONS
Use for curry dishes.

Use as an ingredient in white sauces (for example suprême sauce with curry).

43

Curry Sauce Variation

Currysauce (Ableitung)
Sauce au curry (dérivation)

YIELD: 1 QT 2 OZ (1 L)

Madras curry powder	1 oz	30 g
Butter	1 1/3 oz	40 g
White veal stock	6 3/4 oz	200 ml
Creamed veal velouté sauce (Recipe 45)	1 qt 2 oz	1.0 L
Tomato ketchup	1/3 oz	10 ml
Seasoning	1x	1x

METHOD
Sauté curry powder in butter over low heat for about 1 minute.

Add veal stock and reduce to about 3/4 oz.

Strain mixture through cheesecloth into the *velouté*.

Add ketchup and season to taste.

NOTE: Several curry sauce variations can be made using different basic stocks/sauces and adding the curry essence. For example, Cream Sauce (Recipe 40) can be used in place of the *velouté* sauce.

44

Demi-Glace

Demi-glace
Demi-glace

YIELD: 10 1/2 QT (10 L)

Veal bones	20 lb	9.0 kg
Calves' feet	2 lb 3 oz	1.0 kg
Sachet bag	1	1
Clarified butter	10 1/2 oz	300 g
White wheat flour	12 1/2 oz	360 g
Peanut oil	3 1/3 oz	100 ml
Mirepoix (Recipe 15)	2 lb	900 g
Tomato puree	7 oz	200 g
Dry white wine	1 qt 2 oz	1.0 L
Brown veal stock (Recipe 23)	6 gal 44 oz	24.0 L

[a] Be sure coconut flakes are not sweet.

[b] Use electric hand-held mixer

MISE EN PLACE
Chop veal bones and calves' feet into small pieces.

Make sachet bag consisting of thyme, bay leaves, and peppercorns.

Make a light brown roux with butter and flour; let cool.

METHOD
Heat peanut oil in tilting frying pan or roasting pan; brown bones on all sides.

Pour off any excess oil; add *mirepoix*; continue roasting.

Add tomato puree and continue roasting.

Add white wine and reduce until most liquid has evaporated.

Add 1/2 gallon (2 L) veal stock and reduce again.

Put mixture in suitable kettle or pot and deglaze the pan.

Add remaining stock, bring to a boil, and skim.

Simmer for about 3 hours.

Add sachet bag and let simmer for about 1/2 hour.

Strain through cheesecloth.

Add roux to strained stock and boil until reduced to about 10 1/2 qt.

Strain through fine mesh china cap.

APPLICATIONS
Use as a basic sauce for brown meat dishes.

Dilute with brown veal stock and use to braise meat.

45

*C*reamed Veal Velouté Sauce

Deutsche Sauce
Sauce allemande

YIELD: 1 QT 2 OZ (1 L)

White veal stock (Recipe 28)	13 1/2 oz	400 ml
Veal velouté sauce (Recipe 65)	1 pt 11 oz	800 ml
Egg yolks	2	2
Heavy cream (36%)	6 3/4 oz	200 ml
Seasoning (lemon juice)	1x	1x
Seasoning (salt, cayenne)	1x	1x
Butter, cold	1 2/3 oz	50 g

METHOD
Reduce veal stock quickly to a syrupy consistency, but do not brown.

Add *velouté*; bring to boiling point.

Combine egg yolks with cream and mix into sauce. Do not allow to boil.

Season to taste and strain through fine mesh china cap.

Add cold butter in small nuggets.

APPLICATIONS
Use as an ingredient in white meat sauce variations.

Use as sauce with pasta.

Use with veal fillings for patty shells.

46

*M*ustard Sauce

Dijon-Sauce
Sauce dijonnaise

YIELD: 1 QT 2 OZ (1 L)

Hollandaise sauce (Recipe 60)	1 pt 14 oz	900 ml
Dijon mustard	3 oz	80 g
Seasoning	1x	1x

METHOD
Mix Hollandaise sauce with mustard.

Season to taste.

APPLICATION
Serve with fish poached in *court bouillon*, or with grilled ocean fish.

47

*D*ill Mustard Sauce

Dillsenfsauce
Sauce moutarde à l'aneth

YIELD: 1 QT 2 OZ (1 L)

Prepared mustard, hot	7 oz	200 g
Prepared mustard, mild	2 oz	60 g
Egg yolk[a]	1	1
Sunflower oil	1 pt 4 oz	600 ml
Dill, fresh	1 oz	30 g
Honey	1 oz	30 g
Seasoning (lemon juice)	1x	1x
Seasoning (salt and pepper)	1x	1x

METHOD
Mix hot and mild mustards with egg yolk.

Add oil in thin stream while stirring vigorously.

Remove stems from dill; chop leaves; and add to sauce.

Season with honey, lemon juice, salt and pepper.

APPLICATION
Commonly served with Gravad Lax.

48

*D*uxelles Sauce

Duxelles-Sauce
Sauce duxelles

YIELD: 1 QT 2 OZ (1 L)

Mushrooms, fresh	10 1/2 oz	300 g
Butter	2 oz	60 g
Dry white wine	3 1/3 oz	100 ml
Shallots	1 1/3 oz	40 g
Parsley	2/3 oz	20 g
Tomato puree	1 2/3 oz	50 g
Demi-glace (Recipe 44)	1 pt 4 oz	600 ml
Seasoning	1x	1x

MISE EN PLACE
Clean and wash mushrooms and braise with 1 oz butter and the dry white wine.

Drain off stock and save.

Chop mushrooms fine.

Chop shallots fine.

Chop parsley.

METHOD
Smother chopped shallots in remaining 1 oz butter.

Add tomato paste and continue cooking.

Add mushroom stock and reduce.

Add *demi-glace* and bring to a boil.

Add chopped mushrooms and parsley.

Season to taste.

APPLICATION
Serve with sautéed veal and pork dishes.

49

*H*erb Vinaigrette

Essig-Kräuter-Sauce
Sauce vinaigrette

YIELD: 1 QT 2 OZ (1 L)

Chives, fresh	2/3 oz	20 g
Italian parsley, fresh	1 1/3 oz	40 g
Basil, fresh	1/3 oz	10 g
Chervil, fresh	1/3 oz	10 g
Tarragon, fresh	2/3 oz	20 g
Onions	5 1/3 oz	150 g
Sunflower oil	1 pt 4 oz	600 ml
Herb vinegar	8 1/2 oz	250 ml
Seasoning (salt and pepper)	1x	1x

MISE EN PLACE
Wash chives and cut into small slivers.

Wash herbs and chop leaves.

Chop onions fine.

METHOD
Blend chives, herbs, and onions; add oil and vinegar.

Season to taste.

Stir before each use.

---

[a] Raw egg yolks can cause salmonella food poisoning. Using pasturized egg yolks is recommended.

50

ℱish Sabayon
Fisch-Sabayon
Sabayon de poisson

YIELD: 1 PT 1 OZ (1/2 L)

Shallots	1 2/3 oz	50 g
Herbs, fresh (dill, fennel leaves, and tarragon)	2/3 oz	20 g
White peppercorns	5	5
Dry white wine	5 oz	150 ml
Fish fumet (Recipe 25)	5 oz	150 ml
Chicken stock (Recipe 26)	5 oz	150 ml
Egg yolks[a]	8	8
Butter	2/3 oz	20 g
Seasoning (salt and pepper)	1x	1x

MISE EN PLACE
Chop shallots.

Wash herbs and chop leaves.

Crush peppercorns.

METHOD
Combine dry white wine, fish fumet, chicken stock, shallots, herbs, and peppercorns.

Boil and reduce to 6 3/4 oz (200 ml).

Strain; cool slightly and mix in egg yolks.

Whip mixture over hot water until foamy and thick.

Whip in soft butter in small increments.

Season to taste.

NOTE: If sabayon is used for glazing, 3 1/3 oz (100 ml) of whipped cream should be folded in.

51

ℛich Fish Sauce with Cream
Fisch-Spezialsauce mit Rahm
Sauce poisson spéciale à la crème

YIELD: 1 PT 1 OZ (1/2 L)

Glace de poisson[a]	3 1/3 oz	100 ml
Extra heavy cream (45%)	10 oz	300 ml
Butter, cold	7 oz	200 g
Seasoning (salt and pepper)	1x	1x

METHOD
Combine glace de poisson with cream; bring to a boil and reduce slightly.

Remove from heat and whip in very cold butter in small nuggets.

Season to taste.

Do not allow sauce to return to a boil.

NOTE: Many variations can be created by adding herbs to the sauce or by replacing the plain butter with a flavored butter, such as lobster butter.

52

ℱish Sauce for Glazing
Fisch-Spezialsauce zum Glasieren
Sauce poisson spéciale à glacer

YIELD: 1 PT 1 OZ (1/2 L)

Heavy cream (36%)	5 oz	150 ml
Egg yolks	2	2
Rich fish sauce with cream (Recipe 51)	10 oz	300 ml
Seasoning (salt, cayenne)	1x	1x

METHOD
Whip cream to medium consistency and mix with egg yolks.

Blend into special fish sauce and season to taste.

[a] Raw egg yolks can cause salmonella food poisoning. Using pasturized egg yolks is recommended.

[a] *Glace de poisson*, literally translated "fish glaze," is made by reducing fish fumet to a syrupy consistency. It can taste unpleasant if the fish bones used for the fumet are not very fresh.

53

*F*ish Velouté Sauce

Fisch-Velouté
Velouté de poisson

YIELD: 1 QT 2 OZ (1 L)

White wheat flour	2 oz	60 g
Butter	1 2/3 oz	50 g
Fish stock (Recipe 24)	1 qt 8 oz	1.2 L
Seasoning (salt, cayenne)	1x	1x

METHOD
Roast flour in butter to make a light yellow roux.

Cool roux.

Bring fish stock to a boil and add roux, while stirring.

Bring to a boil.

Simmer for about 30 minutes.

Season to taste.

Strain through fine mesh china cap.

APPLICATIONS
Use as an ingredient in white wine sauce.

Use as a binding sauce for fritters or croquettes. To use as a binding sauce, the amount of roux must be increased by at least 40%.

54

*F*oyot Sauce

Foyot-Sauce
Sauce Foyot

YIELD: 1 QT 2 OZ (1 L)

Tarragon, fresh	2/3 oz	20 g
Chervil, fresh	1/3 oz	10 g
Glace de viande[a]	3 1/2 oz	100 g
Tarragon vinegar	1 2/3 oz	50 ml
Dry white wine	1 oz	30 ml
Hollandaise sauce (Recipe 60)	1 pt 14 oz	900 ml
Seasoning	1x	1x

MISE EN PLACE
Remove stems from tarragon and chop leaves.

Remove stems from chervil and chop leaves.

Melt *glace de viande*.

METHOD
Combine tarragon, tarragon vinegar, and wine and boil until almost reduced.

Blend mixture into Hollandaise sauce.

Blend *glace de viande* into sauce.

Add chopped chervil.

Season to taste.

APPLICATIONS
Serve with sautéed, roasted, or grilled beef dishes.

Use to fill artichoke hearts or tomatoes.

55

*B*rown Veal Juice (thickened)

Gebundener Kalbsjus
Jus de veau lié

YIELD: 1 QT 2 OZ (1 L)

Veal juice (Recipe 64)	2 qts 4 oz	2.0 L
Cornstarch	1/2 oz	15 g
Dry white wine	1 oz	30 ml
Seasoning (salt and pepper)	1x	1x
Butter, cold	1 2/3 oz	50 g

METHOD
Reduce veal stock to about 1 qt.

Mix cornstarch with wine and add to boiling stock to thicken.

Bring to a boil.

Season to taste.

Strain through fine mesh china cap.

Remove from heat and add cold butter in small nuggets.

APPLICATIONS
Serve with roast veal.

Use as an ingredient in other brown sauces.

---

[a] *Glace de viande*, literally translated "meat glaze," is made by reducing meat stock to a syrupy consistency.

56

Chicken Cream Sauce

Geflügelrahmsauce
Sauce suprême

YIELD: 1 QT 2 OZ (1 L)

Chicken stock (Recipe 26)	*10 oz*	*300 ml*
Heavy cream (36%)	*8 1/2 oz*	*250 ml*
Chicken velouté sauce (Recipe 57)	*1 pt 8 oz*	*700 ml*
Seasoning (salt, cayenne)	*1x*	*1x*
Seasoning (lemon juice)	*1x*	*1x*

METHOD
Boil chicken stock until well reduced, but do not brown.

Add reduced stock and cream to chicken *velouté*. Bring to a full boil.

Strain through cheesecloth.

Season with salt, cayenne, and lemon juice.

APPLICATIONS
Use as an ingredient in other white poultry sauces.

Use to bind chicken fillings for patty shells.

Use as a sauce in baked pasta dishes.

NOTE: This sauce is often used with poached poultry dishes. In this case, the poaching stock should be used in place of the chicken stock in the sauce recipe.

57

Chicken Velouté Sauce

Geflügel-Velouté
Velouté de volaille

YIELD: 1 QT 2 OZ (1 L)

White wheat flour	*2 oz*	*60 g*
Butter	*1 2/3 oz*	*50 g*
Chicken stock (Recipe 26)	*1 qt 8 oz*	*1.2 L*
Seasoning (salt, cayenne)	*1x*	*1x*

METHOD
Roast flour in butter to make a light yellow roux.

Cool roux.

Bring chicken stock to boil and add roux.

Bring to a boil, stirring frequently.

Simmer for about 30 minutes.

Season to taste.

Strain through fine mesh china cap.

APPLICATIONS
Use as an ingredient in Chicken Cream Sauce (Recipe 56).

Use as a binding sauce for fritters or croquettes. To use as a binding sauce, the amount of roux must be increased by at least 40%.

58

Vegetable Vinaigrette

Gemüse-Vinaigrette
Vinaigrette aux légumes

YIELD: 1 QT 2 OZ (1 L)

Carrots	*4 1/4 oz*	*120 g*
Leek, white part only	*3 1/2 oz*	*100 g*
Knob celery (celeriac)	*3 1/2 oz*	*100 g*
Zucchini (small)	*4 1/4 oz*	*120 g*
Red bell pepper	*3 1/2 oz*	*100 g*
Yellow bell pepper	*3 1/2 oz*	*100 g*
Chives, fresh	*2/3 oz*	*20 g*
Chervil, fresh	*1/3 oz*	*10 g*
Basil, fresh	*1/3 oz*	*10 g*
Soy sauce	*1 2/3 oz*	*50 ml*
Red wine vinegar	*5 oz*	*150 ml*
Seasoning (salt and pepper)	*1x*	*1x*
Olive oil, cold pressed	*12 oz*	*350 ml*

MISE EN PLACE
Clean and cut vegetables into small dice (*brunoise*).

Lightly parboil vegetables. Drain.

Cut chives into small slivers.

Wash chervil and basil and chop leaves.

METHOD
Mix soy sauce and vinegar.

Add vegetables and herbs.

Season with salt and freshly ground pepper.

Mix in oil. Stir thoroughly to combine.

APPLICATION
Use in composed salads with items such as warm sautéed fish, eggplant, sweetbreads, saddle of hare, chicken breasts.

59

*G*reen Sauce
Grüne Sauce
Sauce verte

YIELD: 1 QT 2 OZ (1 L)

Leaf spinach, frozen	3 1/2 oz	100 g
Tarragon, fresh	1/3 oz	10 g
Chervil, fresh	1/3 oz	10 g
Sorrel	7 oz	200 g
Cress	3 1/2 oz	100 g
Mayonnaise (Recipe 71)	1 lb 12 oz	800 g
Seasoning	1x	1x

METHOD
Defrost spinach; drain and squeeze spinach dry; chop fine.

Wash herbs and chop leaves fine.

Purée herbs and spinach in food processor.

Blend with mayonnaise.

Season to taste.

APPLICATION
Serve with cold poached fish.

60

*H*ollandaise Sauce
Holländische Sauce
Sauce hollandaise

YIELD: 1 QT 2 OZ (1 L)

Butter	2 lb 3 oz	1.0 kg
Shallots	1 2/3 oz	50 g
White peppercorns	10	10
White wine vinegar	1 oz	30 ml
Dry white wine	2/3 oz	20 ml
Water	3 1/3 oz	100 ml
Salt	1/6 oz	5 g
Egg yolks[a]	8	8
Seasoning (salt, cayenne)	1x	1x
Seasoning (lemon juice)	1x	1x

MISE EN PLACE
Clarify butter: Melt it over hot water, remove clear butterfat, and let cool to 115°F (45°C).

Chop shallots.

Crush peppercorns.

METHOD
Boil vinegar, wine, half the water, shallots, peppercorns, and salt until almost completely reduced.

Add remaining water to dilute reduction.

Add egg yolks to reduction and beat over 180°F (80°C) water until thick and foamy.

Add clarified butter in a thin stream, whipping vigorously.

Season with salt, cayenne, and lemon juice.

Strain sauce through a dry cheesecloth.

Keep sauce in covered container in a warm place. For sanitary reasons, the sauce should not be kept longer than 1 hour.

NOTE: If the sauce curdles, beat together 1 egg yolk and a little water over hot water, and beat in sauce in small amounts. As soon as the sauce starts to thicken, the remaining curdled sauce can be added in larger amounts.

APPLICATIONS
Use as basic sauce to make sauce variations.

Serve with boiled or steamed vegetables or with poached fish.

Use to enrich fish sauces.

---

[a] Raw egg yolks can cause salmonella food poisoning. Using pasturized egg yolks is recommended.

61

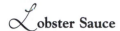obster Sauce

Hummersauce
Sauce amoricaine

YIELD: 1 QT 2 OZ (1 L)

Lobster shells	2 lb 3 oz	1.0 kg
Carrots	2 oz	60 g
Knob celery(celeriac))	1 1/3 oz	40 g
Tomatoes	5 oz	140 g
Garlic clove, peeled	1	1
Shallots	1 1/3 oz	40 g
Olive oil	1 2/3 oz	50 ml
Tomato paste	1 1/3 oz	40 g
Cognac (or any brandy)	2/3 oz	20 ml
Thyme twig, fresh	1	1
Fish fumet (Recipe 25)	1 qt 2 oz	1.0 L
Heavy cream (36%)	1 qt 2 oz	1.0 L
Cornstarch	1/3 oz	10 g
Seasoning (salt, cayenne)	1x	1x
Butter, cold	1 oz	30 g

MISE EN PLACE

Chop lobster shells in mortar or food processor as finely as possible.

Cut carrots and knob celery into small dice.

Cut tomatoes into cubes.

Chop garlic and shallots.

METHOD

Sauté lobster shells in oil.

Add diced carrots and knob celery and continue smothering.

Add tomato paste and continue smothering briefly.

Flame with Cognac.

Add cubed tomatoes, thyme twig, and fish fumet.

Simmer for 30 minutes. Add cream and simmer for 15 minutes more.

Strain without pressure through fine mesh china cap or cheesecloth.

Make a slurry of cornstarch with a little white wine or fish fumet.

Add slurry to boiling sauce to thicken.

Bring to boiling point; season with salt and a little cayenne pepper.

Add cold butter nuggets; blend without boiling further.

APPLICATIONS

Use as an ingredient in fish and crustacean dishes.

Use as base for lobster cream soup.

62

*I*talian Sauce

Italienische Sauce
Sauce italienne

YIELD: 1 QT 2 OZ (1 L)

Mushrooms, fresh	5 1/3 oz	150 g
Butter	2 oz	60 g
Dry white wine	3 1/3 oz	100 ml
Parsley	1/3 oz	10 g
Chervil, fresh	1/6 oz	5 g
Tarragon, fresh	1/6 oz	5 g
Ham, cooked	5 1/3 oz	150 g
Shallots	1 1/3 oz	40 g
Tomato paste	1 2/3 oz	50 g
Demi-glace (Recipe 44)	1 pt 11 oz	800 ml
Seasoning (salt and pepper)	1x	1x

MISE EN PLACE

Clean and wash mushrooms. Braise with half the butter and white wine. Drain off the juice and save stock and mushrooms separately.

Chop mushrooms fine.

Chop parsley, chervil, and tarragon separately.

Cut ham into small dice (*brunoise*).

Peel and chop shallots.

METHOD

Smother shallots in remaining butter.

Add tomato paste and continue cooking.

Add mushroom stock and reduce slightly.

Add *demi-glace* and bring to a boil.

Add ham, mushrooms, and herbs.

Season to taste.

APPLICATIONS

Serve with sautéed meat dishes.

Serve with pasta and vegetables.

63

Hunter's Sauce

Jägersauce
Sauce chasseur

YIELD: 1 QT 2 OZ (1 L)

Mushrooms, fresh	10 1/2 oz	300 g
Butter	3 oz	80 g
Shallots	1 1/3 oz	40 g
Garlic clove, peeled	1/2	1/2
Parsley	1/3 oz	10 g
Tomato paste	2/3 oz	20 g
Dry white wine	3 1/3 oz	100 ml
Demi-glace (Recipe 44)	1 pt 11 oz	800 ml
Butter, cold	1 oz	30 g
Seasoning (salt and pepper)	1x	1x

MISE EN PLACE
Clean, wash, and slice mushrooms.

Braise mushrooms in half the butter in a covered pot.

Drain and save mushroom stock.

Chop shallots and garlic.

Chop parsley.

METHOD
Smother shallots and garlic in remaining butter.

Add tomato paste and continue cooking.

Add wine and reserved mushroom stock and reduce.

Add *demi-glace*, bring to a boil, and simmer for about 5 minutes.

Add cold butter in small nuggets; do not boil any longer.

Add mushrooms and chopped parsley.

Season to taste.

APPLICATION
Serve with sautéed light meat entrees.

64

Veal Juice

Kalbsjus
Jus de veau

YIELD: 10 1/2 QT (10 L)

Veal bones from breast, meaty[a]	11 lb	5.0 kg
Other veal bones	6 lb 10 oz	3.0 kg
Calves' feet	4 lb 7 oz	2.0 kg
Veal trimmings	2 lb 3 oz	1.0 kg
Sachet bag	1	1
Peanut oil	5 oz	150 ml
Mirepoix (Recipe 15)	2 lb 3 oz	1.0 kg
Tomato puree	3 1/2 oz	100 g
Water	4 gal	15.0 L
Dry white wine	2 qt 4 oz	2.0 L
Brown veal stock (Recipe 23)	5 qt 9 oz	5.0 L
Salt	1 oz, or to taste[b]	30 g

MISE EN PLACE
Chop veal bones and veal breast bones into small pieces.

Cut calves' feet into small pieces. Chop veal trimmings.

Make sachet bag consisting of peppercorns, bay leaves, cloves, marjoram, and thyme.

METHOD
Roast veal breast bones, veal bones, calves' feet, and veal trimmings in peanut oil in tilting frying pan or in oven.

Add *mirepoix* and continue roasting.

Drain off excess oil.

Add tomato puree and continue roasting carefully.

Add small amounts of water and reduce two or three times. If bones were roasted in the oven, transfer bones and pan drippings to large pot or kettle.

Add remaining water, wine, and brown veal stock.

Add salt, bring to a boil, and skim. Simmer for 3 to 4 hours.

Add sachet bag for the last hour of simmering.

Strain through cheesecloth.

Reduce stock to 10 1/2 qt (10.0 L). Season to taste.

---

[a] It is important to use enough veal breast bones, as they contain a lot of gelatin. It is important to use meaty bones and trimmings for enough meat flavor.

[b] Since veal juice is used as an ingredient in other recipes, salt sparingly and correct to taste in the final recipe.

65

*V*eal Velouté Sauce

Kalbs-Velouté
Velouté de veau

YIELD: 1 QT 2 OZ (1 L)

Butter	1 2/3 oz	50 g
White wheat flour	2 oz	60 g
White veal stock (Recipe 28)	1 qt 8 oz	1.2 L
Seasoning	1x	1x

METHOD
Make a light yellow roux with butter and flour. Cool the roux.

Bring veal stock to a boil, add roux, and mix well.

Bring to a boil, stirring continuously.

Simmer for about 30 minutes.

Season to taste.

Strain through fine mesh china cap.

APPLICATIONS
Use in Creamed Veal Velouté Sauce (Recipe 45).

Use as a binding sauce for fritters or croquettes. To use as a binding sauce, the amount of roux must be increased by at least 40%.

66

*G*arlic Sauce

Knoblauchsauce
Sauce à l'ail

YIELD: 1 QT 2 OZ (1 L)

Garlic	7 oz	200 g
Red wine	6 3/4 oz	200 ml
Demi-glace (Recipe 44)	1 qt 2 oz	1.0 L
Butter, cold	1 oz	30 g
Seasoning (salt and pepper)	1x	1x

MISE EN PLACE
Peel garlic. Cut into fine slices, lengthwise.

Blanch garlic three times, changing the water each time.

Place garlic slices on a towel to dry.

METHOD
Reduce red wine.

Add *demi-glace*.

Add garlic slices and bring to a boil.

Add cold butter nuggets and do not boil any longer.

Season to taste.

APPLICATION
Serve with sautéed lamb or beef entrees.

67

*H*erb Sauce

Kräutersauce
Sauce aux fines herbes

YIELD: 1 QT 2 OZ (1 L)

Creamed veal velouté sauce (Recipe 45)	1 qt 2 oz	1.0 L
Kitchen herbs, fresh	1 oz	30 g
Butter, cold	2/3 oz	20 g

MISE EN PLACE
Have creamed veal *velouté* ready.

Prepare herbs, such as chervil, dill, parsley, basil, tarragon, cilantro, and chives. Wash herbs and chop leaves. Slice chives into small slivers.

METHOD
Add herbs to *velouté*, and finish sauce with nuggets of cold butter.

APPLICATIONS
The sauce can be varied by using different base sauces.

If only one herb variety is used, the sauce may be named accordingly, for example, chervil sauce or basil sauce.

68

Shrimp Sauce

Krevettensauce
Sauce aux crevettes

YIELD: 1 QT 2 OZ (1 L)

White wine sauce (for fish) (Recipe 103)	1 pt 14 oz	900 ml
Lobster butter (Recipe 11)	3 oz	80 g
Seasoning	1x	1x
Shrimp, canned,[a] small	3 1/2 oz	100 g
Cognac (or any brandy)	1/3 oz	10 ml

METHOD
Bring white wine sauce to a boil. Remove from heat.

Whip lobster butter into sauce.

Season to taste.

Drain shrimp and lightly squeeze out extra packing water.

Warm shrimp in Cognac.

Add shrimp to sauce.

69

Madeira Sauce

Madeirasauce
Sauce madère

YIELD: 1 QT 2 OZ (1 L)

Shallots	1 1/3 oz	40 g
Red wine	6 3/4 oz	200 ml
Demi-glace (Recipe 44)	1 pt 14 oz	900 ml
Madeira wine (sweet or semisweet)	3 1/3 oz	100 ml
Seasoning	1x	1x
Butter, cold	1 2/3 oz	50 g

METHOD
Peel shallots and slice into small slivers.

Boil shallots with red wine until most moisture is evaporated.

Add *demi-glace* and simmer for 5 minutes.

Strain through fine mesh china cap.

Add Madeira wine for flavor.

Season to taste.

Add cold butter in small nuggets; do not allow to boil.

APPLICATIONS
Serve with baked ham or boiled ox tongue.

Serve with sautéed meat or chicken liver dishes.

NOTES: The same method can be used to make other brown sauces with sweet wines.

They should be named for the wine used.

70

Malta Sauce

Malteser Sauce
Sauce maltaise

YIELD: 1 QT 2 OZ (1 L)

Blood oranges	1 lb 5 oz	600 g
Hollandaise sauce (Recipe 60)	1 pt 14 oz	900 ml
Seasoning	1x	1x

MISE EN PLACE
Wash two of the blood oranges and remove thin peel.[a]

Cut peel into fine shreds (zest). Blanch zest.

Squeeze juice from all oranges.

METHOD
Combine juice and zest and reduce.

Add this reduction to Hollandaise sauce.

Season to taste.

APPLICATION
Serve with white asparagus.[b]

[a] drained weight

[a] Remove only the top layer. This is best done with a potato peeler.

[b] In Switzerland, white asparagus are the most common variety.

71

Mayonnaise
Mayonnaise-Sauce
Mayonnaise

YIELD: 1 QT 2 OZ (1 L)

Egg yolks[a]	4	4
Water	2/3 oz	20 ml
Prepared mild mustard	2/3 oz	20 g
Sunflower oil	1 pt 11 oz	800 ml
White wine vinegar	1 oz	30 ml
Seasoning (salt and pepper)	1x	1x
Seasoning (lemon juice)	1x	1x

MISE EN PLACE
Be sure egg yolks and oil are room temperature.

METHOD
Combine egg yolks, water, and mustard; whisk until foamy.

Add oil in a fine and steady stream, while whipping vigorously.

Add vinegar when all oil is incorporated.

Season with salt and pepper and lemon juice.

72

Horseradish Sauce
Meerrettichsauce
Horseradish sauce

YIELD: 1 QT 2 OZ (1 L)

Onions	1 1/3 oz	40 g
Knob celery (celeriac)	2 oz	60 g
Garlic clove, peeled	1	1
Sachet bag	1	1
Horseradish, fresh	1 lb 2 oz	500 g
Butter	1 1/3 oz	40 g
White wheat flour	2 oz	60 g
White veal stock (Recipe 28)	1 pt 11 oz	800 ml
Heavy cream (36%)	3 1/3 oz	100 ml
Seasoning (salt, cayenne)	1x	1x

MISE EN PLACE
Cut onions, knob celery, and garlic into small dice.

Make sachet bag consisting of thyme and bay leaf.

Wash and peel horseradish and grate fine.

METHOD
Sauté vegetables lightly in butter (except horseradish).

Add flour and smother briefly.

Add veal stock and bring to a boil, stirring continuously.

Add sachet bag and boil slowly for 30 minutes.

Strain sauce through fine mesh china cap.

Add heavy cream.

Add grated horseradish; do not allow to boil any longer.

Season to taste.

APPLICATION
Serve with roast beef, boiled ox tongue, or boiled ham.

73

Horseradish Whipped Cream
Meerrettichschaum
Raifort à la neige

YIELD: 1 QT 2 OZ (1 L)

Horseradish, fresh	6 oz	180 g
Lemon	1/2	1/2
Heavy cream (36%)	1 pt 11 oz	800 ml
Seasoning (salt, cayenne)	1x	1x

MISE EN PLACE
Peel horseradish and grate fine.

Blend with lemon juice.

METHOD
Whip cream until stiff.

Carefully fold cream into horseradish.

Season[a] with salt and cayenne.

APPLICATION
Serve with smoked fish.

[a] Raw egg yolks can cause salmonella food poisoning. Using pasturized egg yolks is recommended.

[a] A small amount of sugar can be added, if desired.

74

Morel Cream Sauce

Morchelrahmsauce
Sauce aux morilles

YIELD: 1 QT 2 OZ (1 L)

Morels, fresh	10 1/2 oz	300 g
Shallots	1 oz	30 g
Cream sauce (Recipe 40)	1 pt 11 oz	800 ml
Butter	1 2/3 oz	50 g
Cognac (or any brandy)	2/3 oz	20 ml
Dry white wine	1 2/3 oz	50 ml
Seasoning	1x	1x

MISE EN PLACE
Remove tough portion from morel stems.

Wash morels and cut lengthwise into quarters or sixths.

Wash morels once again to remove any remaining sand.

Blanch morels and let cool.

Chop shallots fine.

Have cream sauce ready.

METHOD
Smother shallots in butter.

Add blanched morels and continue cooking.

Add Cognac and dry white wine and cook briefly.

Drain morels and squeeze out excess stock. Save stock.

Reduce stock to a *glace* consistency.

Add reduced stock and morels to cream sauce.

Simmer mushroom sauce for a few minutes.

Adjust seasoning.

APPLICATIONS
Serve as a second sauce (in addition to roasting juice) with roasted, braised, or lightly glazed entrees.

Serve with lightly sautéed dishes.

Use to fill artichoke bottoms.

Serve with pasta.

75

Mornay Sauce

Mornay-Sauce
Sauce Mornay

YIELD: 1 QT 2 OZ (1 L)

Bechamel sauce (Recipe 34)	1 pt 11 oz	800 ml
Heavy cream (36%)	3 1/3 oz	100 ml
Egg yolks	4	4
Sbrinz, grated[a]	3 1/2 oz	100 g
Seasoning	1x	1x

MISE EN PLACE
Bring Bechamel sauce to a boil and set aside.

METHOD
Whip heavy cream and egg yolks in a steam table until thick.

Add heavy cream/egg yolk mixture to Bechamel sauce (no longer boiling) and stir well.

Fold grated Sbrinz into sauce.

Season to taste.

APPLICATION
Versatile sauce to gratin meat, vegetable, and pasta dishes.

76

Neapolitan Sauce

Neapolitanische Sauce
Sauce napolitaine

YIELD: 1 QT 2 OZ (1 L)

Tomatoes	1 lb 12 oz	800 g
Butter	1 2/3 oz	50 g
Tomato sauce (Recipe 99)	1 pt 8 oz	700 ml
Seasoning (salt and pepper)	1x	1x

MISE EN PLACE
Blanch tomatoes, peel, and cut in half.

Remove seeds from tomatoes and cut into small dice.

---

[a] *Sbrinz* is a hard grating cheese from Switzerland. Parmesan can be substituted.

METHOD

Smother diced tomatoes in butter for about 1 minute.

Add tomatoes to the finished tomato sauce.

Season with salt and freshly ground pepper.

77

Orange Sauce

Orangensauce
Sauce à l'orange

YIELD: 1 QT 2 OZ (1 L)

Oranges	10 1/2 oz	300 g
Crystal sugar	1/3 oz	10 g
Red Port wine	3 1/3 oz	100 ml
Demi-glace (Recipe 44)	1 pt 14 oz	900 ml
Curaçao[a]	2/3 oz	20 ml
Butter, cold	1 oz	30 g
Seasoning	1x	1x

MISE EN PLACE

Peel thin outside layer of skin (zest) from oranges and cut into fine strips.

Boil zest until soft.

Squeeze juice from oranges.

METHOD

Caramelize the sugar.

Add orange juice and Port wine and reduce.

Add *demi-glace*, bring to a boil, and simmer for a few minutes.

Strain through fine mesh china cap.

Add Curaçao. Add cold butter in small nuggets; do not allow to boil.

Season to taste.

Add orange zest.

APPLICATIONS

Serve with sautéed veal dishes.

Serve with poultry and game if roast drippings (*déglaçage*) are used to give character to the sauce.

78

Paprika Sauce (variation)

Paprikasauce (Ableitung)
Sauce au paprika (dérivation)

YIELD: 1 QT 2 OZ (1 L)

Sweet Hungarian paprika	1 1/3 oz	40 g
Butter	1 1/3 oz	40 g
White veal stock (Recipe 28)	6 3/4 oz	200 ml
Creamed veal velouté sauce (Recipe 45)	1 qt 2 oz	1.0 L
Seasoning	1x	1x

METHOD

Smother paprika in butter over low heat for about 1 minute.

Add veal stock and reduce to about 1 2/3 oz (50 ml).

Heat veal *velouté.*

Strain this extract through a cheese cloth into the hot *velouté.*

Season to taste.

NOTE: Depending on the application, the paprika sauce should be made with the *velouté* which corresponds to the dish, for instance, chicken paprika sauce should be made with chicken *velouté.*

VARIATION

In place of the *velouté*, use 1 pt 11 oz (800 ml) of Bechamel sauce (Recipe 34), and add 2/3 oz (20 ml) Red Pepper Coulis (Recipe 79).

---

[a] Curaçao is an orange-flavored liqueur, originally made with bitter oranges which grew wild on the island of the same name. It is now made in many countries. It is available in many colors, the most common being blue. The color has no bearing on taste. For this recipe, an orange color is recommended.

79

ℛed Pepper Coulis

Peperoni-Coulis
Coulis de poivrons

YIELD: 1 QT 2 OZ (1 L)

Onions	7 oz	200 g
Garlic clove, peeled	1	1
Red peppers	4 lb 7 oz	2.0 kg
Sunflower oil	1 2/3 oz	50 ml
Seasoning (salt)	1x	1x
Seasoning	1x	1x
Butter	1 2/3 oz	50 g

MISE EN PLACE
Cut onions and garlic into thin slices.

Split peppers, remove seeds, and wash. Cut into large dice.

METHOD
Sauté onions and garlic briefly in oil.

Add red peppers and continue cooking, season with salt.

Steam mixture for 5 minutes until soft.

Strain vegetables through a fine wire sieve.[a]

Reduce purée to about 1 qt 2 oz (1.0 L).

Season to taste.

Heat butter until foamy and add to sauce. (If coulis is to be used cold, add a little vinegar instead of butter.)

APPLICATIONS
Serve with sautéed or grilled beef dishes.

Serve with grilled ocean fishes and crustaceans.

Use as an ingredient in white sauces.

80

ℳint Sauce

Pfefferminzsauce
Sauce menthe

YIELD: 1 QT 2 OZ (1 L)

Peppermint, fresh	14 oz	400 g
Crystal sugar	5 oz	140 g
White wine vinegar	13 1/2 oz	400 ml
Water	13 1/2 oz	400 ml
Seasoning	1x	1x

MISE EN PLACE
Wash peppermint. Chop leaves fine.

METHOD
Caramelize sugar to light brown color.

Carefully add vinegar and water, while bringing to a boil.

Add boiling liquid to the chopped peppermint leaves. Let cool.

APPLICATION
Serve with roasted lamb.

81

𝒫iquant Sauce

Pikante Sauce
Sauce piquante

YIELD: 1 QT 2 OZ (1 L)

Shallots	1 1/3 oz	40 g
White peppercorns	1/6 oz	5 g
Cornichons,[a] drained	3 oz	80 g
Tarragon, fresh	1/3 oz	10 g
Parsley, fresh	1/3 oz	10 g
Dry white wine	10 oz	300 ml
Demi-glace (Recipe 44)	1 pt 14 oz	900 ml
Sachet bag	1	1
Seasoning (salt, cayenne)	1x	1x
Butter	1 oz	30 g

---

[a] If peppers are peeled before cooking, a food processor can be used to purée them.

[a] Cornichons are tiny, somewhat acidic pickles. Good-quality dill pickles can be substituted, but seeds should be removed.

MISE EN PLACE

Cut shallots into thin slices.

Crush peppercorns.

Chop together cornichons, tarragon and parsley; and reserve for garnish.

METHOD

Combine shallots and peppercorns with wine; reduce to about 1 2/3 oz (50 ml).

Add *demi-glace* and sachet bag and simmer for about 10 minutes.

Strain through fine mesh china cap and season to taste.

Add the butter in small nuggets, without letting the sauce boil.

Add the chopped garnish.

APPLICATIONS

Serve with grilled or sautéed pork dishes.

Serve with boiled ox or veal tongue.

`83`

$\mathcal{P}$ortuguese Sauce

Portugiesische Sauce
Sauce portugaise

YIELD: 1 QT 2 OZ (1 L)

Onions	8 3/4 oz	250 g
Glace de viande[a]	1 2/3 oz	50 g
Parsley	1/3 oz	10 g
Butter	1 2/3 oz	50 g
Tomato concassé (Recipe 97)	1 pt 11 oz	800 ml
Seasoning	1x	1x

MISE EN PLACE

Chop onions fine.

Melt *glace de viande*.

Chop parsley.

METHOD

Smother onions in butter until soft.

Add tomato *concassé* and bring to boil.

Add parsley and *glace de viande*.

Season to taste.

---

[a] *Glace de viande*, literally translated "meat glaze," is made by reducing meat stock to a syrupy consistency.

`83`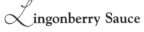

$\mathcal{L}$ingonberry Sauce

Preiselbeersauce
Sauce aux airelles rouges

YIELD: 1 QT 2 OZ (1 L)

Lingonberries, fresh[a]	1 lb 2 oz	500 g
Glucose syrup	3 1/2 oz	100 g
Crystal sugar	10 1/2 oz	300 g
Red wine	3 1/3 oz	100 ml
Red wine vinegar	1 2/3 oz	50 ml

METHOD

Pick over lingonberries and wash.

Combine glucose, sugar, wine, and vinegar. Bring to a boil and skim.

Remove syrup from heat.

Add the berries to the syrup.

Let cool.

APPLICATION

Serve with boiled beef, roast pork, poultry, or game.

`84`

$\mathcal{P}$rovencale Sauce

Provenzalische Sauce
Sauce provençale

YIELD: 1 QT 2 OZ (1 L)

Black canned olives, drained	3 oz	80 g
Parsley	1/3 oz	10 g
Tomato concassé (Recipe 97)	1 pt 14 oz	900 ml
Seasoning	1x	1x

METHOD

Cut olives into slivers, small dice, or slices.

Chop parsley.

Add olives and parsley to tomato *concassé* and bring to a boil.

Season to taste

---

[a] Lingonberries are related to cranberries, but smaller. If cranberries are substituted, they should be boiled for 10 minutes.

85

Cottage Cheese Mayonnaise

Quarkmayonnaise
Mayonnaise au séré

YIELD: 1 QT 2 OZ (1 L)

Mayonnaise (Recipe 71)	1 lb 5 oz	600 g
Cottage cheese, low fat[a]	14 oz	400 g
Seasoning (salt, cayenne)	1x	1x
Seasoning (lemon juice)	1x	1x

METHOD
Combine mayonnaise with cottage cheese and stir until smooth.

Season well with salt, cayenne, and lemon juice.

86

Brown Cream Sauce

Rahmsauce
Sauce à la crème

YIELD: 1 QT 2 OZ (1 L)

Shallots	1 1/3 oz	40 g
Mushrooms, fresh	3 1/2 oz	100 g
Butter	1 1/3 oz	40 g
Dry white wine	3 1/3 oz	100 ml
Demi-glace (Recipe 44)	1 pt 8 oz	700 ml
Heavy cream (36%)	13 1/2 oz	400 ml
Seasoning	1x	1x
Butter, cold	1 oz	30 g

MISE EN PLACE
Chop shallots fine.

Clean, wash, and thinly slice mushrooms.

METHOD
Smother shallots in butter.

Add mushrooms and continue cooking.

Add white wine and reduce.

Add *demi-glace* and simmer for 10 minutes.

Add cream and bring to a rolling boil.

Strain through fine mesh china cap.

Discard mushrooms.

Season to taste.

Add cold butter to sauce in small nuggets, over low flame, without allowing sauce to return to a boil.

APPLICATION
Serve with sautéed white meat dishes.

NOTE: Mushroom trimmings or mushroom stock can be used instead of fresh mushrooms.

87

Ravigote Sauce

Ravigote-Sauce
Sauce ravigote

YIELD: 1 QT 2 OZ (1 L)

Cornichons,[a] canned, drained	4 1/4 oz	120 g
Capers, canned, drained	1 2/3 oz	50 g
Herb vinaigrette (Recipe 49)	1 pt 11 oz	800 ml
Seasoning	1x	1x

METHOD
Chop capers and cornichons and add to herb vinaigrette.

Season to taste.

APPLICATIONS
Serve with cold boiled beef, calves' head, or lamb.

Serve with mussel salad or boiled vegetables.

---

[a] The original recipe calls for *Quark*, a generic German word for cottage cheese. The cottage cheese for this recipe should be fine curd and strained. Skim-milk ricotta cheese makes a good substitute.

[a] Cornichons are tiny, somewhat acidic pickles. Good-quality dill pickles can be substituted, but seeds should be removed.

88

ℛemoulade Sauce

Remouladensauce
Sauce rémoulade

YIELD: 1 QT 2 OZ (1 L)

Anchovy fillets, canned, drained	1/3 oz	10 g
Capers, canned, drained	1 1/3 oz	40 g
Parsley	1/3 oz	10 g
Tarragon, fresh	1/3 oz	10 g
Onions	3 1/2 oz	100 g
Mayonnaise (Recipe 71)	1 lb 5 oz	600 g
Cottage cheese, low fat[a]	3 1/2 oz	100 g
Seasoning (salt, cayenne)	1x	1x

MISE EN PLACE
Purée or mash anchovy fillets.

Chop capers.

Wash herbs; chop leaves fine.

Peel onions and chop fine.

METHOD
Combine all ingredients with the mayonnaise.

Season well with salt and cayenne.

APPLICATION
Serve with deep-fried fish.

NOTE: If pickled onions are used instead of fresh onions, the sauce can be stored longer.

89

ℛed Butter Sauce (for fish)

Rote Buttersauce
Beurre rouge

YIELD: 1 PT 1 OZ (1/2 L)

Butter	12 oz	350 g
Glace de poisson[a]	1 2/3 oz	50 ml
Chicken stock (Recipe 26)	1 2/3 oz	50 ml
Bordeaux red wine	5 oz	150 ml
Lemon	1/2	1/2
Seasoning (salt and pepper)	1x	1x

MISE EN PLACE
Cut butter into cubes and keep cold.

METHOD
Combine *glace de poisson*, chicken stock, and red wine. Reduce to about one-third.

Remove from heat.

Whip cold butter into hot sauce in small quantities until creamy.

Season with lemon juice, salt, and pepper.

APPLICATION
Serve with grilled fish.

---

[a] The original recipe calls for *quark*, a generic German word for cottage cheese. The cottage cheese for this recipe should be fine curd and strained. Skim-milk ricotta cheese makes a good substitute.

[a] *Glace de poisson*, literally translated "fish glaze," is made by reducing fish fumet to a syrupy consistency. It can have an unpleasant taste if the fish bones used for the fumet are not very fresh.

90

Sour Cream Sauce

Sauerrahmsauce
Sauce smitane

YIELD: 1 QT 2 OZ (1 L)

Onions	14 oz	400 g
Garlic cloves, peeled	2	2
Butter	1 2/3 oz	50 g
Thyme sprig, fresh	1	1
Dry white wine	3 1/3 oz	100 ml
White veal stock (Recipe 28)	6 3/4 oz	200 ml
Sour cream[a]	1 qt 2 oz	1.0 L
Cornstarch	1/3 oz	10 g
Seasoning (salt, cayenne)	1x	1x

MISE EN PLACE
Cut onions and garlic into fine slices.

METHOD
Smother onions and garlic in butter and add thyme sprig.

Add wine and reduce completely.

Add veal stock and reduce again almost completely.

Add sour cream, bring to a boil, and simmer for a few minutes.

Strain through fine mesh china cap.

Make a slurry with a little cold wine and cornstarch; add to sauce.

Bring to a boil again. Season with salt and cayenne.

Stir sauce well.[b]

APPLICATION
Serve with sautéed game or veal dishes.

91

Mousseline Sauce

Schaumsauce
Sauce mousseline

YIELD: 1 QT 2 OZ (1 L)

Hollandaise sauce (Recipe 60)	1 pt 14 oz	900 ml
Heavy cream (36%)	3 1/3 oz	100 ml
Seasoning (salt, lemon juice)	1x	1x

METHOD, VARIATION 1
Whip cream until stiff and fold into Hollandaise sauce just before service.

Season with salt and lemon juice.

METHOD, VARIATION 2
Season Hollandaise sauce with additional salt and lemon juice.

Whip cream until stiff. When sauce is ready to be served in sauce boats, pipe a small rosette on top with a pastry bag.

APPLICATION
Serve with hot asparagus or poached fish.

92

Mustard Cream Sauce

Senfrahmsauce
Sauce allemande à la moutarde

YIELD: 1 QT 2 OZ (1 L)

Shallots	2 oz	60 g
Butter	1 2/3 oz	50 g
Dry white wine	3 1/3 oz	100 ml
Creamed veal velouté sauce (Recipe 45)	1 pt 14 oz	900 ml
Prepared mild Dijon-style mustard	3 oz	80 g
Seasoning	1x	1x

METHOD
Chop shallots and smother in butter until cooked.

Add wine and reduce.

Add creamed veal *velouté* and bring to a boil.

---

[a] Swiss sour cream is more liquid than U.S. sour cream. It is advisable to thin U.S. sour cream with about 30% buttermilk.

[b] A hand-held electric mixer should be used to homogenize the sauce.

Cool the sauce slightly and stir in the mustard.

Season to taste. Do not boil the sauce again, as it will curdle.

APPLICATION
Serve with boiled calves' tongue, poached sweetbreads, or boiled lamb.

93

rown Mustard Sauce

Senfsauce
Sauce Robert

YIELD: 1 QT 2 OZ (1 L)

Butter	1 oz	30 g
Dijon mustard	1 oz	30 g
Onions	3 1/2 oz	100 g
Dry white wine	6 3/4 oz	200 ml
Demi-glace (Recipe 44)	1 pt 14 oz	900 ml
Seasoning	1x	1x

MISE EN PLACE
Soften butter.

Combine soft butter with mustard.

Chop onions fine.

METHOD
Combine onions and white wine and reduce.

Add *demi-glace* and boil for 10 minutes.

Strain through fine mesh china cap.

Whip in mustard butter. Do not allow to boil again.

Season to taste.

APPLICATION
Serve with sautéed pork dishes.

94

*M*ustard Sauce for Gravad Lax

Senfsauce für Gravad Lax
Sauce moutarde pour gravad lax

YIELD: FOR 10 SERVINGS

Red currant jelly	2/3 oz	20 g
Prepared mild Dijon-style mustard	3 1/2 oz	100 g
Egg yolk[a]	1	1
Crystal sugar	1 oz	30 g
White wine vinegar	1 2/3 oz	50 ml
Sunflower oil	3 1/3 oz	100 ml
Dill, fresh	2/3 oz	20 g
Seasoning (salt and pepper)	2x	2x

MISE EN PLACE
Melt red currant jelly.

METHOD
Combine mustard, egg yolk, sugar, and vinegar. Stir until sugar is dissolved.

Add oil in a thin stream and mix well until it becomes mayonnaise.

Add the melted red currant jelly and chopped dill.

Season to taste.

[a] Raw egg yolks can cause salmonella food poisoning. Using pasturized egg yolks is recommended.

95

Cream Sauce with Fresh Porcini

Steinpilzrahmsauce
Sauce aux cèpes

YIELD: 1 QT 2 OZ (1 L)

Porcini mushrooms[a]	10 1/2 oz	300 g
Shallots	1 oz	30 g
Cream sauce (Recipe 40)	1 pt 11 oz	800 ml
Butter	1 2/3 oz	50 g
Dry white wine	3 1/3 oz	100 ml
Seasoning	1x	1x

MISE EN PLACE
Clean, wash, and slice mushrooms.

Chop shallots.

Have cream sauce ready.

METHOD
Smother shallots in butter.

Add the prepared mushrooms, and continue cooking.

Add wine and continue cooking.

Drain mushrooms, squeeze out juice, and set aside the mushrooms.

Save juice; reduce mushroom juice to a glaze.

Add cream sauce to the glaze. Add in mushrooms.

Bring sauce to a boil, simmer for a few minutes, and season to taste.

APPLICATIONS
Serve as a second sauce (beside roasting juice) with roasted, braised, or lightly glazed entrees.

Serve with sautéed light dishes, or with vegetable or pasta dishes.

---

[a] Porcini are wild mushrooms, called *cèpes* in French, *Steinpilze* in German, and *porcini* in Italian. These mushrooms are widely available dried, and are increasingly available fresh. Because Italy is a large exporter of these mushrooms, the Italian name is commonly used.

96

Tartar Sauce

Tartarensauce
Sauce tartare

YIELD: 1 QT 2 OZ (1 L)

Eggs	4	4
Cornichons,[a] canned, drained	3 1/2 oz	100 g
Chives, fresh	2/3 oz	20 g
Cottage cheese,[b] low fat	3 1/2 oz	100 g
Mayonnaise (Recipe 71)	1 lb 5 oz	600 g
Seasoning (salt, cayenne)	1x	1x

MISE EN PLACE
Boil eggs. Chill, peel, and chop.

Chop cornichons.

Cut chives into fine slivers.

METHOD
Blend all ingredients with mayonnaise.

Season to taste.

APPLICATION
Serve with cold roasts or cold egg dishes.

97

Tomato Concassé

Tomaten-Concassé
Tomates concassées

YIELD: 1 QT 2 OZ (1 L)

Tomatoes	4 lb 7 oz	2.0 kg
Shallots	1 2/3 oz	50 g
Garlic	1/6 oz	5 g
Olive oil	1 2/3 oz	50 ml
Tomato puree	3 oz	80 g
Seasoning	1x	1x

MISE EN PLACE
Dip tomatoes in boiling water for 3 to 4 seconds, and chill immediately in ice water.

---

[a] Cornichons are tiny, somewhat acidic pickles. Good-quality dill pickles can be substituted, but seeds should be removed.

[b] The original recipe calls for *Quark*, a generic German word for cottage cheese. The cottage cheese for this recipe should be fine curd and strained. Skim-milk ricotta cheese makes a good substitute.

Peel tomatoes, cut in half, remove seeds, and chop into small dice.

Chop shallots.

Crush garlic into a fine paste.

METHOD
Sauté shallots in oil.

Add garlic and tomato puree and continue cooking.

Add diced tomatoes and smother carefully for about 1 minute.

Season with salt and freshly ground pepper.

98

Tomato Coulis

Tomaten-Coulis
Coulis de tomates

YIELD: 1 QT 2 OZ (1 L)

Onions	7 oz	200 g
Garlic clove, peeled	1	1
Tomatoes	5 lb 8 oz	2.5 kg
Olive oil	1 2/3 oz	50 ml
Tomato puree	3 1/2 oz	100 g
Seasoning	1x	1x
Butter	1/6 oz	5 g

MISE EN PLACE
Chop onions and garlic.

Dip tomatoes in boiling water for 3 to 4 seconds and chill immediately in ice water.

Peel tomatoes, cut in half, remove seeds, and chop into cubes.

METHOD
Smother onions and garlic in olive oil.

Add tomato puree and continue cooking.

Add chopped tomatoes, cover pot, and braise in oven for about 15 minutes.

Strain through fine wire sieve.[a]

Reduce resulting puree to about 1 qt 2 oz (1.0 L).

Heat butter until foamy and add to sauce. (If coulis is to be used cold, add a little vinegar instead of butter.)

[a] A food processor can be used.

APPLICATIONS
Serve with sautéed or grilled beef dishes.

Serve with grilled ocean fishes or crustaceans.

99

Tomato Sauce

Tomatensauce
Sauce tomate

YIELD: 1 QT 2 OZ (1 L)

Tomatoes	1 lb 12 oz	800 g
Sachet bag	1	1
Matignon (Recipe 14)	5 1/3 oz	150 g
Butter	3 oz	80 g
Garlic, crushed	1/6 oz	5 g
Tomato puree	8 3/4 oz	250 g
White wheat flour	1/3 oz	10 g
White veal stock (Recipe 28)	1 pt 8 oz	700 ml
Salt (pinch)	1x	1x
Crystal sugar (pinch)	1x	1x
Seasoning	1x	1x

MISE EN PLACE
Dip tomatoes in boiling water for 3 to 4 seconds and chill immediately in ice water.

Peel tomatoes, cut in half, remove seeds, and chop into cubes.

Make sachet bag consisting of basil, thyme, and crushed peppercorns.

METHOD
Braise *matignon* in butter.

Add garlic and tomato puree and continue cooking.

Dust with flour, stir well, and cook briefly.

Add diced tomatoes and veal stock.

Bring to a boil and skim.

Add sachet bag, salt, and sugar.

Simmer for 1 hour.

Season to taste and strain through fine mesh china cap.

NOTE: When tomatoes are not in season, it is advisable to use canned crushed tomatoes instead of lesser quality fresh tomatoes.

100

*T*omato Vinaigrette

Tomaten-Vinaigrette
Vinaigrette aux tomates

YIELD: 1 QT 2 OZ (1 L)

Tomatoes	1 lb 5 oz	600 g
Herb vinaigrette (Recipe 49)	1 pt 8 oz	700 ml
Seasoning	1x	1x

METHOD

Dip tomatoes in boiling water for 3 to 4 seconds and chill immediately in ice water.

Peel tomatoes, cut in half, remove seeds, and chop into cubes.

Add chopped tomatoes to herb vinaigrette.

Season to taste.

APPLICATIONS

Serve with vegetable terrines.

Serve with boiled cold vegetables (asparagus, artichoke bottoms).

Use as a marinade for poached warm fish or fish salad.

101

*T*ruffle Sauce

Trüffelsauce
Sauce Périgueux

YIELD: 1 QT 2 OZ (1 L)

Shallots	1 1/3 oz	40 g
Black truffles	1 oz	30 g
Madeira wine	1 2/3 oz	50 ml
Red wine	6 3/4 oz	200 ml
Demi-glace (Recipe 44)	1 pt 14 oz	900 ml
Butter, cold	1 oz	30 g
Seasoning	1x	1x

MISE EN PLACE

Chop shallots fine.

Chop truffles fine and boil with Madeira wine until reduced.

METHOD

Boil red wine and shallots until reduced.

Add *demi-glace* and bring to boil.

Strain sauce over truffles through fine mesh china cap.

Bring to a boil again and simmer for 5 minutes.

Add cold butter in small nuggets. Do not allow sauce to return to a boil.

Season to taste.

APPLICATION

Serve with roast meat or poultry.

102

*B*eurre Blanc (for fish)

Weisse Buttersauce
Beurre blanc

YIELD: 1 PT 1 OZ (1/2 L)

Butter	12 oz	350 g
Glace de poisson[a]	1 2/3 oz	50 ml
Chicken stock (Recipe 26)	1 2/3 oz	50 ml
Dry white wine	1 2/3 oz	50 ml
Lemon	1/2	1/2
Seasoning (salt and pepper)	1x	1x

MISE EN PLACE

Cut butter into cubes and chill.

METHOD

Combine *glace de poisson*, chicken stock, and white wine. Bring to a boil. Remove from stove.

Add cold butter to sauce in small amounts and whip until creamy.

Season with lemon juice, salt, and pepper.

NOTE: *Beurre blanc* for meat and vegetables is made with reduced chicken stock, but without the *glace de poisson*. *Glace de viande* is not used, as this would make the sauce too brown.

---

[a] *Glace de poisson*, literally translated "fish glaze," is made by reducing fish fumet to a syrupy consistency. It can have an unpleasant taste if the fish bones used for the fumet are not very fresh.

103

$\mathcal{W}$hite Wine Sauce (for fish)

Weissweinsauce
Sauce au vin blanc

YIELD: 1 QT 2 OZ (1 L)

Fish stock,[a] poaching liquid	10 oz	300 ml
Heavy cream (36%)	8 1/2 oz	250 ml
Fish velouté sauce (Recipe 53)	1 pt 8 oz	700 ml
Seasoning (salt, cayenne)	1x	1x
Seasoning (lemon juice)	1x	1x

METHOD
Reduce fish stock to a glaze.

Add glaze and cream to fish *velouté*; boil for 5 minutes.

Strain through cheesecloth.

Season with salt, cayenne, and lemon juice.

APPLICATION
Use as a basic ingredient in white fish sauces.

104

$\mathcal{W}$hite Wine Sauce (made to order)[b]

Weissweinsauce (Zubereitung à la minute)
Sauce au vin blanc (à la minute)

YIELD: 1 QT 2 OZ (1 L)

Heavy cream (36%)	12 oz	350 ml
Cornstarch	2/3 oz	20 g
Egg yolks	2	2
Fish fumet (Recipe 25)	1 qt 2 oz	1.0 L
Appropriate fish stock[c]	10 oz	300 ml
Seasoning	1x	1x
Butter, cold	2 2/3 oz	75 g

MISE EN PLACE
Combine cream, cornstarch, and egg yolks; stir well.

METHOD
Combine fish fumet and fish stock and reduce to about 1 pt 1 oz (500 ml).

Remove from heat. Add cream/cornstarch/egg yolk mixture.

Bring to a boil, stirring with wire whip.

Strain immediately through fine mesh china cap.

Season to taste.

Warm, but do not return to a boil. Add cold butter in small nuggets.

105

$\mathcal{W}$hite Wine Sauce with Saffron (for fish)

Weissweinsauce mit Safranfäden
Sauce vin blanc aux pistils de safran

YIELD: 1 QT 2 OZ (1 L)

Fish fumet (Recipe 25)	1 oz	30 ml
Saffron, dried	1 pinch	1/2 g
White wine sauce (Recipe 103)	1 qt 2 oz	1.0 L

METHOD
Combine fish fumet and saffron; simmer for 10 minutes.

Add strained white wine sauce and boil for 5 minutes.

---

[a] Using the poaching liquid gives the sauce the character of the particular fish.

[b] Because the sauce is *à la minute*, (made at the last minute), keep the fish warm while preparing the sauce.

[c] Using the poaching liquid gives the sauce the character of the particular fish.

106

Game Demi-Glace
Wild Demi-glace
Demi-glace de gibier

YIELD: 10 1/2 QT (10.0 L)

Game bones	22 lb	10.0 kg
Game meat trimmings	2 lb 3 oz	1.0 kg
Sachet bag	1	1
Peanut oil	3 1/3 oz	100 ml
Mirepoix (Recipe 15)	2 lb 3 oz	1.0 kg
Tomato puree	7 oz	200 g
Red wine	1 qt 2 oz	1.0 L
Brown veal stock (Recipe 23)	5 gal 36 oz	20.0 L
Beurre manie[a]	1 lb 2 oz	500 g

MISE EN PLACE

Chop game bones and meat trimmings into small pieces.

Make sachet bag consisting of thyme, bay leaves, peppercorns, juniper berries, and dried porcini.[b]

METHOD

Heat oil in suitable roasting pan and brown bones on all sides.

Add game trimmings and continue to brown.

Drain off excessive oil, add *mirepoix*, and roast for a short time.

Add tomato puree and continue roasting.

Add red wine and boil down until almost reduced.

Add 2 1/2 qt veal stock and reduce again.

Pour mixture into a steam kettle or large pot, including all pan drippings.

Add remaining veal stock, bring to a boil, and skim.

Simmer for 3 hours.

Add sachet bag and simmer 1/2 hour longer.

Strain through fine mesh china cap, and then through cheesecloth.

Add *beurre manie* in small amounts, stirring continuously.

Bring to a boil and reduce to 10 1/2 qt (10.0 L).

Strain through fine mesh china cap.

107

Game Cream Sauce
Wildrahmsauce
Sauce crème gibier

YIELD: 1 QT 2 OZ (1 L)

Shallots	1 1/3 oz	40 g
Mushrooms, fresh	3 1/2 oz	100 g
Butter	1 1/3 oz	40 g
Red wine	3 1/3 oz	100 ml
Game demi-glace (Recipe 106)	1 pt 8 oz	700 ml
Heavy cream (36%)	13 1/2 oz	400 ml
Red currant jelly	1 2/3 oz	50 g
Seasoning	1x	1x
Gin	1/8 oz	25 ml
Butter, cold	1 oz	25 g

MISE EN PLACE

Peel shallots and chop fine.

Clean, wash, and slice mushrooms.

METHOD

Sauté shallots in butter.

Add mushrooms and continue cooking.

Add red wine and reduce.

Add game *demi-glace*, bring to a boil, and simmer for 10 minutes.

Add cream and red currant jelly; bring to a boil again.

Strain through fine mesh china cap.

Add gin; season to taste.

Add cold butter in small nuggets into warm sauce; do not allow sauce to return to a boil.

APPLICATION

Serve with sautéed or oven-roasted game.

---

[a] *Beurre manie* consists of equal parts cold butter and flour, kneaded together. It is used as a thickening agent, and is also called "cold roux."

[b] Porcini are wild mushrooms, called *cèpes* in French, *Steinpilze* in German, and *porcini* in Italian. These mushrooms are widely available dried, and are increasingly available fresh. Because Italy is a large exporter of these mushrooms, the Italian name is commonly used.

108

$\mathcal{O}$nion Sauce

Zwiebelsauce
Sauce lyonnaise

YIELD: 1 QT 2 OZ (1 L)

Onions	1 lb	450 g
Parsley	1/3 oz	10 g
Butter	3 oz	80 g
Dry white wine	3 1/3 oz	100 ml
White wine vinegar	1 2/3 oz	50 ml
Demi-glace (Recipe 44)	1 pt 11 oz	800 ml
Seasoning	1x	1x

MISE EN PLACE
Peel onions, cut in half, and slice.

Chop parsley.

METHOD
Smother onions in butter until about three-quarters cooked.

Add wine and vinegar and boil down until almost reduced.

Add *demi-glace* and simmer for 5 minutes.

Season to taste and add parsley.

APPLICATION
Serve with grilled sausages (bratwurst) or boiled beef gratiné (*miroton de boeuf*).

109

$\mathcal{O}$nion Purée

Zwiebelpüreesauce zum Gratinieren
Sauce Soubise à gratiner

YIELD: 1 QT 2 OZ (1 L)

Onions	3 lb 5 oz	1.5 kg
Rice[a]	5 1/3 oz	150 g
White veal stock (Recipe 28)	1 pt 1 oz	500 ml
Seasoning (salt)	1x	1x
Heavy cream (36%)	3 1/3 oz	100 ml
Egg yolks	4	4
Seasoning (salt, cayenne)	1x	1x

MISE EN PLACE
Cut onions into thin slices.

Precook rice and onions for 3 minutes in plenty of water.

Drain rice; do not rinse.

METHOD
Combine onions and rice with veal stock; salt slightly.

Steam[b] for about 10 minutes (rice and onions must be pre-cooked).

Purée rice mixture and strain through wire sieve.[c]

Boil down puree until no longer runny.

Combine cream and egg yolk and beat in a steam table until creamy.

Fold cream mixture into hot, but not boiling, rice puree.

Season with salt and cayenne.

APPLICATIONS
Use as a component in a number of classical dishes.

Use to gratin vegetables.

---

[a] The recipe specifies Vialone rice, which is a short-grain rice similar to Arborio. Virtually any rice will work.

[b] Be sure the rice is well cooked; 10 minutes cooking time might not be enough for all rice varieties.

[c] A food processor can be used.

Soups

Soups

Cream of Artichoke Soup

Artischokencremesuppe
Crème d'artichauts

YIELD: 2 QT 20 OZ (2.5 L)

Onions	2 oz	60 g
Leeks	2 oz	60 g
Knob celery (celeriac)	2 oz	60 g
Artichokes, large	3	3
Lemon	1/2	1/2
Butter	1 1/3 oz	40 g
White wheat flour	3 oz	80 g
Vegetable bouillon (Recipe 27)	2 qt 20 oz	2.5 L
Milk	3 1/3 oz	100 ml
Heavy cream (36%)	12 oz	350 ml
Seasoning	1x	1x

MISE EN PLACE

Peel onions; cut into small dice.

Wash and trim leeks; be sure sand is cleaned from layers. Cut into small dice.

Trim and wash knob celery and cut into small dice.

Trim artichokes; rub cut parts with lemon juice. Boil in salted water until tender; let cool. Remove center fuzz. Remove leaves and save to make soup.

Reserve tender center artichoke leaves for garnish. Cut artichoke bottoms into small dice for garnish.

Bring vegetable stock to a boil.

METHOD

Sauté diced onions, leeks, and knob celery in butter.

Add artichoke leaves saved for soup (not diced bottoms) and continue cooking.

Sprinkle with flour, stir and cook a few minutes longer, and cool slightly.

Add vegetable stock, bring to a boil, and simmer until vegetables are soft.

Strain, and press vegetable soup through a china cap.

Strain again through cheesecloth.

Add milk and heavy cream, bring to a boil, and season to taste.

Add diced artichoke bottoms.

Garnish with reserved center leaves.

Old-Fashioned Onion Soup

Basler Mehlsuppe[a]

YIELD: 2 QT 20 OZ (2.5 L)

Onions	1 lb 9 oz	700 g
Whole wheat flour	7 oz	200 g
Vegetable shortening	3 oz	80 g
Bouillon (Recipe 22)	3 qt 5 oz	3.0 L
Red wine	6 3/4 oz	200 ml
Seasoning	1x	1x
Sbrinz, grated[b]	3 1/2 oz	100 g

MISE EN PLACE

Peel, slice, or chop onions.

Roast flour in cast iron pan in slow oven until evenly brown; let flour cool.

METHOD

Sauté onions in shortening.

Dust with the roasted flour and mix well; let mixture cool in pot.

Add hot bouillon; stir well until soup starts to boil.

Add red wine, skim, and simmer for at least 1 hour.

Strain through fine mesh china cap.

Season to taste.

Serve with grated cheese on the side.

---

[a] Basel is a city in Switzerland. This soup is a specialty item, always referred to by its Swiss-German name, *Basler Mehlsuppe*.

[b] Sbrinz is a hard grating cheese from Switzerland. Parmesan can be substituted.

112

*P*urée of Cauliflower Soup

Blumekohlpüreesuppe
Purée Dubarry

YIELD: 2 QT 20 OZ (2.5 L)

Cauliflower, fresh	2 lb 3 oz	1.0 kg
Onions	3 1/2 oz	100 g
Knob celery (celeriac)	1 1/3 oz	40 g
Leeks	3 1/2 oz	100 g
Potatoes	10 1/2 oz	300 g
Butter	2 oz	60 g
Bouillon (Recipe 22)	2 qt 20 oz	2.5 L
Seasoning	1x	1x
Heavy cream (36%)	3 1/3 oz	100 ml
Butter, cold	2/3 oz	20 g

MISE EN PLACE

Clean and trim cauliflower and cut into pieces. Save about 3 1/2 oz (100 g) small cauliflower florets for garnish; boil or steam florets.

Cut onions and knob celery into small dice.

Wash and trim leeks; be sure sand is cleaned from layers. Cut into small dice.

Peel and slice potatoes.

METHOD

Sauté onions, knob celery, and leeks in butter.

Add cauliflower (except florets).

Heat bouillon; add to vegetables; bring to a boil; skim; and simmer for 20 minutes.

Add potatoes and simmer for 20 minutes longer.

Purée[a] soup and strain through china cap.

Bring to a boil again; season.

Stir in cream. Add cold butter in small nuggets.

Garnish with cauliflower florets.

---

[a] This is best accomplished with a hand-held electric mixer.

113

*R*ed Beet Soup

Rote-Rüben-Suppe
Borscht

YIELD: 2 QT 20 OZ (2.5 L)

Leeks	7 oz	200 g
Savoy cabbage	5 1/3 oz	150 g
Onions	3 1/2 oz	100 g
Stalk celery[a]	3 1/2 oz	100 g
Fennel bulb (anise)	1 2/3 oz	50 g
Red beets, raw	1 lb 2 oz	500 g
Duckling, young, oven-ready	1 lb 12 oz	800 g
Peanut oil	1 oz	30 ml
Boiled beef[b]	10 1/2 oz	300 g
Bacon, boiled	3 1/2 oz	100 g
Sausages[c]	3 1/2 oz	100 g
Parsley	1/3 oz	10 g
Butter	1 2/3 oz	50 g
Bouillon (Recipe 22)	3 qt 5 oz	3.0 L
Seasoning	1x	1x
Sour cream	5 oz	150 ml

MISE EN PLACE

Wash and trim leeks; be sure sand is cleaned from layers. Cut into fine strips (*julienne*).

Cut cabbage, onions, celery, and fennel into fine strips (*julienne*).

Cut half of the beets into fine strips (*julienne*). Boil in a small amount of water for 10 minutes. Reserve for garnish.

Grate remaining beets and squeeze out juice. A food processor can be used to grate the beets. Squeeze juice by wringing in a wet cloth or rubbing through a fine mesh china cap. Discard the remaining beet pulp.

Season duckling and brown in peanut oil.

Cut boiled beef and bacon into small pieces.

Sauté sausages and cut into small pieces.

Wash parsley, remove stems, and chop leaves.

(continued on next page)

---

[a] The recipe specifies stalk celery, not knob celery. Stalk celery is called *Stangensellerie* in German, and is sometimes referred to in Europe as "English celery." In the United States, it is the standard celery, and is called simply celery.

[b] Any kind of lean boiled beef can be used.

[c] The recipe specifies *chipolata*, small white sausages. English breakfast sausages are a good substitute.

(continued from preceding page)

METHOD

Heat butter and sauté all vegetables, except reserved beet *julienne*.

Add bouillon; bring to a boil; add duckling; and boil until duckling is tender.

Remove duckling from stock, bone, and cut duckling meat into spoon-size pieces.

Return duckling pieces to bouillon, along with diced beef, bacon, and sausages. Bring to a boil once more. Skim.

Add reserved beet *julienne* and beet juice.

Season to taste.

Sprinkle soup with parsley and serve sour cream on the side.

NOTE: Serve immediately so beets will not lose color.

114

$\mathcal{B}$ouillabaisse

Bouillabaisse
Bouillabaisse marseillaise

YIELD: 3 QT 22 OZ (3.5 L)

Red snapper, gutted	1 lb 5 oz	600 g
St. Peter fish (John Dory), gutted	1 lb 5 oz	600 g
Dorade (sea bream), whole, gutted	1 lb 9 oz	700 g
Monkfish, whole, without head	1 lb 5 oz	600 g
Leeks	5 1/3 oz	150 g
Carrots	5 1/3 oz	150 g
Fennel bulb (anise)	5 1/3 oz	150 g
Olive oil	2 3/4 oz	80 ml
Fish stock (Recipe 24)	3 qt 5 oz	3.0 L
Lobster, live	1 lb 2 oz	500 g
Mussels, fresh	14 oz	400 g
Shallots	5 1/3 oz	150 g
Garlic	2/3 oz	20 g
Tomatoes	14 oz	400 g
Dill, fresh	1/6 oz	5 g
Chervil, fresh, chopped	1/6 oz	5 g
French bread (baguette)	7 oz	200 g
Clarified butter	1 1/3 oz	40 g
Saffron, dried	pinch	1/2 g
Dry white wine	10 oz	300 ml
Pernod[a]	1 oz	30 ml
Seasoning	2x	2x

[a] Pernod is an anise-flavored liqueur.

MISE EN PLACE

Bone all fish and cut into small pieces. Save bones and trimmings.

Wash and trim leeks; be sure sand is cleaned from layers. Cut into fine strips (*julienne*).

Cut carrots and fennel into fine strips (*julienne*). Save trimmings.

Sauté fish bones and vegetable trimmings in a small amount of olive oil.

Add fish stock, bring to a boil, and simmer for 20 minutes.

Kill lobster by plunging it head-first into boiling water. Poach lobster in fish stock. Shell lobster and cut meat into pieces.

Scrub mussels, steam separately, and remove from shells. Save mussel stock.

Chop shallots.

Crush garlic into a fine paste.

Blanch and peel tomatoes, remove seeds, and cut into dice.

Slice bread; sauté in butter; add half the garlic paste to butter before bread is brown; sauté until brown.

METHOD

Sauté shallots, remaining garlic, leeks, carrots, and fennel in olive oil.

Add saffron, wine, and the strained fish stock. Add mussel stock.

Simmer until vegetables are almost tender.

Add tomatoes and Pernod; season to taste.

Add fish pieces and mussels, steep for about 5 minutes, but do not boil.

Add lobster pieces.

Adjust seasoning; sprinkle with chopped herbs.

Serve with garlic toast on the side.

115

Cream of Broccoli Soup

Broccolicremesuppe
Crème de brocoli

YIELD: 2 QT 20 OZ (2.5 L)

Broccoli, fresh	2 lb 10 oz	1.2 kg
Vegetable bouillon (Recipe 27)	2 qt 20 oz	2.5 L
Onions	3 1/2 oz	100 g
Knob celery (celeriac)	1 1/3 oz	40 g
Leeks	3 1/2 oz	100 g
Butter	1 1/3 oz	40 g
White wheat flour	1 1/3 oz	40 g
Heavy cream (36%)	6 3/4 oz	200 ml
Milk	3 1/3 oz	100 ml
Seasoning	1x	1x

MISE EN PLACE

Clean and trim broccoli. Select 3 1/2 oz (100 g) broccoli rosettes for garnish; steam rosettes or boil in vegetable stock; save stock. Dice remaining broccoli.

Dice onions and knob celery.

Wash and trim leeks; be sure sand is cleaned from layers. Dice.

METHOD

Sauté onions, knob celery, and leeks in butter, add diced broccoli, and continue cooking.

Sprinkle with flour; let cool slightly.

Add hot stock and bring to a boil, while stirring.

Simmer, skimming occasionally, until vegetables are soft.

Purée[a] and strain through fine mesh china cap.

Bring to a boil again; add cream and milk.

Season to taste.

Garnish with broccoli florets.

---

[a] This is best accomplished with a hand-held electric mixer.

116

Barley Soup

Bündner Gerstensuppe

YIELD: 2 QT 20 OZ (2.5 L)

Great Northern beans[a]	2 2/3 oz	75 g
Onions	5 1/3 oz	150 g
Carrots	3 1/2 oz	100 g
Knob celery (celeriac)	1 2/3 oz	50 g
Leeks, green part only	5 1/3 oz	150 g
Ham, air-dried[b]	1 1/3 oz	40 g
Bündnerfleisch[c]	1 2/3 oz	50 g
Parsley	1/3 oz	10 g
Butter	1 oz	30 g
Barley, medium-size	4 1/4 oz	120 g
Bouillon (Recipe 22)	3 qt 5 oz	3.0 L
Seasoning	2x	2x
Heavy cream (36%)	6 3/4 oz	200 ml

MISE EN PLACE

Soak beans in cold water for 4 to 6 hours.

Peel and chop onions.

Clean carrots and knob celery and cut into small dice (*brunoise*).

Wash and trim leeks; be sure sand is cleaned from layers. Cut into small dice (*brunoise*).

Cut ham and *Bündnerfleisch* into small dice.

Wash parsley, remove stems, and chop.

METHOD

Sauté onions, knob celery, and leeks in butter.

Add barley and drained beans and continue cooking.

Add diced meats, bouillon, and seasoning.

Simmer until barley and beans are tender.

Add cream and adjust seasoning.

Sprinkle with parsley.

NOTE: Instead of bouillon, ham or veal stock can be substituted.

---

[a] Any kind of small white beans, such as Navy beans, can be used.

[b] This is a regional Swiss soup and the recipe calls for *Bündner Rohschinken*, a locally made ham. Prosciutto, or other air-dried ham, can be substituted.

[c] *Bündnerfleisch*, called *viande de grison* in French, is a Swiss air-dried lean beef.

117

Italian Vegetable Soup

Busecca

YIELD: 2 QT 20 OZ (2.5 L)

Borlotti beans[a]	2 oz	60 g
Onions	4 1/4 oz	120 g
Garlic	1/6 oz	5 g
Leeks, white part only	5 1/3 oz	150 g
Savoy cabbage	3 1/2 oz	100 g
Knob celery (celeriac)	3 1/2 oz	100 g
Carrots	5 1/3 oz	150 g
Potatoes	10 1/2 oz	300 g
Tomatoes	5 1/3 oz	150 g
Kalbsgekröse,[b] boiled	1 lb 2 oz	500 g
Marjoram twig, fresh	1	10 g
Parsley	1/3 oz	10 g
Butter	2 oz	60 g
Tomato paste	1 oz	30 g
Bouillon (Recipe 22)	2 qt 20 oz	2.5 L
Seasoning	1x	1x
Parmesan cheese, grated	3 1/2 oz	100 g

MISE EN PLACE

Soak borlotti beans in cold water for 4 to 6 hours. Boil beans in water until tender.

Chop onions.

Purée garlic.

Wash and trim leeks; be sure sand is cleaned from layers. Cut into fine slices (*paysanne*).

Cut cabbage, knob celery, and carrots into fine slices (*paysanne*).

Cut potatoes into fine slices, the same size as the other vegetables.

Peel, seed, and dice tomatoes.

Cut *Kalbsgekröse* into spoon-size pieces.

Chop herbs.

METHOD

Sauté onions and garlic in butter, add leeks and Savoy cabbage, and continue cooking. Add knob celery, carrots, tomato paste, and bouillon.

Bring to a boil, skim, and simmer until vegetables are tender.

Add potatoes and *Kalbsgekröse* and simmer for 10 minutes.

[a] Borlotti beans are dried, pink-speckled beans.

[b] *Kalbsgekröse*, called *fraise de veau* in French, is the net which holds the intestines in place. It is difficult to obtain in many areas, and tripe can be substituted.

Add the cooked borlotti beans. Season to taste.

Add diced tomatoes and herbs.

Serve with grated Parmesan on the side.

118

Cream of Mushroom Soup

Champignoncremesuppe
Crème de champignons

YIELD: 2 QT 20 OZ (2.5 L)

Mushrooms, fresh	1 lb 12 oz	800 g
Leeks, white part only	3 1/2 oz	100 g
Onions	3 1/2 oz	100 g
Knob celery (celeriac)	1 1/3 oz	40 g
Butter	1 1/3 oz	40 g
White wheat flour	3 oz	80 g
Vegetable bouillon (Recipe 27)	2 qt 4 oz	2.0 L
Mushroom stock[a]	1 pt 1 oz	500 ml
Heavy cream (36%)	6 3/4 oz	200 ml
Milk	3 1/3 oz	100 ml
Butter, cold	1/3 oz	10 g
Seasoning	1x	1x
Chervil, fresh, chopped	1/6 oz	5 g

MISE EN PLACE

Clean and wash mushrooms. Cut 3 1/2 oz (100 g) mushroom caps into *julienne* strips and reserve for garnish. Slice remaining mushrooms.

Wash and trim leeks; be sure sand is cleaned from layers. Dice.

Dice onions and knob celery.

Braise mushroom *julienne* quickly in 1/2 oz (13 g) butter.

METHOD

Sauté diced vegetables in remaining 1 oz (27 g) butter.

Add sliced mushrooms and continue cooking. Dust with flour. Let cool.

Heat vegetable stock and mushroom stock. Add to vegetable mixture.

Bring to a boil, skim, and simmer until all vegetables are soft.

Purée,[b] and strain through fine mesh china cap.

[a] Mushroom stock can be made with trimmings.

[b] This is best accomplished with a hand-held electric mixer.

Bring to a boil again and stir in cream and milk. Add 1/3 oz (10 g) cold butter in small nuggets.

Season to taste.

Garnish with mushroom *julienne*. Sprinkle with chervil.

119

Chicken Broth with Rice

YIELD: 2 QT 20 OZ (2.5 L)

Chicken, oven-ready	3 lb 5 oz	1.5 kg
Chicken stock (Recipe 26)	3 qt 5 oz	3.0 L
Onions	3 oz	80 g
Clove	1	1
Bay leaf	1	1
Leeks	7 oz	200 g
Carrots	7 oz	200 g
Knob celery (celeriac)	4 1/4 oz	120 g
Long-grain rice, parboiled	1 oz	30 g
Seasoning	2x	2x
Chervil, fresh, chopped	1 tbsp	2 g

MISE EN PLACE
Blanch chicken.

Bring chicken stock to a boil.

Trim and peel onion. Insert clove and bay leaf.[a]

Wash and trim leeks; be sure sand is cleaned from layers. Cut into fine strips (*julienne*).

Clean carrots and knob celery and cut into fine strips (*julienne*).

METHOD
Add chicken to stock, bring to a boil, and skim.

Add onion studded with clove and bay leaf. Poach until chicken is cooked.

Remove chicken, strain stock through double layer of cheesecloth. Reserve stock.

Skin and bone chicken, cut meat into spoon-size pieces, and keep warm in a little chicken stock.

Sauté vegetables in butter; add rice and chicken stock; bring to a boil; and simmer for 15 minutes. Add hot chicken pieces with the stock.

Season to taste. Sprinkle with chervil.

---

[a] The clove should be pressed into the peeled onion. To insert the bay leaf, a small incision must be made.

120

Clear Oxtail Soup

Klare Ochsenschwanzsuppe
Oxtail clair

YIELD: 2 QT 20 OZ (2.5 L)

Oxtails	2 lb 3 oz	1.0 kg
Calves' feet	10 1/2 oz	300 g
Clarification meat[a]	1 lb	450 g
Water	6 3/4 oz	200 ml
Matignon (Recipe 14)	5 1/3 oz	(150 g)
Tomatoes	1 2/3 oz	(50 g)
Egg whites	2	2
Leeks	3 1/2 oz	100 g
Carrots	5 1/3 oz	150 g
Knob celery (celeriac)	3 1/2 oz	100 g
Peanut oil	1 1/3 oz	40 ml
Mirepoix (Recipe 15)	5 1/3 oz	150 g
Tomato paste	2/3 oz	20 g
Red wine	6 3/4 oz	200 ml
Brown veal stock (Recipe 23)	4 qt 7 oz	4.0 L
Sherry wine, dry	1 2/3 oz	50 ml
Seasoning	1x	1x

MISE EN PLACE
Cut oxtails into pieces at the joints with a strong knife.

Split calves' feet lengthwise.

Grind clarification meat through coarse plate of meat grinder.

Make clarification by combining meat with water, *matignon*, diced tomatoes, and egg whites. Mix well and refrigerate at least 1 hour.

Wash and trim leeks; be sure sand is cleaned from layers.

Cut leeks, carrots, and knob celery into neat dice, a little larger than *brunoise*; boil in water or braise until just done.

METHOD
Roast oxtail pieces and calves' feet in oven until browned evenly.

Add *mirepoix* and continue roasting. Add tomato paste and continue roasting.

Add red wine and reduce.

(continued on next page)

---

[a] The clarification meat should be as lean as possible. Meat from beef shank is preferred because it is very lean and has a high gelatin content.

(continued from preceding page)

Put all above ingredients in a large pot and add veal stock.

Boil until oxtails are tender, about 3 to 4 hours.

Remove oxtails and calves' feet.

Strain stock through cheesecloth, save, and let cool.

Remove meat from oxtails, press into a loaf pan, and chill.

Cut chilled meat into small dice, and reserve for garnish.

Combine cold stock with clarification; stir with a paddle, until mixture starts to boil.

Do not stir any longer and simmer for 1 1/2 hours.

Strain carefully through a double layer of cheesecloth.

Remove all fat from surface with absorbent paper.

Season to taste.

Add sherry wine.

Garnish with oxtail meat and vegetables.

METHOD FOR GARNISH

Blanch tomatoes, peel, cut in half, remove seeds, and cut into small, even dice.

Cook rice in boiling salted water, rinse in cold water, and drain.

METHOD

Sauté leeks, onions, and knob celery in butter.

Dust with flour, continue cooking a short time longer, and let cool.

Add hot veal stock and return to a boil, while stirring.

Skim, and boil for at least 20 minutes.

Strain through fine mesh china cap. Bring to a boil again.

Stir in cream. Add cold butter in little nuggets.

Add tomato paste.

Season to taste.

Garnish with diced tomatoes and cooked rice.

121

Cream Soup with Rice and Tomatoes

Cremesuppe Carmen
Crème Carmen

YIELD: 2 QT 20 OZ (2.5 L)

Leeks, white part only	3 oz	80 g
Onions	3 oz	80 g
Knob celery (celeriac)	1 oz	30 g
White veal stock (Recipe 28)	2 qt 20 oz	2.5 L
Butter	1 2/3 oz	50 g
White wheat flour	3 oz	80 g
Heavy cream (36%)	10 oz	300 ml
Butter, cold	2/3 oz	20 g
Seasoning	1x	1x
Tomato paste	2 oz	60 g

GARNISH

Tomatoes	7 oz	200 g
Long-grain rice	2 oz	60 g

MISE EN PLACE

Wash and trim leeks; be sure sand is cleaned from layers. Cut into large dice.

Cut onions and knob celery into large dice.

Bring veal stock to a boil.

122

Double Consomme

Doppelte Kraftbrühe
Consommé double

YIELD: 2 QT 20 OZ (2.5 L)

Clarification meat[a]	2 lb	900 g
Carrots	3 oz	80 g
Knob celery (celeriac)	2 oz	60 g
Leeks	3 oz	80 g
Tomatoes	1 2/3 oz	50 g
Bay leaf	1/2	1/2
White peppercorns	5	5
Water	6 3/4 oz	200 ml
Bouillon (Recipe 22)	3 qt 5 oz	3.0 L
Seasoning	1x	1x

MISE EN PLACE

Grind clarification meat through coarse plate of meat grinder.

Cut carrots and knob celery into small dice.

Wash and trim leeks; be sure sand is cleaned from layers. Cut into small dice.

Cube tomatoes.

---

[a] The clarification meat should be as lean as possible. Meat from beef shank is preferred because it is very lean and has a high gelatin content.

Make clarification by combining meat, vegetables, spices, tomatoes, and water; refrigerate at least 1 hour.

METHOD

Blend clarification with cold bouillon.

Bring to a boil, stirring carefully with a paddle; do not stir after soup has started to boil.

Skim off fat and other impurities.

Let simmer for 1 1/2 hours. Strain carefully through double layer of cheesecloth.

Remove all fat floating on top with absorbent paper.

Season to taste.

NOTE: No egg whites are needed in this recipe because the amount of clarification meat is double that of a simple consomme.

123

Cold Strawberry Soup

Erdbeerkaltschale
Soupe froide aux fraises

YIELD: 1 QT 19 OZ (1.5 L)

Strawberries, fresh	1 lb 9 oz	700 g
Crystal sugar	3 1/2 oz	100 g
Water	1 pt 1 oz	500 ml
Lemon, zest	1	1
Orange, zest	1	1
Vanilla bean	1/2	1/2
Lemon juice	1 2/3 oz	50 ml
Orange juice	6 3/4 oz	200 ml

MISE EN PLACE

Clean and wash strawberries. Cut a few strawberries into small pieces and reserve as garnish. Purée remaining strawberries.

To make syrup, combine sugar, water, lemon zest, orange zest, and vanilla bean.

Bring to a boil, let cool, and strain.

METHOD

Combine strawberry puree with cold syrup.

Add lemon juice and orange juice.

Garnish with reserved strawberry pieces.

NOTE: If desired, a suitable liqueur (Curaçao, Grand Marnier, or Kirsch) can be added. Serve very cold, in a glass or bowl, with a straw and small spoon.

124

Cream Fish Soup (basic)

Fischcremesuppe (Basis)
Crème de poisson

YIELD: 2 QT 20 OZ (2.5 L)

Leeks, white part only	2 oz	60 g
Onions	2 oz	60 g
Knob celery (celeriac)	1 oz	30 g
Fish stock (Recipe 24)	2 qt 20 oz	2.5 L
Butter	1 2/3 oz	50 g
White wheat flour	3 oz	80 g
Heavy cream (36%)	10 oz	300 ml
Butter, cold	2/3 oz	20 g
Seasoning	1x	1x

MISE EN PLACE

Wash and trim leeks; be sure sand is cleaned from layers. Cut into small dice.

Cut onions and knob celery into small dice.

Bring fish stock to boil.

METHOD

Sauté vegetables in butter.

Dust with flour, continue cooking, and let cool.

Add fish stock to vegetable mixture, and bring to a boil, while stirring.

Skim and simmer for at least 20 minutes.

Strain through fine mesh china cap and bring to a boil again.

Stir in cream. Add cold butter in small nuggets.

Season to taste.

125

*F*ish and Mussels Soup with Cream

Fischcremesuppe mit Muscheln
Crème dieppoise

YIELD: 2 QT 20 OZ (2.5 L)

Leeks	2 oz	60 g
Onions	2 oz	60 g
Knob celery (celeriac)	1 oz	30 g
Fish stock (Recipe 24)	2 qt 20 oz	2.5 L
Butter	1 2/3 oz	50 g
White wheat flour	3 oz	80 g
Heavy cream (36%)	10 oz	300 ml
Butter	2/3 oz	20 g
Seasoning	1x	1x

GARNISH
Mussels, fresh	14 oz	400 g
Shallots	1 2/3 oz	50 g
Dry white wine	5 oz	150 ml
Butter, cold	2/3 oz	20 g
Shrimp, cooked	3 1/2 oz	100 g
Dill, fresh, chopped	1/6 oz	5 g

MISE EN PLACE
Wash and trim leeks; be sure sand is cleaned from layers. Cut into dice.

Cut onions and knob celery into dice.

Bring fish stock to a boil.

METHOD FOR GARNISH
Scrape and wash mussels thoroughly.

Peel and chop shallots.

Stew mussels and shallots in white wine in covered pot.

Remove mussels from stock and reserve stock.

Remove mussels from shells and keep warm in small amount of the stock.

Cut shrimp into bite-size pieces; add to mussels and keep warm.

METHOD
Sauté leeks, onions, and knob celery in butter.

Dust with flour, continue cooking, and let cool.

Heat fish stock, add to vegetables, and bring to a boil, while stirring.

Skim and boil for at least 20 minutes. Add reserved mussels stock.

Strain through fine mesh china cap, then bring to a boil once again.

Stir in cream. Add cold butter in small nuggets.

Season to taste.

Garnish with mussels, shrimp, and dill.

126

*F*ish Consomme

Fischkraftbrühe
Consommé de poisson

YIELD: 2 QT 20 OZ (2.5 L)

Whiting fillets[a]	1 lb	450 g
Leeks, white part only	4 1/4 oz	120 g
Shallots	2 oz	60 g
Mushrooms, fresh	1 oz	30 g
Dill twig, fresh	1	5 g
Egg whites	2	2
Fish stock (Recipe 24)	3 qt 5 oz	3.0 L
Seasoning	1x	1x
Dry vermouth[b]	2/3 oz	20 ml

MISE EN PLACE
Chop fish fillets coarsely with a knife.

Wash and trim leeks; be sure sand is cleaned from layers. Dice.

Dice shallots and mushrooms.

Make clarification by combining chopped fish fillets, leeks, shallots, mushrooms, dill, and egg whites, and refrigerate for at least 1 hour.

METHOD
Mix clarification with cold fish stock.

Bring to a boil, stirring carefully with a paddle.

Simmer for about 30 minutes. (Do not stir after consomme has come to a boil.)

Strain carefully through double layers of cheesecloth.

Remove any surface fat with absorbent paper.

Season to taste, and add dry vermouth.

---

[a] Other lean, white fish can be substituted.

[b] The recipe specifies Noilly Prat, but any brand of dry vermouth can be used. Vermouth comes in dry and sweet varieties; use only dry in this recipe.

127

$\mathscr{B}$eef Broth[a]

Fleischbrühe
Bouillon de viande

Y I E L D : 2 Q T 2 2 O Z (2 . 5 L)

Beef bones	3 lb 5 oz	1.5 kg
Onions	3 1/2 oz	100 g
Leeks	3 1/2 oz	100 g
Savoy cabbage	1 2/3 oz	50 g
Knob celery (celeriac)	1 1/3 oz	40 g
Carrots	1 2/3 oz	50 g
Sachet bag	1	1
Beef brisket, fresh and trimmed	1 lb 2 oz	500 g
Water	5 qt 7 oz	5.0 L
Seasoning	1x	1x

MISE EN PLACE
Cover beef bones with hot water, bring to a boil, drain, and rinse.

Cut onions in half horizontally, leave peel on, and brown cut sides[b].

Wash and trim leeks; be sure sand is cleaned from layers. Cut into quarters.

Clean cabbage, knob celery, and carrots, and tie into a bundle along with leeks.

Make sachet bag consisting of 1/2 bay leaf, 1 clove, some crushed peppercorns, and a little thyme.

METHOD
Cover bones with cold water and bring to a boil. Skim off fat and other impurities.

Add meat and small amount of salt.

After about 2 hours, add vegetable bundle, onions, and sachet bag.

Simmer for about 3 hours; do not overcook meat.

Remove cooked meat with some stock and reserve for further use.

Strain remaining stock through cheesecloth and skim off fat.

Season to taste.

NOTE: Beef stock is also a by-product whenever boiled beef is prepared. If the boiled beef is not needed for another use, inexpensive cow meat or beef scraps can be substituted. These scraps have no further use.

---

[a] This bouillon is a finished soup. When other recipes call for bouillon as an ingredient, it is best to use the Plain Beef Stock (Recipe 22).

[b] The sugar in the onion should be caramelized to color the stock.

128

$\mathscr{C}$rayfish Soup

Flusskrebssuppe
Bisque d'écrevisses

Y I E L D : 1 Q T 1 1 O Z (1 . 5 L)

Crayfish, live	2 lb 3 oz	1.0 kg
Shallots	1 oz	30 g
Butter	2/3 oz	20 g
Cognac (or any brandy)	2/3 oz	20 ml
Onions	1 1/3 oz	40 g
Carrots	1 1/3 oz	40 g
Knob celery (celeriac)	1 oz	30 g
Olive oil	1 oz	30 ml
Tomato paste	1 oz	30 g
White wheat flour	1 1/3 oz	40 g
Dry white wine	3 1/3 oz	100 ml
Fish stock (Recipe 24)	1 qt 13 oz	1.7 L
Heavy cream (36%)	10 oz	300 ml
Butter, cold	1 2/3 oz	50 g
Seasoning (salt, cayenne)	1x	1x

MISE EN PLACE
Wash crayfish, kill by submerging in boiling water, and remove intestines.

Chop shallots and sauté in butter.

Add crayfish and continue cooking.

Add brandy and ignite, remove crayfish, and save stock.

Peel crayfish tails to extract the meat. Cut meat into dice for garnish.

Crush crayfish bodies and shells.[a]

Cut onions, carrots, and knob celery into small dice.

METHOD
Sauté crushed shells in hot olive oil.

Add vegetables and continue cooking.

Add tomato paste and continue cooking.

Dust with flour, add white wine and fish stock.

Bring to a boil and simmer for about 30 minutes.

Add cream and simmer for 15 minutes longer.

Strain soup, without pressure, through fine mesh china cap or cheesecloth.

(continued on next page)

---

[a] The shells are best crushed in a food processor or Buffalo chopper.

(continued from preceding page)

If necessary, reduce soup to desired thickness.

Add cold butter in small nuggets and stir well.

Season to taste with salt and cayenne.

Garnish with diced crayfish tails.

129

Cold Fruit Soup (basic recipe)

Früchtekaltschale (Grundrezept)
Soupe froide aux fruits

YIELD: 1 QT 11 OZ (1.5 L)

Lemon	1	1
Orange	1	1
Pineapple, fresh	7 oz	200 g
Peaches, yellow	7 oz	200 g
Water	10 oz	300 ml
Sugar	3 1/4 oz	90 g
Cinnamon stick	1 small	2 g
Raspberry puree, unsweetened	7 oz	200 g
White wine	12 oz	350 ml
(Sylvaner or Riesling)		
Kirsch	1 oz	30 ml
Champagne (sparkling wine)	8 1/2 oz	250 ml

MISE EN PLACE

Remove a piece of peel from both the lemon and the orange and reserve. Press juice from lemon and orange.

Remove rind from pineapple and cut flesh into small dice.

Blanch peaches, peel, and cut flesh into small dice.

METHOD

Combine water, sugar, cinnamon stick, lemon peel, and orange peel.

Bring to a boil, strain, and let cool.

Add lemon juice, orange juice, raspberry puree, white wine, and kirsch.

Add diced pineapple and peaches and chill.

At the moment of service, add champagne.

Serve in chilled glasses, with drinking straws and small spoons.

130

Gazpacho

YIELD: 2 QT 22 OZ (2.5 L)

Cucumbers	1 lb 5 oz	600 g
Tomatoes	1 lb 5 oz	600 g
Assorted bell peppers	10 1/2 oz	300 g
Onions	3 1/2 oz	100 g
Garlic	1/3 oz	10 g
Mie de pain[a]	3 1/2 oz	100 g
Water	10 oz	300 ml
Bouillon (Recipe 22)	3 1/3 oz	100 ml
Red wine vinegar	1 3/4 oz	50 ml
Olive oil, cold pressed	2 3/4 oz	80 ml
Seasoning (salt and pepper)	1x	1x
Seasoning (Tabasco)	1x	1x

GARNISH

White bread (Pullman loaf)	5 1/3 oz	150 g
Cucumbers	5 1/3 oz	150 g
Tomatoes	5 1/3 oz	150 g
Assorted bell peppers	5 1/3 oz	150 g

MISE EN PLACE

Peel cucumbers and tomatoes, split in half, remove seeds, and cut into chunks.

Split bell peppers, remove seeds, wash, and cut into chunks.

Peel onions and garlic, and cut into thin slices.

Soak *mie de pain* in water.

METHOD FOR GARNISH

Cut bread into small dice and toast croutons in oven.

Peel cucumbers and tomatoes, split in half, remove seeds, and cut into small dice.

Split bell peppers, remove seeds, wash, and cut into small dice.

METHOD

Purée cucumbers, tomatoes, bell peppers, onions, garlic, and soaked *mie de pain*, with cold bouillon.

Add vinegar and oil in small amounts and mix to a homogenous purée.

Season well with salt and pepper and Tabasco.

Chill soup very well, and serve in chilled soup cups.

Serve croutons and diced vegetable garnishes on the side, in small dishes.

---

[a] *Mie de pain* are fresh bread crumbs, made from white Pullman loaves.

131

Cream of Chicken Soup (basic)

Geflügelcremesuppe (Grundrezept)
Crème de volaille

Yield: 2 qt 22 oz (2.5 L)

Leeks, white part only	3 oz	80 g
Onions	3 oz	80 g
Knob celery (celeriac)	1 oz	30 g
Chicken stock (Recipe 26)	3 qt 5 oz	3.0 L
Butter	1 2/3 oz	50 g
White wheat flour	3 oz	80 g
Heavy cream (36%)	10 oz	300 ml
Butter, cold	2/3 oz	20 g
Seasoning	1x	1x

MISE EN PLACE

Wash and trim leeks; be sure sand is cleaned from layers. Cut into small dice.

Cut onions and knob celery into small dice.

Bring chicken stock to a boil.

METHOD

Sauté leeks, onions, and knob celery in butter.

Dust with flour, continue cooking for a short while, and let mixture cool.

Add hot stock and bring to a boil, while stirring.

Simmer for at least 20 minutes.

Strain through fine mesh china cap and bring to a boil again.

Stir in cream. Add cold butter in small nuggets.

Season to taste.

132

Cream of Chicken Soup with Mushrooms and Calves' Tongue

Geflüglecremesuppe Agnes Sorel
Crème Agnès Sorel

Yield: 2 qt 22 oz (2.5 L)

Leeks, white part only	3 oz	80 g
Onions	3 oz	80 g
Knob celery (celeriac)	1 oz	30 g
Chicken stock (Recipe 26)	2 qt 22 oz	2.5 L
Butter	1 2/3 oz	50 g
White wheat flour	3 oz	80 g
Heavy cream (36%)	10 oz	300 ml
Butter, cold	2/3 oz	20 g
Seasoning	1x	1x

GARNISH

Chicken breast, skinless	3 oz	80 g
Veal tongue, boiled and peeled	3 1/2 oz	100 g
Mushrooms, fresh	14 oz	400 g
Butter	2/3 oz	20 g

MISE EN PLACE

Wash and trim leeks; be sure sand is cleaned from layers. Cut into small dice.

Cut onions and knob celery into small dice.

Bring chicken stock to a boil.

METHOD FOR GARNISH

Poach chicken breast in a little chicken stock and let cool. Save poaching stock with rest of chicken stock.

Cut chicken breast and veal tongue into fine strips.

Wash mushrooms, slice, and braise in butter. Add mushroom stock to chicken stock. Purée mushrooms.

METHOD

Sauté leeks, onions, and knob celery in butter.

Dust with flour, continue cooking for a short while, and let mixture cool.

Heat chicken/mushroom stock, add to leek/onion/celery mixture, and bring to a boil, while stirring; skim.

Simmer for at least 20 minutes.

Strain through fine mesh china cap and bring to a boil again.

Stir in cream. Add cold butter in small nuggets.

Season to taste.

Garnish with chicken breast, tongue, and mushroom puree.

133

*C*ream of Chicken Soup with Vegetable Garnish
Geflügelcremesuppe Maria Stuart
Crème Maria Stuart

YIELD: 2 QT 22 OZ (2.5 L)

Leeks, white part only	3 oz	80 g
Onions	3 oz	80 g
Knob celery (celeriac)	1 oz	30 g
Chicken stock (Recipe 26)	2 qt 22 oz	2.5 L
Butter	1 2/3 oz	50 g
White wheat flour	3 oz	80 g
Heavy cream (36%)	10 oz	300 ml
Butter, cold	2/3 oz	20 g
Seasoning	1x	1x

GARNISH
Leek, white part only	1 1/3 oz	40 g
Carrots	1 2/3 oz	50 g
Knob celery (celeriac)	1 oz	30 g
Chicken stock (Recipe 26)	6 3/4 oz	200 ml
Chervil, fresh, chopped	1/6 oz	5 g

MISE EN PLACE
Wash and trim leeks; be sure sand is cleaned from layers. Cut into small dice.

Cut onions and knob celery into small dice.

Bring chicken stock to a boil.

METHOD FOR GARNISH
Clean and trim leek. Cut leeks, carrots, and knob celery into small dice (*brunoise*). Cook in chicken stock.

METHOD
Sauté leeks, onions, and knob celery in butter.

Dust with flour, continue cooking for a short time, and let cool.

Add hot chicken stock and bring to boil while stirring; skim.

Simmer for at least 20 minutes.

Strain through fine mesh china cap and bring to a boil again.

Stir in cream. Add cold butter in small nuggets.

Season to taste.

Garnish with cooked diced vegetables and sprinkle with chervil.

134

*C*hicken Consomme
Geflügelkraftbrühe
Consommé de volaille

YIELD: 2 QT 20 OZ (2.5 L)

Chicken drumsticks	12 oz	350 g
Chicken bones, meaty (necks and backs)	10 1/2 oz	300 g
Clarification meat[a]	5 1/3 oz	150 g
Leeks, white part only	3 oz	80 g
Carrots	3 oz	80 g
Knob celery (celeriac)	2 oz	60 g
Tomatoes	1 2/3 oz	50 g
Egg whites	2	2
Rosemary twig, fresh	1 small	1 g
White peppercorns	5	5
Water	6 3/4 oz	200 ml
Chicken stock (Recipe 26)	3 qt 5 oz	3.0 L
Seasoning	1x	1 x

MISE EN PLACE
Bone chicken drumsticks; save bones.

Coarsely chop chicken bones and roast until light brown.

Grind drumstick meat and clarification meat through coarse plate of meat grinder.

Wash and trim leeks; be sure sand is cleaned from layers. Cut into small dice.

Cut carrots and knob celery into small dice. Cube tomatoes.

Make clarification by thoroughly combining roasted chicken bones, ground chicken and beef, leeks, carrots, knob celery, tomatoes, egg whites, rosemary, white peppercorns, and water. Refrigerate for at least 1 hour.

METHOD
Combine clarification with cold chicken stock and stir well.

Bring to a boil while stirring carefully with a paddle. As soon as consomme starts to boil, do not stir any longer. Skim off fat and impurities. Simmer for 1 hour.

Strain carefully through double layer of cheesecloth.

Remove all fat from surface with absorbent paper.

Season to taste.

---

[a] The clarification meat should be as lean as possible. Meat from beef shank is preferred because it is very lean and has a high gelatin content. Ground turkey meat can also be used.

135

Chicken Consomme with Chicken Quenelles (Dumplings)

Geflügelkraftbrühe Demidow
Consommé de volaille Demidov

YIELD: 2 QT 20 OZ (2.5 L)

Chicken consomme (Recipe 134)	2 qt 20 oz	2.5 L

GARNISH

Leeks, white part only	1 2/3 oz	50 g
Carrots	2 oz	60 g
Knob celery (celeriac)	1 1/3 oz	40 g
Chicken stock (Recipe 26)	1 pt 1 oz	500 ml
Chicken breast, skinless	5 1/3 oz	150 g
Egg white	1	1
Heavy cream (36%)	1 2/3 oz	50 ml
Seasoning	1x	1x

METHOD

Wash and trim leeks; be sure sand is cleaned from layers. Cut into small dice (*brunoise*).

Cut carrots and knob celery into small dice (*brunoise*).

Cook leeks, carrots, and knob celery in chicken stock until cooked but still firm.[a] Drain; reserve chicken broth to poach quenelles.

Remove sinew from chicken breast and cut into dice. Refrigerate until very cold.

Make mousse by combining diced raw chicken with egg white and cream in food processor. Season.[b] Form small quenelles (dumplings) with 2 demi-tasse spoons and poach them in chicken stock.

Add diced vegetables and quenelles to hot chicken consomme and serve.

136

Chicken Consomme with Barley and Chicken

Geflügelkraftbrühe mit Gerste und Geflügelstreifen
Consommé princesse

YIELD: 2 QT 20 OZ (2.5 L)

Chicken consomme (Recipe 134)	2 qt 20 oz	2.5 L

GARNISH

Pearl barley	3 oz	80 g
Chicken breast, skinless	5 1/3 oz	150 g
Chicken stock (Recipe 26)	6 3/4 oz	200 ml

METHOD

Boil barley in plenty of water; drain; discard water.

Rinse barley in cold water; drain again.

Poach chicken breast in chicken stock and cut into strips when cooked.

Add both garnishes to hot chicken consomme.

---

[a] Vegetables could also be steamed to retain vitamins.

[b] Do not taste raw chicken mousse because salmonella bacteria could be present.

137

Chicken Consomme with Chicken Mousse Crepes

Geflügelkraftbrühe Monte Carlo
Consommé Monte-Carlo

YIELD: 2 QT 20 OZ (2.5 L)

Chicken consomme (Recipe 134)	2 qt 20 oz	2.5 L

GARNISH—MOUSSE

Chicken stock (Recipe 26)	1 pt 1 oz	500 ml
Chicken breast, skinless	5 1/3 oz	150 g
Egg white	1	1
Heavy cream (36%)	1 2/3 oz	50 ml
Seasoning	1x	1x

GARNISH—CREPES

White wheat flour	1 2/3 oz	50 g
Milk	3 1/3 oz	100 ml
Egg	1	1
Butter	2/3 oz	20 g
Seasoning	1x	1x

METHOD FOR MOUSSE

Remove sinew from chicken breast and cut into dice. Refrigerate until very cold.

Make mousse by combining diced raw chicken with egg white and cream in food processor. Season.[a]

METHOD FOR CREPES

Mix flour and milk; be sure there are no lumps.

Add egg to batter and mix well.

Melt butter and add to batter.

Season to taste with salt and freshly ground pepper.

Strain batter.

Make thin crepes in an omelette pan; cool on wire rack.

METHOD

Spread mousse on half the number of crepes.

Cover with remaining crepes, sandwich-like. Press lightly.

Cut small disks with 1 1/2-in. cookie cutter. Steam for 3 minutes.

Heat consomme. Serve hot consomme in soup cups, and add crepe disks just before service.

---

[a] Do not taste raw chicken mousse because salmonella bacteria could be present.

138

Chicken Consomme with Tapioca and Chicken Julienne

Geflügelkraftbrühe mit Tapioka und Geflügelstreifen
Consommé reine

YIELD: 2 QT 20 OZ (2.5 L)

Chicken consomme (Recipe 134)	2 qt 20 oz	2.5 L

GARNISH

Chicken breast, skinned	5 1/3 oz	150 g
Chicken stock (Recipe 26)	6 3/4 oz	200 ml
Tapioca	1 1/3 oz	40 g

METHOD

Poach chicken breast in chicken stock and cut into *julienne* strips.

Boil tapioca in plenty of water, drain, rinse with cold water, and drain again.

Add chicken *julienne* and tapioca to hot consomme.

139

Purée of Yellow Split Peas

Gelberbsenpüreesuppe
Purée Victoria

Yield: 2 qt 20 oz (2.5 L)

Yellow split peas	12 oz	350 g
Leeks, white part only	3 1/2 oz	100 g
Onions	3 1/2 oz	100 g
Knob celery (celeriac)	1 1/3 oz	40 g
Potatoes	7 oz	200 g
Bacon rind	1 2/3 oz	50 g
White bread (Pullman loaf)	3 1/2 oz	100 g
Clarified butter	2/3 oz	20 g
Butter	2 oz	60 g
Bouillon (Recipe 22)	3 qt 5 oz	3.0 L
Seasoning	1x	1x
Heavy cream (36%)	3 1/3 oz	100 ml
Butter, cold	2/3 oz	20 g
Chervil, fresh, chopped	1/6 oz	5 g

MISE EN PLACE

Soak yellow split peas in cold water for 4 to 6 hours.

Wash and trim leeks; be sure sand is cleaned from layers. Cut into small dice.

Cut onions and knob celery into small dice.

Peel potatoes and slice.

Tie bacon rind with string, to make removal easier.

Trim crust from bread, cut into small dice, and sauté in clarified butter until croutons are golden brown.

METHOD

Sauté leeks, onions, and knob celery in butter.

Drain split peas; add to leek/onion/celery mixture.

Add bacon rind and cold bouillon. Bring to a boil and skim. Simmer for about 2 hours.

Add potatoes and simmer 1/2 hour longer.

Remove bacon rind, purée,[a] and strain through china cap.

Bring to a boil again; season to taste.

Stir in cream. Add cold butter in small nuggets.

Sprinkle with chervil leaves.

Serve with toasted croutons on the side.

---

[a] This is best accomplished with a hand-held electric mixer.

140

Cream of Vegetable Soup

Gemüsecremesuppe
Crème de légumes

Yield: 2 qt 20 oz (2.5 L)

Leeks, white part only	4 1/4 oz	120 g
Onions	5 1/3 oz	150 g
Knob celery (celeriac)	3 oz	80 g
Carrots	5 1/3 oz	150 g
Vegetable bouillon (Recipe 27)	2 qt 20 oz	2.5 L
Butter	1 1/3 oz	40 g
White wheat flour	3 oz	80 g
Heavy cream (36%)	10 oz	300 ml
Butter, cold	2/3 oz	20 g
Seasoning	1x	1x
Chervil, fresh, chopped	1/6 oz	5 g
Lovage,[a] chopped	1/6 oz	5 g

MISE EN PLACE

Wash and trim leeks; be sure sand is cleaned from layers. Cut into small dice.

Trim onions, knob celery, and carrots, and cut into small dice.

Heat vegetable stock.

METHOD

Sauté vegetables in butter.

Dust with flour, continue cooking for a short while, then let mixture cool.

Add hot stock and bring to a boil, while stirring.

Skim occasionally and boil until vegetables are cooked.

Purée,[b] and strain through fine mesh china cap.

Bring to a boil again. Stir in cream. Add cold butter in small nuggets.

Season to taste.

Add chopped chervil and lovage to soup.

---

[a] Lovage is an herb seldom used outside of Europe. The German name is *Liebstöckel.*

[b] This is best accomplished with a hand-held electric mixer.

141

*V*egetable Soup, Village Style

Gemüsesuppe dörflicher Art
Potage villageoise

YIELD: 2 QT 20 OZ (2.5 L)

Leeks	1 lb 5 oz	600 g
Savoy cabbage	14 oz	400 g
Onions	3 1/2 oz	100 g
Vermicelli (thin spaghetti)	1 1/3 oz	40 g
Butter	1 1/3 oz	40 g
White wheat flour	1 oz	30 g
Vegetable bouillon (Recipe 27)	2 qt 22 oz	2.5 L
Seasoning (salt and pepper)	1x	1x
Chervil, fresh, chopped	1/6 oz	5 g
Sbrinz, grated[a]	3 1/2 oz	100 g

MISE EN PLACE
Wash and trim leeks; be sure sand is cleaned from layers. Cut into fine strips (*julienne*).

Clean cabbage and cut into fine strips (*julienne*).

Peel and chop onions.

Boil vermicelli in salt water, rinse, and drain.

METHOD
Sauté leeks, cabbage, and onions in butter.

Dust with flour.

Add hot vegetable stock, bring to a boil, and skim.

Simmer vegetables until cooked.

Season to taste.

Add cooked vermicelli.

Sprinkle with chervil.

Serve with grated cheese on the side.

142

*G*erminy Soup

Germiny-Suppe
Potage Germiny

YIELD: 1 QT 19 OZ (1.5 L)

Bouillon (Recipe 22)	1 qt 5 1/2 oz	1.1 L
Sorrel, fresh	1 oz	30 g
Butter	2/3 oz	20 g
Heavy cream (36%)	6 3/4 oz	200 ml
Egg yolks	4	4
Seasoning	1x	1x
Butter, cold	1 oz	30 g
Chervil, fresh, chopped	1/6 oz	5 g

MISE EN PLACE
Heat bouillon.

Cut sorrel leaves into thin strips (*chiffonade*).

METHOD
Smother sorrel leaves in butter and place in warm soup cups.

Combine cream and egg yolks and whip in a steam table until warm.

Slowly add hot bouillon and continue stirring.

Pour into soup pot and season to taste.

Heat, stirring constantly, until soup starts to thicken but do not boil.

Strain immediately into another pot through fine mesh china cap .

Add cold butter in small nuggets.

Fill cups with soup and sprinkle with chervil leaves.

Serve immediately.

---

[a] Sbrinz is a hard grating cheese from Switzerland. Parmesan can be substituted.

143

Toasted Semolina Soup

Geröstete Griessuppe
Potage à la semoule grillée

YIELD: 2 QT 20 OZ (2.5 L)

Onions	3 1/2 oz	100 g
Chives, fresh	2/3 oz	20 g
Semolina (hard wheat)	5 1/3 oz	150 g
Sunflower oil	1 1/3 oz	40 ml
Bouillon (Recipe 22)	2 qt 20 oz	2.5 L
Seasoning	1x	1x
Butter, cold	1 1/3 oz	40 g

MISE EN PLACE

Peel onions and chop fine.

Cut chives into small slivers.

METHOD

Sauté semolina in sunflower oil until light brown.

Add onions and continue roasting for a short time; let mixture cool.

Add hot bouillon.

Boil until semolina is soft.

Season to taste.

Add cold butter in small nuggets.

Sprinkle with chives.

144

Cream of Barley Soup

Gerstencremesuppe
Crème d'orge

YIELD: 2 QT 20 OZ (2.5 L)

Leeks, white part only	3 oz	80 g
Onions	3 oz	80 g
Knob celery (celeriac)	1 oz	30 g
Pearl barley	2/3 oz	20 g
White veal stock (Recipe 28)	2 qt 20 oz	2.5 L
Butter	1 2/3 oz	50 g
Barley flour, fine	3 oz	80 g
Heavy cream (36%)	10 oz	300 ml
Salt (pinch)	1x	1x
Chervil, fresh, chopped	1/6 oz	5 g

MISE EN PLACE

Wash and trim leeks; be sure sand is cleaned from layers. Cut into small dice.

Cut onions and knob celery into small dice.

Boil pearl barley in salt water; let cool. Reserve for garnish.

Bring veal stock to a boil.

METHOD

Sauté leeks, onions, and knob celery in butter.

Dust with barley flour; let cool slightly.

Add hot stock and bring to a boil while stirring; skim.

Simmer for at least 20 minutes.

Strain through fine mesh china cap and bring to a boil again.

Add cream and season to taste.

Garnish with boiled barley.

Sprinkle with chervil.

145

*B*arley Soup

Gerstensuppe
Potage d'orge perlé

YIELD: 2 QT 20 OZ (2.5 L)

Leeks	3 oz	80 g
Onions	3 oz	80 g
Carrots	3 oz	80 g
Knob celery (celeriac)	1 2/3 oz	50 g
Chives, fresh	1/6 oz	5 g
White veal stock (Recipe 28)	3 qt 5 oz	3.0 L
Butter	1 1/3 oz	40 g
Pearl barley	5 1/3 oz	150 g
White wheat flour	1 oz	30 g
Heavy cream (36%)	6 3/4 oz	200 ml
Seasoning	1x	1x

MISE EN PLACE

Wash and trim leeks; be sure sand is cleaned from layers. Cut into fine dice (*brunoise*).

Peel onions and chop fine.

Clean carrots and knob celery and cut into fine dice (*brunoise*).

Cut chives into small slivers.

Heat veal stock.

METHOD

Sauté leeks, onions, carrots, and knob celery in butter.

Add barley and continue cooking.

Dust with flour.

Add hot veal stock; boil until barley is tender.[a]

Add cream and season to taste.

Sprinkle with chives.

146

*S*emolina Soup with Sorrel

Griessuppe Leopold
Potage Léopold

YIELD: 2 QT 20 OZ (2.5 L)

Onions	3 1/2 oz	100 g
Sorrel, leaves	2/3 oz	20 g
Butter	1 1/3 oz	40 g
Semolina, hard wheat	3 1/2 oz	100 g
Bouillon (Recipe 22)	3 qt 5 oz	3.0 L
Seasoning	1x	1x
Chervil, fresh, chopped	1/6 oz	5 g

MISE EN PLACE

Peel onions and chop fine.

Cut sorrel leaves into thin strips (*chiffonade*).

METHOD

Sauté onions in butter.

Add semolina and continue cooking.

Add bouillon and stir thoroughly with wire whip.

Bring to a boil and simmer until semolina is soft.

Add sorrel to soup; bring to a boil again.

Season to taste.

Sprinkle soup with chervil leaves.

---

[a] Add more stock if necessary.

147

Purée of Green Peas

Grünerbsen-Püreesuppe
Purée St.-Germain

YIELD: 2 QT 20 OZ (2.5 L)

Split peas, green	10 1/2 oz	300 g
Leeks, white part only	3 1/2 oz	100 g
Onions	3 1/2 oz	100 g
Knob celery (celeriac)	1 1/3 oz	40 g
Potatoes	7 oz	200 g
Bacon rind (skin)	1 2/3 oz	50 g
White bread (Pullman loaf)	3 1/2 oz	100 g
Clarified butter	1 oz	30 g
Butter	2 oz	60 g
Bouillon (Recipe 22)	3 qt 5 oz	3.0 L
Seasoning	1x	1x

MISE EN PLACE

Soak split peas in cold water for 4 to 6 hours.

Wash and trim leeks; be sure sand is cleaned from layers. Cut into small dice.

Cut onions and knob celery into small dice.

Peel potatoes and slice.

Tie bacon rind into a bundle to make it easier to remove.

Trim crust from bread, cut into small cubes, and sauté cubes in clarified butter until croutons are golden brown.

METHOD

Sauté leeks, onions, and knob celery in butter.

Add soaked peas, potatoes, and bacon rind.

Add cold bouillon; season.

Bring to a boil, skim, and simmer for about 2 hours until peas are soft.

Remove bacon rind. Purée.[a]

Bring to a boil once more and season to taste.

NOTE: Croutons can be sprinkled over soup at the last moment, or served on the side.

---

[a] This is best accomplished with a hand-held electric mixer.

148

Hungarian Goulash Soup

Ungarische Gulaschsuppe
Gulyas leves

YIELD: 2 QT 20 OZ (2.5 L)

Beef chuck, trimmed[a]	1 lb 5 oz	600 g
Onions	1 lb 5 oz	600 g
Garlic cloves, peeled	3	3
Caraway seeds, whole	1/2 tsp	2 g
Red bell peppers	10 1/2 oz	300 g
Potatoes	14 oz	400 g
Tomatoes	10 1/2 oz	300 g
Lemon	1/2	1/2
Vegetable shortening	2 oz	60 g
Hungarian sweet paprika	2 oz	60 g
White wheat flour	1 oz	30 g
Bouillon (Recipe 22)	3 qt 5 oz	3.0 L
Seasoning	1x	1x

MISE EN PLACE

Cut beef into 1/2-in. (1 cm) cubes.

Peel onions and chop fine. Purée garlic.

Chop caraway seeds very fine.

Split red peppers in half, remove seeds, and wash. Cut into small dice.

Peel potatoes and cut into small dice.

Peel tomatoes, split, remove seeds, and cut into small dice.

Grate lemon peel.

METHOD

Sauté meat and onions in shortening.

Add garlic, caraway seeds, and paprika and continue cooking.

Dust with flour. Add bouillon and cook until meat is almost tender.

Add red peppers and potatoes and continue cooking until tender.

Add diced tomatoes and grated lemon peel. Season to taste.

NOTE: Additional bouillon may be needed during cooking.

---

[a] The meat should be well trimmed, but not too lean. Other suitable cuts are sirloin tip or knuckle face.

149

Cream of Cucumber Soup

Gurkencremesuppe
Crème de concombres

YIELD: 2 QT 20 OZ (2.5 L)

Cucumbers	3 lb 5 oz	1.5 kg
Vegetable bouillon (Recipe 27)	2 qt 4 oz	2.0 L
Leeks	3 1/2 oz	100 g
Onions	3 1/2 oz	100 g
Knob celery (celeriac)	1 1/3 oz	40 g
Butter	1 1/3 oz	40 g
Dill, fresh	1/6 oz	5 g
White wheat flour	1 1/3 oz	40 g
Heavy cream (36%)	6 3/4 oz	200 ml
Milk	3 1/3 oz	100 ml
Seasoning	1x	1x

MISE EN PLACE

Peel cucumbers, split lengthwise, and remove seeds. Reserve 3 1/2 oz (100 g) for garnish. Cut this portion into small dice and boil in vegetable stock until just about tender. Slice remaining cucumbers.

Wash and trim leeks; be sure sand is cleaned from layers. Cut into dice.

Cut onions and knob celery into dice.

Remove stems from dill and chop leaves.

METHOD

Sauté leeks, onions, and knob celery in butter.

Add cucumbers and dill; continue cooking.

Dust with flour; let cool a little.

Add hot vegetable stock and bring to a boil, stirring constantly.

Boil until vegetables are soft; skim occasionally.

Purée[a] well and strain through fine mesh china cap.

Bring to a boil once more.

Stir in cream and milk. Season to taste.

Add diced cucumbers to soup. Sprinkle with dill.

---

[a] This is best accomplished with a hand-held electric mixer.

150

Oatmeal Soup

Haferflockensuppe
Potage aux flocons d'avoine

YIELD: 2 QT 20 OZ (2.5 L)

Onions	3 1/2 oz	100 g
Leeks, white part only	5 1/3 oz	150 g
White veal stock (Recipe 28)	2 qt 20 oz	2.5 L
Butter	1 1/3 oz	40 g
Oat flakes, small	4 1/4 oz	120 g
Oat flour	2/3 oz	20 g
Heavy cream (36%)	10 oz	300 ml
Seasoning	1x	1x
Chervil, fresh, chopped	1/2 tbsp	2 g

MISE EN PLACE

Peel onions and chop fine.

Wash and trim leeks; be sure sand is cleaned from layers. Cut into fine strips (*julienne*).

Heat veal stock.

METHOD

Sauté onions and leeks in butter.

Add oat flakes and continue cooking.

Dust with oat flour.

Add hot veal stock and simmer until oat flakes are soft.

Add cream. Season to taste. Sprinkle with chervil.

151

Basic Veal Cream Soup

Kalbfleischcremesuppe (Basis)
Crème de veau

YIELD: 2 QT 20 OZ (2.5 L)

Leeks, white part only	3 oz	80 g
Onions	3 oz	80 g
Knob celery (celeriac)	1 oz	30 g
White veal stock (Recipe 28)	2 qt 20 oz	2.5 L
Butter	1 2/3 oz	50 g
White wheat flour	3 oz	80 g
Heavy cream (36%)	10 oz	300 ml
Butter, cold	2/3 oz	20 g
Seasoning	1x	1x

MISE EN PLACE

Wash and trim leeks; be sure sand is cleaned from layers. Cut into dice.

Cut onions and knob celery into dice.

Bring stock to a boil.

METHOD

Sauté vegetables in butter.

Dust with flour, continue cooking a little longer, and then let cool.

Add hot veal stock and bring to a boil, stirring continuously; skim.

Simmer for at least 20 minutes.

Strain through fine mesh china cap and bring to a boil again.

Stir in cream. Add cold butter in small nuggets.

Season to taste.

152

Cold Avocado Soup

Kalte Avocadosuppe
Crème d'avocat froide

YIELD: 2 QT 20 OZ (2.5 L)

Onions	3 1/2 oz	100 g
Garlic clove	1	2 g
Avocado	3	3
Tomatoes	3 1/2 oz	100 g
Oranges	3 1/2 oz	100 g
Butter	2/3 oz	20 g
Chicken stock (Recipe 26)	2 qt 20 oz	2.5 L
Heavy cream (36%)	5 oz	150 ml
Seasoning (salt and pepper)	1x	1x

MISE EN PLACE

Peel and chop onions.

Purée garlic.

Peel and remove pits from avocados, and cut into dice.

Peel tomatoes, remove seeds, and cut into small dice.

Squeeze juice from oranges.

METHOD

Sauté onions and garlic in butter.

Add avocados and continue cooking.

Add chicken stock; bring to a boil.

Simmer for about 10 minutes.

Purée and strain through small-hole china cap.

Add orange juice.

Add cream, season to taste, and chill.

Add diced tomatoes.

Serve in chilled soup cups.

153

Cold Vichyssoise

Kalte Kartoffelsuppe
Vichyssoise

YIELD: 2 QT 20 OZ (2.5 L)

Potatoes	1 lb 2 oz	500 g
Leeks, white part only	10 1/2 oz	300 g
Onions	3 1/2 oz	100 g
Chives, fresh	1/3 oz	10 g
White bread (Pullman loaf)	3 1/2 oz	100 g
Butter	1 2/3 oz	50 g
Bouillon (Recipe 22)	2 qt 20 oz	2.5 L
Heavy cream (36%)	10 oz	300 ml
Seasoning (salt and pepper)	1x	1x

MISE EN PLACE

Peel potatoes and slice.

Wash and trim leeks; be sure sand is cleaned from layers. Cut into medium dice.

Trim onions and cut into medium dice.

Cut chives into small slivers.

Cut bread into cubes and toast under the salamander.

METHOD

Sauté leeks and onions in butter.

Add sliced potatoes.

Add bouillon and boil until all ingredients are soft.

Purée[a] soup, and strain through fine mesh china cap.

Add cream. Season to taste. Bring to a boil again.

Chill, stirring occasionally.

Serve very cold in chilled soup cups.

Sprinkle with chives.

Serve croutons on the side.

---

[a] This is best accomplished with a hand-held electric mixer.

154

$\mathcal{J}$ellied Beef Consomme

Kalte Kraftbrühe
Consommé en gelée

YIELD: 2 QT 20 OZ (2.5 L)

Clarification meat[a]	1 lb 12 oz	800 g
Leeks, green leaves only	3 oz	80 g
Carrots	3 oz	80 g
Knob celery (celeriac)	2 oz	60 g
Tomatoes	1 2/3 oz	50 g
Bay leaf	1/2	1/2
White peppercorns	5	5
Water	6 3/4 oz	200 ml
Seasoning	1x	1x
Bouillon (Recipe 22)	3 qt 5 oz	3.0 L

MISE EN PLACE

Grind meat through coarse plate of meat grinder.

Wash and trim leeks; be sure sand is cleaned from layers. Cut into medium dice.

Trim carrots and knob celery; cut into medium dice.

Cube tomatoes.

Make clarification mixture by combining meat, leeks, carrots, knob celery, tomatoes, bay leaf, and peppercorns, with water; mix thoroughly and refrigerate at least 1 hour.

METHOD

Combine meat mixture with cold bouillon and mix well.

Bring to a boil, stirring carefully with a paddle. Do not stir any longer once consomme starts to boil. Skim off fat and impurities.

Simmer for 1 1/2 hours.

Strain carefully through double layer of cheesecloth.

Remove all fat with absorbent paper.

Season to taste.

Pour into soup cups. Refrigerate until soup is slightly jellied.[b]

---

[a] The meat should be as lean as possible. Meat from beef shank is preferred because it is very lean and has a high gelatin content.

[b] In warm weather, it is advisable to add a small amount of gelatin to the hot soup to ensure that it will gel.

155

$\mathcal{C}$old Tomato Soup

Kalte Tomatensuppe
Crème de tomates froide

YIELD: 2 QT 20 OZ (2.5 L)

Tomatoes	2 lb 3 oz	1.0 kg
Leeks, white part only	3 oz	80 g
Onions	3 1/2 oz	100 g
Knob celery (celeriac)	1 1/3 oz	40 g
Carrots	2 oz	60 g
Garlic	1/6 oz	5 g
Vegetable stock (Recipe 27)	2 qt 20 oz	2.5 L
Butter	1 1/3 oz	40 g
Tomato paste	3 1/2 oz	100 g
White wheat flour	2 1/2 oz	70 g
Heavy cream (36%)	10 oz	300 ml
Seasoning	1x	1x
Basil, fresh, chopped	1 tbsp	2 g
Seasoning (Tabasco)	1x	1x

MISE EN PLACE

Blanch 2 tomatoes, peel, cut in half, remove seeds, and cut into small dice. Reserve for garnish.

Cut remaining tomatoes in half, remove seeds, and cut into large dice.

Wash and trim leeks; be sure sand is cleaned from layers. Cut into medium dice.

Cut all onions, knob celery, and carrots into medium dice.

Purée garlic.

Heat vegetable stock.

METHOD

Sauté vegetables (not including tomatoes) in butter.

Add tomato paste and continue cooking.

Dust with flour and let cool.

Add hot stock, stir well, and bring to a boil.

Add tomatoes (not including those reserved for garnish).

Simmer until ingredients are soft, skimming occasionally.

Purée,[a] and strain through fine mesh china cap.

Bring to a boil again.

Stir in cream. Season to taste (perhaps with a little sugar).

---

[a] This is best accomplished with a hand-held electric mixer.

Add diced tomato garnish. Sprinkle with chopped basil.

Season with Tabasco. Chill.

Taste; adjust seasoning. Serve very cold in chilled soup cups.

Bring to a boil again.

Stir in cream and milk. Season to taste.

Add diced carrots to soup as garnish. Sprinkle with chopped lovage.

156

*C*ream of Carrot Soup

Karottencremesuppe
Crème de carottes

YIELD: 2 QT 20 OZ (2.5 L)

Carrots	2 lb 10 oz	1.2 kg
Vegetable bouillon (Recipe 27)	2 qt 20 oz	2.5 L
Leeks	3 1/2 oz	100 g
Onions	3 1/2 oz	100 g
Knob celery (celeriac)	1 1/3 oz	40 g
Butter	1 1/3 oz	40 g
White wheat flour	1 1/3 oz	40 g
Heavy cream (36%)	6 3/4 oz	200 ml
Milk	3 1/3 oz	100 ml
Seasoning	1x	1x
Lovage,[a] fresh, chopped	1/6 oz	5 g

MISE EN PLACE
Peel carrots. Reserve 3 1/2 oz (100 g) carrots for garnish; cut garnish carrots into small dice; cook or steam in small amount of vegetable bouillon.

Slice remaining carrots.

Wash and trim leeks; be sure sand is cleaned from layers. Cut into medium dice.

Trim onions and knob celery and cut into medium dice.

Heat vegetable bouillon.

METHOD
Sauté leeks, onions, and knob celery in butter.

Add carrot slices and continue cooking.

Dust with flour, stir, and let cool.

Add hot vegetable bouillon and bring to a boil, stirring continuously.

Simmer until all vegetables are soft, skimming occasionally.

Purée,[b] and strain through fine mesh china cap.

---

[a] Lovage is an herb seldom used outside of Europe. The German name is *Liebstöckel.*

[b] This is best accomplished with a hand-held electric mixer.

157

*P*urée of Carrot Soup

Karottenpüreesuppe
Purée Crécy

YIELD: 2 QT 20 OZ (2.5 L)

Leeks	3 1/2 oz	100 g
Onions	3 1/2 oz	100 g
Knob celery (celeriac)	1 1/3 oz	40 g
Carrots	2 lb 3 oz	1.0 kg
Potatoes	10 1/2 oz	300 g
Bouillon (Recipe 22)	2 qt 20 oz	2.5 L
Butter	2/3 oz	20 g
Seasoning	1x	1x
Heavy cream (36%)	3 1/3 oz	100 ml
Butter, cold	2 oz	60 g
Lovage,[a] chopped	1/2 tbsp	2 g

MISE EN PLACE
Wash and trim leeks; be sure sand is cleaned from layers. Cut into medium dice.

Trim onions and knob celery and cut into medium dice.

Peel carrots and potatoes and slice.

Heat bouillon.

METHOD
Sauté leeks, onions, and knob celery in butter.

Add carrots.

Add hot bouillon, bring to a boil, and skim.

Simmer for 20 minutes. Add potatoes and simmer for 20 minutes longer.

Purée,[b] and strain through china cap.

Bring to a boil again.

Stir in cream. Add cold butter in small nuggets.

Season to taste. Sprinkle with lovage.

---

[a] Lovage is an herb seldom used outside of Europe. The German name is *Liebstöckel.*

[b] This is best accomplished with a hand-held electric mixer.

158

𝒫urée of Potato Soup

Kartoffelpüreesuppe
Purée Parmentier

YIELD: 2 QT 20 OZ (2.5 L)

Leeks, white part only	3 1/2 oz	100 g
Onions	3 1/2 oz	100 g
Knob celery (celeriac)	1 1/3 oz	40 g
Potatoes	1 lb 12 oz	800 g
White bread (Pullman loaf)	3 1/2 oz	100 g
Clarified butter	1 oz	30 g
Bouillon (Recipe 22)	2 qt 20 oz	2.5 L
Butter	2 oz	60 g
Bacon rind	1 2/3 oz	50 g
Marjoram twig	1	2 g
Heavy cream (36%)	3 1/3 oz	100 ml
Seasoning	1x	1x
Chervil, fresh, chopped	1/6 oz	5 g

MISE EN PLACE

Wash and trim leeks; be sure sand is cleaned from layers. Cut into medium dice.

Trim onions and knob celery and cut into medium dice.

Peel potatoes and slice.

Remove crust from bread, cut into small cubes, and sauté in clarified butter until croutons are golden brown.

Heat bouillon.

METHOD

Sauté leeks, onions, knob celery, and carrots in butter.

Add potatoes and bacon rind.

Add hot bouillon, bring to a boil, and skim.

Add marjoram twig and simmer for about 45 minutes.

Remove bacon rind.

Purée,[a] and strain through china cap.

Bring to a boil again.

Season to taste. Stir in heavy cream.

Sprinkle with chervil leaves. Serve croutons on the side.

---

[a] This is best accomplished with a hand-held electric mixer.

159

𝒫urée of Chestnut Soup

Kastanienpüreesuppe
Purée Clermont

YIELD: 2 QT 20 OZ (2.5 L)

Leeks	3 1/2 oz	100 g
Onions	3 1/2 oz	100 g
Knob celery (celeriac)	1 1/3 oz	40 g
Potatoes	10 1/2 oz	300 g
Bacon rind	1 2/3 oz	50 g
Bouillon (Recipe 22)	2 qt 20 oz	2.5 L
Shortening	2 oz	60 g
Chestnuts, whole, peeled, frozen	1 lb 5 oz	600 g
Seasoning	1x	1x
Heavy cream (36%)	3 1/3 oz	100 ml
Chervil, fresh, chopped	1/6 oz	2 g

MISE EN PLACE

Wash and trim leeks; be sure sand is cleaned from layers. Cut into medium dice.

Trim onions and knob celery and cut into medium dice.

Peel and slice potatoes.

Tie bacon rind into a bundle to make removal easier.

Heat bouillon.

METHOD

Sauté leeks, onions, and knob celery in shortening.

Add hot potatoes, defrosted chestnuts, bacon rind, and hot bouillon.

Bring to a boil; skim.

Boil until vegetables are soft.

Remove bacon rind.

Purée,[a] and strain through china cap.

Bring to a boil again.

Season to taste. Stir in heavy cream. Sprinkle with chervil leaves.

---

[a] This is best accomplished with a hand-held electric mixer.

160

*C*old Cherry Soup

Kirschenkaltschale
Soupe froide aux cerises

YIELD: 1 QT 19 OZ (1.5 L)

Bing cherries, fresh	4 lb 7 oz	2 kg
Crystal sugar	7 oz	200 g
White wine	6 3/4 oz	200 ml
Maraschino[a]	1 1/3 oz	40 ml
Lemon, juice	1	1
Sour cream	3 1/3 oz	100 ml

MISE EN PLACE
Remove pits from cherries.

METHOD
Purée[b] all ingredients, except lemon juice and sour cream.

Strain through sieve.

Add lemon juice as needed.

Chill thoroughly.

At service, garnish with a spoonful of sour cream.

161

*B*eef Consomme

Kraftbrühe
Consommé

YIELD: 2 QT 20 OZ (2.5 L)

Clarification meat[a]	1 lb	450 g
Carrots	3 oz	80 g
Knob celery (celeriac)	2 oz	60 g
Leeks, green leaves only	3 oz	80 g
Tomatoes	1 2/3 oz	50 g
Egg whites	2	2
Bay leaf	1/2	1/2
White peppercorns	5	5
Water	6 3/4 oz	200 ml
Bouillon (Recipe 22)	3 qt 5 oz	3.0 L
Seasoning (salt)	1x	1x

MISE EN PLACE
Grind meat through coarse plate of meat grinder.

Cut carrots and knob celery into medium dice.

Wash and trim leeks; be sure sand is cleaned from layers. Cut into medium dice.

Cube tomatoes.

Make clarification mixture by combining meat, carrots, knob celery, leeks, tomatoes, egg whites, bay leaf, and white peppercorns with water, mix thoroughly, and refrigerate for at least 1 hour.

METHOD
Thoroughly combine meat mixture with cold bouillon.

Bring to a boil, stirring carefully with paddle. Once consomme starts to boil, do not stir any longer. Skim off fat and impurities. Simmer for 1 hour.

Strain carefully through double layer of cheesecloth.

Remove all fat with absorbent paper.

Season to taste.

---

[a] Maraschino is a white cherry liqueur.

[b] This is best accomplished with a food processor.

[a] The meat should be as lean as possible. Meat from beef shank is preferred because it is very lean and has a high gelatin content.

162

*B*eef Consomme with Custard and Cauliflower

Kraftbrühe Dubarry
Consommé Dubarry

YIELD: 2 QT 20 OZ (2.5 L)

Double consomme (Recipe 122)	*2 qt 20 oz*	*2.5 L*

GARNISH

Butter	*1/3 oz*	*10 g*
Egg	*1*	*1*
Milk	*3 1/3 oz*	*100 ml*
Seasoning (salt, nutmeg)	*1x*	*1x*
Cauliflower, fresh	*10 1/2 oz*	*300 g*

METHOD FOR GARNISH
Butter small souffle cup.

Break egg and stir well. Heat milk, add to egg, and stir well.

Season to taste with salt and nutmeg.

Strain through fine mesh china cap.

Fill souffle cup.

Steam custard in a steamer or a water bath in a low-temperature oven.

Let cool, unmold custard, and cut into attractive shapes.

Wash cauliflower, and divide into small florets. Boil or steam florets until cooked but still firm.

Heat consomme.

Garnish hot consomme with cauliflower florets and custard.

163

*B*eef Consomme with Semolina Quenelles (dumplings)

Kraftbrühe mit Griessklösschen
Consommé aux quenelles de semoule

YIELD: 2 QT 20 OZ (2.5 L)

Double consomme (Recipe 122)	*2 qt 20 oz*	*2.5 L*

GARNISH

Butter	*1 2/3 oz*	*50 g*
Egg	*1*	*1*
Semolina (hard wheat)	*3 1/2 oz*	*100 g*
Parsley, chopped	*1/2 tbsp*	*2 g*
Seasoning (salt and pepper)	*1x*	*1x*
Nutmeg (pinch)	*1x*	*1x*
Bouillon (Recipe 22)	*1 pt 1 oz*	*500 ml*

METHOD
Cream butter and egg.

Add semolina and chopped parsley; mix thoroughly.

Add salt and pepper and nutmeg.

Refrigerate for at least 10 minutes.

Shape small dumplings with 2 demi-tasse spoons.

Poach dumplings for about 12 minutes in bouillon.

Heat consomme.

Serve dumplings in hot consomme.[a]

164

*B*eef Consomme Royal (with egg custard)

Kraftbrühe mit Eierstich
Consommé royale

YIELD: 2 QT 20 OZ (2.5 L)

Double consomme (Recipe 122)	*2 qt 20 oz*	*2.5 L*

GARNISH

Butter	*1/3 oz*	*10 g*
Eggs	*2*	*2*
Milk	*6 3/4 oz*	*200 ml*
Seasoning (salt, nutmeg)	*1x*	*1x*

METHOD
Butter small souffle cups.

Break eggs and stir well. Heat milk, add to eggs, and stir well.

Season to taste.

Strain through fine mesh china cap.

Fill souffle cups.

Steam custard in a steamer or a water bath in low-temperature oven.

Let cool; unmold custard and cut into attractive shapes.

Heat consomme.

Add garnish to hot consomme.

---

[a] Dumplings are fragile and must be placed in soup cups or plates to order.

165

$\mathcal{B}$eef Consomme with Cheese Straws

Kraftbrühe mit Käsestäbchen
Consommé aux paillettes

YIELD: 2 QT 20 OZ (2.5 L)

Double consomme (Recipe 122)	2 qt 20 oz	2.5 L

GARNISH

Puff pastry (Recipe 689)	5 1/3 oz	150 g
Egg	1	1
Parmesan cheese, grated	2/3 oz	20 g
Sweet paprika	1/3 oz	10 g

METHOD

Roll puff pastry into rectangle about 1/16 in. (1.5 mm) thick.

Brush with egg.

Sprinkle with Parmesan and paprika.

Refrigerate for 30 minutes.

Cut into strips about 1/5 in. (5 mm) wide and shape into twists.

Place twists on sheet pan. Let rest again.

Bake at about 400°F (200°C).

Cut baked twists into pieces about 2 1/2 in. (70 mm) long.

Serve twists with the consomme while still fresh.

166

$\mathcal{B}$eef Consomme with Rice and Tomatoes

Kraftbrühe Madrider Art
Consommé madrilène

YIELD: 2 QT 20 OZ (2.5 L)

Double consomme (Recipe 122)	2 qt 20 oz	2.5 L

GARNISH

Long-grain rice	1 1/3 oz	40 g
Tomatoes	7 oz	200 g
Seasoning (salt, cayenne)	1x	1x
Madeira wine[a]	2/3 oz	20 ml

---

[a] A medium-dry sherry can be substituted for the Madeira.

METHOD

Boil rice in salt water, drain, rinse with cold water, and drain again.

Blanch tomatoes, peel, cut in half, remove seeds, and cut into small dice.

Season consomme with salt and cayenne. Add Madeira wine.

Garnish consomme with diced tomatoes and rice just before service.

167

$\mathcal{B}$eef Consomme with Beef Marrow

Karftbühe mit Mark
Consommé à la moelle

YIELD: 2 QT 20 OZ (2.5 L)

Double consomme (Recipe 122)	2 qt 20 oz	2.5 L

GARNISH

Beef marrow (removed from bones)	8 3/4 oz	250 g
Chives, fresh, cut into slivers	1/3 oz	10 g

METHOD

Cut marrow into slices and soak in warm water to remove blood.

Poach marrow to order by dipping briefly in simmering water.

Lift marrow from poaching water and add to consomme at the moment of service.

Sprinkle with chives.

168

Cream of Pumpkin Soup

Kürbiscremesuppe
Crème de potiron

YIELD: 2 QT 20 OZ (2.5 L)

Pumpkin[a]	2 lb 3 oz	1.0 kg
Vegetable bouillon (Recipe 27)	2 qt 20 oz	2.5 L
Leeks	3 1/2 oz	100 g
Onions	3 1/2 oz	100 g
Knob celery (celeriac)	1 1/3 oz	40 g
Butter	1 1/3 oz	40 g
White wheat flour	1 1/3 oz	40 g
Heavy cream (36%)	6 3/4 oz	200 ml
Milk	3 1/3 oz	100 ml
Seasoning	1x	1x
Chervil, fresh, chopped	1/6 oz	5 g

MISE EN PLACE

Peel pumpkin and remove seeds. With melon baller, scoop out 20 small balls to use as garnish, and boil in vegetable stock or steam until cooked. Cut remaining pumpkin into small slices.

Wash and trim leeks; be sure sand is cleaned from layers. Cut into medium dice.

Cut onions and knob celery into medium dice.

METHOD

Sauté leeks, onions, and knob celery in butter.

Add sliced pumpkin and continue cooking.

Dust with flour and let cool.

Add hot vegetable stock, and bring to a boil, stirring continuously.

Boil until vegetables are soft, skimming occasionally.

Purée,[b] and strain through fine mesh china cap.

Bring to a boil again. Stir in cream and milk. Season to taste.

Add pumpkin garnish to soup. Sprinkle with chervil.

169

Lime Soup (Avgolemeno)[a]

Limonensuppe
Crème au citron vert

YIELD: 1 QT 19 OZ (1.5 L)

Double consomme (Recipe 122)	1 qt 2 oz	1.0 L
Limes (green)	3 1/2 oz	100 g
Vialone rice[b]	2/3 oz	20 g
Seasoning	1x	1x
Heavy cream (36%)	6 3/4 oz	200 ml
Egg yolks	4	4
Butter, cold	1 2/3 oz	50 g
Salt (pinch)	1x	1x

MISE EN PLACE

Bring consomme to a boil.

Squeeze juice from limes.

Boil rice in salt water until cooked, drain, rinse with cold water, and drain again.

METHOD

Whip cream and egg yolks with wire whisk in steam table until warm.

Add hot consomme slowly, stirring continuously.

Pour soup into soup pot.

Heat, stirring, until soup starts to thicken (do not allow to boil).

Strain immediately into another soup pot through a fine mesh china cap.

Add cold butter in small nuggets; do not allow the soup to boil again.

Season with lime juice. Season to taste.

Put warm soup into heated cups. Garnish with cooked rice. Serve immediately.

---

[a] The pumpkin flesh should be as red as possible.

[b] This is best accomplished with a hand-held electric mixer.

[a] When made with lemon, this is known as Avgolemono Soup, and is a specialty of Greece.

[b] The recipe specifies Vialone rice, which is a short-grain rice similar to Arborio.

170

Purée of Lentil Soup

Linsenpüreesuppe
Purée Conti

YIELD: 2 QT 20 OZ (2.5 L)

Lentils	12 oz	350 g
Leeks, green leaves only	3 1/2 oz	100 g
Onions	3 1/2 oz	100 g
Knob celery (celeriac)	1 1/3 oz	40 g
Potatoes	7 oz	200 g
Bacon rind (skin), smoked	1 2/3 oz	50 g
White bread (Pullman loaf)	3 1/2 oz	100 g
Clarified butter	2/3 oz	20 g
Butter	2 oz	60 g
Bouillon (Recipe 22)	3 qt 5 oz	3.0 L
Seasoning	1x	1x
Butter, cold	2/3 oz	20 g
Chervil, fresh, chopped	1/2 tbsp	2 g

MISE EN PLACE

Soak lentils in water for 4 to 6 hours.

Wash and trim leeks; be sure sand is cleaned from layers. Cut into medium dice.

Cut onions and knob celery into medium dice.

Peel and slice potatoes.

Tie bacon rind into a bundle to make it easier to remove.

Remove crust from bread, cut into small cubes, and sauté in clarified butter until croutons are golden brown.

METHOD

Sauté leeks, onions, and knob celery in butter. Add drained lentils.

Add cold bouillon and add bacon rind, bring to a boil, and skim.

Boil for about 1 1/2 hours.

Add potatoes and continue boiling 1/2 hour longer.

Remove bacon rind.

Purée,[a] and strain through china cap.

Bring to a boil again.

Season to taste. Add cold butter in small nuggets.

Sprinkle with chervil leaves. Serve bread croutons on the side.

[a] This is best accomplished with a hand-held electric mixer.

171

Cream of Almond Soup

Mandelcremesuppe
Crème dame blanche

YIELD: 2 QT 20 OZ (2.5 L)

Almonds, skinless	3 1/2 oz	100 g
Milk	10 oz	300 ml
Chicken breast, skinless	3 1/2 oz	100 g
Chicken stock (Recipe 26)	2 qt 20 oz	2.5 L
White wheat flour	3 1/2 oz	100 g
Butter	1 2/3 oz	50 g
Heavy cream (36%)	12 oz	350 ml
Seasoning	1x	1x
Chervil, fresh, chopped	1/6 oz	5 g

MISE EN PLACE

Grind almonds very fine, mix with milk, bring to a boil, and steep for 2 hours.

Poach chicken breast in small amount of stock; let cool, and dice.

METHOD

Make white roux with flour and butter; let cool.

Add hot chicken stock and almond milk.

Simmer for at least 20 minutes.

Strain through fine mesh china cap.

Bring to a boil again.

Stir in heavy cream. Season to taste.

Add diced chicken breast. Sprinkle with chervil leaves.

172

Cold Melon Soup

Melonenkaltschale
Soupe froide au melon

YIELD: 1 QT 19 OZ (1.5 L)

Melon (Cavaillon)[a]	4 lb	1.8 kg
Sugar	5 1/3 oz	150 g
White wine	8 1/2 oz	250 ml
Red Port wine	3 1/3 oz	100 ml
Lemon	1	1

MISE EN PLACE
Peel melon, cut in half, and remove seeds. Cut 8 3/4 oz (250 g) of the melon into small dice for garnish. Cut remaining melon into cubes.

METHOD
Purée[b] melon cubes with all other ingredients except lemon. Strain if necessary.

Season with lemon juice.

Add diced melon as garnish.

Serve in chilled glasses with drinking straws and demi-tasse spoons.

173

Minestrone Soup

Minestrone

YIELD: 2 QT 20 OZ (2.5 L)

Borlotti beans[c]	1 2/3 oz	50 g
Onions	3 1/2 oz	100 g
Bacon, smoked	1 2/3 oz	50 g
Leeks, white part only	7 oz	200 g
Savoy cabbage	5 1/3 oz	150 g
Knob celery (celeriac)	3 1/2 oz	100 g
Carrots	5 1/3 oz	150 g
Potatoes	7 oz	200 g
Tomatoes	3 1/2 oz	100 g
Spaghetti	1 2/3 oz	50 g
Fatback, unsalted	1 2/3 oz	50 g
Garlic, peeled	1/3 oz	10 g
Parsley, chopped	1/6 oz	5 g
Basil, chopped	1/6 oz	5 g
Olive oil	1 2/3 oz	50 ml
Tomato paste	1 1/3 oz	40 g
Bouillon (Recipe 22)	2 qt 20 oz	2.5 L
Seasoning	1x	1x
Parmesan cheese, grated	3 oz	80 g

MISE EN PLACE
Soak beans in cold water for 4 to 6 hours, drain, and boil in water until soft.

Chop onions.

Cut bacon into small dice (*brunoise*).

Wash and trim leeks; be sure sand is cleaned from layers.

Cut leeks, cabbage, knob celery, carrots, and potatoes into fine slivers (*paysanne*).

Peel tomatoes halve, remove seeds, and cut into small dice.

Break spaghetti into small pieces by wrapping in a clean kitchen towel and moving towel back and forth over the rim of a table.

Purée fatback, garlic, parsley, and basil in food processor to make pesto.

METHOD
Sauté onions and bacon in olive oil.

Add leeks and cabbage, then remaining knob celery and carrots, and continue cooking.

Add tomato paste and bouillon.

Bring to a boil, skim, and simmer until vegetables are almost tender.

Add potatoes and spaghetti; boil 10 minutes longer.

Add cooked beans, tomatoes, and pesto. Bring to a boil.

Season to taste.

Serve with grated cheese on the side.

---

[a] The recipe specifies Cavaillon melon; another melon can be substituted.

[b] Use a food processor.

[c] Borlotti beans are dried, pink-speckled beans.

174

ℳulligatawny Soup
Mulligatawny

Y I E L D : 2 Q T 20 O Z (2 . 5 L)

Chicken, oven-ready[a]	2 lb	900 g
Chicken stock (Recipe 26)	2 qt 20 oz	2.5 L
Onions	3 oz	80 g
Siam-Patna rice	1 oz	30 g
Butter	1 oz	30 g
Madras curry powder	1 oz	30 g
White wheat flour	3 1/2 oz	100 g
Heavy cream (36%)	6 3/4 oz	200 ml
Seasoning (salt and pepper)	1x	1x

MISE EN PLACE

Blanch chicken in boiling water, rinse, and cook in chicken stock until tender.

Bone and remove skin from boiled chicken; cut meat into small strips.

Peel onions and chop fine.

Strain chicken stock; skim off fat.

Boil rice until cooked but firm.

METHOD

Sauté onions in butter.

Dust with curry powder and continue cooking.

Dust with flour and add the strained chicken stock.

Bring to a boil, skim, and simmer for 45 minutes.

Strain through fine mesh china cap.

Stir in cream. Season to taste.

Add chicken strips and rice.

---

[a] Gutted, with gizzards and neck removed.

175

𝒫etite Marmite Henri IV
Petite Marmite Henri IV

Y I E L D : F O R 10 S E R V I N G S

Chicken, oven ready[a]	4 lb 7 oz	2.0 kg
Beef for boiling[b]	2 lb 10 oz	1.2 kg
Leeks	8 1/3 oz	250 g
Carrots	8 1/3 oz	250 g
Knob celery (celeriac)	7 oz	200 g
Savoy cabbage	8 1/3 oz	250 g
Chives, fresh	1 1/3 oz	50 g
Marrow bones, cut into slices[c]	1 lb 10 oz	750 g
Beef bouillon (Recipe 22)	3 qt 22 oz	3.5 L
Bouquet garni (Recipe 7)	8 oz	250 g
Sachet bag[d]	1	1
Beef bouillon (Recipe 22)	1 qt 2 oz	1.0 L

MISE EN PLACE

Blanch beef and chicken; drain; rinse first in hot, then in cold water.

Wash and trim leeks; be sure sand is cleaned from layers.

Wash and trim carrots, knob celery, and Savoy cabbage.

Cut all four vegetables into strips (*julienne*) or into fine slivers (*paysanne*).

Wash chives; and cut into slivers.

Dip marrow bones in simmering water to blanch.

Make sachet bag.[d]

METHOD

Bring bouillon to boil; add beef, *bouquet garni*, and sachet bag.

Simmer 2 hours; skim; and remove impurities occasionally.

Add chicken; and continue simmering.

Boil leeks, carrots, knob celery, and Savoy cabbage separately in bouillon.

Remove beef and chicken from stock; cut into attractive pieces.

Serve marmite with beef, chicken, vegetables, and marrow bones.

Sprinkle with chives.

---

[a] Boiling beef can be chuck, deckel meat; or knuckle face. It should be trimmed, but not too lean.

[b] Gutted, with gizzards and neck removed. The weight indicates that probably 2 chicken or 1 fowl should be used.

[c] The marrow bones should be sawed across into 1/8-in. sections.

[d] In addition to the usual ingredients, this sachet bag may also include parsley, bay leaf, thyme, cloves, and peppercorns.

176

*C*ream of Rice Soup, German Style

Reiscremesuppe deutsche Art
Crème allemande

YIELD: 2 QT 20 OZ (2.5 L)

Matignon (Recipe 13)	7 oz	200 g
White veal stock (Recipe 28)	2 qt 20 oz	2.5 L
Butter	1 1/3 oz	40 g
Rice flour	3 1/2 oz	100 g
Milk	3 1/3 oz	100 ml
Heavy cream (36%)	8 1/2 oz	250 ml
Seasoning	1x	1x

MISE EN PLACE
Have vegetables and veal stock ready.

METHOD
Heat butter, add *matignon* and sauté.

Dust with rice flour, add veal stock, and simmer for 40 minutes; strain.

Stir in milk and cream.

Season to taste.

177

*P*uréed Red Kidney Bean Soup

Rote Bohnenpüreesuppe
Purée Condé

YIELD: 2 QT 20 OZ (2.5 L)

Red kidney beans	12 oz	350 g
Leeks	3 1/2 oz	100 g
Onions	3 1/2 oz	100 g
Knob celery (celeriac)	1 1/3 oz	40 g
Potatoes	7 oz	200 g
White bread (Pullman loaf)	3 1/2 oz	100 g
Clarified butter	2/3 oz	20 g
Butter	2 oz	60 g
Bouillon (Recipe 22)	3 qt 5 oz	3.0 L
Seasoning	1x	1x
Heavy cream (36%)	3 1/3 oz	100 ml
Butter, cold	2/3 oz	20 g
Chervil, fresh, chopped	1/6 oz	2 g

MISE EN PLACE
Soak red kidney beans in water for 4 to 6 hours.

Wash and trim leeks; be sure sand is cleaned from layers. Cut into medium dice.

Cut onions and knob celery into medium dice.

Peel and slice potatoes.

Remove crust from bread, cut into small cubes, and sauté in clarified butter until croutons are golden brown.

METHOD
Sauté leeks, onions, and knob celery in butter.

Add drained beans.

Add cold bouillon, bring to a boil, and skim.

Simmer for about 2 hours.

Add potatoes and simmer 1/2 hour longer.

Purée[a] and strain through china cap. Bring to a boil once more, and add cream.

Add cold butter in small nuggets. Season to taste.

Sprinkle with chervil. Serve croutons on the side.

---

[a] This is best accomplished with a hand-held electric mixer.

178

*C*ream of Asparagus Soup (vegetarian)

Spargelcremesuppe
Crème d'asperges

YIELD: 2 QT 20 OZ (2.5 L)

White asparagus[a]	14 oz	400 g
Asparagus stock, made from the asparagus (see Mise en place)	2 qt 20 oz	2.5 L
Leeks, white part only	3 1/2 oz	100 g
Onions	3 1/2 oz	100 g
Knob celery (celeriac)	1 1/3 oz	40 g
Butter	1 1/3 oz	40 g
White wheat flour	3 oz	80 g
Heavy cream (36%)	10 oz	300 ml
Seasoning	1x	1x
Chervil, fresh, chopped	1/6 oz	2 g

MISE EN PLACE
Wash and peel asparagus. Cut off tips, cook, and reserve for garnish. (If tips are large, cut into smaller pieces.)

Make asparagus stock: Cut off tough ends of asparagus stalks. Cover with 3 qt 6 oz (3 L) water, bring to a boil, simmer for 20 minutes. Strain and save stock.

Cut asparagus into medium dice.

Wash and trim leeks; be sure sand is cleaned from layers. Cut into medium dice.

Cut onions and knob celery into medium dice.

METHOD
Sauté leeks, onions, and knob celery in butter.

Add diced asparagus and continue cooking.

Dust with flour and continue cooking. Let mixture cool.

Add hot asparagus stock and bring to a boil, stirring.

Boil for at least 20 minutes; skim occasionally.

Strain through china cap. Bring to a boil again.

Stir in cream. Season to taste.

Garnish with asparagus tips. Sprinkle with chervil.

---

[a] In Switzerland, white asparagus is the most common variety. Green asparagus can be substituted.

179

*P*urée of Spinach Soup

Spinatpüreesuppe
Purée florentine

YIELD: 2 QT 20 OZ (2.5 L)

Spinach, fresh	1 lb 12 oz	800 g
Leeks, green leaves only	3 1/2 oz	100 g
Onions	3 1/2 oz	100 g
Knob celery (celeriac)	1 1/3 oz	40 g
Potatoes	10 1/2 oz	300 g
Butter	2 oz	60 g
Bouillon (Recipe 22)	2 qt 20 oz	2.5 L
Heavy cream (36%)	6 3/4 oz	200 ml
Seasoning (salt and pepper)	1x	1x

MISE EN PLACE
Wash and blanch[a] spinach; chop coarsely.

Wash and trim leeks; be sure sand is cleaned from layers. Cut into medium dice.

Cut onions and knob celery into medium dice.

Peel and slice potatoes.

METHOD
Sauté leeks, onions, and knob celery in butter.

Add potatoes and spinach.

Add hot bouillon, bring to a boil, and skim.

Simmer for about 45 minutes.

Purée[b] and strain through china cap.

Bring to a boil again.

Stir in cream. Season to taste.

NOTE: Cream of spinach soup should not be kept in steam table for a long time because taste and color will change.

---

[a] For a more intense spinach flavor, this step can be eliminated.

[b] This is best accomplished with a hand-held electric mixer.

180

Farmer's Soup

Suppe Bauernart
Potage paysanne

YIELD: 2 QT 20 OZ (2.5 L)

Slab bacon, smoked	3 oz	80 g
Onions	3 1/2 oz	100 g
Leeks, green leaves only	5 1/3 oz	150 g
Savoy cabbage	5 1/3 oz	150 g
Carrots	5 1/3 oz	150 g
Knob celery (celeriac)	3 1/2 oz	100 g
Potatoes	5 1/3 oz	150 g
Butter	1 1/3 oz	40 g
White wheat flour	2/3 oz	20 g
Bouillon (Recipe 22)	2 qt 20 oz	2.5 L
Seasoning	1x	1x
Parsley, chopped	1/3 oz	10 g
Sbrinz,[a] grated	3 1/2 oz	100 g

MISE EN PLACE

Cut bacon into small dice.

Chop onions fine.

Wash and trim leeks; be sure sand is cleaned from layers. Cut into small slivers (*paysanne*).

Cut Savoy cabbage, carrots, knob celery, and potatoes into small slivers (*paysanne*).

METHOD

Sauté bacon in butter. Add onions, leeks, Savoy cabbage,[b] and continue cooking.

Add carrots and knob celery and continue cooking.

Dust with flour. Add hot bouillon, bring to a boil, skimming occasionally.

Simmer for about 1 hour. Add potatoes. Simmer for 20 minutes longer.

Season to taste.

Sprinkle with parsley. Serve grated cheese on the side.

181

Brussels Sprouts Soup

Suppe flämische Art
Potage flamande

YIELD: 2 QT 20 OZ (2.5 L)

Onions	3 1/2 oz	100 g
Brussels sprouts	10 1/2 oz	300 g
Leeks	3 1/2 oz	100 g
Potatoes	14 oz	400 g
Butter	1 1/3 oz	40 g
Bouillon (Recipe 22)	2 qt 20 oz	2.5 L
Seasoning	1x	1x
Chervil, fresh, chopped	1/6 oz	5 g

MISE EN PLACE

Chop onions fine.

Trim, wash, and blanch Brussels sprouts. Reserve 3 1/2 oz (100 g) small Brussels sprouts for garnish. Steam and cut into quarters. Coarsely chop remaining Brussels sprouts.

Wash and trim leeks; be sure sand is cleaned from layers. Cut into slivers (*paysanne*).

Cut potatoes into slivers (*paysanne*).

METHOD

Sauté onions and leeks in butter.

Add chopped Brussels sprouts and continue cooking.

Add hot bouillon and bring to a boil, while stirring. Simmer for about 45 minutes.

Add potatoes, skimming occasionally.

Simmer until all ingredients are soft.

Season to taste.

Garnish with reserved Brussels sprouts. Sprinkle with chervil.

---

[a] Sbrinz is a hard grating cheese from Switzerland. Parmesan can be substituted.

[b] Vegetables with high water content are sautéed first in order to cook off some excess moisture.

182

$\mathcal{C}$reamed Potato Soup

Suppe Hausfrauenart
Potage bonne femme

YIELD: 2 QT 20 OZ (2.5 L)

Onions	3 1/2 oz	100 g
Leeks	2 oz	60 g
Baguettes,[a] slices	20	20
Butter	1 oz	30 g
White wheat flour	2/3 oz	20 g
Bouillon (Recipe 22)	2 qt 20 oz	2.5 L
Potatoes	14 oz	400 g
Heavy cream (36%)	3 1/3 oz	100 ml
Seasoning	1x	1x
Chives, cut into slivers	1 tbsp	2 g

MISE EN PLACE

Chop onions fine.

Wash and trim leeks; be sure sand is cleaned from layers. Cut into slivers (*paysanne*).

Toast baguette slices/rounds until golden brown.

METHOD

Sauté onions and leeks in butter.

Dust with flour; let cool slightly.

Add hot bouillon and simmer for 45 minutes.

Add potatoes; boil until all ingredients are soft, skimming occasionally.

Stir in cream just before service.

Season to taste.

Sprinkle with chives.

Serve toasted bread rounds on the side.

[a] Use small loaves of French bread to get small-sized rounds.

183

$\mathcal{V}$egetable Soup

Suppe Pflanzerart
Potage cultivateur

YIELD: 2 QT 20 OZ (2.5 L)

Slab bacon, smoked	1 2/3 oz	50 g
Onions	3 1/2 oz	100 g
Leeks, green leaves only	7 oz	200 g
Carrots	10 1/2 oz	300 g
Turnips (white)	7 oz	200 g
Potatoes	7 oz	200 g
Butter	1 oz	30 g
Bouillon (Recipe 22)	2 qt 20 oz	2.5 L
Seasoning	1x	1x
Parsley, chopped	1/3 oz	10 g
Sbrinz,[a] grated	3 1/2 oz	100 g

MISE EN PLACE

Cut bacon into small dice. Chop onions fine.

Wash and trim leeks; be sure sand is cleaned from layers. Cut into slivers (*paysanne*).

Cut carrots, turnips, and potatoes into fine slivers (*paysanne*).

METHOD

Sauté bacon in butter.

Add onions and leeks and continue cooking.

Add carrots and turnips and continue cooking.

Add hot bouillon and bring to a boil, while stirring. Simmer for 45 minutes.

Add potatoes. Simmer until all ingredients are soft, skimming occasionally.

Stir in cream just before service.

Season to taste.

Sprinkle with parsley.

Serve with grated cheese on the side.

[a] Sbrinz is a hard grating cheese from Switzerland. Parmesan can be substituted.

184

*C*ream of Tomato Soup

Tomatencremesuppe
Crème de tomates

YIELD: 2 QT 20 OZ (2.5 L)

Tomatoes	2 lb 3 oz	1.0 kg
Leeks	3 oz	80 g
Onions	3 1/2 oz	100 g
Knob celery (celeriac)	1 1/3 oz	40 g
Carrots	2 oz	60 g
Butter	1 1/3 oz	40 g
Garlic, crushed	1/6 oz	5 g
Tomato paste	3 1/2 oz	100 g
White wheat flour	2 1/2 oz	70 g
Vegetable bouillon (Recipe 27)	2 qt 20 oz	2.5 L
Heavy cream (36%)	10 oz	300 ml
Seasoning	1x	1x
Basil, fresh, chopped	1/6 oz	2 g

MISE EN PLACE

Blanch 2 tomatoes, peel, halve, remove seeds, and cut into small dice; reserve for garnish.

Cut remaining tomatoes in half, remove seeds, and cut into cubes.

Wash and trim leeks; be sure sand is cleaned from layers. Cut into medium dice.

Cut onions, knob celery, and carrots into medium dice.

METHOD

Sauté leeks, onions, knob celery, carrots, and garlic in butter.

Add tomato paste and continue cooking.

Dust with flour; let cool.

Heat vegetable bouillon, add to vegetable mixture, and bring to a boil, stirring continuously.

Add cubed tomatoes. Boil until all ingredients are soft, skimming occasionally.

Purée and strain through fine mesh china cap.

Bring to a boil again.

Stir in heavy cream.

Season to taste. (If too acidic, add a little sugar.)

Add diced tomato garnish. Sprinkle with basil.

185

*B*aked Onion Soup

Überbackene Zwiebelsuppe
Soup à l'oignon gratinée

YIELD: 2 QT 20 OZ (2.5 L)

Onions	1 lb 2 oz	500 g
French bread (baguette)	5 1/3 oz	150 g
Clarified butter	1 2/3 oz	50 g
Parmesan cheese, grated	3 oz	80 g
Sunflower oil	1 2/3 oz	50 ml
Bouillon (Recipe 22)	2 qt 20 oz	2.5 L
Seasoning (salt and pepper)	1x	1x

MISE EN PLACE

Peel and slice onions.

Cut bread into thin slices, sauté in clarified butter, and sprinkle with half of the Parmesan cheese.

METHOD

Sauté onions in sunflower oil until golden brown.

Add bouillon and simmer until onions are tender (about 20 minutes).

Season to taste.

Fill oven-proof cups or cocottes with soup.

Top with toasted bread slices; sprinkle with remaining grated cheese.

Place under the salamander until cheese is brown (*gratinée*).[a]

---

[a] Soup can also be baked in a water bath in a hot oven.

186

$\mathcal{G}$rape Soup with Auvernier Wine

Weincremesuppe mit Auvernier
Crème au vin d'Auvernier

YIELD: 1 QT 19 OZ (1.5 L)

Onions	2 oz	60 g
Leeks, white part only	1 1/3 oz	40 g
White seedless grapes	7 oz	200 g
Butter	1 1/3 oz	40 g
White wheat flour	1 2/3 oz	50 g
White Auvernier wine[a]	10 oz	300 ml
White veal stock (Recipe 28)	1 qt 19 oz	1.5 L
Heavy cream (36%)	6 3/4 oz	200 ml
Seasoning	1x	1x
Lovage, chopped[b]	1/6 oz	5 g

MISE EN PLACE

Trim onions and cut into medium dice.

Wash and trim leeks; be sure sand is cleaned from layers. Cut into medium dice.

Peel grapes and cut into quarters. Reserve for garnish.

METHOD

Sauté vegetables in butter.

Dust with flour and continue cooking.

Add 5 oz (150 ml) wine and white veal stock. Simmer for 30 minutes.

Strain through fine mesh china cap.

Add remaining wine and bring to a boil.

Add cream and season to taste.

Garnish with grapes.

Serve in hot soup cups, sprinkle with lovage.

---

[a] Auvernier is a Swiss white wine, seldom available outside of Switzerland. It has nothing to do with the wines from Auvergne, a province in central France.

[b] Lovage is an herb seldom used outside of Europe. The German name is *Liebstöckel*.

187

$\mathcal{P}$urée of Navy Beans

Püreesuppe von weissen Bohnen
Purée Faubonne

YIELD: 2 QT 20 OZ (2.5 L)

White Navy beans[a]	12 oz	350 g
Leeks	3 1/2 oz	100 g
Onions	3 1/2 oz	100 g
Knob celery (celeriac)	1 1/3 oz	40 g
Potatoes	7 oz	200 g
Bacon rind (skin)	1 2/3 oz	50 g
White bread (Pullman loaf)	3 1/2 oz	100 g
Clarified butter	2/3 oz	20 g
Butter	2 oz	60 g
Bouillon (Recipe 22)	3 qt 5 oz	3.0 L
Heavy cream (36%)	3 1/3 oz	100 ml
Butter, cold	2/3 oz	20 g
Seasoning	1x	1x
Chervil, fresh, chopped	1/2 tsp	2 g

MISE EN PLACE

Soak beans in cold water for 4 to 6 hours.

Wash and trim leeks; be sure sand is cleaned from layers. Cut into medium dice.

Cut onions and knob celery into medium dice.

Peel and slice potatoes.

Tie bacon rind into a bundle to make removal easier.

Remove crust from bread, cut into small cubes, and sauté in clarified butter until croutons are golden brown.

METHOD

Sauté leeks, onions, and knob celery in butter.

Add drained beans. Add cold bouillon and bacon rind.

Bring to a boil, skim, and simmer for about 2 hours.

Add potatoes, and cook 1/2 hour longer. Remove bacon rind.

Purée[b] soup, and strain through china cap.

Bring to a boil once again.

Stir in cream. Add cold butter in small nuggets.

Season to taste.

Sprinkle with chervil. Serve with bread croutons.

---

[a] Any kind of small white beans can be used.

[b] This is best accomplished with a hand-held electric mixer.

188

$\mathcal{G}$ame Consomme

Wildkraftbrühe
Consommé de gibier

YIELD: 2 QT 20 OZ (2.5 L)

Game trimmings[a]	10 1/2 oz	300 g
Peanut oil	2/3 oz	20 ml
Leeks, green leaves only	3 oz	80 g
Carrots	3 oz	80 g
Knob celery (celeriac)	2 oz	60 g
Tomatoes	1 2/3 oz	50 g
Clarification meat[b]	5 1/3 oz	150 g
Porcini mushrooms, dried[c]	1/3 oz	10 g
Egg whites	2	2
Bay leaf	1/2	1/2
White peppercorns	5	5
Water	6 3/4 oz	200 ml
Game stock (Recipe 29)	3 qt 5 oz	3.0 L
Seasoning	1x	1x

MISE EN PLACE
Roast game trimmings in oil; chill.

Wash and trim leeks; be sure sand is cleaned from layers. Cut into medium dice.

Cut carrots and knob celery into medium dice.

Cube tomatoes.

Make clarification mixture by grinding roasted game trimmings and clarification meat through coarse plate of meat grinder. Thoroughly combine the ground meat, leeks, carrots, knob celery, tomatoes, dried mushrooms, egg whites, bay leaf, white peppercorns, and water. Refrigerate for at least 1 hour.

METHOD
Thoroughly combine clarification mixture with cold game stock.

Bring to a boil, stirring carefully with a paddle. As soon as consomme starts to boil, do not stir any longer.

Skim off fat and impurities and simmer for 1 hour.

Strain carefully through double layer of cheese cloth.

Remove all fat from surface with absorbent paper.

Season to taste.

---

[a] Game trimmings should be lean and without blood.

[b] The meat should be as lean as possible. Meat from beef shank is preferred because it is very lean and has a high gelatin content.

[c] Porcini are wild mushrooms, called *cèpes* in French, *Steinpilze* in German, and *porcini* in Italian. These mushrooms are widely available dried, and are increasingly available fresh. Because Italy is a large exporter of these mushrooms, the Italian name is commonly used.

189

$\mathcal{M}$ille Fanti Soup

Zuppa mille-fanti

YIELD: 2 QT 20 OZ (2.5 L)

Eggs	3	3
Parmesan cheese, grated	1 2/3 oz	50 g
Mie de pain[a]	3 1/2 oz	100 g
Bouillon (Recipe 22)	2 qt 20 oz	(2.5 L)
Chives, fresh	2/3 oz	20 g

MISE EN PLACE
Combine eggs, Parmesan, and *mie de pain* with a small amount of bouillon.

Cut chives into slivers.

METHOD
Bring remaining bouillon to a boil.

Add egg mixture in small threads to simmering stock. Do not stir.

Cover and poach for 10 minutes.

Before service, stir soup carefully with wire whisk to break up garnish.

Sprinkle with chives.

---

[a] *Mie de pain* are fresh bread crumbs, made from white Pullman loaves.

190

$\mathcal{S}$oup, Pavia[a] Style

Zuppa Pavese

Y I E L D : 2 Q T 2 0 O Z (2 . 5 L)

French bread (baguette)	*5 1/3 oz*	*150 g*
Clarified butter	*1 2/3 oz*	*50 g*
Eggs	*10*	*10*
Bouillon (Recipe 22)	*2 qt 20 oz*	*2.5 L*
Seasoning	*1x*	*1x*
Parmesan cheese, grated	*3 oz*	*80 g*

MISE EN PLACE

Slice bread and sauté in clarified butter until golden brown.

Carefully break one egg into each soup cup or cocotte. (If desired, the egg yolk only, unbroken, can be used.)

METHOD

Bring bouillon to a boil and season to taste.

Carefully ladle boiling hot bouillon over the eggs.

Top with bread slices.

Sprinkle with cheese and brown under the salamander.

---

[a] Pavia is a city in Lombardy, Italy.

Appetizers

Cold Appetizers

*A*ssorted Cold Seafood Plate

Allerlei mit Austern und Jacobsmuscheln
Panaché d'huîtres et de coquilles St-Jacques

YIELD: 10 SERVINGS

Broccoli, fresh	1 lb 2 oz	500 g
Leeks, green leaves only	10 1/2 oz	300 g
Oysters, large and flat[a]	30	30
Sea scallops[b]	1 lb 2 oz	500 g
Dry white wine	1 2/3 oz	50 ml
Chervil, fresh for garnish	1/3 oz	10 g

DRESSING

Carrots	3 1/2 oz	100 g
Parsley, Italian, fresh	2/3 oz	20 g
Chervil twig, fresh	1	10 g
Nut oil[c]	3 1/3 oz	100 ml
Herb vinegar	1 1/3 oz	40 ml
Seasoning	1x	1x

METHOD FOR DRESSING

Peel carrots and cut into *julienne*. Steam or boil. Let cool.

Chop parsley and chervil. Save some chervil leaves for garnish.

Combine oil, vinegar, and other dressing ingredients.

Add 2/3 oz (20 ml) cold oyster/scallop stock (fumet).

Season to taste. Mix well.

METHOD

Cut broccoli into small florets. Boil, drain, rinse with cold water, and drain again.

Wash and trim leeks; be sure sand is cleaned from layers. Cut into slivers about 1/5-in. wide, and steam briefly.

Open oysters; save juice.

Clean scallops, cut into thin slices. Poach oysters and scallops briefly in oyster juice and wine. Chill.

Drain chilled seafood and save some stock for dressing.

Blend seafood carefully with small amount of dressing.

PRESENTATION

Make attractive circles on plates with leeks and broccoli.

Place seafood salad in centers.

Drizzle remaining dressing over leeks and broccoli.

Garnish with chervil leaves.

*A*pple and Celery Cocktail

Apfelcocktail mit Sellerie
Cocktail de reinettes au céleri

YIELD: 10 SERVINGS

Apples[a]	4 lb	1.8 kg
Lemon	1	1
Knob celery (celeriac)	10 1/2 oz	300 g
Chives, fresh	1/3 oz	10 g
Walnut halves[b]	3 1/2 oz	100 g
Yogurt, plain	12 oz	350 g
Seasoning (salt and pepper)	1x	1x
Air-dried ham,[c] sliced	10 1/2 oz	300 g
Parsley, sprigs, washed	2/3 oz	20 g

MISE EN PLACE

Wash apples and cut off lids from tops. Save lids.

Remove center cores, then scoop out small balls with small melon baller or other suitable tool. Leave shells whole. Blend apple balls with lemon juice to avoid discoloration.

Cut knob celery into small dice (*brunoise*) and also blend with lemon juice.

Cut chives into slivers.

Chop nuts coarsely.

METHOD

Combine apple balls, knob celery, chives, nuts, and yogurt. Season to taste with salt and pepper.

Fill apple shells with fruit mixture. Replace lids.

Place filled apples onto individual plates.

Garnish each plate with slices of ham and parsley sprigs.

---

[a] Any variety of oysters can be used.

[b] The scallops should be large. If sea scallops are not available, the smaller bay scallops can be substituted. Bay scallops don't have to be sliced.

[c] Any aromatic oil can be used. Good-quality walnut oil is preferable, but good olive oil can be substituted.

---

[a] Golden Delicious apples do not discolor when exposed to air.

[b] Pieces can be used instead of halves. Pecans can be substituted for walnuts.

[c] The recipe specifies air-dried ham from *Graubünden*, a province of Switzerland. *Prosciutto* ham can be substituted.

193

Artichoke Bottoms with Seafood and Vegetable Salad

Artischokenböden mit Krustentier-Gemüse-Salat
Fonds d'artichauts à la salade de crustacé aux légumes

YIELD: 10 SERVINGS

Artichokes, large	10	10
Salt	1/3 oz	10 g
Lemon juice	2/3 oz	20 ml
Shrimp (prawns), large, raw	1 lb 2 oz	500 g
Lobster tail (in shell), raw	5 1/3 oz	150 g
Scampi tails, peeled, raw	7 oz	200 g
Carrots	8 3/4 oz	250 g
Knob celery (celeriac)	8 3/4 oz	250 g
Tomato vinaigrette (Recipe 100)	13 1/2 oz	400 ml
Eggs	3	3
Parsley, Italian, fresh	1/3 oz	10 g
Chervil, fresh	1/3 oz	10 g
Chives, fresh	1/3 oz	10 g
Peanut oil	1 2/3 oz	50 ml
Seasoning (salt and pepper)	1x	1x

MISE EN PLACE

Clean and peel artichokes. Save 20 attractive leaves for garnish.

Trim artichoke bottoms and boil in salted water with lemon juice.

Blanch the reserved 20 artichoke leaves.

Peel shrimp and remove dark veins. Reserve 10 whole shrimp as garnish.

Remove lobster tail from shell.

Cut scampi tails, lobster meat, and shrimp into small dice.

Peel carrots and knob celery. Cut into fine strips (*julienne*).

Blanch vegetables and combine with 2/3 of the tomato vinaigrette.

Hard-boil eggs, chill, peel, and chop.

Chop parsley and chervil. Cut chives into slivers.

METHOD

Heat oil and sauté all seafood, including the 10 reserved shrimp. Season to taste.

Marinate seafood with the tomato vinaigrette/vegetable mixture.

Marinate the 10 reserved shrimp in the remaining 1/3 tomato vinaigrette.

Put drained artichoke bottoms in centers of plates. Fill with seafood/vegetable salad.

Garnish each bottom with a large shrimp.

Fill artichoke leaves with chopped eggs. Place 2 leaves on each plate.

Sprinkle with chopped herbs.

194

Calf Sweetbreads in Aspic

Aspik von Kalbsmilken
Aspic de ris de veau

YIELD: 10 SERVINGS

Meat aspic, fresh (Recipe 5)	1 qt 2 oz	1.0 L
Sweetbreads	1 lb 12 oz	800 g
White veal stock (Recipe 28)	1 qt 2 oz	1.0 L
Onion, studded with cloves[a]	1	1
Dry white wine	3 1/3 oz	100 ml
Horseradish, fresh	1 2/3 oz	50 g
Parsley	2/3 oz	20 g
Assorted bell peppers	2 2/3 oz	75 g
Tomatoes	7 oz	200 g
DRESSING		
Raspberry vinegar	1 oz	30 ml
Hazelnut oil	2/3 oz	20 ml
Sunflower oil	2/3 oz	20 ml
Seasoning	1x	1x

MISE EN PLACE

Coat the inside of a 1 qt 19 oz (1.5 L) mold with aspic.

Soak sweetbreads overnight in cold water. Rinse.

Blanch sweetbreads in salt water for about 3 to 4 minutes. Let cool.

Bring to a boil the veal stock, onion, and wine.

Add blanched sweetbreads and bring to a boil again.

Poach sweetbreads at about 160°F (70°C)[b] for 15 minutes. Skim occasionally. Let sweetbreads cool in the stock.

Peel horseradish and grate fine.

(continued on next page)

---

[a] Two to three cloves should be used.

[b] The suggested poaching temperature could be increased to 180°F (80°C). The poaching time may also need to be increased.

(continued from preceding page)

Wash parsley, remove stems, and chop leaves.

Clean peppers, remove seeds, and cut into small dice. Blanch and let cool.

Peel tomatoes, remove seeds, and cut into small dice.

METHOD FOR DRESSING
Combine raspberry vinegar with oils to make a marinade.

Season to taste.

METHOD
Select the best pieces of sweetbread and cut into thin, even slices.

Line chilled mold attractively with sweetbread slices.

Remove skins from remaining sweetbreads and break into small, even pieces.

Combine sweetbread pieces, horseradish, parsley, peppers, and diced tomatoes.

Add dressing and season to taste.

Fill mold with mixture. Refrigerate.

Pour in cool but still liquid meat aspic.

Refrigerate until thoroughly chilled.

Unmold for service.

NOTE: Instead of using one large mold, individual 5 oz (150 ml) size molds can be used.

195

*P*aupiettes (rolls) of Sole in Aspic
Aspik von Seezungenröllchen
Aspic de paupiettes de sole

YIELD: 10 SERVINGS

Garnish for timbale molds

Fish aspic (Recipe 4)	1 qt 2 oz	1.0 L
Dill sprigs, tops, fresh	10	10
Black olives (canned), drained	1 2/3 oz	50 g
Fish aspic, for topping off (Recipe 4)	3 1/3 oz	100 ml

PAUPIETTES

Fillets of sole	1 lb 2 oz	500 g
Spinach, fresh	2 oz	60 g
Egg whites	1 oz	30 g
Heavy cream	3 1/3 oz	100 ml
Smoked salmon trimmings, diced	1 2/3 oz	50 g
Dill, fresh, chopped	1/3 oz	10 g
Seasoning (salt and pepper)	1x	1x
Butter	2/3 oz	20 g
Fish stock (Recipe 24)	1 2/3 oz	50 ml

FISH MOUSSE

Shallots	1 1/3 oz	40 g
Dry white wine	1 2/3 oz	50 ml
Seasoning (salt and pepper)	1x	1x
Fillets of sole	8 3/4 oz	250 g
Beurre manie[a]	1/3 oz	10 g
Fish aspic (Recipe 4)	3 1/3 oz	100 ml
Heavy cream	3 1/3 oz	100 ml
Dry vermouth[b]	2/3 oz	20 ml
Seasoning	1x	1x

MISE EN PLACE, FOR TIMBALE MOLDS
Coat the inside of 10 small, 5 oz (150 ml) timbale molds with fish aspic.

Garnish attractively with dill leave tops and olives. Refrigerate.

Have fish aspic ready for topping off.

---

[a] *Beurre manie* consists of equal parts cold butter and white wheat flour, kneaded together. It is used as a thickening agent, and is also called a cold roux.

[b] The original recipe specifies Noilly Prat, but any brand of dry vermouth can be used. Vermouth comes in dry and sweet varieties; use only dry in this recipe.

METHOD FOR PAUPIETTES

Reserve the best fish fillets for *paupiettes* (rolls). Trim and flatten the fillets and save trimmings for filling.

Blanch spinach leaves in salt water, drain, chill, and drain again.

Brush fish fillets with egg white and place blanched spinach leaves on top.

Chop remaining fish fillets, trimmings, and egg whites in food processor.

Pass (strain) through wire sieve.[a] Refrigerate.

In a bowl over ice, stir in cream, diced smoked salmon, and chopped dill. Season to taste.

Spread a thin layer of filling on top of the spinach which is on the flattened fish fillets. Roll up tightly.

Roll each fillet in buttered aluminum foil. Poke a few holes with a needle. Poach carefully in fish stock. Let cool. Save stock.

METHOD FOR FISH MOUSSE

Peel and chop shallots.

Combine shallots, fish stock in which the paupiettes were poached, and white wine. Season.

Poach fish fillets in the stock.

Let cool. Remove fish when cold. Save stock.

Thicken fish stock with *beurre manie*. Simmer for 15 minutes and chill resulting *velouté* sauce.

Purée poached fish fillets for mousse and *velouté* in food processor.

Place on ice and combine with cold (but still liquid) fish aspic, lightly whipped cream, and vermouth. Season to taste.

METHOD FOR ASSEMBLY

Cut fish rolls (*paupiettes*) into attractive slices and line the prepared timbale molds.

Fill molds with fish mousse. Refrigerate.

Top off with fish aspic. Chill thoroughly. Unmold for service.

---
[a] If commercial food processor is used, this step can be omitted.

196

*O*ysters on Half Shell

Austern auf Eis
Huîtres sur glace

YIELD: 10 SERVINGS

Oysters	60	60
Lemons	5	5
Butter	3 1/2 oz	100 g
Valais rye bread with nuts[a]	1 lb 12 oz	800 g

MISE EN PLACE

Open oysters carefully. Be sure not to spill the sea water.

Use only closed oysters!

Remove any shell splinters with a wet brush.

PRESENTATION

Serve oysters on ice.

Serve with lemon halves, cold butter,[b] and rye bread.

---
[a] The bread recommended in the original recipe is a specialty bread from a Swiss province. The type of bread (if any) served with oysters varies in different countries.

[b] In many countries, butter is not typically served with oysters.

197

Avocado and Wild Mushroom Plate

Avocadofächer mit Pilzen
Eventails d'avocat aux champignons

YIELD: 10 SERVINGS

Mushrooms, fresh	7 oz	200 g
Chanterelles[a]	5 1/3 oz	150 g
Porcini, fresh[b]	5 1/3 oz	150 g
Shallots	1 oz	30 g
Radishes	1 bunch	1 bunch
Sunflower oil	1 2/3 oz	50 ml
Parsley, chopped	2/3 oz	20 g
Avocados	5	5
Parsley, sprigs	10	20 g

DRESSING		
Parsley	2/3 oz	20 g
Assorted bell peppers	4 1/2 oz	120 g
Olive oil, cold pressed	1 2/3 oz	50 ml
Walnut oil	1 2/3 oz	50 ml
Red wine vinegar	1 2/3 oz	50 ml
Seasoning (salt and pepper)	1x	1x

MISE EN PLACE
Clean all mushrooms. Wash briefly and cut into small pieces.

Chop shallots.

Clean and trim radishes. Cut into slices.

METHOD FOR DRESSING
Wash parsley and chop leaves.

Remove seeds from peppers, cut into small dice, and blanch.

Combine olive oil, walnut oil, and wine vinegar with salt and freshly ground pepper.

Mix about 1/3 of the oil mixture with peppers. Save the remainder.

METHOD
Sauté mushrooms and shallots in sunflower oil. Add chopped parsley.

Remove from heat and combine with reserved 2/3 of the dressing. Season to taste.

Cut avocados in half. Peel and fan (slice fan-like).

---

[a] Chanterelles are yellow wild mushrooms, called *girolles* in French and *Eierschwämme* in German

[b] Porcini are wild mushrooms, called *cèpes* in French, *Steinpilze* in German, and *porcini* in Italian. These mushrooms are widely available dried, and are increasingly available fresh. Because Italy is a large exporter of these mushrooms, the Italian name is commonly used.

Place one avocado fan on each plate; top with dressing/pepper mixture.

Serve marinated mushrooms next to the avocados.

Sprinkle with radish slices and garnish with parsley sprigs.

198

Avocado and Shrimp Salad

Avocados mit Krevetten
Avocats aux crevettes

YIELD: 10 SERVINGS

Avocados, ripe	5	5
Lemon, juice	1	10 ml
Shrimp, drained	1 lb 2 oz	500 g
Cognac (or any brandy)	1 2/3 oz	50 ml
Cocktail sauce (Recipe 39)	8 1/2 oz	250 ml
Sesame seeds (peeled)	3/4 oz	25 g
Lemon	1	1
Black olives, canned, drained	2/3 oz	20 g
Dill leaves, tops	10	10

MISE EN PLACE
Cut avocados in half, remove pits, and sprinkle with lemon juice to prevent oxidation.

Marinate shrimp in Cognac and mix with cocktail sauce.

Toast sesame seeds (without adding any fat) in black cast iron pan.

Cut lemon into 10 very thin slices.

PRESENTATION
Fill avocado halves with shrimp salad.

Sprinkle with sesame seeds. Garnish with a lemon slice, black olive, and dill twig.

199

Terrine of Brook Trout with Dill

Bachforellenterrine mit Dill
Terrine de truite de rivière à l'aneth

YIELD: 20 SERVINGS

Shallots	1 2/3 oz	50 g
Butter	3/4 oz	25 g
White bread (Pullman loaf)	3 1/4 oz	90 g
Heavy cream (36%)	15 oz	450 ml
Egg white	1	1
Trout, gutted, whole	2 lb 3 oz	1.0 kg
Smoked trout fillets, skinless	7 oz	200 g
Seasoning (salt and pepper)	1x	1x
Cayenne pepper, ground	pinch	1 g
Dill, fresh, chopped	1/2 oz	15 g
Dill, sprigs, for garnish	1/2 oz	15 g
SAUCE		
Mayonnaise (Recipe 71)	1 lb 2 oz	500 g
Sour cream, light	6 3/4 oz	200 ml
Dill, fresh, chopped	3/4 oz	25 g
Seasoning (salt and pepper)	1x	1x

MISE EN PLACE
Chop shallots and sauté lightly in butter, without getting color. Let cool.

Remove crust from bread. There should be about 3 oz (80 g) of bread remaining. Cube bread.

Mix 3 1/3 oz (100 ml) cream with egg white and soak cubed bread in mixture.

METHOD
Bone whole trout. Leave skin on, but remove all bones. Cut and trim 6 fillets from the whole fish. There should be about 1 lb 9 oz (700 g) of fillets.

Trim the 6 fillets down to about 1/5-in. thickness. Reserve all trimmings for filling.

Butter a terrine mold. Line the buttered mold with trimmed fish fillets, skin side facing against the sides of the mold.

Remove any skin from leftover trout trimmings, and cut the trimmings into cubes.

Trim *smoked* trout fillets into neat fillets. Set aside. Cut the trimmings into cubes.

Combine all cubed trimmings with shallots and soaked bread. Grind through finest plate of meat grinder.

Purée mixture in food processor with 5 oz (150 ml) cream.

Whip 6 3/4 oz (200 ml) cream and fold into fish farce.

Season to taste and add chopped dill.

Fill terrine mold, which has already been lined with fish fillets, with about half of the fish farce. Place cleaned and trimmed *smoked* trout fillets on top.

Fill mold with remaining mousse. Smooth out top and carefully rap mold on table a few times to settle mousse and eliminate air bubbles.

Cover terrine with aluminum foil and poach in water bath at 185°F (85°C) in oven for about 50 minutes.[a] Let terrine cool.

METHOD FOR SERVICE
To make sauce, blend mayonnaise with sour cream and 1 oz chopped dill. Season to taste.

Cut terrine into slices. Serve plated and garnish with dill twig.

Serve dill mayonnaise on the side.

---

[a] The inside temperature should be at least 140°F (60°C).

200

Smoked Salmon on Puff Pastry Pillow

Blätterteigkissen mit Räucherlachs
Feuilletés au saumon fumé

YIELD: 10 SERVINGS

Puff pastry[a]	10 1/2 oz	300 g
Garden cress[b]	1 2/3 oz	50 g
Smoked salmon, trimmed, boneless	8 3/4 oz	250 g
Onions	5 1/3 oz	150 g
Radishes	1/4 bunch	1/4 bund
Chives, fresh	1/3 oz	10 g
Horseradish whipped cream (Recipe 73)	5 1/3 oz	150 g

MISE EN PLACE

Roll out puff pastry and cut into 3 1/2-in. (9 cm) circles.

Bake until crisp. Let cool and split horizontally. Save tops.

Wash cress.

Slice smoked salmon.

Peel onions and slice into rings.

Trim and wash radishes and cut into small dice.

Cut chives into thin slivers.

PRESENTATION

Fill lower halves of puff pastry circles with cress, horseradish whipped cream, and half of the smoked salmon.

Place puff pastry lids on top.

Place remaining smoked salmon on top of puff pastry.

Garnish with onion rings, diced radishes, and chives.

[a] Puff pastry can be purchased or use Recipe 689.

[b] Garden cress is smaller but more pungent than watercress.

201

Caviar with Blinis

Blinis mit Kaviar
Blinis au caviar

YIELD: 10 SERVINGS

Caviar, Osetra Malossol[a]	10 1/2 oz	300 g
Sour cream, light	13 1/2 oz	400 ml
Butter, melted	3 1/3 oz	100 ml

BLINI BATTER

Yeast, fresh	1 oz	30 g
Milk	1 pt 8 oz	700 ml
White wheat flour	8 3/4 oz	250 g
Buckwheat flour	8 3/4 oz	250 g
Salt	1/3 oz	10 g
Butter	1 2/3 oz	50 g
Egg whites	4	4

METHOD FOR BLINIS

Dissolve yeast in warm milk.

Add white wheat flour, buckwheat flour, and salt. Mix to smooth batter.

Melt butter and add to batter.

Proof batter in warm place for about 2 hours.

Whip egg whites and fold carefully into batter.

Make small blinis (dollar-size pancakes) in small pans.[b]

METHOD

Serve caviar on ice.

Brush blinis with melted butter and serve at once.

Serve sour cream on the side.

[a] Any variety of caviar can be served. Caviar is often served with chopped onions and chopped hard-boiled eggs.

[b] Blinis can be baked on a griddle when no suitable pans are available.

202

$\mathcal{C}$ream Puffs (eclairs) with Game Mousse

Blitzkrapfen mit Wildmousse
Eclairs Saint-Hubert

YIELD: 10 SERVINGS

Puff paste (Recipe 678)	1 lb 5 oz	600 g
Blue figs, fresh	5	5
Chestnuts, peeled, frozen, thawed	8 3/4 oz	250 g
Vegetable bouillon (Recipe 27)	3 1/3 oz	100 ml
Crystal sugar	1 2/3 oz	50 g
Game mousse[a]	1 lb 5 oz	600 g

MISE EN PLACE

With pastry bag, dress 10 eclairs (sticks) about 4 to 5 inches long on pastry sheet pan. Bake and let cool.

Wash and split figs.

Cover chestnuts with vegetable stock. Add sugar and bring to a boil. Reduce liquid until chestnuts are glazed. Let cool.

METHOD

Split eclairs lengthwise. Save lids.

Fill eclairs with game mousse, using a pastry bag with a star tube. Place lids back on.

Plate and garnish with figs and chestnuts.

203

$\mathcal{C}$arpaccio of Salmon Trout and Turbot

Carpaccio von Lachsforelle und Steinbutt
Carpaccio de truite saumonée et de turbot

YIELD: 10 SERVINGS

Salmon trout fillets, skinless[a]	1 lb 2 oz	500 g
Turbot fillets[b]	1 lb 2 oz	500 g
Basil leaves	10	10
Olive oil	4 oz	120 ml
Lime, whole	5 1/3 oz	150 g
Seasoning (salt and pepper)	1x	1x
SALAD		
Cherry tomatoes	10 1/2 oz	300 g
Shallots	1 2/3 oz	50 g
Capers, canned, drained	1 2/3 oz	50 g
Chives, fresh, cut	2/3 oz	20 g
Pumpkin seed oil	1 2/3 oz	50 ml
Balsamic vinegar	2/3 oz	20 ml
Seasoning (salt and pepper)	1x	1x

METHOD FOR SALAD

Cut cherry tomatoes into quarters, cut shallots into thin slices.

Combine with capers and chives.

Add pumpkin seed oil, balsamic vinegar, salt and pepper. Blend and marinate.

METHOD

Remove bones from salmon trout and turbot fillets.

Slice thin and place slices attractively on plates (fan fish alternately).

Drizzle with olive oil and lime juice.

Sprinkle with salt and freshly ground pepper.

Marinate plated fish, refrigerated, for about 15 minutes.

Garnish with bouquets of cherry tomato salad and basil leaves.

---

[a] Use any suitable recipe for game mousse.

[a] Be sure fish is absolutely fresh.

[b] Turbot is a large flat fish from the North Sea or the Eastern part of the Atlantic Ocean. The Pacific turbot is not related.

204

*B*eef Tenderloin Carpaccio

Carpaccio von Rindsfilet
Carpaccio de filet de boeuf

YIELD: 10 SERVINGS

Olive oil, cold pressed	6 3/4 oz	200 ml
Seasoning (salt and pepper)	1x	1x
Beef tenderloin, trimmed[a]	1 lb 12 oz	800 g
Lemons	2	2

GARNISH
Garden cress[b]	2 2/3 oz	75 g
Lemons, quartered	2 1/2	2 1/2
Parmesan cheese shavings[c]	2 oz	60 g

METHOD

Brush plates with olive oil and sprinkle with salt and freshly ground pepper.

Cut chilled, well-trimmed tenderloin into very thin slices.[d] Place slices attractively on plates.

Drizzle with remaining olive oil and with lemon juice.

Season again with salt and pepper.

Sprinkle with Parmesan shavings.

Garnish with garden cress and lemon quarters.

205

*M*ushroom Salad with Hazelnuts

Champignonsalat mit Haselnüssen
Salade de champignons aux noisettes

YIELD: 10 SERVINGS

Mushrooms, fresh	14 oz	400 g
Butter	2/3 oz	20 g
Lemon juice	1/3 oz	10 ml
Seasoning (salt and pepper)	1x	1x
Belgian endive	14 oz	400 g
Hazelnuts, skinless	3 1/2 oz	100 g
Walnut oil	5 oz	150 ml

---

[a] The tenderloin must be first quality, fresh, and completely trimmed.

[b] Garden cress is smaller but more pungent than watercress.

[c] The Parmesan cheese should be shaved, not grated. This is often done in the dining room in front of the customers.

[d] If the tenderloin is well chilled (almost frozen), it can be sliced on the meat slicer.

Cider vinegar	2 oz	60 ml
Seasoning (salt and pepper)	1x	1x
Chives, fresh	1/3 oz	10 g
Garden cress	3 1/2 oz	100 g

MISE EN PLACE

Wash and slice mushrooms.

Sauté with butter and lemon juice. Season to taste. Let cool.

Split endive and cut into small wedges.

Chop hazelnuts coarsely.

Mix walnut oil, cider vinegar, salt and pepper thoroughly to make dressing.

Cut chives into small slivers. Wash garden cress.

PRESENTATION

Place mushrooms, endive wedges, and garden cress on plates. Drizzle with dressing.

Sprinkle with hazelnuts and chives.

206

*C*urry Dip

Curry-Dip-Sauce
Dip au curry

YIELD: 10 SERVINGS

Curry powder, Madras	pinch	2 g
Pineapple juice	1 1/3 oz	40 ml
Cottage cheese, low fat[a]	3 1/2 oz	100 g
Mayonnaise (Recipe 71)	3 1/2 oz	100 g
Yogurt, plain	1 1/3 oz	40 g
Hazelnuts, ground	2/3 oz	20 g
Mango chutney, chopped	2/3 oz	20 g
Walnut oil	1/3 oz	10 ml
Seasoning (salt and pepper)	1x	1x
Sugar (pinch)	1x	1x

METHOD

Mix curry powder with pineapple juice and warm briefly.

Blend thoroughly with remaining ingredients. Season to taste.

---

[a] The original recipe calls for *Quark*, a generic German word for cottage cheese. The cottage cheese for this recipe should be fine curd and strained. Skim-milk ricotta cheese makes a good substitute.

207

*C*old Seafood Platter

Dreierlei aus dem Norden
Trio du nord

YIELD: 10 SERVINGS

Smoked salmon, trimmed	8 3/4 oz	250 g
Garden cress[a]	1 oz	30 g
Smoked trout fillets, skinless	10 1/2 oz	300 g
Lemons	1 1/2	1 1/2
Cucumbers	5 1/3 oz	150 g
Tomatoes	7 oz	200 g
Radishes	1/2 bunch	1/2 bund
Shrimp, cooked	10 1/2 oz	300 g
Cocktail sauce (Recipe 39)	5 oz	150 ml
Parsley, Italian, fresh	2/3 oz	20 g
Boston (butter) lettuce leaves, washed	10	10
Red leaf lettuce[b] leaves, washed	10	10
Horseradish whipped cream (Recipe 73)	7 oz	200 g
Onion rings	10	10
Capers, drained	2/3 oz	20 g

MISE EN PLACE
Cut smoked salmon into 10 thin slices.

Wash cress. Drain well.

Trim smoked trout fillets and cut into 10 even pieces.

Peel lemon carefully with knife to remove rind completely, and cut into thin slices.

Cut cucumbers into 10 slices.

Slice tomatoes and radishes.

Mix shrimp with cocktail sauce.

Wash parsley. Remove stems and chop leaves.

METHOD
Place washed and drained cress in center of plates.

Place smoked salmon slices on top of cress.

Place the smoked trout fillets on lettuce leaves around the salmon. Garnish with sliced radishes.

[a] Garden cress is smaller but more pungent than watercress.

[b] The original recipe calls for *Cicorino-rosso* lettuce.

Place shrimp on red lettuce leaves next to smoked trout. Sprinkle with parsley.

Mound the horseradish cream on top of the cucumber slices. Place around the remaining rim.

Garnish plates with lemon and tomato slices, onion rings, and capers.

208

*E*gg Dip

Eier-Dip-Sauce
Dip aux oeufs

YIELD: 10 SERVINGS

Eggs	3	3
Capers, drained	1/3 oz	10 g
Parsley, Italian, fresh	1/3 oz	10 g
Lemon balm	1 tsp	5 g
Chives, fresh	1/3 oz	10 g
Olive oil, cold pressed	2 1/2 oz	75 ml
White wine vinegar	1 2/3 oz	50 ml
Mustard, prepared, mild	1/3 oz	10 g
Seasoning (salt and pepper)	1x	1x

MISE EN PLACE
Boil eggs. Peel and chop.

Chop capers, parsley, and lemon balm.

Cut chives into thin slivers.

METHOD
Mix olive oil with vinegar, mustard, salt and pepper.

Add remaining ingredients to make dressing.

209

Pheasant Terrine with Red Peppercorns

Fasanenterrine mit roten Pfefferkörnern
Terrine de faisan aux baies rouges

YIELD: 10 SERVINGS

Pheasant, plucked, but not eviscerated	4 lb	1.8 kg
Fatback, fresh (not salted)	13 oz	375 g
Shallots	1 2/3 oz	50 g
Madeira wine[a]	1/3 oz	10 ml
Cognac (or any brandy)	2/3 oz	20 ml
Seasoning (salt and pepper)	1x	1x
Pâté spice[b]	1 tsp	5 g
Heavy cream (36%)	5 oz	150 ml
Pink peppercorns, drained	2/3 oz	20 g

MISE EN PLACE

Eviscerate and clean pheasant. Bone completely.

Reserve pheasant liver and one skinless breast. Cut remaining meat into cubes.

Cut reserved breast into small cubes for garnish.

Cut about 1/3 amount of fatback into thin slices.

Line terrine mold first with transparent wrapper and then with sliced fatback. Reserve some slices for the top.

Cut remaining fatback into small cubes.

Peel and chop shallots.

METHOD

Melt cubed fatback in casserole pan over low heat.

Sauté reserved pheasant liver and shallots lightly in rendered fat.

Add Madeira wine and Cognac and bring to a boil.

Put mixture in a flat pan to cool.

Add pheasant meat. Season to taste with salt, pepper, and pâté spice. Cool mixture thoroughly.

Grind/purée meat mixture in food processor or Buffalo chopper.

Strain (pass) mixture through wire sieve.[c]

Place in bowl on ice and stir in cream, reserved diced pheasant breast, and pink peppercorns. Check seasoning.

Fill prepared terrine mold with farce. Smooth out top.

---

[a] Medium sweet sherry wine can be substituted.

[b] Pâté spice can be purchased commercially, or Seasoning Salt for Poultry (Recipe 10) can be substituted.

[c] If commercial food processor is used, this step can be omitted.

Cover top with fatback slices and then with aluminum foil.

Poach terrine in water bath in oven until center temperature reaches 130°F (55°C).[a]

Weigh down lightly and let cool in mold.

Use when thoroughly cold.

NOTES: Instead of pheasant liver, another game liver or chicken liver can be used.

To serve from the terrine, remove from the mold when cold. Clean the same mold, line with a compatible aspic jelly, put the terrine back in the mold, and glaze with additional aspic.

210

Fresh Figs with Endive Salad

Feigen mit Chicorée
Figues aux endives

YIELD: 10 SERVINGS

Lemon melissa (balm)	1/3 oz	10 g
Sunflower oil	3 1/3 oz	100 ml
Raspberry vinegar	1 1/3 oz	40 ml
Seasoning	1x	1x
Belgian endive	14 oz	400 g
Blue figs, fresh	10	10
Dates	3 1/2 oz	100 g

MISE EN PLACE

Remove stems from lemon balm. Chop leaves.

Combine chopped lemon balm with sunflower oil and raspberry vinegar to make dressing. Season to taste.

Break off leaves from endive (leaves should be whole). Wash and drain.

Cut figs into slices.

Remove pits from dates and quarter lengthwise.

METHOD

Place endive leaves in a circle on plates to form a star pattern.

Place fig slices on top.

Drizzle with dressing.

Garnish with dates.

---

[a] The suggested temperature is low and may not kill harmful bacteria. To be safe, it is recommended to bring the pâté temperature up to at least 140°F (60°C).

211

*F*resh Fig Cocktail (cup) with Port Wine
Feigencocktail mit Porto
Cocktail de figues au porto

YIELD: 10 SERVINGS

Oranges	2	2
Crystal sugar	7 oz	200 g
Water	1 pt 1 oz	500 ml
Red Port wine	6 3/4 oz	200 ml
Cinnamon stick	1	1
Blue figs, fresh	15	15
Yogurt, plain	14 oz	400 g
Seasoning (black pepper)	1x	1x

MISE EN PLACE

Peel some skin from oranges and reserve for syrup.

Halve oranges and press out juice.

Caramelize sugar (brown slightly) in pan. Add water, orange juice, and Port wine. Heat to dissolve sugar. Add cinnamon stick and reserved orange peel. Boil until reduced to syrup consistency.

Wash figs and puncture about 10 small holes in each.

Marinate figs in sugar syrup. Refrigerate for at least 24 hours.

METHOD

Cut figs into wedges and place in cocktail glasses.

Make dressing with yogurt and some fig syrup.

Season dressing to taste with freshly ground black pepper.

Serve dressing over figs.

212

*F*ish Paté
Fischpastete
Pâté de poisson

YIELD: 10 SERVINGS

Paté dough (Recipes 245, 246, or 247)	2 lb	900 g
Smoked salmon, trimmed	5 1/3 oz	150 g
Egg yolk	1	1
Light cream	1/3 oz	10 ml
FISH MOUSSE (FARCE)		
Pike fillets, skinned[a]	10 1/2 oz	300 g
Seasoning (salt and pepper)	1x	1x
Heavy cream	6 3/4 oz	200 ml
Dry vermouth[b]	1/3 oz	10 ml
Egg yolks	2	2
GARNISH		
Salmon fillet, skinned	5 1/3 oz	150 g
Pistachio nuts, peeled	1 oz	30 g
Fish aspic (Recipe 4)	1 pt 1 oz	500 ml
Pernod[c]	1/3 oz	10 ml

MISE EN PLACE FOR MOLD

Line paté mold with paté dough. Save some dough for the lid.

Cut smoked salmon into thin slices.

Line prepared mold with smoked salmon. Save some slices for the top.

Mix egg yolk and light cream thoroughly.

MISE EN PLACE FOR FISH MOUSSE

Cut pike fillets into cubes. Season and refrigerate.

MISE EN PLACE FOR GARNISH

Cut salmon fillet into small cubes and reserve for garnish.

Coarsely chop pistachio kernels.

Melt fish aspic and season with Pernod.

(continued on next page)

[a] It can be difficult to remove the thin skin from pike. It is sufficient to just remove the scales.

[b] The original recipe specifies Noilly Prat, but any brand of dry vermouth can be used. Vermouth comes in dry and sweet varieties; use only dry in this recipe.

[c] Pernod is an anise-flavored liqueur.

(continued from preceding page)

METHOD

Purée/grind thoroughly chilled pike fillets, with small amount of heavy cream, in food processor or Buffalo chopper.

Pass/strain through wire sieve.[a]

Mix in bowl over ice with remaining heavy cream, vermouth, and egg yolks.

Add salmon cubes and pistachio kernels. Season to taste.

Fill dough- and salmon-lined mold. Be sure there are no air bubbles.

Top mold with remaining smoked salmon slices.

Brush dough rim with cream/egg yolk mixture.

Make lid with dough and place on top. Garnish lid attractively with remaining dough.

Make round holes in lid to let steam escape during the baking process.

Brush with cream/egg yolk mixture and refrigerate for 1 hour.

Bake for 10 minutes at 425°F (220°C).

Reduce heat to 360°F (180°C) and continue baking, with steam vent open, until paté has an inside temperature of 115°F (45°C).

When paté is cold, fill with fish aspic jelly and chill thoroughly.

MISE EN PLACE

Line terrine mold carefully with transparent wrapper wrap.

Skin trout fillets. Cube, season, and refrigerate.

MISE EN PLACE FOR GARNISH

Blanch spinach leaves and spread out on absorbent paper to dry.

Cut salmon trout into long strips. Season lightly.

Brush salmon pieces with egg white and wrap in spinach leaves.

METHOD

Purée/grind trout cubes with egg white until smooth.

Pass/strain through wire sieve.[a]

Mix with cream in a bowl over ice. Season to taste.

Fill terrine mold with about 1/3 of trout mousse.

Place salmon trout strips in center of terrine.

Fill terrine with remaining trout mousse. Be sure there are no air bubbles.

Cover with aluminum foil.

Poach in water bath, in oven, until center of terrine has reached 115°F (45°C).

Weigh down slightly and cool in mold.

NOTE: Instead of spinach, Swiss chard can be used to wrap salmon trout fillets.

213

𝒯rout Terrine

Forellenterrine
Terrine de truite

YIELD: 10 SERVINGS

MOUSSE (FARCE)

Trout fillets, skin on	12 oz	350 g
Seasoning (salt and pepper)	1x	1x
Egg white	1 oz	30 g
Heavy cream	8 1/2 oz	250 ml

GARNISH

Spinach, fresh	3 1/2 oz	100 g
Salmon trout fillet, skinless (back pieces are preferred)	10 1/2 oz	300 g
Salt	1 tsp	5 g
Egg white	1/3 oz	10 g

214

𝒫ike Galantine

Galantine von jungem Hecht
Galantine de brocheton

YIELD: 10 SERVINGS

Pike, whole, gutted, and cleaned	3 lb 5 oz	1.5 kg
Heavy cream	6 3/4 oz	200 ml
Butter	1/3 oz	10 g
Pernod	1 oz	30 ml
Coriander, ground	pinch	1 g
Seasoning (salt and pepper)	1x	1x
Fish stock (Recipe 24)	3 qt 5 oz	3.0 L

---

[a] If commercial food processor is used, this step can be omitted.

[a] If commercial food processor is used, this step can be omitted.

GARNISH

Black truffles	2/3 oz	20 g
Red peppers	3 oz	80 g
Pistachio nuts, peeled	1 1/3 oz	40 g

MISE EN PLACE
Remove scales from fish. Rinse and dry with absorbent paper.

Cut off head, and tail at the dorsal fin.

Bone the tail piece.

Bone remaining fish center piece from inside out. Cut off all fins.

Trim fish to get a flat, rectangular piece, about 12-in. x 8-in. and 1/3-in. thick.

Refrigerate fish trimmings and tail fillets. There should be about 8 3/4 oz (250 g) fish.

MISE EN PLACE FOR GARNISH
Cut truffles into small dice.

Clean red peppers. Cut into small dice and blanch.

Coarsely chop pistachio nuts.

METHOD
Purée/grind fish trimmings and tail fillets in food processor or Buffalo chopper until smooth.

Blend mixture in a bowl, placed on ice, and blend in cream.

Season with Pernod, ground coriander, and salt to taste.

Add truffles, diced peppers, and pistachio nuts.

Spread out fish center piece and fill the core evenly with fish mousse.

Roll up fish (to resemble a sausage).

Butter a large piece of aluminum foil. Roll fish up tightly in the foil. Tie with twine to keep roll together.

Poke holes in foil with needle to let steam escape.

Poach in fish stock until center has reached 130°F (55°C).

Let cool in stock. When cool, unroll and roll again tightly in clean aluminum foil. Chill.

NOTES: The fish stock can be prepared with suitable trimmings and fish bones (see Recipe 24).

Depending on use, the galantine can be served whole or sliced. It should be glazed with fish aspic and garnished appropriately.

215

Chicken Liver Mousse
Geflügellebermousse
Mousseline de foie de volaille

YIELD: 10 SERVINGS

Chicken livers, raw	1 lb 2 oz	500 g
Shallots	1 1/3 oz	40 g
Butter	1 2/3 oz	50 g
Cognac (or any brandy)	1 1/3 oz	40 ml
Seasoning (salt and pepper)	1x	1x
Marjoram, fresh, leaves	1/3 oz	10 g
Chicken velouté sauce (Recipe 57)	10 oz	300 ml
Heavy cream	8 1/2 oz	250 ml

GARNISH
Aspic powder[a]	1/3 oz	10 g
Water	6 3/4 oz	200 ml
Cress[b]	2 1/2 oz	70 g
Blood oranges	2 lb 3 oz	1.0 kg

MISE EN PLACE
Trim and clean chicken livers. Wash in hot water. Drain.

Chop shallots and sauté in butter.

Add livers and sauté briefly.

Add Cognac; ignite.

Season with salt and pepper and marjoram leaves.

Reduce chicken *velouté* to about 6 3/4 oz (200 ml).

MISE EN PLACE FOR GARNISH
Make aspic jelly (with powder) according to recipe and chill.

Cut firm aspic into small dice.

Clean and wash cress.

Peel blood oranges and cut into skinless sections.

METHOD
Combine *velouté* and liver mixture while still warm.

Purée in food processor and pass/strain through wire sieve, if necessary.

Fold in lightly whipped heavy cream. Season to taste and chill.

(continued on next page)

---

[a] Aspic powder is available in different flavors. Chicken flavor would probably be best in this recipe. To use, follow directions on can.

[b] The original recipe calls for *Brunnenkresse*, which is a little spicier in flavor than watercress. Watercress can be substituted.

(continued from preceding page)

PRESENTATION

Shape into small dumplings (quenelles) using two spoons.

Serve two dumplings per person.

Garnish with cress, orange wedges, and diced aspic.

216

Chicken Galantine

Geflügelgalantine
Galantine de volaille

YIELD: 10 SERVINGS

Chicken, ready to use[a]	4 lb	1.8 kg
Paté spice[b]	1 tsp	5 g
Seasoning (white pepper)	1x	1x
Dry sherry wine	1 2/3 oz	50 ml
Salt	1/3 oz	10 g
Chicken stock (Recipe 26)	3 qt 5 oz	3.0 L

FARCE

Shallots, chopped	2 oz	60 g
Chicken livers, raw	3 1/2 oz	100 g
Clarified butter	2/3 oz	20 g
Fatback, fresh, unsalted	8 3/4 oz	250 g
Pork neck meat, boneless	7 oz	200 g
Black chanterelles,[c] dried	1 2/3 oz	50 g
Ham, boiled	3 oz	80 g
Heavy cream (36%)	5 oz	150 ml
Ginger, ground	1 pinch	1 g
Seasoning (salt and pepper)	1x	1x

MISE EN PLACE

Bone chicken, starting from the back.

Remove some leg meat and breast fillets. The trimmed chicken should be a rectangular piece about 1/2-in. thick. Reserve removed meat.

Place on sheet pan, skin down.

Season with paté spice, white pepper, and dry Sherry wine. Cover and marinate refrigerated for 30 minutes.

Drain off and reserve the marinade.

Lightly salt chicken rectangle.

MISE EN PLACE FOR FARCE

Sauté shallots and livers in clarified butter. Do not brown.

Remove livers from pan and add reserved marinade to dissolve pan drippings.

Add pan drippings to livers and refrigerate.

Cube fatback and pork meat. Refrigerate.

Soak dried mushrooms, squeeze out liquid, and chop coarsely.

Cut ham into small dice.

METHOD

Grind fatback in food processor or Buffalo chopper. Set aside for next step.

Grind chicken meat, pork neck, and livers. Add in ground fatback last. Process until finely ground.

Pass/strain mixture through wire sieve[a] and refrigerate.

Blend in heavy cream, chopped mushrooms, and diced ham.

Season with ground ginger, salt and pepper.

Place chicken on table,[b] skin down, and fill center evenly with farce.

Roll tightly and sew closed with thin butcher twine.

Wrap tightly in buttered aluminum foil; twist ends or roll up in kitchen towel; tie with twine. Puncture foil.

Poach until center temperature is 150°F (65°C). Let cool in stock until chilled.

Untie, wrap tightly once again, and chill thoroughly.

NOTES: The poaching stock can be made with the resulting chicken bones.

The galantine can be served sliced and garnished appropriately.

---

[a] One large or two small chickens can be used. Two small chickens will result in two galantines.

[b] Paté spice can be purchased commercially, or Seasoning Salt for Poultry (Recipe 10) can be substituted.

[c] Black chanterelles, also known as "trumpets of death," are dark, almost black mushrooms. It is their appearance that gives them their intimidating name; they are quite safe to eat. In German, they are called *Totentrompeten*. If they are not available, other flavorful dried mushrooms can be substituted.

---

[a] If commercial food processor is used, this step can be omitted.

[b] To avoid contamination, work table should be covered with foil or parchment paper and disinfected after chicken is processed.

217

*C*hicken Galantine with Fruits

Geflügelgalantine mit Früchten
Galantine de volaille fruitière

YIELD: 10 SERVINGS

Bananas	6 oz	170 g
Pineapple, fresh	10 1/2 oz	300 g
Apples	7 oz	200 g
White raisins	1 2/3 oz	50 g
Cognac (or any brandy)	1 oz	30 ml
Mango chutney	1 oz	30 g
Seasoning (lemon juice)	1x	1x
Fresh figs	2	2
Walnut halves	1 oz	30 g
Blood oranges	1 lb 5 oz	600 g
Chicken galantine (Recipe 216)	1 lb 12 oz	800 g
Kefir, plain[a]	6 3/4 oz	200 ml
Pineapple leaves	10	10

MISE EN PLACE

Peel bananas[b] and pineapple. Cut into 3/4-in. dice.

Reserve 10 attractive pineapple leaves.

Scoop out small apple balls with melon baller.

Soak white raisins in Cognac.

Chop chutney; add lemon juice.

Blend all above ingredients to marinate fruit.

Cube figs.

Chop walnuts coarsely and set aside for garnish.

Peel oranges and cut into 20 slices.

Cut galantine into 20 slices.

METHOD

Blend marinated fruits with kefir.

Put 2 orange slices on each plate and put fruit salad on top.

Sprinkle with figs and nuts.

Put 2 slices of galantine on each plate.

Garnish with pineapple leaves.

---

[a] Kefir is a liquid yogurt-type milk product.

[b] Bananas can be added at the last moment before service.

218

*E*ggs Filled with Shrimp Salad

Gefüllte Eier mit Krevetten
Oeufs farcis aux crevettes

YIELD: 10 SERVINGS

Eggs	10	10
Cucumbers	10 1/2 oz	300 g
Dill, fresh	1 tsp	5 g
Shrimp, drained	10 1/2 oz	300 g
Yogurt, plain	5 1/3 oz	150 g
Mayonnaise (Recipe 71)	3 1/2 oz	100 g
Seasoning (salt and pepper)	1x	1x
Seasoning (lemon juice)	1x	1x
Broad leaf lettuces, assorted and cleaned	14 oz	400 g
French dressing (Recipe 479)	6 3/4 oz	200 ml
Dill leaves, twigs	10	10

MISE EN PLACE

Cook and peel eggs; split lengthwise.

Remove egg yolks, chop, and set aside for garnish.

Peel cucumbers, remove seeds, and grate coarsely.

Chop dill. Dice shrimp.

Combine shrimp with yogurt, mayonnaise, and grated cucumbers.

Season with chopped dill, salt and pepper, and lemon juice.

PRESENTATION

Place broad leaf lettuces on plates and drizzle with French dressing.

Place two egg white halves on each plate, on top of lettuces, and fill with shrimp salad.

Sprinkle with chopped egg yolks and garnish with dill twig.

219

Stuffed Small Turbot

Gefüllter junger Steinbutt
Turbot farci

YIELD: 10 SERVINGS

Turbot,[a] whole	4 lb	1.8 kg
Fish stock (Recipe 24)	3 qt 5 oz	3.0 L
Black chanterelles,[b] dried	1/3 oz	10 g
Fennel leaves, fresh (anise)	1 tsp	5 g
Spinach, fresh	3 1/2 oz	100 g
Fish aspic, fresh	6 3/4 oz	200 ml
Dry vermouth[c]	1/3 oz	10 ml
Heavy cream	3 1/3 oz	100 ml
Egg white	1	30 g
Seasoning (salt and pepper)	1x	1x
Coriander, ground	pinch	1 g
Butter	1/3 oz	10 g

MISE EN PLACE

Bone turbot; leave head and carcass intact.

Skin and butterfly fillets. Trim fillets.

Flatten fillets carefully between aluminum foil sheets.

Save and refrigerate all trimmings for fish farce.

Poach fish carcass briefly in fish stock. Let cool in stock.

When carcass is cool, remove from stock and place on wire rack. Save stock.

Soak dried chanterelles/mushrooms and chop fine.

Finely chop fennel leaves.

Blanch spinach leaves. Spread on absorbent paper to drain, and chill.

Melt fish aspic and add dry vermouth.

METHOD

Purée/grind chilled fish trimmings with small amount of heavy cream and salt.

Pass/strain through wire sieve.[d]

Place farce in bowl on ice and blend in remaining cream.

---

[a] Turbot is a large flat fish from the North Sea and the Eastern part of the Atlantic Ocean. The Pacific turbot is not related.

[b] Black chanterelles, also known as "trumpets of death," are dark, almost black mushrooms. It is their appearance that gives them their intimidating name; they are called in German, they are called *Totentrompeten*. If they are not available, other flavorful dried mushrooms can be substituted.

[c] The original recipe specifies Noilly Prat, but any brand of dry vermouth can be used. Vermouth comes in dry and sweet varieties; use only dry in this recipe.

[d] If commercial food processor is used, this step can be omitted.

Lightly beat egg white and fold into fish farce.

Season to taste. Add mushrooms and fennel leaves.

Spread fish farce on fish fillets, top with blanched spinach leaves, and roll up lengthwise.

Butter aluminum foil, roll each fillet tightly in foil, and twist ends. Poke holes with needle to let steam escape and prevent air pockets.

Place rolls in shallow pan, cover with fish stock, and poach carefully for about 20 minutes. Let cool in stock.

Unwrap and cut rolls into slices about 1/5-in. thick.

Place slices on wire rack and glaze with fish aspic.

Also glaze fish carcass.

Place slices, slightly overlapping, on fish carcass, starting at tail end with smallest slices.

NOTE: In modern service, the slices are served directly on plates without the fish carcass.

220

Vegetable Cocktail with Yogurt

Gemüsecocktail mit Joghurt
Cocktail de légumes au jogourt

YIELD: 10 SERVINGS

Cauliflower, fresh	14 oz	400 g
Fennel, bulb (anise)	8 3/4 oz	250 g
Tomatoes	10 1/2 oz	300 g
Mushrooms, fresh	5 1/3 oz	150 g
Lemon juice	1/3 oz	10 ml
Chives, fresh	1/3 oz	10 g
White wine vinegar	3/4 oz	25 ml
Sunflower oil	2 oz	60 ml
Seasoning (salt and pepper)	1x	1x
Avocado	1	1
Lemon juice	1/3 oz	10 ml
Artichoke bottoms (large, boiled)	2	2

DRESSING

Oranges	7 oz	200 g
Yogurt, plain	10 1/2 oz	300 g
Olive oil, cold pressed	2 oz	60 ml
Tomato ketchup	2 oz	60 ml
Horseradish, fresh, grated	1/3 oz	10 g
Seasoning (Tabasco)	1x	1x
Seasoning (salt and pepper)	1x	1x

MISE EN PLACE

Clean and trim cauliflower and fennel. Cut cauliflower into florets. Cut fennel into wedges. Steam until cooked, but still firm.

Peel tomatoes, remove seeds, and cube.

Cut mushrooms into quarters. Braise briefly with lemon juice.

Cut chives into small slivers.

Marinate vegetables and chives with vinegar, sunflower oil, salt and pepper.

Peel avocado, remove pit, cut into small wedges, and drizzle with lemon juice to avoid oxidation.

Cut artichoke bottom into 10 slices.

METHOD FOR DRESSING

Peel oranges and cut into small cubes. Blend with yogurt, olive oil, ketchup, grated horseradish, Tabasco, salt and pepper.

PRESENTATION

Fill large cocktail glasses about halfway with dressing.

Add marinated vegetables and top with remaining dressing.

Garnish with avocado wedges and artichoke slices.

221

Vegetable Tartlets with Chicken Mousse

Gemüsetörtchen
Tartelettes jardinière

YIELD: 10 SERVINGS

Pâte brisée (Recipe 710)	12 oz	350 g
Chicken mousse[a]	10 1/2 oz	300 g
Broccoli, fresh	7 oz	200 g
White asparagus	8 3/4 oz	250 g
Peas, frozen	1 2/3 oz	50 g
Stalk celery[b]	3 1/2 oz	100 g
Carrots	3 1/2 oz	100 g
Mushrooms, fresh	1 1/3 oz	40 g
Belgian endive	1 2/3 oz	50 g
Parsley, curly, fresh	2/3 oz	20 g
Chives, fresh	2/3 oz	20 g
Chervil, fresh	1/3 oz	10 g
Vinaigrette dressing (Recipe 487)	6 3/4 oz	200 ml

MISE EN PLACE

Roll out dough and line 10 tartlet molds.

Bake blind[c] and let cool.

Fill with chicken mousse.

Clean and trim vegetables and cut attractively.

Boil or steam vegetables until still firm.

Peel off 10 endive leaves from stem and reserve as garnish. Chop remainder of endive leaves.

Chop herbs.

METHOD

Marinate vegetables with French dressing shortly before service.

Sprinkle plates with herbs.

Place vegetables in center.

Put tartlets on top and garnish each with an endive leaf.

---

[a] Chicken mousse can be made like chicken liver mousse (Recipe 215).

[b] The stalk celery specified in Europe is called *Stangensellerie* in German. In the United States, it is simply referred to as "celery."

[c] To bake blind, the tartlets are lined with aluminum foil and filled with dried beans or rice. This prevents the dough from sliding into the center during the cooking process. After tartlets are baked, the rice or beans are removed.

222

Vegetable and Chicken Terrine

Gemüseterrine
Terrine de légumes

YIELD: 10 SERVINGS

Carrots	7 oz	200 g
String beans, fresh	5 1/3 oz	150 g
Yellow peppers	3 1/2 oz	100 g
Stalk celery[a]	7 oz	200 g
Broccoli, fresh	10 1/2 oz	300 g
Salt	2/3 oz	20 g

FARCE

Chicken breasts, skinless	7 oz	200 g
Paté spice	1 tsp	5 g
Sodium nitrite	1 tsp	5 g
Fatback, fresh, unsalted	3 1/2 oz	100 g
Heavy cream	3 1/3 oz	100 ml
Seasoning (salt and pepper)	1x	1x

MISE EN PLACE

Line terrine mold carefully with transparent wrapper wrap.

Wash and trim vegetables. Cut into small sticks. Cut broccoli into florets.

Boil vegetables in salt water, or steam, until cooked lightly but still firm. Chill in ice water. Salt. Drain and dry on absorbent kitchen paper.

METHOD FOR FARCE

Season chicken breasts with paté spice and sodium nitrite. Refrigerate.

Grind/purée first chicken breasts, and then fatback, in food processor or Buffalo chopper.

Blend chicken meat and fatback; pass/strain through wire sieve.[b]

In a bowl over ice, mix in heavy cream. Season to taste.

METHOD

Line prepared terrine mold with farce.

Fill terrine with layers of vegetables and farce. Be sure there are no air bubbles. The top layer should be farce. Cover with aluminum foil.

Poach in water bath, in oven, until terrine has a center temperature of 150°F (65°C). Place weight on top and let cool.

---

[a] The stalk celery specified in Europe is called *Stangensellerie* in German. In the United States, it is simply referred to as "celery."

[b] If commercial food processor is used, this step can be omitted.

223

Vegetable Terrine with Tomatoes Vinaigrette

Gemüseterrine mit Tomaten-Vinaigrette
Terrine de légumes à la vinaigrette de tomates

YIELD: 10 SERVINGS

Carrots	10 oz	280 g
Stalk celery[a]	5 2/3 oz	160 g
Broccoli, fresh	7 oz	200 g
Peas, frozen	4 1/4 oz	120 g
Artichoke bottoms	2	2
Mushrooms, fresh	2 lb 3 oz	1.0 kg
Water	10 oz	300 ml
Lemon juice	2/3 oz	20 ml
Crystal sugar	1 tsp	5 g
Salt	1 tsp	5 g
Aspic powder[b]	2/3 oz	20 g
Gelatin, leaves[c]	6	9 g
Basil branch, fresh	1	1
Heavy cream	6 3/4 oz	200 ml
Nutmeg (pinch)	1x	1x
Seasoning (salt and pepper)	1x	1x
Tomato vinaigrette (Recipe 100)	13 1/2 oz	400 ml
Chervil, fresh	2/3 oz	20 g

MISE EN PLACE

Wash and trim carrots, celery, and broccoli. Cut into even pieces.

Steam or boil separately until soft.

Boil peas until tender. It is important that all vegetables are well cooked so the finished terrine can be sliced evenly.

Dice artichoke bottoms.

Soak gelatin leaves in cold water.

METHOD FOR MUSHROOM FILLING

Wash mushrooms. Cut in half, and combine with water, lemon juice, sugar, and salt.

Heat casserole pan until very hot.

Add mushrooms and liquid, cover, and braise.

Let mushrooms cool; drain, and save stock.

---

[a] The stalk celery in Europe is called *Stangensellerie* in German. In the United States, it is simply as "celery."

[b] Aspic powder is available in different flavors. Any vegetable flavor can be used in this recipe. To use, follow directions on can.

[c] Powdered unflavored gelatin can be used. It must be dissolved in small amounts of warm water.

Mix 6 3/4 oz (200 ml) hot mushroom stock with aspic powder and soaked, squeezed gelatin leaves to make aspic jelly. Let cool.

Purée cooked mushrooms and basil leaves.

Place mushroom/basil purée in a bowl over ice and blend in cool aspic jelly, heavy cream, nutmeg, and salt and pepper, stirring until cold.

METHOD
Line prechilled terrine mold with mushroom filling. Refrigerate.

Fill terrine mold with layers of vegetables and remaining mushroom mixture. Vegetables should be positioned to create an attractive pattern.

Refrigerate until firm.

Unmold and cut into 20 slices.

Pour tomato vinaigrette in center of each plate and put 2 slices of terrine on top.

Garnish with chervil leaves.

224

Smoked Breast of Duckling with Kumquats

Geräucherte Entenbrust mit Zwergorangen
Magret de canard fumé aux kumquats

YIELD: 10 SERVINGS

Kumquats	1 lb 2 oz	500 g
Crystal sugar	2/3 oz	20 g
Red Port wine	3 1/3 oz	100 ml
Orange juice	3 1/3 oz	100 ml
Water	1 pt 1 oz	500 ml
Lamb's lettuce (mache)	2 oz	60 g
Duckling breast, smoked	1 lb 5 oz	600 g

MISE EN PLACE
Wash kumquats and slice in half.

Caramelize sugar until golden brown; add Port wine, orange juice, and water. Bring to a boil to dissolve sugar.

Add kumquats and simmer for 4 minutes.

Remove kumquats and reduce liquid to thin syrup consistency.

Pour syrup over kumquats. Marinate for at least one day.

Clean and wash lettuce.

PRESENTATION
Trim off fat from duckling breast (if necessary) and cut into thin slices.

Fan out on plates.

Garnish with kumquats and lettuce.

225

Grapefruit Cocktail with Ginger

Grapefruitcocktail mit Ingwer
Cocktail de pamplemousse au gingembre

YIELD: 10 SERVINGS

White grapefruits	10	10
Crystal sugar	3 1/2 oz	100 g
Ginger, fresh, grated	2/3 oz	20 g
Raspberries, fresh	3 1/2 oz	100 g
Mint leaves, fresh	1 tsp	5 g

METHOD
Peel grapefruits and seam out sections (cut wedges away from membranes).

Flavor sections with sugar and grated ginger.

Place sections in glasses.

Top with raspberries.

Garnish with mint.

226

Grapefruit Salad with Cottage Cheese

Grapefruitcocktail mit Quark
Salade de pamplemousse au seré

YIELD: 10 SERVINGS

White grapefruits	5	5
Red grapefruits	5	5
Fennel, bulb (anise)	7 oz	200 g
Sunflower oil	3/4 oz	25 ml
Cider vinegar	1/3 oz	10 ml
Seasoning (salt, cayenne)	1x	1x
Sugar (pinch)	1x	1x
Cottage cheese, low fat[a]	1 lb 2 oz	500 g
Chervil, fresh	1 oz	30 g

(continued on next page)

---

[a] The original recipe calls for *Quark*, a generic German word for cottage cheese. The cottage cheese for this recipe should be fine curd and strained. Skim-milk ricotta cheese makes a good substitute.

(continued from preceding page)

MISE EN PLACE

Peel grapefruits and seam out sections (cut wedges away from membranes).

Trim and clean fennel, cut into slivers, and blanch briefly.

Combine sunflower oil, cider vinegar, salt, cayenne, and sugar to make dressing.

Combine grapefruit wedges with fennel and marinate briefly in about 2/3 of dressing.

Blend cottage cheese, remaining dressing, and some grapefruit juice until smooth.

Remove stems from chervil and wash leaves.

METHOD

Place mound of cottage cheese mixture in the center of each plate.

Surround with grapefruit/fennel salad.

Sprinkle with chervil leaves.

228

Greek Vegetable Salad with Saffron

Griechischer Salat mit Safran
Salade grecque au safran

YIELD: 10 SERVINGS

Artichokes	3	3
Stalk celery[a]	10 1/2 oz	300 g
Cauliflower, fresh	14 oz	400 g
Carrots	14 oz	400 g
Peppers, assorted colors	14 oz	400 g
Mushrooms, fresh	7 oz	200 g
Zucchini[b]	10 1/2 oz	300 g
Olive oil, cold pressed	6 3/4 oz	200 ml
Lemon juice	2 1/2 oz	75 ml
Water	6 3/4 oz	200 ml
Bay leaves	2	2
Fennel leaves, fresh, chopped (anise)	1 tsp	5 g
Thyme twig, fresh, chopped	1	2 g
Saffron, pinch	1x	1x
Seasoning (salt and pepper)	1x	1x

GARNISH

Black olives, canned, drained	7 oz	200 g
Green olives, canned, drained	7 oz	200 g

Peel cucumbers, remove seeds, and dice.

Peel onions and cut into rough slices.

Cube feta cheese.

Boil eggs. Peel and cut into wedges.

Clean and wash lettuce. Separate into leaves; keep leaves whole.

METHOD FOR DRESSING

Chop oregano. Mix with oil, red wine vinegar, salt and pepper.

METHOD

Place lettuce leaves on plates.

Combine all salad ingredients with dressing.

Place salad on top of leaves.

Garnish with black olives and capers.

227

Greek Salad

Griechischer Salat mit Feta-Käse
Salade grecque au feta

YIELD: 10 SERVINGS

Tomatoes	1 lb 5 oz	600 g
Green peppers	14 oz	400 g
Cucumbers	1 lb 5 oz	600 g
Red onions	7 oz	200 g
Feta cheese[a]	14 oz	400 g
Eggs	5	5
Head of lettuce	1	1
Black olives, canned, drained	5 1/3 oz	150 g
Capers, drained	1 2/3 oz	50 g

DRESSING

Oregano, fresh	1/3 oz	10 g
Olive oil, cold pressed	5 oz	150 ml
Red wine vinegar	3 1/3 oz	100 ml
Seasoning (salt and pepper)	1x	1x

MISE EN PLACE

Dice tomatoes and green peppers.

---

[a] Feta is a salty sheep or cow's milk cheese.

[a] The stalk celery specified is known as "English celery" in Europe, and is called *Stangensellerie* in German. In the United States, it is simply referred to as "celery."

[b] In some English-speaking countries, zucchini is referred to as "vegetable marrow."

MISE EN PLACE

Clean and trim artichokes. Save 10 leaves for garnish.

Blanch artichokes and leaves. Set leaves aside.

Remove center fuzz from artichoke bottoms and cut into 20 wedges.

Clean and trim celery, cauliflower, and carrots. Cut into attractive pieces of equal size. Blanch celery, cauliflower, and carrots.

Clean and trim peppers, mushrooms, and zucchini. Cut into attractive pieces of equal size.

METHOD

Sauté all vegetables in olive oil.

Add lemon juice and water.

Season with bay leaves, fennel leaves, thyme, saffron, and salt and pepper.

Cook vegetables until tender but still firm. Let cool in their own juice.

Plate salad. Garnish each plate with one artichoke leaf and black and green olives.

229

*B*asic Terrine

Hausterrine
Terrine maison

YIELD: 10 SERVINGS

Fatback, fresh, unsalted	8 3/4 oz	250 g
Bacon, smoked, whole, skinless	5 1/3 oz	150 g
Pork neck meat, trimmed	7 1/3 oz	210 g
Veal shoulder, trimmed, boneless	5 2/3 oz	160 g
Pork liver	5 1/3 oz	150 g
Seasoning (salt and pepper)	1x	1x
Paté spice	1 tsp	5 g
Sodium nitrite	1 tsp	5 g
Ham, cooked	2 2/3 oz	75 g
Cognac (or any brandy)	1/3 oz	10 ml
Heavy cream (36%)	5 oz	150 ml

GARNISH

Shallots	1 1/3 oz	40 g
Chicken livers, raw	5 1/3 oz	150 g
Clarified butter	2/3 oz	20 g
Cognac (or any brandy)	2/3 oz	20 ml

MISE EN PLACE FOR FARCE

Cut fatback into thin slices and line terrine mold.[a] Save some slices for the top layer.

Cube bacon, pork, veal, and pork liver. Combine with salt and pepper, paté spice, and sodium nitrite. Refrigerate.

Cut ham into small dice and marinate in 1/3 oz (10 ml) Cognac.

MISE EN PLACE FOR GARNISH

Sauté shallots and chicken livers quickly in clarified butter.

Add 2/3 oz (20 ml) Cognac, ignite, and let cool.

Cut livers into large dice.

METHOD

Purée/grind bacon, pork, veal, and pork liver in food processor or Buffalo chopper. Pass/strain through wire sieve.[b]

Place mixture in a bowl on ice and blend in cream and diced, marinated ham.

Fill terrine mold generously with farce.

Place cold chicken livers in center.

Cover with remaining farce. Smooth out top.

Cover with fatback slices.

Poach in water bath, in oven, until center temperature reaches 130°F (55°C).[c] Weight down slightly and let cool in mold.

Serve terrine directly from the mold.[d]

NOTE: The terrine can also be presented coated in aspic jelly. The cooked terrine is removed from the mold, scraped clean of all fat, placed back in the mold, and covered with suitable aspic.

---

[a] It is recommended that the terrine mold be lined first with transparent wrap, in order to make removal easier.

[b] If commercial food processor is used, this step can be omitted.

[c] The suggested temperature may not kill harmful bacteria. To be safe, the center temperature should be at least 140°F (60°C).

[d] The terrine should be an attractive ovenproof ceramic mold.

230

*H*erring in Sour Cream

Heringsfilets mit Sauerrahm
Filets de hareng à la crème acidulée

YIELD: 10 SERVINGS

Eggs	2	2
Matjes herring, cleaned and trimmed, 20 fillets	2 lb 3 oz	1.0 kg
Onion rings	30	30
Dill twigs, tops, fresh	10	10
Parsley, curly, fresh	1/3 oz	10 g

SAUCE

Onions	10 1/2 oz	300 g
Salt	1/2 oz	15 g
Dill pickles, drained	5 1/3 oz	150 g
Apples	12 oz	350 g
Lemon juice	1x	1x
Sour cream (diet)	10 oz	300 ml
Mayonnaise (Recipe 71)	5 1/3 oz	150 g
Chives, fresh, cut	2/3 oz	20 g
Seasoning (lemon juice)	1x	1x
Seasoning (sugar)	pinch	1x
Seasoning (salt and pepper)	1x	1x

MISE EN PLACE
Boil and peel eggs.

METHOD FOR SAUCE
Slice onions into fine slivers and mix thoroughly with salt. Let rest for about 1 hour and press out juice.

Cut dill pickles and apples into strips (large *julienne*).

Reserve some apple *julienne* for garnish. Mix with lemon juice to prevent oxidation.

Combine onions, pickles and remaining apple *julienne* with sour cream, mayonnaise, and chives.

Season to taste with lemon juice, sugar, salt and pepper.

PRESENTATION
Place herring fillets on plates, 2 per person. Cover with sauce.

Sprinkle with reserved apple *julienne*.

Garnish with sliced eggs, onion rings, dill leaves, and parsley.

231

*L*obster Appetizer with Artichoke

Hummervorspeise mit Artischoken
Avant-goût de homard et d'artichauts

YIELD: 10 SERVINGS

Artichokes, large	5	5
Lemon	1	1
Salt	1/3 oz	10 g
Lobsters, boiled (5 small)	5 lb	2 1/4 kg
Butter	2 oz	60 g
Eggs	5	5
Mayonnaise (Recipe 71)	1 1/3 oz	40 g
Mustard, prepared, mild	1 tsp	5 g
Seasoning (salt and pepper)	1x	1x
Worcestershire sauce	1 tsp	5 ml
Black olives, drained	1 1/3 oz	40 g
Wood garlic leaves[a] (ramps)	30	30

DRESSING

Olive oil, cold pressed	4 oz	120 ml
Lemon juice	1 2/3 oz	50 ml
Seasoning (salt and pepper)	1x	1x

MISE EN PLACE
Trim artichokes. Save 30 large, attractive leaves. Trim off all other leaves. Trim bottom.

Boil artichokes in salt water and lemon juice. Let cool in stock. Remove center fuzz.

Blanch the reserved leaves for garnish.

Pull lobster claws from bodies and set aside.

Cut lobsters in half, remove tail meat, and cut tails diagonally into slices.

Cream butter.

Boil eggs. Chill in cold water. Peel.

METHOD FOR DRESSING
Combine olive oil, lemon juice, salt and pepper.

METHOD
Strain eggs through wire sieve.[b]

Blend strained eggs with creamed butter, mayonnaise, mustard, salt and pepper, and Worcestershire sauce.

Fill artichoke leaves with egg mixture using a pastry bag. Garnish leaves with black olives.

---

[a] The original recipe calls for *Bärenlauch*, a wild garlic related to ramps.

[b] A food processor can be used instead.

Cut artichoke bottoms in half crosswise; then cut into crosswise slices.

PRESENTATION

Fan out artichoke bottom halves on plates.

Put each lobster claw on 3 wood garlic leaves (ramps) and place next to artichokes.

Position lobster slices next to claws.

Garnish each plate with 3 filled artichoke leaves.

Drizzle dressing over lobster and artichoke bottoms.

232

Veal Pâté

Kalbfleischpastete
Pâté de veau

YIELD: 10 SERVINGS

Pâte dough	2 lb	900 g
(Recipe 245, 246, or 247)		
Egg yolk	1	1
Light cream	1/3 oz	10 ml

FARCE		
Fatback, fresh, unsalted	7 oz	200 g
Shallots	1 2/3 oz	50 g
Calves' liver	8 3/4 oz	250 g
Veal shoulder, boneless	8 3/4 oz	250 g
Sodium nitrite	1 tsp	5 g
Walnut kernels, halves	1 1/3 oz	40 g
Ham, boiled	3 1/2 oz	100 g
Seasoning (salt and pepper)	1x	1x
Pâté spice[a]	1 tsp	5 g
Heavy cream (36%)	3 1/3 oz	100 ml

ASPIC JELLY		
Aspic powder[b]	1 tsp	5 g
Water	10 oz	300 ml
Madeira wine	1/3 oz	10 ml

MISE EN PLACE

Line pâté mold with dough.

Mix egg yolk into light cream.

Cut fatback into 3/4-in. cubes.

Peel shallots and chop coarsely.

Remove skin from calves' liver, trim, and cut into cubes.

Trim veal shoulder meat and cut into cubes. Sprinkle with sodium nitrate. Refrigerate.

Chop walnuts coarsely.

Cut ham into small dice.

MISE EN PLACE FOR ASPIC JELLY

Make aspic jelly according to instructions on package. Add Madeira wine for additional flavor.

Let jelly cool.

METHOD

Melt fatback over low heat in casserole pan.

Sauté shallots and liver briefly in resulting fat.

Put mixture on sheet pan to cool. Season with salt and pepper and pâté spice.

Purée/grind mixture with chilled veal meat until smooth.

Pass/strain through wire sieve.[a]

Place on ice and blend farce with heavy cream. Add chopped walnuts and ham. Adjust seasoning.

Fill dough-lined mold with farce. Be sure there are no air bubbles.

Brush dough rim with egg yolk-cream mixture.

Cover with dough and cut vent holes (chimneys) to let steam escape.

Decorate top with dough, if desired.

Brush top with egg yolk-cream mixture. Refrigerate for 1 hour.

Bake in oven at 425°F (220°C) for 10 minutes and then at 360°F (180°C), with open vent, until center temperature has reached 150°F (65°C).

Let pâté cool. Pour melted aspic into vent holes until mold is filled.

Refrigerate until thoroughly chilled.

---

[a] Pâté spice can be purchased commercially, or Seasoning Salt for Meat (Recipe 9) can be substituted.

[b] Aspic powder is available in different flavors. Choose a light flavor, such as chicken, for this recipe. To use, follow directions on can.

[a] If commercial food processor is used, this step can be omitted.

233

$\mathcal{C}$heese Dip

Käse-Dip-Sauce
Dip au fromage

YIELD: 10 SERVINGS

Boursin au poivre[a]	5 1/3 oz	150 g
Yogurt, plain	5 1/3 oz	150 g
Seasoning (salt and pepper)	1x	1x

METHOD
Mash cheese with a fork.

Add remaining ingredients and stir until smooth.

234

setra Caviar

Kaviar Osietra, mild gesalzen
Caviar Osciètre Malossol

YIELD: 10 SERVINGS

Caviar, Osetra Malossol[b]	10 1/2 oz	300 g
White bread (Pullman loaf)	1 lb 12 oz	800 g
Butter	1 2/3 oz	50 g

METHOD
Open can and serve caviar on crushed ice.

Serve buttered toast on the side.

NOTES: If desired, caviar can be served with sour cream, chopped egg yolk, chopped egg white, chopped onions, and lemon.

Instead of toast, blinis (Recipe 201) can be served.

235

$\mathcal{S}$alad of Monkfish (lotte) and Green Asparagus

Kleiner Salat mit Seeteufel und grünen Spargeln
Petite salade de baudroie et asperges vertes

YIELD: 10 SERVINGS

Green asparagus (20)	2 lb 3 oz	1.0 kg
Green lentils	3 1/2 oz	100 g
Blood oranges	14 oz	400 g
Vinaigrette dressing (Recipe 487)	6 3/4 oz	200 ml
Monkfish (lotte) tail fillets	1 lb 5 oz	600 g
Seasoning (salt and pepper)	1x	1x
Seasoning (lemon juice)	1x	1x
White wheat flour	1 oz	30 g
Peanut oil	3 1/3 oz	100 ml
Chives, fresh, cut	1/3 oz	10 g

MISE EN PLACE
Peel and trim asparagus, boil until tender. Chill and drain.

Cut off asparagus tips, about 2 in. Split tips in half and reserve as garnish.

Cut the remaining asparagus into 1/2-in. pieces.

Boil lentils in water until tender.

Peel oranges and cut into small dice.

Combine asparagus pieces, drained lentils, and oranges with some French dressing.

METHOD
Season monkfish fillets, dredge in flour, and sauté in peanut oil. Let fish cool, but do not chill.

Cut fish into thin slices.

Arrange fish fillets and asparagus/lentil salad attractively on plates. Garnish with asparagus tips.

Drizzle remaining French dressing over fish.

Sprinkle with chives.

---

[a] Boursin is a soft French cheese available in different flavors/versions. For this recipe, *Boursin au poivre* (with peppercorns) is best. If not available, another soft cheese can be used. Crushed peppercorns can be added.

[b] *Malossol* is a Russian word meaning "little salt."

(clockwise from top): Recipe 113, Red Beet Soup, Recipe 179, Purée of Spinach Soup,
Recipe 163, Beef Consomme with Semolina Quenelles

Recipe 175, Petite Marmite Henri IV

Recipe 193, Artichoke Bottoms with Seafood and Vegetable Salad

Recipe 366, Grilled Scallops with Pistachio Butter

Recipe 371, Turkey Breast with Dried Fruit

Recipe 381, Roast Leg of Lamb with Onions and Potatoes

236

Cream Puffs with Smoked Salmon

Kleine Windbeutel mit Räucherlachs
Choux au saumon fumé

YIELD: 10 SERVINGS

Puff paste (Recipe 678)	14 oz	400 g
Tomatoes	5 1/3 oz	150 g
Hüttenkäse[a]	8 3/4 oz	250 g
Chives, fresh	1/3 oz	10 g
Seasoning (salt and pepper)	1x	1x
Smoked salmon, trimmed	10 1/2 oz	300 g
Egg	1	1
Red lettuce[b]	3 1/2 oz	100 g
Onions	1 1/3 oz	40 g
Italian dressing	1 2/3 oz	50 ml
Parsley	2/3 oz	20 g

MISE EN PLACE

Using a pastry bag, make 20 small puffs of cream puffs, bake, and let cool.

Peel tomatoes, remove seeds, and cut into small cubes.

Blend Hüttenkäse with chives, salt and pepper.

Slice smoked salmon.

Boil egg, peel, and chop.

Clean and wash red lettuce.

Peel onions and cut into rings.

METHOD

Split cream puffs and fill with cheese mixture.

Place smoked salmon on plates.

Place two filled puffs on each plate.

Garnish with red lettuce leaves, onion rings, chopped egg, and parsley.

Drizzle dressing over salad.

[a] Hüttenkäse is a fresh, low-fat, mild cheese. Low-fat ricotta can be substituted.

[b] The original recipe calls for Red Lollo lettuce. Other red leaf lettuce can be substituted.

237

Herb Dip

Kräuter-Dip-Sauce
Dip aux fines herbes

YIELD: 10 SERVINGS

Chives, fresh	1/3 oz	10 g
Parsley, fresh	1 tsp	5 g
Chervil, fresh	1 tsp	5 g
Basil, fresh	1 tsp	5 g
Lovage, fresh[a]	1 tsp	5 g
Cottage cheese, low fat	7 oz	200 g
Yogurt, plain	3 1/2 oz	100 g
Seasoning (salt and pepper)	1x	1x
Seasoning (lemon juice)	1x	1x

MISE EN PLACE

Cut chives into small slivers.

Chop herbs.

METHOD

Mix cottage cheese and yogurt; stir until smooth.

Add herbs and season to taste.

238

Salmon Swirls

Lachsrosetten
Rosettes de saumon

YIELD: 10 SERVINGS

Salmon fillets, skinless	3 lb 5 oz	1.5 kg
Dill, fresh	1 tsp	5 g
Red peppers	2 oz	60 g
Fish aspic, fresh (Recipe 4)	3 1/3 oz	100 ml
Pernod[b]	1 tsp	5 ml
Heavy cream (36%)	2 1/2 oz	75 ml
Seasoning (salt and pepper)	1x	1x
Egg white	3/4 oz	25 g
Butter	1/3 oz	10 g
Black truffle slices (20)	1/3 oz	10 g
Fish stock (Recipe 24)	1 qt 19 oz	1.5 L

(continued on next page)

[a] Lovage is an herb seldom used outside of Europe. The German name is *Liebstöckel*.

[b] Pernod is a licorice-flavored cordial.

(continued from preceding page)

MISE EN PLACE

Trim salmon fillets; cut off tail ends. Reserve trimmings.

Split fillets lengthwise and butterfly. Flatten carefully.

Wash dill. Remove stems and chop leaves.

Clean, wash, trim, and blanch red peppers. Cut into 20 equal pieces.

Melt fish aspic and add Pernod for additional flavor.

METHOD

Purée/grind chilled salmon trimmings in food processor or Buffalo chopper with small amount of cream and salt.

Pass/strain through wire sieve.[a]

Place in a bowl on ice and blend with remaining cream.

Lightly whip egg white and fold into fish farce.

Season to taste and add dill.

Spread fish farce on salmon fillets; roll fillets.

Butter aluminum foil and wrap salmon rolls tightly in foil. Twist ends to close rolls. Poke some holes to let steam escape.

Place salmon rolls in suitable pan, cover with hot fish stock, and poach carefully for 20 minutes. Let cool in stock.

Unwrap, roll tightly in transparent wrap, and chill thoroughly.

Cut salmon rolls with a sharp knife into 20 even slices.

Put slices on wire rack.

Dip truffle slices and red pepper in melted aspic jelly and place on salmon slices. Refrigerate.

Glaze with cool, but still liquid, aspic jelly. Refrigerate.

239

Spiny Lobster (langouste) Parisian Style

Languste Pariser Art
Langouste parisienne

YIELD: 10 SERVINGS

Fish poaching liquid[b]	6 qt 11 oz	6.0 L
Coriander leaves (cilantro)	2/3 oz	20 g
Spiny lobsters, live	6 lb 10 oz	3.0 kg
Fish aspic, fresh (Recipe 4)	1 qt 2 oz	1.0 L
Green olives, stuffed, (canned), drained	1 2/3 oz	50 g
Gelatin leaves, plain	2	30 g
Fish velouté sauce (Recipe 53)	1 1/3 oz	40 ml
Seasoning	1x	1x
Heavy cream (36%)	2 1/2 oz	75 ml
Black truffle slices	1/3 oz	10 g
Chives, fresh	2/3 oz	20 g
Russian salad (Recipe 515)	1 lb 2 oz	500 g
Tartlets, small, made with short pastry (Recipe 710)	10	10

MISE EN PLACE

Add coriander leaves (cilantro) to fish poaching liquid and bring to a boil.

Just before cooking, tie spiny lobsters to small wooden boards so the tail will stay straight. Plunge lobsters, head first, into boiling stock.

Bring to a boil as quickly as possible and poach lobsters at about 170°F (75°C) for about 15 minutes[a], until cooked.

Let lobsters cool in stock.

Line 10 small timbale molds with some melted fish aspic and decorate each with one olive slice. Refrigerate.

Soak gelatin leaves in cold water.

METHOD

Remove lobster tail meat carefully; remove intestines. Keep bodies whole.

Slice tails into 20 even slices (medallions). Save trimmings.

Purée trimmings.[b] There should be about 3 1/2 oz (100 g).

Dissolve soaked gelatin leaves in warm fish velouté. Add velouté to lobster purée, mix thoroughly, and season to taste.

Whip the heavy cream.

Stir gelatin/velouté mixture in a bowl over ice. When it starts to thicken, fold in whipped cream.

Use pastry bag with star tube and dress small mounds of lobster purée on lobster slices.

Garnish each medallion with a cut-out truffle circle and chives. Glaze with fish aspic.

Add small amount of liquid fish aspic to vegetable salad and fill prepared timbale molds.

Seal timbale molds with liquid fish aspic and chill.

Unmold when cold and place inside tartlets.

Cover suitable platter with thin layer of aspic jelly.

Brush cold lobster bodies with aspic jelly, place bodies on platter for decoration.

Place medallions and tartlets attractively on platter.

---

[a] If commercial food processor is used, this step can be omitted.

[b] The poaching liquid is often referred to as *court bouillon*, which is water seasoned with some vegetables and spices.

[a] It is recommended to cook lobsters at a higher temperature.

[b] Use food processor to make lobster mousse.

240

Seafood Cocktail with Balsamic Vinegar

Meeresfrüchtecocktail mit Balsamico
Cocktail de fruits de mer au balsamico

YIELD: 10 SERVINGS

Shrimp, large, raw	14 oz	400 g
Squid	10 1/2 oz	300 g
Mussels, fresh	1 lb 2 oz	500 g
Leaf lettuce, head	1	1
Tomatoes	8 3/4 oz	250 g
Onions	3 1/2 oz	100 g
Parsley, Italian, fresh	2/3 oz	20 g
Scampi tails, peeled, raw	8 3/4 oz	250 g
Olive oil, cold pressed	2 3/4 oz	80 ml
Garlic	1/3 oz	10 g
Seasoning (salt and pepper)	1x	1x

DRESSING

Olive oil, cold pressed	6 3/4 oz	200 ml
Balsamic vinegar	1 2/3 oz	50 ml
Seasoning (salt and pepper)	1x	1x
Shallots	1 1/3 oz	40 g
Basil, fresh	1/3 oz	10 g

MISE EN PLACE

Peel shrimp. Boil 10 tail shell pieces and reserve for garnish.

Remove intestine veins from shrimp.

Clean squid.

Clean and scrape mussels, steam, and remove from shells. Save 10 shell halves for garnish.

Clean lettuce.

Peel tomatoes, remove seeds, and cut into 1/3-in. cubes.

Chop onions and parsley.

METHOD FOR DRESSING

Mix olive oil, balsamic vinegar, salt and pepper.

Chop shallots and basil. Add to oil mixture. Blend thoroughly.

METHOD

Sauté shrimp, scampi tails, and squid with olive oil and garlic. Season and let cool.

Cut the other seafood into small pieces.

Blend tomatoes and onions with some dressing.

Place lettuce leaves on plates.

Place bouquets of tomato salad and seafood salad on leaves.

Drizzle with dressing. Sprinkle with chopped parsley.

Garnish each plate with one shrimp tail shell and one mussel shell.

241

Melon Cocktail

Melonencocktail Cremona
Cocktail de melon Crémona

YIELD: 10 SERVINGS

Cavaillon melons[a]	4 lb 7 oz	2.0 kg
Orange	1	1
Lemon	1	1
Mustard fruits,[b] drained	2 2/3 oz	75 g
Marinade from mustard fruits	3 1/3 oz	100 ml
Dark rum	3 1/3 oz	100 ml
Red Port wine	3 1/3 oz	100 ml

GARNISH

Mint, fresh	1 tsp	5 g

METHOD

Peel melons, remove seeds, and cut into thin slices.

Make orange and lemon zest. Blanch.

Squeeze juice from orange and lemon.

Drain mustard fruits. Save marinade.

Chop mustard fruits.

Combine all ingredients and refrigerate for at least 24 hours.

PRESENTATION

Serve in chilled glasses. Garnish with mint leaves.

[a] *Cavaillon* melons are French melons with red meat. Other melons can be substituted.

[b] Mustard fruits are spiced fruits pickled with mustard. They are available in jars.

242

$\mathcal{S}$alad Niçoise

Nizza-Salat
Salade niçoise

YIELD: 10 SERVINGS

Potatoes	1 lb 5 oz	600 g
Tomatoes	1 lb 5 oz	600 g
String beans (haricots verts), frozen	14 oz	400 g
Onions	7 oz	200 g
Olive oil, cold pressed	6 3/4 oz	200 ml
Herb vinegar	2 1/2 oz	70 ml
Seasoning (salt and pepper)	1x	1x
Capers, drained	1 2/3 oz	50 g
Leaf salad (assorted), cleaned	10 1/2 oz	300 g
Tuna fish (canned, packed in oil)[a]	14 oz	400 g
Anchovy fillets, drained	1 2/3 oz	50 g
Black olives, drained	5 1/3 oz	150 g
Parsley, curly, fresh	2/3 oz	20 g

MISE EN PLACE

Boil potatoes, peel, and cut into slices.

Cut tomatoes into large cubes.

Boil string beans and cut into 1 1/4-in. lengths.

Peel onion and cut into rings.

Make dressing with olive oil, herb vinegar, salt and pepper.

METHOD

Combine potatoes, tomatoes, string beans, half amount of onions, and capers with the dressing.

Place salad leaves on plates and place vegetable salad on top.

Break tuna fish into pieces and place on salad.

Garnish with anchovy fillets, remaining onion rings, olives, and parsley.

[a] The tuna fish should be the best quality.

243

$\mathcal{O}$range Dip

Orangen-Dip-Sauce
Dip à l'orange

YIELD: 10 SERVINGS

Horseradish, fresh	1/3 oz	10 g
Blood oranges	5 1/3 oz	150 g
Mayonnaise (Recipe 71)	5 1/3 oz	150 g
Cottage cheese, low fat[a]	3 1/2 oz	100 g
Yogurt, plain	3 1/2 oz	100 g
Orange juice	1 2/3 oz	50 ml
Dijon-style mustard, prepared, mild	1 tsp	5 g
Seasoning (salt and pepper)	1x	1x
Sugar (pinch)	1x	1x

MISE EN PLACE

Peel and grate horseradish.

Peel oranges and cut into small dice.

METHOD

Combine mayonnaise, cottage cheese, yogurt, and orange juice. Stir until smooth.

Season with horseradish, mustard, salt and pepper, and sugar.

Fold in diced orange.

244

$\mathcal{S}$mall Patty Shells with Smoked Salmon

Pastetchen mit Räucherlachsmousse
Bouchées à la mousse de saumon fumé

YIELD: 10 SERVINGS

Patty shells, baked, small	10	10
Chives, fresh	1/3 oz	10 g
Smoked salmon mousse, made like trout mousse (Recipe 249)	7 oz	200 g
Beluga Malossol caviar	1/3 oz	10 g

[a] The original recipe calls for *Quark*, a generic German word for cottage cheese. The cottage cheese for this recipe should be fine curd and strained. Skim-milk ricotta cheese makes a good substitute.

MISE EN PLACE

Remove lids from patty shells with a sharp knife.

Cut chives into small slivers.

METHOD

Fill patty shells with salmon mousse.

Sprinkle with chives and garnish with caviar.

245

Paté Dough (variation 1)

Pastenteig (Variante 1)
Pâte à pâté

YIELD: 2 LB (900 G)

White wheat flour	1 lb 2 oz	500 g
Butter	3 1/2 oz	100 g
Lard	3 1/2 oz	100 g
Salt	1/3 oz	10 g
Water	3 3/4 oz	130 ml
Egg yolk	1 2/3 oz	50 g

MISE EN PLACE

Sift flour.

Cube butter and lard.

METHOD

Combine flour, butter, and lard (rub together).

Put mixture on pastry board. Make hole in center.

Dissolve salt in water. Put egg yolk and water in center of circle.

Combine (knead) quickly into dough.

Shape into a rectangle. Cover and refrigerate for 1 to 2 hours.

NOTE: All ingredients should be worked together rapidly; otherwise the dough can become crumbly, which is known in the trade as "burnt."

246

Paté Dough (variation 2)

Pastetenteig (Variante 2)
Pâte à pâté

YIELD: 2 LB (900 G)

White wheat flour	1 lb 2 oz	500 g
Lard	5 1/3 oz	150 g
Water	5 oz	150 ml
Salt	1/3 oz	10 g
Egg (whole, shelled)	3 1/4 oz	90 g

MISE EN PLACE

Sift flour.

Cube lard.

METHOD

Combine flour and lard (rub together).

Put mixture on pastry board. Make hole in center.

Dissolve salt in water. Put egg yolk and water in center of circle.

Combine (knead) quickly into dough.

Shape into a rectangle. Cover and refrigerate for 1 to 2 hours.

NOTE: All ingredients should be worked together rapidly; otherwise the dough can become crumbly, which is known in the trade as "burnt."

247

Paté Dough (variation 3)

Pastetenteig (Variante 3)
Pâte à pâté

YIELD: 2 LB (900 G)

White wheat flour	1 lb	450 g
Margarine (for puff paste)[a]	7 oz	200 g
Water	5 oz	150 ml
Salt	1/3 oz	10 g
Egg (whole, shelled)	1 2/3 oz	50 g
Malt (powdered)	1/2 oz	15 g

(continued on next page)

---

[a] There is margarine specially formulated for puff paste. It is available under a number of trade names from bakery suppliers.

(continued from preceding page)

MISE EN PLACE
Sift flour.

Cube margarine.

METHOD
On a pastry board, combine flour and margarine (rub together).

Make hole in center.

Dissolve salt in water. Put egg, malt, and water in center of circle.

Combine (knead) quickly into dough.

Shape into a rectangle. Cover and refrigerate for 1 to 2 hours.

NOTES: The addition of malt will brown the dough evenly during baking.

All ingredients should be worked together rapidly; otherwise the dough can become crumbly, which is known in the trade as "burnt."

248

Fillet of Smoked Trout with Tomato Vinaigrette
Räucherforellenfilets mit Tomaten-Vinaigrette
Filets de truit fumée à la vinaigrette de tomates

YIELD: 10 SERVINGS

Parsley, curly, fresh	2/3 oz	20 g
Chives, fresh	2/3 oz	20 g
Onions	5 1/3 oz	150 g
Lemons	2 1/2	2 1/2
Smoked trout fillets, skinned, boned	1 lb 12 oz	800 g
Tomato vinaigrette (Recipe 100)	13 1/2 oz	400 ml

MISE EN PLACE
Chop parsley.

Cut chives into fine slivers.

Peel onions and slice into rings.

Cut lemons into quarters.

METHOD
Sprinkle individual plates with herbs.

Place a trout fillet in the center of each plate, and cover about 2/3 of the fillet with tomato vinaigrette.

Garnish each plate with some onion rings and 1/4 lemon.

249

Smoked Trout Mousse with Shrimp
Räucherforellenmousse mit Krevetten
Mousse de truit fumée aux crevettes

YIELD: 10 SERVINGS

Trout fillets, smoked, skinless	7 oz	200 g
Gelatin leaves	3	4 1/2 g
Fish velouté sauce (Recipe 53)	3 1/3 oz	100 ml
Dill, fresh	1 oz	30 g
Shrimp, cooked, canned, drained[a]	7 oz	200 g
Sour cream	6 3/4 oz	200 ml
Seasoning (salt and pepper)	1x	1x
Seasoning (lemon juice)	1x	1x
Lime	2 oz	60 g
Heavy cream	10 oz	300 ml
Seasoning (salt and pepper)	1x	1x

MISE EN PLACE
Remove any remaining bones from trout fillets. Purée trout.

Pass/strain through fine wire sieve.[b]

Soak gelatin in cold water. Heat fish velouté.

Dissolve gelatin leaves in velouté.

Reserve 10 dill sprigs for garnish; chop the rest.

Reserve 30 shrimp for garnish; cut the rest into small dice.

Combine shrimp with sour cream, chopped dill, salt and pepper, and lemon juice.

Cut lime into thin slices.

METHOD
Place trout purée in stainless steel bowl on ice.

Combine with almost cold velouté, and stir well.

Whip cream (not very stiff) and fold into mixture.

Season to taste.

Dress trout mousse, with pastry bag and star tube into suitable glasses. Refrigerate.

Top mousse with shrimp salad and garnish with dill and lime slices.

---

[a] The shrimp should be small.

[b] If commercial food processor is used, this step can be omitted.

250

Smoked Salmon Roses with Sour Cream

Räucherlachsrosen mit Sauerrahm
Roses de saumon fumé à la crème acidulée

YIELD: 10 SERVINGS

Smoked salmon, trimmed	1 lb 9 oz	700 g
Tomatoes	7 oz	200 g
Eggs	2	2
Cucumbers	3 1/2 oz	100 g
Lemons	2	2
Parsley, Italian	1 1/3 oz	40 g
Onions	5 1/3 oz	150 g
Sour cream, diet	6 3/4 oz	200 ml
Dill, fresh	1/3 oz	10 g
Seasoning (salt and pepper)	1x	1x
Lettuce, leaves, washed	10	10

MISE EN PLACE

Carve salmon into 30 thin slices.

Cut tomatoes into wedges.

Boil eggs, chill, and peel. Slice eggs.

Slice cucumbers.

Cut lemon into wedges.

Wash parsley and remove leaves from stems.

Peel onions and slice into rings.

Wash dill, remove leaves, chop leaves.

Season sour cream with dill, salt and pepper.

PRESENTATION

Form roses with 3 slices of smoked salmon for each plate.

Place roses on plates and garnish attractively with tomatoes, eggs, cucumbers, lemons, parsley leaves, and onion rings.

Fill salad leaves with seasoned sour cream, or serve the sour cream in small containers.

251

Shrimp Cocktail

Riesenkrevettencocktail
Cocktail de crevette roses

YIELD: 10 SERVINGS

Shrimp, large, raw	1 lb 12 oz	800 g
Court bouillon[a]	1 qt 2 oz	1.0 L
Celery[b]	8 3/4 oz	250 g
Lettuce, leaf, head	1	1
Tomatoes	14 oz	400 g
Avocado	1	1
Heavy cream	3 1/3 oz	100 ml
Cocktail sauce (Recipe 39)	13 1/2 oz	400 ml
Seasoning (salt and pepper)	1x	1x
Seasoning (Tabasco)	1x	1x

MISE EN PLACE

Peel shrimp; remove intestine veins. Poach in court bouillon.[c]

Let shrimp cool in stock. When cold, cut into pieces.

Peel celery and chop.

Wash lettuce and reserve the 10 best center leaves; cut remaining leaves into fine shreds (*chiffonade*).

Peel tomatoes, remove seeds, and dice.

Peel avocado, remove pit, and dice.

Whip cream and fold into cocktail sauce.

Reserve 1/3 of diced tomato and avocado for garnish. Blend remaining vegetables with cocktail sauce mixture.

Season to taste with salt and pepper and Tabasco.

Combine diced shrimp with celery. Season to taste.

PRESENTATION

Distribute lettuce *chiffonade* into 10 suitable glasses.

Add shrimp and celery mixture. Cover with vegetable/cocktail sauce.

Garnish with reserved lettuce leaf, diced tomato, and avocado.

---

[a] Court bouillon is a poaching liquid consisting of water, spices, vinegar, and vegetables, boiled about 20 minutes.

[b] The stalk celery specified is known as "English celery" in Europe, and is called *Stangensellerie* in German. In the United States, it is simply referred to as "celery."

[c] Shrimp are usually boiled in the shell to retain more flavor, and are cleaned when cooked.

252

*G*ravlax

Roh Marinierter Lachs
Gravad Lax

YIELD: 3 LB 5 OZ (1.5 KG)

Salmon fillets, 2, with skin[a]	3 lb 5 oz	1.5 kg
Dill, fresh	1 2/3 oz	50 g
White peppercorns	1 tsp	5 g
Black peppercorns	1 tsp	5 g
Sea salt, coarse	2 oz	60 g
Crystal sugar	1 1/3 oz	40 g

GARNISH

Leaf lettuce, head	1	1
Dill, leaves and blossoms, fresh	1 2/3 oz	50 g
Lemons	2 1/2	2 1/2
Mustard sauce (Recipe 94)	1 lb 5 oz	600 g

METHOD

Trim salmon and remove any remaining bones. (Use tweezers.)

Dry fish fillets with absorbent paper.

Remove dill leaves from stems and chop coarsely.

Crush peppercorns and blend with salt and sugar.

Sprinkle some seasoning mixture in a shallow stainless steel pan.

Place one salmon fillet, skin side down, in pan.

Sprinkle salmon with seasoning mixture and dill.

Put second fillet on top, skin side up.

Sprinkle with remaining seasoning mixture and dill.

Cover with transparent wrap.

Place light weight on top (wooden board).

Marinate for 2 to 3 days.

Turn fish fillets each day, to switch top fillet to bottom.

When ready to serve, dry the fillets.

Wash and trim lettuce.

Cut lemons into wedges.

PRESENTATION

Carve salmon and serve on lettuce leaves.

Garnish with lemon wedge and dill leaves and blossoms.

Serve mustard sauce on the side.

[a] The skin is left on to facilitate slicing.

253

*F*ish Fillets Sauté Vinaigrette

Rotbarben und Petersfishfilet auf Blattsalat
Rouget et saint-pierre sur feuilles de salade

YIELD: 10 SERVINGS

Red snapper, whole, gutted	2 lb 3 oz	1.0 kg
St. Peters fish (John Dory), whole, gutted[a]	3 lb 5 oz	1.5 kg
Assorted lettuces[b]	14 oz	400 g
Seasoning (salt and pepper)	1x	1x
Seasoning (lemon juice)	1x	1x
Soy sauce	1/3 oz	10 ml
White wheat flour	1 oz	30 g
Olive oil, cold pressed	3 1/3 oz	100 ml
Vegetable vinaigrette (Recipe 58)	13 1/2 oz	400 ml
Chervil, fresh, leaves	2/3 oz	20 g
Basil leaves, fresh	20	20

METHOD

Fillet both fish. Remove bones, and cut each fish into 10 portions.

Clean, trim and wash lettuces.

Season fish pieces with salt and pepper, lemon juice, and soy sauce.

Dredge fish pieces into flour and sauté in oil.

PRESENTATION

Place lettuces attractively on plates.

Place fish pieces (one of each kind) on top.

Cover with vegetable vinaigrette.

Sprinkle with chervil leaves and garnish with basil leaves.

[a] John Dory is a fish found in the Eastern Atlantic, Mediterranean, and Black Sea. Any white, firm-fleshed fish can be substituted.

[b] The lettuces should be colorful and seasonal.

254

Sweetbread Salad with Chanterelle Mushrooms

Salat mit Kalbsmilken und Eierschwämmen
Salade au ris de veau et aux chanterelles

YIELD: 10 SERVINGS

Sweetbreads	1 lb 9 oz	700 g
White veal stock (Recipe 28)	1 qt 8 oz	1.2 L
Chanterelles, fresh[a]	1 lb 5 oz	600 g
Potatoes	14 oz	400 g
Leaf lettuce, head	1	1
Lamb's lettuce (mache)	3 1/2 oz	100 g
Shallots	3 1/2 oz	100 g
Garlic	1/3 oz	10 g
Chives, fresh	2/3 oz	20 g
Olive oil, cold pressed	3 1/3 oz	100 ml
Seasoning (salt and pepper)	1x	1x

DRESSING

Thyme, fresh	1 tsp	5 g
Parsley, curly, fresh	2/3 oz	20 g
Cornichons, drained[b]	1 2/3 oz	50 g
Herb vinegar	3 1/3 oz	100 L
Sunflower oil	8 1/2 oz	250 ml
Seasoning (salt and pepper)	1x	1x

METHOD FOR DRESSING

Remove stems from thyme and parsley. Wash, dry, and chop.

Chop cornichons.

Blend with vinegar and sunflower oil.

Season to taste.

MISE EN PLACE

Soak sweetbreads in cold water overnight. Wash in hot water to remove blood.

Cover with veal stock. Bring to a boil and poach for 20 minutes.

Let cool in stock. When cold, remove membranes and break into small clusters.

Clean and wash chanterelle mushrooms.

Boil potatoes, peel, and slice.

Clean and wash lettuces.

Peel and chop shallots and garlic.

Slice chives into slivers.

---

[a] Chanterelles are wild yellow mushrooms, called *girolles* in French and *Eierschwämme* in German.

[b] Cornichons are tiny, rather acidic pickles. Good-quality dill pickles can be substituted, but seeds should be removed.

METHOD

Sauté shallots and garlic in olive oil. Add mushrooms and continue cooking over high heat.

Add sweetbreads and continue cooking until thoroughly heated and blended, season to taste. Let cool.

Line plates with lettuce leaves. Place sweetbread salad in centers.

Surround with sliced potatoes and lamb's lettuce.

Drizzle dressing over potatoes and salads.

Sprinkle with chives.

255

Lobster and Sweetbread Salad

Salatvorspeise mit Hummer und Kalbsmilke
Avant-goût d'homard et de ris de veau

YIELD: 10 SERVINGS

Sweetbreads	1 lb 12 oz	800 g
White veal stock (Recipe 28)	1 qt 19 oz	1.5 L
Lobster, freshly cooked	2 lb	900 g
Olive oil, cold pressed	3 1/3 oz	100 ml
Lettuce, leaf, assorted, cleaned and washed	1 lb 5 oz	600 g
Herb vinaigrette (Recipe 49)	8 1/2 oz	250 ml
Chervil	1 tsp	5 g
Marinade for sweetbreads		
Egg yolks	2	2
Mustard, prepared, coarsegrain	1 oz	30 g
Coriander leaves (cilantro), chopped	1 tbsp	2 g
Seasoning (salt and pepper)	1x	1x
Seasoning (lemon juice)	1x	1x

MISE EN PLACE

Soak sweetbreads in cold water overnight. Wash in hot water to remove blood.

Cover with stock. Bring to a boil and poach for 20 minutes.

Let cool in stock. When cold, cut into 20 even slices.

Cut lobster (including claws) into 10 even portions. Save legs for garnish.

(continued on next page)

(continued from preceding page)

METHOD FOR MARINADE
Combine egg yolks, mustard, and chopped coriander leaves. Season with salt and pepper and lemon juice.

METHOD
Brush sweetbread slices with marinade.

Sauté sweetbread slices in oil.

Line 10 plates with assorted lettuces.

Place lukewarm sweetbread slices and lobster[a] in center.

Sprinkle salads with herb vinaigrette.

Garnish with lobster legs and chervil leaves.

256

Salmon Tartar with Salad

Salm-Tartar mit kleinem Salat
Tartare de saumon et petite salade

YIELD: 10 SERVINGS

Salmon fillet, skinless, very fresh!	1 lb 12 oz	800 g
Seasoning (salt and pepper)	1x	1x
Lemons	2	2
Dill, fresh	2/3 oz	20 g
Shallots	1 2/3 oz	50 g
Olive oil, cold pressed	1 2/3 oz	50 ml

SALAD

Frisée salad (curly chicorée)	4 1/4 oz	120 g
Red lettuce	7 oz	200 g
String beans (haricots verts), fresh or frozen	10 1/2 oz	300 g

DRESSING

Walnut oil	3 1/3 oz	100 ml
White wine vinegar	1 2/3 oz	50 ml
Seasoning (salt and pepper)	1x	1x

GARNISH

Tomatoes	7 oz	200 g
Shallots	1 1/3 oz	40 g
Parsley, Italian, fresh	1/3 oz	10 g

MISE EN PLACE
Remove all small bones from salmon fillet.

Chop fish with sharp knife. *Do not squash or mash fish!*

Season with salt and pepper and lemon juice.

Remove dill leaves from stems and chop.

Peel shallots and chop.

Wash and drain frisée and red lettuce.

Boil string beans, chill, and drain. If beans are too large, cut into pieces.

Prepare dressing: Mix walnut oil, vinegar, and salt and pepper.

Prepare garnish: Peel tomatoes, remove seeds, and cut into small dice. Peel shallots and slice into fine rings. Wash parsley.

METHOD
Mix chopped salmon with dill, shallots, and olive oil. Refrigerate for at least 15 minutes.

PRESENTATION
Place salmon tartar into center of plates; shape attractively.

Garnish with diced tomatoes and shallot rings.

Place salads and beans around and drizzle with dressing.

Garnish with parsley leaves.

257

Ham Mousse with Green Asparagus

Schinkenmousse mit grünen Spargeln
Mousse de jambon aux asperges verts

YIELD: 10 SERVINGS

Green asparagus	2 lb 3 oz	1.0 kg
Radishes	1/2 bunch	1/2 bund
Chives, fresh	2/3 oz	20 g
Herb vinaigrette (Recipe 49)	6 3/4 oz	200 ml
Ham, boiled	2 oz	60 g
Eggs	2	2
Chervil, fresh leaves	1 tsp	5 g
Ham mousse[a]	14 oz	400 g

MISE EN PLACE
Peel and trim asparagus. Boil until cooked, but firm. Chill in cold water, drain. If asparagus are very thick, split lengthwise.

---

[a] This salad should be served while sweetbreads and lobster are still warm.

[a] Use recipe for Smoked Trout Mousse with Shrimp (Recipe 249), but replace trout with ham and replace fish *velouté* with Bechamel Sauce (Recipe 34).

Trim and wash radishes. Cut into fine dice (*brunoise*).

Cut chives into slivers.

Combine radishes and chives with herb vinaigrette.

Cut ham into fine strips (*julienne*).

Boil eggs. Peel and cut into slices.

PRESENTATION

Place asparagus in centers of individual plates.

Shape mousse into oval quenelles using 2 soup spoons, or with oval scoop. Place on top of asparagus.

Sprinkle with ham *julienne*.

Drizzle radish chive vinaigrette over asparagus.

Garnish with egg slices and chervil leaves.

258

Cold Fillet of Sole with Mango Sauce

Seezungencocktail mit Mango
Cocktail de la sole à la mangue

YIELD: 10 SERVINGS

Fillets of sole	1 lb 9 oz	700 g
Court bouillon[a]	1 qt 2 oz	1.0 L
Knob celery (celeriac)	8 3/4 oz	250 g
Seasoning (lemon juice)	1x	1x
Red oak lettuce	5 1/3 oz	150 g
Strawberries, fresh	5 1/3 oz	150 g
Green peppercorns (canned, drained)	1/3 oz	10 g

DRESSING

Mango, ripe	1	1
Heavy cream (36%)	3 1/3 oz	100 ml
Mayonnaise (Recipe 71)	3 1/3 oz	100 ml
Mango chutney, chopped	2/3 oz	20 g
Orange juice	1 1/3 oz	40 ml
Cider vinegar	1 tsp	5 ml
Seasoning (salt and pepper)	1x	1x
Seasoning lemon juice)	1x	1x

METHOD FOR DRESSING

Peel mango. Purée about 2/3 and cut the rest into small dice.

Combine with all other dressing ingredients. Season well.

[a] Court bouillon is a poaching liquid consisting of water, spices, vinegar, and vegetables, boiled for about 20 minutes.

METHOD

Cut sole fillets into strips and poach in court bouillon.

Peel knob celery and cut into *julienne*. Season with lemon juice.

Clean and wash lettuce.

Dice strawberries.

PRESENTATION

Line serving dishes with lettuce, put knob celery in center.

Place poached fish on top, fish should still be warm.

Cover with dressing and sprinkle with diced strawberries and green peppercorns.

259

Bouquet of White Asparagus with Herb Cheese

Spargelbukett mit Hüttenkäse
Bouquet d'asperges au fromage frais

YIELD: 10 SERVINGS

White asparagus	6 lb 10 oz	3.0 kg
Radishes	1 bunch	1 bund
Assorted bell peppers	3 1/2 oz	100 g
Hüttenkäse[a]	14 oz	400 g
Chives, sliced	2/3 oz	20 g
Sunflower oil	1 2/3 oz	50 ml
White wine vinegar	2/3 oz	20 ml
Seasoning (salt and pepper)	1x	1x
Eggs	2	2
Tomato vinaigrette (Recipe 100)	10 oz	300 ml
Parsley, Italian, fresh	2/3 oz	20 g

MISE EN PLACE

Peel asparagus, boil, and let cool.

Cut radishes and peppers into small dice.

Make cheese spread by combining cheese with radishes, peppers, cut chives, oil, vinegar and salt and pepper.

Boil eggs, peel, and cut into slices.

PRESENTATION

Place asparagus on plates.

Drizzle with tomato vinaigrette.

Place mound of cheese spread next to asparagus and garnish with sliced eggs and parsley twigs.

[a] Hüttenkäse is a fresh, low-fat mild cheese. Low-fat ricotta cheese can be substituted.

260

Asparagus Mousse with Crayfish

Spargelmousse mit Krebsen
Mousse d'asperges aux écrevisse

YIELD: 10 SERVINGS

Green asparagus	1 lb 2 oz	500 g
Salt	1/3 oz	10 g
Crayfish tails, cooked and peeled	8 3/4 oz	250 g
Vegetable vinaigrette (Recipe 58)	10 oz	300 ml
Parsley, curly, fresh	1/3 oz	10 g
Red leaf lettuce	10 1/2 oz	300 g
Asparagus mousse, ready[a]	1 lb 5 oz	600 g

MISE EN PLACE

Peel and trim asparagus, boil in salted water, chill in cold water, and let cool. Cut asparagus into pieces. Save tips for garnish.

Carefully combine asparagus with crayfish tails and vegetable vinaigrette.

Chop parsley.

Trim and wash lettuce.

PRESENTATION

Line plates with lettuce.

Place asparagus/crayfish salad in the centers.

Place 3 small quenelles (dumplings) of asparagus mousse on top. Use 2 table spoons or oval scoop to shape the dumplings.

Garnish with asparagus tips and chopped parsley.

---

[a] Asparagus mousse can be made like Tomato Mousse with Quail Eggs (Recipe 265), but replace tomatoes with cooked green asparagus and omit sugar.

261

Asparagus Salad with Oranges and Ham

Spargelsalat Mikado
Salade d'asperges mikado

YIELD: 10 SERVINGS

White asparagus	5 lbs 8 oz	2.5 kg
Salt	1/3 oz	10 g
Ham, boiled	5 1/3 oz	150 g
Oranges	14 oz	400 g
Assorted peppers	8 3/4 oz	250 g
Red leaf lettuce leaves	20	20
Chives, fresh	2/3 oz	20 g

DRESSING

Madras curry powder	pinch	2 g
Orange juice	3 1/3 oz	100 ml
Cottage cheese, low fat	8 3/4 oz	250 g
Salad dressing[a]	6 3/4 oz	200 ml
Seasoning (salt and pepper)	1x	1x

METHOD FOR DRESSING

Blend curry powder with warm orange juice. Combine all ingredients; mix until smooth.

MISE EN PLACE

Peel asparagus, trim and boil in salted water, let cool. Reserve tips for garnish, cut the rest into pieces.

Cut ham into strips (*julienne*).

Peel oranges and remove sections between membranes.

Trim peppers, cut into strips (*julienne*), and blanch.

Clean lettuce.

Cut chives into slivers.

PRESENTATION

Combine asparagus pieces, ham *julienne*, orange sections, and peppers with about 2/3 of the dressing.

Place 2 lettuce leaves on each plate.

Mound asparagus tips on one leaf and asparagus salad on the other.

Drizzle dressing over asparagus tips.

Sprinkle with chives.

---

[a] Any homogenized salad dressing can be used.

*F*ruit Salad Plate with Celery

Stangensellerie-Rohkost mit Früchten
Crudité de céleri en branches aux fruits

YIELD: 10 SERVINGS

Stalk celery (with some leaves)[a]	2 lb 3 oz	1.0 kg
Lemon	1	1
Orange juice	5 oz	150 ml
Honey	1 1/3 oz	40 g
Seasoning (salt and pepper)	1x	1x
Oranges, blood	14 oz	400 g
Apples	10 1/2 oz	300 g
Melon, Cavaillon[b]	10 1/2 oz	300 g
Pineapple, fresh	10 1/2 oz	300 g
Raisins, golden	1 2/3 oz	50 g
Hazelnuts (filberts), shelled, skins removed	1 2/3 oz	50 g

MISE EN PLACE

Peel and wash celery. Save some leaves for garnish. Cut celery into fine strips (*julienne*).

Combine lemon and orange juice, warm, and mix with honey. Season with salt and freshly ground black pepper.

Combine celery and half the dressing.

Peel and trim fruits and cut into large dice.

Blend oranges, apples, melon, and pineapple with remaining dressing.

Soak raisins in a little dressing.

Chop hazelnuts coarsely.

PRESENTATION

Place celery salad in center of plate and top with diced fruit.

Garnish with raisins, hazelnuts, and chopped reserved celery leaves.

*B*eefsteak Tartar

Tartar-Beefsteak
Beefsteak Tartare

YIELD: 10 SERVINGS

Tartar meat[a]	2 lb 10 oz	1.2 kg
Pickles, drained	3 1/2 oz	100 g
Onions	3 1/2 oz	100 g
Capers, drained	2 2/3 oz	75 g
Anchovies, drained	2/3 oz	20 g
Parsley	2/3 oz	20 g
Egg yolks[b]	6	6
Dijon mustard	3/4 oz	25 g
Sunflower oil	1 2/3 oz	50 ml
Tomato ketchup	5 oz	150 ml
Paprika (sweet)	2/3 oz	20 g
Cognac (or any brandy)	1 2/3 oz	50 ml
Lemon	1	1
Seasoning (salt and pepper)	1x	1x
Seasoning (Tabasco)	1x	1x

METHOD

Grind meat through medium plate of meat grinder.[c]

Chop pickles, onions, capers, anchovies, and parsley.

Mix egg yolks, mustard, and oil.

Combine meat, chopped ingredients, egg-oil mixture, tomato ketchup, paprika, Cognac, and lemon juice.

Season to taste. It should be somewhat tangy.

Shape into 10 patties,[d] and serve with toast and butter.

---

[a] The stalk celery sometimes referred to as "English celery" in Europe, is called *Stangensellerie* in German. In the United States it is referred to simply as "celery."

[b] *Cavaillon* melons are French melons with red meat. Other melons can be substituted.

---

[a] Use lean, fresh beef such as top sirloin.

[b] It is safest to use pasteurized egg yolks.

[c] The grinder should be chilled and the meat ground as close to service time as practical.

[d] Shape on sanitary surface and do not touch meat with hands.

264

Beefsteak Tartar Canapes

Tartar-Canapés
Canapés tartare

YIELD: 10 SERVINGS

Bread, white (Pullman loaf)	7 oz	200 g
Butter	1 oz	30 g
Cornichons, drained	1/3 oz	10 g
Radishes	3	3
Beefsteak tartar, prepared (Recipe 263)	7 oz	200 g

METHOD

Remove crust from bread, slice, and toast.

Butter toast. Let cool.

Slice cornichons and clean radishes for garnish.

Spread tartar meat on toast.

Cut into canape-size pieces.

Garnish each canape with cornichon and radish slices.

265

Tomato Mousse with Quail Eggs

Tomatenmousse mit Wachteleiern
Mousse de tomates aux oeufs de caille

YIELD: 10 SERVINGS

Quail eggs	20	20
Tomatoes, ripe	1 lb 12 oz	800 g
Veal velouté sauce (Recipe 65)	2 oz	60 ml
Gelatin, leaves	4	6 g
Heavy cream	8 1/2 oz	250 ml
Seasoning (salt and pepper)	1x	1x
Seasoning (Tabasco)	1x	1x
Seasoning[a] (lemon juice)	1x	1x
Cress	3 1/2 oz	100 g
Cherry tomatoes	7 oz	200 g
Vinaigrette dressing (Recipe 487)	5 oz	150 ml

METHOD

Boil quail eggs, peel, and slice in half.

Peel tomatoes, remove seeds, and purée.[a] There should be a 1 lb 2 oz (500 g) of mixture.

Warm *velouté*.

Soak gelatin leaves in water and add to warm *velouté* to dissolve.

Whip cream.

Put tomato purée in a bowl on ice and mix with *velouté*. When mixture starts to thicken, fold in whipped cream and season to taste. Refrigerate.

Wash cress.

Cut cherry tomatoes in half.

PRESENTATION

Place cress in center of plates and drizzle with French dressing.

Place 3 small quenelles (dumplings) of tomato mousse on top. Use 2 tablespoons or oval scoop to shape dumplings.

Garnish with quail eggs and cherry tomatoes.

266

Tomatoes with Mozzarella and Basil

Tomaten mit Mozzarella und Basilikum
Tomates au mozzarella et au basilic

YIELD: 10 SERVINGS

Tomatoes, large and very ripe[b]	3 lb 5 oz	1.5 kg
Mozzarella cheese, fresh[c]	14 oz	400 g
Basil leaves	20	20
Onions	5 1/3 oz	150 g

DRESSING

Red wine vinegar	2 3/4 oz	80 ml
Olive oil, cold pressed	6 3/4 oz	200 ml
Basil, chopped	1/2 oz	15 g
Seasoning (salt and pepper)	1x	1x

METHOD FOR DRESSING

Combine all ingredients.

---

[a] If tomatoes are not very ripe, a pinch of sugar should be added.

[a] If very ripe and meaty tomatoes are not available, some good-quality tomato juice can be added, but mixture should not exceed 1 lb 2 oz (500 g).

[b] Tomatoes should be vine-ripened.

[c] Buffalo mozzarella cheese is preferred.

METHOD

Wash and slice tomatoes and spread slices on plates.

Slice mozzarella and place on tomato slices.

Wash basil and place leaves between tomatoes and cheese.

Peel onions and cut into thin slices. Break slices into rings and sprinkle over tomatoes.

Drizzle dressing over tomatoes.

267

*C*razy Salad

Verrückter Salat
Salade folle

YIELD: 10 SERVINGS

Shrimp, large, raw (5)	10 1/2 oz	300 g
Veal kidney, trimmed of fat	7 oz	200 g
Smoked salmon, trimmed	6 1/3 oz	180 g
Quail eggs	20	20
Tête de Moine[a]	5 1/3 oz	150 g
Radishes	1 bunch	1 bund
Walnuts, chopped	1 1/3 oz	40 g
Assorted leaf lettuces, washed and trimmed	1 lb 5 oz	600 g
Italian dressing	10 oz	300 ml
Seasoning (salt and pepper)	1x	1x
Peanut oil	1 2/3 oz	50 ml
Cherry tomatoes, halved	7 oz	200 g
Pear, fresh	3 1/2 oz	100 g
Parsley, curly, fresh, chopped	1/3 oz	10 g
Chives, fresh, cut into slivers	1/3 oz	10 g

MISE EN PLACE

Peel and split shrimp.

Cut veal kidney into 10 slices.

Carve salmon into thin slices.

Boil quail eggs, peel, and halve.

Shave 10 bouquets (curls) from the *Tête de Moine*.[b]

Slice radishes.

METHOD

Mix lettuce with Italian dressing and divide onto plates.

---

[a] *Tête de Moine* is a semi-hard, round cheese from the Swiss canton Berne. It is served shaved.

[b] A *girolle* can be used to shave cheese.

Season shrimp and kidney slices and sauté quickly in oil. Place on top of lettuce.

Add sliced salmon.

Put halved quail eggs, *Tête de Moine* curls, sliced radishes, walnuts, and halved cherry tomatoes on top of salad.

Cut pear into fine strips (*julienne*),[a] and sprinkle over salad.

Sprinkle salad with parsley and chives.

268

*W*ild Mushroom Salad

Waldpilzecocktail
Cocktail de champignons des bois

YIELD: 10 SERVINGS

White mushrooms, fresh[b]	10 1/2 oz	300 g
Chanterelle mushrooms, fresh[c]	7 oz	200 g
Porcini mushrooms,[d] fresh	7 oz	200 g
Shallots	1 2/3 oz	50 g
Parsley, curly, fresh	2/3 oz	20 g
Sunflower oil	1 2/3 oz	50 ml
Seasoning (salt and pepper)	1x	1x
Herb vinegar	1 2/3 oz	50 ml
Red leaf lettuce	7 oz	200 g
Scallions	3–5	3–5

DRESSING

Herb vinegar	1 2/3 oz	50 ml
Sunflower oil	3 1/3 oz	100 ml
Seasoning (salt and pepper)	1x	1x

METHOD FOR DRESSING

Combine all ingredients.

METHOD

Trim and wash mushrooms.

Peel and chop shallots.

Chop parsley.

Sauté shallots in oil. Add mushrooms. Season to taste and cook briefly.

(continued on next page)

---

[a] The original recipe suggests grating the pear over the salad.

[b] White mushrooms are the standard cultivated mushrooms used in the United States.

[c] Chanterelles are yellow wild mushrooms, called *girolles* in French and *Eierschwämme* in German.

[d] Porcini are wild mushrooms, called *cèpes* in French, *Steinpilze* in German, and *porcini* in Italian. These mushrooms are widely available dried and are increasingly available fresh. Because Italy is a large exporter of these mushrooms, the Italian name is commonly used.

(continued from preceding page)

Season with salt and pepper and vinegar while still warm.

Add about half the amount of chopped parsley.

Wash lettuce.

Slice scallions crosswise into rings.

Line glasses with lettuce. Place mushrooms on top.

Sprinkle with scallion rings and remaining parsley.

Drizzle with dressing.

269

$\mathcal{G}$ame Paté

Wildpastete
Pâté de gibier

YIELD: 10 SERVINGS

Pâté dough	2 lb	900 g
(Recipe 245, 246, or 247)		
Egg yolk	1	1
Coffee cream/light cream	1/3 oz	10 ml

FARCE

Fatback, fresh, unsalted	7 oz	200 g
Venison meat,[a] boneless and trimmed	10 1/2 oz	300 g
Veal shoulder, boneless and trimmed	3 1/2 oz	100 g
Calves' liver	5 1/3 oz	150 g
Juniper berries	4 to 5	3 g
Paté spice	1 tsp	5 g
Cognac (or any brandy)	1 oz	30 ml
Seasoning (salt and pepper)	1x	1x
Apples[b]	2 1/2 oz	70 g
Black truffles	2/3 oz	20 g
Heavy cream	3 1/3 oz	100 ml
Seasoning (salt and pepper)	1x	1x

GARNISH

Fatback, fresh, unsalted	1 2/3 oz	50 g
Venison tenderloin	3 1/2 oz	100 g
Clarified butter	1/3 oz	10 g
Aspic powder[c]	1/2 oz	15 g
Water	10 oz	300 ml
Cognac (or any brandy)	1/3 oz	10 ml

---

[a] Venison meat in Switzerland is likely to be roebuck.

[b] Granny Smith apples are recommended.

[c] Aspic powder is available commercially.

MISE EN PLACE
Line paté mold with dough.

Mix egg yolk with coffee cream.

Cut fatback for farce into 3/4-in. cubes.

Cut venison meat, veal shoulder, and calves' liver into cubes.

Marinate meat with juniper berries, paté spice, and Cognac.

Peel apples, core, and cut into slices.

Dice truffle.

MISE EN PLACE FOR GARNISH
Cut fatback for garnish into thin, large slices on meat slicer.

Sauté venison tenderloin for garnish in clarified butter and let cool.

Wrap venison tenderloin in the sliced fatback.

Make aspic jelly according to recipe on package; add Cognac for additional flavor.

METHOD
Melt cubed fatback over low heat in casserole pan.

Sauté venison, veal, and liver cubes briefly in resulting fat.

Spread mixture on sheet pan to let cool and season with some salt and pepper. Add apples.

Purée/grind mixture until smooth.

Pass/strain through wire sieve.[a]

Place in a bowl on ice and blend farce with heavy cream and diced truffles. Season to taste.

Fill lined pâté mold about 1/3 high with farce. Be sure there are no air bubbles.

Put venison tenderloin in center and cover with remaining farce.

Brush dough rim with egg yolk-cream mixture.

Cover with dough and cut holes (chimneys) to let steam escape.

Decorate top with dough pieces.

Brush top with egg yolk-cream mixture. Refrigerate for 1 hour.

Bake in oven at 425°F (220°C) for 10 minutes and then at 360°F (180°C), with open vent, until center temperature has reached 130°F (55°C).[e]

Let paté cool. Pour cool, but liquid, aspic jelly through chimney holes and refrigerate until completely chilled.

---

[a] If commercial food processor is used, this step can be omitted.

[b] The suggested temperature does not kill harmful bacteria. The center temperature should be at least 140°F (60°C).

270

Cream Puffs with Cheese and Ham Filling

Windbeutel mit Käse-Schinken Füllung
Choux vaudoise

YIELD: 10 SERVINGS

Pâte à choux (Recipe 678)	14 oz	400 g
Tomme vaudoise[a]	14 oz	400 g
Ham, boiled	7 oz	200 g
Fennel, bulb (anise)	8 3/4 oz	250 g
Pear	8 3/4 oz	250 g
Walnut oil	2 oz	60 ml
Herb vinegar	1 1/3 oz	40 ml
Seasoning (salt and pepper)	1x	1x
Yogurt, plain	4 1/4 oz	120 g
Seasoning (salt and pepper)	1x	1x

METHOD

Make 10 cream puffs using pastry bag, and bake until golden brown and fully cooked.

Dice cheese and ham into 1/5-in. cubes.

Clean and trim fennel. Save some fennel leaves for garnish.

Peel and core pear.

Cut fennel and pear into even wedges.

Make dressing with walnut oil, vinegar, salt and pepper.

Combine cheese, ham, and yogurt; season with salt and pepper.

Split cream puffs; save lids.

Fill cream puffs with ham and cheese mixture.

Warm puffs in oven for 5 to 7 minutes until cheese starts to melt.

Place lids on top and place on plates.

Surround cream puffs attractively with fennel and pear wedges.

Drizzle dressing on top.

[a] *Tomme vaudoise* is a semi-soft cheese from the Swiss canton Vaud.

Hot Appetizers

271

Moussaka

Auberginengratin
Moussaka

YIELD: 10 SERVINGS

Eggplants	1 lb 12 oz	800 g
Salt	2/3 oz	20 g
Tomatoes	1 lb 2 oz	500 g
Onions	7 oz	200 g
Garlic	1 tsp	5 g
Oregano, fresh	2/3 oz	20 g
Lamb chuck, boneless, well trimmed	1 lb 5 oz	600 g
Egg yolks	4	4
Sour cream, diet	6 3/4	200 ml
Parmesan cheese, grated	1 2/3	50 g
White wheat flour	1 2/3 oz	50 g
Olive oil	6 3/4 oz	200 ml
Seasoning (salt and pepper)	1x	1x

MISE EN PLACE

Wash and dry eggplants. Do not peel. Cut into 1/4-in. slices.

Sprinkle eggplant slices with salt; let stand 30 minutes.

Peel tomatoes, remove seeds, and dice.

Peel and chop onions and garlic.

Chop oregano leaves.

Grind lamb meat through medium-size plate of meat grinder.

Combine egg yolks with sour cream and Parmesan cheese.

METHOD

Pat dry eggplant slices; dredge in flour and sauté in oil.

Sauté ground lamb in oil; stir frequently to keep pieces separate.

Add onions and garlic and continue cooking.

Add tomatoes and oregano and continue cooking.

Season to taste.

Oil ovenproof dish and line with half the amount of eggplant slices.

Cover slices with lamb mixture.

Top with remaining eggplant slices.

Pour egg/sour cream mixture over top.

Bake for 30 minutes until golden brown.

272

*B*asel[a] Onion Tart

Basler Zwiebelwähe
Tarte au fromage bâloise

YIELD: 10 SERVINGS

Short pastry (Recipe 710)	1 lb 9 oz	700 g

FILLING

Emmenthal cheese[b]	14 oz	400 g
Onions	1 lb 5 oz	600 g
Butter	1 2/3 oz	50 g

CUSTARD

Milk	13 1/2 oz	400 ml
Heavy cream	6 3/4 oz	200 ml
Eggs	4	4
White wheat flour	3 oz	80 g
Seasoning (salt and pepper)	1x	1x

MISE EN PLACE
Line 2 tart molds about 11 inches in diameter with dough; poke some holes in dough.

Grate cheese coarsely.

Peel and slice onions.

METHOD
Sauté onions in butter until golden.

Let onions cool and place evenly in molds.

Combine custard ingredients; do not beat so no air bubbles will be created.

Strain through fine mesh china cap.

Fill molds with custard.

Bake in lower part of oven at 425°F (220°C) for 30 to 40 minutes.

273

*P*uff Pastry Pillow with Fois Gras and Truffles

Blätterteigkissen mit Entenleber und Trüffel
Feuilletés au foie de canard et aux truffes

YIELD: 10 SERVINGS

Puff pastry (Recipe 689)	1 lb 5 oz	600 g
Egg	1	1
Truffle, canned, drained	2/3 oz	20 g
Duck livers, raw[a]	1 lb 2 oz	500 g
Butter, cold	2/3 oz	20 g
Seasoning (salt and pepper)	1x	1x
Cognac (or any brandy)	1 oz	30 ml
Brown veal juice, thickened (Recipe 55)	6 3/4 oz	200 ml

MISE EN PLACE
Roll out puff pastry about 1/8-in. thick and cut 10 rectangles 5 1/2 in. x 4 in. (14 cm x 10 cm).

Put rectangles on pastry sheet and refrigerate for 30 minutes.

Beat egg with small amount of cold water and brush onto rectangles.

Bake at 400°F (200°C).

When baked, slice off top layer as lid; keep pillows warm.

Cut truffles into thin slices.

METHOD
Slice duck liver; sauté slices quickly in half the butter.

Season and place slices on puff pastry pillows.

Add Cognac to pan, ignite, add veal juice, and reduce.

Add remaining cold butter in small nuggets. Do not allow to boil any more.

Add truffle slices.

Cover liver slices with sauce and place lids on top catty-corner.

---

[a] Basel is a Swiss city near the German and French borders.

[b] Emmenthal is the genuine Swiss cheese.

[a] The liver in this recipe is fresh *foie gras*.

274

$\mathscr{P}$uff Pastry Pillow with Spring Vegetables

Blätterteigkissen mit feinem Gemüse
Feuilletés jardinière

YIELD: 10 SERVINGS

Puff pastry (Recipe 689)	1 lb 5 oz	600 g
Egg	1	1
Baby carrots	7 oz	200 g
Kohlrabi	7 oz	200 g
Snow peas, fresh	5 1/3 oz	150 g
Peas (petits pois), frozen	3 1/2 oz	100 g
Scallions	3–5	3–5
Butter	1 2/3 oz	50 g
White veal stock (Recipe 28)	10 oz	300 ml
Heavy cream (36%)	6 3/4 oz	200 ml
Egg yolks	2	2
Cornstarch	1/3 oz	10 g
Crystal sugar	1 tsp	5 g
Seasoning (salt and pepper)	1x	1x
Chives, fresh, cut into slivers	2/3 oz	20 g

MISE EN PLACE
Roll out puff pastry about 1/8-in. thick and cut 10 rectangles 5 1/2 in. x 4 in. (14 cm x 10 cm).

Put rectangles on pastry sheet and refrigerate for 30 minutes.

Beat egg with small amount of cold water and brush onto rectangles.

Bake at 400°F (200°C).

When baked, slice off top layer as lid; keep pillows warm.

Peel and trim carrots and kohlrabi and slice into large strips (*julienne*).

Trim snow peas and blanch.

Thaw *petits pois*.

Cut scallions in 1-in. pieces.

METHOD
Sauté carrots and kohlrabi in butter and add veal stock.

Cook until just done; remove vegetables and reduce stock.

Combine cream, egg yolks, and cornstarch.

Add to stock, stirring continuously, and heat carefully until thick.

Add all vegetables; season to taste with sugar, salt and pepper. Bring to boil.

Ladle vegetables over puff pastry pillows.

Sprinkle with chives and place lids on top catty-corner.

275

$\mathscr{P}$uff Pastry Turnover with Seafood

Blätterteigkrapfen mit Meeresfrüchten
Rissoles aux fruits de mer

YIELD: 10 SERVINGS

Puff pastry, lean (Recipe 715)	1 lb 12 oz	800 g
Monkfish, fillets	10 1/2 oz	300 g
Mussels, fresh	1 lb 2 oz	500 g
Mushrooms, fresh	7 oz	200 g
Shallots	2/3 oz	20 g
Butter	2/3 oz	20 g
Dry white wine	3 1/3 oz	100 ml
Fish fumet (Recipe 25)	6 3/4 oz	200 ml
Shrimp, small cooked	3 1/2 oz	100 g
Fish velouté sauce (Recipe 53)	10 oz	300 ml
Heavy cream (36%)	3 1/3 oz	100 ml
Seasoning (lemon juice)	1x	1x
Seasoning (salt and pepper)	1x	1x
Egg	1	1

MISE EN PLACE
Roll out puff pastry and cut 10 circles about 5 1/2 in. in diameter. Refrigerate circles.

Cut monkfish fillets into cubes.

Scrape and clean mussels, steam, and remove from shells.

Wash and trim mushrooms and cut into quarters.

Peel and chop shallots.

METHOD
Sauté shallots in butter; add mushrooms and continue cooking.

Add wine and fish fumet; add monkfish; bring to a boil; and poach fish. Add mussels and shrimp and return to a boil.

Remove seafood. Reserve stock. Boil down stock until almost reduced. Add fish *velouté* and cream. Reduce until thick.

Add all seafood, bring to a boil, and season. Chill mixture.[a]

Break egg and mix with small amount of cold water.

Brush dough circle rims with egg. Place cold seafood in centers; fold over tops. Press rims down and seal with fork. Brush with egg.

Poke holes to let steam escape.

Bake at 400°F (200°C) for 20 to 30 minutes.

Serve each portion on a paper doily, with lobster sauce (Recipe 61) on the side.

---

[a] Mixture should be fairly thick. If too runny, thicken with a little cornstarch.

276

$\mathscr{P}$uff Pastry Turnover with Wild Mushrooms

Blätterteigkrapfen mit Pilzfüllung
Rissoles forestière

YIELD: 10 SERVINGS

Puff pastry, lean (Recipe 715)[a]	1 lb 12 oz	800 g
Mushrooms, fresh	7 oz	200 g
Chanterelles[b]	7 oz	200 g
Porcini, fresh[c]	7 oz	200 g
Shallots	1 oz	30 g
Parsley, curly, fresh	2/3 oz	20 g
Thyme twig, fresh	1	1
Basil leaves, fresh	1 oz	30 g
Butter	1 oz	30 g
Dry white wine	3 1/3 oz	100 ml
Demi-glace (Recipe 44)	1 pt 4 oz	600 ml
Heavy cream	3 1/3 oz	100 ml
Seasoning (salt and pepper)	1x	1x
Egg	1	1

MISE EN PLACE
Roll out puff pastry and cut 10 circles about 5 1/2 in. in diameter. Refrigerate circles.

Trim and wash mushrooms and cut into cubes or quarters.

Peel and chop shallots.

Clean, wash, and chop herbs.

METHOD
Sauté shallots in butter; add all mushrooms.

Add wine, bring to a boil and remove mushrooms. Save juice.

Reduce juice with *demi-glace* and cream to about half.

Add mushrooms and herbs and season to taste. Let mixture cool.[d]

Break egg and mix with small amount of cold water.

Brush rims of dough circles with egg.

Place cold mushroom filling in centers and fold over tops.

---

[a] Puff pastry can also be purchased ready to use.

[b] Chanterelles are yellow wild mushrooms, called *girolles* in French and *Eierschwämme* in German

[c] Porcini are wild mushrooms, called *cèpes* in French, *Steinpilze* in German, and *porcini* in Italian. These mushrooms are widely available dried, and are increasingly available fresh. Because Italy is a large exporter of these mushrooms, the Italian name is commonly used.

[d] Mixture should be fairly thick. If too runny, thicken with a little cornstarch.

Press rims down and seal with fork. Brush with egg.

Poke holes to let steam escape.

Bake at 400°F (200°C) for 20 to 30 minutes.

Serve each portion on a paper doily with Madeira sauce (Recipe 69) on the side.

277

$\mathscr{P}$uff Pastry Turnover with Game

Blätterteigkrapfen mit Wildfüllung
Rissoles au salpicon de gibier

YIELD: 10 SERVINGS

Puff pastry, lean (Recipe 715)[a]	1 lb 12 oz	800 g
Venison roast, trimmed[b]	1 lb 5 oz	600 g
Game stock (Recipe 29)	10 oz	300 ml
Cornstarch	2/3 oz	20 g
Shallots	2/3 oz	20 g
Mushrooms, fresh	7 oz	200 g
Butter	2/3 oz	20 g
Cognac (or any brandy)	2/3 oz	20 ml
Seasoning (salt and pepper)	1x	1x
Egg	1	1
Parsle, sprigs, curly, fresh, washed	10	10

MISE EN PLACE
Roll out puff pastry and cut 10 circles about 5 1/2 in. in diameter. Refrigerate circles.

Roast the venison meat.

Reduce game stock. Thicken with cornstarch. The sauce should be very thick.

Peel and chop shallots.

Wash and trim mushrooms. Cut into dice or quarter.

Cut roasted venison into small dice.

METHOD
Sauté shallots in butter; add mushrooms.

---

[a] Puff pastry can also be purchased ready to use.

[b] Boneless leg meat or lean shoulder is recommended.

Add Cognac, ignite, and add game sauce and diced meat.

Reduce until thick; season. If mixture is still runny, thicken with additional cornstarch. Chill mixture.

Break egg and mix with small amount of cold water.

Brush rims of dough circles with egg.

Place cold game mushroom filling in centers. Fold down tops to form crescent shapes.

Press rims down and seal with fork. Brush with egg.

Poke holes to let steam escape.

Bake at 400°F (200°C) for 20 to 30 minutes.

Serve each portion on a paper doily with a sprig of parsley.

NOTE: Madeira sauce (Recipe 69) or any other brown sauce should be served on the side.

278

Baked Shrimp and Broccoli

Broccoli-Krevetten-Gratin
Gratin de brocoli et de crevettes roses

YIELD: 10 SERVINGS

Broccoli, fresh	1 lb 12 oz	800 g
Shrimp, large tails, raw	1 lb 12 oz	800 g
Heavy cream (36%)	4 oz	120 ml
Puff pastry (Recipe 689)[a]	7 oz	200 g
Egg	1	1
Butter	1 1/3 oz	40 g
Seasoning (salt and pepper)	1x	1x
Dry white wine	6 3/4 oz	200 ml
Fish velouté sauce (Recipe 53)	13 1/2 oz	400 ml
Hollandaise sauce (Recipe 60)	4 oz	120 ml

MISE EN PLACE
Trim and clean broccoli, cut into florets, boil or steam, and keep warm.

Peel shrimp, split, and de-vein.

Whip cream.

Make 20 *fleurons*[b] with puff pastry, brush with egg, and bake.

METHOD
Sauté shrimp in butter, remove, season, and keep warm.

Add wine and reduce about one third. Add velouté, bring to a boil, and season to taste. Remove from stove.

---

[a] Puff pastry can also be purchased ready to use.

[b] *Fleurons* are puff pastry half-moons. Other shapes can be used.

Fold in whipped cream and Hollandaise sauce. Do not boil any longer.

Place warm broccoli and shrimp in 10 deep (soup) plates.

Cover with sauce and brown under the salamander.

Garnish each portion with 2 *fleurons*.

279

Mushroom Toast

Champignonschnitten
Croûtes aux champignons à la crème

YIELD: 10 SERVINGS

Bread, white (Pullman loaf)	1 lb 2 oz	500 g
Clarified butter	3 oz	80 g
Mushrooms, fresh	1 lb 12 oz	800 g
Shallots	1 2/3 oz	50 g
Butter	3 1/2 oz	100 g
Dry white wine	6 3/4 oz	200 ml
Lemon	1	1
Seasoning (salt and pepper)	1x	1x
Cream sauce (Recipe 40)	8 1/2 oz	250 ml
Heavy cream	6 3/4 oz	200 ml
Seasoning	1x	1x
Chives, cut into slivers	1 oz	30 g

MISE EN PLACE
Remove crust from bread and cut into 10 slices.

Sauté slices in clarified butter until brown on each side.

Trim and wash mushrooms and cut into slices.

Peel and chop shallots.

METHOD
Sauté shallots in butter; add mushrooms, wine, and lemon juice.

Season with salt and pepper, cover, and cook a few minutes.

Remove mushrooms; save juice (stock).

Reduce stock to about 8 1/2 oz (250 ml).

Stir in cream sauce and heavy cream; reduce sauce until thick.

Add mushrooms and adjust seasoning.

Serve mushrooms over toast and sprinkle with chives.

NOTE: Instead of cultivated mushrooms, any kind of wild mushrooms can be used.

𝓑atter-fried Vegetables with Tomato Sauce

Fritot von Gemüse
Fritot de légumes

Y I E L D : 10 S E R V I N G S

Cauliflower, fresh	14 oz	400 g
Broccoli, fresh	14 oz	400 g
Salsify (oyster plants), fresh	14 oz	400 g
Celery,[a] fresh	10 1/2 oz	300 g
Mushrooms, small, fresh	7 oz	200 g
Parsley, curly, fresh	1 2/3 oz	50 g
Seasoning (salt and pepper)	1x	1x
Seasoning (lemon juice)	1x	1x
White wheat flour	1 2/3 oz	50 g
Frying batter (Recipe 672)	1 lb 9 oz	700 g
Oil for frying (10% oil loss)	6 1/4 oz	180 ml
Tomato sauce (Recipe 99)	1 pt 1 oz	500 ml

MISE EN PLACE

Clean and trim cauliflower and broccoli and cut into florets.

Peel and trim salsify and celery, split if thick, and cut into 2-in. pieces.

Boil or steam each vegetable (cauliflower, broccoli, salsify, and celery) separately; keep vegetables firm. Drain.

Trim and wash mushrooms; cut in half if large.

Wash and chop parsley.

Season vegetables with salt and pepper, lemon juice, and chopped parsley.

Dredge vegetables in flour, dip in batter, and deep-fry at 360°F (180°C). Keep vegetables separated.

Drain vegetables on absorbent paper.

Serve on a paper doily. Serve tomato sauce on the side.

𝓗am Fritters

Gebackene Brandteig-Schinkenkrapfen
Beignets soufflés au jambon

Y I E L D : 10 S E R V I N G S

Water	13 1/2 oz	400 ml
Butter	3 1/2 oz	100 g
Seasoning (salt, nutmeg)	1x	1x
Paprika, mild	1 tsp	5 g
White wheat flour, sifted	8 1/2 oz	240 g
Eggs	6	6
Ham, boiled	10 1/2 oz	300 g
Parsley sprigs, curly, fresh	10	20 g
Madeira sauce (Recipe 69)	1 pt 1 oz	500 ml
Oil for frying (10% oil loss)	4 oz	120 ml

METHOD FOR CREAM PUFF PASTE

Combine water, butter, salt, nutmeg, and paprika and bring to a boil.

Add sifted flour all at once; stir over heat until the paste is smooth, thick, and no longer clings to the pot.

Let cool slightly. Stir in eggs, one by one.

Cut ham into small dice (*brunoise*) and add to paste.

METHOD FOR FRYING

Make strips of parchment paper about 2 1/2 in. (6 cm) wide. Lightly oil the strips.

Pipe dumplings, about 2/3 oz (20 g) in weight, onto the parchment strips, using a pastry bag with a smooth tip.

Dip strips in hot fat (the dumplings will come loose) and deep-fry at medium heat 325°F (160°C) until brown and cooked thoroughly. The dumplings should double in size.

Drain on absorbent paper.

Serve on a doily and garnish with parsley sprigs.

Serve with Madeira sauce on the side.

---

[a] The stalk celery specified is known as "English celery" in Europe, and is called *Stangensellerie* in German. In the United States it is simply referred to as "celery."

282

Calve's Brain Fritters

Gebackene Hirnkrapfen
Beignets de cervelle

YIELD: 10 SERVINGS

Calve's brains	2 lb 3 oz	1.0 kg
Cold soaking water	1x	1x
Hot soaking water	1x	1x
Water	2 qt 5 oz	2.0 L
Matignon (Recipe 13)	7 oz	200 g
Dry white wine	6 3/4 oz	200 ml
White wine vinegar	3 1/3 oz	100 ml
Sachet bag	1	1
Seasoning (salt and pepper)	1x	1x
Lemon	1	1
Parsley	2/3 oz	20 g
White wheat flour	1 2/3 oz	50 g
Frying batter (Recipe 672)	1 pt 1 oz	500 ml
Oil for frying (10% oil loss)	5 oz	140 ml
Tomato sauce (Recipe 99)	1 pt 1 oz	500 ml

MISE EN PLACE

Soak calves' brains overnight in cold water.

Place in hot water and carefully remove all blood vessels and skin.

Combine water, flavoring vegetables, dry white wine, white wine vinegar, and sachet bag.

Bring to a boil and simmer for 10 minutes.

Place brains in stock, carefully bring to boiling temperature, and poach for 10 minutes. Let cool in the stock.

Wash and clean parsley and chop fine.

METHOD

Remove brains from stock, drain, and cut into slices about 1/3-in. thick.

Sprinkle with salt and pepper, lemon juice, and parsley.

Carefully dredge brain slices in flour, dip in batter, and deep-fry at 360°F (180°C).

Drain on absorbent paper.

Serve on a doily with tomato sauce on the side.

283

Braised Mushrooms

Gedünstete Champignons
Champignons étuvés

YIELD: 10 SERVINGS

Mushrooms, fresh	3 lb 5 oz	1.5 kg
Butter	1 1/3 oz	40 g
Seasoning (salt and pepper)	1x	1x
Seasoning (lemon juice)	1x	1x
Dry white wine	3 1/3 oz	100 ml

METHOD

Clean, trim, and wash mushrooms.

Cut into slices, quarters, or halves, depending on size.

Heat butter and add mushrooms.

Season with salt and pepper.

Add lemon juice and wine. Cover and cook until done.

284

Chicken and Ham Croquettes

Geflügelkroketten
Croquettes de volaille

YIELD: 10 SERVINGS

White chicken stock (Recipe 26)	1 qt 2 oz	1.0 L
Chicken breasts, skinless	1 lb 5 oz	600 g
Butter	1 1/3 oz	40 g
White wheat flour	2 oz	60 g
Shallots	1 1/3 oz	40 g
Mushrooms, fresh	3 1/2 oz	100 g
Ham, boiled	3 1/2 oz	100 g
Butter	2/3 oz	20 g
Heavy cream	1 2/3 oz	50 ml
Semolina, hard wheat[a]	2/3 oz	20 g
Seasoning (salt and pepper)	1x	1x
Egg yolks	4	4
White wheat flour	3 1/2 oz	100 g
Eggs	2	2
Bread crumbs, fine	7 oz	200 g
Oil for frying (10% oil loss)	3 1/3 oz	100 ml

(continued on next page)

[a] Cream of Wheat can be used.

(continued from preceding page)

MISE EN PLACE

Reduce chicken stock by half.

Add chicken breasts and poach for about 10 minutes. Let breasts cool in stock. Remove chicken. Reserve stock.

Dice cold chicken into small cubes (brunoise).

Make white roux with butter and flour and let cool slightly.

Slowly add in chicken stock to make velouté sauce. Bring to a boil, stirring continuously. Boil sauce for 10 minutes. There should be about 1 pt 1 oz (500 ml). Keep sauce hot.

Chop shallots and mushrooms.

Cut ham into small dice (brunoise).

METHOD

Sauté shallots and mushrooms in 1 oz (30 g) butter.

Add diced chicken and ham and continue cooking.

Add hot velouté sauce and cream and bring mixture to a boil.

Stir in semolina, keep stirring until mixture is thick. Season to taste. Stir in egg yolks and cook until mixture is thick.

Spread croquette mixture about 1/2-in. thick on an oiled sheet pan.

Cover with oiled parchment paper and chill.

Turn sheet pan upside down and drop croquette mixture on floured kitchen table.

Cut croquette mixture into rectangles.

Break eggs and mix with a little cold water.

Dredge croquettes in flour, eggs, and bread crumbs.

Deep-fry at 350°F (175°C). Drain on absorbent paper. Serve on a doily.

NOTE: Croquettes can be served with Truffle Sauce (Recipe 101) or Madeira Sauce (Recipe 69).

285

Stuffed Mushrooms

Gefüllte Champignons
Champignons farcis

YIELD: 10 SERVINGS

Mushrooms, fresh (40)	2 lb 3 oz	1.0 kg
Butter	2/3 oz	20 g
Dry white wine	3 1/3 oz	100 ml
Shallots	1 2/3 oz	50 g
Ham, boiled	3 1/2 oz	100 g
Parsley, Italian, fresh	1/3 oz	10 g
Butter	2/3 oz	20 g
Mie de pain[a]	2/3 oz	20 g
Demi-glace (Recipe 44)	3 1/3 oz	100 ml
Seasoning (salt and pepper)	1x	1x
Seasoning (lemon juice)	1x	1x
Sbrinz,[b] grated	1 2/3 oz	50 g
Butter	2/3 oz	20 g
Madeira sauce (Recipe 69)	1 pt 1 oz	500 ml

MISE EN PLACE

Wash mushrooms and twist off stems. Chop stems and reserve.

Braise mushroom caps in butter and wine and set aside.

Remove mushroom caps; reserve stock.

Peel and chop shallots.

Cut ham into fine dice (brunoise).

Wash and chop parsley.

Butter ovenproof dish (gratin dish).

METHOD

Place braised mushroom caps in ovenproof dish, cavities facing up.

Sauté shallots in butter, add chopped mushroom stems, and continue cooking.

Add ham, parsley, reserved mushroom stock, mie de pain, and demi-glace.

Cook over high heat until mixture is rather dry (duxelles).

Season with salt and pepper and lemon juice.

Fill mushroom caps with duxelles, sprinkle with cheese and butter, and bake until brown and hot.

Serve Madeira sauce on the side.

---

[a] Mie de pain are fresh bread crumbs, made from white Pullman loaves.

[b] Sbrinz is a hard grating cheese from Switzerland. Parmesan can be substituted.

286

$\mathcal{S}$tuffed Morels

Gefüllte Morcheln
Morilles farcies

YIELD: 10 SERVINGS

Morels, fresh	1 lb 5 oz	600 g
Chervil, fresh	1/3 oz	10 g
Parsley, curly, fresh	1/3 oz	10 g
Mousseline farce, veal or poultry (Recipe 17)[a]	7 oz	200 g
Shallots	1 2/3 oz	50 g
Butter	1 2/3 oz	50 g
Cognac (or any brandy)	2 3/4 oz	80 ml
White veal stock (Recipe 28)	5 1/4 oz	150 ml
Heavy cream (36%)	8 1/2 oz	250 ml
Seasoning (salt and pepper)	1x	1x
Lemon juice	1/3 oz	10 ml

MISE EN PLACE
Wash morels carefully and remove stems.[b] Blanch morel caps. Trim stems and cut into small dice.

Wash and chop chervil and parsley.

Blend farce with diced morel stems and herbs.

Fill morel caps with mixture, using pastry bag with straight tube.

Peel and chop shallots.

METHOD
Sauté shallots in butter in a wide casserole pan, large enough to hold all morel heads.

Carefully place filled morel caps on top of shallots.

Heat and add Cognac; ignite.

Add veal stock, bring to a boil, and simmer for 3 minutes.

Remove morels with slotted spoon; keep warm.

Reduce stock, stir in cream, and reduce to creamy consistency.

Season with salt and pepper and lemon juice.

Arrange morels on a plate and cover with sauce.

NOTE: If morels are large, they can be split after they are filled and cooked, and served on top of sauce for an attractive presentation.

---

[a] Recipe 17 is made with veal, but it can also be made with poultry.

[b] Morels are often sandy and must be washed thoroughly.

287

$\mathcal{S}$tuffed Zucchini (vegetable marrow) Boats

Gefüllte Zucchetti
Courgettes farcies

YIELD: 10 SERVINGS

Zucchini, 5 pieces	2 lb 3 oz	1.0 kg
Onions	5 2/3 oz	160 g
Garlic	1 tsp	5 g
Mushrooms, fresh	10 1/2 oz	300 g
Tomatoes	14 oz	400 g
Oregano, fresh	1 tsp	5 g
Parsley	2/3 oz	20 g
Butter	1 oz	30 g
Sbrinz, grated[a]	2 oz	60 g
Seasoning (salt and pepper)	1x	1x
Butter	2/3 oz	20 g

MISE EN PLACE
Wash zucchini and split lengthwise. Scoop out and chop centers and reserve.

Blanch zucchini shells. Chill in cold water and drain. Do not overcook zucchini.

Peel and chop onions and garlic.

Trim, wash, and chop mushrooms.

Peel tomatoes, remove seeds, and dice.

Chop oregano and parsley.

Butter ovenproof dish (gratin platter).

METHOD
Sauté onions and garlic in butter.

Add chopped zucchini, mushrooms, tomatoes, and herbs and cook until somewhat dry.

Add half of the grated cheese and season with salt and pepper.

Season zucchini boats and fill with mixture.

Sprinkle with remaining cheese, dot with butter, and bake until zucchini are tender and brown.

---

[a] Sbrinz is a hard grating cheese from Switzerland. Parmesan can be substituted.

288

$\mathcal{S}$tuffed Onions with Beef

Gefüllte Zwiebeln
Oignons farcis

YIELD: 10 SERVINGS

Beef, stew meat, trimmed	14 oz	400 g
Onions (20)	4 lb 7 oz	2.0 kg
Ham, boiled	7 oz	200 g
Parsley	2/3 oz	20 g
Butter	3 1/2 oz	100 g
Mie de pain[a]	3 1/2 oz	100 g
Seasoning (salt and pepper)	1x	1x
Sbrinz, grated[b]	3 1/2 oz	100 g
Bouillon (Recipe 22)	13 1/2 oz	400 ml

MISE EN PLACE

Grind meat through medium-size plate of meat grinder.

Peel onions. Each onion should weigh about 3 1/2 oz (100 g).

Boil onions for 15 minutes in salt water; let cool in stock.

Cut ham into fine dice (*brunoise*).

Chop parsley.

Butter an ovenproof dish (gratin platter).

Cut off onion tops; scoop out centers with melonballer. The onion shells should have about 3 layers left standing. Reserve scooped out centers.

Place onion shells in gratin pan.

METHOD

Chop onion centers and sauté with 1 2/3 oz (50 g) butter. Add ham and parsley. Let cool completely.

Blend ground meat, onion/ham mixture, and 2 1/2 oz (75 g) *mie de pain*; season to taste.

Fill onion shells with meat mixture; sprinkle with remaining *mie de pain*, grated cheese, and melted butter.

Bring bouillon to a boil on top of stove and pour around onions in gratin pan.

Cover dish and bring to a boil on top of stove.

Bake for 10 minutes with lid and 10 minutes without lid (or until brown).

[a] *Mie de pain* are fresh bread crumbs, made from white Pullman loaves.

[b] Sbrinz is a hard grating cheese from Switzerland. Parmesan can be substituted.

289

$\mathcal{A}$rtichoke Bottoms Stuffed with Wild Mushrooms

Gefüllte Artischokenböden mit Steinpilzen
Fonds d'artichauts farcis aux cèpes

YIELD: 10 SERVINGS

Artichoke bottoms, large, trimmed, cooked	10	10
Porcini,[a] fresh	1 lb 2 oz	500 g
Shallots	1 2/3 oz	50 g
Chives, fresh	2/3 oz	20 g
Butter	1 1/3 oz	40 g
Dry white wine	3 1/3 oz	100 ml
Heavy cream (36%)	8 1/2 oz	250 ml
Seasoning (salt and pepper)	1x	1x
Seasoning (lemon juice)	1x	1x

MISE EN PLACE

Heat artichoke bottoms in their stock.

Trim, wash, and slice porcini.

Peel and chop shallots.

Cut chives into small slivers.

METHOD

Sauté porcini and shallots in butter.

Add white wine and cook for 2 to 3 minutes.

Remove porcini; reserve stock.

Reduce stock, stir in cream, and boil until thick.

Return porcini to pan and season to taste with salt and pepper and lemon juice.

Drain the warm artichoke bottoms. Fill with mushroom mixture.

Sprinkle filled artichoke bottoms with chives.

[a] The original recipe calls for *Steinpilze*, a mushroom readily available in Switzerland during the summer. Porcini are wild mushrooms, called *cepés* in French, and *porcini* in Italian. These mushrooms are widely available dried and are increasingly available fresh. Because Italy is a large exporter of these mushrooms, the Italian name is commonly used. Other wild mushrooms can be substituted.

290

Carrot and Onion Flan

Gemüse-Flan
Flan de légumes

YIELD: 10 SERVINGS

Carrots	1 lb 5 oz	600 g
Onions	3 oz	80 g
Butter	2/3 oz	20 g
Butter	1 1/3 oz	40 g
Heavy cream (36%)	6 3/4 oz	200 ml
Bechamel sauce (Recipe 34)	6 3/4 oz	200 ml
Eggs	2	2
Seasoning (salt, nutmeg)	1x	1x

MISE EN PLACE

Peel, trim, and slice carrots. Boil or steam until soft, drain, and discard cooking liquid.

Peel onions and cut into thin slices.

Butter 10 timbale molds.

METHOD

Sauté onions in butter, add carrots, and continue cooking.

Purée onion/carrot mixture with cream in food processor.

Add purée to hot cream sauce, add eggs, mix well, season to taste.

Fill buttered timbale molds with puree/cream mixture.

Place molds in water bath, cover, and bring to a boil on top of stove.

Poach for 30 minutes in 325°F (165°C) oven.

Let rest in a warm place for 15 minutes before unmolding.

NOTE: This recipe can be used for other vegetables. If the vegetables contain a lot of water (such as spinach and cabbage), be sure they are well drained and the amount of eggs is increased.

291

Vegetable Croquettes

Gemüsekroketten
Croquettes de légumes

YIELD: 10 SERVINGS

Carrots	3 oz	80 g
Knob celery (celeriac)	5 1/3 oz	150 g
Zucchini (vegetable marrow)	5 1/3 oz	150 g
Tomatoes	7 oz	200 g
Milk	1 pt 4 oz	600 ml
Butter	1 oz	30 g
Seasoning (salt and pepper)	1x	1x
Nutmeg	pinch	1x
Semolina, hard wheat[a]	5 1/3 oz	150 g
Egg yolks	2	2
Sbrinz,[b] grated	2 oz	60 g
Eggs	2	2
White wheat flour	3 1/2 oz	100 g
Bread crumbs	3 1/2 oz	100 g
Oil for frying (10% oil loss)	4 oz	120 ml
Tomato sauce (Recipe 99)	1 pt 1 oz	500 ml

MISE EN PLACE

Wash and trim carrots, knob celery, and zucchini. Cut into small dice. Boil or steam until tender, but not soft. Drain vegetables.

Peel tomatoes, remove seeds, and dice.

METHOD

Combine milk with butter, season with salt and pepper and nutmeg.

Bring milk to a slow boil and gradually stir in semolina. Stir with wire whisk to break up lumps. Bring to a slow boil, stirring continuously. Simmer for 5 minutes over low heat.

Add diced vegetables. Add egg yolks. Stir over low heat until mixture is heated through and stiff.

Add grated cheese and adjust seasoning.

Spread croquette mixture about 1/2-in. thick on oiled sheet pan.

Cover with oiled parchment paper and chill.

Break eggs and mix with a little cold water.

Turn sheet pan upside down and drop croquette mixture onto floured table. Cut croquette mixture into rectangles. Dredge rectangles in flour, dip in eggs, coat with bread crumbs.

Deep-fry rectangles at 340°F (170°C). Drain on absorbent paper.

Serve on a doily with tomato sauce on the side.

---

[a] Cream of Wheat can be used.

[b] Sbrinz is a hard grating cheese from Switzerland. Parmesan can be substituted.

292

Batter-Fried Gruyere Cheese

Genfer Malakow
Malakov genevoise

YIELD: 10 SERVINGS

Gruyere[a] cheese (in one piece)	1 lb 2 oz	500 g
Mustard, prepared, mild	1 2/3 oz	50 g

BATTER

White wheat flour	8 3/4 oz	250 g
Beer	10 oz	300 ml
Peanut oil	3/4 oz	25 ml
Seasoning (salt and pepper)	1x	1x
Nutmeg	pinch	1x
Egg whites	3	3
Oil for frying	as needed	as needed

MISE EN PLACE

Remove rind from cheese and cut into sticks about 3 in. long and 3/4-in. thick.

Carefully spread sticks with mustard.

Make batter with flour, beer, peanut oil, salt and pepper, and nutmeg.

Let batter rest at room temperature for at least 1 hour.

METHOD

Shortly before use, whip egg whites and fold into batter.

Dip cheese sticks in batter and fry at 340°F (170°C) until golden.

Drain on absorbent paper.

NOTE: This dish can be served with a tomato sauce (Recipe 99) on the side.

293

Creamed Sweetbreads in Patty Shells

Kalbsmilkenpastetchen
Bouchées au ris de veau

YIELD: 10 SERVINGS

Sweetbreads	1 lb 5 oz	600 g
Puff pastry (Recipe 689)[b]	2 lb 10 oz	1.2 kg
Egg	1	1
Mushrooms	10 1/2 oz	300 g
Shallots	2/3 oz	20 g
Butter	2 oz	60 g
White wheat flour	2 oz	60 g
White veal stock (Recipe 28)	1 qt 19 oz	1.5 L
Dry white wine	3 1/3 oz	100 ml
Seasoning (lemon juice)	1x	1x
Butter	2/3 oz	20 g
Heavy cream	6 3/4 oz	200 ml
Egg yolks	2	2
Seasoning (salt and pepper)	1x	1x

MISE EN PLACE

Soak sweetbreads in cold water overnight.

Blanch sweetbreads in boiling water; chill; and drain.

Use puff pastry to make 20 small patty shells about 2 1/2 in. in diameter.

Brush patty shells with egg and refrigerate for at least 1 hour.

Bake patty shells and keep warm.

Trim and wash mushrooms and cut into quarters.

Chop shallots.

Make a roux with 2 oz butter and 2 oz flour.

METHOD

Bring veal stock and white wine to a boil; add sweetbreads.

Return to a boil, skim, and poach sweetbreads for 20 minutes. Let cool in stock. Drain sweetbreads; reserve stock.

Remove skin and break sweetbreads into small pieces.

Sauté mushrooms with shallots and lemon juice in 2/3 oz butter. Add sweetbreads, cover, heat mixture, and keep warm.

Combine roux with 1 qt 2 oz (1 L) reserved stock. Bring to a boil, stirring continuously. Simmer for 10 minutes and keep hot.

Drain off juices from mushroom/sweetbreads mixture. Reduce to a glaze consistency and add to stock.

Mix heavy cream and egg yolks, and stir into boiling sauce, but do not allow to boil any longer.

Combine sauce with sweetbreads and season to taste.

Using a sharp knife, cut lids from patty shells; reserve lids.

Fill warm patty shells with sweetbreads and place lids on top.

Serve immediately.

Serve any remaining sweetbread filling on the side.

---

[a] This Swiss cheese is sometimes referred to as Greyerzer.

[b] Puff pastry can be purchased commercially.

294

$\mathcal{S}$eafood Quiche

Meeresfrüchtekuchen mit Safran
Quiche marseillaise

Yield: 10 servings

Butter, melted	1/3 oz	10 g
Flour	2/3 oz	20 g
Puff pastry, lean (Recipe 715)	14 oz	400 g
Leeks	7 oz	200 g
Onions	3 1/2 oz	100 g
Monkfish, fillets	10 1/2 oz	300 g
Mussels, fresh	1 lb 2 oz	500 g
White wine, dry	6 3/4 oz	200 ml
Butter	1 1/3 oz	40 g
Saffron	pinch	1x
Milk	6 3/4 oz	200 ml
Heavy cream (36%)	3 1/3 oz	100 ml
Eggs	2	2
Seasoning (salt and pepper)	1x	1x

MISE EN PLACE

Brush rimmed baking sheet 10 inches square[a] with melted butter. Dust baking sheet with flour.

Roll out puff pastry and line baking sheet. Poke holes at random to let steam escape. Prebake 10 minuits.

Wash and trim leeks; be sure sand is cleaned from layers. Cut into fine *julienne*.

Peel and clean onions and cut into fine *julienne*.

Cube fish fillets.

Scrape mussels, wash, and braise in white wine.

Drain mussels; reserve stock.

Break mussels out of shells; remove strings.

METHOD

Braise onions and leeks in butter; add cubed fish, saffron, and reserved mussel stock. Cover and simmer briefly. Add cooked mussels and heat. Drain off and reserve stock.

Let drained fish, mussels, and vegetables cool.

When cool, place seafood evenly in mold lined with dough.

Reduce reserved fish stock and let cool slightly.

Blend milk, cream, and eggs. Mix with reduced fish stock. Strain through fine mesh china cap. Season to taste.

Pour custard over seafood; bake at low heat for about 30 minutes, until center is firm.[b]

---

[a] Quiche is often made in a round mold, which is easier to portion than quiche made in a square.

[b] Quiche should be baked at low temperature, 375°F (190°C) or less, and should rest 1/2 hour before service.

295

$\mathcal{S}$weetbreads au Gratin with Green Asparagus

Milkengratin mit Spargeln
Gratin de ris de veau aux asperges

Yield: 10 servings

Veal sweetbreads	2 lb 3 oz	1.0 kg
White veal stock (Recipe 28)	1 qt 2 oz	1.0 L
White wine, dry	6 3/4 oz	200 ml
Green asparagus	1 lb 5 oz	600 g
Salt	2/3 oz	20 g
Butter	1 oz	30 g
White wheat flour	1 oz	30 g
Seasoning (salt and pepper)	1x	1x
Hollandaise sauce (Recipe 60)	4 oz	120 ml
Heavy cream (36%)	4 oz	120 ml

MISE EN PLACE

Soak sweetbreads in cold water, then in warm water to wash out blood.

Blanch, chill, then poach sweetbreads in veal stock and wine until cooked. Let cool in stock.

Remove sweetbreads and reserve stock.

Trim sweetbreads, remove skin, and break into small pieces. Keep warm in a little veal stock.

Trim asparagus, peel if necessary, and boil until tender, but still firm. Cool in cold water and drain. Cut into 3/4-in. pieces; save tips for garnish. Keep warm.

Make roux with butter and flour.

Whip cream.

METHOD

Reduce sweetbreads stock to about 13 1/2 oz (400 ml).

Add roux, bring to a boil, and simmer sauce for 20 minutes. Season to taste. Remove sauce from heat and blend in Hollandaise sauce and whipped cream.

Place warm sweetbreads and asparagus pieces in 10 soup plates. Be sure sweetbreads and asparagus are well drained.

Cover sweetbreads and asparagus with sauce and glaze under the salamander until brown.

Garnish with warm asparagus tips.

296

$\mathcal{V}$egetarian Patty Shells

Pastetchen mit feinem Gemüse
Bouchées fermière

YIELD: 10 SERVINGS

Puff pastry (Recipe 689)[a]	2 lb 10 oz	1.2 kg
Egg	1	1
Carrots, small, young	7 oz	200 g
Kohlrabi	7 oz	200 g
Cauliflower, fresh	7 oz	200 g
String beans (haricots verts), fresh	7 oz	200 g
Chives	2/3 oz	20 g
Peas (petits pois), frozen	7 oz	200 g
Butter	1 2/3 oz	50 g
White veal stock (Recipe 28)	6 3/4 oz	200 ml
Bechamel sauce (Recipe 34)	1 pt 11 oz	800 ml
Heavy cream (36%)	6 3/4 oz	200 ml
Seasoning	1x	1x

MISE EN PLACE

Use puff pastry to make 20 small patty shells about 2 1/2 in. in diameter. Brush with egg and refrigerate for at least 1 hour.

Bake patty shells and keep warm.

Clean, trim, and wash vegetables, except frozen peas.

Dice carrots and kohlrabi. Break cauliflower into small florets. Break string beans into 1 1/3-in. pieces.

Cut chives into small slivers.

METHOD

Braise vegetables (except peas) in butter and veal stock. Do not overcook. Remove vegetables; save stock.

Reduce stock and stir in cream sauce; bring to a boil.

Add heavy cream and cooked vegetables, add peas, and bring to a boil. Add chives, season to taste.

With a sharp knife, slice tops from patty shells, and keep warm in oven.

Fill hot patty shells with vegetables and place lids on top.

Serve immediately.

Serve any remaining filling on the side.

---

[a] Puff pastry can also be purchased ready to use.

297

$\mathcal{S}$pinach Crepes

Pfannkuchen mit Spinatfüllung
Crêpes florentine

YIELD: 10 SERVINGS

BATTER

Milk	10 oz	300 ml
Eggs	4	4
White wheat flour, sifted	5 oz	140 g
Seasoning (salt, nutmeg)	1x	1x
Butter	2 oz	60 g

FILLING

Spinach, fresh, trimmed	2 lb 3 oz	1.0 kg
Shallots	1 2/3 oz	50 g
Garlic	1/3 oz	10 g
Butter	1 oz	30 g
Seasoning (salt and pepper)	1x	1x
Seasoning (nutmeg)	1x	1x
Cream sauce (Recipe 40)	1 pt 1 oz	500 ml
Sbrinz,[a] grated	1 2/3 oz	50 g
Butter	1 oz	30 g

MISE EN PLACE

Make batter with milk, eggs, and flour. Season with salt and nutmeg. Strain batter through china cap.

Make 20 crepes (thin pancakes) in butter. Cover pancakes with aluminum foil to keep them moist.

Wash spinach, boil in salted water, and drain. Chill spinach with cold water and drain again. Squeeze dry. Chop spinach coarsely.

Peel and chop shallots. Purée (crush) garlic.

METHOD

Sauté shallots and garlic in butter.

Add spinach. Season with salt and pepper and nutmeg.

Fill crepes with spinach mixture and roll up or fold over.

Place crepes in buttered ovenproof dish (gratin platter).

Cover with hot cream sauce; sprinkle with cheese and melted butter.

Bake in oven until brown.

---

[a] Sbrinz is a hard grating cheese from Switzerland. Parmesan can be substituted.

298

Ham Souffle

Schinkenauflauf
Soufflé au jambon

YIELD: 10 SERVINGS

Butter	3 1/2 oz	100 g
White wheat flour	3 1/2 oz	100 g
Ham, boiled	8 3/4 oz	250 g
Milk	1 pt 1 oz	500 ml
Seasoning (salt and pepper)	1x	1x
Seasoning, paprika	1x	1x
Egg yolks	8	8
Egg whites	8	8
Cornstarch	1/3 oz	10 g

MISE EN PLACE

Butter souffle molds[a] and dust with flour.

Purée ham in food processor or Buffalo chopper.

Heat milk.

METHOD

Melt butter in heavy casserole pan and add flour.

Add hot milk. Stir well with wire whisk. When mixture starts to thicken, stir with wooden paddle. Bring to a boil.

Season paste with salt and pepper and a pinch of paprika.

Let cool slightly.

Blend in egg yolks one by one. Blend in puréed ham.

Whip egg whites and fold in cornstarch.

Fold about 25% of beaten egg whites into batter to soften.

Gradually fold in the rest of the beaten egg whites into batter.

Fill prepared souffle molds about three-quarters full.

Place mold in water bath for 30 minutes to prewarm mixture.

Bake first at 360°F (180°C) and finish at 400°F (200°C).

Place souffle on a paper doily. Serve at once.

NOTES: Baking times for prewarmed mixtures are as follows: for large souffle molds, about 20 to 25 minutes, for individual molds, about 10 to 12 minutes.

The ham souffle can be served with a Madeira Sauce (Recipe 69).

The same proportions and method can be used to make poultry and game souffles.

[a] Two large molds for 5 servings each or individual molds can be used.

299

Spinach Souffle

Spinatauflauf
Soufflé aux épinards

YIELD: 10 SERVINGS

Butter	3 1/2 oz	100 g
White wheat flour	3 1/2 oz	100 g
Garlic, chopped	1/3 oz	10 g
Spinach, frozen, chopped	8 3/4 oz	250 g
Milk	13 1/2 oz	400 ml
Egg yolks	8	8
Seasoning (salt and pepper)	1x	1x
Egg whites	8	8
Cornstarch	1/3 oz	10 g

MISE EN PLACE

Butter souffle molds[a] and dust with flour.

Purée/crush garlic.

Defrost spinach and squeeze out juice.

Heat milk.

METHOD

Melt butter in heavy casserole pan and add flour.

Add hot milk. Stir well with wire whisk. When mixture starts to thicken, stir with wooden paddle. Let cool slightly.

Blend in egg yolks one by one. Add garlic and spinach.

Season paste with salt and pepper.

Whip egg whites and fold in cornstarch.

Fold about 25% of beaten egg whites into the paste.

Gradually fold in the rest of the beaten egg whites.

Fill prepared souffle molds about three quarters full.

Place molds in water bath for 30 minutes to prewarm mixture.

Bake first at 375°F (180°C) and finish at 400°F (200°C).

Place souffle on a paper doily. Serve at once.

NOTES: Baking times for pre-warmed mixtures are as follows: for large souffle molds, about 20 to 25 minutes; for individual molds, about 10 to 12 minutes.

Spinach souffle can be served with a Madeira sauce (Recipe 69).

The same proportions and method can be used for other vegetable puree souffles.

[a] Two large molds for 5 servings each or individual molds can be used.

300

𝒫orcini Mushroom Sauté

Steinpilze Bordeleser Art
Cèpes bordelaise

YIELD: 10 SERVINGS

Porcini[a]	3 lb 5 oz	1.5 kg
Shallots	1 2/3 oz	50 g
Parsley	1 oz	30 g
Butter	1 2/3 oz	50 g
Seasoning (salt and pepper)	1x	1x
Lemon	1/2	1/2
Mie de pain[b]	1 2/3 oz	50 g

MISE EN PLACE

Trim and wash porcini and cut into slices.

Peel and chop shallots.

Wash parsley and chop leaves.

METHOD

Sauté porcini in butter and season with salt and pepper.

Add shallots and continue cooking.

Before serving, season with lemon juice and sprinkle with parsley and *mie de pain*.

301

𝒫orcini Mushrooms with Garlic and Herbs

Steinpilze mit Knoblauch und Kräutern
Cèpes provençale

YIELD: 10 SERVINGS

Porcini,[a] fresh	2 lb 3 oz	1.0 kg
Shallots	3 1/2 oz	100 g
Garlic	1 oz	30 g
Chervil, fresh	1/3 oz	10 g
Basil, fresh	1/3 oz	10 g
Parsley	1/3 oz	10 g
Thyme	1 tsp	5 g
Marjoram	1/3 oz	10 g
Tomatoes	7 oz	200 g
Butter	3 1/2 oz	100 g
Dry white wine	3 1/3 oz	100 ml
Seasoning (salt and pepper)	1x	1x

MISE EN PLACE

Trim and wash porcini and cut into slices or dice.

Peel and chop shallots and garlic.

Wash and chop herbs.

Peel tomatoes, remove seeds, and cut into small dice.

METHOD

Sauté shallots in butter. Add porcini and continue cooking.

Add wine. Cook until the resulting liquid is reduced and porcini start to brown slightly.

Add garlic, herbs, and tomatoes.

Season to taste.

[a] The original recipe calls for *Steinpilze*, a mushroom readily available in Switzerland during the summer. Porcini are wild mushrooms called *cèpes* in French and *porcini* in Italian. These mushrooms are widely available dried, and are increasingly available fresh. Because Italy is a large exporter of these mushrooms, the Italian name is commonly used. Other wild mushrooms can be substituted.

[b] *Mie de pain* are fresh bread crumbs, made from white Pullman loaves.

[a] The original recipe calls for *Steinpilze*, a mushroom readily available in Switzerland during the summer. Porcini are wild mushrooms, called *cèpes* in French and *porcini* in Italian. These mushrooms are widely available dried, and are increasingly available fresh. Because Italy is a large exporter of these mushrooms, the Italian name is commonly used. Other wild mushrooms can be substituted.

302

*B*aked Endives with Ham

Überbackener Chicorée mit Schinken
Endives westphalienne

Yield: 10 servings

Belgian endive	2 lb 3 oz	1.0 kg
Veal kidney fat (suet)	1 2/3 oz	50 g
Butter	2/3 oz	20 g
Matignon (Recipe 13)	3 1/2 oz	100 g
Vegetable bouillon (Recipe 27)	1 pt 1 oz	500 ml
Seasoning (lemon juice)	1x	1x
Seasoning (salt and pepper)	1x	1x
Ham, boiled[a]	8 3/4 oz	250 g
Cream sauce (Recipe 40)	1 pt 11 oz	800 ml
Sbrinz,[b] grated	3 1/2 oz	100 g
Butter	2/3 oz	20 g

MISE EN PLACE

Trim endive if necessary. Remove cores, but be sure leaves stay together.

Chop veal suet.

Sauté flavoring vegetables in butter; place endives on top.

Add vegetable bouillon and chopped suet.

Season with lemon juice and salt and pepper.

Bring to a boil on top of stove.

Cover and braise in oven until endives are tender. Let cool.

Slice ham.

METHOD

Remove endives from cooking liquid and drain.

Wrap each endive in one slice of ham.

Butter a suitable ovenproof dish (gratin platter). Place endives in dish.

Heat cream sauce and cover endives.

Sprinkle with cheese and melted butter.

Bake until hot and brown on top.

---

[a] The French recipe title suggests that a smoked Westphalian ham is used.

[b] Sbrinz is a hard grating cheese from Switzerland. Parmesan can be substituted.

Eggs and Cheese

Egg Dishes

303

Eggs in Cocotte with Chicken Livers

Eier in Töpfchen mit Geflügelleber
Oeufs en cocotte chasseur

YIELD: 10 SERVINGS

Butter	2/3 oz	20 g
Eggs[a]	10	10
Chicken livers, raw	10 1/2 oz	300 g
Shallots	1 2/3 oz	50 g
Mushrooms	3 1/2 oz	100 g
Sage, fresh	1/3 oz	10 g
Chives	2/3 oz	20 g
Butter	1 oz	30 g
Seasoning (salt and pepper)	1x	1x
Madeira wine	1 2/3 oz	50 ml
Demi-glace (Recipe 44)	6 3/4 oz	200 ml
Seasoning (salt and pepper)	1x	1x

MISE EN PLACE

Butter 10 individual cocottes (china souffle cups).

Break one egg into each of the 10 cocottes. Be sure not to break egg yolks.

Trim and clean chicken livers and cut into pieces.

Peel and chop shallots.

Trim and wash mushrooms and cut into quarters.

Chop sage leaves.

Cut chives into small slivers.

METHOD

Sauté chicken livers briefly in butter, remove from pan, and season with salt and pepper.

Sauté shallots in the same pan, add mushrooms and sage, and continue cooking.

Add Madeira wine and reduce. Add *demi-glace*, reduce again if necessary, and season to taste.

Reserve small amount of sauce and combine remaining sauce with chicken livers.

Place livers in cocottes and carefully slide eggs on top.

Poach cocottes in water bath in slow oven until the egg white is cooked but the egg yolk is still soft.[b]

Drizzle remaining sauce on top.

Sprinkle with chives.

[a] The eggs must be very fresh.

[b] There is concern about eating raw or undercooked egg yolks because they could be contaminated with salmonella bacteria.

304

Eggs in Cocotte with Chicken

Eier in Töpfchen mit Geflügelwürfelchen
Oeufs en cocotte reine

YIELD: 10 SERVINGS

Butter	2/3 oz	20 g
Eggs[a]	10	10
Shallots	2/3 oz	20 g
Chicken breast, boneless and skinless	10 1/2 oz	300 g
Chicken stock (Recipe 26)	1 pt 4 oz	600 ml
Butter	1 oz	30 g
White wheat flour	1 oz	30 g
Mushrooms	3 1/2 oz	100 g
Chives, fresh	2/3 oz	20 g
Heavy cream (36%)	3 1/3 oz	100 ml
Butter	1 oz	30 g
Dry white wine	1 2/3 oz	50 ml
Seasoning (lemon juice)	1x	1x
Seasoning (salt and pepper)	1x	1x

MISE EN PLACE

Butter 10 individual cocottes (china souffle cups).

Break one egg into each of the 10 cocottes. Be sure not to break egg yolks.

Peel and chop shallots.

Poach chicken breasts in stock, let cool, and cut into small dice. Reserve stock.

Make white roux with the 1 oz butter and 1 oz flour.

Trim and wash mushrooms and cut into quarters.

Cut chives into small slivers.

METHOD

Make cream sauce by combining roux and reserved chicken stock. Bring to a boil, stirring continuously, stir in cream, and simmer for 20 minutes.

Sauté shallots in butter, add mushrooms, wine, and lemon juice. Remove mushrooms; save stock.

Reduce mushroom stock. Add in cream sauce. Return to a boil and season to taste. Reserve small amount and combine the rest with mushrooms and cooked chicken meat.

Bring to a boil and season to taste.

Place mixture in cocottes and slide eggs on top.

Poach cocottes in water bath in slow oven until the egg white is cooked but the egg yolk is still soft.[b]

Drizzle remaining sauce on top and sprinkle with chives.

[a] The eggs must be very fresh.

[b] There is concern about eating raw or undercooked egg yolks because they could be contaminated with salmonella bacteria.

305

Bacon and Mushroom Omelette

Omelette mit Speck und Champignons
Omelette bonne femme

YIELD: 10 SERVINGS

Eggs	20	20
Seasoning (salt and pepper)	1x	1x
Parsley, Italian, fresh	1 oz	30 g
Onions	7 oz	200 g
Bacon	10 1/2 oz	300 g
Mushrooms, fresh	10 1/2 oz	300 g
Butter	3 1/2 oz	100 g
Butter	2/3 oz	20 g

MISE EN PLACE

Break eggs, season, and stir well. Strain through fine mesh china cap.

Wash and chop parsley and add to egg mixture.

Peel onions and cut into thin slices.

Cut bacon into thin slices.

Trim and wash mushrooms and cut into thin slices.

METHOD

Melt butter in omelette pan (nonstick pan preferred).

Add onions and bacon and sauté. Add mushrooms and continue cooking.

Add egg mixture and stir until mixtures starts to thicken.

Tilt pan and let mixture slide toward rim of pan.

Roll egg mixture with spatula into an oval shape.

Turn pan over to slide omelette onto hot china platter.

Brush with melted butter.

NOTES: It is recommended that omelettes be made individually or in no more than 4 servings at a time.

When making several omelettes, the filling for all should be made ahead of time.

306

Scrambled Eggs with Tomatoes

Rühreier mit Tomatenwürfeln
Oeufs brouillés portugaise

YIELD: 10 SERVINGS

Eggs	20	20
Seasoning (salt and pepper)	1x	1x
Shallots	1 2/3 oz	50 g
Tomatoes	1 lb 2 oz	500 g
Parsley	2/3 oz	20 g
Butter	1 2/3 oz	50 g
Seasoning (salt and pepper)	1x	1x
Butter	1 oz	30 g
Heavy cream	1 2/3 oz	50 ml

MISE EN PLACE

Break eggs, season, and stir well. Strain through fine mesh china cap.

Peel and chop shallots.

Peel tomatoes, remove seeds, and cut into cubes.

Wash and chop parsley leaves.

METHOD

Sauté shallots in butter. Add tomatoes and cook briefly. Season to taste. Keep warm.

Melt butter in heavy stainless steel casserole or saucepan.

Add eggs. Cook over low heat or in steam table, stirring continuously with wooden paddle.

Cook until mixture is creamy. Add cold cream to stop the cooking.

Turn scrambled eggs onto plate or service dish.

Place tomatoes in center, on top of eggs.

Sprinkle with chopped parsley.

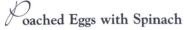

307

Poached Eggs with Spinach

Verlorene Eier mit Spinat
Oeufs pochés florentine

YIELD: 10 SERVINGS

Spinach, fresh	2 lb 3 oz	1.0 kg
Shallots	1 oz	30 g
Garlic	1/3 oz	10 g
Eggs, very fresh	10	10
Butter	1 oz	30 g
Seasoning (salt and pepper)	1x	1x
Water	2 qt 4 oz	2.0 L
White wine vinegar	6 3/4 oz	200 ml
Cream sauce (Recipe 40)	1 pt 1 oz	500 ml
Sbrinz,[a] grated	3 1/2 oz	100 g
Butter	2/3 oz	20 g

MISE EN PLACE

Trim and wash spinach, blanch, and drain.

Peel and chop shallots and garlic.

Break eggs carefully into 10 individual cups.[b] Be sure not to break egg yolks.

METHOD

Sauté shallots and garlic in butter. Add spinach and continue cooking. Season to taste.

Butter suitable ovenproof platter (gratin dish). Spread spinach evenly in dish.

Combine water and vinegar and bring to a boil.

Slide eggs into lightly boiling vinegar water; poach for 3 to 4 minutes. The egg white should be firm; the egg yolk should be soft.

Remove eggs with slotted spoon. Place eggs briefly in warm salt water to cool.

Trim each egg and place on top of spinach.

Heat cream sauce and blend with half of the grated cheese.

Ladle sauce over eggs, sprinkle with remaining grated cheese and with melted butter.

Brown under the salamander.

NOTE: Eggs can be poached ahead of time, chilled in salt water, and warmed to order in salt water.

---

[a] Sbrinz is a hard grating cheese from Switzerland. Parmesan can be substituted.

[b] Eggs should be kept separate so that, if one yolk breaks, it will not ruin the rest of the eggs. Keeping them separate also makes it easier to slide them into the poaching liquid.

Cheese Dishes

308

Swiss Fondue

Fondue vaudoise

YIELD: 10 SERVINGS

Gruyere cheese[a]	3 lb 14 oz	1.75 kg
Bread, baguette	3 lb 5 oz	1.5 kg
Garlic, cloves	2	2
Dry white wine	1 qt 2 oz	1.0 L
Kirsch[b]	3 1/3 oz	100 ml
Cornstarch	1 1/3 oz	40 g
Seasoning (white pepper)	1x	1x
Seasoning (nutmeg)	1x	1x

MISE EN PLACE

Grate cheese.

Cut bread into cubes.[c]

Peel and mash garlic.

METHOD

Rub inside of a *caquelon*[d] pot with the mashed garlic cloves.

Add wine and bring to a boil.

Add cheese and melt over heat, stirring continuously, until smooth.

Make a slurry with Kirsch and cornstarch; add to boiling[e] cheese to thicken. Season with pepper and nutmeg.

Put *caquelon* on *rechaud* (food warmer).

Serve bread with fondue.

---

[a] This Swiss cheese is sometimes referred to as Greyerzer.

[b] Kirsch is the German word for a dry cherry brandy. Kirsch made in Switzerland is renowned.

[c] It is important that each cube has some crust for stability because the cubes are speared and dipped in the cheese. It is best to select a slender loaf of French bread.

[d] A *Caquelon* is a ceramic heat-proof pot made specifically for fondue.

[e] Cheese should not be exposed to high heat for a prolonged period. The cornstarch should be added when the cheese mixture is just below the boiling point; then the mixture should barely simmer.

309

Fried Camembert Cheese
Gebackener Camembert
Camembert frit

YIELD: 10 SERVINGS

Camembert cheese, ripe, chilled	1 lb 2 oz	500 g
Parsley	1 2/3 oz	50 g
White wheat flour	1 2/3 oz	50 g
Frying batter (Recipe 672)	10 1/2 oz	300 g
Oil for frying (10% oil loss)	2 3/4 oz	80 ml

MISE EN PLACE

Cut ripe, chilled cheese into wedges.

Wash parsley and drain well.

METHOD

Dredge cheese wedges in flour, dip in batter, and deep-fry at 360°F (180°C).

Drain on absorbent paper.

Serve on a doily and garnish with parsley sprigs.

310

Fried Cheese Puffs
Gebackene Brandteig-Käsekrapfen
Beignets soufflés au fromage

YIELD: 10 SERVINGS

Water	13 1/2 oz	400 ml
Butter	3 1/2 oz	100 g
Seasoning (salt, nutmeg)	1x	1x
Paprika, mild	1 tsp	5 g
White wheat flour	8 1/2 oz	240 g
Eggs	6	6
Gruyere cheese[a]	10 1/2 oz	300 g
Seasoning (salt and pepper)	1x	1x
Parsley, curly, fresh	2/3 oz	20 g
Tomato sauce (Recipe 96)	1 pt 1 oz	500 ml
Oil for frying (10% oil loss)	4 oz	120 ml

[a] This Swiss cheese is sometimes referred to as Greyerzer.

MISE EN PLACE

Combine water, butter, and seasoning. Bring to a boil.

Add flour all at once and stir over heat until paste is smooth and does not cling to the sides of the pot.

Let cool slightly; mix in eggs, one by one.

Cut cheese into small dice.

Blend cheese and cream puff paste. Adjust seasoning.

METHOD FOR FRYING

Cut strips of parchment paper about 2 1/2 in. (6 cm) wide. Oil strips lightly.

Pipe dumplings weighing 2/3 oz (20 g) each on paper, using pastry bag with smooth tip.

Dip parchment strips in hot fat (the dumplings will come loose) and deep-fry at medium heat, 325°F (165°C), until brown and cooked thoroughly. The dumplings should double in size.

Drain on absorbent paper.

Serve on doilies and garnish with parsley sprigs.

Serve with tomato sauce on the side.

311

Cheese Souffle
Käseauflauf
Soufflé au fromage

YIELD: 10 SERVINGS

Butter for molds	1 oz	30 g
Flour for molds	1x	1x
Butter	1 2/3 oz	50 g
Gruyere cheese[a]	8 3/4 oz	250 g
Milk	1 pt 1 oz	500 ml
Butter	3 1/2 oz	100 g
White wheat flour	3 1/2 oz	100 g
Seasoning (salt and pepper)	1x	1x
Seasoning (paprika)	1x	1x
Egg yolks	8	8
Egg whites	8	8
Cornstarch	1/3 oz	10 g

(continued on next page)

[a] This Swiss cheese is sometimes referred to as Greyerzer.

(continued from preceding page)

MISE EN PLACE
Butter souffle molds and dust with flour.

Grate cheese.

Heat milk.

METHOD
Melt butter, add flour, and stir until smooth.

Add hot milk and stir well with wire whisk. When mixture starts to thicken, stir with wooden paddle.

Season with salt and pepper and a pinch of paprika.

Let cool slightly and blend in egg yolks, one by one, and grated cheese.

Whip egg whites and fold in cornstarch.

Fold about 25% of the beaten egg whites into batter first, then add the remaining egg whites.

Fill souffle molds about three-quarters full.

Place molds in water bath for 30 minutes to warm mixture.

Bake first at 325°F (160°C) and finish at 400°F (200°C).

Place souffle molds on a paper doily and serve at once.

NOTE: Baking time for warm mixtures are: large souffle molds, about 20 to 25 minutes; small, individual molds, about 10 to 12 minutes.

312

Grilled Cheese Toast with Tomatoes and Green Peppers

Käseschnitte mit Tomaten und Peperoni
Croûte au fromage portugaise

YIELD: 10 SERVINGS

Bread, white (Pullman loaf)	1 lb 2 oz	500 g
Gruyere cheese[a]	1 lb 2 oz	500 g
Tomatoes	14 oz	400 g
Green peppers	7 oz	200 g
Oregano, fresh	1/3 oz	10 g
Parsley	2/3 oz	20 g
Butter	3 1/2 oz	100 g
Garlic	1 tsp	5 g
Seasoning (salt and pepper)	1x	1x
Dry white wine	3 1/3 oz	100 ml

---
[a] This Swiss cheese is sometimes referred to as Greyerzer.

MISE EN PLACE
Cut bread into 10 slices.

Cut cheese into thin slices.

Peel tomatoes, remove seeds, and cut into cubes.

Trim and dice peppers.

Chop oregano and parsley separately.

METHOD
Smother tomatoes and peppers in a small amount of butter; add oregano.

Peel and purée garlic, add to smothered vegetables, and season to taste.

Spread bread slices with remaining butter and sauté on both sides until brown.

Sprinkle toast slices with wine and top with cheese.

Melt cheese under the salamander.

Garnish the center of each slice with vegetables and sprinkle with parsley.

313

Quiche Lorraine

Lothringer Käsekuchen
Quiche lorraine

YIELD: 10 SERVINGS

Butter	2/3 oz	20 g
White wheat flour	2/3 oz	20 g
Short pastry (Recipe 710)	14 oz	400 g
Onions	7 oz	200 g
Bacon, smoked	7 oz	200 g
Butter	1 2/3 oz	50 g
Gruyere cheese[a]	8 3/4 oz	250 g
Milk	6 3/4 oz	200 ml
Heavy cream	3 1/3 oz	100 ml
Eggs	2	2
White wheat flour	2/3 oz	20 g
Seasoning (salt and pepper)	1x	1x
Seasoning (nutmeg)	pinch	1x

MISE EN PLACE
Butter a tart mold 11 inches in diameter and dust with flour.

Roll out short pastry and line mold.

---
[a] This Swiss cheese is sometimes referred to as Greyerzer.

Peel onions and cut into thin slices. Cut bacon into thin strips.

Smother onions and bacon in butter and let cool.

Grate cheese.

Combine milk, cream, eggs, and flour. Strain through fine mesh china cap.

Season with salt and pepper and nutmeg, and add cheese.

METHOD

Spread onion and bacon mixture evenly in tart mold.

Fill mold with custard.

Bake at 400°F (200°C)[a] for about 30 minutes.

314

aked Cheese Crepes

Pfannkuchen mit Käsefüllung
Crêpes au fromage

YIELD: 10 SERVINGS

Milk	10 oz	300 ml
Eggs	4	4
White wheat flour, sifted	5 oz	140 g
Seasoning (salt, nutmeg)	1x	1x
Butter	2 oz	60 g
Gruyere cheese[b]	7 oz	200 g
Cream sauce (Recipe 40)	1 qt 2 oz	1.0 L
Egg yolks	2	2
Sbrinz[,c] grated	1 2/3 oz	50 g
Butter	1 oz	30 g

MISE EN PLACE

Combine milk and eggs, add sifted flour, and season with salt and nutmeg.

Strain batter through fine mesh china cap.

Bake 20 thin crepes (pancakes), cover with aluminum foil to keep from drying out, and let cool.

Cut Gruyere cheese into small dice.

Butter suitable ovenproof platter (gratin dish).

METHOD

Heat cream sauce and divide in half.

Stir egg yolks and cheese into half amount of sauce.[a]

Fill crepes with cheese sauce, roll or fold, and place on platter.

Cover with remaining sauce, sprinkle with grated cheese and melted butter.

Bake until golden brown.

315

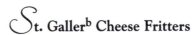t. Galler[b] Cheese Fritters

St. Galler Käsekugeln
Boulettes au fromage saint-galloise

YIELD: 10 SERVINGS

Tilsiter cheese[c]	1 lb 10 oz	750 g
White wheat flour	5 1/3 oz	150 g
Egg yolks	10	10
Seasoning (white pepper)	1x	1x
Seasoning (paprika)	1x	1x
Egg whites	10	10
White wheat flour	3 1/2 oz	100 g
Oil loss (frying)	3 1/3 oz	100 ml

MISE EN PLACE

Remove rind from cheese and grate fine.

METHOD

Blend grated cheese, flour, and egg yolks.

Season with pepper and paprika.

Whip egg whites and fold into cheese mixture.

Form walnut-size balls with the egg/cheese mixture and roll in flour.

Deep-fry at 400°F (200°C) until golden brown.

NOTE: This dish can be served with Tomato Sauce (Recipe 99).

---

[a] The crust can be prebaked.

[b] This Swiss cheese is sometimes referred to as Greyerzer.

[c] Sbrinz is a hard grating cheese from Switzerland. Parmesan can be substituted.

---

[a] Sauce should *not* be very hot, or else cheese will start to melt and sauce will become stringy, making it difficult to fill the crepes.

[b] St. Gallen is a city in eastern Switzerland.

[c] Tilsiter is a semisoft cheese.

316

$\mathcal{W}$elsh Rarebits

Walisische Käseschnitte
Croûte au fromage tartiné

YIELD: 10 SERVINGS

Butter	5 1/3 oz	150 g
Bread, white (Pullman loaf)	1 lb 2 oz	500 g
Cheddar cheese	14 oz	400 g
Beer	3 1/3 oz	100 ml
Mustard powder	1/3 oz	10 g
Worcestershire sauce	2/3 oz	20 ml
Seasoning (salt and pepper)	1x	1x

MISE EN PLACE
Reserve 1 2/3 oz (50 g) butter.

Slice bread into 10 slices and sauté in the rest of the butter until golden brown.

Grate cheese.

METHOD
Combine grated cheese with reserved butter, beer, mustard powder, and Worcestershire sauce, and season to taste. The mixture should have the consistency of dough.

Spread cheese mixture onto bread slices in a pyramid shape. Cut each slice in half diagonally.

Brown under the salamander.

Fish and Shellfish

Fish Dishes

ℬraised Whole Turbot in White Wine Sauce

Braisierter Steinbutt
Turbotin braisé

YIELD: 10 SERVINGS

Turbot,[a] whole, gutted	8 lb 13 oz	4.0 kg
Butter	3 oz	80 g
Matignon (Recipe 13)	10 1/2 oz	300 g
Dill, fresh	1/3 oz	10 g
Tarragon, fresh	1/3 oz	10 g
Bay leaf	1	1
Seasoning (salt and pepper)	1x	1x
Dry white wine	1 pt 1 oz	500 ml
Fish fumet (Recipe 25)	1 qt 19 oz	1.5 L
White wine sauce (Recipe 103)	1 pt 1 oz	500 ml
Lemon, juice	1/2	1/2
Seasoning	1x	1x

MISE EN PLACE
Wash and clean turbot.

Butter the insert of a turbot poacher.

METHOD
Smother *matignon* in butter and spread on bottom of turbot poacher.[b] Add dill, tarragon, and bay leaf.

Season turbot with salt and pepper.

Place turbot on buttered insert and lower into poacher on top of vegetables.

Add wine and fish fumet. The fish should be about one-quarter submerged.

Bring to a boil on top of stove, cover lightly, and braise in oven at low temperature.

Baste occasionally with its own juices.

Remove fish with insert when done. Cover and keep warm.

Strain stock through fine mesh china cap; boil stock until almost totally reduced.

Add white wine sauce and lemon juice. Season to taste.

Serve fish whole[c] on buttered, hot platter. Brush with melted butter to give it a sheen. Serve sauce on the side.

[a] Turbot is a large flat fish from the North Sea or the Eastern part of the Atlantic. It is somewhat scarce and expensive. Halibut can be substituted, although the texture and flavor may be inferior. The Pacific turbot is not related.

[b] There is a diamond-shaped fish poacher made specifically for turbot. The insert has handles so the fish can easily be removed after cooking.

[c] The black top skin is often removed before service.

ℬraised Sea Bass with Vermouth[a]

Braisierter Wolfsbarsch mit Noilly Prat
Loup de mer braisé au Noilly Prat

YIELD: 10 SERVINGS

Sea bass, whole, gutted, trimmed	6 lb 10 oz	3.0 kg
Butter	3 oz	80 g
Matignon (Recipe 13)	10 1/2 oz	300 g
Dill, fresh	1/3 oz	10 g
Tarragon, fresh	1/3 oz	10 g
Bay leaf	1	1
Seasoning (salt and pepper)	1x	1x
Dry vermouth	10 oz	300 ml
Fish stock (Recipe 24)	2 qt 20 oz	2.5 L
Heavy cream	10 oz	300 ml
Hollandaise sauce (Recipe 60)	3 1/3 oz	100 ml
Seasoning (lemon juice)	1x	1x
Seasoning (salt and pepper)	1x	1x
GARNISH		
Vegetables julienne	1 lb 2 oz	500 g
Butter	1 oz	30 g
Mushrooms, fresh	7 oz	200 g

MISE EN PLACE
Wash and clean sea bass.

Butter fish poacher insert.

MISE EN PLACE FOR GARNISH
Braise vegetables *julienne* in butter.

Trim and wash mushrooms and cut into slices. Braise in butter.

METHOD
Braise *matignon* in butter and spread on bottom of fish poacher. Add dill, tarragon, and bay leaf. Spread on bottom of fish poacher.

Season fish with salt and pepper and place on poacher insert. Lower insert into poacher on top of vegetables.

Add dry vermouth and fish stock. The fish should be about one-quarter submerged.

Bring to a boil on top of stove, cover lightly, and braise in oven at low temperature.

Baste occasionally with its own juices.

When done, remove fish with insert. Cover and keep warm.

[a] The original recipe specifies Noilly Prat, but any brand of dry vermouth can be used. Vermouth comes in dry and sweet varieties; use only dry in this recipe.

Strain braising stock through fine mesh china cap.

Reduce braising stock to about 10 oz (300 ml).

Add cream and return to a boil. Remove from heat and fold in Hollandaise sauce.

Season with lemon juice and adjust seasoning.

Place fish on lightly buttered serving platter and cover with small amount of sauce.

Sprinkle with vegetables *julienne* and mushrooms. Serve remaining sauce on the side.

319

*B*atter-Fried Wide-Mouth Bass Fillets

Im Backtaig fritierte Eglifilets[a]
Filet de perchette frit Orly

YIELD: 10 SERVINGS

Bass fillets, skinless	2 lb 10 oz	1.2 kg
Lemon, juice	1	1
Seasoning (pepper)	1x	1x
Salt	1/3 oz	10 g
White wheat flour	1 2/3 oz	50 g
Oil for frying (10% oil loss)	5 oz	150 ml

BATTER
White wheat flour	5 2/3 oz	160 g
Beer	5 oz	150 ml
Water	3 1/3 oz	100 ml
Peanut oil	1 oz	30 ml
Seasoning (salt and pepper)	1x	1x
Egg white	1	1

GARNISH
Lemon, cut into wedges	2	2
Parsley, curly, fresh	1 2/3 oz	50 g
Tomato sauce (Recipe 99)	1 pt 1 oz	500 ml

MISE EN PLACE
Marinate fish fillets with lemon juice, salt, and pepper.

METHOD FOR BATTER
Combine flour, beer, water, oil, salt and pepper and mix into a smooth batter. Strain through china cap. Let rest in a warm place for 1 hour.

Shortly before use, beat egg white until foamy and fold into batter.

METHOD
Salt fish fillets and dredge in flour.

Dip in batter and fry at 360°F (180°C) until golden brown.

Drain on absorbent paper.

Garnish with lemon wedges and parsley.

Serve with tomato sauce on the side.

320

*W*ide-Mouth Bass Fillets with Porcini Mushrooms

Eglifilets[a] mit Steinpilzen
Filet de perch aux cèpes

YIELD: 10 SERVINGS

Bass fillets, skinless	2 lb 10 oz	1.2 kg
Lemon, juice	1	1
Seasoning (pepper)	1x	1x
Porcini mushrooms[b]	14 oz	400 g
Shallots	1 2/3 oz	50 g
Garlic	1 tsp	5 g
Chives, fresh	2/3 oz	20 g
Salt	1/3 oz	10 kg
White wheat flour	1 2/3 oz	50 g
Peanut oil	3 1/3 oz	100 ml
Butter	1 2/3 oz	50 g
Seasoning (salt and pepper)	1x	1x

MISE EN PLACE
Marinate fish fillets with lemon juice and pepper.

Trim and wash porcini mushrooms and cut into slices.

Chop shallots and garlic.

Cut chives into fine slivers.

METHOD
Salt fish fillets and dredge in flour.

Sauté fish in oil until golden brown on each side; remove from pan and keep warm.

Add butter to pan and sauté shallots and garlic.

Add porcini mushrooms and continue cooking.

Place mushrooms over fish. Sprinkle with chives.

[a] Egli are small bass found in Swiss lakes. They are called *Kretzer* in the Lake Constance area.

[b] Porcini are wild mushrooms, called *cèpes* in French, *Steinpilze* in German, and *porcini* in Italian. These mushrooms are widely available dried, and are increasingly available fresh. Because Italy is a large exporter of these mushrooms, the Italian name is commonly used.

321

ℳarinated Halibut Fillets (cold)

Marinierte Heilbuttfilets
Escabèche

YIELD: 10 SERVINGS

Halibut fillets, skinless	3 lb 8 oz	1.6 kg
Olive oil	6 3/4 oz	200 ml
Leaf lettuce, washed	1 head	1 kopf

MARINADE

Onions	5 1/3 oz	150 g
Red peppers	3 1/2 oz	100 g
Carrots	3 1/2 oz	100 g
Garlic	1/3 oz	10 g
White wine vinegar	13 1/2 oz	400 ml
Bay leaf	1	1
Cayenne	pinch	2 g
Seasoning	1x	1x

MISE EN PLACE FOR MARINADE
Peel, and trim onions, red peppers, and carrots. Cut into strips (*julienne*).

Chop garlic.

METHOD
Sauté fish fillets in oil.[a] Transfer fish to china or stainless steel dish.

Add onions, peppers, carrots, and garlic to sauté pan and cook briefly.

Add vinegar, bay leaf, and cayenne and season to taste.

Boil for 10 minutes.

Pour hot vegetable marinade over fish.

Let cool, cover, and marinate one day in refrigerator.

Serve fish on lettuce leaves and top with marinade.

---

[a] Fish could be dredged in flour to make sautéing easier.

322

𝒲hitefish Fillets with Tomatoes

Felchenfilets Dugléré
Filets de féra Dugléré

YIELD: 10 SERVINGS

Shallots	2 oz	60 g
Butter, melted	1 oz	30 g
Tomatoes	1 lb 5 oz	600 g
Heavy cream (36%)	3 1/3 oz	100 ml
Whitefish,[a] freshwater, fillets	3 lb	1.4 kg
Seasoning (salt and pepper)	1x	1x
Melted butter	1 oz	30 g
Lemon	1/2	1/2
Dry white wine	10 oz	300 ml
Fish fumet (Recipe 25)	10 oz	300 ml
Fish velouté sauce (Recipe 53)	6 3/4 oz	200 ml
Hollandaise sauce (Recipe 60)	3 1/3 oz	100 ml

MISE EN PLACE
Chop shallots. Butter a shallow pan (*sautoir*) with melted butter and sprinkle with shallots.

Blanch and peel tomatoes. Cut in half, remove seeds, and dice.

Lightly whip heavy cream, but not too stiff.

METHOD
Season whitefish fillets with salt and pepper, brush with melted butter, and place side by side in the *sautoir*. Sprinkle with lemon juice.

Add diced tomatoes, white wine, and fish fumet.

Cover with buttered parchment paper and bring to a boil on top of stove.

Lower heat and poach[b] for about 5 minutes until done.

Remove fish and as much tomato as possible. Keep fish warm.

Reduce poaching liquid. Add fish *velouté* to poaching liquid and boil until the desired consistency is reached.

Remove from heat. Fold in the Hollandaise sauce first. Then fold in the lightly whipped cream.

Place drained fish and tomatoes on a serving dish.

Cover with Hollandaise/cream sauce and brown under the salamander.

---

[a] The original recipe calls for *felchen*, a somewhat rare fish found in Swiss lakes. Great Lakes whitefish can be substituted.

[b] The fish can be poached in the oven as well as on top of the stove. Oven poaching is more common in commercial kitchens.

323

$\mathcal{W}$hitefish Fillets Luzern[a] Style

Felchenfilets Luzerner Art
Filets de féra lucernoise

Yield: 10 servings

Whitefish,[b] freshwater, fillets	3 lb	1.4 kg
Lemon, juice	1	1
Seasoning (white pepper)	1x	1x
Onions	10 1/2 oz	300 g
Tomatoes	1 lb 5 oz	600 g
Salt	1/3 oz	10 g
White wheat flour	1 2/3 oz	50 g
Peanut oil	3 1/3 oz	100 ml
Butter	2 2/3 oz	75 g
Capers	3 1/2 oz	100 g
Brown veal juice, thickened (Recipe 55)	3 1/3 oz	100 ml
Parsley, chopped	1 2/3 oz	50 g

MISE EN PLACE
Marinate fish fillets with lemon juice and white pepper.

Chop onions.

Peel tomatoes, cut in half, remove seeds, and dice.

METHOD
Salt fish, dredge lightly in flour, and sauté in oil. Keep fish fillets warm.

In another pan, sauté chopped onions in butter, add tomatoes and capers, and cook briefly.

Pour veal juice into serving dish and place fish fillets on top.

Top fish with onions, tomatoes, and capers.

Sprinkle with parsley.

[a] Luzern is a city in Switzerland, on the lake of the same name.

[b] The original recipe calls for *felchen*, a somewhat rare fish found in Swiss lakes. Great Lakes whitefish can be substituted.

324

$\mathcal{F}$illets of Flounder with Lemon and Capers

Flundern Grenobler[a] Art
Filets grenobloise

Yield: 10 servings

Flounder, fillets	3 lb 8 z	1.6 kg
Lemon, juice	1	1
Seasoning (white pepper)	1x	1x
Lemons	3	3
Cress[b]	3 1/2 oz	100 g
Seasoning (salt)	1x	1x
White wheat flour	1 2/3 oz	50 g
Peanut oil	3 1/3 oz	100 ml
Butter	1 2/3 oz	50 g
Capers, drained	3 1/2 oz	100 g
Worcestershire sauce	1/3 oz	10 ml
Parsley, chopped	1 oz	30 g

MISE EN PLACE
Marinate flounder fillets with lemon juice and ground white pepper.

Peel lemons with knife,[c] remove all skin and pith, cut flesh from sections, and cut into fine dice.

Wash and drain cress.

METHOD
Salt flounder fillets, dredge with flour, and sauté in oil until golden brown on both sides. Be sure fish is cooked. Keep fish warm.

Heat butter and sauté diced lemon and capers.

Add Worcestershire sauce and chopped parsley and heat until foamy.

Pour foaming sauce over fish. Garnish with cress.

[a] Grenoble is a French town near the Swiss border.

[b] The original recipe calls for *Brunnenkresse*, which is a little spicier in flavor than watercress. Watercress can be substituted.

[c] Both the yellow rind and white membrane should be removed.

325

Poached Blue Brook Trout
Forelle blau
Truite au bleu

YIELD: 10 SERVINGS

Matignon (Recipe 13)	8 3/4 oz	250 g
Parsley stems, fresh	1 oz	30 g
Bay leaf	1/2	1/2
White peppercorns	1/3 oz	10 g
Thyme twig, fresh	1	5 g
Salt	2 oz	60 g
Water	1 gal 24 oz	4.5 L
Trout, live, 10 whole fish	5 lb 8 oz	2.5 kg
White wine vinegar	8 1/2 oz	250 ml
Dry white wine	8 1/2 oz	250 ml
Lemon, sliced	1	1
Butter	5 1/3 oz	150 g
Lemons, cut into wedges	2	2

MISE EN PLACE

Combine *matignon*, parsley, bay leaf, white peppercorns, thyme, and salt with water. Boil for 10 minutes to prepare stock.

Kill the trout,[a] gut, and sprinkle with a small amount of the vinegar.

METHOD

Add remaining vinegar, wine, and sliced lemon to stock.

Slide trout into stock and poach for 8 minutes at 170°F (75°C).

Melt butter. Serve trout with melted butter and lemon wedges.

---

[a] Handling is key to this dish: The fish must be handled carefully with wet hands in order to keep as much natural film on fish as possible. The film turns blue when exposed to acidity.

Killing the trout humanely requires a special technique. Hold live fish with wet hand behind the gills and strike with the back of a heavy knife. That will stun the fish. Gut and cook right away.

326

Poached Brook Trout Fillets with Nettle Sauce
Forellenfilets mit Brennesselsauce
Filets de truite aux orties

YIELD: 10 SERVINGS

Nettles	3 1/2	100 g
Butter	1 2/3 oz	50 g
Trout fillets	3 lb	1.4 kg
Seasoning (salt and pepper)	1x	1x
Glace de poisson[a]	5 oz	150 ml
Heavy cream (36%)	10 oz	300 ml
Butter, cold	5 1/3 oz	150 g
Seasoning (salt and pepper)	1x	1x

GARNISH

Puff pastry[b] (Recipe 689)	3 1/2 oz	100 g
Egg yolk	1	1

MISE EN PLACE

Prepare garnish: Roll out puff pastry and cut 20 *fleurons*[c] with a cookie cutter. Brush *fleurons* with egg yolk mixed with small amount of water and bake.

Remove nettle leaves[d] from stems, wash, blanch, and chop coarsely.

METHOD

Melt butter and brush on bottom and sides of a shallow ovenproof dish.

Season the trout with salt and pepper and place in a shallow pan (*sautoir*); brush fish with butter.

Place dish under salamander to cook fish. Do not overcook.

Mix *glace de poisson* and heavy cream, bring to a boil, and reduce slightly.

Remove from heat. Add butter in small nuggets. Do not allow sauce to boil again.

Add nettles. Adjust seasoning.

Pour sauce into a hot serving dish; place fish on top.

Place *fleurons* around fish.

---

[a] *Glace de poisson*, literally translated "fish glaze," is made by reducing fish fumet to a syrupy consistency. It can have an unpleasant taste if the fish bones used for the fumet are not very fresh.

[b] Puff pastry can also be purchased ready to use.

[c] *Fleurons* are puff pastry half-moons. Other shapes can be used.

[d] European nettle leaves sting, and gloves must be worn to pick them before they are cooked. Also, they have a distinct flavor.

327

*P*oached Fillets of Brook Trout with Mushroom Sauce

Forellenfilets Hausfrauenart
Filets de truite bonne femme

YIELD: 10 SERVINGS

Shallots	2 oz	60 g
Butter	1 oz	30 g
Heavy cream (36%)	3 1/3 oz	100 ml
Mushrooms, fresh	1 lb 2 oz	500 g
Trout fillets	3 lb	1.4 kg
Seasoning (salt and pepper)	1x	1x
Lemon, juice	1/2	1/2
Melted butter	1 oz	30 g
Dry white wine	10 oz	300 ml
Fish fumet (Recipe 25)	10 oz	300 ml
Fish velouté sauce (Recipe 53)	6 3/4 oz	200 ml
Hollandaise sauce (Recipe 60)	3 1/3 oz	100 ml
Seasoning	1x	1x

GARNISH

Puff pastry[a] (Recipe 689)	3 1/2 oz	100 g
Egg yolk	1	1
Mushrooms, fresh, 20 caps	7 oz	200 g
Butter	2/3 oz	20 g
Seasoning (salt and pepper)	1x	1x
Lemon, juice	1/2	1/2

MISE EN PLACE FOR GARNISH

Roll out puff pastry, and cut 20 *fleurons*[b] with a cookie cutter. Brush *fleurons* with egg yolk mixed with small amount of water and bake.

Wash mushroom caps. Braise with butter, salt and pepper, and lemon juice. Keep warm.

MISE EN PLACE

Chop shallots. Butter a shallow pan (*sautoir*) and sprinkle with shallots.

Whip heavy cream, but not too stiff.

Wash and slice mushrooms.

METHOD

Season trout fillets with salt and pepper and lemon juice.

Place fillets side by side in prepared casserole.

Brush with melted butter to keep fillets separated. Sprinkle fish with sliced mushrooms.

---

[a] Puff pastry can also be purchased ready to use.

[b] *Fleurons* are puff pastry half-moon shapes. Other shapes can be used.

Add wine and fish fumet to casserole.

Cover with aluminum foil and bring to a slow boil. Simmer for 5 minutes.

Remove fish and mushrooms and keep warm. Reduce fish stock.

Add *velouté* sauce. Add any stock that drains from fish fillets.

Boil until the sauce has reached desired consistency.

Remove sauce from stove and fold in lightly whipped cream and Hollandaise sauce. Adjust seasoning.

Cover fish with sauce and brown under the salamander.

Garnish with *fleurons* and mushroom caps.

328

*D*eep-Fried Fish Fillets

Fritierte Fischstreifen mit Zitrone
Goujons[a] de poisson frits au citron

YIELD: 10 SERVINGS

Whiting fillets	1 lb 2 oz	500 g
Flounder fillets	1 lb 2 oz	500 g
Halibut fillets	1 lb 2 oz	500 g
Lemons, juice	1 1/2	1 1/2
Seasoning (white pepper)	1x	1x
Lemons	5	5
Salt	1/3 oz	10 g
White wheat flour	1 lb 10 oz	750 g
Oil for frying (10% oil loss)	5 oz	150 ml

MISE EN PLACE

Cut fish fillets into strips.

Marinate fish with lemon juice and white pepper.

Slice the whole lemons in half.

METHOD

Salt fish and dredge in flour, piece by piece.[b] Press flour into each strip by rolling the strip lightly. Shake off excess flour.

Deep-fry at 360°F (180°C).

Drain on absorbent paper and salt lightly.

Serve on platter with a paper doily or on individual plates.

Garnish with lemon halves.

NOTE: Other kinds of fish can be prepared in the same manner.

---

[a] The French name *goujons* refers to small fish, fried whole. The fish strips should resemble small fish. Large fillets should be cut on a bias.

[b] Fish must be floured to order, piece by piece. If floured ahead of time, the fish will stick together.

329

Grilled Salmon with Red Wine Butter
Grillierter Lachs mit Rotweinbutter
Saumon grillée au beurre de vin rouge

YIELD: 10 SERVINGS

Salmon fillets, skinless	3 lb 5 oz	1.5 kg
Lemon, juice	1	1
Seasoning (ground white pepper)	1x	1x
Peanut oil	3 1/3 oz	100 ml
Seasoning (salt)	1/3 oz	10 g

RED WINE BUTTER
Red wine, dark and strong	6 3/4 oz	200 ml
Butter	7 oz	200 g
Seasoning (salt and pepper)	1x	1x

MISE EN PLACE FOR RED WINE BUTTER
Reduce wine almost completely. Let cool.

Cream butter and blend with reduced wine.

Season to taste.

METHOD
Cut fish fillets into 20 slices 2 2/3 oz (75 g) each.

Marinate fish with lemon juice and pepper.

Salt fish, dredge in oil, and grill[a] to order.

Garnish with red wine butter.[b]

330

Grilled Monkfish (lotte) with Leeks
Grillierte Seeteufelschnitten auf Lauchbett
Tranches de baudroie grillées sur lit de poireaux

YIELD: 10 SERVINGS

Monkfish, gutted, whole, without head	4 lb 7 oz	2.0 kg
Lemon, juice	1	1
Seasoning (white pepper)	1x	1x
Seasoning (salt)	1x	1x
Peanut oil	3 1/3 oz	100 ml

GARNISH
Leeks, white part only	2 lb 14 oz	1.3 kg
Onions	4 1/4 oz	120 g
Cottage cheese, rich[a]	14 oz	400 g
Egg yolks	6	6
Vegetable shortening	1 1/3 oz	40 g
White veal stock (Recipe 28)	10 oz	300 ml
Seasoning (salt and pepper)	1x	1x

MISE EN PLACE
Trim and wash fish and cut into steaks.

Marinate fish with lemon juice and white pepper.

MISE EN PLACE FOR GARNISH
Wash and trim leeks; be sure sand is cleaned from layers. Cut into fine strips (*julienne*).

Chop onions.

Combine cottage cheese with egg yolks and blend thoroughly.

METHOD
Sauté onions in shortening; add leeks and veal stock. Cover and braise until leeks are soft and all liquid has evaporated.[b]

Salt fish steaks, brush with oil, and grill on both sides until cooked, but still moist.

Combine hot leek mixture with cottage cheese/egg yolk mixture. Season to taste.

Place leek/cheese mixture on service platter and brown under the salamander.

Place fish on top.

---

[a] Fish can be grilled or cooked on a very hot griddle. It should be brown and crisp outside, yet still underdone inside.

[b] Red wine butter can be served a number of ways: piped into small rosettes and chilled, rolled in parchment paper to make a cylinder about 1 in. (25 mm) thick, chilled, and sliced, served room temperature and spooned onto warm fish. The butter will melt by the time the dish arrives at the table.

---

[a] The recipe calls for *Rahm Quark*, which is a fine-curd cottage cheese with a high fat content.

[b] It might be necessary to remove the lid to let the liquid evaporate.

331

*G*rilled Fillets of Sole with Fresh Noodles
Grillierte Seezungenfilets auf frischen Nudeln
Filets de sole grillés aux nouillettes fraîches

YIELD: 10 SERVINGS

Fillets of sole	2 lb 14 oz	1.3 kg
Lemon, juice	1	1
Seasoning (white pepper)	1x	1x
Seasoning (salt)	1x	1x
Peanut oil	3 1/3 oz	100 ml

GARNISH

Fresh noodles, narrow	14 oz	400 g
Salt	3/4 oz	25 g
Tomatoes	14 oz	400 g
Shallots	1 1/3 oz	40 g
Butter	2 oz	60 g
Seasoning (salt)	1/3 oz	10 g
Nutmeg	1x	1x
Garlic, chopped	1/4 tsp	5 g
Olive oil	2/3 oz	20 ml
Seasoning (salt and pepper)	1x	1x
Basil, fresh	2/3 oz	20 g

MISE EN PLACE
Marinate sole fillets with lemon juice and white pepper.

Boil noodles *al dente* in salt water; rinse and drain.

Peel tomatoes, remove seeds, and cut into small dice.

Chop shallots.

METHOD
Salt fish, dredge in peanut oil, and cook on hot grill or griddle.

Melt butter in a pan, add noodles, toss until hot, and season with salt and nutmeg.

Sauté shallots and garlic in olive oil, add tomatoes, and season to taste.

Plate noodles, place fish fillets on top, and garnish with tomatoes and basil leaves.

332

*S*almon Scallopini with Calvados
Lachsschnitzel mit Calvados
Aiguillettes de saumon au calvados

YIELD: 10 SERVINGS

Salmon fillets, skinless	2 lb 14 oz	1.3 kg
Lemon, juice	1	1
Seasoning (white pepper)	1x	1x
Shallots	1 oz	30 g
Apples[a]	10 1/2 oz	300 g
Chanterelle mushrooms[b]	10 1/2 oz	300 g
Chives, fresh	2/3 oz	20 g
Salt	1/3 oz	10 g
White wheat flour	1 2/3 oz	50 g
Peanut oil	2 3/4 oz	80 ml
Butter	1 oz	30 g
Calvados[c]	2 3/4 oz	80 ml
Fish velouté sauce (Recipe 53)	10 oz	300 ml
Heavy cream (36%)	6 3/4 oz	200 ml
Seasoning (salt and pepper)	1x	1x

MISE EN PLACE
Cut salmon fillets into 20 cutlets and flatten lightly.

Marinate cutlets with lemon juice and pepper.

Chop shallots.

Peel apples and cut into small dice.

Trim and wash chanterelle mushrooms.

Cut chives into small slivers.

METHOD
Salt salmon cutlets and dredge in flour. Sauté salmon in oil and keep warm.

Sauté shallots in butter; add diced apples and mushrooms. Continue to cook for a short time. Add Calvados; ignite and reduce.

Bring fish *velouté* to a boil, reduce, add cream, and reduce again.

Add apples and mushrooms to *velouté* sauce and season to taste.

Plate salmon cutlets, top with sauce, and sprinkle with chives.

[a] Any cooking apple, such as Granny Smith, can be used.

[b] Chanterelle's are yellow wild mushrooms, called *girolles* in French and *Eierschwämme* in German. When not available fresh, canned mushrooms can be substituted, but the flavor will not be the same.

[c] Calvados is an apple brandy from the Normandy region of France. Applejack can be substituted.

Salmon Scallopini in Parchment

Lachsschnitzel in der Papierhülle
Escalopes de saumon en papillote

YIELD: 10 SERVINGS

Salmon fillets, skinless	2 lb 14 oz	1.3 kg
Seasoning (salt and pepper)	1x	1x
Lemon juice	2/3 oz	20 ml
Butter	2 oz	60 g
Spinach, fresh	14 oz	400 g
Chives, fresh	2/3 oz	20 g
Shallots	1 2/3 oz	50 g
Garlic, chopped	1/4 tsp	5 g
Butter	2/3 oz	20 g
Seasoning (salt and pepper)	1x	1x
Nutmeg	1x	1x
Parchment paper		
Butter	2 oz	60 g
Dry duxelles (Recipe 20)	10 1/2 oz	300 g

MISE EN PLACE

Cut salmon fillets into 20 cutlets. Season with salt and pepper and lemon juice. Sauté salmon cutlets briefly in butter. Let cool.

Boil spinach, drain, and rinse in cold water. Drain again and squeeze out excess liquid. Chop spinach coarsely.

Cut chives into small slivers.

Chop shallots.

METHOD

Sauté shallots and garlic in butter, add spinach, and season with salt and pepper and nutmeg.

Cut parchment paper into circles about 12 in. (300 mm) in diameter; fold over once to crease.

Melt butter and brush onto center of lower paper half.

Layer the spinach, sautéed salmon, and duxelles on buttered parchment and sprinkle with chives.

Fold over the top paper half. Crimp rim with double fold to make an airtight seam.

Brush sealed bags with butter. Place bags on baking sheets and puff up[a] to order in a very hot oven. Serve at once.[b]

---

[a] One dependable method for puffing bags is to place them in shallow sauté pans, in about 1/2 in. (12 mm) of *hot* oil. Then place the pan in a very hot oven.

[b] It is important that the bag color lightly and get some stability, but it should not be brittle; otherwise the paper pieces will fall into the food when the bag is opened.

Salmon Cutlets with Whisky Cream Sauce

Lachsschnitzel schottische Art
Aiguillettes de saumon écossaise

YIELD: 10 SERVINGS

Salmon fillets, skinless	2 lb 14 oz	1.3 kg
Shallots	2 oz	60 g
Butter	1 2/3 oz	50 g
Diced vegetables (brunoise)	7 oz	200 g
Seven-grain pilaf (See Recipe 340)	7 oz	200 g
Smoked salmon, trimmed	8 3/4 oz	250 g
Salmon caviar	2 2/3 oz	75 g
Melted butter	1 oz	30 g
Seasoning (salt and pepper)	1x	1x
Lemon, juice	1/2	1/2
Dry white wine	10 oz	300 ml
Fish fumet (Recipe 25)	10 oz	300 ml
Fish velouté sauce (Recipe 53)	6 3/4 oz	200 ml
Heavy cream (36%)	5 oz	150 ml
Seasoning (salt and pepper)	1x	1x
Whisky	2 oz	60 ml
Dill sprigs, fresh	10	10

MISE EN PLACE

Cut salmon into 20 cutlets.

Chop shallots.

Butter a low-sided casserole pan; sprinkle with shallots.

Braise or steam vegetable *brunoise*.

Make seven-grain pilaf.

Slice smoked salmon and shape the slices into roses. Fill rose centers with salmon caviar.

METHOD

Place salmon cutlets in prepared casserole and brush with melted butter to keep cutlets separated.

Season with salt and pepper and lemon juice. Add white wine and fish fumet.

Cover casserole with aluminum foil; bring to a boil and poach for 5 minutes.

Remove salmon cutlets to a warm platter; cover and keep warm.

Reduce the salmon stock, add fish *velouté*, and bring to a boil.

Stir in heavy cream and reduce sauce to desired consistency.

Season sauce and strain through a fine mesh china cap.

Add whisky and heat sauce. Add drained vegetable *brunoise* and simmer briefly.

Plate salmon cutlets and cover with sauce.

Garnish each portion with a smoked salmon rose and dill sprig.

Serve with seven-grain pilaf on the side.

335

Salmon Cutlets with Mustard Cream Sauce

Lachsschnitzel mit Senfsauce
Aiguillettes de saumon à la moutarde

YIELD: 10 SERVINGS

Salmon fillets, skinless	2 lb 10 oz	1.2 kg
Dry white wine	1 2/3 oz	50 ml
Glace de poisson[a]	1 2/3 oz	50 ml
Chicken stock (Recipe 26)	1 2/3 oz	50 ml
Butter, cold	12 oz	350 g
Heavy cream (36%)	5 oz	150 ml
Mustard seeds	1 2/3 oz	50 g
Seasoning (salt and pepper)	1x	1x
Lemon, juice	1/2	1/2
Butter, melted	1/3 oz	10 g
Seasoning (salt and pepper)	1x	1x
Seasoning (lemon juice)	1x	1x
Dijon-style mustard, mild	1 oz	30 g

GARNISH
Cucumbers	10 1/2 oz	300 g
Tomatoes	10 1/2 oz	300 g
Butter	1 oz	30 g
Dill, fresh, chopped	1/3 oz	10 g
Seasoning (salt and pepper)	1x	1x

MISE EN PLACE FOR GARNISH
Peel cucumbers, remove seeds, and dice.

Peel tomatoes, remove seeds, and dice.

MISE EN PLACE
Cut salmon fillets into 20 cutlets.

Combine white wine, *glace de poisson*, and chicken stock, bring to a boil, and reduce about one-third. Remove mixture from stove and add cold butter in small nuggets. Do not allow the sauce to return to a boil.

Whip the heavy cream to a soft foam.

Crush the mustard seeds.

[a] *Glace de poisson*, literally translated "fish glaze," is made by reducing fish fumet to a syrupy consistency.

METHOD
Season the salmon cutlets with salt and pepper and lemon juice.

Brush fish with melted butter, place in a steamer basket,[a] and steam. Keep warm.

Finish garnish: Sauté cucumbers in butter; add diced tomatoes and dill. Season to taste.

Finish sauce: Season the sauce with salt and pepper and lemon juice. Fold in lightly whipped cream, crushed mustard seeds, and prepared mustard.

Plate salmon. Cover with sauce. Garnish with cucumber/tomato mixture.

336

Sautéed Hake in Egg Batter

Im Ei sautierte Meerhechttranchen
Tranches de colin sautées à l'oeuf

YIELD: 10 SERVINGS

Hake[b] steaks	3 lb 5 oz	1.5 kg
Seasoning (white pepper)	1x	1x
Lemons, juice	1 1/2	1 1/2
Eggs	3	3
Salt	1/3 oz	10 g
White wheat flour	2 2/3 oz	75 g
Peanut oil	4 oz	120 ml
Butter	3 oz	80 g

GARNISH
Lemons	2 1/2	2 1/2

MISE EN PLACE
Marinate hake steaks with white pepper and lemon juice.

Break eggs and mix thoroughly.

Quarter lemons for garnish to make 10 wedges.

METHOD
Salt hake steaks, dredge in flour, and shake off excess.

Dip into eggs (shake off excess).

Sauté fish in oil until golden brown.[c]

Plate the fish. Brown the butter and pour over fish at moment of service.

Garnish with lemon wedges.

[a] A steamer basket or any low-pressure steamer can be used.

[b] The French name for hake is *colin*; the German name is *Meerhecht*. The fish is closely related to cod, which can be substituted.

[c] If oil is too hot, the egg coating may burn.

Poached Hake with Capers

Pochierte Meerhechttranchen mit Kapern
Tranches de colin pochées aux câpres

YIELD: 10 SERVINGS

Lemon	1/2	1/2
White peppercorns	1/3 oz	10 g
Water	3 qt 5 oz	3.0 L
Milk	10 oz	300 ml
Salt	1 1/3 oz	40 g
Bay leaf	1	1
Dill, sprig, fresh, chopped	1	5 g
Hake[a] steaks	3 lb 5 oz	1.5 kg
Butter	3 1/2 oz	100 g
Capers, drained	1 2/3 oz	50 g
Parsley, chopped	2/3 oz	20 g

MISE EN PLACE

Peel lemon and cut into slices.

Crush white peppercorns.

Combine water, milk, salt, bay leaf, dill, and peppercorns, and bring to a boil.

METHOD

Reduce temperature of water mixture to 170°F (75°C).

Place hake steaks and lemon slices into water mixture.

Poach fish at 170°F (75°C) for about 8 minutes.

Carefully remove fish steaks from stock; drain.

Place fish on serving platter and keep warm.

Heat butter in cast iron pan until brown. Add capers[b] and pour mixture over fish steaks.

Sprinkle with parsley.

[a] The French name for hake is *colin*; the German name is *Meerhecht*. The fish is closely related to cod, which can be substituted.

[b] Be sure the pan is deep because the butter will foam.

Fillets of Flounder[a] Sauté with Potatoes, Mushrooms, and Asparagus

Rotzungenfilets schöne Müllerin
Filets de limande sole belle meunière

YIELD: 10 SERVINGS

Flounder fillets	2 lb 14 oz	1.3 kg
Lemon	1	1
Seasoning (salt, white pepper)	1x	1x
White wheat flour	1 2/3 oz	50 g
Peanut oil	2 3/4 oz	80 ml
Butter	1 2/3 oz	50 g
Lemon, juice	1/2	1/2
Worcestershire sauce	dash	5 ml
Parsley, chopped	1 1/3 oz	40 g

GARNISH

Potatoes	2 lb 3 oz	1.0 kg
Salt	1/3 oz	10 g
Mushrooms, fresh	10 1/2 oz	300 g
Green asparagus	1 lb 2 oz	500 g
Butter	1 oz	30 g
Seasoning (salt and pepper)	1x	1x
Butter	2/3 oz	20 g

MISE EN PLACE FOR GARNISH

Peel potatoes and scoop out balls with melon baller. Par-boil potato balls for about 5 minutes in salt water. Drain.

Trim and wash mushrooms and cut into quarters or halves, depending on size.

Peel and trim asparagus; cut to about 5-in. (120 mm) lengths. Boil asparagus and keep warm.

METHOD

Flatten flounder fillets, if necessary. Season with lemon juice, salt, and white pepper.

Dredge fillets in flour and shake off excess.

Sauté fillets in oil until golden brown on both sides. Keep fish warm.

Finish garnish: Sauté potato balls in 1 oz (30 g) butter until light brown; season with salt and white pepper. Sauté mushrooms in 2/3 oz (20 g) butter. Combine with potatoes.

Heat 1 2/3 oz (50 g) butter in cast iron pan until brown.[b] Add lemon juice, Worcestershire sauce, and chopped parsley and heat until foamy.

Pour foaming butter over fish.

Arrange potato/mushroom garnish and asparagus garnish around fish.

[a] The German recipe calls for *Rotzunge*, a fish of the flounder family with dry, soft flesh.

[b] Be sure the pan is deep because the butter will foam.

339

Stuffed Fillets of Flounder[a] with Asparagus

Rotzungenröllchen mit Spargelspitzen
Paupiettes de limande sole aux pointes d'asperges

YIELD: 10 SERVINGS

Green asparagus	1 lb 5 oz	600 g
Salt	1/3 oz	10 g
Flounder fillets	2 lb 14 oz	1.3 kg
Shallots	2 oz	60 g
Butter	2/3 oz	20 g
Melted butter	1 oz	30 g
Lemon juice	1/2	1/2
Heavy cream (36%)	1 2/3 oz	50 ml
Dry white wine	10 oz	300 ml
Fish fumet (Recipe 25)	10 oz	300 ml
Fish velouté sauce (Recipe 53)	6 3/4 oz	200 ml
Hollandaise sauce (Recipe 60)	3 1/3 oz	100 ml
Seasoning (salt and pepper)	1x	1x

FARCE (STUFFING)

Pike fillets, skinless and boneless	3 1/2 oz	100 g
Heavy cream (36%)	3 1/3 oz	100 ml
Egg white	1/2	1/2
Sherry, dry	2/3 oz	20 ml
Mushrooms, fresh	4 1/4 oz	120 g
Shallots	2/3 oz	20 g
Butter	2/3 oz	20 g
Seasoning (salt and pepper)	1x	1x

METHOD FOR FARCE

Cut pike fillets into cubes and freeze lightly.

In food processor, purée the semi-frozen fish with heavy cream, egg white, and sherry. Strain or pass through fine wire sieve.[b]

Wash mushrooms, peel shallots, and chop both. Sauté mushroom and shallot mixture in butter over high heat until all moisture is evaporated. Let mixture cool and add to fish farce.

Season to taste.

MISE EN PLACE

Peel and trim asparagus. Cut to 5-in. (120 mm) lengths. Boil asparagus in salted water and keep warm.

Flatten fish fillets lightly, spread with fish farce, and roll up tightly. Fasten with toothpicks or roll in buttered aluminum foil strips.

Chop shallots.

Butter a shallow casserole pan and sprinkle with the shallots.

Place fish rolls tightly in casserole, brush with melted butter to keep rolls separated, and sprinkle with lemon juice.

Whip heavy cream to a light foam.

METHOD

Add wine and fish fumet to fish rolls. Cover with aluminum foil.

Bring to a boil and poach carefully for about 10 minutes.

Remove fish rolls, remove toothpicks; and keep fish warm.

Reduce fish stock to about one-third, add *velouté*, and boil until the desired consistency is reached.

Strain sauce through fine mesh china cap. Fold lightly whipped cream and Hollandaise sauce into strained sauce. Season to taste.

Cover fish with sauce and brown under the salamander.

Garnish platter with asparagus.

340

Poached Saibling with Seven-Grain Pilaf

Saibling auf Bett von Getreidekörnern
Omble chevalier sur lit de grains céréales

YIELD: 10 SERVINGS

Saibling fillets[a]	3 lb	1.4 kg
Seasoning (salt and pepper)	1x	1x
Butter	2/3 oz	20 g
Melted butter	1 oz	30 g
Fish fumet (Recipe 25)	10 oz	300 ml
Dry white wine	10 oz	300 ml
Kitchen herbs, fresh	1 oz	30 g
Fish velouté sauce (Recipe 53)	6 3/4 oz	200 ml
Heavy cream (36%)	1 3/4 oz	50 ml
Hollandaise sauce (Recipe 60)	10 oz	300 ml
Seasoning (salt and pepper)	1x	1x

(continued on next page)

---

[a] The German recipe calls for *Rotzunge*, a fish of the flounder family with dry, soft flesh.

[b] This step can be omitted if the fish is puréed in a high-speed food processor.

[a] Saibling is a freshwater trout-like fish, sometimes known as "golden trout."

(continued from preceding page)

GARNISH

Tomatoes	12 oz	350 g
Butter	2/3 oz	20 g
Seasoning (salt and pepper)	1x	1x
Dill, sprig, fresh, top leaves	10	10

SEVEN-GRAIN PILAF

Buckwheat kernels	2 2/3 oz	75 g
Spelt kernels[a]	2 2/3 oz	75 g
Pearl barley	2 2/3 oz	75 g
Millet	2 2/3 oz	75 g
Rye kernels	2 2/3 oz	75 g
Wheat kernels	2 2/3 oz	75 g
Oat kernels	2 2/3 oz	75 g
Butter	1 2/3 oz	50 g
Vegetable bouillon (Recipe 27)	1 qt 2 oz	1.0 L
Butter	1 oz	30 g
Seasoning salt and pepper	1x	1x

MISE EN PLACE FOR GARNISH

Peel tomatoes, remove seeds, and cut into cubes. Smother tomatoes in butter and keep warm.

Season with salt and pepper.

Wash dill sprigs.

METHOD FOR PILAF

Sauté the seven grains in butter.

Add hot vegetable bouillon, bring to a boil, cover, and cook in slow oven, 325°F (165°C), for about 45 minutes.

Mix in cold butter, in small nuggets, with a fork. Season to taste.

METHOD

Remove any remaining bones from fillets. Season with salt and pepper and fold over.

Butter a steamer basket, place saibling in basket, and brush with melted butter.

Put fish fumet, white wine, and herbs in a casserole pan. Place steamer basket on top; cover and steam until fish is done.

Keep fish warm.

Reduce stock, add *velouté*, and reduce to desired consistency.

Strain through fine mesh china cap.

Fold in lightly whipped cream and Hollandaise sauce. Season to taste.

Serve fish on top of pilaf, cover with sauce, and brown under the salamander.

Garnish with tomatoes and dill sprigs.

---

[a] Spelt is a type of wheat, known as *Dinkel* in German.

341

Poached Saibling with Herbs

Saibling auf Zuger Art
Omble chevalier zougoise

YIELD: 10 SERVINGS

Fresh herbs[a]	1 2/3 oz	50 g
Shallots	2 oz	60 g
Butter	1 oz	30 g
Seasoning (salt and pepper)	1x	1x
Saibling fillets[b]	2 lb 14 oz	1.3 kg
Melted butter	1 oz	30 g
Lemon	1/2	1/2
Dry white wine	10 oz	300 ml
Fish fumet (Recipe 25)	10 oz	300 ml
Cold roux, beurre manié	1 2/3 oz	50 g
Heavy cream (36%)	5 oz	150 ml
Seasoning (salt and pepper)	1x	1x

GARNISH

Puff pastry (Recipe 689)	3 1/2 oz	100 g
Egg yolk	1	1

MISE EN PLACE

Wash and chop herbs.

Peel and chop shallots.

Butter a shallow casserole pan and sprinkle with shallots.

MISE EN PLACE FOR GARNISH

Roll out puff pastry with a cookie cutter and cut 10 half-moons (*fleurons*) or other desired shapes.[c]

Brush *fleurons* with egg yolk mixed with small amount of water and bake until golden brown.

METHOD

Season saibling fillets, fold fillets, and place tightly in the buttered casserole.

Brush fish with melted butter to keep moist and to keep fillets separated.

Sprinkle with herbs. Squeeze lemon over fish.

Add white wine and fish fumet.

Cover with aluminum foil, bring to a simmer, and poach carefully for about 5 minutes.

---

[a] A suggested herb mixture can include chervil, dill, tarragon, parsley, chives, thyme, sage, and fennel leaves.

[b] Saibling is a freshwater trout-like fish, sometimes known as "golden trout."

[c] Instead of half-moons, the dough can be cut into diamonds, which eliminates dough trimmings.

Remove saibling and keep warm. Reduce fish stock.
Add cold roux in small nuggets. Stir in heavy cream.
Boil sauce to desired consistency; adjust seasoning.
Cover saibling fillets with sauce. Garnish with *fleurons*.

342

$\mathcal{B}$readed Fillets of Sole Sautéed with Bananas

Sautierte Seezungenfilets mit Bananen
Filets de sole panés sautés aux bananes

YIELD: 10 SERVINGS

Fillets of sole[a]	3 lb	1.4 kg
Lemon	1	1
Seasoning (white pepper)	1x	1x
Seasoning (salt)	1x	1x
White wheat flour	1 2/3 oz	50 g
Eggs	2	2
Mie de pain[b]	7 oz	200 g
Clarified butter	3 1/2 oz	100 g

GARNISH

Bananas (5)	1 lb 14 oz	850 g
White wheat flour	1 oz	30 g
Butter	1 2/3 oz	50 g

MISE EN PLACE

Marinate sole fillets with lemon juice and white pepper.

Salt fish, dredge in flour, in eggs, and then in *mie de pain*.
Press *mie de pain* lightly on fish.

METHOD

Sauté fish in clarified butter until brown on both sides. Keep
fish warm.

Peel bananas, split lengthwise (there should be 10 halves),
roll in flour, and sauté in butter.

Serve bananas with fish.

343

$\mathcal{S}$hredded Monkfish Fillets in Cucumber Cream Sauce

Seeteufel-Geschnetzeltes mit Gurkencremesauce
Emincé de baudroie à la crème de concombres

YIELD: 10 SERVINGS

---

[a] The sole most commonly used in Switzerland is known as Dover sole in the United States. Flounder fillets can be substituted.

[b] *Mie de pain* are fresh bread crumbs, made from white Pullman loaves.

Monkfish fillets	3 lb	1.4 kg
Lemon, juice	1	1
Seasoning (white pepper)	1x	1x
Dill, fresh, chopped	2/3 oz	20 g
Salt	1x	1x
White wheat flour	1 2/3 oz	50 g
Clarified butter	3 oz	80 g
Worcestershire sauce	1 tsp	5 ml
Lemon	1/2	1/2

SAUCE

Cucumbers	10 1/2 oz	300 g
Fish velouté sauce (Recipe 53)	10 oz	300 ml
Heavy cream (36%)	10 oz	300 ml
Seasoning (salt and pepper)	1x	1x

GARNISH

Cucumbers	1 lb 5 oz	600 g
Butter	2/3 oz	20 g
Seasoning (salt and pepper)	1x	1x
Pink peppercorns, canned, drained	1 oz	30 g

MISE EN PLACE FOR SAUCE

Peel 10 1/2 oz (300 g) cucumbers for sauce, remove seeds,
and cut into small dice.

Add fish *velouté* to cucumbers; bring to a boil, and reduce.

Stir in heavy cream and reduce to desired consistency.

Purée sauce; adjust seasoning.

MISE EN PLACE FOR GARNISH

Peel 1 lb 5 oz (600 g) cucumbers for garnish and remove
seeds. Scoop out small pearl-size balls with melon baller.[a]

Sauté cucumber pearls in butter until tender and season to
taste.

MISE EN PLACE

Cut monkfish fillets into small slices. Season with lemon
juice and white pepper.

METHOD

Salt monkfish and dredge in flour.[b] Sauté quickly in clarified
butter until golden brown.

Season with Worcestershire sauce and lemon. Garnish with
chopped dill.

Put cucumber sauce into serving dish and mound fish on top.

Sprinkle with cucumber pearls and pink peppercorns.

---

[a] Melon ballers (scoops) are available in many sizes. This recipe calls for
rather small balls.

[b] The shredded fish should be floured in small amounts, and just before
sautéing. If the shredded fish is floured ahead of time, the pieces will stick
together.

344

Monkfish in Red Wine Sauce with Mushrooms and Pearl Onions

Seeteufel Matrosenart
Baudroie en matelote

YIELD: 10 SERVINGS

Shallots	2 oz	60 g
Butter	1 oz	30 g
Seasoning (salt and pepper)	1x	1x
Monkfish fillets	3 lb	1.4 kg
Melted butter	1 oz	30 g
Lemon	1/2	1/2
Red wine	13 1/2 oz	400 ml
Fish fumet (Recipe 25)	6 3/4 oz	200 ml
Cold roux, beurre manié	1 2/3 oz	50 g
Glace de poisson[a]	1 2/3 oz	50 ml
Seasoning (salt and pepper)	1x	1x
Butter	1 2/3 oz	50 g
Lemon, juice	1	1

GARNISH

Mushrooms, fresh	10 1/2 oz	300 g
Butter	2/3 oz	20 g
Pearl onions, fresh	10 1/2 oz	300 g
Vegetable bouillon (Recipe 27)	6 3/4 oz	200 ml
Sugar	1x	1x
Crayfish tails (peeled)	5 1/3 oz	150 g
Butter	2/3 oz	20 g
Seasoning (salt and pepper)	1x	1x
White bread (Pullman loaf)	5 1/3 oz	150 g

MISE EN PLACE
Chop shallots. Butter a shallow casserole pan and sprinkle with shallots.

MISE EN PLACE FOR GARNISH
Wash and trim mushrooms and cut into quarters. Sauté in butter.

Peel pearl onions and braise in vegetable stock with a pinch of sugar to glaze.

Sauté crayfish tails in butter.

Combine mushrooms, glazed onions, and crayfish tails. Season to taste. Keep warm.

Cut bread into slices and cut out 10 heart-shaped croutons. Toast croutons.

METHOD
Season monkfish, fold over if necessary, and place in prepared casserole pan. Brush fillets with melted butter to keep pieces separated.

Add lemon juice, red wine, and fish fumet.

Cover with aluminum foil, bring to a boil, and poach for about 5 minutes.

Remove fish to warm platter. Reduce fish stock.

Add *beurre manié* in pinches, bring to a boil, and boil to desired consistency. Add *glace de poisson*. Adjust seasoning.

Add cold butter in small nuggets. Do not allow the sauce to return to a boil.

Season with lemon juice.

Cover the fish with sauce. Add garnishes.

345

Monkfish in Broccoli Cream Sauce

Seeteufelmedaillons mit Broccolicremesauce
Médaillons de baudroie à la crème de brocoli

YIELD: 10 SERVINGS

Monkfish fillets	3 lb	1.4 kg
Lemon, juice	1	1
Seasoning (white pepper)	1x	1x
Salt	1x	1x
White wheat flour	1 2/3 oz	50 g
Peanut oil	2 1/2 oz	75 ml
Butter	3 1/2 oz	100 g

SAUCE

Broccoli, fresh	7 oz	200 g
Glace de poisson[a]	5 oz	150 ml
Heavy cream (36%)	10 oz	300 ml
Seasoning (salt and pepper)	1x	1x

GARNISH

Shallots	1 oz	30 g
Tomatoes	14 oz	400 g
Butter	1 oz	30 g
Seasoning (salt and pepper)	1x	1x
Almonds, sliced	1 oz	30 g
Broccoli, fresh	14 oz	400 g

---

[a] *Glace de poisson*, literally translated "fish glaze," is made by reducing fish fumet to a syrupy consistency. It can have an unpleasant ta e if the fish bones used for the fumet are not very fresh.

[a] *Glace de poisson*, literally translated "fish glaze," is made by reducing fish fumet to a syrupy consistency. It can have an unpleasant taste if the fish bones used for the fumet are not very fresh.

MISE EN PLACE FOR GARNISH

Chop shallots.

Peel tomatoes, remove seeds, and cut into small cubes.

Sauté shallots and tomatoes in butter, season, and keep warm.

Toast almonds.

Divide 14 oz (400 g) broccoli for garnish into small florets; discard any woody parts of stems; reserve tender trimmings. Blanch broccoli florets and keep warm.

MISE EN PLACE FOR SAUCE

Trim any woody stems from 7 oz (200 g) broccoli; cut florets, tender stems, and reserved trimmings from garnish into small pieces and steam until soft. Purée broccoli in food processor.

MISE EN PLACE

Trim fish fillets and cut into medallions for 10 portions. Season with lemon juice and white pepper.

METHOD

Flatten fish fillets, season with salt, dredge in flour and press lightly, and sauté in oil and butter. Keep warm.

Finish sauce: Combine *glace de poisson* and heavy cream and bring to a boil. Add puréed broccoli; reduce sauce if necessary. Season to taste.

Put sauce into flat serving dish. Place fish on top of sauce.

Arrange tomato and broccoli garnishes attractively around fish.

Sprinkle with almonds.

346

$\mathcal{M}$onkfish with Coriander Seeds

Seeteufel mit Korianderkörnern
Baudroie aux grains de coriandre

YIELD: 10 SERVINGS

Monkfish fillets	3 lb	1.4 kg
Lemon	1	1
Seasoning (white pepper)	1x	1x
Coriander seeds	1 oz	30 g
Salt	1x	1x
Olive oil	2 oz	60 ml
Coriander leaves (cilantro), fresh	1 oz	30 g
SAUCE		
Red peppers	1 lb 12 oz	800 g
Shallots	1 2/3 oz	50 g
Butter, cold	1 oz	30 g
White veal stock (Recipe 28)	6 3/4 oz	200 ml
Butter, cold	3 1/2 oz	100 g
Seasoning (salt and pepper)	1x	1x

MISE EN PLACE

Trim monkfish fillets and cut into thin slices, about 1/8-in. (3 mm) thick.

Marinate monkfish with lemon and white pepper.

Crush coriander seeds.

METHOD FOR SAUCE

Wash red peppers, remove seeds, and cut into cubes.

Peel and chop shallots.

Sauté peppers and shallots in butter, add veal stock, cover and braise until peppers are soft.

Purée peppers in food processor and strain sauce through fine mesh china cap.

Bring sauce to a boil, remove from heat, and add cold butter in small nuggets. Do not allow sauce to return to a boil.

Season to taste.

METHOD

Brush monkfish with oil, salt, and sprinkle with crushed coriander seeds.

Place on heat-proof dish and broil quickly under the salamander until just about done.

Put sauce on serving plates; place monkfish on top.

Garnish with coriander leaves.

347

*P*oached Fillets of Sole with Asparagus

Seezungenfilets Argenteuil
Filets de sole Argenteuil

YIELD: 10 SERVINGS

Shallots	2 oz	60 g
Butter	2/3 oz	20 g
Fillets of sole[a]	2 lb 14 oz	1.3 kg
Melted butter	1 oz	30 g
Seasoning (salt and pepper)	1x	1x
Lemon	1/2	1/2
Dry white wine	10 oz	300 ml
Fish fumet (Recipe 25)	10 oz	300 ml
Fish velouté sauce (Recipe 53)	6 3/4 oz	200 ml
Heavy cream (36%)	3 1/3 oz	100 ml
Seasoning (salt and pepper)	1x	1x

GARNISH

White asparagus	2 lb 3 oz	1.0 kg
Salt	1/3 oz	10 g
Puff pastry (Recipe 689)	3 1/2 oz	100 g
Egg yolk	1	1
Dill tops, fresh	10	10

MISE EN PLACE FOR GARNISH
Peel asparagus and boil in salt water until tender. Trim asparagus to 5-in. (120 mm) lengths.

Roll out puff pastry and cut out 10 half-moons (*fleurons*) or other desired shapes.[b] Mix egg yolk with small amount of water. Brush fleurons with egg yolk mixture. Bake *fleurons* until golden brown. Keep warm.

METHOD
Peel and chop shallots.

Butter shallow casserole pan and sprinkle with shallots.

Fold sole fillets; and place on top of shallots. Brush with melted butter.

Season with salt and pepper and lemon juice.

Add wine and fish fumet. Cover with aluminum foil and bring to a boil. Poach for about 8 minutes. Remove fish to warm platter.

---

[a] The sole commonly used in Switzerland is known as Dover sole in the United States. Local sole can be substituted.

[b] Instead of half-moons, the dough can be cut into diamonds, which eliminates dough trimmings.

Reduce fish stock, add *velouté*, and reduce. Stir in heavy cream and reduce to desired consistency. Season to taste and strain through fine mesh china cap.

Warm the asparagus.

Cover fish with sauce. Garnish with warm asparagus, *fleurons*, and dill.

348

*P*oached Fillets of Sole and Lobster in Champagne Sauce

Seezungenfilets in Champagner
Filets de sole au Champagne

YIELD: 10 SERVINGS

Shallots	2 oz	60 g
Butter	2/3 oz	20 g
Fillets of sole[a]	2 lb 14 oz	1.3 kg
Melted butter	1 oz	30 g
Seasoning (salt, white pepper)	1x	1x
Lemon, juice	1/2	1/2
Champagne[b]	6 3/4 oz	200 ml
Fish fumet (Recipe 25)	10 oz	300 ml
Cold roux (beurre manié)	1 2/3 oz	50 g
Heavy cream (36%)	5 oz	150 ml
Seasoning (salt and pepper)	1x	1x

Garnish

Puff pastry (Recipe 689)	3 1/2 oz	100 g
Egg yolk	1	1
Dill tops, fresh	10	10
Lobster, cooked	1 lb 10 oz	750 g
Truffle, canned, drained	1/3 oz	10 g

METHOD FOR GARNISH
Roll out puff pastry and cut 10 half-moons (*fleurons*) or other desired shapes.[c] Mix egg yolk with small amount of water. Brush *fleurons* with egg yolk mixture. Bake pastry until golden brown. Keep warm.

Break out lobster meat. Cut tail into 10 slices; cut claws into small pieces. Keep warm in small amount of champagne.

Cut truffles into 10 thin slices. Cover, to prevent drying out.

---

[a] The sole commonly used in Switzerland is known as Dover sole in the United States Because this dish includes lobster and truffles, the best quality fish seems called for.

[b] Other sparkling wine can be substituted. The sparkling wine should be dry (brut).

[c] Instead of half-moons, the dough can be cut into diamonds, which eliminates dough trimmings.

METHOD

Peel and chop shallots. Butter suitable shallow casserole pan and sprinkle with shallots.

Fold fish fillets and place on top of shallots. Brush with butter. Season with salt, white pepper, and lemon juice.

Add champagne and fish fumet. Cover with aluminum foil, bring to a boil, and poach for 8 minutes.

Remove fish to warm platter, cover, and keep warm.

Reduce fish stock, add *beurre manié* in pinches, and reduce.

Stir in heavy cream and reduce to desired consistency.

Season to taste and strain sauce through fine mesh china cap.

Cover fish with sauce.

Garnish with lobster medallions and claw meat, truffle slices, *fleurons*, and dill.

349

$\mathcal{F}$**ried Whole Sole with Tarragon Butter**

Seezunge Colbert
Sole Colbert

YIELD: 10 SERVINGS

Sole,[a] whole, 10 fish	6 lb 10 oz	3.0 kg
Seasoning (salt, white pepper)	1x	1x
Lemons	1 1/2	1 1/2
Eggs	3	3
White wheat flour	2 2/3 oz	75 g
Mie de pain[b]	8 3/4 oz	250 g
Oil for frying (10% oil loss)	8 1/2 oz	250 ml

TARRAGON BUTTER

Butter	7 oz	200 g
Tarragon, fresh	2/3 oz	20 g
Glace de viande[c]	1/3 oz	10 g
Lemon, juice	1	1
Seasoning (salt and pepper)	1x	1x

GARNISH

Lemons, quartered	2 1/2	2 1/2
Parsley	1 2/3 oz	50 g

METHOD FOR TARRAGON BUTTER

Cream butter. Wash and chop tarragon; melt *glace de viande*.

Combine creamed butter with tarragon and *glace de viande*.

Season with lemon juice, salt and pepper. Mix thoroughly.

Spread butter mixture onto a piece of parchment paper, shape butter into a roll about 1-in. (25 mm) thick. Roll up and refrigerate.

Slice butter into 20 slices, keep refrigerated.

METHOD

Remove skin from sole; remove head. Place fish on table, top side[a] up. Make incision along the center. Carefully fold back the top fillet to create an open pocket. Season with salt, white pepper, and lemon juice.

Break eggs and mix with 2 tbsp water. Dredge fish in flour, then in eggs. Then dredge in *mie de pain*. Press *mie de pain* onto fish; be sure to keep the pocket open.

Deep-fry at 170°F (75°C) until golden brown.

Place fish on hot plates and remove center bone without breaking fish.

At the moment of service, put 2 tarragon butter slices into each pocket. Garnish with lemon quarters and parsley.

---

[a] The sole commonly used in Switzerland is known as Dover sole in the United States Local sole can be substituted.

[b] *Mie de pain* are fresh bread crumbs, made from white Pullman loaves.

[c] *Glace de viande*, literally translated "meat glaze," is made by reducing meat stock to a syrupy consistency.

---

[a] The top side of the fish is the plumper side which had the eyes on it, before the head was removed.

350

*P*oached Fillets of Sole with Mussels and Shrimp

Seezungenfilets Marguery
Filets de sole Marguery

YIELD: 10 SERVINGS

Shallots	2 oz	60 g
Butter	1 oz	30 g
Fillets of sole[a]	2 lb 14 oz	1.3 kg
Melted butter	1 oz	30 g
Mussels, fresh	1 lb 12 oz	800 g
Heavy cream (36%)	3 1/3 oz	100 ml
Lemon, juice	1/2	1/2
Seasoning (salt and pepper)	1x	1x
Dry white wine	10 oz	300 ml
Fish fumet (Recipe 25)	10 oz	300 ml
Shrimp, cooked	8 3/4 oz	250 g
Fish velouté sauce (Recipe 53)	6 3/4 oz	200 ml
Hollandaise sauce (Recipe 60)	3 1/3 oz	100 ml
Seasoning (salt and pepper)	1x	1x

GARNISH

Puff pastry (Recipe 689)	3 1/2 oz	100 g
Egg yolk	1	1

METHOD FOR GARNISH

Roll out puff pastry and cut out 10 half-moons (*fleurons*) or other desired shapes.[b]

Mix egg yolk with small amount of water. Brush puff pastry with egg yolk mixture.

Bake until golden brown. Keep warm.

MISE EN PLACE

Chop shallots.

Butter a fish poacher and sprinkle with shallots.

Fold sole fillets and place on top of shallots. Brush with melted butter.

Scrape mussels, steam, and reserve mussels stock. Remove mussels from shells, clean, and keep warm in a little stock.

Whip cream to a soft foam.

METHOD

Season fish with lemon juice, salt and pepper.

Add wine and fish fumet to poaching pan. Cover with aluminum foil. Bring to a boil and poach for about 8 minutes.

Remove fish to warm ovenproof platter.

Add shrimp to fish stock and bring to a boil. Remove from heat, add in mussels, just long enough to warm them. Remove shrimp and mussels from stock and keep warm.

Add reserved mussels stock to the fish stock. Bring to a boil and reduce.

Add *velouté* and reduce to desired consistency.

Strain through fine mesh china cap.

Fold Hollandaise sauce and lightly whipped cream into sauce. Adjust seasoning.

Place shrimp and mussels on platter around fish; cover with sauce.

Glaze (brown) under the salamander.

Garnish with fleurons.

351

*F*illets of Sole Sautéed with Artichokes and Potatoes

Seezungenstreifen Murat
Goujons[a] de sole Murat

YIELD: 10 SERVINGS

Potatoes	2 lb 3 oz	1.0 kg
Artichoke bottoms, large, cooked	5	5
Brown veal stock, thickened (Recipe 23)	6 3/4 oz	200 ml
Peanut oil for vegetables	1 2/3 oz	50 ml
Seasoning (salt and pepper)	1x	1x
Fillets of sole[b]	2 lb 14 oz	1.3 kg
Lemon, juice	1	1
Seasoning (white pepper)	1x	1x
White wheat flour	2 2/3 oz	75 g
Peanut oil for fish	1 2/3 oz	50 ml
Salt	1x	1x
Butter	2 1/2 oz	70 g
Worcestershire sauce	1 tbsp	5 ml

---

[a] The sole commonly used in Switzerland is known as Dover sole in the United States. Local sole can be substituted.

[b] Instead of half-moons, the dough can be cut into diamonds, which eliminates dough trimmings.

[a] The name *goujons* refers to small fish, fried whole. The fish strips should resemble small fish. Large fillets should be cut on a bias.

[b] The sole commonly used in Switzerland is known as Dover sole in the United States. Local sole can be substituted.

Lemon, juice	1/2	1/2
Kitchen herbs,[a] fresh, chopped	1 oz	30 g

MISE EN PLACE

Peel potatoes. Using a melon baller, scoop out round balls about 1/2 in. (12 mm) in diameter. Blanch potato balls, drain, and let cool.

Quarter artichoke bottoms. If bottoms are large, cut into eighths.

Bring veal stock to a boil.

METHOD

Sauté potato balls in oil until cooked and brown. Add artichoke pieces and sauté together until they are heated. Season to taste.

Cut sole into small, finger-size slivers (goujons). Season with lemon juice and white pepper.

Roll fish pieces in flour in the palms of your hands. Shake off excess flour.

Sauté fish quickly in hot oil. Be sure pieces stay separated.

Carefully mix fish with potato and artichoke mixture. Be sure fish pieces do not break. Salt to taste.

Put veal stock in bottom of serving dish; heap fish and vegetables on top.

Heat butter until brown; add Worcestershire sauce, lemon juice, and chopped herbs.[b] Pour hot butter mixture over fish.

352

Poached Turbot in Red Wine Sauce with Sesame Seeds

Steinbuttfilets mit Sesam
Filets de turbot aux grains de sésame

YIELD: 10 SERVINGS

Turbot[c] fillets	2 lb 14 oz	1.3 kg
Shallots	2 oz	60 g
Butter	2/3 oz	20 g
Sesame seeds	1 2/3 oz	50 g
Seasoning (salt and pepper)	1x	1x
Melted butter	1 oz	30 g

Lemon, juice	1/2	1/2
Red wine	13 1/2 oz	400 ml
Fish fumet (Recipe 25)	6 3/4 oz	200 ml
Cold roux (beurre manié)	1 2/3 oz	50 g
Glace de poisson[a]	1 pt 1 oz	500 ml
Lemon, juice	1	1
Butter, cold	3 1/2 oz	100 g
Chervil leaves, fresh	2/3 oz	20 g

MISE EN PLACE

Cut turbot fillets into 10 portions.

Chop shallots. Butter suitable shallow casserole pan and sprinkle with shallots.

Toast sesame seeds under the salamander until golden brown.

METHOD

Season turbot and place on top of shallots.

Brush with butter and sprinkle with lemon juice.

Add red wine and fish fumet. Cover with aluminum foil; bring to a boil and poach for about 10 minutes, until just cooked.

Remove fish to warm platter, cover, and keep warm.

Reduce fish stock. Thicken with *beurre manié* and boil until the desired consistency is reached.

Strain sauce through fine mesh china cap. Add *glace de poisson*.

Bring to a boil. Season with lemon juice.

Whip in cold butter in small nuggets; do not allow the sauce to return to a boil.

Cover fish with sauce; sprinkle with sesame seeds.

Garnish with chervil leaves.

---

[a] The original recipe does not specify the composition of the herb mixture. A mixture of parsley, tarragon, dill, and chervil would be good in this recipe.

[b] The butter will foam when the liquids and herbs are added. Be sure the pan is large enough.

[c] Turbot is a large flat fish from the North Sea or the Eastern part of the Atlantic. Halibut can be substituted, although the texture and flavor may be inferior. Pacific turbot is not related.

---

[a] *Glace de poisson*, literally translated "fish glaze," is made by reducing fish fumet to a syrupy consistency. It can have an unpleasant taste if the fish bones used for the fumet are not very fresh.

353

Poached Turbot in Saffron Cream Sauce

Steinbutt mit Safranfäden
Turbot aux pistils de safran

YIELD: 10 SERVINGS

Turbot[a] fillets	2 lb 14 oz	1.3 kg
Shallots	2 oz	60 g
Butter	1 2/3 oz	50 g
Leeks, green leaves only	5 1/3 oz	150 g
Knob celery (celeriac)	3 1/2 oz	100 g
Carrots	5 1/3 oz	150 g
Tomatoes	10 1/2 oz	300 g
Butter	1 oz	30 g
Seasoning (salt and pepper)	1x	1x
Melted butter	2/3 oz	20 g
Lemon, juice	1/2	1/2
Dry white wine	10 oz	300 ml
Fish fumet	10 oz	300 ml
Cold roux (beurre manié)	1 2/3 oz	50 g
Heavy cream (36%)	5 oz	150 ml
Seasoning	1x	1x
Saffron threads	1x	1x

MISE EN PLACE
Cut fish fillets into 10 portions.

Chop shallots. Butter a shallow casserole pan and sprinkle with the shallots.

Wash and trim leeks; be sure sand is cleaned from layers. Cut into fine strips (*julienne*).

Trim knob celery and carrots and cut into fine strips (*julienne*).

Braise or steam leeks, knob celery, and carrots until tender, but not soft.

Keep vegetables warm.

Peel tomatoes, remove seeds, and cut into small dice. Smother tomatoes in butter. Keep warm; reserve for garnish.

METHOD
Season fish fillets and place them on top of shallots.

Brush with some melted butter and sprinkle with lemon juice.

Add white wine and fish fumet. Cover with aluminum foil, bring to a boil, and poach fish for about 10 minutes until just cooked.

Remove fish. Place on serving platter, atop vegetables *julienne*, and keep warm.

Reduce fish stock. Thicken with *beurre manié*, and reduce again.

Add heavy cream and boil again until the desired consistency is reached.

Strain through fine mesh china cap. Adjust seasoning.

Add saffron[a] to sauce. Pour over fish. Garnish with tomatoes.

354

Steamed Turbot in Carrot Cream Sauce

Steinbuttschnitzel mit Karottencreme
Aiguillettes de turbot à la crème de carottes

YIELD: 10 SERVINGS

Turbot[b] fillets	2 lb 14 oz	1.3 kg
Butter	1 oz	30 g
Seasoning (salt and pepper)	1x	1x
Lemon	1/2	1/2
SAUCE		
Carrots	1 lb 2 oz	500 g
Butter	1 oz	30 g
Shallots	1 1/3 oz	40 g
White wine, Sautérnes[c]	5 oz	150 ml
Fish stock (Recipe 24)	6 3/4 oz	200 ml
Heavy cream (36%)	6 3/4 oz	200 ml
Seasoning (salt and pepper)	1x	1x
Lemon, juice	1	1
GARNISH		
Baby carrots	1 lb 2 oz	500 g
Spinach, fresh	7 oz	200 g
Butter	2/3 oz	20 g
Lemon, juice	1	1
Seasoning (salt and pepper)	1x	1x

---

[a] Turbot is a large flat fish from the North Sea or the Eastern part of the Atlantic. Halibut can be substituted, although the texture and flavor may be inferior. Pacific turbot is not related.

[a] Saffron can be added along with the fish fumet instead.

[b] Turbot is a large flat fish from the North Sea or the Eastern part of the Atlantic. Halibut can be substituted, although the texture and flavor may be inferior. Pacific turbot is not related.

[c] Sautérnes is a sweet wine from France. Another sweet white wine can be substituted.

METHOD FOR SAUCE
Peel carrots and cut into small cubes.

Braise carrots with butter, shallots, 3 1/3 oz (100 ml) Sautérnes, and fish stock.

Purée carrots when tender.

Stir heavy cream and remaining sautérnes into carrot puree. Bring to a boil and season with lemon juice, salt and pepper.

METHOD FOR GARNISH
Trim and peel baby carrots, but leave some green stem. Braise or steam. Keep warm.

Trim, wash, and blanch spinach. Sauté in butter and season to taste. Keep warm.

METHOD FOR TURBOT
Cut turbot into 20 slices.

Butter steamer basket, position fish slices side by side in basket, brush with butter. Steam fish until done.

Pour carrot sauce onto bottom of serving dish; place fish on top.

Garnish with bouquets of baby carrots and spinach.

355

*P*oached St. Peter's Fish with Vodka Cream Sauce
St. Petersfisch Moskauer Art
Filets de saint-pierre moscovite

YIELD: 10 SERVINGS

St. Peter's Fish,[a] whole, gutted	8 lb 13 oz	4.0 kg
Shallots	2 oz	60 g
Butter	1 oz	30 g
Seasoning (salt and pepper)	1x	1x
Melted butter	1 oz	30 g
Lemon, juice	1/2	1/2
Dry white wine	10 oz	300 ml
Fish fumet (Recipe 25)	10 oz	300 ml
Cold roux (beurre manié)	1 2/3 oz	50 g
Heavy cream (36%)	5 oz	150 ml
Vodka	2 oz	60 ml
Osetra caviar	1 2/3 oz	50 g
Dill tops, fresh	10	10

[a] St. Peter's fish, *Tilapia Galilee*, is an Israeli fish found in the Sea of Galilee. Also known as John Dory, tilapia, or in French as *Saint-Pierre*. It is unattractive in appearance, but delicious in taste. There are many species of *tilapia*, found in many locations around the world, mostly in tropical waters. It is a firm-textured, lean, mild-tasting, saltwater and freshwater fish.

GARNISH

Puff pastry (Recipe 689)	3 1/2 oz	100 g
Egg yolk	1	1

METHOD FOR GARNISH
Roll out puff pastry and cut out 10 half-moons (*fleurons*) or other desired shapes.[a]

Mix egg yolk with small amount of water. Brush puff pastry with egg yolk mixture.

Bake until golden brown. Keep warm.

MISE EN PLACE
Bone fish. Cut fillets into 10 portions.

Chop shallots. Butter a shallow casserole pan and sprinkle with the shallots.

METHOD
Season fish fillets and place them on top of shallots.

Brush with butter and sprinkle with lemon juice.

Add wine and fish fumet. Cover with aluminum foil, bring to a boil, and poach for about 8 minutes. Remove fish to warm platter.

Reduce fish stock. Thicken with *beurre manié* and reduce again.

Stir in heavy cream and boil again until the desired consistency is reached.

Strain through fine mesh china cap. Adjust seasoning.

Add vodka and caviar to sauce at the moment of service.

Cover fish with sauce and garnish with *fleurons* and dill.

[a] Instead of half-moons, the dough can be cut into diamonds, which eliminates dough trimmings.

356

Poached Perch Fillets with Crayfish Sauce

Zanderfilets Joinville
Filets de sandre joinville

YIELD: 10 SERVINGS

Shallots	2 oz	60 g
Butter	1 oz	30 g
Perch fillets	2 lb 14 oz	1.3 kg
Seasoning (salt and pepper)	1x	1x
Melted butter	1 oz	30 g
Lemon	1/2	1/2
Dry white wine	10 oz	300 ml
Fish fumet	10 oz	300 ml
Cold roux (beurre manié)	1 2/3 oz	50 g
Heavy cream (36%)	5 oz	150 ml
Lobster butter[a] (Recipe 11)	1 oz	30 g

GARNISH

Live crayfish	2 lb 3 oz	1.0 kg
Salt	1/3 oz	10 g
Mushrooms, fresh	10 1/2 oz	300 g
Butter	1 oz	30 g
Seasoning (salt and pepper)	1x	1x
Truffle, canned, drained	1/3 oz	10 g
Tarragon, fresh, chopped	2/3 oz	20 g

MISE EN PLACE
Chop shallots. Butter shallow casserole pan and sprinkle with shallots.

METHOD FOR GARNISH
Boil crayfish in salted water. Break out tails and keep warm. Save shells for future use.[a]

Cut mushrooms into quarters and braise in butter. Season to taste.

Cut truffles into 10 slices.

METHOD
Season perch fillets and place them on top of shallots. Brush with melted butter and sprinkle with lemon juice.

Add white wine and fish fumet. Cover with aluminum foil, bring to a boil, and poach about 8 minutes until just cooked. Remove fish to warm platter.

Reduce fish stock. Thicken with *beurre manié* and reduce again.

Stir in cream and boil again until the desired consistency is reached.

Strain through fine mesh china cap; adjust seasoning.

Whip lobster butter into sauce.

Cover fish with sauce. Garnish with bouquets of crayfish tails, mushrooms, and chopped tarragon.

357

Poached Perch Fillets on Spinach with Red Wine Sauce

Zanderfilets in Rotwein pochiert, auf Blattspinat
Filets de sandre pochés au vin rouge sur feuilles d'épinards

YIELD: 10 SERVINGS

Shallots	2 oz	60 g
Butter	1 oz	30 g
Perch fillets	2 lb 14 oz	1.3 kg
Seasoning (salt and pepper)	1x	1x
Melted butter	2/3 oz	20 g
Lemon, juice	1/2	1/2
Red wine	13 1/2 oz	400 ml
Fish fumet	6 3/4 oz	200 ml
Cold roux (beurre manié)	1 2/3 oz	50 g
Glace de poisson[a]	1 2/3 oz	50 ml
Butter, cold	1 2/3 oz	50 g
Seasoning (salt and pepper)	1x	1x
Lemon	1/2	1/2

GARNISH

Spinach, fresh	3 lb 5 oz	1.5 kg
Shallots	1 2/3 oz	50 g
Butter	2/3 oz	20 g
Seasoning (salt and pepper)	1x	1x

MISE EN PLACE
Chop 2 oz (60 g) shallots.

Butter a shallow casserole pan and sprinkle with shallots.

Season perch fillets and place them on top of shallots.

METHOD FOR GARNISH
Wash and blanch spinach.

Chop 1 2/3 oz (50 g) shallots and sauté in butter. Add the spinach and season to taste.

---

[a] The crayfish shells can be saved and used to make crayfish butter by the same method as for Lobster Butter (Recipe 11). They can also be used for crayfish bisque.

[a] *Glace de poisson*, literally translated "fish glaze," is made by reducing fish fumet to a syrupy consistency. It can have an unpleasant taste if the fish bones used for the fumet are not very fresh.

METHOD

Brush perch fillets with melted butter and sprinkle with lemon juice.

Add red wine and fish fumet. Cover with aluminum foil, bring to a boil, and poach for about 8 minutes. Remove fish to warm platter.

Reduce fish stock. Thicken with *beurre manié* and reduce again.

Add *glace de poisson* and boil again until the desired consistency is reached.

Strain through fine wire china cap. Adjust seasoning.

Whip in cold butter in small nuggets. Do not allow the sauce to return to a boil.

Season with salt and pepper and lemon juice.

Serve fish on a bed of spinach, cover with sauce, and serve some sauce on the side.

Shellfish Dishes

358

Crayfish in Bordelaise Cream Sauce
Flusskrebse Bordeleser Art
Ecrevisse bordelaise

YIELD: 10 SERVINGS

Crayfish, live	8 lb 13 oz	4.0 kg
Matignon (Recipe 13)	8 3/4 oz	250 g
Butter	1 2/3 oz	50 g
Seasoning (salt, cayenne)	1x	1x
Seasoning (white pepper)	1x	1x
Cognac	1 2/3 oz	50 ml
Dry white wine	6 3/4 oz	200 ml
Fish stock (Recipe 24)	3 1/3 oz	100 ml
Fish velouté sauce (Recipe 53)	3 1/3 oz	100 ml
Heavy cream (36%)	3 1/3 oz	100 ml
Lobster butter/crayfish butter[a] (Recipe 11)	1 2/3 oz	50 g
Parsley, chopped	2/3 oz	20 g

MISE EN PLACE

Plunge crayfish head first into large amount of boiling water to kill them quickly. Boil for about 3 minutes.

Remove intestine by twisting the center scale of the tail and gently pulling out the dark intestinal vein.

METHOD

Sauté *matignon* in butter.

Add prepared crayfish; season with salt, cayenne, and white pepper.

Add Cognac and ignite. When flames have stopped, add wine and fish stock.

Bring to a boil and boil for about 5 minutes.

Remove crayfish from stock. Remove the meat from tails and claws.

Reduce crayfish stock; add *velouté* and heavy cream.

Boil until a saucelike consistency is reached. Strain through fine mesh china cap.

Whip lobster butter into hot sauce.

Add crayfish to sauce; heat gently. Do not allow sauce to return to a boil.

Serve sprinkled with parsley.

[a] Crayfish butter can be used in this recipe instead of lobster butter. It is made the same way, but uses crayfish shells instead of lobster shells.

359

Crayfish in Cream Sauce

Flusskrebse Matrosenart
Ecrevisse marinière

YIELD: 10 SERVINGS

Crayfish, live	8 lb 13 oz	4.0 kg
Shallots	1 2/3 oz	50 g
Butter	1 2/3 oz	50 g
Bay leaf	1	1
Thyme twig, fresh	1	1
Dry white wine	6 3/4 oz	200 ml
Fish stock (Recipe 24)	1 qt 19 oz	1.5 L
Heavy cream (36%)	6 3/4 oz	200 ml
Seasoning (salt and pepper)	1x	1x
Lemon, juice	1	1
Parsley, chopped	2/3 oz	20 g

MISE EN PLACE

Plunge crayfish head first into large amount of boiling water to kill them quickly. Boil for about 3 minutes.

Remove intestine by twisting the center scale of the tail and gently pulling out the dark intestinal vein.

Peel and chop shallots.

METHOD

Sauté shallots in butter.

Add prepared crayfish. Add bay leaf, thyme, and white wine. Bring to a boil.

Add fish stock and boil for 5 minutes.

Remove crayfish from stock. Remove meat from tails and claws.[a]

Reduce crayfish stock.[b] Add heavy cream.

Boil until the desired consistency is reached. Strain through fine mesh china cap.

Season with salt, pepper and lemon juice.

Add crayfish to sauce. Sprinkle with parsley.

---

[a] Save shells and carcasses to make Crayfish Butter (Recipe 11) or Crayfish Soup (Recipe 128).

[b] This recipe does not list any thickening agents so the stock should be well reduced before the heavy cream is added.

360

Lobster in Herb, Wine, and Tomato Sauce

Hummer amerikanische Art
Homard américaine

YIELD: 10 SERVINGS

Lobsters, live	11 lb	5.0 kg
Shallots	5 1/3 oz	150 g
Garlic clove, peeled	1	1
Tomatoes	1 lb 5 oz	600 g
Seasoning (salt and pepper)	1x	1x
Peanut oil	1 2/3 oz	50 ml
Thyme sprig, fresh	1	5 g
Parsley stems, fresh	3/4 oz	25 g
Cognac (or any brandy)	1 2/3 oz	50 ml
Dry white wine	8 1/2 oz	250 ml
Fish fumet (Recipe 25)	1 pt 1 oz	500 ml
Glace de viande[a]	3 1/2 oz	100 g
Cayenne	1x	1x
Butter, cold	5 1/3 oz	150 g

MISE EN PLACE

Kill lobsters by plunging them, head first, into large amount of boiling water. Remove lobsters before they are cooked.

Twist off tails. Cut tails, still in shells, into slices about 1–in. (25 mm) thick.

Crack claws, but leave meat in shells.

Split the bodies. Remove the coral and tomalley (liver), mash with fork, and set aside for sauce. Remove and discard the sac near the top of the head.

Chop shallots. Crush garlic.

Peel tomatoes, halve, remove seeds, and cut into medium-size dice.

METHOD

Season lobster (tail slices, claws, and bodies) and sauté in oil over high heat.

Add shallots, garlic, thyme, and parsley. Lower the heat and smother the vegetables until cooked.

Add Cognac and ignite. When flames have stopped, add white wine, fish fumet, and *glace de viande*. Reduce stock.

Add tomatoes, season with cayenne, cover, and braise slowly for 10 minutes.

---

[a] *Glace de viande*, literally translated "meat glaze", is made by reducing meat stock to a syrupy consistency.

Remove lobster from stock. Remove lobster meat from shells. Discard shells.

Remove thyme sprig and parsley stems from stock and reduce stock to desired consistency.

Add mashed coral and tomalley to sauce, stirring vigorously with wire whisk.

Add cold butter in small nuggets, stirring vigorously. Do not allow the sauce to return to a boil.

Serve lobster tail meat covered with sauce. Garnish with lobster claw meat.

361

Shelled Lobster in Chervil and Tarragon Sauce

Hummerblankett mit Kerbel und Estragon
Blanquette de homard au cerfeuil et à l'estragon

YIELD: 10 SERVINGS

Lobsters, live	10 lb	4.5 kg
Stock (court bouillon)[a]	5 qts 9 oz	5.0 L
Carrots	8 3/4 oz	250 g
Celery[b]	10 1/2 oz	300 g
Shallots	7 oz	200 g
Tarragon, fresh	2/3 oz	20 g
Chervil, fresh	2/3 oz	20 g
Butter	3 1/2 oz	100 g
Cognac (or any brandy)	3 1/3 oz	100 ml
Dry vermouth[c]	5 oz	150 ml
Fish fumet (Recipe 25)	12 oz	350 ml
Heavy cream (36%)	1 pt 11 oz	800 ml
Butter, cold	3 1/2 oz	100 g
Seasoning (salt, cayenne)	1x	1x

GARNISH
Puff pastry (Recipe 689)	3 1/2 oz	100 g
Egg yolk	1	1

MISE EN PLACE FOR GARNISH

Roll out puff pastry and cut into 10 half-moons (*fleurons*) or other desired shapes.

Mix egg yolk with small amount of water, brush mixture on *fleurons*, and bake until golden brown.[a]

MISE EN PLACE

Plunge lobsters head first into boiling stock (court bouillon) and poach for 10 minutes.

Shell lobster tails and claws. Reserve shells and carcasses. Reserve some legs for garnish. Cut lobster meat into bite-size pieces.

Peel and trim carrots and celery and cut into medium-size dice.

Chop shallots.

Wash and chop tarragon and chervil.

METHOD

Sauté carrots, celery, and shallots in butter.

Add lobster shells and carcasses and smother for 5 minutes.

Add Cognac and ignite. When flames have stopped, add vermouth and fish fumet. Reduce to about half.

Add heavy cream and boil for 15 minutes.

Remove lobster shells and carcasses and strain sauce through fine mesh china cap.

Reduce sauce further to desired consistency.

Heat lobster meat in sauce and place meat in deep serving dish.

Whip cold butter into sauce in small nuggets.

Season sauce with salt and cayenne. Add chopped herbs.

Serve sauce over lobster pieces. Garnish with *fleurons* and reserved lobster legs.

---

[a] Court bouillon is a poaching liquid consisting of water, spices, vinegar, and vegetables, boiled about 20 minutes.

[b] The celery specified in the original recipe is stalk celery, *Stangensellerie* in German. This was further specified as the expensive form, *gebleicht*, which is grown partially underground, so the stalks stay white and keep the dish white.

[c] The original recipe specifies Noilly Prat, but any brand of dry vermouth can be used. Vermouth comes in dry and sweet varieties; use only dry in this recipe.

[a] Instead of half-moons, the dough can be cut into diamonds, which eliminates dough trimmings.

362

Lobster Fricassee with Vermouth

Hummerfrikasse mit Noilly Prat
Fricassée de homard au Noilly Prat

YIELD: 10 SERVINGS

Lobsters, live	10 lb	4.5 kg
Butter, cold	2 2/3 oz	75 g
Shallots	5 1/3 oz	150 g
Seasoning (salt, cayenne)	1x	1x
Olive oil	2 3/4 oz	80 ml
Butter	2 1/2 oz	70 g
Cognac (or any brandy)	3 1/3 oz	100 ml
Dry vermouth[a]	6 3/4 oz	200 ml
Fish fumet (Recipe 25)	8 1/2 oz	250 ml
Heavy cream (36%)	1 pt 1 oz	500 ml
Lemon juice	2/3 oz	20 ml

MISE EN PLACE

Kill lobsters by plunging them first into boiling water. Remove from water before it is cooked.

Remove lobster from shells[b] and cut into pieces.

Blend lobster coral and tomalley (liver) with cold butter. Strain/pass through a fine wire sieve.

Peel and chop shallots.

METHOD

Season lobster pieces and sauté in olive oil.

Drain off oil and replace it with butter.

Add shallots and sauté together with lobster pieces.

Add Cognac and ignite. When flames have stopped, add vermouth. Reduce to about half.

Remove lobster pieces.

Add fish fumet and heavy cream to pan and reduce to desired consistency.

Strain through a fine mesh china cap. Season with lemon juice.

Heat lobster pieces in sauce. When hot, place in serving dish.

Whip coral/tomalley butter into hot sauce, but do not allow to boil.

Pour sauce over lobster pieces.

---

[a] The original recipe specifies Noilly Prat, but any brand of dry vermouth can be used. Vermouth comes in dry and sweet varieties; use only dry in this recipe.

[b] Shells can be saved to make Lobster Butter (Recipe 11) or Crayfish Soup (Recipe 128).

363

Boiled Lobster

Hummer im Sud
Homard au court-bouillon

YIELD: 10 SERVINGS

Water	5 qts 9 oz	5.0 L
Matignon (Recipe 13)	1 lb 2 oz	500 g
Parsley stems, fresh	1 oz	30 g
Bay leaf	1	1
White peppercorns	1/3 oz	10 g
Caraway seeds	1/8 oz	3 1/2 g
Salt	2 2/3 oz	75 g
Dry white wine	1 pt 11 oz	800 ml
White wine vinegar	8 1/2 oz	250 ml
Lobsters, live	10 lb	4.5 kg

MISE EN PLACE

Make court bouillon by combining water with *matignon* and next five ingredients. Boil for 10 minutes. Add white wine and vinegar and bring to a boil again.

METHOD

Plunge lobsters head first into boiling stock (court bouillon) and bring to a boil.

Poach lobsters for 12 minutes at 170°F (75°C).

Serve lobsters in *poissonniere*,[a] with some vegetables and lobster stock.

---

[a] A *poissonniere* is a fish kettle. In fine restaurant service, the kettle is brought to the table. The lobster is presented and then shelled in front of the guests.

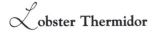

`364`

Lobster Thermidor

Hummer Thermidor
Homard thermidor

YIELD: 10 SERVINGS

Lobsters, live	11 lb	5.0 kg
Stock (court bouillon)[a]	4 qts 7 oz	4.0 L
Dry white wine	3 1/3 oz	100 ml
Mustard, powder	1 2/3 oz	50 g
Peanut oil	1 2/3 oz	50 ml
Butter	1 2/3 oz	50 g
Black truffles, sliced	1 2/3 oz	50 g

SAUCE

Fish sauce for glazing (Recipe 52)	1 pt 1 oz	500 ml
Dijon mustard	3/4 oz	25 g

MISE EN PLACE

Boil lobsters in court bouillon.

Make a paste with white wine and mustard powder.

METHOD

Split lobster. Roast halves lightly in oil and butter.

Remove meat from tails and slice diagonally.

Crack claws, set aside, and keep warm.

Remove stomachs from carcasses and discard stomachs.

Brush carcasses with wine/mustard paste.

Place lobster slices, alternating with truffle slices, in carcasses.

Add Dijon mustard to fish sauce.

Cover lobster slices with fish sauce, heat, and glaze in hot oven or under the salamander.

Garnish with reserved warm lobster claws.

---

[a] Court bouillon is a poaching liquid consisting of water, spices, vinegar, and vegetables, boiled about 20 minutes.

`365`

Ragout of Spiny Lobsters with Cress Purée

Langusteragout mit Kressecreme
Ragoût de Langouste à la crème de cresson

YIELD: 10 SERVINGS

Spiny lobster tails[a]	5 lb	2.25 kg
Mushrooms, fresh	10 1/2 oz	300 g
Shallots	1 2/3 oz	50 g
Butter	1 2/3 oz	50 g
Cognac (or any brandy)	3 1/3 oz	100 ml
Dry white wine	6 3/4 oz	200 ml
Fish stock (Recipe 24)	6 3/4 oz	200 ml
Heavy cream (36%)	5 oz	150 ml
Lobster butter, cold (Recipe 11)	3 1/2 oz	100 g
Tarragon, fresh, chopped	1/3 oz	10 g
Seasoning (salt and pepper)	1x	1x

CRESS PURÉE

Watercress[b]	1 lb 2 oz	500 g
Butter	3/4 oz	25 g
Heavy cream (36%)	5 oz	150 ml
Seasoning (salt and pepper)	1x	1x

GARNISH

Tarragon leaves, fresh	1/2 oz	15 g

MISE EN PLACE FOR CRESS PURÉE

Blanch watercress; drain, chill, and squeeze out excess moisture. Purée.

MISE EN PLACE

Cut lobster tails, still in shell, into 1–in. (25 mm) slices.

Trim and wash mushrooms (reserve trimmings) and cut into quarters. Sauté mushrooms in half the butter and keep warm.

Chop shallots.

METHOD

Smother lobster pieces in remaining half of the butter; add reserved mushroom trimmings and chopped shallots.

Add Cognac and ignite. When flames stop, add white wine, fish stock, and heavy cream. Steep/poach lobster for a few minutes.

(continued on next page)

---

[a] Spiny lobster tails are often marketed as frozen rock lobster tails.

[b] The original recipe calls for *Brunnenkresse*, which is a little spicier in flavor than watercress. Watercress can be substituted. The flavor of watercress varies. Sometimes it has a very pungent taste. Cress can be blended with spinach if a milder taste is desired.

(continued from preceding page)

Remove lobster pieces. Remove meat from shells and keep warm.

Strain sauce through fine mesh china cap.

Reduce sauce, if necessary, and whip in cold lobster butter in small nuggets.

Add chopped tarragon. Season to taste.

Finish cress puree: Heat watercress purée in butter. Heat heavy cream and add to watercress. Season to taste. Place purée in centers of serving plates.

Place bouquets of lobster and mushrooms around the watercress, cover with sauce, and garnish with tarragon leaves.

NOTE: The same recipe can be made with Maine or Scandinavian lobster.

366

Grilled Scallops with Pistachio Butter

Grillierte Jakobsmuscheln
Coquilles Saint-Jacques grillées

YIELD: 10 SERVINGS

Scallops, shucked[a]	3 lb	1.4 kg
Seasoning (salt and pepper)	1x	1x
Olive oil, cold pressed	1 2/3 oz	50 ml
Dill tops, fresh	10	10

PISTACHIO BUTTER

Butter	7 oz	200 g
Pistachio nuts, shelled, finely chopped	1 2/3 oz	50 g
Pernod[b]	2/3 oz	20 ml
Seasoning (salt, cayenne)	1x	1x

MISE EN PLACE FOR PISTACHIO BUTTER
Cream butter with finely chopped pistachio nuts, Pernod, and seasoning.

Dress small rosettes on parchment paper[c] with a pastry bag and refrigerate.

METHOD
Season scallops and brush with oil.

Grill scallops. Give them a half turn during the grilling process to create an attractive grid pattern.

Serve with a rosette of pistachio butter. Garnish with dill.

---

[a] The scallops should be large sea scallops.

[b] Pernod is an anise-flavored liqueur.

[c] The butter can also be shaped into a roll and cut into small slices when cold. Rosette shapes aren't necessary since the butter should melt anyway.

367

Scallops au Gratin (Coquilles St. Jacques)

Jakobsmuscheln Pariser Art
Coquilles Saint-Jacques parisienne

YIELD: 10 SERVINGS

Fish stock (Recipe 24)	1 qt 2 oz	1.0 L
Dry white wine	1 pt 1 oz	500 ml
Shallots, sliced	10 1/2 oz	300 g
Parsley stems, fresh	1 2/3 oz	50 g
Knob celery (celeriac), sliced	3 1/2 oz	100 g
Bay leaf	1	1
Mushrooms, fresh	1 lb 7 oz	650 g
Scallops, shucked[a]	3 lb 5 oz	1.5 kg
Butter	1 1/3 oz	40 g
White wheat flour	1 oz	30 g
Heavy cream (36%)	6 3/4 oz	200 ml
Egg yolks	2	2
Lemon	1	1
Seasoning (salt and pepper)	1x	1x
Gruyere cheese, grated	3 1/2 oz	100 g

MISE EN PLACE
Combine fish stock, white wine, shallots, parsley stems, knob celery, and bay leaf. Bring to a boil and boil for 20 minutes.

Strain stock through fine mesh china cap. Reduce stock by about half.

Clean mushrooms and cut into halves or quarters.

METHOD
Poach scallops and mushrooms in reduced stock. Remove scallops and mushrooms and drain. Save stock.

Make a roux in a pan with butter and flour. Add reserved stock, bring to a boil, and simmer for about 10 minutes.

Mix heavy cream and egg yolks thoroughly. Add to simmering sauce, mix well, and do not allow sauce to return to a boil.

Season with lemon juice, salt and pepper.

Fill coquille shells with well-drained scallops and mushrooms.

Cover with sauce, sprinkle with cheese, and brown under the salamander.

---

[a] Small scallops (bay scallops) are recommended for this dish.

368

Steamed Mussels with Wine and Herbs

Muscheln Seemansart
Moules marinière

YIELD: 10 SERVINGS

Mussels, fresh	8 lb 13 oz	4.0 kg
Shallots	3 1/2 oz	100 g
Dill, fresh	3/4 oz	25 g
Thyme, fresh	2/3 oz	20 g
Butter	1 2/3 oz	50 g
Dry white wine	1 pt 1 oz	500 ml
Seasoning (white pepper)	1x	1x
Lemon, juice	1/2	1/2
Butter, cold	3 1/2 oz	100 g
Parsley, chopped	1 oz	30 g

MISE EN PLACE

Clean mussels thoroughly; scrape off encrustation, beards, and strings.

Chop shallots, dill, and thyme.

METHOD

Sauté shallots in butter; add mussels, dill, and thyme.

Add white wine and season with white pepper.

Cover pot and cook over high heat until mussels are open (about 8 minutes).

Remove mussels and keep warm.

Strain the stock through doublelayer cheesecloth.

Reduce stock to about one-third and season with lemon juice.

Whip cold butter into stock in small nuggets; do not allow sauce to return to a boil.

Break off top shells of mussels.

Serve each mussel on half shell and cover with sauce.

Sprinkle with parsley.

NOTE: Start with only completely closed mussels. Open mussels can be spoiled and even toxic.

369

Glazed Oysters Flavored with Sherry

Warme Austern mit Sherry
Huîtres chaudes au xérès

YIELD: 10 SERVINGS

Oysters (flat)	60	60
Shallots	3 1/2 oz	100 g
Heavy cream (36%)	5 oz	150 ml
Butter	1 2/3 oz	50 g
Sherry, dry	5 oz	150 ml
Fish fumet (Recipe 25)	3 1/3 oz	100 ml
Heavy cream (36%)	3 1/3 oz	100 ml
Butter, cold	5 1/3 oz	150 g
Hollandaise sauce (Recipe 60)	1 2/3 oz	50 ml

MISE EN PLACE

Shuck oysters carefully. Save juice and bottom shells.

Strain oyster juice. Clean and dry oyster shells and keep warm.

Chop shallots.

Whip cream and set aside for finishing the sauce.

METHOD

Carefully poach oysters in their juice. Do not allow to boil.

Remove oysters from hot juice, reserve juice,[a] and keep oysters warm and moist.

Sauté shallots in butter, add reserved oyster juice, sherry, fish fumet, and heavy cream.

Reduce stock and strain through fine mesh china cap. Heat stock again.

Whip cold butter, in small nuggets, into the hot stock.

Fold in whipped cream and Hollandaise sauce.

Place one poached oyster on each warm halfshell, cover with sauce, and glaze under the salamander.

---

[a] Pour liquid off from sand, or strain out sand.

C H A P T E R

Meat

Cold Meat Dishes

370

Poularde with Exotic Fruits

Bresse-Poularde mit exotischen Früchten
Poularde de Bresse aux fruits exotiques

YIELD: 10 SERVINGS

Poularde de Bresse,[a] oven-ready	4 lb	1.8 kg
Matignon (Recipe 14)	5 1/3 oz	150 g
Seasoning (salt and pepper)	1x	1x
Clarified butter	1 2/3 oz	50 g
Dry white wine	3 1/3 oz	100 ml
Chicken stock (Recipe 26)	6 3/4 oz	200 ml
Poultry aspic (Recipe 6)	3 1/3 oz	100 ml

FARCE (STUFFING)

Shiitaki mushrooms, dried	1/3 oz	10 g
Butter	2/3 oz	20 g
Shallots	1 1/4 oz	35 g
Chicken livers, raw	1 2/3 oz	50 g
Pork shoulder, trimmed, boneless	2 oz	60 g
Fatback, unsalted	1 2/3 oz	50 g
Butter	2/3 oz	20 g
Pine nuts, shelled	1 oz	30 g
Seasoning salt for poultry (Recipe 10)	1/3 oz	10 g
Cognac (or any brandy)	2/3 oz	20 ml
Heavy cream (36%)	1 2/3 oz	50 ml
Papaya, candied, diced	1 oz	30 g

MISE EN PLACE

Remove giblets from poularde and reserve. Prepare poularde for roasting.

Remove legs from poularde. Bone legs from inside out without puncturing skin.

Remove and reserve leg meat for farce.

METHOD FOR FARCE (STUFFING)

Soak shiitaki mushrooms in cold water overnight.

Chop shallots. Trim chicken livers. Sauté shallots and chicken livers in butter. Refrigerate.

Cube pork meat and fatback and add to shallots and chicken livers.

Add reserved poularde leg meat and chill mixture.

Cut soaked shiitaki mushrooms into small dice and braise with butter until tender.

Toast pine nuts until golden brown.

Add seasoning salt to chilled meat mixture and purée/grind in food processor to a smooth paste.

Pass/press through wire sieve.[a]

Put mixture in a bowl over ice and mix in Cognac, heavy cream, papaya, shiitaki mushrooms, and toasted pine nuts.

METHOD

Fill leg skins with stuffing and tie or sew skin with kitchen twine.

Spread flavoring vegetables leg bones, and giblets in deep Dutch oven (*braisiere*).

Place poularde breast and stuffed legs on top of vegetables. Season with salt and pepper.

Heat clarified butter and pour over poultry.

Cook, covered, in slow oven until done.

Remove breast and legs to a wire rack and let cool.

Add wine to roast drippings, scrape the bottom, and bring to a boil to dissolve.

Add chicken stock, boil, strain, and remove fat.

Reduce stock to a glaze consistency.

Add melted chicken aspic. Strain, and remove fat again. Let cool.[b]

Remove meat from breast. Slice breast meat and leg meat into 10 equal portions.

Brush meat with cool but still liquid aspic.

NOTE: Suitable garnishes would be: tartlets with tropical curry-fruit salad, pineapple slices with litchi nuts and Maraschino cherries, mango slices with ginger cottage cheese and papaya pearls.

---

[a] A poularde is a specially bred, large fat roasting hen. *Poularde de Bresse* is considered the best poularde on the market.

[a] If sinews are removed from drumsticks, and a powerful food processor is used, this step could be eliminated.

[b] Before aspic is cold, check the consistency by dripping a small amount on a chilled plate. If the jelly is too soft, it must be heated and some soaked gelatin leaves added.

371

*T*urkey Breast with Dried Fruits

Brust von jungem Truthahn mit Dörrfrüchten
Suprême de dindonneau aux fruits secs

YIELD: 10 SERVINGS

Turkey breast, boneless and oven-ready	2 lb 14 oz	1.3 kg
Apricots, dried	1 2/3 oz	50 g
Prunes, dried, pitted	1 2/3 oz	50 g
Figs, dried	3 1/2 oz	100 g
Walnut kernels	3 1/2 oz	100 g
Seasoning salt for poultry (Recipe 10)	2/3 oz	20 g
Clarified butter	2 2/3 oz	75 g
Dry white wine	3 1/3 oz	100 ml
Poultry aspic, fresh (Recipe 6)	10 oz	300 ml

MISE EN PLACE

Poke two holes lengthwise into the turkey breast. Start with a sharp, slender, long knife, and enlarge the opening with a sharpening steel.

Dice the dried fruits. Chop the nuts if they are not already chopped. Blend fruits and nuts.

Stuff turkey breast cavities with the fruit and nut mixture.

Tie breast with butcher twine to get an elongated, even piece.

METHOD

Season breast with seasoning salt.

Brown breast in clarified butter on top of stove, and roast in oven until the center temperature reaches 160°F (70°C). (The turkey breast can also be cooked in a low temperature oven, eliminating the top of the stove browning.)

Remove breast, place on wire rack, and chill.

Carefully drain off fat. Add white wine, scrape bottom, and boil to dissolve pan drippings.

Reduce pan drippings. Add poultry aspic, bring to a boil, then strain through doublelayer of cheesecloth. Remove all remaining fat.[a]

Cover chilled breast with aspic.[b]

Cut breast into 20 even slices and garnish as desired.

NOTE: Suitable garnishes are: poached apple halves with red currant jelly, poached apple slices with chestnut purée and glazed chestnuts, pear halves poached in red wine.

---

[a] The most efficient way to remove fat is to cool the aspic and peel off the hardened fat from the top.

[b] The whole breast can be glazed, or the individual slices can be glazed.

372

*P*heasant Galantine with Grapes

Fasan mit Trauben
Faisan vigneronne

YIELD: 10 SERVINGS

Pheasant, whole, in feathers[a]	5 lb 8 oz	2.5 kg
Bacon, smoked	3 1/2 oz	100 g
Mirepoix for brown stock (Recipe 15)	5 1/3 oz	150 g
Seasoning salt for poultry (Recipe 10)	2/3 oz	20 g
Clarified butter	1 2/3 oz	50 g
Red port wine	2 oz	60 ml
Chicken stock (Recipe 26)	13 1/2 oz	400 ml
Poultry aspic, fresh (Recipe 6)	6 3/4 oz	200 ml

FARCE (STUFFING)

Fatback, unsalted	3 oz	80 g
Pheasant breast filet meat[b]	3 1/2 oz	100 g
Seasoning (salt and pepper)	1x	1x
Pâté seasoning[c]	1/2 tsp	2 g
Dark sultana raisins	2/3 oz	20 g
Shallots	1 1/3 oz	40 g
Clarified butter	2/3 oz	20 g
Cognac (or any brandy)	2/3 oz	20 ml
Heavy cream (36%)	1 2/3 oz	50 ml
Seasoning (salt and pepper)	1x	1x

GARNISH

Puff pastry (Recipe 689)	10 1/2 oz	300 g
Egg yolk	1	1
Seedless red or blue grapes	3 1/2 oz	100 g
Seedless white grapes	3 1/2 oz	100 g
White wine jelly (Recipe 783)	3 1/3 oz	100 ml

MISE EN PLACE

Pluck pheasant. Remove innards and reserve the liver.

Singe pheasant to remove all hair, wash well, and dry.

(continued on next page)

---

[a] A whole pheasant this size might be tough, so it is better to use two smaller birds. Plucked and eviscerated pheasant can also be used; the total eviscerated weight of one or two birds, for this recipe, should be about 4 lb (1.8 kg).

[b] The pheasant breast fillet meat is from a separate bird. Chicken breast can be substituted.

[c] Pâté spice can be purchased commercially, or seasoning salt for poultry (Recipe 10) can be substituted.

(continued from preceding page)

Remove legs. Bone legs from inside out without puncturing skin. Remove and reserve leg meat for farce.

METHOD FOR FARCE (STUFFING)
Cut fatback and pheasant breast and leg meat into dice. Keep fatback separate. Chill diced meats. Season with salt and pepper and pâté seasoning.

Blanch sultanas and drain.

Chop shallots. Sauté shallots and pheasant liver in clarified butter. Add Cognac and ignite. Chill mixture.

Purée fatback in food processor; add shallot/liver mixture and pheasant filet breast meat.

Strain/pass through a fine wire sieve. If sinews were removed from the pheasant meat, this step could be eliminated.

Place mixture in a bowl over ice and incorporate cream. Add blanched sultanas. Check seasoning.

METHOD FOR GARNISH
Roll out puff pastry and cut out 10 oval leaves.

Mix egg yolk with small amount of water and brush leaves. Make a decorative vein pattern on leaves with the back of a fork.

Refrigerate dough for 1 hour. Bake until golden brown.

Cut grapes in half (if grapes are not seedless, the seeds should be removed).

Close to service time, split the puff pastry leaves horizontally.

Place grapes on bottom part of the leaves and brush with wine jelly.

Put lids back catty-corner so that grapes are visible.

METHOD
Fill pheasant legs with farce (stuffing). Tie or sew legs with kitchen twine to get two even-size rolls.

Line roasting pan or Dutch oven with smoked bacon slices and sprinkle with *mirepoix*.

Season pheasant meat (whole breast and legs) with poultry seasoning and place on top of *mirepoix*.

Melt clarified butter and pour over pheasant meat.

Cover pan and roast in oven for about 20 minutes.

Remove lid and increase heat to brown meat slightly.

Put pheasant breast and legs on wire rack to let cool. Roast until done

Drain off all fat. Add wine and chicken stock. Scrape bottom and boil to dissolve pan drippings.

Strain through double layer of cheesecloth. Skim and reduce to glaze consistency.

Add 3 1/3 oz (100 ml) poultry aspic. Bring to a boil again and skim. Let aspic cool.

Remove breast carefully from carcass. Cut meat into attractive slices.

Glaze pheasant breast slices and legs with cool aspic. Refrigerate to solidify aspic.

Serve meat with puff pastry leaves.

373

Top Sirloin with Mixed Pickles
Gebratener Rindshuftspitz mit Essiggemüse
Pointe de culotte de boeuf rôtie aux mixed pickles

YIELD: 10 SERVINGS

Top sirloin[a]	4 lb 7 oz	2.0 kg
Aspic powder	1/3 oz	10 g
Water	6 3/4 oz	200 ml
Seasoning salt for meat (Recipe 9)	1 oz	30 g
Peanut oil	1 2/3 oz	50 ml
Green lollo lettuce[b]	8 3/4 oz	250 g

MIXED PICKLE VEGETABLES

Celery, bleached[c]	8 3/4 oz	250 g
Cauliflower, fresh	8 3/4 oz	250 g
Bell peppers, assorted colors	12 oz	350 g
Carrots	12 oz	350 g
Pearl onions, fresh	8 3/4 oz	250 g

MARINADE

Water	1 pt 1 oz	500 ml
Herb vinegar	6 3/4 oz	200 ml
Mustard seeds	1/6 oz	5 g
Coriander seeds	1/6 oz	5 g
Salt	1/3 oz	10 g
Bay leaf	1	1
Thyme twig, fresh	1	1

MISE EN PLACE
Prepare sirloin for roasting. Tie with butcher twine to retain its shape.

Combine aspic powder with cold water, bring to a boil, and let cool.

Clean, wash, and trim vegetables for pickles. Cut into any desired shape, into even-size pieces.

---

[a] Meat should be well trimmed but have a thin fat cover.

[b] Any lettuce can be substituted.

[c] The celery specified in the original recipe is stalk celery, *Stangensellerie* in German. This was further specified as the expensive form, *gebleicht*, which is grown partially underground, so the stalks stay white.

Combine marinade ingredients and bring to a boil.

Add vegetables to marinade; boil until vegetables are just about tender, but not overcooked. Let vegetables cool in the marinade.

METHOD
Season the sirloin. Brown in oil in very hot oven, 445°F (230°C), on both sides.

Roast at 360°F (180°C) to 400°F (200°C), basting occasionally.

Roast to desired degree of doneness. Check with meat thermometer.

Put roast on wire rack and let cool completely.

Trim, if necessary, and cut into 20 slices.

Brush slices with aspic jelly.

Serve meat with mixed pickle on lettuce leaves.

NOTE: Serve with Tartar Sauce (Recipe 96).

374

$\mathcal{B}$eef Brisket with Marinated Vegetables

Kaltes Siedfleisch mit marinierten Gemüsen
Boeuf bouilli grecque

YIELD: 10 SERVINGS

Brisket, fresh, trimmed	4 lb	1.8 kg
Aspic powder	1/3 oz	10 g
Water	6 3/4 oz	200 ml
Bouillon (Recipe 22)	4 qt 7 oz	4.0 L
Bouquet garni (Recipe 7)	7 oz	200 g
Sachet bag[a]	1	1

VEGETABLES FOR GARNISH

Knob celery (celeriac)	2 lb 10 oz	1.2 kg
Cauliflower, fresh	14 oz	400 g
Stalk celery, bleached[b]	14 oz	400 g
Zucchini	14 oz	400 g
Red peppers	5 1/3 oz	150 g

MARINADE FOR GARNISH

Shallots	2 oz	60 g
Olive oil, cold pressed	3 1/3 oz	100 ml
Thyme twig, fresh	1	1

---

[a] For this recipe, use bay leaf, peppercorns, marjoram, thyme, and cloves.

[b] The celery specified in the original recipe is stalk celery, *Stangensellerie* in German. This was further specified as the expensive form, *gebleicht*, which is grown partially underground, so the stalks stay white.

Bay leaf	1	1
Seasoning (salt and pepper)	1x	1x
Dry white wine	6 3/4 oz	200 ml
White wine vinegar	1 2/3 oz	50 ml
Bouillon (Recipe 22)	10 oz	300 ml
Saffron	1x	1x

MISE EN PLACE
Blanch brisket in boiling water. Remove, and wash meat first in hot water then in cold water.

Combine aspic powder with 6 3/4 oz (200 ml) cold water, bring to a boil, and let cool.

MISE EN PLACE FOR GARNISH
Peel knob celery and cut into 10 slices about 3/4-in. (18 mm) thick. Cut rounds as large as possible with a pastry cutter.[a] Lightly scoop out center.

Divide cauliflower into small rosettes.

Cut celery into strips about 1 in. (25 mm) long.

Cut zucchini into strips the same size, or cut into ovals.

Trim red peppers and cut into dice.

METHOD FOR GARNISH
Peel shallots and sauté in olive oil.

Add all marinade ingredients, except saffron.

Bring to a boil and boil for 10 minutes.

Add celery slices and boil for 10 additional minutes. Remove celery slices and place them on a wire rack to cool.

Add the remaining vegetables (not the celery) and saffron to marinade.

Bring to a boil and boil for 10 minutes. Let vegetables cool and marinate in their stock, preferably overnight.

Remove vegetables and drain well.

METHOD
Bring bouillon to a boil, add *bouquet garni* and sachet bag. Skim.

Add blanched meat and simmer until tender, skimming occasionally.

When meat is tender, let it cool in its broth.

Remove meat, trim, and cut into 20 slices.

Glaze slices with aspic jelly.

Fill celery slices with marinated vegetables.

Serve meat with celery slices.

NOTE: Serve with Horseradish Whipped Cream (Recipe 73) or with Lingonberry Sauce (Recipe 83).

---

[a] Save trimmings for other uses.

375

Rack of Veal with Mushrooms
Poeliertes Kalbskarree mit Pilzen
Carré de veau poêlé aux champignons

YIELD: 10 SERVINGS

Rack of veal	4 lb 7 oz	2.0 kg
Aspic powder	1/3 oz	10 g
Water	6 3/4 oz	200 ml
Mirepoix for brown stock (Recipe 15)	7 oz	200 g
Thyme twig, fresh	1	1
Rosemary twig, fresh	1	1
Bay leaf	1	1
Seasoning salt for meat (Recipe 9)	1 oz	30 g
Clarified butter	3 1/2 oz	100 g
Dry white wine	3 1/3 oz	100 ml
Brown veal stock (Recipe 23)	1 pt 1 oz	500 ml
Lettuce leaves, Boston or buttercup	10	10

GARNISH

Chanterelles mushrooms[a]	10 1/2 oz	300 g
Porcini mushrooms, fresh[b]	10 1/2 oz	300 g
Cultivated mushrooms, fresh[c]	10 1/2 oz	300 g
White wine vinegar	3 1/3 oz	100 ml
White peppercorns	3	3
Bay leaf	1	1
Shallots	2 oz	60 g
Salt	1x	1x

MISE EN PLACE
Trim and bone veal. Tie with butcher twine to retain its shape.

Combine aspic powder with water, bring to a boil, and let cool.

METHOD FOR GARNISH
Trim, clean, and wash all mushrooms. Cut into thick, even chunks.

Combine vinegar, white peppercorns, bay leaf, shallots, and salt.

---

[a] Chanterelles are yellow wild mushrooms, called *girolles* in French and *Eierschwämme* in German. Canned chanterelles can be substituted, but they will probably not be as flavorful.

[b] Porcini are wild mushrooms, called *cèpes* in French, *Steinpilze* in German, and *porcini* in Italian. These mushrooms are widely available dried, and are increasingly available fresh. Because Italy is a large exporter of these mushrooms, the Italian name is commonly used.

[c] Use the standard American cultivated mushrooms or Cremini mushrooms.

Add mushrooms, cover, bring to a boil, and boil for 5 minutes. Let mixture cool.

METHOD
Put *mirepoix*, thyme, rosemary, and bay leaf in deep roasting pan or Dutch oven.

Season meat with seasoning salt and place on top. Melt clarified butter and pour over meat.

Cook briefly in oven at 325°F (165°C).

Cover and roast at 285°F (140°C) to 325°F (165°C), basting frequently.

About 10 minutes before the meat is cooked, remove the lid to brown the meat.

Remove meat and place on wire rack to cool.

Drain off all fat.

Add wine and veal stock. Scrape bottom and boil to dissolve pan drippings.

Boil for about 5 minutes and strain through double layer of cheesecloth.

Skim off all fat and reduce stock to glaze consistency.

Add aspic, bring to a boil, and let cool.[a]

Glaze roast with aspic jelly and cut into 10 slices. (Instead of glazing the whole piece of meat, it can be sliced first and the slices glazed.)

Drain mushrooms and put into lettuce cups.

Serve meat with mushrooms.

376

Rack of Lamb with Leek and Bacon Salad
Lamkarree ländliche Art
Carré d'agneau campagnarde

YIELD: 10 SERVINGS

Rack of lamb with loin, oven-ready	4 lb 7 oz	2.0 kg
Aspic powder	1/3 oz	10 g
Water	6 3/4 oz	200 ml
Seasoning salt for meat (Recipe 9)	1 oz	30 g

---

[a] The aspic must be absolutely fat-free. Fat can be easily removed when the aspic is cold and solid. The accumulated fat on top can be peeled off.

Rosemary leaves, fresh	2/3 oz	20 g
Peanut oil	1 2/3 oz	50 ml

GARNISH

Short pastry (Recipe 710)	8 3/4 oz	250 g
Shallots	1 2/3 oz	50 g
Bacon, smoked	5 1/3 oz	150 g
Leeks, white part only	1 lb 5 oz	600 g
Sunflower oil	3 1/3 oz	100 ml
Marjoram, fresh, chopped	1/3 oz	10 g
White wine vinegar	2 3/4 oz	80 ml
Seasoning (salt and pepper)	1x	1x

MISE EN PLACE

Trim lamb and tie loin end with butcher twine.

Combine aspic powder with water, bring to a boil, and let cool.

METHOD FOR GARNISH

Roll out dough. Cut out 10 circles and place into tartlet forms.

Blind-bake tartlets, remove from molds, and let cool.

Chop shallots. Cut bacon into slivers.

Wash and trim leeks; be sure sand is removed from the layers. Cut into strips (julienne).

Sauté shallots in oil, add bacon and cook until bacon is done, but not crisp.

Add leeks and chopped marjoram leaves. Cook for 15 minutes longer.

Add vinegar. Season to taste. Let mixture cool.

METHOD

Season lamb meat with seasoning salt and rosemary leaves.

Roast lamb, turning it in peanut oil to brown both sides, in hot oven, about 445°F (230°C).

Continue roasting at 400°F (200°C), basting frequently.

When meat has reached the desired inside temperature, remove meat to a wire rack and let cool.

Cut meat into attractive slices, chill on wire rack, and glaze slices with aspic jelly.

Fill tartlets with leek salad.

Serve meat slices with tartlets.

NOTE: Serve with Mint Sauce (Recipe 80).

Hot Meat Dishes

377

Beef Stew, Bourguignonne
Boeuf bourguignonne

YIELD: 10 SERVINGS

Beef shoulder clod, trimmed	4 lb 7 oz	2.0 kg
Sachet bag[a]	1	1
White wheat flour	2 2/3 oz	75 g
Clarified butter	1 2/3 oz	50 g
Seasoning	1x	1x
Mirepoix (Recipe 15)	5 1/3 oz	150 g
Bacon rind (skin)	1 2/3 oz	50 g
Tomato paste	3 1/2 oz	100 g
Garlic cloves, peeled	2	2
Red wine	1 pt 1 oz	500 ml
Brown veal stock (Recipe 23)	13 1/2 oz	400 ml
Seasoning (salt and pepper)	1x	1x

GARNISH INGREDIENTS

Slab bacon, smoked (not sliced)	10 1/2 oz	300 g
Mushrooms, fresh	1 lb 2 oz	500 g
Pearl onions	5 1/3 oz	150 g
Butter	3 1/2 oz	100 g
Seasoning (salt and pepper)	1x	1x

MISE EN PLACE

Cut beef into stew-size pieces, 1 1/3–oz (40 g) cubes.

Prepare sachet bag.

Lightly brown (dry roast) flour in skillet until pale yellow.

METHOD FOR GARNISH

Remove rind (skin) from bacon and cut into 1/4–in. (7 mm) slivers (lardons). Blanch bacon and set aside.

Wash mushrooms and cut into halves or quarters, depending on size.

Peel and blanch pearl onions.

Sauté bacon, mushrooms, and pearl onions in butter.

METHOD

Heat clarified butter.

Sauté beef in hot clarified butter until browned on all sides. When beef is brown, lift out and set aside. Season beef.

(continued on next page)

---

[a] For this recipe, use thyme, bay leaf, crushed peppercorns, and parsley stems.

(continued from preceding page)

Add *mirepoix* and bacon rind and sauté briefly.

Add tomato paste and crushed garlic cloves and continue cooking.

Sprinkle with toasted flour, mix well, and add wine.

Add meat, veal stock, and herbs. Adjust seasoning.

Cover and stew until meat is tender.

Serve stew topped with bacon/mushroom/onion garnish.

378

Assorted Boiled Meats

Bollito misto

YIELD: 10 SERVINGS

Beef for boiling	2 lb 3 oz	1.0 kg
Veal shoulder, boned	2 lb 3 oz	1.0 kg
Boiling fowl, oven-ready	3 lb	1.4 kg
Carrots	1 lb 10 oz	750 g
Knob celery (celeriac)	1 lb 10 oz	750 g
Onion, studded with 3 to 4 cloves	1	1
White peppercorns	10	10
Bouillon (Recipe 22)	4 qt 7 oz	4.0 L
Veal tongue, fresh	1 lb 2 oz	500 g
Zampone,[a] fresh, uncooked	1 lb 2 oz	500 g
Vegetable bouillon (Recipe 27)	1 qt 2 oz	1.0 L

MISE EN PLACE
Blanch beef, veal, and fowl. Rinse first with hot water, then with cold water.

Peel and trim carrots and knob celery and cut into sticks.

METHOD
Add clove-studded onion and white peppercorns to bouillon and bring to a boil.

Add beef, veal, and fowl to bouillon and simmer until done. Be aware that the meats will be done at different times. Remove each meat and set aside as it is done.

Simmer veal tongue and zampone, each in a separate pot of water.

Boil carrots and knob celery in vegetable stock.

Serve assorted meats and vegetables with some stock.

---

[a] Zampone is an Italian sausage specialty. It is a stuffed pig's foot, available raw, as for this recipe, or fully cooked.

379

Lamb Stew Emmenthal Style

Emmentaler Lammvoressen
Blanquette d'agneau emmentaloise

YIELD: 10 SERVINGS

Lamb stew meat,[a] cut into 1 1/3–oz (40 g) cubes	4 lb 7 oz	2.0 kg
Pearl onions	10 1/2 oz	300 g
Carrots	10 1/2 oz	300 g
White turnips	7 oz	200 g
Knob celery (celeriac)	5 1/3 oz	150 g
White veal stock (Recipe 28)	1 qt 19 oz	1.5 L
Dry white wine	8 1/2 oz	250 ml
Sachet bag[b]	1	1
Butter	1 oz	30 g
White wheat flour	1 2/3 oz	50 g
Heavy cream (36%)	3 1/3 oz	100 ml
Saffron	1x	1x
Seasoning	1x	1x

MISE EN PLACE
Blanch lamb and rinse first in hot water, then in cold water.

Peel pearl onions.

Trim and peel carrots, turnips, and knob celery. Cut into small dice or small sticks.

METHOD
Heat veal stock and white wine. Add blanched lamb, bring to a boil, and skim.

Add sachet bag and simmer until almost done. Before the lamb is fully cooked, add the pearl onions and diced vegetables.

Remove lamb and vegetables when cooked, and keep warm in a little stock. Reserve remaining stock.

Melt butter and add flour to make a white roux. Let cool slightly.

Heat 1 qt 2 oz (1.0 L) reserved stock. Add hot stock to cool roux; stir to dissolve roux; bring to a boil, stirring constantly. Simmer for 20 to 30 minutes.

Strain through double layer of cheesecloth.

Add cooked lamb and vegetables.

Stir in heavy cream and saffron[c] and adjust seasoning.

NOTE: This dish is traditionally served with boiled potatoes and beet salad. If desired, the vegetables can be cooked separately from the meat.

---

[a] The stew meat should be cut from the shoulder and neck, and should be lean and well trimmed.

[b] For this recipe, use bay leaf, peppercorns, thyme, and rosemary.

[c] The saffron can also be added during the cooking process.

380

$\mathcal{S}$irloin Steak Sautéed with Red Wine Sauce

Entrecôte mit Rotweinsauce
Entrecôte marchand de vin

YIELD: 10 SERVINGS

Sirloin steaks[a]	3 lb 5 oz	1.5 kg
Seasoning (salt and pepper)	1x	1x
Peanut oil	3 1/3 oz	100 ml
Shallots, chopped	2 1/2 oz	70 g
Red wine	10 oz	300 ml
Demi-glace (Recipe 44)	13 1/2 oz	400 ml
Butter, cold	3 1/2 oz	100 g

METHOD

Season sirloin steaks with salt and pepper. Sauté steaks quickly on both sides in hot peanut oil.

Remove steaks,[b] and keep warm.

Drain off fat, add shallots, and sauté.

Add red wine and reduce completely.

Add *demi-glace* and bring to a boil. Strain sauce through fine mesh china cap.

Add half the cold butter to sauce, in small nuggets.

Melt remaining butter; turn steaks in butter to heat on both sides.

Serve with sauce[c] on top, and some sauce on the side.

NOTE: Use a full-bodied red wine.

381

$\mathcal{R}$oast Leg of Lamb with Onions and Potatoes

Gebratene Lammkeule Bäckerinart
Gigot d'agneau rôti boulangère

YIELD: 10 SERVINGS

Garlic	1 oz	30 g
Leg of lamb, oven-ready	5 lb	2.25 kg
Seasoning salt for meat (Recipe 9)	2/3 oz	20 g
Rosemary, fresh, chopped	1/3 oz	10 g
Peanut oil	2 3/4 oz	80 ml
Matignon (Recipe 14)	7 oz	200 g
Dry white wine	6 3/4 oz	200 ml
Brown veal stock (Recipe 23)	1 pt 1 oz	500 ml

GARNISH

Potatoes	5 lb 8 oz	2.5 kg
Peanut oil	3 1/3 oz	100 ml
Onions	12 oz	350 g
Seasoning (salt, nutmeg)	1x	1x
Seasoning (white pepper)	1x	1x
Butter	1 2/3 oz	50 g

MISE EN PLACE

Crush garlic and rub onto leg of lamb.

METHOD FOR GARNISH

Peel potatoes, cut into slices, and blanch.

Peel onions and cut into slices.

Sauté potatoes in peanut oil; add onions.

Season with salt, nutmeg, and white pepper.

Add butter and sauté potatoes and onions together until done.

METHOD

Season leg of lamb with seasoning salt and rosemary.

Roast with peanut oil in hot oven, at 425°F (220°C), turning to brown on all sides.

Lower heat and roast at 360°F (180°C), basting occasionally with drippings, until desired doneness. (Check with meat thermometer.)

Remove lamb from pan and keep warm on wire rack.

Drain off fat from pan, add vegetables, and sauté for a few minutes. Add wine and reduce. Add brown veal stock, bring to a boil, and boil for 10 minutes.

Strain sauce through a fine mesh china cap. Skim off any remaining fat.

PRESENTATION

Slice meat and serve on top of potato and onion garnish.

Serve sauce on the side.

NOTE: When small quantities are needed, the meat is often cooked on top of the sliced potatoes. The meat juice flavors the potatoes.

---

[a] Steak portion sizes vary from country to country.

[b] Steaks should be cooked to order. The degree of doneness should be decided by the customer. If steaks are cooked ahead of time and kept warm, they could become dry and overcooked.

[c] In the United States, most customers eat steak without sauce. It is best to serve the sauce on the side.

382

Roast Rack of Veal with Bouquet of Vegetables

Gebratenes Kalbskarree mit Gemüse
Carré de veau rôti bouquetière

YIELD: 10 SERVINGS

Rack of veal, oven-ready	5 lb 5 oz	2.4 kg
Seasoning salt for meat (Recipe 9)	2/3 oz	20 g
Peanut oil	2 3/4 oz	80 ml
Matignon (Recipe 14)	7 oz	200 g
Dry white wine	6 3/4 oz	200 ml
Brown veal stock (Recipe 23)	1 pt 1 oz	500 ml
Madeira wine	1 2/3 oz	50 ml
Seasoning	1x	1x

GARNISH

Cauliflower, fresh	1 lb 12 oz	800 g
Lemon, juice	1/2	1/2
Butter	3/4 oz	25 g
Seasoning (salt and pepper)	1x	1x
Green beans, fresh[a]	1 lb 2 oz	500 g
Bouillon (Recipe 22)	6 3/4 oz	200 ml
Onions, chopped	1 2/3 oz	50 g
Savory, fresh	1/4 oz	7 g
Kohlrabi	1 lb 12 oz	800 g
White veal stock (Recipe 28)	10 oz	300 ml
Butter	3/4 oz	25 g
Onions, chopped	1 2/3 oz	50 g
Sugar	1x	1x
Tomatoes (5 whole)	14 oz	400 g
Seasoning (salt and pepper)	1x	1x
Butter	3/4 oz	25 g
Hollandaise sauce (Recipe 60)	6 3/4 oz	200 ml

MISE EN PLACE
Trim rack of veal and tie with butcher twine to keep meat together.

METHOD
Season rack of veal, coat with oil, and start roasting in very hot oven. Lower heat and continue roasting. Baste occasionally.

While meat cooks, prepare garnish.

When meat is cooked, remove to a wire rack and keep warm.

Drain off all fat from roasting pot, add flavoring vegetables, and roast.

---

[a] In Europe, green beans are usually small and slender, and are called *haricots verts*. They cook quickly, and it is important to keep them crisp and green.

Add white wine to dissolve pan drippings, and reduce.

Add brown veal stock, add any drippings from veal, bring to a boil, and boil for 15 minutes.

Skim, strain through fine mesh china cap, and skim off any remaining fat.

Add Madeira wine and adjust seasoning.

METHOD FOR GARNISH
Divide cauliflower into small rosettes. Braise cauliflower with lemon juice, butter, and a small amount of water. Season to taste.

Snip off ends of green beans. Braise in bouillon with onions and savory. Do not overcook.

Peel kohlrabi and cut into attractive wedges or sticks. Braise kohlrabi in white veal stock with butter, chopped onions, and a pinch of sugar. Reduce stock and glaze kohlrabi.

Cut tomatoes in half horizontally. Season, top with butter, and brown under the broiler or salamander until the tops are brown and the tomatoes are hot.

PRESENTATION
Cut rack of veal into 10 slices.

Surround veal slices with bouquets of vegetables. Cover cauliflower with Hollandaise sauce.

383

Roast Beef Tenderloin with Glazed Vegetables

Gebratenes Rindsfilet mit glasiertem Gemüse
Filet de boeuf rôti nivernaise

YIELD: 10 SERVINGS

Beef tenderloin, peeled, trimmed, oven-ready	4 lb	1.8 kg
Seasoning salt for meat (Recipe 9)	2/3 oz	20 g
Peanut oil	2 3/4 oz	80 ml
Matignon (Recipe 14)	7 oz	200 g
Dry white wine	6 3/4 oz	200 ml
Brown veal stock (Recipe 23)	1 pt 1 oz	500 ml

GARNISH

Carrots	1 lb 2 oz	500 g
Turnips, white, small	1 lb 2 oz	500 g
Pearl onions, fresh	1 lb 2 oz	500 g
Butter	3 1/2 oz	100 g
Sugar, pinch	3x	3x
White veal stock (Recipe 28)	1 pt 9 oz	750 ml
Seasoning (salt and pepper)	1x	1x

MISE EN PLACE
Tie tenderloin with kitchen twine to keep its shape during the roasting process.

METHOD FOR GARNISH
Peel carrots and turnips. Cut into attractive shapes, such as sticks, wedges, or barrel shapes.

Peel pearl onions and blanch.

When meat is almost ready, braise each vegetable separately with butter and sugar in veal stock.

Be sure all braising liquid is evaporated and the vegetables have a nice sheen.

Season with salt and pepper.

METHOD
Season tenderloin. Roast with peanut oil, starting with very high heat, then lower heat. Check the inside temperature frequently with meat thermometer. When the desired degree of doneness is reached, remove meat to wire rack and keep warm.

Carefully drain off all fat from pan, add *matignon* and sauté briefly.

Add wine and reduce completely.

Add brown veal stock and bring to a boil.

Skim, and strain sauce through fine mesh china cap.

Return stock to stove and reduce until the desired consistency is reached.

Adjust seasoning.

PRESENTATION
Slice beef. Serve sliced beef with bouquets of glazed vegetables.

Serve sauce on the side.

384

tuffed Breast of Veal

Gefüllte Kalbsbrust
Poitrine de veau farcie

YIELD: 10 SERVINGS

Breast of veal,[a] oven-ready	3 lb 5oz	1.5 kg
Seasoning salt for meat (Recipe 9)	1/3 oz	10 g
Peanut oil	3 1/3 oz	100 ml
Mirepoix for brown stock (Recipe 15)	10 1/2 oz	300 g
Tomato paste	1 oz	30 g
Dry white wine	3 1/3 oz	100 ml
Brown veal stock (Recipe 23)	1 qt 19 oz	1.5 L

[a] Veal breast for stuffing should be boned carefully so the muscle layer is not punctured.

Rosemary twig, fresh	1	1
Thyme twig, fresh	1	1
Basil, fresh	1/3 oz	10 g
Cornstarch	2/3 oz	20 g

STUFFING
Onions	3 1/2 oz	100 g
Parsley	1 1/3 oz	40 g
White bread (Pullman loaf)	7 oz	200 g
Milk	3 1/3 oz	100 ml
Butter	2/3 oz	20 g
Veal shoulder, boneless, trimmed	10 1/2 oz	300 g
Fatback (unsalted)	3 1/2 oz	100 g
Egg	1	1
Seasoning (salt and pepper)	1x	1x

MISE EN PLACE
Make pocket in veal breast.

METHOD FOR STUFFING
Chop onions and parsley.

Cut bread into cubes and soak in milk.

Sauté onions in butter. Add soaked bread and mix well over heat until it forms a paste (*panade*). Let cool.

Grind veal shoulder and fatback through fine plate of meat grinder.

Combine ground meat, the cold *panade*, egg, and chopped parsley. Season.

METHOD
Fill veal breast with stuffing and close pocket with butcher's twine.

Season veal with seasoning salt and brown lightly in peanut oil in Dutch oven (*braisiere*). Remove meat from pan.

Drain off fat from pan. Add *mirepoix* and roast lightly.

Add tomato paste and continue roasting for a short time.

Return veal to pan and add wine and a small amount of veal stock.

Braise meat, in uncovered pan, in the oven. Baste frequently.

Allow liquid to reduce to syrup consistency.

Add enough veal stock to come to one-fourth of the height of the veal breast. Add herbs (rosemary, thyme, and basil). Cover and braise until veal is cooked. Baste veal frequently, especially when it is close to being done.

Remove veal and keep warm.

Add remaining veal stock to braising liquid, bring to a boil, and thicken with cornstarch.

Strain sauce through fine mesh china cap, skim, and adjust seasoning.

PRESENTATION
Slice meat. Brush the sliced meat with butter for a more attractive appearance, and pour veal sauce around it.

385

Stuffed Lamb Shoulder

Gefüllte Lammschulter
Epaule d'agneau farcie

Y I E L D :   1 0   S E R V I N G S

Lamb shoulder, boneless, no shank	3 lb 8 oz	1.6 kg
Seasoning (salt and pepper)	1x	1x
Peanut oil	2 3/4 oz	80 ml
Mirepoix for brown stock (Recipe 15)	7 oz	200 g
Tomatoes, cubed	3 1/2 oz	100 g
Dry white wine	3 1/3 oz	100 ml
Brown veal stock (Recipe 23)	1 pt 4 oz	600 ml
Sachet bag[a]	1	1
Cornstarch	2/3 oz	20 g

STUFFING (FARCE)

Veal shoulder meat, trimmed	5 1/3 oz	150 g
Lamb shoulder meat, no shank	5 1/3 oz	150 g
Fatback (unsalted)	5 1/3 oz	150 g
Seasoning (salt and pepper)	1x	1x
Garlic	1/3 oz	10 g
Onions	1 2/3 oz	50 g
Parsley, fresh	1 oz	30 g
Black chanterelles, dried[b]	2/3 oz	20 g
Egg	1	1
Heavy cream (36%)	3 1/3 oz	100 ml
Seasoning (salt and pepper)	1x	1x

METHOD FOR STUFFING (FARCE)

Cube veal, lamb, and fatback. Season and refrigerate.

Peel garlic and onions.

Strip parsley leaves from stems.

Grind meats, fatback, garlic, onions, and parsley through medium plate of meat grinder.

Soak black chanterelles in cold water for 2 hours. Drain the chanterelles, discard water, and chop coarsely.

Add chopped chanterelles, egg, and heavy cream to farce, mix well, and adjust seasoning.

METHOD

Spread boned lamb shoulder on work table, place stuffing in the center, and shape into an even roll. Tie securely with butcher's twine.

Season shoulder and brown lightly on all sides, in peanut oil, in Dutch oven (*braisiere*). Remove meat from pot.

Drain off fat from pot. Add *mirepoix* and sauté.

Add cubed tomatoes and return the browned lamb shoulder to the pot.

Add white wine and a small amount of veal stock. Braise, basting frequently, until liquid is reduced to syrup consistency.

Add more veal stock and the sachet bag. (The stock should cover about one-third of the meat.) Cover and braise in oven, basting frequently with the stock.

When meat is cooked (it should be welldone), remove and keep warm.

Add remaining veal stock, bring to a boil, and skim.

Strain through fine mesh china cap; skim again.

Thicken sauce with cornstarch and adjust seasoning.

Slice meat and serve with sauce.

386

Smoked Ox Tongue with White Beans

Geräucherte Rindszunge auf weissen Bohnen
Langue de boeuf fumée bretonne

Y I E L D :   1 0   S E R V I N G S

Ox tongue, smoked	3 lb 5 oz	1.5 kg
White beans[a]	1 lb 5 oz	600 g
Onions	1 2/3 oz	50 g
Garlic	1/4 oz	7 g
Bouquet garni (Recipe 7)	7 oz	200 g
Bacon rind (skin)	3 1/2 oz	100 g
Sachet bag[b]	1	1
Butter	3/4 oz	25 g
Tomato concassé (Recipe 97)	6 3/4 oz	200 ml
Demi-glace (Recipe 44)	6 3/4 oz	200 ml
Parsley, chopped	2/3 oz	20 g

[a] For this recipe, use bay leaf, peppercorns, thyme, and rosemary.

[b] Black chanterelles, also known as "trumpets of death," are dark, almost black mushrooms. It is their appearance that gives them their intimidating name; they are quite safe to eat. In German, they are called *Totentrompeten*. If they are not available, other flavorful dried mushrooms can be substituted.

[a] Any white beans can be used, such as navy beans or Great Northern beans.

[b] Suggestions for this recipe are bay leaf, peppercorns, thyme, and savory.

SAUCE

Demi-glace (Recipe 44)	13 1/2 oz	400 ml
Madeira wine	3 1/3 oz	100 ml

MISE EN PLACE

Soak ox tongue[a] in cold water to remove salt.

Soak beans in cold water for 4 to 6 hours.

Peel onions and garlic and chop fine.

METHOD

Put tongue in large amount of cold water and bring to a boil. Boil, without any seasoning, until tender. Reserve stock.

Put tongue in cold water, peel, and trim. Place trimmed tongue in small amount of boiling stock and keep warm.

Bring beans to a boil in the soaking water. Add *bouquet garni*, bacon rind, and the sachet bag.

Boil beans until tender, drain, and discard water.

Sauté chopped onions in butter and add chopped garlic and tomatoes *concassé*.

Add beans and chopped parsley.

METHOD FOR SAUCE

Combine *demi-glace* and Madeira wine. Boil until the desired consistency is reached. Strain through fine mesh china cap.

PRESENTATION

Slice tongue and serve on a bed of beans, covered with Madeira sauce.

387

Shredded Calves' Liver with Madeira Sauce

Geschnetzelte Kalbsleber mit Madeirasauce
Emincé de foie de veau au madère

YIELD: 10 SERVINGS

Calves' liver	3 lb 5 oz	1.5 kg
Onions	8 3/4 oz	250 g
Parsley	1 2/3 oz	50 g
Peanut oil	2 3/4 oz	80 ml
Seasoning (salt and pepper)	1x	1x
Butter	1 2/3 oz	50 g
Madeira wine	5 oz	150 ml
Demi-glace (Recipe 44)	1 pt 4 oz	600 ml

MISE EN PLACE

Skin and trim liver. Cut into slivers.

Peel and chop onions.

Wash parsley and chop leaves.

METHOD

Sauté liver in peanut oil over high heat[a] until still rare. Do not overcook.

Season with salt and pepper and put the liver in a colander to drain.

Add butter to the pan and sauté onions.

Add Madeira wine and bring to a boil. Add *demi-glace* and bring to a boil.

Remove from heat, add liver just to warm it, and blend with sauce. Do not allow to boil.

Serve sprinkled with chopped parsley.

---

[a] The salt content of smoked ox tongue varies. In some countries the tongue can be boiled without prior soaking.

[a] The dish is usually made to order. If more than one portion is made, it is advisable to sauté the liver in small amounts to keep it rare.

388

$\mathscr{B}$raised Beef Top Sirloin with Vegetables

Geschmorter Rindshuftspitz mit Gemüse
Pointe de coulotte de boeuf à la mode

YIELD: 10 SERVINGS

Top sirloin, trimmed, with thin fat cover[a]	4 lb 7 oz	2.0 kg
Seasoning salt for meat (Recipe 9)	2/3 oz	20 g
Calves' feet[b]	1 lb 10 oz	750 g
Peanut oil	3 1/3 oz	100 ml
Mirepoix for brown stock (Recipe 15)	7 oz	200 g
Bacon rind (skin)	7 oz	200 g
Tomato paste	1 2/3 oz	50 g
Red wine	10 oz	300 ml
Sachet bag[c]	1	1
Brown veal stock (Recipe 23)	1 qt 12 1/3 oz	1.3 L
Demi-glace (Recipe 44)	1 pt 8 oz	700 ml
Madeira wine	1 2/3 oz	50 ml
Cornstarch	2/3 oz	20 ml

GARNISH

Carrots	7 oz	200 g
Knob celery (celeriac)	7 oz	200 g
White turnips (small)	7 oz	200 g
Pearl onions	5 1/3 oz	150 g
Butter	1 2/3 oz	50 g
White veal stock	6 3/4 oz	200 ml
Sugar	1x	1x
Seasoning (salt and pepper)	1x	1x
Parsley, Italian, fresh, chopped	1 1/3 oz	40 g

METHOD

Season sirloin with seasoning salt.

Brown sirloin and calves' feet, in oil, in Dutch oven (*braisiere*).

Remove sirloin and calves' feet.

Drain off oil from pan. Add *mirepoix* and bacon rind to pan and roast both.

Add tomato paste and continue roasting.

Return sirloin and calves' feet to *braisiere*.

Add wine and reduce almost completely.

Add sachet bag, some brown veal stock, and all *demi-glace*. Braise in oven. Baste, turning the meat occasionally. If necessary, add veal stock to keep the liquid level to about one-third of the sirloin.

When sirloin is tender, remove and keep warm.

Remove calves' feet. Bone feet and cut into strips.

Strain the sauce through a fine mesh china cap. Skim. Add Madeira wine to sauce and bring to a boil. Adjust seasoning and thicken with cornstarch.

METHOD FOR GARNISH

Peel and trim carrots, knob celery, and white turnips. Cut into wedges, sticks, or other uniform shapes.

Peel pearl onions.

Braise each vegetable separately, with butter and a little white veal stock. Season with sugar, salt and pepper.

Allow liquid to reduce to give vegetables a nice sheen.

Wash and chop parsley.

PRESENTATION

Serve beef, covered with sauce, and garnished with calves' feet and glazed vegetables.

Serve some sauce on the side.

389

$\mathscr{B}$raised Beef Roulades with Tomatoes

Geschmorte Rindsröllchen mit Tomaten
Paupiettes de boeuf braisées aux tomates

YIELD: 10 SERVINGS

Beef top round,[a] trimmed	3 lb 5 oz	1.5 kg
Onions	8 3/4 oz	250 g
Ham, boiled	7 oz	200 g
Dill pickles, drained	8 3/4 oz	250 g
Butter	1 oz	30 g
Mustard, prepared, mild	2/3 oz	20 g
Paprika	1/4 oz	7 g
Seasoning salt for meat (Recipe 9)	1/3 oz	10 g
Peanut oil	2 3/4 oz	80 ml
Matignon (Recipe 14)	7 oz	200 g
Tomato paste	1 2/3 oz	50 g
Red wine	6 3/4 oz	200 ml
Brown veal stock (Recipe 23)	1 qt 2 oz	1.0 L
Demi-glace (Recipe 44)	1 pt 1 oz	500 ml

[a]The names of beef cuts and butchering methods vary from region to region.
[b] The calves' feet should be blanched and split.
[c] For this recipe, use bay leaf, peppercorns, thyme, and marjoram.

[a] The names of beef cuts and butchering methods vary from region to region.

GARNISH

Tomatoes	1 lb 5 oz	600 g
Basil, fresh	2/3 oz	20 g
Thyme, fresh	1/3 oz	10 g
Butter	1 2/3 oz	50 g
Seasoning	1x	1x

MISE EN PLACE

Cut beef into 10 even slices and flatten. They should be about 1/4-in. (6 mm) thick.

Peel and slice onions.

Cut ham into coarse strips (*julienne*).

Cut pickles into spears for 10 even portions.

METHOD FOR GARNISH

Peel tomatoes, halve, remove seeds, and cut into medium-size dice.

Clean and chop basil and thyme.

Sauté tomatoes in butter, add basil and thyme, and season to taste.

Cook for 5 minutes over high heat, remove from stove, and keep warm.

METHOD

Sauté onions in butter, add ham, and sauté lightly. Let mixture cool.

Place flattened beef slices on work table. Brush with mustard and dust with paprika.

Top each meat slice with onion/ham mixture and one portion of pickle.

Fold in ends, roll up meat, and secure with kitchen twine.

Season meat. Brown in oil on all sides. Remove from pot.

Drain off excess oil from pot. Add *matignon* and sauté.

Add tomato paste and continue cooking.

Add wine and reduce completely.

Return meat to pot, add veal stock and *demi-glace* to just about cover meat. Bring to boil, cover, and braise in oven. Baste occasionally.

Check liquid level; if necessary, add more veal stock.

Remove meat when it is fully cooked.

Strain sauce through fine mesh china cap, skim, and reduce if necessary. Adjust seasoning.

PRESENTATION

Remove strings from beef rolls (*roulades*).

Serve meat covered with sauce. Garnish with sautéed tomatoes.

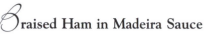

390

Braised Ham in Madeira Sauce

Geschmorter Schinken mit Madeira
Jambon braisé au madère

YIELD: 20 SERVINGS

Ham, bone in, raw[a]	13 lb 4 oz	6.0 kg
Matignon (Recipe 14)	1 lb 2 oz	500 g
Butter	1 2/3 oz	50 g
Madeira wine	10 oz	300 ml
Dry white wine	10 oz	300 ml
Brown veal stock (Recipe 23)	1 qt 19 oz	1.5 L
Cornstarch	2/3 oz	20 g
Powdered sugar	1 2/3 oz	50 g

MISE EN PLACE
Boil ham until about three-quarters done.

Remove skin and aitchbone. Trim off most fat. Score remaining fat layer diagonally.

METHOD
Sauté *matignon* in butter, in Dutch oven (*braisiere*).

Place ham on top of vegetables and add Madeira wine and white wine.

Add veal stock to about one fourth the height of the ham.

Braise in slow oven, basting frequently, until ham is cooked.

Remove ham and keep warm.

Strain sauce through fine mesh china cap; skim off all fat.

Bring sauce to a boil, add remaining veal stock, and reduce. Thicken sauce with cornstarch.

Sprinkle ham with powdered sugar and brown in very hot oven.

Serve sauce on the side.

NOTE: The ham can be brushed with honey instead of sugar.

[a] The ham should be a mild cured and smoked ham.

391

*B*reast of Veal Slices with Ratatouille

Glasierte Kalbsbrustschnitten mit Ratatouille
Tendrons de veau glacés à la ratatouille

YIELD: 10 SERVINGS

Breast of veal, oven-ready[a]	4 lb	1.8 kg
Seasoning salt for meat (Recipe 9)	1/3 oz	10 g
White wheat flour	1 oz	30 g
Peanut oil	2 3/4 oz	80 ml
Mirepoix for brown stock (Recipe 15)	7 oz	200 g
Bacon rind (skin)	5 1/3 oz	150 g
Tomato paste	1 oz	30 g
Dry white wine	6 3/4 oz	200 ml
Brown veal stock (Recipe 23)	1 qt 19 oz	1.5 L
Cornstarch	2/3 oz	20 g

GARNISH

Onions	2 2/3 oz	75 g
Garlic	1/4 oz	7 g
Eggplants	8 3/4 oz	250 g
Zucchini	8 3/4 oz	250 g
Tomatoes	10 1/2 oz	300 g
Bell peppers, assorted	10 1/2 oz	300 g
Kitchen herbs, fresh[b]	2/3 oz	20 g
Olive oil	1 2/3 oz	50 ml
Seasoning (salt and pepper)	1x	1x

MISE EN PLACE
Cut veal breast into 10 even slices. Fold each slice into a hairpin-shaped piece, and tie with kitchen twine.

METHOD FOR GARNISH
Chop onions and garlic.

Trim and wash eggplants and zucchini and cut into cubes.

Peel tomatoes, halve, remove seeds, and cut into cubes.

Split peppers, remove stems and seeds, and cut into cubes.

Wash and chop herbs.

Sauté onions and garlic in oil.

Add peppers, eggplants, and zucchini. Season to taste.

Add herbs, cover, and braise until vegetables are almost tender.

Add tomatoes and braise briefly. Keep ratatouille warm.

---

[a] The veal breast should be boneless and welltrimmed.

[b] Herbs such as thyme, rosemary, and parsley should be used in this recipe.

METHOD
Season veal slices, dust with flour, and brown in oil on all sides in Dutch oven (*braisiere*). Remove meat from pan.

Drain off excess oil. Add *mirepoix* and bacon rind to pan and roast briefly.

Add tomato paste and continue roasting.

Return meat to *braisiere*; add wine and small amount of veal stock. Reduce stock, basting meat frequently.

Add remaining stock, cover, and braise in oven until meat is tender. Turn meat and baste occasionally with the reducing sauce. It should get a nice glaze. Add more stock if necessary.

Remove meat, strain sauce through fine mesh china cap, skim off all fat.

Reduce sauce further if necessary and thicken with cornstarch.

PRESENTATION
Remove twine from meat.

Serve meat on top of ratatouille, with some sauce around.

Serve remaining sauce on the side.

392

*G*lazed Veal Shank with Vegetables

Glasierte Kalbshaxe bürgerliche Art
Jarret de veau glacé bourgeoise

YIELD: 10 SERVINGS

Veal shanks, bone in, trimmed, oven-ready	7 lb 12 oz	3.5 kg
Seasoning salt for meat (Recipe 9)	2/3 oz	20 g
Peanut oil	3 1/3 oz	100 ml
Mirepoix for brown stock (Recipe 15)	12 oz	350 g
Tomato paste	1 2/3 oz	50 g
Thyme twig, fresh	1	1
Sage, fresh	1/3 oz	10 g
Rosemary twig, fresh	1	1
Dry white wine	6 3/4 oz	200 ml
Brown veal stock	1 qt 19 oz	1.5 L
Cornstarch	1/3 oz	10 g

GARNISH

Carrots	1 lb	450 g
Turnips, white, small	12 oz	350 g
Pearl onions	7 oz	200 g
Butter	1 2/3 oz	50 g
White veal stock (Recipe 28)	6 3/4 oz	200 ml

Sugar	1x	1x
Seasoning (salt and pepper)	1x	1x
Peas, frozen	3 1/2 oz	100 g
Parsley, chopped	1 1/3 oz	40 g

METHOD

Season veal shanks and roast lightly on all sides, in peanut oil, in Dutch oven (*braisiere*). Remove veal from pan.

Drain excess oil from pan. Add *mirepoix* and roast briefly.

Add tomato paste and continue roasting. Add herbs.

Return meat to *pan*; add wine and a small amount of veal stock. Reduce stock, basting meat frequently.

Add remaining stock, cover, and braise in oven until meat is tender. Turn meat and baste occasionally with the reducing sauce. It should get a nice glaze. Add more stock if necessary.

Remove veal and keep warm.

Strain sauce through fine mesh china cap; skim off all fat.

Reduce sauce further if necessary; and thicken with cornstarch.

Take meat off the bones and cut into attractive slices.

METHOD FOR GARNISH

Peel carrots, turnips, and pearl onions. Braise each vegetable separately in butter and veal stock. Season with sugar and salt and pepper. Let braising liquid reduce to glaze vegetables.

Thaw peas.

Combine all vegetables. Heat briefly. Add chopped parsley.

PRESENTATION

Brush veal slices with melted butter to give a nice sheen. Serve veal slices with vegetables, surrounded with some sauce.

Serve remaining sauce on the side.

393

͟Glazed Veal Sweetbreads with Tarragon

Glasierte Kalbsmilken mit Estragon
Ris de veau glacés à l'estragon

YIELD: 10 SERVINGS

Veal sweetbreads	3 lb 8 oz	1.6 kg
Onion	1 2/3 oz	50 g
Bay leaf	1	1
Clove	1	1
White veal stock (Recipe 28)	2 qt 20 oz	2.5 L
Dry white wine	6 3/4 oz	200 ml
Shallots	1 oz	30 g
Tarragon, fresh	3/4 oz	25 g
Butter	1 oz	30 g
Madeira wine	6 3/4 oz	200 ml
Brown veal stock (Recipe 23)	1 pt 1 oz	500 ml
Cornstarch	1/3 oz	10 g
Tarragon vinegar	1/3 oz	10 ml
Seasoning	1x	1x
Butter	1 oz	30 g

MISE EN PLACE

Soak sweetbreads in cold water overnight.

Peel onion; make incision and insert bay leaf; press clove into onion.

Add onion to white veal stock and white wine. Bring to a boil. Add sweetbreads.

Poach sweetbreads, for about 20 minutes, until about three-quarters cooked.

Chop shallots.

Strip leaves from tarragon and chop leaves.

METHOD

Sauté shallots in butter.

Place sweetbreads on top of shallots; add 5 oz (150 ml) Madeira wine and some of the brown veal stock to about one-fourth the height of sweetbreads. Cover pot and braise in oven, basting sweetbreads frequently.

When almost done, remove lid and continue basting to give sweetbreads a nice sheen.

Remove sweetbreads and keep warm.

Add remaining veal stock, bring to a boil, skim, and strain sauce through a fine mesh china cap.

Thicken sauce with cornstarch.

Add remaining Madeira wine, chopped tarragon leaves, and tarragon vinegar. Season to taste.

Add cold butter in small nuggets. Do not allow the sauce to return to a boil.

Slice sweetbreads on a bias and serve covered with sauce.

394

Glazed Veal Sweetbreads with White Port Wine

Glasierte Kalbsmilken mit weissem Porto
Ris de veau glacés au porto blanc

YIELD: 10 SERVINGS

Veal sweetbreads	3 lb 8 oz	1.6 kg
Onions	1 2/3 oz	50 g
Bay leaf	1	1
Clove	1	1
White veal stock (Recipe 28)	2 qt 20 oz	2.5 L
Dry white wine	6 3/4 oz	200 ml
Shallots	1 oz	30 g
Butter	1 oz	30 g
White Port wine	6 3/4 oz	200 ml
Brown veal stock (Recipe 23)	1 pt 1 oz	500 ml
Cornstarch	1/3 oz	10 g
Seasoning	1x	1x
Butter	1 oz	30 g

MISE EN PLACE

Soak sweetbreads in cold water overnight.

Peel onion; make incision and insert bay leaf; press clove into onion.

Add onion to white veal stock and wine. Bring to a boil. Add sweetbreads.

Poach sweetbreads until about three-quarters cooked; this will take about 20 minutes.

Chop shallots.

METHOD

Sauté shallots in butter.

Place sweetbreads on top of shallots; add 5 oz (150 ml) white Port wine and some of the brown veal stock to about one fourth the height of sweetbreads. Cover pot and braise in oven, basting sweetbreads frequently.

When almost done, remove lid and continue basting to give sweetbreads a nice sheen.

Remove sweetbreads and keep warm.

Add remaining veal stock, bring to a boil, skim, and strain sauce through a fine mesh china cap.

Thicken sauce with cornstarch.

Add remaining Port wine. Season to taste.

Add cold butter in small nuggets. Do not allow the sauce to return to a boil.

Slice sweetbreads on a bias and serve covered with sauce.

395

Glazed Pork Shoulder Roast with Apples

Glasierte Schweinsschulter Mirza
Epaule de porc glacée Mirza

YIELD: 10 SERVINGS

Pork shoulder, boneless, oven-ready	3 lb 8 oz	1.6 kg
Rosemary twig, fresh	1	1
Seasoning salt for meat (Recipe 9)	1/3 oz	10 g
Peanut oil	2 3/4 oz	80 ml
Mirepoix for brown stock (Recipe 15)	7 oz	200 g
Bacon rind (skin)	3 1/2 oz	100 g
Tomato paste	2/3 oz	20 g
Dry white wine	3 1/3 oz	100 ml
Brown veal stock (Recipe 23)	1 qt 19 oz	1.5 L
Cornstarch	1/3 oz	10 g

GARNISH

Apples, 5 each	1 lb 10 oz	750 g
Dry white wine	6 3/4 oz	200 ml
Water	6 3/4 oz	200 ml
Lemon, juice	1/2	1/2
Crystal sugar	1 2/3 oz	50 g
Red currant jelly	3 1/2 oz	100 g

MISE EN PLACE FOR GARNISH

Peel apples, cut in half, and scoop out core.

Combine white wine, water, lemon juice, and sugar. Poach apples very carefully; do not overcook. Keep apples warm in poaching liquid.

METHOD

Place rosemary twig on pork. Tie pork with butcher twine to give it an even shape.

Season pork and brown lightly on all sides, in peanut oil, in a Dutch oven (*braisiere*). Remove pork from pan.

Pour off excess oil from pan, add *mirepoix* and bacon rind, and roast lightly.

Add tomato paste and continue roasting.

Return pork to pan, and add white wine and small amount of veal stock. Reduce stock, basting meat frequently.

Add sufficient stock to reach to about one-quarter the level of the meat. Cover and cook in the oven.

When almost done, remove lid. Baste pork with the reduced liquid to give the pork a nice sheen. Remove pork and keep warm.

Add remaining stock, bring to a boil, and skim.

Strain through a fine mesh china cap; skim off all fat.

Bring sauce to a boil and thicken with cornstarch. Adjust seasoning.

Remove apples from poaching liquid and let drain on wire rack.

Slice meat; brush slices with melted butter. Serve sauce around meat.

Fill apples with currant jelly and serve with meat.

396

Grilled Veal Kidneys with Mustard

Grillierte Kalbsnierenschnitten mit Senf
Tranches de rognon de veau grillées dijonnaise

YIELD: 10 SERVINGS

Veal kidneys, not peeled[a]	3 lb	1.4 kg
Shallots	5 1/3 oz	150 g
Peanut oil	3 1/3 oz	100 ml
Seasoning (salt and pepper)	1x	1x
Butter	5 1/3 oz	150 g
Dijon-style mustard[b]	3 oz	80 g
Lemon, juice	1/2	1/2
Parsley, chopped	1 1/3 oz	40 g
Seasoning (pepper, freshly ground)	1x	1x

MISE EN PLACE

Trim kidneys, but leave a thin fat cover of about 1/5 in. (5 mm). Cut kidneys into slices.

Peel shallots and chop very fine.

METHOD

Just before service, season kidney slices. Brush kidneys with oil and grill to order, medium rare [c]

While kidneys are cooking, sauté shallots in butter; add mustard, lemon juice, and half the chopped parsley; season with freshly ground pepper.

Serve kidneys with mustard spread, and sprinkle with remaining parsley.

397

Grilled Spare Ribs

Grillierte Schweinsbrustrippen
Spareribs

YIELD: 10 SERVINGS

Breast spareribs (pork)	5 lb 8 oz	2.5 kg
Salt	2/3 oz	20 g

MARINADE
Garlic	1/3 oz	10 g
Pepper, white, ground	1 pinch	1 g
Paprika	1/8 oz	3 1/2 g
Ginger, dry, ground	1/8 oz	3 1/2 g
Coriander seeds, ground	1/8 oz	3 1/2 g
Honey	1 2/3 oz	50 g
Soy bean oil	5 oz	150 ml

MISE EN PLACE

Crush garlic to a smooth paste and combine with all other marinade ingredients.

Brush spareribs with marinade and refrigerate for at least 2 hours.

METHOD

Drain spareribs on wire rack. Season with salt.

Grill ribs over high heat, on both sides.[a]

Reduce heat and grill for about 20 to 30 minutes.

Before serving, let ribs rest, covered, for 5 to 10 minutes.

NOTE: Spareribs may require a longer cooking time.

---

[a] The size of kidneys, and their fat content, varies greatly. After trimming, before cooking, there should be at least 5 oz (140 g) of meat per person.

[b] There are many different versions of Dijon mustard. The mustard for this recipe should be smooth and flavorful, but not sharp.

[c] Kidneys should be cooked to order, according to the customer's request. Although kidneys cooked well done can be dry, some people may prefer them this way.

[a] Many chefs prefer to omit the high heat at the beginning; instead, they roast the meat in a slow oven for about 1 hour or more.

398

$\mathcal{G}$rilled Chateaubriand with Bearnaise Sauce

Grillierte Chateaubriands mit Bearner Sauce
Chateaubriands grillés béarnaise

YIELD: 10 SERVINGS

Beef tenderloin heads, trimmed (5)[a]	4 lb	1.8 kg
Thyme, fresh	1/3 oz	10 g
Rosemary, fresh	1/3 oz	10 g
White peppercorns	1/4 oz	7 g
Peanut oil	3 1/3 oz	100 ml
Salt	1/3 oz	10 g

GARNISH

White bread (Pullman loaf)	8 3/4 oz	250 g
Butter	1 2/3 oz	50 g
Bearnaise sauce (Recipe 33)	13 1/2 oz	400 ml

MISE EN PLACE

Trim and slightly flatten tenderloins.

Remove stems from herbs and chop leaves. Crush white peppercorns.

Mix herbs and peppercorns with peanut oil.

Brush mixture on steaks and marinate for 1 to 2 hours (if possible).

Cut bread into 5 slices and trim off crust.

METHOD

Salt meat and place on very hot grill. Cook the more attractive side of the tenderloins first.

Turn steaks 60 degrees after a short time to sear in an attractive diamond pattern.

Turn steaks over and proceed in the same manner; brush steaks occasionally with the oil mixture.

Place steaks in medium-hot oven to cook further, if necessary.[b]

When the steaks are done, keep warm for a short while, to allow the juices to circulate and to minimize juice loss when they are cut.

Sauté bread in butter.

Slice meat to order and serve on top of the bread slices (croûtons).

Serve Bearnaise sauce on the side.

---

[a] Chateaubriand is a large tenderloin steak. One steak generally serves two customers. This steak is cut from the "head" (thick end) of the tenderloin.

[b] Steaks should be cooked according to customers' specifications. If the steaks are ordered medium-well or well done, it is necessary to cook them further in the oven.

399

$\mathcal{G}$rilled Veal Chops with Basil Butter

Grillierte Kalbskoteletts mit Basilikumbutter
Côtes de veau grillées au beurre de basilic

YIELD: 10 SERVINGS

Veal chops, completely trimmed, 10[a]	4 lb	1.8 kg
Salt	1/3 oz	10 g

MARINADE

Basil, fresh	1/3 oz	10 g
Thyme, fresh	1/3 oz	10 g
Peanut oil	3 1/3 oz	100 ml
Seasoning (white pepper)	1x	1x
Lemon juice	2/3 oz	20 ml

BASIL BUTTER

Basil, fresh	1 2/3 oz	50 g
Butter	5 1/3 oz	150 g
Lemon juice	1 2/3 oz	50 ml
Glace de viande[b]	1 2/3 oz	50 g
Seasoning (salt and pepper)	1x	1x

GARNISH

Cress[c]	1 2/3 oz	50 g
Lemon wedges	10	10

METHOD FOR MARINADE

Chop basil and thyme and mix with peanut oil, white pepper, and lemon juice.

METHOD FOR BASIL BUTTER

Remove stems from basil and chop.

Cream butter, add chopped basil, lemon juice, melted *glace de viande*, and salt and pepper.

Shape butter with pastry bag on parchment paper into 10 rosettes and chill. (Butter can also be shaped into a roll, wrapped in foil, chilled, and sliced.)

METHOD

Marinate veal chops for at least 2 hours.

Place chops on hot grill.

Turn chops 60 degrees after a short time to sear in an attractive diamond pattern.

---

[a] The size of veal chops varies. A single bone-in chop, completely trimmed, can weigh 7 oz (200 g) or more.

[b] *Glace de viande*, literally translated "meat glaze," is made by reducing meat stock to a syrupy consistency.

[c] The original recipe calls for *Brunnenkresse*, which is a little spicier in flavor than watercress. Watercress can be substituted.

Turn chops over and proceed in the same manner, brushing meat occasionally with marinade.

Place chops in oven to cook completely.[a]

PRESENTATION

Serve chops garnished with cress and a lemon wedge.

Serve butter rosettes, or butter slices, on the side.

400

Grilled Veal Paillards[b] with Lemon

Grillierte Kalbs-Paillards mit Zitrone
Paillards de veau grillés au citron

YIELD: 10 SERVINGS

Veal, top round,[c] completely trimmed	3 lb 5 oz	1.5 kg
Seasoning salt for meat (Recipe 9)	2/3 oz	20 g
Peanut oil	3 1/3 oz	100 ml

GARNISH

Lemons	5	5
Parsley sprigs, curly, fresh	1 2/3 oz	50 g

MISE EN PLACE

Cut 10 thin cutlets from veal top round. Flatten between two sheets of plastic wrap. The cutlets should be very thin.

Cut lemons in half.

Wash parsley, break off and discard the large stems.

METHOD

Season veal cutlets with seasoning salt and brush with peanut oil.

Place cutlets—to order—on very hot grill. After a short time, turn meat 60 degrees to sear in an attractive diamond pattern.

Turn cutlets over and proceed in the same manner. Brush with oil to keep veal moist.

Serve immediately, garnished with lemon half and parsley sprigs.

401

Grilled Double Lamb Chops with Thyme

Grillierte doppelte Lammchops mit Thymian
Doubles chops d'agneau grillés au thym

YIELD: 10 SERVINGS

Basil, fresh	1/3 oz	10 g
Thyme, fresh	1 oz	30 g
Peanut oil	3 oz	80 g
Seasoning (white pepper)	1x	1x
Double lamb chops, trimmed, 10	4 lb	1.8 kg
Garlic	1/4 oz	7 g
Salt	1/3 oz	10 g
Butter	1 2/3 oz	50 g

GARNISH

Cress[a]	1 2/3 oz	50 g

MISE EN PLACE

Chop basil and thyme leaves.

Blend the basil and 1/3 oz (10 g) thyme with peanut oil and white pepper.

Marinate lamb chops.

Crush or chop garlic and blend with remaining thyme.

METHOD

Salt lamb chops and place on hot grill, best side down first.

After a short time, turn chops 60 degrees to sear in an attractive diamond pattern.

Turn chops over and grill until done,[b] basting with marinade to keep lamb moist.

Just before serving, brown the butter in a deep-sided skillet, add garlic and thyme,[c] and pour foaming hot over lamb chops.

Garnish with cress.

---

[a] It is advisable to cook the chops briefly in the oven to be sure the tissues around the bone are cooked.

[b] Paillards are very thin cutlets, cut across the grain.

[c] The names of meat cuts vary from country to country. "Top round" is called *Eckstück* or *Bäggli* in Switzerland, and *Oberschale* in Germany.

[a] The recipe calls for *Brunnenkresse*, which is a little spicier in flavor than watercress. Watercress can be substituted.

[b] Lamb should be cooked to the customer's specifications; in most cases, it is served medium-rare.

[c] Be sure the pan is deep enough; the butter will foam up when garlic and thyme are added.

402

Grilled Porterhouse Steaks with Herb Butter

Grillierte Porterhouse-Steaks mit Kräuterbutter
Steaks Porterhouse grillés maître d'hôtel

YIELD: 10 SERVINGS

Thyme, fresh	1/3 oz	10 g
Rosemary	1/3 oz	10 g
White peppercorns	1/4 oz	7 g
Peanut oil	3 1/3 oz	100 ml
Porterhouse steaks,[a] trimmed, oven-ready, 5	6 lb 10 oz	3.0 kg
Salt	pinch	2 g

GARNISH

Cress[b]	3 1/2 oz	100 g
Lemons	2 1/2	2 1/2
Herb butter (Use maitre d'hotel butter, Recipe 444)	7 oz	200 g

MISE EN PLACE

Wash thyme and rosemary and chop leaves. Crush white peppercorns.

Blend herbs and crushed pepper with oil and marinate steaks.

Wash cress. Cut lemons into quarters.

METHOD

Place steaks, best side down first, on hot grill. After a short time, turn steaks 60 degrees to sear in an attractive diamond pattern.

Turn steaks over and proceed in the same manner, brushing with marinade to keep meat moist.

Put steaks in hot oven[c] if additional cooking is required.

If no further cooking is needed, keep steaks warm to let the juices settle.

Serve steaks garnished with cress and lemon wedges.

Serve *maitre d'hotel* butter on the side.

NOTE: Porterhouse steaks are normally sized for 2 to 4 portions. In fine restaurants, the steaks are often carved at the table.

---

[a] The size of meat portions varies greatly from country to country. In some places, the portion size is 1 lb (450 g).

[b] The recipe calls for *Brunnenkresse*, which is a little spicier in flavor than watercress. Watercress can be substituted.

[c] The meat should be cooked to the customer's specifications. If the steak is ordered medium-well or welldone, it is necessary to cook them further in the oven.

403

Grilled Club Steak with Tomatoes and Fried Onion Rings

Grillierte Rumpsteaks mit Tomaten und gebackenen Zwiebelringen
Rumpsteaks grillés tyrolienne

YIELD: 10 SERVINGS

Sirloin butt, trimmed	3 lb 8 oz	1.6 kg
Thyme, fresh	1/4 oz	7 g
Rosemary, fresh	1/4 oz	7 g
White peppercorns	1/8 oz	3 1/2 g
Peanut oil	2 3/4 oz	80 ml
Salt	1/3 oz	10 g

GARNISH

Onions	1 lb 2 oz	500 g
Shallots	3 1/2 oz	100 g
Tomatoes	2 lb 3 oz	1.0 kg
Kitchen herbs,[a] fresh	1/3 oz	10 g
Butter	1 oz	30 g
Seasoning (salt and pepper)	1x	1x
White wheat flour	1 2/3 oz	50 g
Oil for frying (10% oil loss)	1 2/3 oz	50 ml
Cress[b]	7 oz	200 g

MISE EN PLACE

Cut sirloin butt into 10 steaks.

Chop thyme and rosemary leaves. Crush peppercorns.

Add herbs and crushed pepper to peanut oil.

Marinate the steaks in oil mixture.

METHOD FOR GARNISH

Peel onions and cut into rings.[c]

Peel and chop shallots.

Peel tomatoes, cut in half, remove seeds, and cut into dice.

Wash and chop herbs.

Sauté shallots in butter, add tomatoes and herbs, season, and cook briefly. Keep warm.

Dredge onion rings in flour[d] and deep-fry until golden brown.

Wash cress.

---

[a] Herbs such as parsley and chives would be good for this garnish.

[b] The original recipe calls for *Brunnenkresse*, which is a little spicier in flavor than watercress. Watercress can be substituted.

[c] A meat slicer can be used to cut even onion rings.

[d] The onions can be dipped in cream and then dredged in flour. The cream makes the flour adhere to the onions, and also helps to brown the rings evenly.

METHOD
Season steaks and place on hot grill.

After a short time, turn steaks about 60 degrees to sear in an attractive diamond pattern.

Turn steaks over and proceed in the same manner, brushing with marinade. Cook to desired doneness.

Serve steaks topped with stewed tomatoes and onion rings.

Garnish with cress.

404

Veal Rouladen with Ham, Tomatoes, and Sage
Involtini cacciatore
Paupiettes de Veau

YIELD: 10 SERVINGS

Veal top round,[a] trimmed	2 lb 10 oz	1.2 kg
Parma ham[b]	3 1/2 oz	100 g
Shallots	1 2/3 oz	50 g
Sage, fresh	2/3 oz	20 g
Parsley	1 oz	30 g
Chicken livers, raw, trimmed	8 3/4 oz	250 g
Butter	1 oz	30 g
Seasoning (salt and pepper)	1x	1x
White wheat flour	1 2/3 oz	50 g
Clarified butter	1 2/3 oz	50 g
Marsala wine[c]	3 1/3 oz	100 ml
Bouillon (Recipe 22)	1 pt 1 oz	500 ml
Butter, cold	1 2/3 oz	50 g

MISE EN PLACE
Cut veal into 10 thin cutlets. Flatten between two sheets of aluminum foil.

Cut ham into small dice.

Chop shallots, sage, and parsley.

METHOD
Sauté chicken livers in butter, remove, and let cool.

Add ham, shallots, sage, and parsley; season with salt and pepper.

Chop mixture, including livers, coarsely.

---

[a] The names of meat cuts vary from country to country. "Top round" is called *Eckstück* or *Bäggli* in Switzerland, and *Oberschale* in Germany.

[b] Parma ham is an air-dried ham from Parma, Italy. The ham is often marketed as prosciutto ham.

[c] Marsala is a sweet wine from Sicily. Sweet sherry can be substituted.

Place a mound of chopped liver on each cutlet.

Fold in ends, roll up tightly, and tie with butcher's twine.

Dredge rolls in flour and brown on all sides in clarified butter.

Remove veal rolls, add Marsala wine and bouillon, and bring to a boil.

Return veal to casserole. Braise in oven, without lid, for about 10 minutes, basting frequently.

Remove veal rolls and keep warm.

Add cold butter to hot sauce in small nuggets. Do not allow sauce to return to a boil.

Remove twine from veal rolls. Serve covered with sauce.

405

Irish Stew
Irish Stew

YIELD: 10 SERVINGS

Lamb stew meat,[a] cut into 1 1/3-oz (40 g) cubes	4 lb 7 oz	2.0 kg
Onions	2 lb 3 oz	1.0 kg
Potatoes	5 lb 8 oz	2.5 kg
Garlic	1/3 oz	10 g
Salt	2/3 oz	20 g
Sachet bag[b]	1	1
White veal stock (Recipe 28)	3 qt 5 oz	3.0 L
Worcestershire sauce	3 1/3 oz	100 ml

MISE EN PLACE
Blanch lamb, drain, and wash, first in hot water, then in cold water. Drain again.

Peel onions and cut into thin slices.

Peel potatoes and cut into thin slices.

Peel and chop garlic.

METHOD
Layer lamb, onions, and potatoes in a stew pot.

Add garlic, salt, and sachet bag.

(continued on next page)

---

[a] The stew meat should be cut from the shoulder and neck, and should be lean and well trimmed.

[b] For this recipe, use bay leaf, peppercorns, thyme, and rosemary.

(continued from preceding page)

Fill with veal stock.

Cover pot and simmer slowly until meat is tender.

Remove sachet bag.

Sprinkle with Worcestershire sauce just before serving.

NOTE: In some instances, Irish stew recipes also call for vegetables, such as savoy cabbage, carrots, celery, or leeks. When this is the case, the amount of onions and potatoes should be reduced accordingly.

406

*V*eal Blanquette with Mushrooms and Pearl Onions

Kalbsblankett mit Champignons und Perlzwiebeln
Blanquette de veau ancienne

YIELD: 10 SERVINGS

Veal shoulder, cut into 1 1/3-oz (40 g) cubes	3 lb 8 oz	1.6 kg
White veal stock (Recipe 28)	1 qt 19 oz	1.5 L
Dry white wine	10 oz	300 ml
Bouquet garni (Recipe 8)	10 1/2 oz	300 g
Sachet bag[a]	1	1

SAUCE

Butter	1 1/3 oz	40 g
White wheat flour	1 2/3 oz	50 g
Egg yolks	3	3
Heavy cream (36%)	6 3/4 oz	200 ml
Lemon	1/2	1/2
Seasoning (salt and pepper)	1x	1x

GARNISH

Pearl onions	10 1/2 oz	300 g
Mushrooms, fresh	8 3/4 oz	250 g
Butter	3/4 oz	25 g
Lemon, juice	1/4	1/4
Seasoning (salt and pepper)	1x	1x

MISE EN PLACE
Blanch veal cubes, drain, and wash, first in hot water, then in cold water. Drain again.

METHOD FOR GARNISH
Peel pearl onions and blanch.

Wash and trim mushrooms. Leave mushrooms whole, or cut into halves or quarters, depending on size.

Smother onions and mushrooms in butter and lemon juice. Season to taste.

METHOD
Combine veal stock and white wine; heat.

Add veal, bring to a boil, and skim.

Add *bouquet garni* and sachet bag; simmer until veal is tender.

Remove veal (use a skimmer) and keep warm in small amount of stock. Reserve remaining stock.

Melt butter; add flour to make a white roux. Let cool slightly.

Heat 1 qt 2 oz (1.0 L) reserved stock. Add hot stock to cool roux, stir to dissolve roux, bring to a boil, stirring constantly. Simmer for 30 minutes.

Strain sauce through double layer of cheesecloth.

Blend egg yolks thoroughly with heavy cream.

Put sauce back onto stove and bring to a boil. Remove from heat and add egg yolk cream mixture (*liaison*).

Add veal, heat, but do not allow sauce to return to a boil. Season with lemon juice, salt and pepper.

Serve with mushroom/onion garnish.

407

*B*oiled Calf's Head Turtle Style

Kalbskopf Schildkrötenart
Tête de veau en tortue

YIELD: 10 SERVINGS

Calf's head,[a] boned	5 lb 8 oz	2.5 kg
White veal stock (Recipe 28)	5 qt 9 oz	5.0 L
White wine vinegar	3 1/3 oz	100 ml
Lemon	1	1
Bouquet garni (Recipe 8)	14 oz	400 g
Onion, studded with 2 cloves	1	1
Sachet bag[b]	1	1
Seasoning (salt)	1x	1x

---

[a] For this recipe, use bay leaf, peppercorns, and thyme.

[a] The calf's head is normally sold blanched, all hair removed, the brain removed, and in some cases, without the tongue.

[b] For this recipe, use bay leaf, peppercorns, and thyme.

SAUCE

Madeira sauce (Recipe 69)	1 qt 26 3/4 oz	1.7 L
Tomato sauce	10 oz	300 ml
Kitchen herbs,[a] fresh, chopped	1 1/3 oz	40 g
Seasoning (salt, cayenne)	1x	1x

GARNISH

Mushrooms, fresh	7 oz	200 g
Butter	3/4 oz	25 g
Eggs	5	5
Black olives, drained	3 1/2 oz	100g
Cornichons,[b] drained	3 1/2 oz	100 g
White bread (Pullman loaf)	5 1/3 oz	150 g
Parsley, chopped	2/3 oz	20 g

MISE EN PLACE

Blanch calf's head, drain, and wash, first in hot water, then in cold water.

Trim and cut calf's head meat into stew-size pieces.

METHOD FOR GARNISH

Trim mushrooms and cut into halves or quarters, depending on size. Sauté mushrooms in butter and keep warm.

Boil eggs, peel, and cut into quarters.

Remove pits from black olives. Cut cornichons into fans.

Dice bread and toast under the salamander.

METHOD

Bring veal stock to a boil and add calf's head pieces.

Add vinegar, lemon, *bouquet garni*, onion, sachet bag, and salt.

Skim occasionally and simmer until calf's head meat is tender.

Make sauce by combining Madeira sauce with tomato sauce. Bring to boil and reduce to desired consistency. Season sauce with herbs, salt, and cayenne.

Be sure calf's head meat is well drained; add meat to sauce.

Serve meat in sauce. Place garnishes on top; sprinkle with parsley.

NOTE: This dish can also be garnished with small quenelles (dumplings) made with Mousseline Farce (Recipe 17).

---

[a] Herbs such as sage, marjoram, rosemary, basil, and thyme could be used in this sauce.

[b] Cornichons are small, somewhat acidic pickles. Do not use gherkins (sweet pickles).

408

Veal Fricasse with Mushrooms

Kalbsfrikassee mit Champignons
Fricassée de veau aux champignons

YIELD: 10 SERVINGS

Veal shoulder meat, cut into 1 1/3-oz (40 g) cubes	3 lb 8 oz	1.6 kg
Salt	1/3 oz	10 g
White pepper, ground	pinch	2 g
White wheat flour	2 1/2 oz	70 g
Onions	8 3/4 oz	250 g
Clarified butter	3 1/2 oz	100 g
Dry white wine	10 oz	300 ml
White veal stock (Recipe 28)	1 qt 19 oz	1.5 L
Sachet bag[a]	1	1
Heavy cream (36%)	6 3/4 oz	200 ml
Lemon	1/2	1/2
Seasoning (salt and pepper)	1x	1x

GARNISH

Mushrooms, fresh	10 1/2 oz	300 g
Butter	3/4 oz	25 g
Lemon	1/2	1/2

METHOD FOR GARNISH

Wash and trim mushrooms and cut into halves or quarters, depending on size. Sauté mushrooms in butter, season with lemon juice and keep warm.

METHOD

Season veal with salt and pepper and dust veal with small amount of flour.

Peel and chop onions.

Heat clarified butter in wide, heavy saucepan (*rondeau*). Add meat and chopped onions; smother over low heat until the meat juices have reduced to syrup consistency. Do not allow veal or juices to brown.

Dust with remaining flour, add wine and veal stock and bring to a boil.

Skim and add sachet bag. Simmer until veal is tender.

Remove veal with skimmer and keep warm.

Purée sauce and strain through a small-hole china cap.

Bring sauce to a boil, stir in heavy cream, and season with lemon juice. (If sauce is too liquid, thicken with a small amount of cornstarch.)

Return veal to sauce and heat. Add mushroom garnish to sauce.

---

[a] For this recipe, use bay leaf, peppercorns, and thyme.

409

$\mathcal{V}$eal Cutlet Cordon Bleu (stuffed with ham and cheese)

Kalbsschnitzel Cordon Bleu
Escalopes de veau Cordon bleu

YIELD: 10 SERVINGS

Veal top round,[a] trimmed	3 lb	1.4 kg
Ham, cooked	7 oz	200 g
Gruyere cheese[b]	7 oz	200 g
Eggs	4	4
White bread (Pullman loaf)	10 1/2 oz	300 g
Seasoning salt for meat (Recipe 9)	1/3 oz	10 g
White wheat flour	1 2/3 oz	50 g
Clarified butter	5 1/3 oz	150 g
Lemon wedges	10	10

MISE EN PLACE

Cut veal into 20 cutlets 2 1/2 oz (70 g). Flatten between two sheets of aluminum foil.

Slice ham into 10 thin slices. Cut Gruyere into 10 slices.

Layer ham slices and cheese slices on top of 10 veal cutlets and cover with remaining cutlets.

Break eggs and mix well.

Remove crusts from bread and grate[c] into fresh bread crumbs.

METHOD

Season veal cutlets. Dredge in flour, then in eggs, and then in fresh bread crumbs.

Press crumbs on lightly; shake off excess.

Sauté veal in clarified butter, on both sides, until golden brown.

Serve with lemon wedges.

NOTE: The meat can also be cut into 10 *thick* cutlets, a pocket cut into the side, and the filling inserted.

410

$\mathcal{V}$eal Cutlet Holstein (with fried eggs and anchovy)

Kalbsschnitzel Holstein
Escalopes de veau Holstein

YIELD: 10 SERVINGS

Veal top round,[a] trimmed	3 lb 5 oz	1.5 kg
Seasoning salt for meat (Recipe 9)	1/3 oz	10 g
White wheat flour	1 2/3 oz	50 g
Peanut oil	3 1/3 oz	100 ml

GARNISH

Eggs	10	10
Butter	3 1/2 oz	100 g
Seasoning (salt and pepper)	1x	1x
Anchovy fillets, drained	5 1/3 oz	150 g
Parsley, sprigs, washed	1 oz	30 g

MISE EN PLACE

Cut veal into 10 cutlets. Pound lightly to tenderize the meat.

METHOD

Season veal cutlets, dredge in flour, and sauté, on both sides, in peanut oil.

Fry eggs, sunny-side up, in butter; season eggs. Place one egg on each cutlet.

Split anchovy fillets lengthwise and place on cutlets in an attractive geometric pattern.

Garnish with parsley sprigs.

---

[a] The names of meat cuts vary from country to country. "Top round" is called *Eckstück* or *Bäggli* in Switzerland, and *Oberschale* in Germany.

[b] Gruyere cheese is referred to as Greyerzer in some parts of Switzerland.

[c] The best way to make fresh bread crumbs is in the food processor.

---

[a] The names of meat cuts vary from country to country. "Top round" is called *Eckstück* or *Bäggli* in Switzerland, and *Oberschale* in Germany.

411

Veal Cutlet in Cream Sauce

Kalbsschnitzel mit Rahmsauce
Escalopes de veau à la crème

YIELD: 10 SERVINGS

Veal top round or Kalbsnuss,[a] trimmed	3 lb 5 oz	1.5 kg
Shallots	2 1/2 oz	70 g
Heavy cream (36%)	13 1/2 oz	400 ml
Seasoning (salt and pepper)	1x	1x
White wheat flour	1 2/3 oz	50 g
Peanut oil	3 1/3 oz	100 ml
Dry white wine	6 3/4 oz	200 ml
Brown veal juice (Recipe 55)	10 oz	300 ml
Seasoning (salt)	1x	1x
Lemon juice	1/3 oz	10 ml

MISE EN PLACE

Cut veal into 20 cutlets; pound cutlets lightly to tenderize and flatten them.

Peel and chop shallots.

Whip half the heavy cream into soft peaks.

METHOD

Season cutlets and dust with flour.

Heat peanut oil; sauté cutlets in hot oil, on both sides, until light golden.

Remove cutlets and keep warm.

Pour off excess oil.

Add shallots and sauté in the pan drippings.

Add wine and reduce completely.

Add veal juice and remaining heavy cream and bring to a boil.

Strain sauce through a fine mesh china cap.

Fold the whipped cream into the sauce.

Season with salt and lemon juice.

Serve cutlets covered with sauce and serve some sauce on the side.

---

[a] The names of meat cuts very from country to country. The cut recommended in the original recipe is called Nuss in German and "noix" in French. Top round can also be used.

412

Veal Stew with Spring Vegetables

Kalbsvoressen mit Frühlingsgemüse
Sauté de veau aux primeurs

YIELD: 10 SERVINGS

Onions	1 2/3 oz	50 g
Garlic	1/3 oz	10 g
Veal stew meat,[a] cut into 1 1/3 oz (40 g) cubes	3 lb 8 oz	1.6 kg
Seasoning salt for meat (Recipe 9)	1/3 oz	10 g
White wheat flour	3/4 oz	25 g
Peanut oil	3 1/3 oz	100 ml
Tomato paste	1 2/3 oz	50 g
Dry white wine	6 3/4 oz	200 ml
Brown veal stock (Recipe 23)	6 3/4 oz	200 ml
Demi-glace (Recipe 44)	1 pt 1 oz	500 ml
Sachet bag	1	1
Cornstarch	1/3 oz	10 g

GARNISH

Carrots	7 oz	200 g
White turnips (small)	7 oz	200 g
Knob celery (celeriac)	7 oz	200 g
Pearl onions	5 1/3 oz	150 g
Butter	1 2/3 oz	50 g
White veal stock (Recipe 28)	10 oz	300 ml
Crystal sugar	1x	1x
Seasoning (salt and pepper)	1x	1x
Peas, frozen	5 1/3 oz	150 g

MISE EN PLACE

Peel and chop onions and garlic.

METHOD FOR GARNISH

Peel and trim carrots, white turnips, and knob celery. Cut into wedges, sticks, or barrel shapes.

Peel pearl onions.

Braise vegetables—except peas—with butter, veal stock, sugar, and seasoning.

Add peas when vegetables are almost cooked. Keep warm.

(continued on next page)

---

[a] The stew meat should be cut from the shoulder, and should be lean and well trimmed.

(continued from preceding page)

METHOD

Season veal and dust lightly with flour.

Brown veal, on all sides, in peanut oil. Use large, heavy saucepan (*rondeau*) or Dutch oven (*braisiere*). Pour off excess oil.

Add onions to veal and cook briefly.

Add tomato paste and continue cooking.

Add white wine and reduce.

Add veal stock and *demi-glace*. (The liquid should just about cover the meat.)

Add sachet bag and garlic. Bring to a boil.

Cover and braise stew in the oven, stirring occasionally. Add more veal stock, if necessary.

When the meat is tender, remove pan from oven.

Remove meat with skimmer and keep warm.

Strain sauce through fine mesh china cap; skim off all fat.

Bring sauce to a boil. (Thicken with cornstarch, if necessary.)

Return meat to sauce and heat. Season to taste.

Serve vegetables over meat.

413

Grandmother's Veal Stew

Kalbsvoressen Grossmutterart
Sauté de veau grand-mère

YIELD: 10 SERVINGS

Onions	1 2/3 oz	50 g
Garlic	1/3 oz	10 g
Veal stew meat,[a] cut into 1 1/3–oz (40 g) cubes	3 lb 8 oz	1.6 kg
Seasoning salt for meat (Recipe 9)	1/3 oz	10 g
White wheat flour	1 oz	30 g
Peanut oil	3 1/3 oz	100 ml
Tomato paste	1 2/3 oz	50 g
Dry white wine	6 3/4 oz	200 ml
Brown veal stock (Recipe 23)	1 qt 2 oz	1.0 L
Demi-glace (Recipe 44)	1 pt 1 oz	500 ml
Sachet bag[b]	1	1
Cornstarch	1/3 oz	10 g

[a] The stew meat should be cut from the shoulder, and should be lean and well trimmed.

[b] For this recipe, bay leaf, peppercorns, and thyme could be used.

GARNISH

Pearl onions	7 oz	200 g
Slab bacon, smoked (not sliced)	5 1/3 oz	150 g
Mushrooms, fresh	7 oz	200 g
Butter	2/3 oz	20 g
White veal stock (Recipe 28)	3 1/3 oz	100 ml
Lemon, juice	1/2	1/2
Seasoning (salt and pepper)	1x	1x

MISE EN PLACE

Peel and chop onions and garlic.

METHOD FOR GARNISH

Peel pearl onions and blanch.

Cut bacon into sticks about 1/4–in (7 mm) thick and blanch.

Trim and wash mushrooms and cut into quarters or halves, depending on size.

Braise pearl onions with 1/3 oz (10 g) butter and veal stock.

Sauté bacon and mushrooms in remaining 1/3 oz (10 g) butter; season with lemon juice, salt and pepper.

Combine bacon and mushrooms with pearl onions and keep warm.

METHOD

Season veal and dust lightly with flour.

Brown veal, on all sides, in peanut oil. Use large, heavy saucepan (*rondeau*) or Dutch oven (*braisiere*).

Pour off excess oil.

Add onions to veal and cook briefly.

Add tomato paste and continue cooking.

Add white wine and reduce.

Add veal stock and *demi-glace*. (The liquid should just about cover the meat.)

Add sachet bag and garlic. Bring to a boil.

Cover and braise stew in the oven, stirring occasionally. Add more veal stock, if necessary.

When the meat is tender, remove pot from oven.

Remove meat with skimmer and keep warm.

Strain sauce through fine mesh china cap; skim off all fat.

Bring sauce to a boil. (Thicken with cornstarch, if necessary.)

Return meat to sauce and heat. Season to taste.

Serve garnish over meat.

414

Boiled Calves' Tongue with Cream Sauce

Kalbszunge mit weisser Sauce
Langue de veau allemande

YIELD: 10 SERVINGS

Calves' tongues, fresh	3 lb 5 oz	1.5 kg
White veal stock (Recipe 28)	2 qts 4 oz	2.0 L
Bouquet garni (Recipe 8)	10 1/2 oz	300 g
Sachet bag[a]	1	1
Dry white wine	6 3/4 oz	200 ml
Butter	1 1/3 oz	40 g
White wheat flour	1 2/3 oz	50 g
Egg yolk	1	1
Heavy cream (36%)	3 1/3 oz	100 ml
Seasoning (salt and pepper)	1x	1x
Dill, fresh, tops	10	10

MISE EN PLACE
Blanch calves' tongues, drain, and wash, first in hot water, then in cold water, drain again.

METHOD
Bring veal stock to a boil and add the calves' tongues, *bouquet garni*, sachet bag, and white wine. Simmer, skimming occasionally.

Remove calves' tongues when tender and keep warm. Reserve stock.

Melt butter; add flour to make a white roux. Let cool slightly.

Heat 1 qt 2 oz (1.0 L) reserved stock. Add hot stock to cool roux, stir to dissolve roux, bring to a boil, stirring constantly. Simmer for 30 minutes. Remove from heat.

Blend egg yolk with cream. Add to sauce, but do not allow to return to a boil.

Strain through a fine mesh china cap. Season to taste.

Slice tongues lengthwise. Cover with sauce and garnish with dill.

[a] For this recipe, use bay leaf, peppercorns, thyme, and rosemary.

415

Pork Cutlets Braised in Beer

Karbonade von Schweinefleisch flämischer Art
Carbonnade de porc flamande

YIELD: 10 SERVINGS

Pork butt, boneless and trimmed[a]	3 lb	1.4 kg
Onions	5 1/3 oz	150 g
White wheat flour	2 oz	60 g
Savoy cabbage	3 lb 14 oz	1.75 kg
Onions	5 1/3 oz	150 g
Slab bacon, smoked (not sliced)	5 1/3 oz	150 g
Salt	1/3 oz	10 g
White pepper, ground	pinch	2 g
Paprika	1/4 oz	7 g
Peanut oil	3 1/3 oz	100 ml
Beer	1 pt 1 oz	500 ml
Brown veal stock (Recipe 23)	1 pt 1 oz	500 ml
Sachet bag[b]	1	1
Vegetable shortening	1 2/3 oz	50 g
Bouillon (Recipe 22)	6 3/4 oz	200 ml
Marjoram, ground	pinch	1 g
Seasoning (salt and pepper)	1x	1x

MISE EN PLACE
Cut pork into 10 cutlets.

Peel 5 1/3 oz (150 g) onions and cut into thin slices.

Dry toast flour until golden brown.

Trim cabbage, cut into large dice, wash, and drain. Blanch cabbage and drain well.

Peel remaining 5 1/3 oz (150 g) onions and chop.

Cut bacon into small dice, blanch, and drain.

METHOD
Season pork cutlets with salt, white pepper, and paprika.

Brown cutlets, on both sides, in hot peanut oil.

Remove pork from pan and pour off excess fat.

Add sliced onions and sauté. Dust with toasted flour.

Add beer and bring to a boil.

Return pork cutlets to pan. Add sufficient veal stock to cover cutlets. Add sachet bag. Bring to a boil; cover pot, and braise cutlets in the oven until tender.

(continued on next page)

[a] The names of meat cuts vary from region to region. The meat specified in the original recipe is called *Schweinshuft* in German.

[b] Bay leaf, peppercorns, and thyme can be used in this recipe.

(continued from preceding page)

Remove pork cutlets and keep warm. Remove sachet bag.

Strain sauce through fine mesh china cap, skim, and adjust seasoning.

Cover meat with sauce and keep warm.

Sauté chopped onions and bacon in shortening.

Add cabbage and smother until cabbage has wilted.

Add bouillon; season with marjoram, salt and pepper.

Cover and braise until cabbage is cooked.

Serve meat covered with sauce, and garnished with cabbage.

416

Meatballs in Caper Sauce
Königsberger Klopse

YIELD: 10 SERVINGS

White bread (Pullman loaf)	2 oz	60 g
Milk	3 1/3 oz	100 ml
Beef, chuck, trimmed	13 oz	375 g
Veal shoulder meat, trimmed	13 oz	375 g
Pork neck meat, trimmed	13 oz	375 g
Anchovy fillets, drained	1 2/3 oz	50 g
Parsley, chopped	1 2/3 oz	50 g
Onions	1 2/3 oz	50 g
Butter	1 1/3 oz	40 g
Lemon	1	1
Eggs	5	5
Seasoning (salt and pepper)	1x	1x
Bouillon (Recipe 22)	2 qt 4 oz	2.0 L

CAPER SAUCE
Reserved bouillon/stock
  from cooking meat

Butter	4 1/4 oz	120 g
White wheat flour	3 1/2 oz	100 g
Capers, drained	3 1/2 oz	100 g
Egg yolks	5	5
Sour cream, light	3 1/3 oz	100 ml

MISE EN PLACE
Cut bread into cubes and soak in hot milk. Let cool.

Grind beef, veal, pork, anchovy fillets, parsley, and the soaked bread through the fine plate of the meat grinder.

Peel and chop onions, sauté in butter, and let cool.

Grate lemon rind; save lemon juice for the sauce.

Combine ground meats, onions, grated lemon peel, and eggs. Season mixture.

Shape mixture into 20 meatballs.

METHOD
Bring bouillon to a boil. Add meatballs, and poach for 20 minutes.

Remove meatballs with skimmer and keep warm. Strain and skim stock and reserve for sauce.

METHOD FOR CAPER SAUCE
Melt butter and add flour to make a white roux. Let cool slightly.

Heat reserved stock. Add hot stock to cool roux, stir to dissolve roux, and bring to a boil, stirring constantly.

Simmer sauce until the desired consistency is reached.

Add capers and lemon juice. Remove from heat.

Mix egg yolks with sour cream and add to sauce. Do not allow the sauce to return to a boil.

PRESENTATION
Heat meatballs in sauce. Do not return to a boil.

417

White Lamb Stew with Tomatoes and Herbs
Lammblankett mit Tomaten und Kräutern
Blanquette d'agneau aux tomates et aux herbes

YIELD: 10 SERVINGS

Lamb stew meat,[a] cut into 1 1/3–oz (40 g) cubes	3 lb 8 oz	1.6 kg
White veal stock (Recipe 28)	1 qt 19 oz	1.5 L
Dry white wine	10 oz	300 ml
Bouquet garni (Recipe 8)	10 1/2 oz	300 g
Sachet bag[b]	1	1
Butter	1 oz	30 g
White wheat flour	1 2/3 oz	50 g
Heavy cream (36%)	6 3/4 oz	200 ml
Egg yolks	3	3
Lemon	1/2	1/2
Seasoning (salt and pepper)	1x	1x

---

[a] The stew meat should be cut from the shoulder and neck, and should be lean and well trimmed.

[b] For this recipe, bay leaf, peppercorns, and thyme can be used.

GARNISH

Tomatoes	1 lb 2 oz	500 g
Shallots	1 2/3 oz	50 g
Garlic	1/4 oz	7 g
Thyme, fresh	1/3 oz	10 g
Oregano, fresh	1/3 oz	10 g
Parsley	2/3 oz	20 g
Butter	3/4 oz	25 g
Seasoning (salt and pepper)	1x	1x

MISE EN PLACE

Blanch lamb, drain, and wash, first in hot water, then in cold water. Drain again.

METHOD FOR GARNISH

Peel tomatoes, cut in half, remove seeds, and chop coarsely.

Chop shallots and garlic.

Chop thyme, oregano, and parsley.

Sauté shallots and garlic in butter, add tomatoes and herbs, and season to taste with salt and freshly ground pepper. Smother tomatoes until cooked; keep warm.

METHOD

Combine veal stock and white wine and bring to a boil.

Add blanched lamb, bring to a boil, and skim.

Add *bouquet garni* and sachet bag. Simmer until lamb is tender.

Remove lamb with skimmer and keep warm. Reserve stock.

Melt butter; add flour to make a white roux. Let cool slightly.

Heat 1 qt 2 oz (1.0 L) reserved stock. Add hot stock to cool roux, stir to dissolve roux and bring to a boil, stirring constantly. Simmer for 20 to 30 minutes. Remove from heat.

Strain sauce through double layer of cheesecloth.

Bring sauce to a boil again; remove from heat.

Mix heavy cream and egg yolks, add to hot sauce, mix well, but do not allow sauce to return to a boil.

Heat lamb in sauce. Season with lemon juice. Adjust seasoning.

Serve lamb stew, topped with tomato garnish.

418

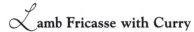

$\mathcal{L}$amb Fricasse with Curry

Lammfrikassee mit Curry
Fricassée d'agneau au curry

YIELD: 10 SERVINGS

Lamb stew meat,[a] lean	3 lb 8 oz	1.6 kg
Salt	1/3 oz	10 g
White pepper, ground	pinch	2 g
White wheat flour	1 2/3 oz	50 g
Onions	8 3/4 oz	250 g
Apples	8 3/4 oz	250 g
Clarified butter	3 1/2 oz	100 g
Curry powder[b]	1 2/3 oz	50 g
Dry white wine	10 oz	300 ml
White veal stock (Recipe 28)	1 qt 8 oz	1.2 L
Sachet bag[c]	1	1
Heavy cream (36%)	6 3/4 oz	200 ml
Cornstarch	1/3 oz	10 g
Seasoning (salt and pepper)	1x	1x

METHOD

Season lamb with salt and white pepper and dust with a small amount of flour.

Peel onions and cut into thin slices.

Peel and core apples and cut into thin slices.

Heat clarified butter in a wide, heavy saucepan (*rondeau*), add lamb and onions, and smother together without allowing to brown.

Add apples and continue cooking.

Dust with remaining flour and the curry powder.

Add white wine and veal stock and bring to a boil. Add sachet bag, cover, and simmer until lamb is tender.

Remove lamb with skimmer and keep warm. Discard sachet bag.

Purée sauce[d] and strain through a fine mesh china cap.

Bring sauce to a boil, stir in heavy cream, thicken with cornstarch.

Add lamb and heat.

---

[a] The stew meat should be cut from the shoulder and neck, and should be lean and well trimmed.

[b] The quality of the curry powder is important. The original recipe specifies Madras curry powder.

[c] For this recipe, bay leaf, peppercorns, and thyme can be used.

[d] This is best accomplished with a hand-held electric mixer.

419

*B*oiled Leg of Lamb with Vegetables and Caper Sauce

Lammkeule englische Art
Gigot d'agneau anglaise

YIELD: 10 SERVINGS

Leg of lamb, oven-ready	6 lb 10 oz	3.0 kg
Bouillon (Recipe 22)	4 qt 7 oz	4.0 L
Bouquet garni (Recipe 8)	10 1/2 oz	300 g
Sachet bag	1	1
Caper sauce (See Recipe 416)	13 1/2 oz	400 ml

GARNISH
Carrots	1 lb 2 oz	500 g
White turnips, small	1 lb 2 oz	500 g
Savoy cabbage	1 lb 2 oz	500 g
Green beans, fresh	1 lb	450 g
Seasoning (salt and pepper)	1x	1x

MISE EN PLACE
Tie leg of lamb with butcher's twine to retain its shape.

Blanch, drain, and wash, first in hot water, then in cold water. Drain again.

MISE EN PLACE FOR GARNISH
Peel carrots and cut into even sticks or barrel shapes.

Peel white turnips and cut into even sticks or barrel shapes.

Trim Savoy cabbage and cut into large dice.

Snip off green bean ends.

METHOD
Bring bouillon to a boil, add *bouquet garni*, sachet bag, and lamb.

Simmer, skimming occasionally, until lamb is tender and well-done.[a] Strain stock, skim, and reserve to poach garnish vegetables and to make caper sauce.

Poach each garnish vegetable separately in small amounts of reserved stock.

Make caper sauce using sauce ingredients and method for Meatballs in Caper Sauce (Recipe 416).

Serve lamb with bouquets of vegetables.

Serve caper sauce on the side.

NOTE: The vegetables can also be puréed.

---

[a] Boiled lamb is normally cooked well-done. The service staff should be informed of this.

420

*B*rown Lamb Stew with Vegetables

Lammragout mit kleinem Gemüse
Navarin d'agneau aux petits légumes

YIELD: 10 SERVINGS

Onions	5 1/3 oz	150 g
Garlic	2/3 oz	20 g
Tomatoes	10 1/2 oz	300 g
Lamb stew meat,[a] cut into 1 1/3 oz (40 g) cubes	3 lb 8 oz	1.6 kg
Seasoning salt for meat (Recipe 9)	1/3 oz	10 g
Peanut oil	3 1/3 oz	100 ml
Tomato paste	1 2/3 oz	50 g
Dry white wine	6 3/4 oz	200 ml
Brown veal stock (Recipe 22)	1 qt 2 oz	1.0 L
Demi-glace (Recipe 44)	1 pt 1 oz	500 ml

GARNISH
Pearl onions	8 3/4 oz	250 g
Carrots	1 lb 2 oz	500 g
Turnips, white, small	1 lb 2 oz	500 g
Potatoes	1 lb 2 oz	500 g
Seasoning (salt and pepper)	1x	1x

MISE EN PLACE
Peel and chop onions.

Peel and chop garlic.

Peel tomatoes, cut in half, remove seeds, and dice.

MISE EN PLACE FOR GARNISH
Peel and trim pearl onions.

Peel and trim carrots and turnips and cut into sticks or barrel shapes.

Peel potatoes and scoop out small balls.

Blanch all vegetables and potatoes, and drain.

METHOD
Season meat and brown in hot oil in wide saucepan (*rondeau*) or in Dutch oven (*braisiere*).

Drain off excess fat.

Add chopped onions and sauté.

Add tomato paste, stir in, and cook briefly.

Add garlic and cook briefly.

Add diced tomatoes and wine. Reduce.

---

[a] The stew meat should be cut from the shoulder and neck, and should be lean and well trimmed.

Add sufficient veal stock and *demi-glace* to cover meat.

Cover pan and braise meat until about three-fourths done.

Remove meat with skimmer. Strain sauce through a fine mesh china cap. Skim off all fat.

Add blanched vegetables and cooked meat to sauce. Simmer until done.

NOTE: When large amounts are prepared, cook the vegetables separately and place them over the meat at the time of service. This will better control the cooking and will make portioning easier.

421

*P*uff Pastry House with Veal and Pork Luzern Style

Luzerner Chügelipastete

YIELD: 10 SERVINGS

| Puff pastry (Recipe 689) | 1 lb 12 oz | 800 g |
| Egg yolks | 2 | 2 |

FILLING

Apple wine (cider)	6 3/4 oz	200 ml
White veal stock (Recipe 28)	1 qt 19 oz	1.5 L
Veal shoulder meat, trimmed	1 lb 2 oz	500 g
Pork butt, trimmed	1 lb 2 oz	500 g
Onion studded with 3 cloves	1	1
Veal sausage stuffing[a]	1 lb 2 oz	500 g
Apples, for cooking[b]	10 1/2 oz	300 g
Mushrooms, fresh	10 1/2 oz	300 g
Butter	2 oz	60 g
White wheat flour	2 1/2 oz	70 g
Butter	2/3 oz	20 g
Golden sultanas	3 1/2 oz	100 g
Heavy cream (36%)	6 3/4 oz	200 ml
Seasoning (salt and pepper)	1x	1x

MISE EN PLACE

Make a puff pastry house or large patty shell.[c]

Combine apple wine and veal stock.

Add veal, pork, and onion studded with cloves. Bring to a boil and boil until veal and pork are tender. Remove meat from stock, cut into small dice, and set aside.

---

[a] Veal sausage stuffing is readily available from butchers in some areas. Mousseline farce (Recipe 17), could be substituted.

[b] Granny Smith apples are suitable for this dish. It is best to sprinkle a small amount of lemon juice over the diced apples to prevent oxidation.

[c] Puff pastry house is a local specialty of Luzern, Switzerland.

Strain stock and reserve.

Form veal sausage stuffing into small balls.

Peel and core apples and cut into small dice.

Trim and wash mushrooms and cut into slices.

METHOD

Poach sausage meatballs in reserved stock. Reserve stock again for sauce.

Make sauce by melting butter and adding flour to make a white roux. Let cool slightly. Heat 1 qt 2 oz (1.0 L) reserved stock. Add hot stock to cool roux, stir to dissolve roux, bring to a boil, stirring constantly, and simmer for 30 minutes. Remove from heat.

Sauté mushrooms, apples, and sultanas in butter.

When sauce is cooked, add veal and pork, meatballs, mushrooms, apples, and sultanas. Bring to a boil and stir in heavy cream. Season to taste.

Fill pastry house at the moment of service.

422

*O*sso Buco (braised veal shanks)

Ossi-buchi Cremolata

YIELD: 10 SERVINGS

Veal shanks, cut into portions[a]	5 lb	2.25 kg
Onions	7 oz	200 g
Carrots	7 oz	200 g
Knob celery (celeriac)	5 1/3 oz	150 g
Leeks, green leaves only	5 1/3 oz	150 g
Garlic	1/3 oz	10 g
Tomatoes	10 1/2 oz	300 g
Seasoning salt for meat (Recipe 9)	2/3 oz	20 g
White wheat flour	3/4 oz	25 g
Peanut oil	3 1/3 oz	100 ml
Tomato paste	1 2/3 oz	50 g
Sage, fresh	1/3 oz	10 g
Oregano, fresh	1/3 oz	10 g
Dry white wine	6 3/4 oz	200 ml
Brown veal stock (Recipe 23)	1 qt 2 oz	1.0 L
Demi-glace (Recipe 44)	1 pt 1 oz	500 ml

(continued on next page)

---

[a] The veal shanks should be cut from the leg and should be completely trimmed.

(continued from preceding page)

GARNISH (CREMOLATA)

Lemon	1	1
Garlic cloves	2	2
Parsley, washed	1 1/3 oz	40 g

MISE EN PLACE

Make incision into the skins of the veal shanks to prevent curling.

Peel and chop onions.

Peel and trim carrots, knob celery, and leeks and cut into small dice (*brunoise*).

Peel and chop garlic.

Peel tomatoes, cut in half, remove seeds, and dice.

MISE EN PLACE FOR GARNISH

Remove peel from lemon with vegetable peeler.

Mince garlic, lemon peel, and parsley and set aside.

METHOD

Season veal shanks and dust lightly with flour. Brown cut veal shanks, on both cut sides, in peanut oil. Remove meat and pour off excess oil.

Add chopped onions and sauté. Add chopped carrots, knob celery, and leeks and continue cooking.

Add tomato paste and chopped garlic. Add veal shanks and sauté briefly.

Add sage, oregano, and white wine and reduce almost completely.

Add sufficient veal stock and *demi-glace* to cover meat.

Cover pot and braise meat in oven. Turn meat and baste occasionally.

Add diced tomatoes shortly before veal is tender.

Check sauce consistency and reduce if necessary. Adjust seasoning.

Serve veal shanks covered with sauce; sprinkle with garnish.

NOTE: The marrow in the center of the bone is a delicacy. A marrow spoon or an oyster fork should be provided to customers so the marrow can be eaten.

423

Spanish Paella
Paëlla

YIELD: 10 SERVINGS

Pork butt, trimmed	10 1/2 oz	300 g
Chorizos (garlic sausages), 2 links	5 1/3 oz	150 g
Squid, cleaned	7 oz	200 g
Onions	3 1/2 oz	100 g
Bell peppers, assorted colors	5 1/3 oz	150 g
Tomatoes, fresh, peeled and seeded	7 oz	200 g
Mussels, fresh	10 1/2 oz	300 g
Chicken drumsticks and thighs	2 lb 10 oz	1.2 kg
Olive oil	3 1/3 oz	100 ml
Arborio rice[a]	1 lb 5 oz	600 g
Saffron	pinch	1 g
Dry white wine	6 3/4 oz	200 ml
Chicken stock (Recipe 26)	1 qt 8 oz	1.2 L
Shrimp, large, raw	10 1/2 oz	300 g
Peas, frozen	7 oz	200 g

MISE EN PLACE

Cut pork butt into small cubes.

Cut sausages into 3/4–in. (200 mm) slices.

Cut squid across into rings.

Peel and dice onions.

Split bell peppers, remove seeds, and cut into 1 1/2–in. (35 mm) squares.

Cut tomatoes into large dice.

Scrape and clean mussels.

METHOD

Sauté chicken drumsticks and thighs and diced pork butt in oil.

Add sliced *chorizos* and squid and continue cooking.

Add onions and bell peppers and continue cooking.

Add tomatoes and rice. Add saffron. Add white wine and poultry stock and lightly mix, just to distribute ingredients.

Scatter mussels, shrimp, and peas evenly over the top.

Cover and simmer until all liquid is absorbed and rice is cooked.

---

[a] Arborio rice is an Italian rice with a round kernel. Other rice varieties can be substituted.

NOTE: Paella is a Spanish national dish, with many local variations. Inland, chicken, rabbit, other meats, and other local ingredients are used. In coastal provinces, seafood is predominant. The name *paella* refers to a black iron pan with two handles in which the paella is prepared and also served.

424

Veal Piccata
Piccata milanese

YIELD: 10 SERVINGS

Veal tenderloins, trimmed[a]	2 lb 10 oz	1.2 kg
Eggs	4	4
Parmesan cheese, grated	3 1/2 oz	100 g
Clarified butter	3 1/2 oz	100 g
Seasoning salt for meat (Recipe 9)	1/3 oz	10 g
White wheat flour	1 2/3 oz	50 g

GARNISH

Ox tongue, smoked, cooked and trimmed	3 1/2 oz	100 g
Ham, boiled	3 1/2 oz	100 g
Mushrooms, fresh	3 1/2 oz	100 g
Butter	1 2/3 oz	50 g

SAUCE

Madeira wine	1 2/3 oz	50 ml
Demi-glace (Recipe 44)	13 1/2 oz	400 ml

MISE EN PLACE
Cut veal into 30 thin cutlets, about 1 1/3 oz (40 g) each. Pound cutlets lightly.

METHOD FOR GARNISH
Cut ox tongue and ham into strips (*julienne*).

Trim and wash mushrooms and cut into strips (*julienne*).

Sauté mushrooms in butter and add tongue and ham. Keep warm.

METHOD FOR SAUCE

Combine Madeira wine with *demi-glace*. Bring to a boil and keep warm.

METHOD
Break eggs and mix with Parmesan.

Heat clarified butter in cast iron pan.

Season cutlets, dredge first in flour, then in egg/cheese mixture.

Sauté cutlets in hot butter. (Be sure butter is not too hot, because the egg batter will burn.)

Serve three pieces of piccata per person.

Surround with sauce. Top with *julienne* garnish.

425

Poached Calves' Brains with Capers
Poschiertes Kalbshirn mit Kapern
Cervelle de Veau pochée aux câpres

YIELD: 10 SERVINGS

Calves' brains	3 lb 8 oz	1.6 kg
White veal stock (Recipe 28)	2 qt 4 oz	2.0 L
Dry white wine	6 3/4 oz	200 ml
Matignon (Recipe 13)	7 oz	200 g
Parsley stems, fresh	2/3 oz	20 g
Tarragon, fresh	2/3 oz	20 g
Thyme twig, fresh	1	1
Capers, drained	1 2/3 oz	50 g
Parsley, chopped	1 oz	30 g
Butter	3 1/2 oz	100 g

MISE EN PLACE
Soak calves' brains in cold water overnight.

Carefully drain off water and replace with warm water. While brains are submerged, peel off skin and blood vessels. Do not break brains. Change water frequently during the process.

METHOD
Combine veal stock, white wine, *matignon*, parsley, tarragon, and thyme. Bring to a boil and boil for 10 minutes. Let stock cool.

Add calves' brains to cold stock. Bring to a slow boil and poach for 10 minutes.

Remove brains with skimmer. Place on serving platter.[a]

Heat butter in cast iron pan until brown, add capers and chopped parsley, and pour over brains.

---

[a] It might be difficult to obtain veal tenderloins in some markets. Veal top round, cut from the leg, can be substituted. This meat might have to be tenderized by pounding.

[a] Large brains should be cut in half.

426

*B*raised Veal Tenderloin with Porcini

Poeliertes Kalbsfilet mit Steinpilzen
Filet mignon de veau poêle aux cèpes

YIELD: 10 SERVINGS

Matignon (Recipe 14)	10 1/2 oz	300 g
Bay leaf	1	1
Clove	1	1
Rosemary twig, fresh	1	1
Thyme twig, fresh	1	1
Veal tenderloins, trimmed[a]	4 lb	1.8 kg
Seasoning (salt and pepper)	1x	1x
Clarified butter	3 1/2 oz	100 g
Dry white wine	1 2/3 oz	50 ml
Brown veal stock (Recipe 23)	1 pt 4 oz	600 ml
Cornstarch	1/3 oz	10 g
Madeira wine	1 2/3 oz	50 ml
Seasoning (white pepper)	1x	1x

GARNISH

Porcini mushrooms, fresh[b]	1 lb 12 oz	800 g
Onions	2 2/3 oz	75 g
Garlic	2/3 oz	20 g
Parsley, fresh	2/3 oz	20 g
Butter	1 2/3 oz	50 g
Lemon	1/2	1/2
Seasoning (salt and pepper)	1x	1x
Butter, melted	2/3 oz	20 g

MISE EN PLACE FOR GARNISH
Trim, wash, and slice mushrooms.

Peel and chop onions and garlic.

Chop parsley leaves.

METHOD
Line suitable Dutch oven (*braisiere*) or wide, heavy saucepan (*rondeau*) with *matignon*.

Add bay leaf, clove, rosemary, and thyme. Place veal on top. Sprinkle veal with salt and pepper.

Heat clarified butter and pour over veal.

Place in oven and roast briefly at 325°F (165°C).

Cover and roast[a] at 285°F (140°C) to 325°F (165°C), basting veal occasionally with its own juices.

Remove the lid 10 minutes before the meat is cooked and let the veal brown lightly.

Remove meat from pot and keep warm.

Add white wine and veal stock, bring to a boil, and boil for 5 minutes.

Strain stock through a fine mesh china cap; skim off all fat.

Bring stock to a boil and thicken with cornstarch. Reduce to desired consistency.

Add Madeira wine. Adjust seasoning.

Make garnish by sautéing onions and garlic in butter. Add mushrooms and sauté over high heat until mushrooms are cooked. Season mushrooms with lemon juice, salt and pepper. Add chopped parsley and small amount of veal stock.

Slice meat and brush with melted butter to give it a nice sheen.

Serve sauce and mushrooms around meat. Serve remaining sauce on the side.

427

*R*oast Saddle of Veal Orloff

Poelierter Kalbsrücken Orlow
Selle de veau poêlée Orlov

YIELD: 10 SERVINGS

Loin of veal, whole,[b] bone in, trimmed	8 lb 4 oz	3.75 kg
Seasoning salt for meat (Recipe 9)	2/3 oz	20 g
Mirepoix (Recipe 15)	10 1/2 oz	300 g
Thyme twig, fresh	1	1
Rosemary twig, fresh	1	1
Bay leaf	1	1
Clarified butter	3 1/2 oz	100 g
Brown veal stock (Recipe 23)	1 pt 4 oz	600 ml
Cornstarch	1/3 oz	10 g
Madeira wine	1 2/3 oz	50 ml
Truffle, canned, drained	2/3 oz	20 g
Bechamel sauce (Recipe 34)	8 1/2 oz	250 ml

[a] It might be difficult to obtain veal tenderloins in some markets. Boneless veal loin can be substituted.

[b] Porcini are wild mushrooms, called *cèpes* in French, *Steinpilze* in German, and *porcini* in Italian. These mushrooms are widely available dried, and are increasingly available fresh. Because Italy is a large exporter of these mushrooms, the Italian name is commonly used. The recipe calls for *Steinpilze*, which are readily available in Switzerland during the summer.

[a] The proper term is *poêler*, which is a combination of roasting and braising in a meat's own juices. There is no exact English language equivalent.

[b] Veal loin is also sold under the name "saddle" in many places. It must be well trimmed, flanks and first ribs removed, center bone flattened (so loin can sit flat), and the rest of the carcass intact.

Parmesan cheese, grated	2 2/3 oz	75 g
Hollandaise sauce (Recipe 60)	6 3/4 oz	200 ml

ONION PURÉE (SOUBISE)

Onions	1 lb 2 oz	500 g
Arborio rice[a]	7 oz	200 g
Salt	1/3 oz	10 g
Milk	1 pt 1 oz	500 ml
Bay leaf	1	1
Clove	1	1
Seasoning (salt and pepper)	1x	1x
Goose liver mousse, canned	5 1/3 oz	150 g

MISE EN PLACE

Remove tendon from the top of the veal saddle. Tie saddle with butcher's twine to retain its shape during roasting.

METHOD FOR ONION PURÉE (SOUBISE)

Peel and slice onions.

Blanch rice for 3 minutes in ample salt water. Drain off water.

Combine onions, blanched rice, milk, bay leaf, and clove. Steam in pressure cooker or in covered pot until rice is very soft. Add more milk if necessary. (The onion puree should be thick so it will hold together atop the veal. Exact milk amounts may vary, due to the moisture content of the onions.)

Remove bay leaf and clove.

Purée mixture in food processor. Strain through fine wire sieve.

Season purée to taste. Let cool but do not chill.

METHOD FOR ROASTING MEAT

Line Dutch oven (braisiere) or wide, heavy saucepan (rondeau) with mirepoix.

Add thyme, rosemary, and bay leaf.

Place meat on top and sprinkle meat with seasoning salt.

Heat clarified butter and pour over meat.

Place in oven and roast briefly at 325°F (165°C).

Cover and roast at 285°F (140°C) to 325°F (165°C), basting veal occasionally with its own juices.

Remove the lid 10 minutes before veal is cooked and let the meat brown lightly.

Remove meat and keep warm.

Add veal stock. Bring to a boil and boil for 5 minutes.

Strain stock through a fine mesh china cap; skim off all fat.

Bring stock to a boil, thicken with cornstarch mixed with Madeira wine, and reduce to desired consistency.

Add Madeira wine. Adjust seasoning.

METHOD

Bone veal saddle by removing the 2 loins from the carcass.[a] Let veal cool slightly. Cut each veal loin into 10 slices.

Cut truffle into 20 thin slices.

Blend goose liver mousse with onion purée.[b]

Spread small amount of onion/liver mousse purée on the carcass.

Spread a small amount of onion/liver mousse purée on each meat slice. Top with one truffle slice.

Place the meat slices back on the carcass. When all slices are replaced, the saddle should be in its original shape.

Blend hot Bechamel sauce with Hollandaise sauce and grated Parmesan.

Place veal saddle on wire rack and cover with Bechamel/Parmesan sauce.

Place meat in hot oven to heat and to brown.

Serve whole to a group of 10. The dining room staff will present the dish and serve it from a gueridon (serving table).

---

[a] Arborio is an Italian rice, with a round kernel. Another rice suitable for this dish would be Vialone.

---

[a] A classic way to assemble this dish is to leave on the carcass a thin slice of the front and back of each loin. This will form a box on each side, so that the reassembled saddle will hold together. To serve the veal, slices are lifted from the box, and the end slices are not served at the table.

[b] If mixture is not thick enough to hold together atop veal, an egg can be added.

428

*B*eef Stew with Vegetables

Rindsdünstragout mit kleinem Gemüse
Estouffade de boeuf aux petits légumes

YIELD: 10 SERVINGS

Onions	14 oz	400 g
Garlic	1/3 oz	10 g
Slab bacon, smoked (not sliced)	10 1/2 oz	300 g
Beef stew meat, chuck, cut into 1 1/3-oz (40 g) cubes	3 lb 8 oz	1.6 kg
Seasoning salt for meat (Recipe 9)	1/3 oz	10 g
Clarified butter	2 oz	60 g
Tomato paste	1 oz	30 g
White wheat flour	1 oz	30 g
Red wine	10 oz	300 ml
Brown veal stock (Recipe 23)	1 qt 2 oz	1.0 L
Sachet bag[a]	1	1
Cornstarch, if necessary	1x	1x
Seasoning	1x	1x

GARNISH

Carrots	10 1/2 oz	300 g
Turnips, white, small	10 1/2 oz	300 g
Pearl onions	7 oz	200 g
Butter	3 1/2 oz	100 g
Vegetable bouillon (Recipe 27)	10 oz	300 ml
Sugar	1x	1x
Seasoning (salt and pepper)	1x	1x

MISE EN PLACE

Peel and chop onions and garlic.

Cut bacon into cubes about 1/2–3/4 in. (20–30 mm) thick and blanch.

METHOD FOR GARNISH

Peel and trim carrots and turnips. Cut into sticks or small barrel shapes.

Peel pearl onions.

Braise each vegetable separately in butter, vegetable stock, and sugar. Let stock reduce to give vegetables a nice sheen.

Mix vegetables together after they are cooked. Season with salt and pepper. Keep warm.

---

[a] For this recipe, bay leaf, thyme, and marjoram could be used.

METHOD

Season stew meat with seasoning salt, combine with chopped onions and garlic, and smother mixture in clarified butter without browning. Cook until the meat juices reach a syrupy consistency.

Add blanched bacon cubes and tomato paste and continue cooking.

Dust with flour, add red wine, add veal stock to cover meat, bring to a boil, and skim.

Add sachet bag, simmer, covered, on top of stove or in the oven until meat is tender, and add stock when necessary.

Remove meat and bacon cubes with skimmer and keep warm.

Remove sachet bag and strain sauce through a fine mesh china cap.

Skim again, bring to a boil, reduce if necessary, or thicken with a small amount of cornstarch.

Return meat and bacon cubes to pot and bring to a boil. Adjust seasoning.

Serve glazed vegetables over the stew.

429

*B*eef Stew with Tomatoes and Olives

Rindsdünstragout mit Tomaten und Oliven
Estouffade de boeuf aux tomates et aux olives

YIELD: 10 SERVINGS

Onions	14 oz	400 g
Garlic	2/3 oz	20 g
Slab bacon, smoked (not sliced)	10 1/2 oz	300 g
Black olives, drained	3 1/2 oz	100 g
Tomatoes	14 oz	400 g
Beef stew meat, chuck, cut into 1 1/3-oz (40 g) cubes	3 lb 8 oz	1.6 kg
Seasoning salt for meat (Recipe 9)	1/3 oz	10 g
Clarified butter	1 oz	30 g
Tomato paste	1 oz	30 g
White wheat flour	1 oz	30 g
Red wine	10 oz	300 ml
Brown veal stock (Recipe 23)	1 qt 2 oz	1.0 L
Sachet bag	1	1
Cornstarch, if necessary	1x	1x
Seasoning (salt and pepper)	1x	1x
Butter	1 oz	30 g

MISE EN PLACE

Peel and chop onions and garlic.

Cut bacon into cubes about 1/2–3/4 in. (20–30 mm) thick and blanch.

Remove pits from olives and cut olives into halves or slivers.

Peel tomatoes, cut in half, remove seeds, and chop coarsely.

METHOD

Season stew meat with seasoning salt, combine with chopped onions and garlic, and smother mixture in clarified butter without browning. Cook until the meat juices reach a syrupy consistency.

Add blanched bacon cubes and tomato paste and continue cooking.

Dust with flour, add red wine, add veal stock to cover meat, bring to a boil, and skim.

Add sachet bag, simmer, covered, on top of stove or in the oven until meat is tender, and add stock when necessary.

Remove meat and bacon cubes with skimmer and keep warm.

Remove sachet bag and strain sauce through a fine mesh china cap.

Skim again, bring to a boil, and reduce if necessary, or thicken with a small amount of cornstarch.

Add meat and bacon cubes to pot and bring to a boil. Adjust seasoning.

Sauté tomatoes and olives in butter and serve on top of the stew.

430

Beef Stroganoff

Rindsfiletgulasch Stroganow
Filet de boeuf Stroganov

YIELD: 10 SERVINGS

Beef tenderloin, trimmed[a]	3 lb 8 oz	1.6 kg
Onions	5 1/3 oz	150 g
Dill pickles, drained	3 1/2 oz	100 g
Mushrooms, fresh	3 1/2 oz	100 g
Clarified butter	2 2/3 oz	75 g
Seasoning (salt and pepper)	1x	1x
Paprika	pinch	2 g
Red wine	6 3/4 oz	200 ml
Demi-glace (Recipe 44)	1 pt 1 oz	500 ml
Sour cream	3 1/3 oz	100 ml
Seasoning (salt and pepper)	1x	1x

MISE EN PLACE

Cut beef tenderloin into small cubes or strips.

Peel and chop onions.

Cut pickles into fine *julienne*.

Trim and wash mushrooms and cut into slices.

METHOD

Sauté meat[b] quickly in hot clarified butter and season with salt and pepper.

Put meat in colander to drain.

Add onions to pan and smother. Add pickles and mushrooms.

Dust with paprika. Add red wine and *demi-glace*.

Bring to a boil and boil briefly.

Stir in sour cream thoroughly, but do not allow the sauce to return to a boil.

Add meat and heat.

---

[a] Tenderloin heads and tails and other clean trimmings can be used.

[b] It is advisable to sauté the meat in two or three batches to be sure it will brown.

431

eef Wellington

Rindsfilet Wellington
Filet de boeuf Wellington

YIELD: 10 SERVINGS

Beef tenderloin, center piece, trimmed[a]	2 lb 14 oz	1.3 kg
Salt	2/3 oz	20 g
Seasoning (white pepper)	1x	1x
Peanut oil	1 2/3 oz	50 ml
FARCE		
Veal shoulder meat, trimmed and lean	3 oz	80 g
Bacon, smoked (not sliced)	3 1/2 oz	100 g
Chicken liver, raw	3 oz	80 g
Morels, dried (no stems)	1/3 oz	10 g
Mushrooms, fresh	1 oz	30 g
Shallots	2/3 oz	20 g
Thyme twig, fresh	1	5 g
Black truffle, canned	1/3 oz	10 g
Seasoning (salt and pepper)	1x	1x
Pâté spice[b]	pinch	1 g
Butter	1/3 oz	10 g
Cognac (or any brandy)	2/3 oz	20 ml
Madeira wine	2/3 oz	20 ml
Brown veal juice, thickened (Recipe 55)	2/3 oz	20 ml
Butter	2/3 oz	20 g
Fresh bread crumbs (mie de pain)[c]	1 oz	30 g
Goose liver mousse (canned)	1 2/3 oz	50 g
Egg yolks	2	2
Seasoning	1x	1x
DOUGH		
Fatback, unsalted	10 1/2 oz	300 g
Half puff pastry (Recipe 715)	1 lb 9 oz	700 g
Egg yolks	2	2
SAUCE		
Truffle sauce (Recipe 101)	13 1/2 oz	400 ml

---

[a] The tenderloin should be an even-shaped center piece.

[b] Pâté spice can be purchased commercially, or Seasoning Salt for Meat (Recipe 9) can be substituted.

[c] Mie de pain are fresh bread crumbs, made from white Pullman loaves.

MISE EN PLACE
Trim and tie tenderloin. (It should be without head and tail.)

Season tenderloin with salt and white pepper, brush with peanut oil, and roast in 485°F (250°C) oven for 5 to 7 minutes depending on meat thickness.

Place tenderloin on wire rack and let cool. Save juice drippings for farce.

MISE EN PLACE FOR FARCE
Cube veal, bacon, and chicken liver.

Soak morels in cold water until soft.

Trim and wash mushrooms and cut into slices.

Chop shallots.

Chop thyme leaves.

Chop truffles.

METHOD FOR FARCE
Drain morels and chop coarsely. (Some of the soaking juice can be added to the farce for more flavor.)

Season cubed veal, bacon, and chicken liver with salt and pepper and pâté spice and sauté in butter.

Add morels, sliced mushrooms, shallots, and thyme and continue cooking.

Add Cognac, Madeira wine, and tenderloin juice drippings. Add veal juice and boil mixture thoroughly.

Let mixture cool and grind through fine plate of meat grinder.

Put resulting paste in a shallow sauté pan (*sautoir*).

Add butter and stir over heat to evaporate more moisture.

Add *mie de pain* and mashed goose liver mousse; stir to bind mixture.

Remove from heat and add egg yolks and chopped truffles. Adjust seasoning.

Let mixture cool.

METHOD FOR PRE-ASSEMBLY
Remove strings from tenderloin.

Spread cold meat paste all around tenderloin. The cover should be about 1/4-in. (12 mm) thick. Chill the tenderloin.

METHOD FOR FINAL ASSEMBLY
Cut unsalted fatback into thin sheets on a meat slicer. The sheets should be very thin, but as large as possible.

Roll puff pastry into a rectangle large enough to completely cover the tenderloin. Mix egg yolks with small amount of cold water. Brush dough with some of the egg yolk mixture to make dough adhere to meat.

Place tenderloin in center of dough and wrap completely. Place, seam side down, on baking sheet. Decorate the top with dough trimmings. Brush with remaining egg yolk mixture. Poke small holes in pastry to let steam escape.

Refrigerate package for 1 hour.

Bake at 400°F (200°C) for 30 to 40 minutes.

Check inside temperature frequently, until it registers 120°F (50°C) to 130°F (55°C).[a]

Let meat rest for 20 to 30 minutes before it is carved.

Heat truffle sauce and serve on the side.

432

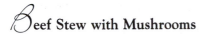 eef Stew with Mushrooms

Rindsragout mit Champignons
Sauté de boeuf aux champignons de Paris

YIELD: 10 SERVINGS

Onions	1 2/3 oz	50 g
Garlic	2/3 oz	20 g
Beef stew meat, chuck, cut into 1 1/3-oz (40 g) cubes	3 lb 8 oz	1.6 kg
Seasoning salt for meat (Recipe 9)	1/3 oz	10 g
Peanut oil	3 1/3 oz	100 ml
Tomato paste	1 2/3 oz	50 g
Red wine	10 oz	300 ml
Brown veal stock (Recipe 23)	1 qt 8 oz	1.2 L
Demi-glace (Recipe 44)	1 pt 4 oz	600 ml
Sachet bag[b]	1	1
Paprika	1/3 oz	10 g
Bouquet garni (Recipe 7)	1 bundle	1
Cornstarch	1/3 oz	10 g

GARNISH

Mushrooms, fresh	10 1/2 oz	300 g
Butter	1 2/3 oz	50 g
Lemon	1/2	1/2
Dry white wine	1 2/3 oz	50 ml
Seasoning (salt and pepper)	1x	1x

MISE EN PLACE
Peel and chop onions and garlic.

METHOD FOR GARNISH
Trim and wash mushrooms, and cut into halves or quarters, depending on size.

Braise mushrooms with butter, lemon juice, and white wine.

Season to taste and keep warm.

METHOD
Season stew meat with seasoning salt and brown in peanut oil in a shallow sauce pan (*rondeau*) or Dutch oven (*braisiere*).

Pour off excess oil. Add onions and garlic and smother with meat.

Add tomato paste and continue cooking.

Add red wine and reduce.

Add sufficient veal stock and *demi-glace* to cover meat.

Add sachet bag, paprika, and *bouquet garni*.

Cover pot and simmer on top of the stove or in the oven.

Add more stock as needed; the meat should always be covered with stock.

Remove stew meat with skimmer, skim stock, and strain through a fine mesh china cap.

Bring stock to a boil and thicken with cornstarch.

Add stew meat and adjust seasoning.

Heat mushrooms and serve over stew.

---

[a] The suggested inside temperature may not kill all harmful bacteria. A slightly higher temperature of 140°F (60°C) is recommended, although the meat would be medium, rather than medium-rare.

[b] Bay leaf, peppercorns, and thyme could be used in this recipe.

433

Braised Beef (Pot Roast) Bourguignonnne

Rindsschmorbraten Burgunder Art
Pièce de boeuf bourguignonne

YIELD: 10 SERVINGS

Beef shoulder clod,[a] larded if desired	5 lb	2.25 kg
Red wine	1 pt 1 oz	500 ml
Mirepoix (Recipe 15)	10 1/2 oz	300 g
Kitchen herbs, fresh[b]	2/3 oz	20 g
Seasoning (salt and pepper)	1x	1x
Peanut oil	1 2/3 oz	50 ml
Tomato paste	3 oz	80 g
Brown veal stock (Recipe 23)	1 qt 2 oz	1.0 L
Demi-glace (Recipe 44)	1 pt 1 oz	500 ml
Sachet bag[c]	1	1

GARNISH

Pearl onions	7 oz	200 g
Slab bacon, smoked (not sliced)	5 1/3 oz	150 g
Mushrooms, fresh	7 oz	200 g
White bread (Pullman loaf)	3 1/2 oz	100 g
Parsley	2/3 oz	20 g
Butter	2 2/3 oz	75 g
Vegetable bouillon (Recipe 27)	3 1/3 oz	100 ml
Sugar	1x	1x
Seasoning (salt)	1x	1x

MISE EN PLACE
Tie beef with butcher's twine to retain its shape.

Marinate beef for at least 24 hours with wine, *mirepoix*, and kitchen herbs.

METHOD FOR GARNISH
Peel and blanch pearl onions.

Cut bacon into sticks, blanch, and set aside.

Trim and wash mushrooms and cut into halves or quarters, depending on size.

Remove crust from bread, cut into cubes (*croûtons*), and toast under the salamander.

Chop parsley leaves.

Glaze pearl onions in butter, vegetable stock, and sugar.

Sauté bacon sticks and add mushrooms. Mix with pearl onions and season to taste.

METHOD
Remove beef from marinade and drain. Remove mirepoix from marinade and set aside. Reserve marinade.

Season beef with salt and pepper and brown in peanut oil on all sides.

Pour off excess oil. Add *mirepoix* and roast in the oven until light brown.

Add tomato paste and continue roasting. Return beef to pot.

Bring reserved marinade to a boil, strain, and add to beef.

Reduce marinade to syrupy consistency.

Add veal stock and *demi-glace*. The liquid should cover about two-thirds of the meat.

Add sachet bag. Cover pot and braise in oven until beef is tender, turning meat and basting it occasionally. Remove meat, cover, and keep warm.

Strain sauce through a fine mesh china cap. Skim sauce.

Reduce the sauce and thicken with cornstarch if necessary. Skim off all fat.

Slice beef and cover with sauce.

Serve bacon, mushroom, and pearl onion garnish over beef. Sprinkle with croûtons and parsley.

434

Smoked Ox Tongue with Madeira Sauce

Rindszunge mit Madeirasauce
Langue de boeuf au madère

YIELD: 10 SERVINGS

Ox tongue, smoked	3 lb 8 oz	1.6 kg

SAUCE

Demi-glace (Recipe 44)	1 pt 8 oz	700 ml
Madeira wine	3 1/3 oz	100 ml
Seasoning	1x	1x

MISE EN PLACE
Soak[a] tongue in cold water.

---

[a] Shoulder clod is a juicy cut of meat, suitable for braising; however, the cut is rather small. If large quantities are needed, beef top round can be used; however, top round is rather dry and should be larded.

[b] Herbs such as parsley, thyme, and rosemary would be good in this dish.

[c] Bay leaf, peppercorns, marjoram, savory, allspice, and cloves could be used in this recipe.

---

[a] Soaking will remove some of the smoky flavor. In some countries, smoked tongue does not require soaking, because it is less salty.

METHOD

Boil tongue in water, without any additional spices, until tender.

Remove tongue from water and reserve stock.

Immediately plunge tongue into cold water and peel off skin.

Trim tongue and heat in small amount of reserved boiling stock. Keep warm.

Combine *demi-glace* and Madeira wine, bring to a boil, and reduce to desired consistency. Adjust seasoning.

Slice tongue. Serve covered with sauce.

435

Roast Sirloin of Beef, English-Style[a]

Roastbeef englische Art
Roastbeef anglaise

YIELD: 10 SERVINGS

Roast sirloin[b] of beef, boneless and trimmed	4 lb 7 oz	2.0 kg
Seasoning salt for meat (Recipe 9)	2/3 oz	20 g
Peanut oil	2 3/4 oz	80 ml
Matignon (Recipe 14)	7 oz	200 g
Red wine	6 3/4 oz	200 ml
Brown veal stock (Recipe 23)	1 pt 4 oz	600 ml
Seasoning	1x	1x

METHOD

Season beef sirloin with seasoning salt.

Brown sirloin on both sides in peanut oil in a hot 440°F (230°C) oven.

Continue roasting at 360°F (180°C) to 400°F (200°C), basting frequently.

Remove meat 50°F (10°C) below the desired inside temperature.

Place meat on wire rack and keep warm.

Pour off all excess fat. Add *matignon* and roast briefly.

Add red wine and reduce completely.

Add veal stock, bring to a boil, and skim.

Strain stock through a fine mesh china cap; skim again.

Boil sauce down to the desired consistency.

Serve meat with sauce on the side.

436

Veal Scallopini with Ham and Sage

Saltimbocca alla romana

YIELD: 10 SERVINGS

Veal, top round[a]	3 lb 5 oz	1.5 kg
Air-dried ham[b]	4 1/4 oz	120 g
Sage, fresh	1 2/3 oz	50 g
Seasoning salt for meat (Recipe 9)	1/3 oz	10 g
White wheat flour	1 2/3 oz	50 g
Peanut oil	2 3/4 oz	80 ml
Marsala wine[c]	3 1/3 oz	100 ml
Brown veal juice, thickened (Recipe 55)	13 1/2 oz	400 ml
Butter	1 2/3 oz	50 g

MISE EN PLACE

Cut veal into 30 small cutlets, about 1 1/3 oz (40 g) each.

Cut ham, on meat slicer, into 30 small slices.

Trim and wash sage; pluck leaves from stems.

Place one sage leaf on each cutlet and top with ham.

Fasten ham with wood skewers.

METHOD

Season cutlets with seasoning salt and dust with flour.

Sauté cutlets on both sides in peanut oil.

Place cutlets on a warm platter.

Pour off excess oil; add wine to pan to dissolve pan drippings.

Add veal juice and boil for a few minutes.

Add cold butter in small nuggets. Do not allow sauce to return to a boil.

At the moment of service remove skewers.

Serve a small amount of sauce over meat; serve the rest of the sauce on the side.

---

[a] In Switzerland and some other parts of Europe, beef is typically served medium to well-done. "English-Style" in the title of this dish refers to the fact that the beef is usually served medium-rare or rare.

[b] In Switzerland, sirloin is used for roast beef. In the United States, prime rib is used.

[a] The names of meat cuts vary from country to country. "Top round" is called *Eckstück* or *Bäggli* in Switzerland, and *Oberschale* in Germany.

[b] The recipe specifies *Bündner Rohschinken*, which is a local ham from a Swiss province. Prosciutto can be substituted.

[c] Marsala is a sweet fortified wine from Sicily. Sweet sherry can be substituted.

437

Garlic Sausage Baked in Brioche

Saucissons im Briocheteig
Saucissons en brioche

YIELD: 10 SERVINGS

Garlic sausage[a]	2 lb 14 oz	1.3 kg
Dry white wine	1 pt 1 oz	500 ml
Garlic, crushed	2/3 oz	20 g
Bay leaf	1	1
Clove	1	1
Shallots	3 1/2 oz	100 g
Butter	1 2/3 oz	50 g
Egg yolks	2	2
Heavy cream (36%)	6 3/4 oz	200 ml
Brioche dough (Recipe 680)	3 lb	1.4 kg
Egg	1	1

MISE EN PLACE

Prick sausage with a toothpick or a fork.

Steam sausage with white wine, garlic, bay leaf, and clove, over medium heat, for about 30 minutes. Let sausage cool. Save stock; peel sausage.

Strain stock, skim, and reserve for sauce.

Peel and chop shallots. Sauté shallots in butter and let cool.

Blend egg yolks thoroughly with heavy cream (*liaison*) and set aside.

METHOD

Roll out brioche dough to about 1/2-in. (12 mm) thick.

Sprinkle dough with half the shallots.

Place sausage in center of dough and sprinkle with remaining shallots.

Wrap sausage in dough to form a loaf. Place dough, seam side down, in buttered and flour-dusted loaf mold.

Proof dough for about 20 minutes.

Mix egg with 1 tbsp of water and brush dough with egg mixture.

Bake at 425°F (220°C) for about 35 minutes. Lower heat if brioche browns too quickly.

Bring reserved sausage stock to a boil. Remove from heat.

Add egg yolk/cream *liaison* to hot stock, stirring vigorously. Do not allow the sauce to return to a boil.

Slice sausages and serve sauce on the side.

[a] The recipe calls for *Waadländer* sausages, a local Swiss specialty. Other garlic sausages can be substituted, but they should not be too fatty.

438

Veal Filet Mignon with Porcini Cream Sauce and Asparagus

Sautierte Kalbsfilet-Mignons mit Steinpilzrahmsauce
Mignons de veau sautés aux cèpes à la crème

YIELD: 10 SERVINGS

Veal tenderloins,[a] trimmed, center part only	3 lb	1.4 kg
Porcini[b] mushrooms, fresh	14 oz	400 g
Shallots	1 2/3 oz	50 g
Garlic clove, peeled	1	1
Heavy cream (36%)	6 3/4 oz	200 ml
Seasoning salt for meat (Recipe 9)	1/3 oz	10 g
Peanut oil	3 1/3 oz	100 ml
Butter	1 2/3 oz	50 g
Butter	8 3/4 oz	250 g
Egg yolks	12	12
Veal juice (Recipe 64)	6 3/4 oz	200 ml
Dry white wine	10 oz	300 ml
Seasoning	1x	1x

GARNISH

White asparagus	2 lb 3 oz	1.0 kg
Green asparagus	2 lb 3 oz	1.0 kg
Chervil, fresh	2/3 oz	20 g
Salt	2/3 oz	20 g

MISE EN PLACE

Cut 20 medallions, 2 1/2 oz (70 g) each, from veal tenderloins.

Trim and wash porcini mushrooms and cut into slices.

Peel and chop shallots and garlic.

Whip the heavy cream.

MISE EN PLACE FOR GARNISH

Peel the asparagus and trim to about 5-in. (125 mm) lengths.

Tie white and green asparagus, separately, into bundles.

Remove chervil leaves from stems.

METHOD

Season veal medallions with seasoning salt and sauté in peanut oil briefly on both sides. Be sure veal is still pink.

[a] It might be difficult to obtain veal tenderloins in some markets. Boneless veal loin can be substituted.

[b] Porcini are wild mushrooms, called *cepes* in French, *Steinpilze* in German, and *porcini* in Italian. These mushrooms are widely available dried, and are increasingly available fresh. Because Italy is a large exporter of these mushrooms, the Italian name is commonly used. The recipe calls for *Steinpilze*, which are readily available in Switzerland during the summer.

Sauté porcini mushrooms with shallots and garlic in 1 2/3 oz (50 g) butter, drain off all juices, and keep warm.

Melt 8 3/4 oz (250 g) butter.

Combine egg yolks with veal juice and white wine. Whip the mixture with a whisk, in steam table, until it is foamy and hot (as in making Hollandaise sauce). Then whip in the melted butter and fold in the whipped cream.

Fold sautéed mushrooms gently into cream sauce mixture. Season to taste.

Boil asparagus in salted water, remove strings from bundles, and keep asparagus warm.

Place cream sauce in centers of serving plates and brown under the salamander.

Place veal medallions on top.

Garnish with white and green asparagus and chervil leaves.

Wash basil, thyme, and parsley and chop leaves.

Remove pits from olives.

METHOD

Season lamb chops with thyme and salt and pepper. Sauté chops in peanut oil until medium-rare,[a] set aside on wire rack and keep warm.

Pour off excess oil and add butter to pan.

Sauté shallots and garlic in butter.

Add white wine and reduce.

Add veal juice and reduce to the desired consistency.

Add mushrooms, tomatoes, herbs, and olives. Bring to a boil.

Adjust seasoning.

Serve sauce with lamb chops.

439

Lamb Chops Sautéed with Mushrooms and Tomatoes

Sautierte Lammchops provenzalische Art
Chops d'agneau sautés provençale

YIELD: 10 SERVINGS

Shallots	1 2/3 oz	50 g
Garlic	2/3 oz	20 g
Mushrooms, fresh	3 1/2 oz	100 g
Tomatoes	8 3/4 oz	250 g
Basil, fresh	2/3 oz	20 g
Thyme, fresh	1/3 oz	10 g
Parsley	2/3 oz	20 g
Black olives, drained	3 1/2 oz	100 g
Thyme, fresh, chopped	2/3 oz	20 g
Seasoning (salt and pepper)	1x	1x
Lamb chops, trimmed, ready to cook (10)	3 lb 8 oz	1.6 kg
Peanut oil	3 1/3 oz	100 ml
Butter	1 2/3 oz	50 g
Dry white wine	6 3/4 oz	200 ml
Veal juice, thickened (Recipe 55)	13 1/2 oz	400 ml
Seasoning	1x	1x

MISE EN PLACE

Peel and chop shallots and garlic.

Trim and wash mushrooms and cut into slices.

Peel tomatoes, cut in half, remove seeds, and cut into dice.

440

Beef Tenderloin Medallions with Marrow and Red Wine Sauce

Sautierte Rindsfilet-Mignons mit Mark
Mignons de boeuf sautés bordelaise

YIELD: 10 SERVINGS

Beef tenderloin, trimmed	3 lb	1.4 kg
Beef marrow	10 1/2 oz	300 g
Shallots	3 1/2 oz	100 g
White peppercorns	1/2 oz	15 g
Thyme, fresh	1/3 oz	10 g
Salt	2/3 oz	20 g
Seasoning (white pepper, ground)	1x	1x
Peanut oil	3 1/3 oz	100 ml
Butter	2/3 oz	20 g
Red wine (Bordeaux)	10 oz	300 ml
Brown veal juice, thickened (Recipe 55)	13 1/2 oz	400 ml
Butter, cold	1 2/3 oz	50 g

MISE EN PLACE

Cut 20 beef medallions, 2 1/2 oz (70 g) each.

Soak marrow, first in cold water, then in tepid water, to remove blood.

Dice marrow and keep in ice water.

Peel and chop shallots.

(continued on next page)

---

[a] Customers should be asked how they would like their lamb chops cooked.

(continued from preceding page)

Crush white peppercorns.

Chop thyme leaves.

METHOD

Season beef medallions with salt and ground white pepper and sauté quickly in hot oil on both sides. Keep meat rare to medium-rare.

Place beef on wire rack and keep warm.

Pour off excess oil.

Add butter to pan and sauté shallots.

Add crushed peppercorns, thyme, and red wine and reduce to about one-third.

Add veal juice, bring to a boil, and boil to desired consistency.

Strain through a fine mesh china cap.

Bring to a boil again and add cold butter in small nuggets. Do not allow the sauce to return to a boil.

Dip marrow briefly into simmering water. Add marrow to sauce at the moment of service.

Serve meat covered with marrow sauce.

441

Pork Medallions Sautéed with Apples and Calvados

Sautierte Schweinsfiletmedaillons auf Apfelschnitzen
Médaillons de filet mignon de porc sautés normande

YIELD: 10 SERVINGS

Pork tenderloin, trimmed[a]	3 lb	1.4 kg
Apples[b]	1 lb 12 oz	800 g
Seasoning (salt and pepper)	1x	1x
White wheat flour	1 2/3 oz	50 g
Peanut oil	3 1/3 oz	100 ml
Butter	1 1/3 oz	40 g
Crystal sugar	2 oz	60 g
Dry white wine	6 3/4 oz	200 ml
Golden sultanas	1 2/3 oz	50 g
Lemon, juice and grated peel	1	1
Calvados (or any apple brandy)	1 2/3 oz	50 ml

MISE EN PLACE

Cut tenderloin into 20 medallions (steaks) about 2 1/2 oz (70 g) each.

Peel and core apples and cut into even-sized wedges.

---

[a] It might not be possible to obtain pork tenderloins in some markets. Boneless pork loin, well trimmed, can be substituted.

[b] Granny Smith or other cooking apples should be used.

METHOD

Season pork medallions with salt and pepper and dust with flour.

Sauté golden brown on both sides in peanut oil. Keep meat warm.

Combine butter and sugar. Heat until sugar is light brown (caramelized).

Add white wine, apples, sultanas, lemon juice, and grated peel. Bring to a boil, cover, and stew briefly. Add Calvados.

Put apples on plates; serve pork medallions on top.

442

Beef Tournedos Sautéed with Crushed Peppercorns

Sautierte Tournedos mit zerdrücktem Pfeffer
Tournedos de boeuf sautés au poivre écrasé

YIELD: 10 SERVINGS

Beef tenderloin, trimmed[a]	3 lb 5 oz	1.5 kg
White peppercorns	1/2 oz	15 g
Salt	1/3 oz	10 g
Peanut oil	3 1/3 oz	100 ml
Butter	1 2/3 oz	50 g
Cognac (or any brandy)	3 1/3 oz	100 ml
Red wine	6 3/4 oz	200 ml
Demi-glace (Recipe 44)	1 pt 1 oz	500 ml
Butter, cold	1 oz	30 g

MISE EN PLACE

Cut beef into 10 tournedos (steaks) of 5 1/3 oz (150 g) each.

Crush white peppercorns.

METHOD

Sprinkle crushed peppercorns on both sides of tournedos; press on lightly.

Season beef with salt and sauté in peanut oil to desired doneness.

Pour off excess oil and add butter to pan. Turn beef in melting butter.

Add Cognac and ignite.

Remove tournedos, place on wire rack, and keep warm.

Add red wine and bring to a boil. Add *demi-glace* and boil thoroughly.

Add cold butter in small nuggets; do not allow the sauce to return to a boil.

Serve sauce over meat.

---

[a] The tenderloin should be well trimmed.

443

Boneless Loin of Lamb with Fennel Purée

Sautierte Lammrückenfilets auf Fenchelpüree
Filets d'agneau sautés à la purée de fenouil

YIELD: 10 SERVINGS

Loin of lamb, boneless and trimmed	3 lb 5 oz	1.5 kg
Seasoning (salt and pepper)	1x	1x
Olive oil	3 1/3 oz	100 ml
GARNISH		
Shallots	1 2/3 oz	50 g
Fennel bulbs (anise)	1 lb 9 oz	700 g
Peppermint, fresh	2/3 oz	20 g
Butter	1 1/3 oz	40 g
Chicken stock (Recipe 26)	1 pt 11 oz	800 ml
Seasoning (salt and pepper)	1x	1x
Seasoning (lemon juice)	1x	1x
Cold roux (beurre manie)	2/3 oz	20 g

MISE EN PLACE FOR GARNISH

Peel and chop shallots.

Trim fennel, wash, and slice.

Chop peppermint leaves.

METHOD FOR GARNISH

Sauté shallots in butter; add sliced fennel and chicken stock.

Cover and bring to a boil. Simmer until the fennel is soft.

Purée[a] and strain through a small hole china cap.

Season with salt and pepper and lemon juice.

Bring to a boil and thicken with *beurre manie*.

Add chopped peppermint leaves.

METHOD FOR MEAT

Season the lamb with salt and pepper and roast in olive oil in very hot oven for 10 minutes.

Remove from pan and keep warm. Let rest for 10 minutes to allow the juices to circulate.

Slice meat into 3/4-in. (19 mm) thick slices and place on top of fennel puree.

---

[a] The fennel can be puréed in a food processor. It is best to drain off the excess stock first. Some stock can be added back later, when the puree is heated.

444

Club Steaks Sautéed with Herb Butter

Sautierte Rumpsteaks mit Kräuterbutter
Rumpsteak sautés maître d'hôtel

YIELD: 10 SERVINGS

Top sirloin butt[a]	3 lb 8 oz	1.6 kg
Seasoning (salt and pepper)	1x	1x
Peanut oil	1 2/3 oz	50 ml
HERB BUTTER		
Butter	5 1/3 oz	150 g
Parsley	1 oz	30 g
Chives, fresh	2/3 oz	20 g
Glace de viande[b]	2/3 oz	20 g
Lemon	1/2	1/2
Seasoning (salt and pepper)	1x	1x
GARNISH		
Cress, trimmed and washed	1 2/3 oz	50 g

METHOD FOR HERB BUTTER

Cream the butter.

Chop parsley. Cut chives into small slivers.

Melt *glace de viande*.

Combine all ingredients; season with lemon juice, salt and pepper.

Shape butter into a roll about 1-in. (25 mm) thick; roll in parchment paper or aluminum foil and refrigerate.

METHOD

Cut sirloin into 10 steaks, about 5 2/3 oz (160 g) each. Pound steaks lightly to tenderize and season with salt and pepper.

Sauté[c] steaks in hot oil on both sides to the desired degree of doneness.

Serve with a slice of herb butter on top. Garnish with cress.

---

[a] Meat terminology varies from country to country. The original recipe calls for *Rindshuft*.

[b] *Glace de viande*, literally translated "meat glaze," is made by reducing meat stock to a syrupy consistency.

[c] The steaks can also be broiled. If this is the case, the menu terminology has to be revised.

445

Pork Chops Sauté with Mustard Sauce

Sautierte Schweinskotletts mit Senfsauce
Côtes de porc sautées Robert

YIELD: 10 SERVINGS

Pork loin, rib end, trimmed	3 lb 8 oz	1.6 kg
Shallots	1 2/3 oz	50 g
Seasoning (salt and pepper)	1x	1x
White wheat flour	1 2/3 oz	50 g
Peanut oil	3 1/3 oz	100 ml
Dry white wine	6 3/4 oz	200 ml
Demi-glace (Recipe 44)	1 pt 1 oz	500 ml
Dijon mustard[a]	1 2/3 oz	50 g
Lemon	1/2	1/2

MISE EN PLACE

Cut meat into 10 chops, 5 2/3 oz (160 g) each, including bone.

Peel and chop shallots.

MISE EN PLACE

Season pork chops with salt and pepper, and dust with flour.

Sauté in hot peanut oil on both sides. Remove and keep warm.

Pour off excess fat, add shallots to pan, and sauté.

Add white wine and reduce completely.

Add *demi-glace* and bring to a boil. Season sauce with mustard and lemon juice. (Do not allow the sauce to return to a boil after mustard has been added.)

Serve chops covered with sauce.

446

Pork Cutlets Sautéed with Paprika Cream Sauce

Sautierte Schweinssteaks mit Paprikarahmsauce
Steaks de porc sautés à la crème au paprika

YIELD: 10 SERVINGS

Pork loin, boneless	3 lb 5 oz	1.5 kg
Bell peppers, assorted	8 3/4 oz	250 g
Butter	1 oz	30 g
Seasoning salt for meat (Recipe 9)	1/3 oz	10 g
White wheat flour	1 2/3 oz	50 g
Peanut oil	3 1/3 oz	100 ml
Paprika	1/3 oz	10 g
Dry white wine	6 3/4 oz	200 ml
Madeira wine	1 2/3 oz	50 ml
Demi-glace (Recipe 44)	1 pt 4 oz	600 ml
Heavy cream (36%)	6 3/4 oz	200 ml
Seasoning (salt and pepper)	1x	1x

MISE EN PLACE

Cut pork loin into 10 cutlets, 5 1/3 oz (150 g) each. Pound cutlets lightly.

Split bell peppers in half and remove seeds. Wash peppers and cut into fine strips (*julienne*). Braise peppers lightly in butter; do not overcook. Keep peppers warm.

METHOD

Season cutlets with seasoning salt and dust with flour.

Sauté pork in hot peanut oil on both sides, remove, and keep warm.

Pour off excess fat.

Add paprika and immediately add white wine and Madeira wine; do not allow paprika to burn.

Reduce wine to about half and add *demi-glace*.

Reduce sauce to desired consistency. Strain through a fine mesh china cap.

Stir in heavy cream, heat sauce, and adjust seasoning.

Add cutlets to sauce to heat, but do not allow to boil.

Serve pork cutlets with sauce.

Sprinkle bell pepper *julienne* over meat as garnish.

[a] There are different versions of Dijon mustard. The mustard for this recipe should be smooth textured and sharp tasting.

447

Pork Cutlets Sautéed Gypsy Style

Sautierte Schweinssteaks Zigeunerart
Steaks de porc sautés zingara

Y I E L D :   1 0   S E R V I N G S

Pork loin, boneless	3 lb 5 oz	1.5 kg
Seasoning salt for meat (Recipe 9)	1/3 oz	10 g
Peanut oil	3 1/3 oz	100 ml
Shallots, chopped	1 2/3 oz	50 g
Paprika	1 pinch	2 g
Dry white wine	3 1/3 oz	100 ml
Demi-glace (Recipe 44)	13 1/2 oz	400 ml
Cayenne	pinch	1 g

GARNISH

Ox tongue, smoked, cooked, and trimmed	3 1/2 oz	100 g
Mushrooms, fresh	8 3/4 oz	250 g
Butter	1 oz	30 g
Lemon juice	1/3 oz	10 ml

MISE EN PLACE
Cut pork loin into 10 even-sized cutlets.

METHOD FOR GARNISH
Cut ox tongue into fine strips (*julienne*).

Trim and wash mushrooms and cut into slices.

Smother mushrooms with butter and lemon juice.

METHOD
Season pork cutlets with seasoning salt and sauté in hot peanut oil on both sides. Keep warm.

Pour off excess oil.

Add chopped shallots to pan and sauté lightly.

Dust with paprika, add white wine, and reduce completely.

Add *demi-glace*, bring to a boil, and season with cayenne.

Add ox tongue/mushroom garnish and bring to a boil.

Serve pork cutlets with sauce.

448

Ham Baked in Bread Dough

Schinken im Brotteig
Jambon en croûte

Y I E L D :   3 0   S E R V I N G S

Ham, smoked, bone in	17 lb 10 oz	8.0 kg

DOUGH

Yeast, fresh	3 1/2 oz	100 g
Baker's malt, powdered	1 1/3 oz	40 g
Water	1 qt 19 oz	1.5 L
Whole wheat flour[a]	5 lb 8 oz	2.5 kg
Salt	1 2/3 oz	50 g

MISE EN PLACE
Poach ham in plenty of water for about 3 1/2 hours at 160°F (70°C) to 180°F (80°C). Let ham cool in its stock.

METHOD FOR DOUGH
Dissolve yeast and malt in small amount of warm, 95°F (38°C), water.

Sift flour and combine with yeast, malt, water, and salt to make a stiff dough.

Knead dough thoroughly on pastry board.

Cover dough and proof for 1 hour in a warm place. Punch dough down, allow to rise, and punch down again.

Remove ham from stock. Trim off skin and fat; remove aitchbone; trim shank.

Roll out dough and place ham in center. Be sure ham is dry.

Wrap ham in dough. Place, seam side down, on pastry sheet. Decorate with dough trimmings.

Proof dough-wrapped ham in temperatures not above 86°F (30°C) for 30 minutes.

Bake dough-wrapped ham at 400°F (200°C) for the first 45 minutes. Lower heat to 360°F (180°C) and bake 5 hours longer.

Let ham rest at least 30 minutes before serving.

---

[a] The original recipe calls for *Ruchmehl*. The best translation is whole wheat flour. Flour grades and quality levels can vary; it is advisable to use hard wheat flour (high gluten) in this recipe.

449

Roast Pork Loin with Dried Prunes

Schweinsbraten mit Dörrpflaumen
Rôti de porc suédoise

YIELD: 10 SERVINGS

Pork loin, boneless	4 lb	1.8 kg
Dried prunes	8 3/4 oz	250 g
Seasoning salt for meat (Recipe 9)	2/3 oz	20 g
Peanut oil	2 3/4 oz	80 ml
Matignon (Recipe 14)	7 oz	200 g
Rosemary twig, fresh	1	1
Sage, fresh	1/6 oz	5 g
Dry white wine	6 3/4 oz	200 ml
Brown veal stock (Recipe 23)	1 pt 11 oz	800 ml
Madeira wine	3 1/3 oz	100 ml
Seasoning (salt and pepper)	1x	1x

MISE EN PLACE

Make pocket lengthwise in pork loin. Make hole first with sharpening steel, and then carefully enlarge pocket with knife.

Remove pits from prunes. Stuff pork cavity with prunes.

Tie pork loin with butcher's, twine to retain its shape; tie aluminum foil at the ends to prevent prunes from falling out.

METHOD

Season pork with seasoning salt. Roast in peanut oil, first at 425°F (220°C), then at 360°F (180°C).

When meat is fully cooked, remove and keep warm.

Pour off excess fat.

Add *matignon*, rosemary, and sage, roast for a few minutes, add white wine, and reduce.

Add veal stock, bring to a boil, and boil thoroughly to dissolve the pan drippings.

Skim sauce and strain through a fine mesh china cap.

Reduce the sauce[a] to desired consistency, skimming frequently.

Add Madeira wine. Adjust seasoning.

Slice meat. Serve sauce separately.

---

[a] Technically it is not a sauce, because it is not thickened.

450

Pork Chops Baked with Tomatoes and Cheese

Schweinskoteletts Walliser Art
Côtes de porc valaisanne

YIELD: 10 SERVINGS

Pork loin, rib end, trimmed, oven-ready	3 lb 12 oz	1.7 kg
Shallots	3 1/2 oz	100 g
Garlic	1/6 oz	5 g
Kitchen herbs, fresh[a]	2/3 oz	20 g
Raclette cheese[b]	1 lb 2 oz	500 g
Seasoning salt for meat (Recipe 9)	2/3 oz	20 g
Peanut oil	1 2/3 oz	50 ml
Butter	1 2/3 oz	50 g
Tomato concassé, fresh (Recipe 97)	13 1/2 oz	400 ml
Seasoning (salt and pepper)	1x	1x
Rosemary twig, fresh	10	10

MISE EN PLACE

Cut pork loin into 10 chops.

Peel and chop shallots and garlic.

Trim and wash kitchen herbs and chop.

Cut raclette cheese into 10 slices.

METHOD

Season pork chops with seasoning salt and sauté in hot peanut oil on both sides, until chops are fully cooked.

Remove chops and keep warm. Pour off excess oil.

Add butter to pan and sauté shallots and garlic.

Add tomato concassé, bring to a boil, add kitchen herbs, and season to taste.

Put small mound of tomatoes on each cutlet and top with raclette cheese.

Melt cheese under the salamander.

Garnish with rosemary twigs.

---

[a] Oregano and sage would be good in this dish.

[b] Raclette cheese is a local Swiss cheese from the province of Valais. It is specified in this dish because it melts evenly.

451

Boiled Beef with Sauerkraut and Bacon

Siedfleisch Elsässer Art
Boeuf bouilli alsacienne

YIELD: 10 SERVINGS

Rib eye,[a] trimmed	5 lb	2.25 kg
Beef bones	5 lb 8 oz	2.5 kg
Onion, 1 large	4 1/3 oz	125 g
Bouquet garni (Recipe 7)	1 lb 2 oz	500 g
Sachet bag[b]	1	1
Salt	1/3 oz	10 g

GARNISH

Onions	6 1/3 oz	180 g
Vegetable shortening	2 2/3 oz	75 g
Sauerkraut, fresh	3 lb 5 oz	1.5 kg
Dry white wine	6 3/4 oz	200 ml
Bouillon (Recipe 22)	1 qt 2 oz	1.0 L
Sachet bag[b]	1	1
Slab bacon, smoked (not sliced)	3 oz	80 g

MISE EN PLACE
Tie rib eye with butcher's twine. Put rib eye in hot water, bring to a boil, and drain. Wash rib eye, first in hot water, then in cold water.

Soak beef bones in cold water; drain. Add more cold water, bring bones to a boil, and drain. Wash beef bones, first in hot water, then in cold water.

Cut onion (not peeled) in half horizontally and place, cut side down, on hot stove top. Brown onion.

METHOD
Cover beef bones with ample amount of cold water, bring to a boil, skim, and simmer for about 1 1/2 hours.

Add *bouquet garni*, sachet bag, and browned onion.

Add rib eye and salt and simmer until meat is tender, skimming occasionally.

Remove rib eye and keep hot in small amount of stock.

METHOD FOR GARNISH
Peel and chop onions. Sauté in shortening.

Add sauerkraut, white wine, and bouillon.

Add sachet bag and bacon.

---

[a] The names of meat cuts vary from country to country. Rib eye is sometimes called prime rib, before the bones are removed. The cut is also sometimes called "Spencer roll."

[b] For this recipe, bay leaf, peppercorns, thyme, and rosemary could be used.

Cover pot and simmer for about 1 hour, or until bacon is tender.

PRESENTATION
Slice rib eye and bacon. Serve with sauerkraut.

NOTE: The sauerkraut can be thickened by adding 5 oz (150 g) grated raw potatoes at the beginning of the cooking process.

452

Glazed Calves' Sweetbreads with Porcini Mushrooms

Überbackene Kalbsmilken mit Steinpilzen
Gratin de ris de veau aux cèpes

YIELD: 10 SERVINGS

Sweetbreads	3 lb 12 oz	1.7 kg
White veal stock (Recipe 28)	2 qt 4 oz	2.0 L
Dry white wine	6 3/4 oz	200 ml
Onion studded with 1 clove	1	1
Seasoning (salt and pepper)	1x	1x
White wheat flour	1 oz	30 g
Peanut oil	3 1/3 oz	100 ml
Butter	1 2/3	50 g

SAUCE

Shallots	2 2/3 oz	75 g
Garlic	1/6 oz	5 g
Porcini mushrooms,[a] fresh	14 oz	400 g
Butter	1 1/3 oz	40 g
Dry white wine	2 1/2 oz	75 ml
Heavy cream (36%)	3 1/3 oz	100 ml
Veal velouté sauce (Recipe 65)	13 1/2 oz	400 ml
Seasoning	1x	1x
Heavy cream (36%)	5 oz	150 ml
Egg yolks	3	3

GARNISH

Chives, fresh, cut into slivers	2/3 oz	20 g

MISE EN PLACE
Soak sweetbreads overnight. Wash in warm water; remove any fat and membranes.

(continued on next page)

---

[a] Porcini are wild mushrooms, called *cèpes* in French, *Steinpilze* in German, and *porcini* in Italian. These mushrooms are widely available dried, and are increasingly available fresh. Because Italy is a large exporter of these mushrooms, the Italian name is commonly used. The recipe calls for *Steinpilze*, which are readily available in Switzerland during the summer.

(continued from preceding page)

METHOD

Combine veal stock and white wine, add clove-studded onion, and bring to a boil.

Add sweetbreads and bring to a boil again. Skim.

Lower heat to about 160°F (70°C) and poach sweetbreads for 15 minutes. Let sweetbreads cool in the stock.

Remove skin and trim sweetbreads. Cut into slices.

Season sweetbread slices with salt and pepper and dust with flour. Sauté in peanut oil, on one side, until brown.

Pour off oil and replace with butter.

Turn sweetbreads and sauté on the other side. Keep warm.

METHOD FOR SAUCE

Peel and chop shallots and garlic.

Trim and wash porcini mushrooms and cut into slices.

Sauté shallots and garlic in butter in a shallow sauté pan.

Add mushrooms, cover pot, smother, and remove mushrooms with skimmer.

Remove lid, add white wine, and reduce over high heat.

Add 3 1/3 oz (100 ml) heavy cream; reduce sauce to about one-third.

Add *velouté* and bring to a boil. Adjust seasoning.

Return mushrooms to sauce and bring to a boil.

Blend 5 oz (150 ml) heavy cream thoroughly with egg yolks to make *liaison*. Stir liaison into hot sauce, but do not allow to return to a boil.

Serve sweetbread slices covered with sauce. Brown sauce under the salamander.

Sprinkle with chives.

453

Boiled Beef with Onion Sauce

Überbackenes Siedfleish mit Zwiebelsauce
Miroton de boeuf

YIELD: 10 SERVINGS

Rib eye,[a] trimmed	5 lb	2.25 kg
Beef bones	5 lb 8 oz	2.5 kg
Bouquet garni (Recipe 7)	1 lb 2 oz	500 g
Onion, 1 large	4 1/3 oz	125 g
Sachet bag	1	1
Salt	1/3 oz	10 g
Mie de pain[a]	4 1/4 oz	150 g
Butter	1 2/3 oz	50 g
SAUCE		
Onions	2 oz	60 g
Butter	1 2/3 oz	50 g
Demi-glace (Recipe 44)	1 pt 1 oz	500 ml
White wine vinegar	1 2/3 oz	50 ml
Seasoning	1x	1x

MISE EN PLACE

Tie rib eye with butcher's twine. Put rib eye in hot water, bring to a boil, and drain. Wash rib eye, first in hot water, then in cold water.

Soak beef bones in cold water; drain. Add more cold water, bring bones to a boil, and drain. Wash beef bones, first in hot water, then in cold water.

Cut onion (not peeled) in half horizontally and place, cut side down, on hot stove top. Brown onion.

METHOD

Cover beef bones with ample amount of cold water, bring to a boil, skim, and simmer for about 1 1/2 hours.

Add *bouquet garni*, sachet bag, and browned onion.

Add rib eye and salt and simmer until meat is tender, skimming occasionally.

Remove rib eye and keep hot in small amount of stock.

METHOD FOR SAUCE

Peel and slice onions. Sauté onions in butter.

Add *demi-glace*. Add vinegar, bring to a boil, and simmer until onions are fully cooked.

Adjust seasoning.

PRESENTATION

Place half of the onion sauce in a gratin dish. Slice the rib eye and place on top. Cover with remaining onion sauce.

Sprinkle with *mie de pain* and melted butter.

Brown under the salamander.

---

[a] The names of meat cuts vary from country to country. Rib eye is sometimes called prime rib, before the bones are removed. The cut is also sometimes called "Spencer roll."

[a] *Mie de pain* are fresh bread crumbs, made from white Pullman loaves.

454

*H*ungarian Beef Goulash

Ungarisches Gulasch
Goulache hongroise

YIELD: 10 SERVINGS

Onions	2 lb 12 oz	1.25 kg
Bell peppers, assorted	1 lb	450 g
Tomatoes	1 lb 2 oz	500 g
Garlic	1/3 oz	10 g
Caraway seeds, whole	1/3 oz	10 g
Potatoes	2 lb 3 oz	1.0 kg
Beef stew meat,[a] cut into 1 1/3-oz (40 g) cubes	3 lb 8 oz	1.6 kg
Clarified butter	3 1/2 oz	100 g
Hungarian sweet paprika	3 1/2 oz	100 g
Red wine	6 3/4 oz	200 ml
Bouillon (Recipe 22)	1 qt 2 oz	1.0 L
Seasoning (salt and pepper)	1x	1x

MISE EN PLACE

Peel and slice onions.

Split bell peppers in half, remove seeds, and wash. Cut peppers into thin strips (*julienne*).

Peel tomatoes, cut in half, remove seeds, and dice into small cubes.

Peel garlic and chop along with caraway seeds.[b]

Peel potatoes and cut into medium-size cubes.

METHOD

Sweat beef stew meat and onions in clarified butter, until the meat juices reach a syrupy consistency.

Add bell peppers, paprika, and tomatoes and continue cooking.

Add garlic, caraway seeds, red wine, and bouillon. Bring to a boil, cover, and braise until beef is almost tender.

Add cubed potatoes and simmer until potatoes are tender. Adjust seasoning.

NOTES: For restaurant service, the potatoes should be cooked separately.

In Hungary, the goulash is often served with small flour dumplings, known as *Spätzle* in German and *Csipetke* in Hungarian.

[a] Beef stew meat can come from many different cuts of meat. The meat should be lean, but have flavor. It is important that all meat pieces be from the same cut, so the meat will cook evenly. The preferred meat for Hungarian goulash is from beef shanks.

[b] Chopping the caraway seeds along with the garlic will help to keep the seeds together.

455

*V*iennese Veal Goulash

Wiener Gulasch
Goulache viennoise

YIELD: 10 SERVINGS

Onions	2 lb 3 oz	1.0 kg
Garlic	1/4 oz	7 g
Caraway seeds, whole	1/8 oz	3 1/2 g
Tomatoes	1 lb 2 oz	500 g
Clarified butter	3 1/2 oz	100 g
Veal shoulder meat, cut into 1 1/3-oz (40 g) cubes	3 lb 8 oz	1.6 kg
Salt	1/3 oz	10 g
Seasoning (white pepper)	1x	1x
Hungarian sweet paprika	1 2/3 oz	50 g
White veal stock (Recipe 28)	1 qt 2 oz	1.0 L
Sour cream, light	10 oz	300 ml
Lemon, juice	1	1
Seasoning	1x	1x

MISE EN PLACE

Peel onions and cut into fine slices.

Peel garlic and chop along with caraway seeds.[a]

Peel tomatoes, cut in half, remove seeds, and cut into small cubes.

METHOD

Sauté onions in clarified butter, but do not brown.

Add veal and sweat until the meat juices reach a syrupy consistency.

Season with salt and white pepper.

Add paprika, garlic, and tomatoes and continue cooking.

Add veal stock, bring to a boil, cover, and braise until veal is tender.

Add caraway seeds, sour cream, and lemon juice. Adjust seasoning.

NOTE: If less chopped onions are used, the onions can be dusted with flour to thicken the sauce. The sauce can also be puréed, in which case the veal must first be removed.

[a] Chopping the caraway seeds along with the garlic will help to keep the seeds together.

456

Breaded Veal Cutlets

Wiener Schnitzel
Escalope de veau viennoise

YIELD: 10 SERVINGS

Veal, top round [a]	3 lb 5 oz	1.5 kg
Lemons	2 1/2	2 1/2
Eggs	2	2
Seasoning salt for meat (Recipe 9)	1/3 oz	10 g
White wheat flour	1 2/3 oz	50 g
Mie de pain [b]	12 oz	350 g
Clarified butter	10 1/2 oz	300 g
Butter	3 1/2 oz	100 g
Parsley, washed	1 2/3 oz	50 g

MISE EN PLACE

Cut veal into 10 cutlets of 5 1/3 oz (150 g) each; pound/flatten the cutlets slightly.

Cut lemons into 10 wedges.

Break eggs and mix well.

METHOD

Season veal cutlets with seasoning salt.

Dredge cutlets in flour, then in egg mixture, and then in *mie de pain*. Press crumbs on meat lightly.

Fry cutlets in clarified butter; drain.

At the moment of service, brown the butter and pour over cutlets.

Serve garnished with lemon wedges and parsley.

---

[a] The original recipe calls for *Huft*, which is the tenderest part of the veal leg.

[b] *Mie de pain* are fresh bread crumbs, made from white Pullman loaves.

457

Calves' Liver Brochettes with Bacon, Zurich Style

Zürcher Leberspiessli
Brochettes de foie de veau zurichoise

YIELD: 10 SERVINGS

Calves' liver, skinned	2 lb 7 oz	1.1 kg
Bacon, smoked, sliced	1 lb 2 oz	500 g
Sage, fresh	2/3 oz	20 g
Wooden skewers	10	10
Veal juice, thickened	13 1/2 oz	400 ml
Seasoning (salt and pepper)	1x	1x
Clarified butter	1 2/3 oz	50 g
GARNISH		
Green beans, fresh	2 lb 14 oz	1.3 kg
Salt	1/3 oz	10 g
Onions	1 2/3 oz	50 g
Butter	1 2/3 oz	50 g
Bouillon (Recipe 22)	10 oz	300 ml
Savory, fresh	1/3 oz	10 g
Seasoning (salt and pepper)	1x	1x

MISE EN PLACE

Cut liver into cubes or into sticks about 1/2 in. (12 mm) x 1 1/2 in. (40 mm). There should be 50 pieces.

Cut bacon slices in half. There should be 50 slices. Blanch bacon.

Put one small sage leaf on each piece of liver and wrap in bacon.

Put 5 liver pieces on each of 10 skewers.

METHOD FOR GARNISH

Trim green beans, blanch in ample boiling salted water, drain, chill, and drain again.

Chop onions and sauté in butter.

Add beans and bouillon and bring to a boil.

Chop savory leaves and add to beans.

Cover pot and braise beans until tender, but still firm. Season to taste.

METHOD

Bring veal juice to a boil and keep hot.

Season skewered meat and sauté in clarified butter.

Serve skewers on top of beans. Serve veal juice on the side.

7

Poultry and Game

Poultry Dishes

Roast Duckling with Oranges

Gebratene junge Ente mit Orangen
Caneton à l'orange

YIELD: 10 SERVINGS

Young ducklings, oven-ready, 2 birds[a]	7 lb 12 oz	3.5 kg
Oranges	3	3
Seasoning salt for poultry (Recipe 10)	1 oz	30 g
Peanut oil	2 1/2 oz	75 ml
Matignon (Recipe 14)	10 1/2 oz	300 g
Dry white wine	3 1/3 oz	100 ml
Brown chicken stock[b]	6 3/4 oz	200 ml
Orange juice	5 oz	150 ml
Red Port wine	3 1/3 oz	100 ml
Demi-glace (Recipe 44)	1 pt 4 oz	600 ml
Curaçao	3 1/3 oz	100 ml
Cayenne	pinch	1 g
Seasoning	1x	1x
Butter	1 2/3 oz	50 g

MISE EN PLACE
Truss ducklings to retain their shape during roasting.

Peel oranges and seam out the wedges.

METHOD
Season duckling with seasoning salt, pour peanut oil over duckling, and roast in hot oven until tender and crisp, basting occasionally. Remove duckling and keep warm.

Pour off excess fat.

Add *matignon* and roast briefly.

Add white wine and brown chicken stock and bring to a boil to dissolve pan drippings.

Add orange juice and Port wine. Reduce stock.

Add *demi-glace* and Curaçao and season with cayenne.

Reduce sauce to desired consistency and skim.

Strain sauce through a fine wire china cap and skim again. Adjust seasoning.

Heat orange wedges in butter.

[a] These portions are small because of the weight loss in cooked duck. You may wish to increase the serving size.

[b] Brown chicken stock can be made like brown veal stock (Recipe 23), but using chicken bones instead of veal bones.

Carve duckling and serve with orange wedges and some sauce.

Serve remaining sauce on the side.

Chicken Blanquette with Chives

Geflügelblankett mit Schnittlauch
Blanquette de volaille à la ciboulette

YIELD: 10 SERVINGS

Chicken, 3 birds	6 lb 10 oz	3.0 kg
Chicken stock (Recipe 26)	1 qt 19 oz	1.5 L
Dry white wine	10 oz	300 ml
Bouquet garni (Recipe 8)	10 1/2 oz	300 g
Sachet bag	1	1
Salt	1/3 oz	10 g
SAUCE		
Chives, fresh	1 2/3 oz	50 g
Butter	1 oz	30 g
White wheat flour	1 2/3 oz	50 g
Heavy cream (36%)	6 3/4 oz	200 ml
Egg yolks	2	2
Lemon, juice	1/4	1/4
Seasoning	1x	1x

MISE EN PLACE
Cut up chicken as for chicken sauté.[a]

Blanch chicken pieces and drain. Wash, first in hot water, then in cold water.

METHOD
Combine chicken stock, white wine, *bouquet garni*, sachet bag, and salt. Bring to a boil and skim.

Add chicken pieces and poach until tender. Remove chicken pieces when cooked. (Note that breast pieces will cook faster than leg pieces, and must be removed sooner.) Reserve stock.

Keep chicken pieces warm in small amount of stock.

METHOD FOR SAUCE
Cut chives into small slivers.

Melt butter, add flour, and make roux; allow roux to cool.

[a] The chickens are cut into 8 pieces each, consisting of 2 drumsticks, 2 thighs with bone left in, 4 breast pieces with wing bones still attached to two of them.

Heat 1 qt 2 oz (1.0 L) reserved stock; add hot stock to cool roux and bring to a boil, stirring continuously. Simmer for 20 minutes.

Strain through double layer of cheesecloth.

Bring sauce back to a boil, remove from heat.

Mix heavy cream and egg yolks (*liaison*) and add *liaison* to sauce; stir well. Do not allow sauce to return to a boil.

Add lemon juice and adjust seasoning.

Heat chicken in sauce, but do not allow to boil.

Add chives.

460

Chicken Fricassee with Tarragon

Geflügelfrikassee mit Estragon
Fricassée de volaille à l'estragon

YIELD: 10 SERVINGS

Chicken, 3 birds	6 lb 10 oz	3.0 kg
Onions	7 oz	200 g
Tarragon, fresh	2/3 oz	20 g
Tarragon vinegar	2/3 oz	20 ml
Salt	1 oz	30 g
Seasoning (white pepper)	1x	1x
White wheat flour	2 1/2 oz	70 g
Butter, clarified	2 1/2 oz	70 g
White wheat flour	1 2/3 oz	50 g
Dry white wine	6 3/4 oz	200 ml
Chicken stock (Recipe 26)	1 qt 2 oz	1.0 L
Sachet bag[a]	1	1
Heavy cream (36%)	6 3/4 oz	200 ml

MISE EN PLACE
Cut up chicken as for chicken sauté.[b]

Peel and chop onions.

Remove tarragon leaves from stems. Blanch leaves in tarragon vinegar and reserve both together.

METHOD
Season chicken pieces with salt and white pepper and dust with flour.

Heat clarified butter in wide, heavy saucepan (*rondeau*); add chicken pieces and chopped onions. Sweat until the meat juices are syrupy.

Dust with remaining flour.

Add white wine and chicken stock, bring to a boil, and skim. The liquid should just about cover the chicken pieces.

Add the sachet bag, cover, and braise at low heat on top of stove or in the oven.

Remove chicken pieces when cooked. (Note that breast pieces cook faster than leg pieces and must be removed sooner.) Remove sachet bag. Reserve stock.

Keep chicken pieces warm in small amount of stock.

Purée sauce.[a] Strain sauce through a fine mesh wire china cap.

Heat sauce again, stir in heavy cream, and reduce sauce to desired consistency.

Add chicken pieces and tarragon leaves and vinegar.

Heat and serve.

461

Chicken Fricassee with Vegetables

Geflügelfrikassee mit Gemüse
Fricassée de volaille aux légumes

YIELD: 10 SERVINGS

Chicken, 3 birds	6 lb 10 oz	3.0 kg
Onions	8 3/4 oz	250 g
Seasoning salt for poultry (Recipe 10)	2/3 oz	20 g
White wheat flour	2 1/2 oz	70 g
Clarified butter	3 1/2 oz	100 g
Dry white wine	10 oz	300 ml
Chicken stock (Recipe 26)	1 qt 2 oz	1.0 L
Sachet bag	1	1
Heavy cream (36%)	6 3/4 oz	200 ml
Lemon, juice	1/2	1/2
Seasoning	1x	1x

GARNISH

Carrots	5 1/3 oz	150 g
Knob celery (celeriac)	3 1/2 oz	100 g
Leeks, green leaves only	3 1/2 oz	100 g
Butter	1 2/3 oz	50 g

(continued on next page)

---

[a] This one should contain tarragon, peppercorns, bay leaf, and thyme.

[b] The chickens are cut into 8 pieces each, consisting of 2 drumsticks, 2 thighs with bone left in, 4 breast pieces with wing bones still attached to two of them.

[a] This is best accomplished with a commercial hand-held electric mixer.

(continued from preceding page)

MISE EN PLACE
Cut up chicken as for chicken sauté.[a]

Peel and chop onions.

METHOD FOR GARNISH
Trim and wash carrots, and knob celery and cut into fine strips (*julienne*).

Trim and wash leeks; be sure sand is cleaned from layers. Cut into fine strips (*julienne*).

Braise vegetable *julienne* in butter until tender and keep warm.

METHOD
Season chicken pieces with seasoning salt and dust with some of the flour.

Heat clarified butter in wide, heavy saucepan (*rondeau*); add chicken pieces and chopped onions. Sweat until the meat juices are syrupy.

Dust with remaining flour.

Add white wine and chicken stock, bring to a boil, and skim. The liquid should just about cover the chicken pieces.

Add sachet bag, cover, and braise at low heat on top of stove or in the oven.

Remove chicken pieces when cooked. (Note that breast pieces cook faster than leg pieces, and must be removed sooner.) Remove sachet bag. Reserve stock.

Keep chicken pieces warm in small amount of stock.

Purée sauce.[b] Strain sauce through a fine mesh wire china cap.

Reheat sauce, stir in heavy cream and lemon juice, and adjust seasoning.

Thicken sauce, if necessary, with a small amount of cornstarch.

Heat chicken pieces in sauce.

Garnish with vegetable *julienne*.

---

[a] The chickens are cut into 8 pieces each, consisting of 2 drumsticks, 2 thighs with bone left in, 4 breast pieces with wing bones still attached to two of them.

[b] This is best accomplished with a commercial hand-held electric mixer.

462

Chicken Curry

Geschmorter Hahn mit Curry Rahmsauce
Coq à la crème au curry

YIELD: 10 SERVINGS

Chicken, 3 birds	6 lb 10 oz	3.0 kg
Apples	8 3/4 oz	250 g
Onions	12 oz	350 g
Coconut flakes, dried, unsweetened	1 2/3 oz	50 g
Milk	3 1/3 oz	100 ml
Seasoning salt for poultry (Recipe 10)	2/3 oz	20 g
White wheat flour	1 oz	30 g
Clarified butter	3 1/2 oz	100 g
Curry powder, Madras[a]	1 2/3 oz	50 g
Chicken stock (Recipe 26)	1 qt 2 oz	1.0 L
Bay leaf	1	1
Heavy cream (36%)	8 1/2 oz	250 ml
Seasoning (salt)	1x	1x
Lemon, juice	1/2	1/2

MISE EN PLACE
Cut up chicken as for chicken sauté.[b]

Peel and core apples and cut into thin slices.

Peel onions and cut into thin slices.

Soak coconut flakes in hot milk.

METHOD
Season chicken pieces with seasoning salt and dust with flour.

Heat clarified butter in wide, heavy saucepan (*rondeau*), add chicken pieces, and roast in oven until light brown on both sides.

Remove chicken pieces before they are completely cooked and keep warm.

Add apples and onions to pan and sauté.

Add curry powder, chicken stock, bay leaf, and coconut flakes soaked with the milk. Bring to a boil and simmer for 20 minutes.

Purée sauce[c] and strain through a small hole china cap.

---

[a] The quality of curry powder is important. The original recipe specifies Madras curry.

[b] The chickens are cut into 8 pieces each, consisting of 2 drumsticks, 2 thighs with bone left in, 4 breast pieces with wing bones still attached to two of them.

[c] This is best accomplished with a commercial hand-held electric mixer.

Return sauce to stove, bring to a boil, and stir in heavy cream. Reduce to desired consistency.

Return chicken thighs and drumsticks to sauce and simmer.

Before thighs and drumsticks are fully cooked, add in the breast pieces, and continue simmering until all pieces are fully cooked.

Season with salt and lemon juice.

463

Chicken in Red Wine

Geschmorter Hahn in Rotwein
Coq au vin rouge

YIELD: 10 SERVINGS

Chicken, 3 birds	6 lb 10 oz	3.0 kg
Shallots	3 1/2 oz	100 g
Seasoning salt for poultry (Recipe 10)	2/3 oz	20 g
White wheat flour	1 2/3 oz	50 g
Peanut oil	3 1/3 oz	100 ml
Cognac (or any brandy)	3/4 oz	25 ml
Butter	1 2/3 oz	50 g
Red wine	10 oz	300 ml
Brown chicken juice, thickened[a]	1 pt 1 oz	500 ml
Seasoning	1x	1x
Butter	1 oz	30 g

MISE EN PLACE
Cut up chicken as for chicken sauté.[b]

Peel and chop shallots.

METHOD
Season chicken pieces with seasoning salt and dust with flour.

Heat peanut oil in wide, heavy saucepan (*rondeau*), add chicken pieces, and roast, turning to roast on both sides, but do not cook completely.

Pour off excess oil, add Cognac, and ignite.

Remove chicken pieces and keep warm.

Add butter and chopped shallots and sauté.

Add red wine and reduce.

Add brown chicken juice, bring to a boil to dissolve pan drippings, and skim.

Strain sauce through a fine mesh wire china cap. Adjust seasoning.

Return chicken thighs and drumsticks to sauce and simmer.

Before thighs and drumsticks are fully cooked, add in the breast pieces and continue simmering until chicken is fully cooked.

Transfer chicken pieces to a deep serving dish, such as a *cocotte*, and keep warm.

Reduce the sauce to desired consistency. Finish sauce by adding cold butter in small nuggets. Do not allow sauce to return to a boil.

Serve sauce over chicken.

464

Grilled Chicken with Bacon and Grilled Tomatoes

Grilliertes Hähnchen amerikanische Art
Poulet grillé américaine

YIELD: 10 SERVINGS

Chicken,[a] broilers, oven-ready, 5 birds	7 lb 12 oz	3.5 kg
Salt	2/3 oz	20 g
Mie de pain[b]	5 1/3 oz	150 g
Butter	3 1/2 oz	100 g
Brown chicken juice[c]	13 1/2 oz	400 ml

MARINADE

Mustard powder	1/3 oz	10 g
Rosemary, fresh	1/6 oz	5 g
Peanut oil	3 1/2 oz	100 g
Cayenne, ground	pinch	2 g
White pepper, ground	pinch	1 g

GARNISH

Tomatoes, 5 each	1 lb 12 oz	800 g
Seasoning (salt and pepper)	1x	1x
Bacon slab, smoked, whole	7 oz	200 g

(continued on next page)

---

[a] Brown chicken juice can be made like Brown Veal Juice (Recipe 55), but use chicken ingredients in place of the veal ingredients.

[b] The chickens are cut into 8 pieces each, consisting of 2 drumsticks, 2 thighs with bone left in, 4 breast pieces with wing bones still attached to two of them.

---

[a] The size of the chicken varies. In the United States, a broiler weighs about 2 lb 7 oz (1.1 kg).

[b] *Mie de pain* are fresh bread crumbs, made from white Pullman leaves.

[c] Brown chicken juice can be made like Brown Veal Juice (Recipe 55), but use chicken ingredients in place of the veal ingredients.

(continued from preceding page)

METHOD FOR MARINADE

Stir mustard powder with 1/2 tbsp of cold water.

Chop rosemary leaves and combine with all marinade ingredients (mustard powder, peanut oil, cayenne, and white pepper).

MISE EN PLACE FOR EACH CHICKEN

Butterfly the chicken; remove back bone and breast bone cartillage.

Pound chicken lightly to flatten. Make incision in skin at the base of the breast and tuck in legs to truss.

Brush chicken on both sides with marinade and let chicken marinate, refrigerated, for 30 minutes or more.

METHOD FOR GARNISH

Remove stem end from tomatoes and cut tomatoes horizontally in half. Season halves with salt and pepper.

Cut bacon into 10 slices.

METHOD

Salt chicken and place, skin side down, on hot grill.

Turn chicken 60 degrees after a few minutes to sear in an attractive diamond pattern. Turn over and proceed the same way on the other side.

Sprinkle chicken with some *mie de pain* and melted butter. (Save remaining crumbs and butter for the tomatoes.)

Put chicken in hot oven to brown and cook through.

Bring chicken juice to a boil and keep warm.

Grill bacon slices until crisp.

Sprinkle tomatoes with remaining bread crumbs and butter and brown under the salamander.

Cut chicken in half, remove breast bones.

Serve chicken with grilled tomatoes and bacon. Serve chicken juice on the side.

465

Grilled Chicken with Mustard

Grilliertes Hähnchen Teufelsart
Poulet grillé diable

YIELD: 10 SERVINGS

Chicken,[a] broilers, oven-ready, 5 birds	7 lb 12 oz	3.5 kg
Peanut oil	3 1/2 oz	100 g
Mustard powder	1 oz	30 g
Dry white wine	2/3 oz	20 ml
Seasoning salt for chicken	1 1/3 oz	40 g
Mie de pain[b]	4 1/2 oz	130 g
Butter	2 1/2 oz	70 g
SAUCE		
Kitchen herbs,[c] fresh	2/3 oz	20 g
Shallots	2 2/3 oz	75 g
White peppercorns	1/4 oz	7 g
Dry white wine	3 1/3 oz	100 ml
Brown chicken juice, thickened[d]	13 1/2 oz	400 ml
Tomato sauce (Recipe 99)	3 1/3 oz	100 ml
Seasoning (salt, cayenne)	1x	1x
GARNISH		
Cress, washed	3 1/2 oz	100 g
Lemon halves	10	10

MISE EN PLACE FOR EACH CHICKEN

Butterfly chicken; remove back bone and breast bone cartillage.

Pound chicken lightly to flatten. Make incision in skin at the base of the breast and tuck in legs to truss.

Brush chicken on both sides with peanut oil.

Combine mustard powder with white wine into a smooth paste.

METHOD FOR SAUCE

Wash and trim herbs and chop leaves.

Peel and chop shallots and crush peppercorns.

Combine shallots, wine, and peppercorns. Reduce almost completely.

Add chicken juice and tomato sauce. Bring to a boil and strain through a fine mesh wire china cap.

---

[a] The size of the chicken varies. In the United States, a broiler weighs about 2 lb 7 oz (1.1 kg).

[b] *Mie de pain* are fresh bread crumbs, made from white Pullman leaves.

[c] Rosemary and tarragon could be used.

[d] Brown chicken juice can be made like brown veal juice (Recipe 55), but use chicken ingredients in place of the veal ingredients.

Season sauce with cayenne and chopped herbs. Keep sauce hot.

METHOD

Brush chicken with peanut oil, sprinkle with seasoning salt, and place, skin side down, on hot grill.

Turn chicken 60 degrees after a few minutes to sear in an attractive diamond pattern. Turn over and proceed the same way on the other side.

Brush skin side with mustard, sprinkle with *mie de pain* and melted butter.

Put chicken in hot oven to brown and cook through.

Split chicken and remove breast bone.

Garnish with cress and lemon halves. Serve sauce on the side.

METHOD

Combine chicken stock and *bouquet garni* and bring to a boil.

Add chicken and giblets. Poach until chicken is tender. Remove chicken and keep hot in small amount of stock. Reserve stock. Discard giblets.

Make roux with butter and flour. Let cool.

Heat 1 pt 9 oz (750 ml) stock, add hot stock to cool roux, and bring to a boil, stirring continuously.

Reduce sauce to about 1 pt 1 oz (500 ml). Melt *glace de viande*.

Stir in heavy cream, lemon juice, and most melted *glace de viande* to sauce, and adjust seasoning.

Remove skin from chicken and carve.

Serve covered with sauce and drizzled with the rest of the melted *glace de viande*.

466

*P*oached Poularde with Cream Sauce

Poschiertes Masthuhn Albufera
Poularde pochée Albuféra

YIELD: 10 SERVINGS

Poulardes,[a] oven-ready, 2 birds with giblets	7 lb 12 oz	3.5 kg
White chicken stock (Recipe 26)	3 qt 22 oz	3.5 L
Bouquet garni (Recipe 8)	8 3/4 oz	250 g
Butter	1 1/3 oz	40 g
White wheat flour	1 oz	30 g
Glace de viande[b]	3/4 oz	25 g
Heavy cream (36%)	1 2/3 oz	50 ml
Lemon juice	1/2	1/2
Seasoning	1x	1x

MISE EN PLACE

Truss chicken with butcher's twine.

Cover chicken and giblets (except livers)[c] with water and bring to a boil. Drain. Wash first in hot water, then in cold water. Drain again.

467

*O*ven-Roasted Poularde with Morel Sauce

Poeliertes Masthuhn mit Morcheln
Poularde poêlée aux morilles

YIELD: 10 SERVINGS

Poulardes,[a] oven-ready, 2 birds	7 lb 12 oz	3.5 kg
Bacon slab, lean, boiled	5 1/3 oz	150 g
Onions	2 2/3 oz	75 g
Morels, fresh	1 lb 2 oz	500 g
Parsley, curly, fresh	1 2/3 oz	50 g
Matignon (Recipe 14)	7 oz	200 g
Rosemary twig, fresh	1	1
Sage, fresh	1/3 oz	10 g
Salt	2/3 oz	20 g
Seasoning (white pepper)	1x	1x
Clarified butter	3 1/2 oz	100 g
Dry white wine	3 1/3 oz	100 ml
Brown chicken stock[b]	1 pt 4 oz	600 ml
Cornstarch	1/3 oz	10 g
Butter	1 2/3 oz	50 g
Seasoning	1x	1x

(continued on next page)

---

[a] A poularde is a specially bred, large fat roasting hen. Most poulardes are heavier than the weight specified here.

[b] *Glace de viande*, literally translated "melt glaze," is made by reducing meat stock to a syrupy consistency.

[c] Livers are not needed in this recipe. Save for other uses.

---

[a] A poularde is a specially bred, large fat roasting hen. Most poulardes are heavier than the weight specified here.

[b] Brown chicken stock can be made like Brown Veal Stock (Recipe 23), but use chicken bones instead of veal bones.

(continued from preceding page)

MISE EN PLACE

Truss the poulardes with butcher's twine.

Cut bacon into small dice.

Peel and chop onions.

Trim morels, wash very well, and cut into halves or quarters. Blanch.

Trim and wash parsley and chop leaves.

METHOD

Line a Dutch oven (*braisiere*) with diced bacon, *matignon*, rosemary, and sage.

Season the poulardes with salt and white pepper and place on top.

Heat clarified butter and pour over poulardes.

Cover and start cooking in the oven at 325°F (165°C). Continue cooking at 285°F (140°C) to 315°F (160°C), basting frequently with the pan juices.

Remove lid about 10 minutes before poulardes are cooked to brown them lightly.

Remove the poulardes and keep warm.

Add white wine and brown chicken stock and bring to a boil to dissolve pan drippings. Skim. Thicken with cornstarch.

Strain sauce through a fine wire china cap.

Sauté chopped onions in butter. Add morels and cook briefly. Add parsley and a small amount of sauce.

Carve chicken and top with morels. Serve sauce on the side.

468

*O*ven-Roasted Guinea Hen with Tiny Vegetables

Poeliertes junges Perlhuhn mit kleinem Gemüse
Pintadeau poêlé aux petits légumes

YIELD: 10 SERVINGS

Guinea hens, 2 birds	6 lb 10 oz	3.0 kg
Fatback, unsalted	7 oz	200 g
Salt	pinch	2 g
Seasoning (white pepper)	1x	1x
Matignon (Recipe 14)	7 oz	200 g
Clarified butter	3 1/2 oz	100 g
Brown veal stock (Recipe 23)	1 pt 1 oz	500 ml

GARNISH

Carrots	10 1/2 oz	300 g
Turnips, white, small	10 1/2 oz	300 g
Pearl onions	7 oz	200 g
Butter	3 1/2 oz	100 g
Vegetable stock	10 oz	300 ml
Sugar	1x	1x
Seasoning (salt and pepper)	1x	1x

MISE EN PLACE

Truss guinea hens.

Cut fatback into thin slices and tie slices to guinea hen breasts (*barde*).

METHOD FOR GARNISH

Peel carrots and turnips. Cut into sticks or barrel shapes.

Peel pearl onions.

Braise vegetables separately with butter, vegetable stock, sugar, and seasoning.

Keep warm.

METHOD

Line a Dutch oven (*braisiere*) with *matignon*.

Season guinea hens with salt and white pepper and place on top.

Heat clarified butter and pour over hens.

Cover and start cooking in the oven at 325°F (165°C). Continue cooking at 285°F (140°C) to 300°F (150°C), basting frequently.

Remove lid about 10 minutes before hens are cooked. Remove fatback and reserve (see note).

Allow the hens to brown. Remove hens, turn upside down, and keep warm.

Add veal stock to pot and reduce to about half. Skim.

Strain sauce through a fine mesh wire china cap. Skim again.

Carve guinea hens and serve with bouquets of vegetables.

Serve sauce on the side.

NOTE: The removed fatback can be cut into strips, sautéed, and added to the garnish.

469

Chicken Sautéed with Peppers, Garlic, and Tomatoes

Pollo a la chilindrón

YIELD: 10 SERVINGS

Chickens, oven-ready, 3 each	7 lb 12 oz	3.5 kg
Onions	7 oz	200 g
Bell peppers, assorted	10 1/2 oz	300 g
Garlic	2/3 oz	20 g
Tomatoes	5 lb 8 oz	2.5 kg
Ham, cured, air-dried[a]	3 1/2 oz	100 g
Seasoning salt for poultry (Recipe 10)	2/3 oz	20 g
Olive oil, cold pressed	3 1/3 oz	100 ml
Green olives, canned, drained, pitted	3 1/2 oz	100 g
Seasoning	1x	1x

MISE EN PLACE

Cut up chicken as for chicken sauté.[b]

Peel onions and cut into slices.

Remove seeds from peppers, wash, and cut into strips (julienne).

Crush garlic.

Peel tomatoes, cut in half, remove seeds, and cut into dice.

Dice ham.

METHOD

Season chicken pieces with seasoning salt and sauté in olive oil. Before chicken pieces are fully cooked, remove from pan.

Add onions, peppers, and garlic to pan and sauté.

Add tomatoes and return chicken to pan. Cover and simmer until all chicken pieces are cooked through.

Add diced ham and olives. Adjust seasoning.

Serve chicken covered with vegetables.

[a] Any air-dried ham, such as prosciutto, can be used.

[b] The chickens are cut into 8 pieces each, consisting of 2 drumsticks, 2 thighs with bone left in, 4 breast pieces with wing bones still attached to two of them.

470

Chicken Breasts Sautéed with Cucumbers

Sautierte Geflügelbrüstchen mit Gurken
Suprêmes de volaille sautées Doria

YIELD: 10 SERVINGS

Shallots	1 2/3 oz	50 g
Chicken breast cutlets, boneless and skinless, 10	3 lb	1.4 kg
Seasoning salt for poultry (Recipe 10)	2/3 oz	20 g
Peanut oil	3 1/3 oz	100 ml
Butter	2/3 oz	20 g
Dry white wine	6 3/4 oz	200 ml
Brown chicken juice, thickened[a]	13 1/2 oz	400 ml
Seasoning	1x	1x
Butter, cold	1 oz	30 g

GARNISH

Dill, fresh	2/3 oz	20 g
Cucumbers	10 1/2 oz	300 g
Butter	3/4 oz	25 g
Seasoning (salt and pepper)	1x	1x

MISE EN PLACE

Peel and chop shallots.

METHOD FOR GARNISH

Wash dill and chop leaves.

Peel cucumbers and cut into even sticks, cubes, or barrel shapes.

Braise cucumbers in butter, season with salt and pepper, and add chopped dill leaves.

METHOD

Season chicken breasts with seasoning salt and sauté in peanut oil. Remove and keep warm.

Pour off excess oil. Add butter and sauté shallots in butter.

Add white wine and reduce.

Add chicken juice and reduce sauce to desired consistency.

Adjust seasoning and add cold butter in small nuggets. Do not allow the sauce to return to a boil.

Serve chicken covered with sauce. Garnish with cucumbers.

[a] Brown chicken juice can be made like Brown Veal Juice (Recipe 55), but use chicken ingredients in place of the veal ingredients.

Game Dishes

Roast Leg of Venison with Fresh Figs

Gebratene Rehkeule mit frischen Feigen
Gigue de chevreuil rôtie aux figues fraîches

YIELD: 10 SERVINGS

Venison leg, oven-ready[a]	5 lb 5 oz	2.4 kg
Seasoning (salt and pepper)	1x	1x
Peanut oil	1 2/3 oz	50 ml
Matignon (Recipe 14)	7 oz	200 g
Red wine	6 3/4 oz	200 ml
Game demi-glace (Recipe 106)	1 pt 1 oz	500 ml
Crystal sugar	5 1/3 oz	150 g
Red wine	3 1/3 oz	100 ml
Butter, melted	2/3 oz	20 g

GARNISH

Blue figs, fresh	20	20
Red Port wine	6 3/4 oz	200 ml

METHOD FOR GARNISH
Wash figs and cut into halves.

Combine figs and Port wine, bring to a slow boil, cover, and simmer for 5 minutes.

Keep figs warm.

METHOD
Season venison leg with salt and pepper.

Roast venison with peanut oil in hot oven at 425°F (220°C) for about 10 minutes. Lower heat to 360°F (180°C) to 400°F (200°C); and continue roasting, basting frequently.

Remove venison from oven at an inside temperature 10 degrees lower than desired.[b] The inherent heat will continue to cook the meat.

Pour off fat, add *matignon*; and roast lightly.

Add half the red wine and game *demi-glace*. Bring to a boil, reduce slightly, and skim.

Strain sauce through a fine mesh wire china cap.

Put sugar in heavy casserole and melt (caramelize) until brown.

Carefully add Port wine and remaining red wine and reduce to about one-third.

Add the game sauce, bring to a boil, and reduce to desired consistency.

Carve venison and brush sliced meat with butter to retain its sheen.

Serve with poached figs. Serve sauce on the side.

Roast Quails with Grapes

Gebratene Wachteln mit Trauben
Cailles rôtiees vigneronne

YIELD: 10 SERVINGS

Fatback, unsalted	10 1/2 oz	300 g
Quails, farm raised, oven-ready, 20 pieces	8 lb	3.6 kg
Salt	2/3 oz	20 g
Seasoning (white pepper)	1x	1x
Peanut oil	3 1/3 oz	100 ml
Matignon (Recipe 14)	10 1/2 oz	300 g
Red wine	6 3/4 oz	200 ml
Game stock (Recipe 29)	1 pt 4 oz	600 ml
Seasoning	1x	1x

GARNISH

White grapes[a]	5 1/3 oz	150 g
Red grapes[a]	5 1/3 oz	150 g
Butter	1 oz	30 g

MISE EN PLACE
Cut fatback, on meat slicer, into thin slices. There should be 20 slices.

Truss quails to retain their shape and cover breasts with fatback. Tie fatback to birds with butcher's twine (*barde*).

METHOD FOR GARNISH
Remove grapes from stems and wash. Peel grapes; if grapes are large, cut in half. Remove pits.

Sauté grapes in butter at the moment of service.

METHOD
Season quails with salt and white pepper and roast in peanut oil in hot oven for about 15 minutes, basting frequently.

After 10 minutes, remove fatback and allow breasts to brown. Save fatback.

---

[a] The original recipe calls for roebuck, a small European deer.

[b] Game meat is often served medium-rare.

---

[a] Seedless, thin-skinned grapes can be substituted.

Remove quails (the quails should still be pink) and keep warm.

Add *matignon* and roast briefly.

Pour off excess oil.

Add red wine and reduce. Add game stock and boil thoroughly. Skim stock.

Strain stock through a fine mesh wire china cap. Adjust seasoning.

Remove trussing twine from quails. Serve birds with grapes.

NOTE: The fatback can be cut into strips, sautéed until crisp, and served with the quails.

473

$\mathcal{R}$oast Pheasant with Sauerkraut

Gebratener Fasan mit Sauerkraut
Faisan rôti à la choucroute

YIELD: 10 SERVINGS

Fatback, unsalted	7 oz	200 g
Pheasants, oven-ready, 2 birds	5 lb 12 oz	2.6 kg
Salt	2/3 oz	20 g
Seasoning (white pepper)	1x	1x
Peanut oil	3 1/3 oz	100 ml
Matignon (Recipe 14)	7 oz	200 g
Madeira wine	3 1/3 oz	100 ml
Game stock (Recipe 29)	10 oz	300 ml
Seasoning	1x	1x

GARNISH

Braised sauerkraut (Recipe 563)	2 lb 3 oz	1.0 kg
Sausages[a]	14 oz	400 g
Slab bacon (not sliced), smoked, boiled	14 oz	400 g
Potatoes	2 lb 3 oz	1.0 kg
Salt	1/3 oz	10 g

MISE EN PLACE

Cut fatback, on meat slicer, into thin slices. Truss pheasants to retain their shape and cover breasts with fatback. Tie fatback to birds with butcher's twine (*barde*).

METHOD FOR GARNISH

Combine sauerkraut, sausages, and bacon, heat thoroughly, and keep warm.

Peel potatoes and cut into even quarters or barrel shapes (turned). Boil potatoes in salt water, or steam for about 20 minutes before service.

METHOD

Season pheasants with salt and white pepper and roast with peanut oil in hot oven. Reduce heat and roast until medium-rare, basting frequently.

About 5 minutes before the birds are done, remove fatback, and allow the pheasant breasts to brown. Reserve fatback.

Remove pheasants and keep warm.

Pour off excess oil. Add *matignon*; and roast briefly.

Add Madeira wine and reduce.

Add game stock, bring to a boil, boil briefly, and skim.

Strain stock through a fine mesh wire china cap. Skim again.

Cut reserved fatback into slivers and sauté until crisp.

Carve pheasant, sausages, and boiled bacon.

Serve meats on sauerkraut, sprinkled with crisp fatback.

Serve potatoes and game juice on the side.

474

$\mathcal{R}$oast Saddle of Venison with Pears and Lingonberries

Gebratener Rehrücken mit Preiselbeerbirne
Selle de chevreuil Baden-Baden

YIELD: 10 SERVINGS

Venison saddle, center piece,[a] trimmed	7 lb	3.2 kg
Seasoning (salt and pepper)	1x	1x
Peanut oil	3 1/3 oz	100 ml
Red wine	6 3/4 oz	200 ml
Game demi-glace (Recipe 106)	13 1/2 oz	400 ml
Gin	3 1/3 oz	100 ml
Heavy cream (36%)	3 1/3 oz	100 ml
Seasoning	1x	1x

(continued on next page)

---

[a] The recipe calls for *Zungenwurst*. Another boiling sausage can be substituted.

[a] The game indicated is roebuck.

(continued from preceding page)

GARNISH

Pears, ripe, 5 pieces	1 lb 12 oz	800 g
Dry white wine	6 3/4 oz	200 ml
Water	6 3/4 oz	200 ml
Lemon	1/2	1/2
Crystal sugar	3 1/2 oz	100 g
Lingonberries,[a] stewed, ready to eat	7 oz	200 g

MISE EN PLACE

Prepare venison for roasting. Trim if necessary; remove tendons along the back.[b]

METHOD FOR GARNISH

Peel pears, split in half lengthwise, and remove cores.

Combine white wine, water, lemon, and sugar. Bring to a boil.

Add pears and poach until done. Keep warm.

Just before serving meat, drain poached pears, and fill with lingonberries.

METHOD

Season venison with salt and pepper and roast with peanut oil, starting in a hot 450°F (230°C) oven. Lower temperature and continue roasting, basting frequently.

Remove venison[c] and keep warm.

Pour off excess oil. Add red wine and reduce completely.

Add game *demi-glace*, bring to a boil, and boil thoroughly. Skim, and strain sauce through a fine mesh wire china cap. Skim again.

Add gin and heavy cream to sauce and bring to a boil. Adjust seasoning.

Carve venison. Serve with pears filled with lingonberries.

Serve sauce on the side.

---

[a] Lingonberries are related to cranberries. They are available canned. Cranberries can be substituted.

[b] If desired, the meat can be covered with thin slices of fatback to prevent drying during the roasting process.

[c] Game meat is often served medium-rare.

475

Venison Stew Hunter Style

Rehpfeffer Jägerart
Civet de chevreuil chasseur

YIELD: 10 SERVINGS

Venison shoulder meat, trimmed, boneless[a]	4 lb 7 oz	2.0 kg
Seasoning (salt and pepper)	1x	1x
Peanut oil	3 1/3 oz	100 ml
Game stock (Recipe 29)	1 qt 2 oz	1.0 L
Game demi-glace (Recipe 106)	1 pt 1 oz	500 ml
Heavy cream (36%)	1 2/3 oz	50 ml
Pig's blood[b]	6 3/4 oz	200 ml
Seasoning (salt and pepper)	1x	1x

MARINADE

Red wine	1 qt 2 oz	1.0 L
Red wine vinegar	6 3/4 oz	200 ml
Mirepoix for brown stock (Recipe 15)	5 1/3 oz	150 g
Bay leaf	1	1
Clove	1	1
White peppercorns	1/6 oz	5 g
Juniper berries	1/6 oz	5 g
Thyme twig, fresh	1	1
Rosemary twig, fresh	1	1

GARNISH

Pearl onions	7 oz	200 g
Mushrooms, fresh	7 oz	200 g
Butter	1 2/3 oz	50 g
Bacon slab, smoked	6 oz	170 g
Bread, white (Pullman loaf)	7 oz	200 g

METHOD

Cut venison into stew-size pieces, about 1 2/3 oz (50 g) each.

Combine all marinade ingredients.

Add venison and marinate, refrigerate, for 8 to 10 days.

METHOD FOR GARNISH

Peel pearl onions.

Trim and wash mushrooms. Cut into halves or quarters, depending on size.

---

[a] The original recipe calls for roebuck, a small European deer.

[b] In some countries, it is illegal to purchase and use blood in retail establishments. In this case, just eliminate the blood; there is no substitute.

Smother pearl onions and mushrooms in butter and keep warm.

Cut bacon into sticks (*lardons*) and blanch. Sauté bacon until crisp and keep warm.

Cut bread into 5 slices. Cut each slice diagonally and trim into heart-shaped croûtons. Toast croûtons and keep warm.

METHOD

Drain off marinade from venison and vegetables and reserve marinade.

Sort out venison pieces and set aside. Reserve vegetables and spices separately.

Bring marinade liquid to a boil and keep hot.

Season venison with salt and pepper and brown[a] on all sides in hot peanut oil. Remove venison.

Add drained marinade vegetables and spices and sauté.

Add back the venison and the marinade liquid and reduce.

Add game stock and game *demi-glace*. The liquid should cover the meat.

Cover the pot and braise until the venison is tender.

Remove venison with skimmer and separate meat pieces from sauce vegetables.

Purée sauce and vegetables and strain sauce through a fine mesh wire china cap. Skim sauce.

Stir in heavy cream and pig's blood, add to hot sauce, and stir. Do not allow the sauce to return to a boil.

Add venison and heat. Adjust seasoning.

Combine garnish of pearl onions, mushrooms, and bacons; and serve over meat. Garnish with croûtons.

476

Venison Chops Sautéed with Blueberries

Sautierte Hirschkotletts mit Heidelbeeren
Côtelettes de cerf sautées aux myrtilles

YIELD: 10 SERVINGS

Venison chops,[a] trimmed, 10 chops	4 lb	1.8 kg
Blueberries,[b] fresh	4 1/4 oz	120 g
Seasoning (salt and pepper)	1x	1x
Peanut oil	3 1/3 oz	100 ml
Butter	2/3 oz	20 g
Red wine	6 3/4 oz	200 ml
Game demi-glace (Recipe 106)	13 1/2 oz	400 ml
Red currant jelly	1 2/3 oz	50 g
Sour cream	6 3/4 oz	200 ml
Butter, cold	1 2/3 oz	50 g
Seasoning	1x	1x

MISE EN PLACE

Trim chops, if necessary, and prepare for cooking.

Wash and drain blueberries.

METHOD

Season venison chops and sauté in peanut oil. Keep chops medium-rare.

Remove chops and place on wire rack; keep warm.

Pour off excess fat. Add butter to pan.

Add blueberries and cook briefly. Add red wine and reduce.

Add game *demi-glace* and boil to desired consistency.

Strain sauce through a china cap.

Heat sauce and add red currant jelly and sour cream.

Add cold butter in small nuggets; do not allow the sauce to return to a boil.

Adjust seasoning.

Serve chops covered with sauce. Serve remaining sauce on the side.

---

[a] Since the meat is very wet, it must be browned in small amounts, or it will sweat rather than brown.

---

[a] This recipe specifically calls for venison, not roebuck.

[b] Wild blueberries, called huckleberries in the United States, are available in Switzerland. They are generally more flavorful than cultivated blueberries.

477

Venison Cutlets with Mushrooms and Brussels Sprouts

Sautierte Rehnüsschen Jägerart
Noisettes de chevreuil sautées chasseur

YIELD: 10 SERVINGS

Venison[a] leg meat, boneless, trimmed	3 lb 5 oz	1.5 kg
Salt	1/3 oz	10 g
White pepper, ground	pinch	2 g
White wheat flour	1 2/3 oz	50 g
Peanut oil	3 1/3 oz	100 ml
Red wine	6 3/4 oz	200 ml
Game demi-glace (Recipe 106)	10 oz	300 ml
Heavy cream (36%)	6 3/4 oz	200 ml
Cayenne	pinch	1 g
Lemon juice	1/3 oz	10 ml

GARNISH

Mushrooms, fresh	8 3/4 oz	250 g
Brussels sprouts, fresh	1 lb 5 oz	600 g
Turnips, white, small	1 lb 5 oz	600 g
Butter	2 2/3 oz	75 g
Lemon	1/4	1/4
Seasoning (salt and pepper)	1x	1x

MISE EN PLACE
Cut venison into 30 small cutlets, 1 2/3 oz (50 g) each.

METHOD FOR GARNISH
Trim and wash mushrooms. Cut into halves or quarters, depending on size.

Trim Brussels sprouts. Peel turnips and cut into sticks or oval shapes.

Sauté mushrooms in 1 oz (30 g) butter and lemon juice. Season and keep warm.

Boil or steam Brussels sprouts and turnips. Sauté separately in remaining butter and season.

Keep garnish vegetables warm.

METHOD
Season venison cutlets with salt and white pepper and dust with flour.

Sauté quickly in peanut oil, to medium-rare. Remove cutlets to a wire rack and keep warm.

Pour off excess oil. Add red wine and reduce.

Add game *demi-glace* and boil thoroughly.

Stir in heavy cream. Season with cayenne and lemon juice.

Serve venison cutlets with garnish vegetables. Serve the sauce on the side.

478

Venison Cutlets with Apples

Sautierte Rehnüsschen Mirza
Noisettes de chevreuil Mirza

YIELD: 10 SERVINGS

Venison[a] leg meat, boneless, trimmed	3 lb 5 oz	1.5 kg
Salt	1/3 oz	10 g
White pepper, ground	pinch	1x
White wheat flour	1x	1x
Peanut oil	3 1/3 oz	100 ml
Red wine	10 oz	300 ml
Game demi-glace (Recipe 106)	10 oz	300 ml
Heavy cream (36%)	6 3/4 oz	200 ml
Cayenne, ground	pinch	1 g
Lemon juice	1/3 oz	10 ml

GARNISH

Apples, 5	1 lb 12 oz	800 g
Dry white wine	6 3/4 oz	200 ml
Water	6 3/4 oz	200 ml
Crystal sugar	1 2/3 oz	50 g
Red currant jelly	3 1/2 oz	100 g

MISE EN PLACE
Cut venison into 30 small cutlets, 1 2/3 oz (50 g) each.

METHOD FOR GARNISH
Peel apples, cut in half, and remove cores.

Combine white wine, water, and sugar, bring to a boil, poach apples, and keep warm.

Just before serving venison, drain apple halves, and fill with red currant jelly.

---

[a] The game specified is roebuck, a small European deer. If regular venison is used, it is best to use the boneless loin, because the leg might be tough and dry. If the loin is used, two pieces, at 2 1/2 oz (75 g) each, should be cut for each portion.

[a] The game specified is roebuck, a small European deer. If regular venison is used, it is best to use the boneless loin, because the leg might be tough and dry. If the loin is used, two pieces, at 2 1/2 oz (75 g) each, should be cut for each portion.

METHOD

Season venison cutlets with salt and white pepper and dust with flour.

Sauté quickly in peanut oil, to medium-rare. Remove cutlets to a wire rack and keep warm.

Pour off excess oil. Add red wine and reduce.

Add game *demi-glace* and boil thoroughly.

Stir in heavy cream. Season with cayenne and lemon juice.

Cover cutlets with sauce and serve with currant-filled apples.

CHAPTER

Salads

479

*F*rench Dressing

Amerikanische Salatsauce
Sauce à salade américaine

YIELD: 1 QT 2 OZ (1.0 L)

Onions	5 1/3 oz	150 g
Mustard, mild, prepared	2 oz	60 g
Egg yolks[a]	2	2
Cayenne, ground	pinch	1 g
White pepper, ground	pinch	1 g
Crystal sugar	pinch	1x
Worcestershire sauce	1/6 tsp	5 g
Lemon juice	2/3 oz	20 ml
White wine vinegar	3/4 oz	25 ml
Sunflower oil	1 pt 1 oz	500 ml

METHOD
Peel and chop onions.

Combine onions, mustard, egg yolks, cayenne, white pepper, sugar, Worcestershire sauce, lemon juice, and half amount of vinegar in food processor. Process mixture to thick puree.

Add sunflower oil and remaining vinegar in a thin stream, processing at high speed, into a homogenous sauce.

Thin dressing with water, if necessary. Adjust seasoning.

NOTE: If the dressing is made ahead of time, it is advisable to use 1 1/3 oz (40 g) onion powder instead of fresh onions.

480

*A*pple Dressing

Apfelsalatsauce
Sauce à salade aux pommes

YIELD: 1 QT 2 OZ (1.0 L)

Apples	7 oz	200 g
Onions	3 1/2 oz	100 g
Horseradish, fresh	1 oz	30 g
Apple cider vinegar	8 1/2 oz	250 ml
Salt	1/3 oz	(10 g)
Cayenne pepper, ground	pinch	2 g
Sunflower oil	13 1/2 oz	400 ml

[a] It is a good idea to use pasteurized egg yolks because this dressing isn't cooked.

METHOD
Peel and core apples and cut in chunks.

Peel onions and cut into chunks.

Peel and grate horseradish.

Put apples, onions, and horseradish in food processor and purée.

Add salt and cayenne.

Add oil and vinegar in a thin stream, processing at high speed, into a homogenous sauce.

481

*A*rtichoke Salad

Artischokensalat
Salade d'artichauts

YIELD: 10 SERVINGS

Artichokes, fresh, small	20	20
Lemon juice	1 2/3 oz	50 ml
Salt	2/3 oz	20 g

DRESSING

Onions	1 2/3 oz	50 g
Kitchen herbs, fresh	1 oz	30 g
White wine vinegar	3 1/3 oz	100 ml
Sunflower oil	6 3/4 oz	200 ml
Seasoning (salt and pepper)	1x	1x

MISE EN PLACE
Cut off stems from artichokes. Cut off about one-third from top and discard outer leaves.

Trim off the tips of remaining leaves.

Cut artichokes into quarters.

Keep cut artichokes in cold water with lemon juice and salt.

METHOD FOR DRESSING
Peel and chop onions.

Trim, wash, and chop herbs (such as chives and parsley).

Combine all dressing ingredients.

METHOD
Boil artichokes in salt water and drain well.

Save tender center leaves for garnish.

Trim off the fuzzy, inedible straw in the center.

Marinate artichokes in dressing. Artichokes will absorb the dressing better while still fresh and warm.

NOTES: Small, pointed, purple Italian artichokes are recommended for this salad.

Vegetable salads should be mixed with dressing while still warm, and they should never be served directly from the refrigerator.

Italian Dressing (Recipe 493) is also suitable for this salad.

482

*A*vocado, Orange, and Grapefruit Salad

Avocadosalat
Salade aux avocats

YIELD: 10 SERVINGS

Avocados, ripe	5	5
Lemon	1/2	1/2
White grapefruits	2	2
Oranges	2	2

DRESSING
Lemon verbena, fresh	1 oz	30 g
Apple vinegar	2 1/2 oz	75 ml
Lemon, juice	1/2	1/2
Cottage cheese, creamy[a]	10 1/2 oz	300 g
Seasoning (salt, cayenne pepper)	1x	1x

MISE EN PLACE
Split avocados and remove pits. Peel, cube, and sprinkle with lemon juice.

Peel oranges and grapefruits. Remove sections with a sharp knife between the seams.

Wash and chop verbena leaves.

METHOD
Combine dressing ingredients into a smooth sauce. Season to taste.

Carefully combine avocado with orange and grapefruit sections.

Place in serving dishes and cover with dressing.

NOTE: This salad should be made right before service.

---

[a] The original recipe calls for *Rahm Quark*, which is a fine-curd cottage cheese with a high fat content.

483

*C*auliflower Salad

Blumenkohlsalat
Salade de chou-fleur

YIELD: 10 SERVINGS

Cauliflower	3 lb 8 oz	1.6 kg
Salt	2/3 oz	20 g
Lemon juice	1 2/3 oz	50 ml
Chervil	2/3 oz	20 g

DRESSING
Seasoning (salt and pepper)	1x	1x
White wine vinegar	3 1/3 oz	100 ml
Heavy cream (36%)	3 1/3 oz	100 ml
Sunflower oil	3 1/3 oz	100 ml

MISE EN PLACE
Trim and wash cauliflower and divide into small rosettes.

Combine 3 1/2 qt (3.5 L) water with salt and lemon juice.

Add cauliflower and boil until tender, but still crisp.

Wash and chop chervil leaves.

METHOD
Mix dressing ingredients.

Drain cauliflower and toss, while still warm, with the dressing.

Let salad marinate for 2 hours before service.

Sprinkle with chervil.

NOTES: Vegetable salads should be mixed with dressing while still warm, and they should never be served directly from the refrigerator.

Other suitable dressings are Yogurt Dressing (Recipe 494) and Vinaigrette Dressing (Recipe 484).

484

Vinaigrette Dressing

Einfache Salatsauce
Sauce à la salade simple

YIELD: 1 QT 2 OZ (1.0 L)

Salt	1/3 oz	10 g
White pepper, ground	pinch	1 g
Mustard, prepared	1/6 oz	5 g
White wine vinegar, mild[a]	12 oz	350 ml
Sunflower oil	1 pt 6 oz	650 ml

METHOD

Combine salt, white pepper, mustard, and white wine vinegar first.

Add sunflower oil and stir well.

Stir dressing before use.

485

Diet Salad Dressing

Energiereduzierte Salatsauce
Sauce à salade régime

YIELD: 1 QT 2 OZ (1.0 L)

Kitchen herbs, fresh	1 1/2 oz	40 g
Yogurt, plain	10 1/2 oz	300 g
Cottage cheese, diet, creamy	5 2/3 oz	160 g
Sour cream, diet	6 3/4 oz	200 ml
Orange juice	6 3/4 oz	200 ml
Apple cider vinegar	3 1/3 oz	100 ml
Thistle oil[b] or safflower oil	3 1/3 oz	100 ml
Seasoning (salt and pepper)	1x	1x

METHOD

Wash and chop herbs (such as chives, parsley, and chervil).

Combine all ingredients into a smooth dressing.

NOTE: This dressing is suitable for a reduced-fat diet. If the salt is eliminated, it can be appropriate for other diets.

---

[a] If the vinegar is not very mild, the amount may need to be reduced.

[b] The original recipe calls for *Distelöl*. Another low-cholesterol oil can be substituted.

486

Fennel Salad

Fenchelsalat
Salade de fenouil

YIELD: 10 SERVINGS

Fennel bulbs (anise)	3 lb 5 oz	1.5 kg
DRESSING		
Garlic clove, peeled	1	1
Seasoning (salt and pepper)	1x	1x
Saffron, ground	pinch	1/4 g
White wine vinegar	3 1/3 oz	100 ml
Lemon	1/2	1/2
Olive oil, cold pressed	3 1/3 oz	100 ml
Sunflower oil	3 1/3 oz	100 ml

MISE EN PLACE

Trim and wash fennel, cut bulbs into thin strips, and chop leaves.

METHOD

Chop garlic, add fennel greens and all other dressing ingredients, and blend well.

Mix dressing with fennel and let marinate for one-half hour before service.

NOTES: Crisp bacon bits can be added.

Other suitable dressings are Roquefort Dressing (Recipe 508), Creamy Salad Dressing (Recipe 502), and Yogurt Dressing (Recipe 494).

487

French Vinaigrette Dressing

Französische Salatsauce
Sauce à salade française

YIELD: 1 QT 2 OZ (1.0 LITER)

Shallots	5 1/3 oz	150 g
Tarragon, fresh	1/3 oz	10 g
Chervil, fresh	1/3 oz	10 g
Mustard, prepared	3 oz	80 g
Salt	1/3 oz	10 g
White pepper, ground	pinch	2 g
White wine vinegar	8 1/2 oz	250 ml
Sunflower or walnut oil	1 pt 1 oz	500 ml
Season to taste	1x	1x

METHOD

Peel and chop shallots.

Wash and trim tarragon and chervil and chop leaves.

Combine all ingredients except oil.

Add oil in small increments and mix well.

Season to taste.

Stir dressing before use.

488

ℱruit Salad with Curry

Früchtesalat mit Curry
Salade de fruits au curry

YIELD: 10 SERVINGS

Pineapple, fresh	1 lb 9 oz	700 g
Oranges	2	2
Papaya	1	1
Apples	1 lb 2 oz	500 g
Bananas	1 lb 2 oz	500 g
DRESSING		
Ginger, fresh	1/3 oz	10 g
Lemon juice	1 2/3 oz	50 ml
Madras curry powder	2/3 oz	20 g
Mayonnaise (Recipe 71)	10 1/2 oz	300 g
Sour cream, light	6 3/4 oz	200 ml
GARNISH		
Pine nuts, peeled	1 2/3 oz	50 g
Peppermint, fresh	1 oz	30 g

MISE EN PLACE

Trim and peel pineapple, remove core, and cut into dice.

Peel oranges; seam out sections with a sharp knife.

Peel papaya, remove seeds, and cut into dice.

Peel and core apples. Dice apples and carefully mix in with other fruits.[a]

Peel and grate ginger.

Warm the lemon juice, add curry powder, and stir until smooth.

Toast pine nuts in oven or under the salamander until light brown.

Wash peppermint.

---

[a] Mix the apple with the other fruits immediately, so the acidity in the other fruits will keep the apple from turning brown.

METHOD

Mix mayonnaise with sour cream, grated ginger, and curried lemon juice.

Add prepared fruits to dressing and blend.

AT SERVICE TIME

Peel bananas, cut into slices, and carefully fold in.

Sprinkle salad with toasted pine nuts.

Garnish with peppermint leaves.

489

𝒞ooked Carrot Salad[a]

Gekochter Karottensalat
Salade de carottes cuites

YIELD: 10 SERVINGS

Carrots	3 lb 5 oz	1.5 kg
DRESSING		
Onions	3 1/2 oz	100 g
Seasoning (salt and pepper)	1x	1x
Sugar	1x	1x
White wine vinegar	3 1/3 oz	100 ml
Sunflower oil	5 oz	150 ml
GARNISH		
Chives, fresh	2/3 oz	20 g

MISE EN PLACE

Peel and wash carrots and steam or simmer until just tender. Do not overcook.

Cut carrots into slices or cubes.

METHOD FOR DRESSING

Chop onions and mix with all dressing ingredients.

METHOD

Cut chives into small slivers.

Marinate carrots in dressing while still warm.

Serve salad at room temperature.

Sprinkle with chives.

NOTES: Vegetable salads should be mixed with dressing while still warm, and they should never be served directly from the refrigerator.

Other suitable dressings are Italian Dressing (Recipe 493) and Yogurt Dressing (Recipe 494).

---

[a] Also see Raw Carrot Salad (Recipe 503).

490

ℬoiled Beets and Onion Salad[a]

Gekochter Randensalat (Rote Beete oder Rüben)
Salade de betteraves rouges cuits

YIELD: 10 SERVINGS

Red beets, steamed	3 lb 5 oz	1.5 kg
DRESSING		
Onions	1 lb 2 oz	500 g
Herb vinegar	5 oz	150 ml
Sunflower oil	6 3/4 oz	200 ml
Seasoning (salt and pepper)	1x	1x

MISE EN PLACE
Peel beets while still warm and cut into dice, coarse strips (*julienne*), or slices.

METHOD
Peel onions and chop fine.

Combine beets with all dressing ingredients.

Season to taste.

NOTES: To extend the storage life of the cooked beets, they can be refrigerated in the following pickling marinade:

Combine equal amounts of red wine vinegar and white wine vinegar, add a clove-studded onion, salt and sugar to taste, and bring to a boil.

Boil for 10 minutes and pour, still boiling hot, over the cooked, sliced beets.

Cool and refrigerate. (These pickled beets should be served cold.)

Oil and chopped onions should be added when the beets are served.

491

𝒢reen Bean Salad

Salat von grünen Bohnen
Salade de haricots verts

YIELD: 10 SERVINGS

Green beans, fresh	2 lb 10 oz	1.2 kg
Salt	2/3 oz	20 g
DRESSING		
Onions	3 1/2 oz	100 g
Garlic cloves	2	2
Savory, fresh	1/3 oz	10 g
Seasoning (salt and pepper)	1x	1x
White wine vinegar	3 1/3 oz	100 ml
Sunflower oil	5 oz	150 ml

MISE EN PLACE
Snip off ends of green beans, break in half if large, and wash.

Boil beans in ample salt water and drain. (Beans can also be steamed.)

METHOD FOR DRESSING
Peel and chop onions and garlic cloves.

Chop the savory leaves.

Combine all dressing ingredients and mix well.

METHOD
Combine beans,[a] while still warm, with the dressing.

NOTES: Vegetable salads should be mixed with dressing while still warm, and they should never be served directly from the refrigerator.

Italian Dressing (Recipe 493) is also suitable for this salad.

---

[a] Also see Raw Beet Salad (Recipe 504).

---

[a] Beans will turn gray from the vinegar in the dressing. To keep their bright green color, the salad should be mixed just before serving.

492

Cucumber Salad with Yogurt Dressing

Gurkensalat
Salade de concombres

YIELD: 10 SERVINGS

Cucumbers	2 lb 10 oz	1.2 kg

DRESSING

Dill, fresh	1/3 oz	10 g
Mustard powder	1/6 oz	5 g
Seasoning (salt and pepper)	1x	1x
Herb vinegar	3 1/3 oz	100 ml
Yogurt, plain	3 1/2 oz	100 g
Sunflower oil	3 1/3 oz	100 ml

GARNISH

Dill top leaves, fresh	10	10

MISE EN PLACE
Wash cucumbers, peel completely or score partially as desired, split lengthwise, and remove seeds.

Cut cucumbers into thin slices or strips (*julienne*).

METHOD FOR DRESSING
Chop dill.

Combine all dressing ingredients.

Mix well.

METHOD
Combine cucumbers with dressing just before serving.

Garnish with dill leaves.

NOTES: Seedless or young cucumbers do not need to be split and can be left whole.

Blend dressing and cucumbers close to service time. Cucumbers have a high water content, and, if mixed too early, the dressing will become diluted.

Other suitable dressings are Vinaigrette Dressing (Recipe 484), Cottage Cheese Dressing (Recipe 500), and French Dressing (Recipe 479).

493

Italian Dressing

Italienische Salatsauce
Sauce à salade italienne

YIELD: 1 QT 2 OZ (1.0 L)

Onions	5 1/3 oz	150 g
Salt	1/3 oz	10 g
Seasoning (white pepper)	1x	1x
Red wine vinegar	6 3/4 oz	200 ml
Balsamic vinegar	3 1/3 oz	100 ml
Olive oil, cold pressed	1 pt 4 oz	600 ml

METHOD
Peel and chop onions.

Combine onions, salt, white pepper, and both vinegars.

Add oil in a thin stream, stirring constantly. Mix well.

Stir dressing before use.

494

Yogurt Dressing

Joghurtsalatsauce
Sauce à salade au yogourt

YIELD: 1 QT 2 OZ (1.0 L)

Kitchen herbs, fresh	2 oz	60 g
Yogurt, plain	1 lb 10 oz	750 g
Salt	1/3 oz	10 g
White pepper, ground	pinch	1 g
Orange juice	3 1/3 oz	100 ml
Lemon juice	1 2/3 oz	50 ml
Seasoning	1x	1x

METHOD
Wash and chop herbs, such as parsley, chives, and chervil.

Combine all ingredients into a smooth dressing.

495

*P*otato Salad

Kartoffelsalat
Salade de pommes de terre

YIELD: 10 SERVINGS

Potatoes, waxy[a]	5 lb 8 oz	2.5 kg
Salt	2/3 oz	20 g
Onions	7 oz	200 g
Bouillon (Recipe 22)	13 1/2 oz	400 ml

DRESSING
Sunflower oil	6 3/4 oz	200 ml
Herb vinegar	3 1/3 oz	100 ml
Seasoning (salt and pepper)	1x	1x

GARNISH
Chives, cut	2/3 oz	20 g

MISE EN PLACE
Wash potatoes and boil in salt water. (Potatoes can also be steamed).

Peel potatoes, while still warm, and cut into 1/6-in. (4 mm) slices.

Peel and chop onions.

METHOD
Heat bouillon and pour over potatoes.

Add chopped onions.

Stir together oil, herb vinegar, and salt and pepper.

Add dressing to potatoes and blend carefully.

Allow dressing to penetrate the potatoes.

Serve sprinkled with chives.

NOTES: Do not serve potato salad directly from the refrigerator.

The amount of dressing needed varies depending on the type of potatoes used.

Potato salad should be made fresh daily.

Potato Salad can also be made with Mayonnaise (Recipe 71), yogurt, or light/low-fat sour cream.

496

*L*eek Salad

Lauchsalat
Salade de poireaux

YIELD: 10 SERVINGS

Leeks	3 lb 5 oz	1.5 kg
Salt	2/3 oz	20 g

DRESSING
Seasoning (salt and pepper)	1x	1x
Lemon juice	1 2/3 oz	50 ml
Sunflower oil	5 oz	150 ml

MISE EN PLACE
Wash and trim leeks; be sure sand is cleaned from layers. Cut the leaves crosswise into fine strips (*julienne*).

Blanch leeks briefly and drain well.

METHOD
Combine dressing ingredients and mix thoroughly.

Blend leeks, while still warm, with dressing ingredients.

NOTE: Vegetable salads should be mixed with dressing while still warm, and they should never be served directly from the refrigerator.

497

*C*orn Salad

Maissalat
Salade de maïs

YIELD: 10 SERVINGS

Corn, canned, drained	1 lb 12 oz	800 g
Bell peppers, red	3 1/2 oz	100 g
Apples	5 1/3 oz	150 g

DRESSING
Cayenne pepper, ground	pinch	1 g
White wine vinegar	1 2/3 oz	50 ml
Mayonnaise (Recipe 71)	1 2/3 oz	50 g
Sunflower oil	3 1/3 oz	100 ml
Seasoning (salt and pepper)	1x	1x

[a] The potatoes should not be mealy (russet type) potatoes. Use waxy varieties such as "Type A" Nicola or Stella potatoes.

METHOD

Rinse corn with cold water and drain well.

Cut peppers in half, remove seeds, and cut into small dice.

Peel[a] and core apples and cut into small dice.

Combine dressing ingredients and mix with salad. Let salad marinate.

NOTE: Italian Dressing (Recipe 493) is also suitable for this salad.

498

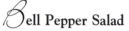ell Pepper Salad

Peperonisalat
Salade de poivrons

YIELD: 10 SERVINGS

| Assorted peppers | 2 lb 10 oz | 1.2 kg |
| Onions | 3 1/2 oz | 100 g |

DRESSING

Garlic, chopped	1/6 oz	5 g
Seasoning (salt and pepper)	1x	1x
Red wine vinegar	3 1/3 oz	100 ml
Olive oil, cold pressed	5 oz	150 ml

MISE EN PLACE

Split peppers, remove seeds, and cut into fine strips (julienne).

Peel and chop onions.

METHOD

Mix peppers and onions.

Combine dressing ingredients and blend well.

Marinate peppers in dressing.

499

*M*ushroom Salad

Pilzsalat
Salade de champignons

YIELD: 10 SERVINGS

Mushrooms,[a] fresh	1 lb 5 oz	600 g
Chanterelles,[b] fresh	7 oz	200 g
Oyster mushrooms,[c] fresh	10 1/2 oz	300 g
Olive oil, cold pressed	3/4 oz	25 ml
Lemon, juice	1/2	1/2
Seasoning (salt and pepper)	1x	1x
Shallots	1 2/3 oz	50 g
Lemon, juice	1/2	1/2
Kitchen herbs, fresh	1 2/3 oz	50 g

DRESSING

Red wine vinegar	6 3/4 oz	200 ml
Olive oil, cold pressed	13 1/2 oz	400 ml
Seasoning (salt and pepper)	1x	1x
Chives, fresh, cut in slivers	1 2/3 oz	50 g

MISE EN PLACE

Trim, wash, and slice or quarter all of the mushrooms.

Braise mushrooms with oil and lemon juice, season to taste, and let cool.

Peel and chop shallots and add to mushrooms. Season with lemon juice.

Wash and chop herbs, such as parsley, chervil, and tarragon.

METHOD

Combine dressing ingredients and mix with mushrooms, shallots, and herbs.

Let mixture marinate.

---

[a] Apples can also be diced unpeeled. Green varieties, such as Granny Smith, will add a little green color to the salad.

[a] Use the standard American cultivated mushrooms.

[b] Chanterelles are yellow wild mushrooms, called *girolles* in French and *Eierschwämme* in German.

[c] Oyster mushrooms are called *pleurotte* in French and *Austernseitlinge* in German. If not available, cremini or portobello mushrooms can be substituted.

500

Cottage Cheese Dressing

Quarksalatsauce
Sauce à salade au séré

YIELD: 1 QT 2 OZ (1.0 L)

Kitchen herbs, fresh	2 oz	60 g
Cottage cheese, low fat	1 lb 5 oz	600 g
Salt	1/3 oz	10 g
White pepper, ground	pinch	1 g
Lemon juice	6 3/4 oz	200 ml
White wine vinegar	5 oz	150 ml
Seasoning	1x	1x

MISE EN PLACE
Wash and chop herbs, such as chives, chervil, and lovage.

METHOD
Blend cottage cheese with herbs, and all other dressing ingredients.

Adjust seasoning.

501

Radish Salad

Radieschensalat
Salade de radis roses

YIELD: 10 SERVINGS

Radishes	8 bunches	8 bu
Chives, fresh	1 2/3 oz	50 g
DRESSING		
Horseradish mustard	dash	2 g
Seasoning (salt and pepper)	1x	1x
White wine vinegar	3 1/3 oz	100 ml
Sunflower oil	5 oz	150 ml

MISE EN PLACE
Trim and wash radishes. Cut into fine slices or thin strips (*julienne*).

Cut chives into thin strips (*julienne*).

METHOD
Blend together all dressing ingredients and combine with radishes.

Sprinkle with chives.

NOTES: Combine radishes with dressing at the last moment, otherwise the salad will become too wet.

Other suitable dressings are French Dressing (Recipe 479) and Cottage Cheese Dressing (Recipe 500).

502

Creamy Salad Dressing

Rahmsalatsauce
Sauce à salade à la crème

YIELD: 1 QT 2 OZ (1.0 L)

Vegetable bouillon (Recipe 27)	6 3/4 oz	200 ml
Heavy cream (36%)	3 1/3 oz	100 ml
Sour cream, light	6 3/4 oz	200 ml
Lemon juice	3 1/3 oz	100 ml
White wine vinegar	6 3/4 oz	200 ml
Sunflower oil	6 3/4 oz	200 ml
Seasoning (salt and pepper)	1x	1x
Sugar	1x	1x

METHOD
Combine all ingredients into a smooth dressing.

Season to taste with salt and pepper and sugar.

503

Raw Carrot Salad[a]

Roher Karottensalat
Salade de carottes crues

YIELD: 10 SERVINGS

Carrots	2 lb 10 oz	1.2 kg
Oregano, fresh	1/3 oz	10 g
DRESSING		
Lemon juice	1 2/3 oz	50 ml
Orange juice	1 2/3 oz	50 ml
Sugar	1x	1x
Seasoning (salt and pepper)	1x	1x
Sunflower oil	5 oz	150 ml

[a] Also see Cooked Carrot Salad (Recipe 489).

MISE EN PLACE

Peel carrots and grate coarsely or cut into fine strips (*julienne*).

Chop oregano leaves.

METHOD

Blend dressing ingredients and mix with carrots.

NOTE: Other suitable salad dressings are Yogurt Dressing (Recipe 494), Cottage Cheese Dressing (Recipe 500), and Creamy Salad Dressing (Recipe 502).

504

 aw Beet Salad[a]

Roher Randensalat
Salade de betteraves rouges crues

YIELD: 10 SERVINGS

Beets, raw	2 lb 3 oz	1.0 kg
Apples	8 3/4 oz	250 g
DRESSING		
Horseradish, fresh	2/3 oz	20 g
Seasoning (salt and pepper)	1x	1x
Herb vinegar	5 oz	150 ml
Sunflower oil	6 3/4 oz	200 ml

MISE EN PLACE

Wash and peel beets and grate coarsely or cut into fine strips (*julienne*).

Peel and core apples and cut into fine dice.

METHOD

Peel and grate horseradish and combine with all dressing ingredients.

Marinate beets and apples with dressing.

NOTES: This salad can also be seasoned with caraway seeds or caraway essence. (The essence is made by steeping caraway seeds in a small amount of boiling water.)

Other suitable dressings are Italian Dressing (Recipe 493) and Creamy Salad Dressing (Recipe 502).

---

[a] Also see Boiled Beets and Onion Salad (Recipe 490).

505

Knob Celery Salad

Roher Selleriesalat
Salade de céleri cru

YIELD: 10 SERVINGS

Knob celery (celeriac)	2 lb 10 oz	1.2 kg
Lemon	1/2	1/2
DRESSING		
Mayonnaise (Recipe 71)	7 oz	200 g
Sour cream, light	3 1/3 oz	100 ml
Seasoning (salt, cayenne pepper)	1x	1x

MISE EN PLACE

Wash, trim, and peel knob celery. Cut into fine strips (*julienne*) or grate coarsely. Blend knob celery with lemon juice.

METHOD

Combine dressing ingredients and mix with the celery.

NOTE: Other suitable dressings are French Dressing (Recipe 479), Cottage Cheese Dressing (Recipe 500), and Yogurt Dressing (Recipe 494).

506

Salad with Apples, Carrots, and Sultanas

Rohkostsalat mit Äpfeln, Karotten, and Sultaninen
Salade de pommes et de carottes aux raisins secs

YIELD: 10 SERVINGS

Apples	1 lb 5 oz	600 g
Lemon juice	1 1/3 oz	40 ml
Carrots	1 lb 5 oz	600 g
Blue sultanas (raisins)	1 2/3 oz	50 g
Belgian endive	5 1/3 oz	150 g
Sunflower seeds, peeled	1 2/3 oz	50 g
Heavy cream (36%)	5 oz	150 ml
Horseradish, fresh	2 2/3 oz	75 g
Ginger, fresh[a]	2/3 oz	20 g
Orange juice	5 oz	150 ml
Seasoning (salt and pepper)	1x	1x
Sugar	1x	1x
Seasoning (cayenne pepper)	1x	1x

(continued on next page)

---

[a] Powdered ginger can be substituted.

(continued from preceding page)

MISE EN PLACE

Peel and core apples and cut into quarters. Grate apples coarsely and blend immediately with lemon juice to prevent oxidation.

Peel carrots and grate coarsely, the same size as the apples.

Blanch sultanas, drain, and let cool.

Trim Belgian endives and divide into individual leaves.

Toast sunflower seeds under the salamander until golden brown.

Whip heavy cream.

Peel and grate horseradish and fold into the whipped cream.

Peel and grate ginger and fold into the whipped cream.

METHOD

Combine apples, carrots, and orange juice. Add sultanas.

Season horseradish/ginger cream with salt and pepper, sugar, and cayenne.

Arrange Belgian endive leaves on plates and place salad in center.

Top with horseradish/ginger cream, using a pastry bag or spoon.

Sprinkle with sunflower seeds.

507

Salad of Red Cabbage,[a] Apples, and Grapes

Rohkostsalat mit Rotkabis, Äpfeln, and Trauben
Salade de chou rouge et de pommes aux raisins

YIELD: 10 SERVINGS

Red cabbage	1 lb 12 oz	800 g
Apples	1 lb 5 oz	600 g
Lemon juice	1 1/3 oz	40 ml
White grapes, seedless preferred	10 1/2 oz	300 g
Walnut halves[b]	1 2/3 oz	50 g
Cider, sweet	8 1/2 oz	250 ml
Seasoning (salt and pepper)	1x	1x
Sugar	1x	1x
Red currant jelly	5 1/3 oz	150 g
Walnut oil	1 1/3 oz	40 ml

[a] Also see recipe for Cabbage Salad (Recipe 525).

[b] Walnut pieces can be substituted.

MISE EN PLACE

Wash red cabbage, quarter, remove trunk, and cut into very thin slices.

Peel and core apples, cut into thin slices, and mix immediately with lemon juice to prevent oxidation.

Pluck white grapes from stems, cut in half, and remove seeds, if any.

Chop walnuts.

MISE EN PLACE

Marinate red cabbage and apples in cider for 6 hours.

Season with salt and pepper and sugar.

Add grapes.

Melt red currant jelly and blend with walnut oil. Add to salad.

Sprinkle the salad with nuts just before serving.

508

Roquefort Dressing

Roquefort-Salatsauce
Sauce à salade au roquefort

YIELD: 1 QT 2 OZ (1.0 L)

Roquefort cheese (genuine)	10 1/2 oz	300 g
Shallots	3 oz	80 g
Cottage cheese, low fat[a]	7 oz	200 g
Mustard, prepared, mild	2 oz	60 g
Cayenne pepper, ground	pinch	1 g
White wine vinegar	3 1/3 oz	100 ml
Sunflower oil	6 3/4 oz	200 ml
Salt	1/6 oz	5 g

MISE EN PLACE

Cube roquefort cheese.

Peel shallots and chop coarsely.

METHOD

Combine all ingredients, except half the vinegar and half the oil.

Purée ingredients in food processor to a smooth paste.

Incorporate remaining vinegar and oil into a homogenous dressing, while machine is operating at high speed.

If necessary, thin dressing with a small amount of warm water.

[a] The original recipe calls for *Quark*, a generic German word for cottage cheese. The cottage cheese for this recipe should be fine and strained. Skim-milk ricotta is a good substitute.

509

Artichoke and Tomato Salad

Salat Aida
Salade Aïda

Yield: 10 Servings

Curly endive[a]	10 1/2 oz	300 g
Tomatoes	1 lb 12 oz	800 g
Artichokes, large	3	3
Lemon juice	1 2/3 oz	50 ml
Salt	1/6 oz	5 g
Bell peppers, assorted	10 1/2 oz	300 g
Eggs	2	2

DRESSING
Mustard, prepared, mild	1 oz	30 g
Seasoning (salt and pepper)	1x	1x
White wine vinegar	5 oz	150 ml
Sunflower oil	8 1/2 oz	250 ml

MISE EN PLACE

Trim and wash curly endive.

Peel tomatoes, halve, and cut into wedges.

Peel off all outer leaves from artichokes and remove center fuzz.

Trim bottoms, cut into wedges, and sprinkle artichoke bottoms with lemon juice.

Boil artichoke bottoms immediately in salt water until tender, let cool, and cut into thin slices.

Cut peppers in half, remove seeds, and cut into fine strips (*julienne*).

Boil eggs, chill in cold water, and peel. Chop eggs coarsely.

METHOD

Combine dressing ingredients.

Arrange salad ingredients attractively in bouquets.

Sprinkle with chopped eggs and top with dressing.

---

[a] Also called frisee or chicory.

510

Rice and Pepper Salad

Salat andalusische Art
Salade andalouse

Yield: 10 servings

Tomatoes	14 oz	400 g
Yellow peppers	7 oz	200 g
Green peppers	7 oz	200 g
Long-grain rice, converted	7 oz	200 g
Kitchen herbs, fresh (parsley and basil)	2/3 oz	20 g

DRESSING
Garlic, crushed	1/6 oz	5 g
Seasoning (salt and pepper)	1x	1x
Seasoning (Tabasco)	1x	1x
Sherry wine vinegar	1 2/3 oz	50 ml
White wine vinegar	3 1/3 oz	100 ml
Olive oil	6 3/4 oz	200 ml

MISE EN PLACE

Peel tomatoes, halve, and cut in wedges.

Cut peppers in half, remove seeds, and cut into fine strips (*julienne*).

Boil rice in ample water, drain, rinse in cold water, drain again, and let cool.

Chop parsley and basil.

METHOD

Combine tomato wedges, peppers, and rice.

Combine all dressing ingredients and mix well.

Add dressing to tomatoes, peppers, and rice and let marinate for at least 2 hours.

Sprinkle salad with herbs.

511

Cucumber and Tomato Salad

Salat Emma
Salade Emma

YIELD: 10 SERVINGS

Cucumbers	2 lb 3 oz	1.0 kg
Tomatoes	1 lb 2 oz	500 g
Chives	3/4 oz	25 g

DRESSING
Dill, fresh	3/4 oz	25 g
Mustard, prepared, mild	2/3 oz	20 g
Seasoning (salt and pepper)	1	1
Herb vinegar	5 oz	150 ml
Sunflower oil	6 3/4 oz	200 ml
Red wine vinegar	3 1/3 oz	100 ml
Seasoning (salt and pepper)	1x	1x
Olive oil, cold pressed	3 1/3 oz	100 ml

MISE EN PLACE
Wash cucumbers and peel partially. Split, remove seeds if necessary, and cut into fine strips (*julienne*).

Peel tomatoes (optional), halve, and cut into slices.

Chop dill.

Combine dill, mustard, salt and pepper, herb vinegar, and sunflower oil.

METHOD
Just before serving, blend cucumbers with the dill oil mixture.

Make mounds of cucumber salad in the centers of plates.

Place tomato slices around.

Combine red wine vinegar with salt and pepper and add olive oil. Drizzle red wine vinegar olive oil dressing over tomatoes.

Sprinkle with chives.

512

Vegetable Salad with Ham

Salat Italienische Art
Salade italienne

YIELD: 10 SERVINGS

Carrots	14 oz	400 g
Turnips, white, small	8 3/4 oz	250 g
Potatoes	8 3/4 oz	250 g
Green beans, fresh	8 3/4 oz	250 g
Peas, frozen	8 3/4 oz	250 g
Onions	3 1/2 oz	100 g
Ham, boiled	7 oz	200 g
Anchovy fillets, drained	1 oz	30 g
Capers, drained	1 oz	30 g
Mayonnaise (Recipe 71)	10 1/2 oz	300 g
Seasoning (salt and pepper)	1x	1x

GARNISH
Eggs	3	3
Italian parsley	2/3 oz	20 g

MISE EN PLACE
Wash and peel carrots, turnips, and potatoes. Cut into small dice. Boil or steam each vegetable separately.

Trim green beans, boil in ample water, drain, chill, and drain again. Cut beans into 1/2-in. lengths.

Blanch peas, drain, chill, and drain again.

Peel and chop onions.

Cut ham into small dice.

Chop anchovy fillets coarsely.

MISE EN PLACE FOR GARNISH
Boil eggs, chill in cold water, peel, and cut into slices.

Wash and chop parsley.

METHOD
Combine boiled vegetables, chopped onions, diced ham, anchovy fillets, and capers.

Combine salad with mayonnaise and season to taste with salt and pepper.

Garnish salad with egg slices. Sprinkle with parsley.

513

Celery and Cauliflower Salad with Walnuts

Salat Marie-Louise
Salade Marie-Louise

YIELD: 10 SERVINGS

Celery, white, bleached[a]	1 lb 5 oz	600 g
Cauliflower, fresh	1 lb 5 oz	600 g
Kitchen herbs, fresh	2/3 oz	20 g
Head lettuce	2 1/2	2 1/2
Walnut halves[b]	1 2/3 oz	50 g
Vinaigrette dressing (Recipe 484)	5 oz	150 ml

DRESSING FOR CELERY

Walnut oil	1 2/3 oz	50 ml
Sunflower oil	1 2/3 oz	50 ml
Sherry wine vinegar	1 1/3 oz	40 ml
Seasoning (salt and pepper)	1x	1x

DRESSING FOR CAULIFLOWER

Sour cream, low fat	5 oz	150 ml
Lemon juice	1 2/3 oz	50 ml
Seasoning (salt and pepper)	1x	1x

MISE EN PLACE
Peel and wash celery and cut into small strips. Blanch celery, drain, chill quickly in cold water, and drain again immediately.

Divide cauliflower into small rosettes. Boil or steam until tender, but not too soft; drain.

Wash and chop herbs (such as chervil, chives, and parsley).

Wash and trim lettuce. Reserve the large outer leaves and cut the centers into quarters.

Chop nuts coarsely.

METHOD
Combine celery dressing ingredients and mix with the drained celery.

Combine cauliflower dressing ingredients and add kitchen herbs.

Put lettuce leaves on plates and make bouquets of celery salad and cauliflower salad on top of lettuce. Cover cauliflower with the sour cream dressing.

Add one lettuce quarter to each plate.

Drizzle herb vinaigrette on lettuce leaves.

Sprinkle salad with chopped nuts.

[a] Bleached celery is available in Switzerland. The celery sticks are kept covered with soil during the growing process, so they stay white.
[b] Chopped nuts can be substituted.

514

Black Beans, Corn, and Pepper Salad

Salat mexikanische Art
Salade mexicaine

YIELD: 10 SERVINGS

Black beans	10 1/2 oz	300 g
Salt	2/3 oz	20 g
Red peppers	7 oz	200 g
Green peppers	7 oz	200 g
Green beans, fresh	7 oz	200 g
Corn, canned, drained	10 1/2 oz	300 g
Salt	2/3 oz	20 g

DRESSING

Garlic	1/6 oz	5 g
Savory, fresh	1/3 oz	10 g
Seasoning (salt and pepper)	1x	1x
Chili sauce	1 2/3 oz	50 ml
White wine vinegar	3 1/3 oz	100 ml
Sunflower oil	6 3/4 oz	200 ml

MISE EN PLACE
Soak black beans in cold water for 4 to 6 hours.

Bring to a boil, cover, and boil until tender. Add salt, drain, and let cool.

Split red and green peppers in half, remove seeds, and cut into fine strips (*julienne*).

Trim green beans, boil in salted water until still crisp, drain, chill, and drain again. Cut green beans into 1 1/2-in. (35 mm) lengths.

METHOD
Peel and chop garlic. Chop savory.

Combine all dressing ingredients.

Marinate all vegetables with dressing.

NOTE: Kidney beans can be substituted.

515

ℛussian Salad

Salat russische Art
Salade russe

YIELD: 10 SERVINGS

Carrots	14 oz	400 g
Knob celery (celeriac)	7 oz	200 g
Potatoes	14 oz	400 g
Green beans, fresh	14 oz	400 g
Salt	1x	1x
Peas, frozen	7 oz	200 g

DRESSING

Mayonnaise (Recipe 71)	7 oz	200 g
Yogurt, plain	3 1/2 oz	100 g
Seasoning (salt and pepper)	1x	1x

MISE EN PLACE

Wash, trim, and peel carrots and knob celery. Cut vegetables into small dice. Boil each separately until still crisp, drain, chill in cold water, and drain again.

Wash and peel potatoes, cut into small dice, and steam or boil until tender. Do not overcook.

Trim green beans, boil in salted water until still crisp, drain, chill, and drain again. Cut into 1 1/2-in. (35 mm) lengths.

Blanch peas, chill in cold water, and drain.

METHOD

Mix cooked vegetables together.

Mix mayonnaise and yogurt and add to vegetables.

Blend together to coat vegetables and season to taste.

NOTE: Steaming the vegetables is preferable to boiling.

516

Salad of Green Beans, Tomatoes, and Mushrooms

Salat spanische Art
Salade espagnole

YIELD: 10 SERVINGS

Green beans, fresh	1 lb 5 oz	600 g
Tomatoes	1 lb 5 oz	600 g
Mushrooms, fresh	8 3/4 oz	250 g
Lemon juice	2/3 oz	20 ml
Bell peppers, assorted colors	7 oz	200 g
Onions	3 1/2 oz	100 g
Romaine lettuce heads	2	2

DRESSING

Garlic	1/6 oz	5 g
Thyme, fresh	1/6 oz	5 g
Basil, fresh	1/6 oz	5 g
Olive oil, cold pressed	5 oz	150 ml
Sunflower oil	3 1/3 oz	100 ml
White wine vinegar	5 oz	150 ml
Seasoning (salt and pepper)	1x	1x

MISE EN PLACE

Trim green beans, boil in salted water until still crisp, drain, chill, and drain again. Cut into 1 1/2-in. (35 mm) lengths.

Cut tomatoes in half; cut each half into eight wedges.

Trim and wash mushrooms, slice, and braise with lemon juice.

Wash peppers, cut in half, and remove seeds. Cut peppers into fine strips (*julienne*).

Peel onions and slice into thin rings.

Trim and wash lettuce; separate leaves.

METHOD

Crush garlic. Wash and chop thyme and basil.

Make dressing with garlic, herbs, oils, vinegar, and seasoning.

Combine green beans and tomato wedges and season with half the dressing.

Arrange lettuce leaves on plates. Place a bouquet of green bean/tomato salad in the center of each plate, atop lettuce.

Place bouquets of mushrooms and peppers around green bean/tomato salad.

Drizzle remaining dressing over the mushrooms and the peppers.

Garnish with onion rings.

517

Sauerkraut Salad

Sauerkrautsalat
Salade de choucroute

YIELD: 10 SERVINGS

Sauerkraut[a]	2 lb 3 oz	1.0 kg
Apples	7 oz	200 g
Golden sultanas (raisins)	3 1/2 oz	100 g

DRESSING
Sugar	1x	1x
Seasoning (ground black pepper)	1x	1x
Sour cream, low fat	6 3/4 oz	200 ml
Lemon, juice	1/2	1/2

MISE EN PLACE
Wash the raw sauerkraut, drain, and squeeze out excess moisture.

Peel and core apples and cut into small dice.

METHOD
Combine sauerkraut, apples, and sultanas.

Add dressing ingredients and blend thoroughly.

NOTES: This salad is suitable for diet menus.

Another suitable dressing for this salad is Yogurt Dressing (Recipe 494).

518

Sour Cream Dressing

Sauerrahmsalatsauce
Sauce à salade à la crème acidulée

YIELD: 1 QT 2 OZ (1.0 L)

Kitchen herbs, fresh	3 oz	80 g
Sour cream, low fat	1 pt 11 oz	800 ml
Salt	1/3 oz	10 g
Cayenne pepper, ground	pinch	2 g
Lemon juice	4 oz	120 ml

METHOD
Wash and chop herbs, such as chives, parsley, dill, tarragon, and basil.

Mix all dressing ingredients. Stir to blend well.

519

Soy Bean Sprouts Salad

Sojasprossensalat
Salad de germes de soja

YIELD: 10 SERVINGS

Soybean sprouts	2 lb 3 oz	1.0 kg

DRESSING
Lemon juice	1 2/3 oz	50 ml
Soy sauce	2/3 oz	20 ml
Soybean oil	1/3 oz	10 ml
Sunflower oil	3 1/3 oz	100 ml
Seasoning (salt and pepper)	1x	1x

METHOD
Wash soybean sprouts, blanch, and drain well.

Combine all dressing ingredients and blend with soybean sprouts.

Let salad marinate.

NOTE: To be completely sure the sprouts do not harbor unhealthy organisms, it is recommended that the sprouts be blanched briefly.

---

[a] In Switzerland, sauerkraut is commonly sold raw (fresh). If canned sauerkraut is used, washing might not be necessary.

520

$\mathscr{A}$sparagus Salad

Spargelsalat
Salad de pointes d'asperges

YIELD: 10 SERVINGS

White asparagus[a]	5 lb 8 oz	2.5 kg
Salt	2/3 oz	20 g
Sugar	pinch	1x
Parsley, fresh, curly	2/3 oz	20 g

DRESSING

Mayonnaise (Recipe 71)	7 oz	200 g
Herb vinegar	1 2/3 oz	50 ml
Yogurt, plain	3 1/2 oz	100 g
Seasoning (salt and pepper)	1x	1x

MISE EN PLACE

Peel asparagus and trim off tough ends.

Tie asparagus into bundles and boil in salted water[b] with a pinch of sugar. Remove, chill in cold water immediately, and drain.

Wash and chop parsley.

METHOD

Combine all dressing ingredients.

Cover asparagus with dressing and sprinkle with parsley.

521

$\mathscr{S}$pinach Salad

Spinatsalat
Salade de feuilles d'épinards

YIELD: 10 SERVINGS

Spinach, fresh	1 lb 12 oz	800 g

DRESSING

Shallots	1 2/3 oz	50 g
Garlic	1/6 oz	5 g
Seasoning (salt and pepper)	1x	1x
White wine vinegar	3 1/3 oz	100 ml
Sunflower oil	6 3/4 oz	200 ml

GARNISH

Eggs	2	2
Garlic	1/6 oz	5 g
White bread (Pullman loaf)	3 1/2 oz	100 g
Butter	1 oz	30 g

MISE EN PLACE

Trim and wash spinach and drain thoroughly.

METHOD FOR DRESSING

Peel and chop shallots and garlic.

Combine all dressing ingredients.

METHOD FOR GARNISH

Boil eggs, chill in cold water, peel, and chop.

Peel and chop garlic.

Remove crust from bread and cut into small cubes.

Heat butter, sauté garlic briefly, add bread cubes, and sauté until bread cubes are golden brown (croûtons).

METHOD

Just before serving, blend raw spinach with dressing.

Sprinkle with croutons and chopped eggs.

NOTE: Another suitable dressing would be Italian Dressing (Recipe 493).

---

[a] Green asparagus can be substituted.

[b] Asparagus can also be steamed.

522

Tomato Salad

Tomatensalat
Salade de tomates

YIELD: 10 SERVINGS

Tomatoes (10)	2 lb 10 oz	1.2 kg
Onions	3 1/2 oz	100 g
Basil, fresh	2/3 oz	20 g
Chives, fresh	2/3 oz	20 g
Seasoning (salt and pepper)	1x	1x
Red wine vinegar	3 1/3 oz	100 ml
Olive oil, cold pressed	5 oz	150 ml

MISE EN PLACE

Wash tomatoes and remove stem end. Cut into slices.

Peel and chop onions.

Chop basil leaves.

Cut chives into small slivers.

METHOD

Arrange tomato slices, in sequence,[a] on plates.

Season with salt and pepper.

Sprinkle with chopped onions.

Drizzle with vinegar and oil.

Sprinkle with chopped basil and chives.

NOTES: The classic method calls for peeled tomatoes. This is no longer recommended in commercial establishments for health reasons.

Another suitable dressing is herb vinaigrette dressing. Use Vinaigrette Dressing (Recipe 484) and add kitchen herbs.

---

[a] Place the tomato slices on plates in the order in which they were cut.

523

Waldorf Salad

Waldorf-Salat
Salade Waldorf

YIELD: 10 SERVINGS

Knob celery (celeriac)	2 lb 10 oz	1.2 kg
Apples	10 1/2 oz	300 g
DRESSING		
Mayonnaise (Recipe 71)	7 oz	200 g
Sour cream, low fat	3 1/3 oz	100 ml
Lemon	1/2	1/2
Seasoning (salt and cayenne pepper)	1x	1x
GARNISH		
Walnut halves	3 1/2 oz	100 g
Pineapple slices, canned, drained[a]	3	3

MISE EN PLACE

Wash, trim, and peel knob celery. Cut into fine strips (julienne).

Peel and core apples and cut into small dice.

Dice pineapple slices.

METHOD

Blend dressing ingredients.

Mix dressing with salad ingredients.

Garnish with walnut halves and pineapple pieces.

---

[a] Pineapple is optional. The original recipe for Waldorf Salad did not call for pineapple

524

*W*hite Bean Salad

Salat von weissen Bohnen
Salade bretonne

YIELD: 10 SERVINGS

Small white beans[a]	1 lb 5 oz	600 g
Salt	2/3 oz	20 g
Slab bacon, boiled	5 1/3 oz	150 g
Onions	3 1/2 oz	100 g
DRESSING		
Garlic cloves, peeled	2	2
Savory, fresh	1/3 oz	10 g
Thyme, fresh	1/6 oz	5 g
Seasoning (salt and pepper)	1x	1x
White wine vinegar	5 oz	150 ml
Sunflower oil	6 3/4 oz	200 ml

MISE EN PLACE
Soak white beans in cold water for 4 to 6 hours. Bring to a boil and boil until tender; add salt.

Cut bacon into small dice and sauté lightly.

Peel and chop onions.

METHOD FOR DRESSING
Chop garlic. Wash and chop savory and thyme.

Blend all dressing ingredients.

METHOD
Combine beans, while still warm, with diced bacon, chopped onions, and dressing, and let marinate, refrigerated. Stir occasionally to cool mixture evenly.

Remove beans from refrigerator some time before serving. This salad should not be served too cold.

NOTE: Italian Dressing (Recipe 493) is also suitable for this salad.

---

[a] Navy beans or great Northern beans can be used.

525

*C*abbage Salad

Weisskohlsalat
Salade de chou blanc

YIELD: 10 SERVINGS

Cabbage[a]	3 lb 5 oz	1.5 kg
Slab bacon, smoked	7 oz	200 g
Onions	5 1/3 oz	150 g
Seasoning (salt, nutmeg)	1x	1x
Caraway seeds, whole	1/3 oz	10 g
Seasoning (black pepper)	1x	1x
Bouillon (Recipe 22)	6 3/4 oz	200 ml
DRESSING		
Mustard, prepared, mild	2/3 oz	20 g
Herb vinegar	5 oz	150 ml
Sunflower oil	5 oz	150 ml

MISE EN PLACE
Trim cabbage and cut into thin slices.

Cut bacon into small dice.

Peel and chop onions.

METHOD
Put cabbage in a large bowl.

Sauté bacon, add onions, and sauté lightly. Add to cabbage.

Season cabbage with salt, nutmeg, caraway seeds, and pepper.

Bring bouillon to a boil and pour over cabbage. Let cabbage marinate until cool.

Mix all dressing ingredients and add to cabbage. Toss to mix well.

NOTE: Red cabbage salad can be made by substituting red cabbage, and by using red wine vinegar. Also see recipe for Salad of Red Cabbage, Apples, and Grapes (Recipe 507).

---

[a] The recipe calls for white (winter) cabbage.

526

Chicken, Ox Tongue, and Knob Celery Salad

Windsor-Salat
Salade Windsor

YIELD: 10 SERVINGS

Knob celery (celeriac)	1 lb 12 oz	800 g
Mushrooms, fresh	10 1/2 oz	300 g
Peanut oil	3 1/3 oz	100 ml
Lemon	1/2	1/2
Chicken breasts, boneless, skinless	1 lb 2 oz	500 g
Chicken stock (Recipe 26)	6 3/4 oz	200 ml
Ox tongue, boiled	7 oz	200 g
DRESSING		
Mayonnaise (Recipe 71)	7 oz	200 g
Yogurt, plain	3 1/2 oz	100 g
Seasoning (salt and pepper)	1x	1x
GARNISH		
Field salad (mache), trimmed and washed	7 oz	200 g
Black truffles, sliced	1/8 oz	3 g

MISE EN PLACE

Trim, wash, and peel knob celery. Cut into fine strips (*julienne*).

Trim and wash mushrooms and cut in thin slices. Braise with peanut oil and lemon juice and let cool.

Poach chicken breasts in chicken stock and let cool in stock.

Cut chicken breast and ox tongue into fine strips (*julienne*).

Cut truffle slices into a very fine *julienne*.

METHOD

Combine knob celery, mushrooms, chicken, and ox tongue.

Combine dressing ingredients and mix thoroughly. Add to celery/meat mixture. If necessary, add small amount of cold chicken stock to thin dressing.

Serve vegetable/meat salad in centers of plates.

Surround with field salad and sprinkle with truffle *julienne*.

527

Zucchini (vegetable marrow) Salad

Zucchettisalat
Salade de courgettes

YIELD 10 SERVINGS

Zucchini	2 lb 10 oz	1.2 kg
DRESSING		
Garlic	1/6 oz	5 g
White wine vinegar	5 oz	150 ml
Olive oil, cold pressed	3 1/3 oz	100 ml
Sunflower oil	3 1/3 oz	100 ml
Seasoning (salt and pepper)	1x	1x
GARNISH		
Basil, fresh	1/3 oz	10 g

MISE EN PLACE

Wash zucchini and trim off stems; cut into thin slices or strips (*julienne*).

Chop or crush garlic, or press through a garlic press.

METHOD

Combine garlic, vinegar, and oils. Season to taste with salt and pepper.

Blend dressing with zucchini.

Cut basil into very fine *julienne* and sprinkle on salad.

NOTE: Other suitable dressings are Italian Dressing (Recipe 493) and Yogurt Dressing (Recipe 494).

CHAPTER

Vegetables

Vegetables

528

*W*hole Artichokes

Artischoken
Artichauts

YIELD: 10 SERVINGS

Artichokes, large	10	10
Lemon juice	3 1/3 oz	100 ml
Salt	2/3 oz	20 g

MISE EN PLACE
Cut off stems from artichokes.

Trim bottoms with a sharp knife.

Cut off tops about one-third of the way down.

Trim remaining leaves with scissors.

As soon as each artichoke is trimmed, drizzle with some lemon juice or place in acidulated water.

METHOD
Boil artichokes in salted water, flavored with lemon juice, or steam artichokes until cooked. To check for doneness, insert the point of a knife into the bottom.

Remove with skimmer and drain well. Twist out the center leaves to remove them, and reserve.

Remove the exposed center straw with a melon baller or a teaspoon.

Return center leaves back to artichoke, but place them upside down to form a flower.

Artichokes can be served hot, warm, or cold.

529

*A*rtichoke Bottoms

Artischokenböden
Fonds d'artichauts

YIELD: 10 SERVINGS

Artichokes	20	20
Lemon juice	3 1/3 oz	100 ml
Veal kidney fat	3 1/2 oz	100 g
Salt	2/3 oz	20 g
White wheat flour	1 2/3 oz	50 g

MISE EN PLACE
Cut off stems from artichokes.

Trim bottoms with a sharp knife.

Cut off tops about one-third of the way down.

Trim bottom and remove center straw.

Trim remaining leaves with scissors.

As soon as each artichoke is trimmed, drizzle with some lemon juice or place in acidulated water.

Coarsely chop kidney fat.

METHOD
Combine remaining lemon juice, salt, kidney fat, and 2 qt 4 oz (2.0 L) water; bring to a boil.

Make a slurry with a small amount of cold water and flour. Pour into boiling water while stirring.

Boil artichoke bottoms in the resulting stock. Let cool, and store artichokes in stock until serving.

NOTE: The veal kidney fat adds flavor, but may be eliminated if there are dietary concerns.

530

*B*aked Eggplants with Tomatoes

Auberginengratin
Gratin d'aubergines

YIELD: 10 SERVINGS

Eggplants	3 lb 5 oz	1.5 kg
Seasoning (salt and pepper)	1x	1x
Lemon juice	1/3 oz	10 ml
Tomatoes	10 1/2 oz	300 g
White wheat flour	1 2/3 oz	50 g
Olive oil	3 1/3 oz	100 ml
Heavy cream (36%)	8 1/2 oz	250 ml
Egg yolks	4	4
Sbrinz, grated[a]	2 oz	60 g
Seasoning (salt and pepper)	1x	1x
Nutmeg	1x	1x

MISE EN PLACE
Wash and trim eggplants. If eggplant skins are tough, peel them. (Small eggplants usually have more tender skins.)

Cut eggplants into slices about 1/3-inch (10 mm) thick.

Marinate eggplants with salt and pepper and lemon juice.

[a] Sbrinz is a hard grating cheese from Switzerland. Parmesan can be substituted.

Peel tomatoes, halve, remove seeds, and cut into dice.

METHOD

Dry eggplant slices on absorbent paper.

Dredge in flour and sauté on both sides, in olive oil, until golden brown.

Place eggplant slices, like shingles, in an oiled, ovenproof serving dish (*gratin* platter).

Sprinkle with diced tomatoes.

Whip heavy cream to a medium stiff foam. Fold in egg yolks and grated Sbrinz.

Spread mixture over eggplant slices.

Bake in oven, with strong top heat, until brown.

531

$\mathcal{L}$eaf Spinach with Anchovies

Blattspinat mit Sardellen
Epinards italienne

YIELD: 10 SERVINGS

Spinach, fresh	3 lb 5 oz	1.5 kg
Salt	2/3 oz	20 g
Shallots	3 oz	80 g
Garlic	1/2 oz	15 g
Anchovy fillets, canned, drained	1 oz	30 g
Butter	3 oz	80 g
Nutmeg	1x	1x
Seasoning (salt and pepper)	1x	1x

MISE EN PLACE

Trim and wash spinach. Blanch in ample salted water, drain, and chill immediately; drain again.

Peel and chop shallots and garlic.

Chop anchovy fillets coarsely.

METHOD

Sauté shallots and garlic in butter.

Add spinach,[a] season with nutmeg, salt and pepper, and heat.

Blend chopped anchovies with spinach.

---

[a] If leaves are very large, chop spinach coarsely.

532

$\mathcal{C}$hinese Cabbage and Veal Roll

Chinakohlroulade
Roulade de chou chinois

YIELD: 10 SERVINGS

Chinese cabbage (Nappa cabbage)	2 lb 10 oz	1.2 kg
Salt	1/3 oz	10 g
Pork caul[a]	10 1/2 oz	300 g
White bread (Pullman loaf)	5 1/3 oz	150 g
Bouillon (Recipe 22)	10 oz	300 ml
Butter	2/3 oz	20 g
Bacon, smoked, sliced	10 1/2 oz	300 g

STUFFING

Shiitake mushrooms, dried	9 oz	250 g
Shallots	2 oz	60 g
Red bell peppers	3 1/2 oz	100 g
Butter	1 1/3 oz	40 g
Veal sausage stuffing[b]	14 1/4 oz	400 g
Seasoning (salt and pepper)	1x	1x

MISE EN PLACE

Trim Chinese cabbage and separate leaves.

Blanch leaves in salted water, drain, chill, and drain again.

Spread a sheet of aluminum foil on table.

Spread out caul to cover the surface.

Place cabbage leaves on top, slightly overlapping.

Dab leaves with absorbent paper to dry them.

Remove crust from bread and cut into small dice. Toast under the salamander until golden brown (*croutons*).

MISE EN PLACE FOR STUFFING

Soak shiitake mushrooms for 1 hour. Discard soaking water and remove stems. Chop mushrooms coarsely.

Peel and chop shallots.

Split red peppers, remove seeds, and cut into small dice. Blanch peppers and drain.

Sauté shallots in butter and add shiitake mushrooms and red peppers. Let cool.

Blend veal sausage stuffing with mushroom mixture. Season to taste.

(continued on next page)

---

[a] Caul is the netting that holds the intestines together. Available from butcher shops, it is often salted and must be soaked in cold water to remove the salt.

[b] Veal sausage stuffing is readily available in Switzerland. Mousseline farce (Recipe 17) can be substituted.

(continued from preceding page)

METHOD

Cover cabbage leaves evenly with bacon slices.

Spread stuffing uniformly on top.

Sprinkle with *croûtons*.

Roll up tightly; tie with butcher's twine to form a sausage.

Place roll in a shallow pot.

Add bouillon. Place heavy plate on top to keep roll submerged.

Cover and braise in oven at 325°F (165°C), until center has reached 180°F (80°C).

Let cool slightly and unroll. Cut into slices to serve.

533

atter-Fried Eggplant Slices

Fritierte Auberginen
Aubergines frites

YIELD: 10 SERVINGS

Eggplants	2 lb 10 oz	1.2 kg
Garlic	1/3 oz	10 g
Thyme, fresh	1/3 oz	10 g
Oregano, fresh	1/3 oz	10 g
Lemon	1/2	1/2
Eggs	3	3
Seasoning (salt and pepper)	1x	1x
White wheat flour	3 1/2 oz	100 g
Oil for frying (10% oil loss)	4 oz	120 ml

MISE EN PLACE

Wash eggplants, remove stems, and cut into 1/3-in. (10 mm) thick slices.

Chop or crush garlic into a fine paste.

Wash thyme and oregano and chop leaves.

Marinate eggplant slices with garlic, herbs, and lemon juice.

Break eggs and mix well.

METHOD

Season eggplant slices and dredge in flour.

Dip in eggs and scrape off excess eggs.

Deep-fry until golden brown. Drain on absorbent paper.

534

*F*ried Knob Celery (celeriac)

Fritierter Knollensellerie
Céleri-rave frit

YIELD: 10 SERVINGS

Knob celery (celeriac)	3 lb 5 oz	1.5 kg
Lemon	1	1
Salt	1/3 oz	10 g
White wheat flour	3 1/2 oz	100 g

BATTER

White wheat flour	12 oz	350 g
Milk	6 3/4 oz	200 ml
Water	6 3/4 oz	200 ml
Egg yolk	1	1
Seasoning (salt and pepper)	1x	1x
Nutmeg	1x	1x
Egg whites	3	100 g
Oil for frying (10% oil loss)	5 oz	150 ml

MISE EN PLACE

Wash, trim, and peel knob celery.

Cut knob celery into halves or quarters, depending on size. Cut pieces into 1/3-in. (10 mm) thick slices or into wedges.

Boil knob celery until tender (but not soft) in water with lemon and salt. Celery can also be steamed.

Drain knob celery and spread out to cool.

METHOD FOR BATTER

Sift flour. Combine milk, water, and egg yolk.

Add milk/egg mixture to sifted flour and mix into a smooth batter. Season to taste with salt and pepper and nutmeg.

Whip egg whites and fold into batter.

METHOD

Dredge knob celery slices in flour, dip in batter, and deep-fry at 360°F (180°C).

Drain on absorbent paper and serve.

535

Fresh Stewed Tomatoes

Gedünstete Tomatenwürfel/Tomaten-Concassé
Tomates concassées

YIELD: 10 SERVINGS

Tomatoes	3 lb 5 oz	1.5 kg
Shallots	2 2/3 oz	75 g
Olive oil	1 2/3 oz	50 ml
Seasoning (salt and pepper)	1x	1x

MISE EN PLACE
Wash tomatoes, remove stem ends, make cross-shaped incision on the other side to facilitate peeling. Dip tomatoes in boiling water for a few seconds. Peel with small knife, starting where the incision was made.

Cut tomatoes in half horizontally and squeeze out seeds.

Cut into small cubes.

Peel and chop shallots.

METHOD
Sauté shallots in olive oil in a wide, shallow saucepan.

Add tomatoes and cook quickly over high heat until tomatoes are melted.

NOTES: Depending on use, garlic and kitchen herbs such as thyme, marjoram, basil, and others can be added.

If the tomatoes are pale, a small amount of tomato paste can be added for color.

536

Stuffed Eggplants

Gefüllte Auberginen
Aubergines farcies

YIELD: 10 SERVINGS

STUFFING

Rice, long-grain, parboiled	7 oz	200 g
Onions	5 1/3 oz	150 g
Red bell peppers	5 1/3 oz	150 g
Blue sultanas (raisins)	2 oz	60 g
Marjoram, fresh	1/3 oz	10 g
Peppermint, fresh	1/3 oz	10 g
Bananas	10 1/2 oz	300 g
Olive oil	1 2/3 oz	50 ml
Seasoning (salt and pepper)	1x	1x
Eggplants, 5	2 lb 10 oz	1.2 kg
Lemon	1	1
Olive oil	2/3 oz	20 ml
Salt	1/3 oz	10 g
Bouillon (Recipe 22)	10 oz	300 ml
Butter	2 oz	60 g

MISE EN PLACE FOR STUFFING
Boil rice, drain, and let cool.

Peel and chop onions.

Cut peppers in half, remove seeds, and cut into small dice.

Blanch sultanas and drain.

Wash and chop marjoram and peppermint.

MISE EN PLACE
Wash eggplants, remove stems, and cut in half lengthwise.

Sprinkle immediately with lemon juice to prevent oxidation.

Make a few incisions on cut sides and brush with olive oil.

Place eggplants, cut-side down, on baking sheet, and bake for 10 minutes in medium-hot oven.

Remove from oven, turn cut-side up, and scoop out pulp, leaving a shell about 1/6-in (5 mm) thick. Sprinkle shell with salt. Reserve pulp for stuffing.

METHOD FOR STUFFING
Chop reserved eggplant pulp coarsely.

Peel bananas and cut into dice.

Sauté chopped onions in olive oil, add diced peppers, and continue cooking.

Add chopped eggplant pulp and continue cooking.

Add rice, sultanas, and bananas.

Season robustly with marjoram, peppermint, and salt and pepper.

METHOD
Butter an ovenproof serving platter (*gratin* dish).

Fill eggplants and place in serving dish. Add bouillon and butter.

Bake in oven, with strong bottom heat, until eggplants are done.

537

Stuffed Cucumbers
Gefüllte Gurken
Concombres farcies

YIELD: 10 SERVINGS

Cucumbers	2 lb 10 oz	1.2 kg
Butter	3/4 oz	25 g
Dill seed, ground	2/3 oz	20 g
Seasoning (salt and pepper)	1x	1x
Onions	3 1/2 oz	100 g
Pork shoulder meat, trimmed	1 lb 2 oz	500 g
Olive oil	1 1/3 oz	40 ml
Seasoning (salt and pepper)	1x	1x
Bay leaf	1	1
Cloves, ground	1x	1x
Dry white wine	3 1/3 oz	100 ml
Demi-glace (Recipe 44)	6 3/4 oz	200 ml
Bouillon (Recipe 22)	6 3/4 oz	200 ml
Parmesan cheese, grated	3 1/2 oz	100 g
Butter	2/3 oz	20 g

MISE EN PLACE
Peel cucumbers and cut off ends. Reserve ends.

Split in half lengthwise, scoop out seeds and discard, scoop out some flesh and reserve.

Cut cucumbers into even lengths, about 2 1/2-in (60 mm) long. Reserve trimmings.

Butter a suitable ovenproof platter (*gratin* dish) and arrange cucumber lengths, cut-side up.

Dice all reserved cucumber ends and trimmings.

Season with ground dill seed and salt and pepper.

Peel and chop onions.

Cut pork meat into very small dice.

METHOD
Sauté onions in olive oil. Add diced pork and season with salt and pepper, bay leaf, and ground cloves. Continue cooking.

Add white wine and reduce. Add *demi-glace* and bring to a boil.

Add diced cucumbers and let mixture reduce until rather thick.

Remove bay leaf. Fill cucumber lengths with stuffing.

Pour bouillon around cucumbers.

Sprinkle stuffing with cheese and drizzle stuffing with melted butter.

Bake in oven until cucumbers are tender and brown on top.

538

Stuffed Peppers
Gefüllte Peperoni
Poivrons farcies

YIELD: 10 SERVINGS

Green peppers, large	10	10
Seasoning (salt and pepper)	1x	1x
STUFFING		
Onions	3 1/2 oz	100 g
Parsley	1/3 oz	10 g
Butter	2/3 oz	20 g
Rice[a]	10 1/2 oz	300 g
Bouillon (Recipe 22)	10 oz	300 ml
Beef, shoulder clod, lean, chopped (or ground lean chuck)	1 lb 5 1/2 oz	600 g
Peanut oil	1 oz	30 ml
Seasoning (salt and pepper)	1x	1x
Dry white wine	3 1/3 oz	100 ml
Brown veal stock (Recipe 23)	10 oz	300 ml
SAUCE		
Onions	5 1/3 oz	150 g
Butter	1 oz	30 g
Fresh stewed tomatoes (Recipe 535)	6 3/4 oz	200 ml
Bouillon (Recipe 22)	6 3/4 oz	200 ml
Seasoning (salt and pepper)	1x	1x

MISE EN PLACE
Wash peppers and trim the stem to about 1/3in. (10 mm).

Slice off tops with stems attached and save.

Carefully scoop out seeds from pepper cups and wash out peppers.

Briefly blanch the pepper cups and lids and turn upside down to drain.

Turn pepper cups upright and season inside.

Arrange pepper cups in tightly fitting casserole.

METHOD FOR STUFFING
Peel and chop onions. Wash and chop parsley.

Sauté onions in butter.

Add rice and cook briefly, stirring.

Add bouillon, bring to a boil, and simmer until all liquid is absorbed, but rice is not fully cooked.

---

[a] The recipe specifies Vialone rice, which is a short-grain rice similar to Arborio; Arborio can be substituted.

Sauté chopped beef in peanut oil, stirring often to break up meat.

Season beef with salt and pepper and add white wine.

Add brown veal stock and the parboiled rice.

Add chopped parsley and blend well.

METHOD FOR SAUCE
Peel onions and slice thin.

Sauté sliced onions in butter. Add stewed tomatoes and bouillon.

Season to taste with salt and pepper.

METHOD
Fill peppers with the still somewhat liquid stuffing. Place pepper lids on top.

Pour sauce around stuffed peppers.

Cover and braise in the oven for about 45 minutes.

Spoon sauce over peppers when serving.

539

Stuffed Onions

Gefüllte Zwiebeln
Oignons farcies

YIELD: 10 SERVINGS

Onions, 10 large, uniform in size	3 lb	1.4 kg
Salt	1/2 oz	15 g
Bouillon (Recipe 22)	10 oz	300 ml
Sbrinz cheese, grated[a]	3 oz	80 g

STUFFING

Bacon, smoked, sliced	10 1/2 oz	300 g
Parsley	2/3 oz	20 g
Marjoram, fresh	2/3 oz	20 g
White bread (Pullman loaf)	10 1/2 oz	300 g
Butter	3 oz	80 g
Seasoning (salt and pepper)	1x	1x

MISE EN PLACE
Peel onions, cut off tops, and leave root end in tact. Blanch briefly in salted water or steam onions lightly.

Carefully scoop out centers to form cups. Be sure onions are held together at the root ends. The cups should be at least 2 layers thick.

---

[a]Sbrinz is a hard grating cheese from Switzerland. Parmesan can be substituted.

Chop scooped out onion and reserve.

METHOD FOR STUFFING
Cut bacon into small dice.

Chop parsley and marjoram leaves.

Remove crust from bread and slice into small cubes. Toast cubes under the salamander until golden brown (*croûtons*).

Sauté diced bacon in butter.

Add parsley, marjoram, *croûtons*, and reserved chopped onions.

Season to taste with salt and pepper.

METHOD
Arrange onion cups in an ovenproof dish (*gratin* platter).

Fill onion cups with stuffing. Pour bouillon around onions, and cover with buttered aluminum foil.

Bake in oven at 325°F (165°C) until onions are tender.

Remove foil and sprinkle with cheese.

Brown in hot oven or under the salamander.

540

Stuffed Cabbage

Gefüllter Kohl
Chou farci

YIELD: 10 SERVINGS

Green cabbage	3 lb 8 oz	1.6 kg
Salt	1/3 oz	10 g
Butter	2/3 oz	20 g
Bouillon (Recipe 22)	10 oz	300 ml

STUFFING

Slab bacon, smoked	12 oz	350 g
Onions	7 oz	200 g
Vegetable shortening	1 2/3 oz	50 g
Marjoram, ground	1/6 oz	5 g
Caraway seeds	1/6 oz	5 g
Seasoning (salt and pepper)	1x	1x

MISE EN PLACE
Remove damaged outer leaves from cabbage; remove center core without splitting cabbage and discard.

Bring ample amount of salted water to a boil.

Dip cabbage in water for about 30 seconds.

(continued on next page)

(continued from preceding page)

Remove cabbage with skimmer and carefully peel off outer leaves. Repeat process until most leaves are peeled off. There should be 20 leaves. If leaves are large, cut in half.

Quarter the remaining center into four wedges.

Blanch leaves and center wedges to make them pliable. Drain.

METHOD FOR STUFFING
Cut bacon into small dice. Peel and chop onions.

Coarsely chop blanched cabbage wedges.

Sauté bacon and onions in shortening.

Add chopped cabbage and season robustly with marjoram, caraway, and salt and pepper.

Sauté thoroughly to blend and heat ingredients. Let cool.

METHOD
Spread cabbage leaves on table and fill with stuffing. Roll leaves into sausage shapes. (Or place leaves, one at a time, on a kitchen towel, add filling, close towel, and twist into ball shape.)

Butter suitable shallow pan, and pack cabbage rolls/balls tightly, seam side down.

Pour bouillon over cabbage, cover, and braise at 325°F (165°C) until cabbage is tender.

Remove cabbage and keep warm.

Reduce braising liquid and serve over cabbage.

MISE EN PLACE
Wash and trim Belgian endive, if necessary.

With a pointed knife, remove the bitter center core from the base end. Be sure endive leaves do not separate.

Blanch endives in salt and lemon water. Drain.

Chop veal kidney fat coarsely.

METHOD
Butter a suitable shallow pan.

Add kidney fat and *matignon*. Sauté over low heat until fat starts to melt.

Place endive tightly, side by side, on top.

Add vegetable stock and lemon juice. The stock should cover about one-third of the vegetables.

Season with salt and pepper. Cover with buttered aluminum foil.

Place a plate on top (to prevent endive from floating) and bring to a boil.

Braise in oven at 325°F (165°C) until Belgian endive are tender.

Remove from stock.

Lightly flatten endive and fold over. Brush with hot butter and serve.

NOTE: The veal kidney fat adds flavor, but may be eliminated if there are dietary concerns.

541

 raised Belgian Endive

Geschmorte Brüsseler Endivien
Endives braisées

YIELD: 10 SERVINGS

Belgian endive	3 lb 5 oz	1.5 kg
Salt	1/3 oz	10 g
Lemon	1/2	1/2
Veal kidney fat	5 1/3 oz	150 g
Butter	1 oz	30 g
Matignon (Recipe 14)	7 oz	200 g
Vegetable bouillon (Recipe 27)	6 3/4 oz	200 ml
Lemon	1/2	1/2
Seasoning (salt and pepper)	1x	1x
Butter	1 2/3 oz	50 g

542

 raised Green Beans

Geschmorte grüne Bohnen
Haricots verts braisés

YIELD: 10 SERVINGS

Green beans, fresh	3 lb 5 oz	1.5 kg
Salt	2/3 oz	20 g
Slab bacon, smoked	3 1/2 oz	100 g
Onions	3 1/2 oz	100 g
Butter	3 oz	80 g
Seasoning (salt and pepper)	1x	1x
Savory, fresh, twig	1/3 oz	10 g
Bouillon (Recipe 22)	10 oz	300 ml

MISE EN PLACE
Wash and trim beans. If beans are large, break in half.

Blanch in salted water and drain.

Cut bacon into small dice.

Peel and chop onions.

METHOD

Sauté bacon and onions in butter.

Add green beans, season with salt and pepper, and sauté briefly.

Add savory and bouillon, cover, and braise in oven until beans are tender.

Remove savory. Remove beans with skimmer.

Reduce stock to a syrupy consistency. Pour over beans.

543

 raised Red Cabbage

Geschmortes Rotkraut
Chou rouge braisé

YIELD: 10 SERVINGS

Red cabbage	3 lb 5 oz	1.5 kg
Apples	5 1/3 oz	150 g
Red wine	10 oz	300 ml
Onions	5 1/3 oz	150 g
Sachet bag	1	1
Bacon rind (skin)	3 1/2 oz	100 g
Vegetable shortening	1 2/3 oz	50 g
Red wine vinegar	1 oz	30 ml
Bouillon (Recipe 22)	1 pt 11 oz	800 ml
Vialone rice[a]	1 oz	30 g
Red currant jelly	1 oz	30 g
Seasoning (salt and pepper)	1x	1x

MISE EN PLACE

Trim cabbage, cut into quarters, and remove core. Cut cabbage into thin slices on a slicer or with a mandolin.

Peel apples, core, and cut into thin slices.

Combine cabbage and apples and marinate in red wine for a few hours.

Peel and slice onions.

Make sachet bag with bay leaf, cloves, juniper berries, and peppercorns.

METHOD

Sauté onions and bacon rind in shortening.

Add marinated cabbage and apples.

---

[a] The recipe specifies Vialone rice which is a short-grain rice similar to Arborio; Arborio rice can be substituted. The rice should be sticky.

Add red wine vinegar, bouillon, sachet bag, and rice.

Cover and braise until cabbage is tender.

Remove sachet bag and bacon rind.

Add red currant jelly and season to taste with salt and pepper.

NOTE: Instead of rice, the red cabbage can be thickened with potato.

544

$\mathcal{B}$raised Fennel (anise) with Beef Marrow

Geschmorter Fenchel mit Mark
Fenouil braisé à la moelle

YIELD: 10 SERVINGS

Fennel bulb (anise)	3 lb 8 oz	1.6 kg
Salt	2/3 oz	20 g
Marrow bones[a]	14 1/4 oz	400 g
Butter	2/3 oz	20 g
Matignon (Recipe 14)	7 oz	200 g
Bacon rinds (skins) and trimmings	1 2/3 oz	50 g
Seasoning (salt and pepper)	1x	1x
Bouillon (Recipe 22)	1 qt 2 oz	1.0 L
SAUCE		
Shallots	1 1/3 oz	40 g
Red wine	8 1/2 oz	250 ml
Peppercorns, black	5	5
Bay leaf	1/4	1/4
Thyme twig, fresh	1/2	1/2
Seasoning (pepper)	1x	1x
Butter, cold	2/3 oz	20 g

MISE EN PLACE

Wash and trim fennel bulbs, make incision on stem ends, and cut large bulbs in half. Blanch fennel in salted water.

Remove marrow from bones; slice or dice marrow; and soak in cold water.

METHOD

Butter suitable shallow saucepan.

Add *matignon* and bacon rinds and trimmings. Smother lightly.

(continued on next page)

---

[a] Marrow bones should be cut into 2-in. (500 mm) slices, so the marrow can be pushed out easily.

(continued from preceding page)

Place fennel bulbs on top. Season to taste with salt and pepper.

Add bouillon. It should cover about two-thirds of the fennel.

Cover with buttered aluminum foil. Put weight on top to prevent fennel bulb from floating. Bring to a boil.

Cover and braise in oven at 325°F (165°C) until fennel is tender. Keep fennel warm in stock.

METHOD FOR SAUCE
Peel and chop shallots.

Combine shallots with red wine, peppercorns, bay leaf, thyme, and pepper. Bring to a boil and reduce.

Drain off 1 pt 4 oz (600 ml) of the fennel stock and add to shallot/spice mixture. Simmer for about 5 minutes.

Strain stock through a fine mesh wire china cap. Adjust seasoning.

Add cold butter in small nuggets. Do not allow the sauce to return to a boil.

With a perforated ladle, dip marrow in hot water to poach. Add marrow to the sauce.

Cover fennel with sauce and serve at once.

545

*B*raised **Romaine Lettuce with Bacon**

Geschmorter Lattich mit Speck
Laitue romaine braisé au lard

YIELD: 10 SERVINGS

Romaine lettuce	*3 lb 8 oz*	*1.6 kg*
Salt	*2/3 oz*	*20 g*
Butter	*2/3 oz*	*20 g*
Matignon (Recipe 14)	*7 oz*	*200 g*
Bacon, smoked, sliced	*7 oz*	*200 g*
Seasoning (salt and pepper)	*1x*	*1x*
Bouillon (Recipe 22)	*10 oz*	*300 ml*

MISE EN PLACE
Trim and wash lettuce. Blanch in salted water, drain, and cool.

METHOD
Butter a shallow pan.

Add *matignon* and sliced bacon.

Place lettuce on top, season with salt and pepper, and add bouillon.

Cover with buttered aluminum foil. Place weight on top to prevent lettuce from floating. Bring to a boil on top of stove.

Cover and braise in oven at 325°F (165°C) until lettuce is tender.

Remove lettuce and let cool.

Remove bacon and cut into strips.

Reduce braising liquid.

Trim and portion lettuce into 10 even-sized packages and keep warm.

Pour reduced braising liquid over lettuce packages. Sprinkle with bacon.

546

raised **Cabbage**

Geschmorter Weisskohl
Chou blanc braisé

YIELD: 10 SERVINGS

Cabbage	*3 lb 8 oz*	*1.6 kg*
Vegetable shortening	*1 2/3 oz*	*50 g*
Onions	*5 1/3 oz*	*150 g*
Bacon rind (skin)	*3 1/2 oz*	*100 g*
Bouillon (Recipe 22)	*1 pt 11 oz*	*800 ml*
Sachet bag	*1*	*1*
Seasoning (salt and pepper)	*1x*	*1x*

MISE EN PLACE
Trim cabbage, cut into quarters, and remove core. Cut cabbage into thin slices.[a]

Make sachet bag with bay leaf, clove, lovage, and caraway seeds.

Peel and chop onions.

METHOD
Sauté onions and bacon rind in shortening.

Add cabbage and continue cooking.

Add bouillon and sachet bag. Cover and braise in oven. Add more bouillon if necessary. Remove bacon rind and sachet bag.

Season with salt and pepper.

NOTE: The same method can be used for other vegetables in the cabbage family. Caraway seeds are often used alone as seasoning, in place of the sachet bag.

---

[a] The cabbage can be cut on a slicer, or manually with a mandolin.

547

$\mathcal{G}$lazed Carrots
Glasierte Karotten
Carottes glacées

YIELD: 10 SERVINGS

Carrots	4 lb	1.8 kg
Butter	1 1/3 oz	40 g
Sugar	1x	1x
Water or bouillon (Recipe 22)	1 pt 1 oz	500 ml
Salt	1/3 oz	10 g

MISE EN PLACE
Wash and peel carrots. Cut into small sticks or small barrel shapes.

Blanch carrots if very large (or they will be tough).

METHOD
Butter shallow saucepan (*sauteuse*).

Add carrots and sugar. Smother carrots lightly.

Add water or bouillon to barely cover carrots.

Season with salt, cover, and braise until carrots are tender.

Remove lid and reduce liquid rapidly to a syrupy consistency.

Toss carrots in syrup to glaze.

548

$\mathcal{G}$lazed Chestnuts
Glasierte Kastanien
Marrons glacés

YIELD: 10 SERVINGS

Crystal sugar	3 oz	80 g
Vegetable bouillon (Recipe 27)	10 oz	300 ml
Chestnuts, whole, peeled, frozen	2 lb 3 oz	1.0 kg
Butter	1 oz	30 g

METHOD
Melt sugar (caramelize) until light brown.

Carefully add vegetable stock and bring to a boil.

Add chestnuts and butter.

Cover and cook until liquid is reduced to a syrupy consistency.

Turn chestnuts carefully in syrup to glaze evenly.

NOTE: If fresh chestnuts are used, they must be peeled first. To peel nuts, make small incisions with a sharp knife on the round sides of the nuts. Place nuts with a small amount of water on a sheet pan and bake in the oven for 10 minutes.

549

$\mathcal{G}$lazed Pearl Onions
Glasierte Perlzwiebeln
Petits oignons glacés

YIELD: 10 SERVINGS

Pearl onions	2 lb 3 oz	1.0 kg
Butter	2 oz	60 g
Sugar	1x	1x
Seasoning (salt and pepper)	1x	1x
Vegetable bouillon (Recipe 27)	6 3/4 oz	200 ml
Parsley, chopped	1 oz	30 g

MISE EN PLACE
Peel onions,[a] blanch, and drain.

METHOD
Melt butter in a shallow saucepan (*sauteuse*).

Add onions and season with sugar and salt and pepper.

Add vegetable stock. Cover and braise until onions are tender.

Remove onions with skimmer.

Reduce stock to a syrupy consistency.

Add onions and toss in syrup to glaze evenly.

Serve sprinkled with parsley.

---

[a] Pearl onions peel more easily in hot water.

550

aked Belgian Endive

Gratinierte Brüsseler Endivien
Endives gratinées

YIELD: 10 SERVINGS

Belgian endive	3 lb 5 oz	1.5 kg
Onions	5 1/3 oz	150 g
Veal kidney fat	5 1/3 oz	150 g
Ham, boiled	7 oz	200 g
Clarified butter	1 2/3 oz	50 g
Vegetable bouillon (Recipe 27)	8 1/2 oz	250 ml
Seasoning (salt and pepper)	1x	1x
Lemon juice	1/3 oz	10 ml
Bechamel sauce (Recipe 34)	10 oz	300 ml
Heavy cream (36%)	3 1/3 oz	100 ml
Sbrinz, grated[a]	3 1/2 oz	100 g
Butter, melted	1 2/3 oz	50 g

MISE EN PLACE
Wash endives; trim if necessary. With a pointed knife, remove the bitter core. Be sure endive leaves do not separate.

Blanch endives in salt and lemon water, drain, and chill immediately.

Peel and chop onions.

Chop veal kidney fat coarsely.

Cut ham into 10 slices.

METHOD
Smother onions in kidney fat and clarified butter in a saucepan (*sauteuse*).

Place endives on top. Add vegetable stock. It should reach to about two-thirds the height of the vegetables.

Season with salt and pepper; and sprinkle with lemon juice.

Cover with buttered aluminum foil. Place a weight on top to prevent endives from floating. Bring to a boil on top of stove.

Braise in oven at 325°F (165°C) until endives are tender.

Remove endives from braising stock; reserve braising stock and let endives cool.

Wrap each endive in a ham slice.

Strain and reduce braising stock, stir in *Bechamel*, and bring to a boil.

Place endives in a buttered ovenproof dish (*gratin* dish).

Mix sauce with heavy cream and half the grated cheese.

Cover endives with sauce, sprinkle with remaining cheese, and drizzle with melted butter.

Bake in hot oven until heated and brown on top.

NOTE: The veal kidney fat adds flavor, but may be eliminated if there are dietary concerns.

551

Cauliflower au Gratin

Gratinierter Blumenkohl
Chou-fleur Mornay

YIELD: 10 SERVINGS

Cauliflower, fresh	3 lb 8 oz	1.6 kg
Salt	1/3 oz	10 g
Butter	1/3 oz	10 g
Bechamel sauce (Recipe 34)	1 pt 11 oz	800 ml
Heavy cream (36%)	3 1/3 oz	100 ml
Egg yolks	4	4
Sbrinz,[a] grated	3 1/2 oz	100 g
Seasoning (salt and pepper)	1x	1x
Butter	1 2/3 oz	50 g

MISE EN PLACE
Wash and trim cauliflower. Divide into small rosettes.

Boil in salted water or steam. Drain well.

Butter ovenproof serving dish (*gratin* platter).

METHOD
Bring *bechamel* sauce to a boil.

Mix heavy cream with egg yolks and half the grated cheese.

Add to *bechamel* sauce and stir well; do not allow sauce to return to a boil.

Adjust seasoning.

Place cauliflower in gratin dish.

Cover with sauce, sprinkle with remaining cheese, and drizzle with melted butter.

Bake until hot and brown. (Finish under broiler or salamander if desired.)

NOTE: If cauliflower is steamed, salt is not necessary.

---

[a] Sbrinz is a hard grating cheese from Switzerland. Parmesan can be substituted.

[a] Sbrinz is a hard grating cheese from Switzerland. Parmesan cheese can be substituted.

552

$\mathcal{L}$eeks au Gratin

Gratinierter Lauch
Gratin de poireaux

YIELD: 10 SERVINGS

Leeks, white part only	3 lb 8 oz	1.6 kg
Seasoning (salt and pepper)	1x	1x
Butter	3 oz	80 g
Sbrinz,[a] grated	3 1/2 oz	100 g

MISE EN PLACE
Trim leeks and split in half. Wash out sand between layers.

Tie into bundles.

METHOD
Steam, boil, or braise leeks.

Remove twine and trim leeks into portion-size lengths.

Butter suitable ovenproof dish (*gratin* dish) with some of the butter.

Place leeks in dish, season with salt and pepper, and sprinkle with cheese and remaining butter.

Bake in oven until hot and brown.

NOTE: Instead of cheese and butter, the leeks can be topped with Mornay Sauce (Recipe 75).

553

$\mathcal{C}$ucumbers in Cream Sauce with Dill

Gurken in Rahmsauce
Concombres à la crème

YIELD: 10 SERVINGS

Cucumbers	3 lb 8 oz	1.6 kg
Dill, fresh	2/3 oz	20 g
Butter	1 2/3 oz	50 g
Seasoning (salt and pepper)	1x	1x
Sugar	1x	1x
Bechamel sauce (Recipe 34)	8 1/2 oz	250 ml
Heavy cream (36%)	3 1/3 oz	100 ml

MISE EN PLACE
Wash cucumbers; peel if desired. Split in half lengthwise and remove seeds. Cut into small sticks or barrel shapes.

Wash dill and chop leaves.

METHOD
Braise cucumbers, in a covered pot, with butter, salt and pepper, and sugar.

Remove lid and reduce braising liquid.

Add *bechamel* sauce and heavy cream. Bring to a boil.

Sprinkle with dill.

NOTE: Cucumbers can also be steamed, seasoned, and then mixed with the cream sauce.

554

$\mathcal{S}$mall Peas with Lettuce and Pearl Onions

Junge Erbsen Französische Art
Petits pois à la française

YIELD: 10 SERVINGS

Small peas, frozen	2 lb 3 oz	1.0 kg
Pearl onions	10 1/2 oz	300 g
Head lettuce	1/2	1/2
Butter	3 oz	80 g
Seasoning (salt and pepper)	1x	1x
Sugar	1 pinch	
Bouillon (Recipe 22)	6 3/4 oz	200 ml
Cold roux (beurre manie)[a]	2/3 oz	20 g

MISE EN PLACE
Peel pearl onions,[b] boil or steam for 5 minutes. Drain.

Wash lettuce and cut into fine strips (*chiffonade*).

METHOD
Smother peas and pearl onions in butter. Season with salt and pepper and sugar.

Add bouillon, cover, and braise until done.

Thicken with *beurre manie*.

Add lettuce, and bring to a boil.

Remove from heat and serve immediately.

---

[a] Sbrinz is a hard grating cheese from Switzerland. Parmesan can be substituted.

[a] *Beurre manie* is a combination of equal amounts of flour and cold butter. It is added to boiling stock in small, pea-size nuggets.

[b] Pearl onions peel more easily in hot water.

555

*C*ardoons[a] with Toasted Bread Crumbs

Kardy polnische Art
Cardons polonaise

YIELD: 10 SERVINGS

Cardoons	3 lb 8 oz	1.6 kg
Lemon juice	1 oz	30 ml
Veal kidney fat	3 1/2 oz	100 g
Eggs	3	3
Parsley	2/3 oz	20 g
Salt	2/3 oz	20 g
Lemon juice	2 oz	60 ml
White wheat flour	1 2/3 oz	50 g
Butter	3 1/2 oz	100 g
Fresh bread crumbs (mie de pain)[b]	2 2/3 oz	75 g

MISE EN PLACE

Wash cardoons, strip away the tough fibers, and peel with an asparagus or potato peeler.

Put cardoons in lemon water to prevent oxidation.

Chop veal kidney fat coarsely.

Boil eggs, rinse in cold water, peel, and chop.

Wash and chop parsley leaves.

METHOD

Bring to a boil 2 qt 5 oz (2.0 L) water. Add kidney fat, salt, and 2 oz (60 ml) lemon juice.

Make a slurry with flour and small amount of cold water. Pour into boiling water while stirring.

Add cardoons and simmer until tender.

Remove from stock, let cool, and cut into 2-in. (50 mm) lengths.

Heat cardoons and put into suitable serving dish (*gratin* dish).

Sprinkle with chopped eggs and parsley.

Brown the butter in deep iron pan,[c] add *mie de pain*, sauté briefly, and pour over cardoons.

---

[a] The cardoon is a vegetable of the thistle family, related to artichokes, but resembling celery in appearance.

[b] *Mie de pain* are fresh bread crumbs, made from white Pullman loaves.

[c] Be sure pan is deep enough, because the butter will foam when the bread crumbs are added.

556

*S*now Peas

Kefen
Pois mange-tout

YIELD: 10 SERVINGS

Snow peas, fresh	2 lb 14 oz	1.3 kg
Salt	1/3 oz	10 g
Shallots	3 1/2 oz	100 g
Garlic	1/6 oz	5 g
Butter	3 oz	80 g
Seasoning (salt and pepper)	1x	1x
Bouillon (Recipe 22)	6 3/4 oz	200 ml

MISE EN PLACE

Wash snow peas and remove stem ends.

Blanch in salted water, plunge in ice water, and drain.

Peel and chop shallots.

Peel and chop garlic.

METHOD

Sauté shallots briefly in butter.

Add snow peas and garlic. Season to taste.

Add bouillon, cover, and braise briefly. Snow peas should be crisp when served.

NOTES: Snow peas should be served immediately after cooking or they will become limp and will lose color.

If desired, 3 1/2 oz (100 g) bacon, blanched and cut into small dice, can be added when the shallots are sautéed.

557

*K*ohlrabi Sauté

Kohlrabi mit Butter
Choux-raves au beurre

YIELD: 10 SERVINGS

Kohlrabi	4 lb	1.8 kg
Kitchen herbs, fresh	1 oz	30 g
Salt	1/3 oz	10 g
Butter	3 oz	80 g
Seasoning (pepper)	1x	1x

MISE EN PLACE

Remove leaves and stems from kohlrabi. Reserve tender center leaves.

Peel kohlrabi and cut into sticks or barrel shapes.

Wash and chop tiny center leaves and set aside for garnish.

Wash and chop kitchen herbs (such as parsley and chives).

METHOD

Boil kohlrabi in salted water (or steam) until tender and drain thoroughly.

Brown the butter. Toss kohlrabi in the brown butter and season with pepper.

Garnish with chopped center kohlrabi leaves and kitchen herbs.

NOTE: If kohlrabi are steamed, salt is not necessary.

558

Corn on the Cob

Maiskolben
Epis de maïs

YIELD: 10 SERVINGS

Corn on the cob, fresh[a]	10	10
Salt	2/3 oz	20 g
Butter	3 1/2 oz	100 g

MISE EN PLACE

Shuck corn, remove silks and stems.

Method

Boil in salted[b] water or steam.

Drain and serve with hot butter.

---

[a] Corn loses quality rapidly. It is best eaten the same day it is picked.

[b] Many chefs choose to eliminate the salt when cooking corn.

559

Corn Sauté

Maiskörner mit Butter
Grains de maïs au beurre

YIELD: 10 SERVINGS

Corn kernels, canned, drained	2 lb 3 oz	1.0 kg
Butter	3 oz	80 g
Seasoning (salt and pepper)	1x	1x
Sugar	1x	1x

METHOD

Wash and drain corn.

Sauté in butter and season to taste.

NOTES: Frozen corn can be used, but it should be braised for a few minutes.

Corn can also be blended with cream sauce (Recipe 40).

560

Okra with Tomatoes

Okra mit Tomaten
Gombos aux tomates

YIELD: 10 SERVINGS

Okra, fresh	3 lb 5 oz	1.5 kg
Salt	1/3 oz	10 g
Shallots	3 1/2 oz	100 g
Garlic	1/3 oz	10 g
Parsley	2/3 oz	20 g
Butter	1 2/3 oz	50 g
Seasoning (salt and pepper)	1x	1x
Fresh stewed tomatoes (Recipe 535)	6 3/4 oz	200 ml

MISE EN PLACE

Wash okra. Remove stems, but do not cut okra open.

Blanch okra in salted water and drain.

Peel and chop shallots and garlic.

Wash and chop parsley.

METHOD

Sauté shallots and garlic in butter.

Add okra, season with salt and pepper, cover, and braise. Add small amount of Bouillon (Recipe 22) if necessary.

Add stewed tomatoes and heat briefly.

Sprinkle with parsley.

561

Fried Knob Celery with Pepper Coulis

Panierter Knollensellerie au Peperoni-Coulis
Céleri-rave pané sur coulis de poivrons

YIELD: 10 SERVINGS

Knob celery (celeriac)	3 lb 5 oz	1.5 kg
Lemon	1/2	1/2
Salt	1/3 oz	10 g
Lemon	1/2	1/2
Eggs	3	3
White wheat flour	1 2/3 oz	50 g
Seasoning (salt and pepper)	1x	1x
Bread crumbs	5 1/3 oz	150 g
Clarified butter	3 1/2 oz	100 g
Butter	1 2/3 oz	50 g

PEPPER COULIS

Yellow peppers	9 oz	250 g
Red peppers	9 oz	250 g
Shallots	3 oz	80 g
Garlic	2/3 oz	20 g
Olive oil	2 oz	60 ml
Seasoning (salt and pepper)	1x	1x

MISE EN PLACE FOR CELERY
Wash and peel knob celery. Cut into halves or quarters. Place in lemon water while you work to prevent discoloration.

Cut into 1/2-in. (12 mm) slices.

Boil in salt and lemon water. Do not overcook; the slices should be firm. Drain thoroughly and spread out to cool and dry.

Break eggs and mix with small amount of water.

Season flour with salt and pepper.

Dredge knob celery slices, first in flour, then in eggs, and then in bread crumbs.

METHOD FOR PEPPER COULIS
Split peppers in half, remove seeds, and wash. Cut peppers[a] into small dice, keeping the two colors separate.

Peel and chop shallots and garlic.

Braise each pepper color separately in olive oil, with half the shallots and garlic.

Purée each pepper color separately in food processor, season to taste, and keep warm.

---

[a] The peppers are best peeled.

METHOD
Sauté knob celery slices in clarified butter and fresh butter.

Drain knob celery slices on absorbent paper.

Arrange the two pepper coulis on plates and place the celery slices on top.

562

Ratatouille

Ratatouille
Ratatouille

YIELD: 10 SERVINGS

Onions	5 1/3 oz	150 g
Garlic	1/3 oz	10 g
Bell peppers, assorted	1 lb 5 1/2 oz	600 g
Eggplants	1 lb 2 oz	500 g
Zucchini	1 lb 2 oz	500 g
Marjoram twig, fresh	1	10 g
Thyme twig, fresh	1	10 g
Basil, fresh	2/3 oz	20 g
Olive oil, cold pressed	3 1/3 oz	100 ml
Seasoning (salt and pepper)	1x	1x
Stewed tomatoes, fresh (Recipe 535)	10 oz	300 ml

MISE EN PLACE
Peel and chop onions and garlic.

Cut peppers in half, remove seeds, and wash. Cut peppers into dice.

Trim and wash eggplants and zucchini and cut into dice.

Wash marjoram and thyme and chop leaves.

Wash basil and chop leaves.

METHOD
Sauté onions, garlic, and diced peppers in olive oil.

Add eggplant and zucchini, marjoram, and thyme, and salt and pepper. Cover and braise. (Vegetables should contain sufficient moisture to braise without adding liquid.)

When vegetables are tender, add stewed tomatoes and basil. Heat and serve.

563

Braised Sauerkraut

Sauerkraut
Choucroute

YIELD: 10 SERVINGS

Onions	5 1/3 oz	150 g
Potatoes	5 1/3 oz	150 g
Sachet bag	1	1
Bacon rinds (skins)	7 oz	200 g
Vegetable shortening	3 oz	80 g
Sauerkraut[a]	3 lb 5 oz	1.5 kg
Dry white wine	6 3/4 oz	200 ml
Bouillon (Recipe 22)	1 qt 2 oz	1.0 L
Dry white wine	3 1/3 oz	100 ml
Seasoning (salt and pepper)	1x	1x

MISE EN PLACE
Peel and chop onions.

Peel potatoes.

Make a sachet bag with juniper berries, mustard seeds, coriander seeds, peppercorns, and bay leaf.

METHOD
Sauté onions and bacon rind in vegetable shortening.

Add sauerkraut, 6 3/4 oz (200 ml) white wine, bouillon, and sachet bag.

Bring to a boil, cover, and braise in oven for 1 hour.

Grate potatoes and mix with remaining 3 1/3 oz (100 ml) white wine.

Add potato mixture to sauerkraut to thicken it.

Continue cooking for 30 minutes.

Remove sachet bag; season with salt and pepper; and serve.

NOTES: To preserve nutritional value, the sauerkraut should not be washed, and should be braised only a short time.

If cured or smoked meat is served with the sauerkraut, it should be boiled separately, and the resulting stock used instead of bouillon.

564

Eggplant Slices Sautéed with Egg Batter

Sautierte Auberginen im Ei mit Kräutern
Aubergines romaine aux herbs

YIELD: 10 SERVINGS

Kitchen herbs, fresh (chervil, thyme and marjoram)	1 oz	30 g
Eggplants	3 lb 5 oz	1.5 kg
Lemon, juice	1/2	1/2
Seasoning (salt and pepper)	1x	1x
Eggs	3	3
White wheat flour	1 2/3 oz	50 g
Clarified butter	3 oz	80 g
Butter	1 2/3 oz	50 g
Parsley, sprigs	1 1/3 oz	40 g

MISE EN PLACE
Wash and chop herbs.

Wash and trim eggplants.

Cut eggplants into 1/3-in. (8 mm) thick slices.

Marinate slices with lemon juice, salt and pepper, and half the amount of chopped herbs.

Beat eggs and mix with small amount of cold water.

METHOD
Drain eggplant and remove moisture with absorbent paper towel.

Dust eggplant with flour, dredge in egg mixture, and sauté in clarified butter until golden brown on both sides.

Add fresh butter to pan, brown the butter, and add remaining herbs. Pour foaming butter over eggplants.

Garnish eggplant with parsley sprigs.

[a] In Switzerland sauerkraut is commonly sold raw (fresh).

565

Sautéed Morels

Sautierte Morcheln
Morilles sautées

YIELD: 10 SERVINGS

Morels, fresh	1 lb 5 oz	600 g
Shallots	1 2/3 oz	50 g
Butter	3 oz	80 g
Seasoning (salt and pepper)	1x	1x
Parsley	2/3 oz	20 g

MISE EN PLACE
Trim morels and split or quarter, depending on size.

Wash thoroughly.

Blanch morels and drain.

Peel and chop shallots.

Wash and chop parsley leaves.

METHOD
Sauté shallots in butter, add morels, season with salt and pepper, and sauté.

Sprinkle with chopped parsley.

NOTE: Fresh morels must always be blanched and the water discarded.

566

Sautéed Red Pepper Quarters

Sautierte Peperoni Viertel
Quartiers de poivrons sautés

YIELD: 10 SERVINGS

Red peppers	3 lb 5 oz	1.5 kg
Oil for frying(10% oil loss)	4 oz	120 ml
Shallots	3 oz	80 g
Garlic	2/3 oz	20 g
Olive oil	1 1/3 oz	40 ml
Seasoning (salt and pepper)	1x	1x
Sugar	1x	1x

MISE EN PLACE
Wash and dry red peppers.

Dip in hot fat in deep fat fryer until skin starts to blister.

Put in a bowl and cover. The developing steam will soften the peppers.

Wash and peel red peppers in warm water.

Split in half and remove seeds; cut each half into quarters.

Peel and chop shallots and garlic.

METHOD
Sauté shallots and garlic in olive oil.

Add peppers and sauté carefully until peppers are cooked.

Season with salt and pepper and sugar.

567

Sautéed Brussels Sprouts

Sautierter Rosenkohl
Choux de Bruxelles sautés

YIELD: 10 SERVINGS

Brussels sprouts	3 lb 8 oz	1.6 kg
Salt	1/3 oz	10 g
Shallots	2 2/3 oz	75 g
Garlic	1/6 oz	5 g
Butter	3 oz	80 g
Seasoning (salt and pepper)	1x	1x

MISE EN PLACE
Wash and trim Brussels sprouts.

Boil in salted water (or steam) until almost done. Drain.

Peel and chop shallots.

Peel and chop garlic.

METHOD
Sauté shallots in butter.

Add Brussels sprouts and garlic, season with salt and pepper, and sauté until hot and blended.

NOTES: Diced, cooked ham or blanched bacon can be added if desired.

If the Brussels sprouts are steamed, salt is not needed.

568

$\mathcal{W}$hite Asparagus with Parmesan Cheese

Spargeln Mailänder Art
Asperges milanaise

YIELD: 10 SERVINGS (APPETIZER SIZE)

White asparagus[a]	11 lb	5.0 kg
Salt	2/3 oz	20 g
Sugar	1x	1x
Parmesan cheese, grated	7 oz	200 g
Butter	3 1/2 oz	100 g

MISE EN PLACE
Wash asparagus and peel carefully. Tie with kitchen twine into 10 bundles.

Cut off dry and tough ends and trim asparagus to equal lengths.

METHOD
Boil asparagus until tender in salted water, with a pinch of sugar, for about 20 minutes. Do not overcook asparagus; check frequently. (Asparagus can also be steamed.)

Drain and place hot asparagus on serving dishes. Remove strings from bundles.

Sprinkle with Parmesan and melted butter.

569

$\mathcal{C}$reamed Spinach

Spinat in Rahmsauce
Epinards à la crème

YIELD: 10 SERVINGS

Spinach, fresh	4 lb 7 oz	2.0 kg
Salt	2/3 oz	20 g
Shallots	3 1/2 oz	100 g
Garlic	1/6 oz	5 g
Bechamel sauce (Recipe 34)	6 3/4 oz	200 ml
Butter	1 2/3 oz	50 g
Heavy cream (36%)	3 1/3 oz	100 ml
Seasoning (salt and pepper)	1x	1x

MISE EN PLACE
Trim spinach and rinse several times to remove all sand.

Blanch spinach in salt water, drain, chill, and drain again.

Squeeze out excess water. Grind, puree, or chop spinach.

Peel and chop shallots and garlic.

Heat *bechamel* sauce.

METHOD
Sauté shallots and garlic in butter.

Add spinach and heat.

Add *bechamel* sauce to spinach mixture and heat thoroughly.

Add heavy cream and season to taste with salt and pepper.

570

$\mathcal{S}$tuffed Tomatoes Provençale

Tomaten provenzalischer Art
Tomates farcies provençale

YIELD: 10 SERVINGS (2 PIECES PER PERSON)

Tomatoes, 10	2 lb 10 oz	1.2 kg
Butter	2/3 oz	20 g
Seasoning (salt and pepper)	1x	1x

STUFFING

Anchovy fillets, canned, drained	2/3 oz	20 g
Parsley	1 oz	30 g
Thyme, fresh	1/3 oz	10 g
Oregano, fresh	1/3 oz	10 g
Onions	3 1/2 oz	100 g
Garlic	1/3 oz	10 g
Olive oil, cold pressed	3 1/3 oz	100 ml
Fresh bread crumbs (mie de pain)	5 1/3 oz	150 g
Seasoning (salt and pepper)	1x	1x
Sbrinz,[a] grated	1 2/3 oz	50 g
Butter, melted	1 2/3 oz	50 g

MISE EN PLACE
Wash tomatoes, remove stem ends, and cut in half horizontally.

Carefully scoop out seeds.

Butter suitable ovenproof service platter (*gratin* dish).

(continued on next page)

---

[a] Green asparagus can be substituted, but cooking time should be reduced to 7 to 10 minutes.

[a] Sbrinz is a hard grating cheese from Switzerland. Parmesan can be substituted.

(continued from preceding page)

Season tomatoes with salt and pepper and arrange in dish, cut-side up.

METHOD FOR STUFFING

Chop anchovy fillets.

Wash parsley, thyme, and oregano and chop leaves.

Peel and chop onions and garlic and sauté in olive oil.

Add chopped anchovies, herbs, and bread crumbs. Season to taste.

METHOD

Fill tomato halves with stuffing. Sprinkle with cheese and melted butter.

Bake until brown, but do not overcook. The tomatoes should still hold their shape.

571

Jerusalem Artichokes

Topinambur
Topinambours

YIELD: 10 SERVINGS

Jerusalem artichokes	4 lb 7 oz	2.0 kg
Kitchen herbs, fresh	1/3 oz	10 g
Salt	1/3 oz	10 g
Butter	3 1/2 oz	100 g
Seasoning (salt and pepper)	1x	1x

METHOD

Clean Jerusalem artichokes thoroughly with a brush. Peel; remove dirt in crevices with a scraper. Cut Jerusalem artichokes into slices.

Wash kitchen herbs (such as parsley, tarragon, chives, and chervil) and chop leaves.

METHOD

Boil Jerusalem artichokes in salted water, or steam, until tender.

Drain and sauté with butter and herbs. Season to taste with salt and pepper.

NOTE: Jerusalem artichokes can also be blended with *Bechamel* Sauce (Recipe 34) or blended with heavy cream, sprinkled with cheese, and browned.

572

Braised Sliced Carrots

Vichy-Karotten
Carottes Vichy

YIELD: 10 SERVINGS

Carrots	2 lb 10 oz	1.2 kg
Shallots	1 2/3 oz	50 g
Parsley	2/3 oz	20 g
Butter	1 2/3 oz	50 g
Seasoning (salt and pepper)	1x	1x
Sugar	1x	1x
Vichy[a] water	1 pt 1 oz	500 ml

MISE EN PLACE

Trim, peel, and wash carrots. Cut carrots into 1/10-in. (12 mm) slices.

Peel and chop shallots.

Wash parsley and chop leaves.

METHOD

Sauté shallots in butter. Add carrots and season with salt and pepper and sugar.

Fill pot with water until carrots are just about covered.

Cover pot and braise until carrots are tender.

Serve sprinkled with parsley.

---

[a] Vichy is a mineral water spa in southwest France. Plain water or Vegetable Bouillon (Recipe 27) can be substituted.

573

*Z*ucchini Provençale

Zuchetti provenzalischer Art
Courgettes provençale

YIELD: 10 SERVINGS

Zucchini	2 lb 14 oz	1.3 kg
Onions	1 2/3 oz	50 g
Garlic	1/6 oz	5 g
Thyme, fresh	1/3 oz	10 g
Oregano, fresh	1/3 oz	10 g
Rosemary, fresh	1/6 oz	5 g
Sage, fresh	1/6 oz	5 g
Olive oil, cold pressed	1 1/3 oz	40 ml
Vegetable bouillon (Recipe 27)	3 1/3 oz	100 ml
Seasoning (salt and pepper)	1x	1x

MISE EN PLACE

Wash and trim zucchini and cut into sticks or barrel shapes.

Peel and chop onions and garlic.

Wash thyme, oregano, rosemary, and sage and chop leaves.

METHOD

Sauté onions and garlic in olive oil.

Add zucchini and sauté briefly. Add vegetable stock.

Cover and braise until zucchini are tender, but still firm.

Remove zucchini with skimmer.

Remove pot lid and reduce cooking liquid rapidly.

Return zucchini to reduced liquid and heat.

Add chopped herbs and season to taste.

NOTE: If zucchini are cut into barrel shapes, there will be more waste, so about 3 lb 8 oz (1.6 kg) will be needed.

10

Potatoes, Pasta, Rice,
and Grains

Potato Dishes

Oven-Roasted Potatoes with Onions

Bäckerinkartoffeln
Pommes boulangère

YIELD: 10 SERVINGS

Potatoes	3 lb 5 oz	1.5 kg
Salt	2/3 oz	20 g
Onions	10 1/2 oz	300 g
Parsley	2/3 oz	20 g
Peanut oil	3 1/3 oz	100 ml
Seasoning (salt and pepper)	1x	1x
Butter	1 2/3 oz	50 g

MISE EN PLACE
Wash and peel potatoes. Cut into 1/10-in. (25 mm) slices.

Bring ample amount of salted water to a boil. Add potatoes and blanch.

Drain and spread out on sheet pan to cool quickly and to prevent further cooking.

Peel and slice onions.

Wash parsley and chop leaves.

METHOD
Heat peanut oil in roasting pan. Add potatoes, season with salt and pepper, and start browning on top of stove.

Continue roasting in oven, turning potatoes occasionally.

Drain off excess oil and brown the sliced onions in this oil.

Combine onions with potatoes and add butter.

Continue roasting briefly, turning potatoes to blend with onions.

Sprinkle with chopped parsley leaves.

Rösti Potatoes[a]

Berner Rösti
Pommes bernoise

YIELD: 10 SERVINGS

Potatoes, boiled in their skins	3 lb 5 oz	1.5 kg
Onions	5 1/3 oz	150 g
Slab bacon, smoked (unsliced)	3 1/2 oz	100 g
Clarified butter	5 1/3 oz	150 g
Seasoning (salt and pepper)	1x	1x

MISE EN PLACE
Peel potatoes and shred coarsely.[b]

Peel and chop onions fine.

Cut bacon into small dice.

METHOD
Sauté onions and bacon in clarified butter, in a well-seasoned cast iron skillet.

Add potatoes. Season to taste with salt and pepper.

Sauté and turn potatoes until heated; then flatten potatoes like a pancake.

Brown and crisp the bottom, then turn potato pancake over in one piece and brown on the other side.

Slide potato cake onto a warm platter, or cut into wedges for individual portions.

NOTE: Potatoes are best if boiled the day before; this will keep them from sticking together when grated.

---

[a] Also see Rösti Potatoes made with raw potatoes Recipe 616.

[b] In Switzerland, a special grater is used to tear the potatoes into long shreds.

576

*P*ear-Shaped Potato Croquettes

Birnenkartoffeln
Pommes Williams

YIELD: 10 SERVINGS

Potatoes, russet type	3 lb 5 oz	1.5 kg
Salt (optional)	1/3 oz	10 g
Egg yolks	3	3
Seasoning (salt, nutmeg)	1x	1x
Eggs	2	2
White wheat flour	1 2/3 oz	50 g
Bread crumbs, fine[a]	3 1/2 oz	100 g
Almond slivers or spaghetti	2/3 oz	20 g
Oil for frying (10% oil loss)	5 oz	150 ml

MISE EN PLACE
Wash and peel potatoes and cut into even-sized chunks.

Steam potatoes or cook in lightly salted water and drain well.

When cooked, dry potatoes briefly in the oven.

Pass potatoes through a wire sieve or ricer.[b]

METHOD
Add egg yolks to potatoes and season to taste with salt and nutmeg.

Mold the potato mixture into small, pear-shaped croquettes.

Break whole eggs and mix with small amount of water.

Dredge croquettes first in flour, then in egg mixture, and then in bread crumbs. Shake off excess crumbs and pat crumbs to croquettes. Remold croquettes into pearshapes, if necessary.

Insert an almond sliver, or small spaghetti piece, into tops of croquettes to imitate the pear stem.

Deep-fry at 350°F (175°C) until golden brown.

Drain on absorbent paper and serve on a paper doily, or use as a garnish with meat.

---

[a] Use more bread crumbs as needed. Bread crumbs can be dry or fresh, but must be finely grated.

[b] Potatoes should not be puréed in a food processor, or will become gummy.

577

*B*ouillon Potatoes

Bouillonkartoffeln
Pommes au bouillon

YIELD: 10 SERVINGS

Potatoes	3 lb 5 oz	1.5 kg
Salt	2/3 oz	20 g
Parsley	2/3 oz	20 g
Onions	3 1/2 oz	100 g
Diced vegetables[a] (brunoise)	3 1/2 oz	100 g
Butter	2/3 oz	20 g
Bouillon (Recipe 22)	1 qt 2 oz	1.0 L
Seasoning (salt and pepper)	1x	1x

MISE EN PLACE
Wash and peel potatoes. Cut into medium-size cubes or slices.

Blanch potatoes in salted water, drain, and spread out to cool quickly and to prevent further cooking.

Wash parsley and chop leaves.

Peel and chop onions.

METHOD
Sauté onions and vegetables in butter.

Add potatoes and hot bouillon. Bring to a boil and skim.

Cover pot and simmer slowly until potatoes are tender.

Season to taste wih salt and pepper.

Sprinkle with chopped parsley leaves.

---

[a] The vegetables *brunoise* should consist of equal amounts of carrots, celery, and leeks, cut into small dice.

578

Bouillon Potatoes with Paprika

Bouillonkartoffeln mit Paprika
Pommes hongroise

YIELD: 10 SERVINGS

Potatoes	3 lb 5 oz	1.5 kg
Salt	2/3 oz	20 g
Onions	7 oz	200 g
Parsley	2/3 oz	20 g
Butter	2/3 oz	20 g
Paprika	1/2 oz	15 g
Bouillon (Recipe 22)	1 qt 2 oz	1.0 L
Stewed tomatoes, fresh (Recipe 535)	5 oz	150 ml
Seasoning (salt and pepper)	1x	1x

MISE EN PLACE
Wash and peel potatoes. Cut into medium-size cubes or slices.

Blanch potatoes in salted water, drain, and spread out to cool quickly and to prevent further cooking.

Peel and chop onions.

Wash parsley and chop leaves.

METHOD
Sauté onions in butter; add potatoes and paprika.

Add hot bouillon, bring to a boil, and skim.

Cover pot and simmer slowly until potatoes are tender.

Add stewed tomatoes and simmer together for a few minutes.

Season to taste with salt and pepper and sprinkle with chopped parsley leaves.

579

Oven-Roasted Potatoes

Bratkartoffeln
Pommes rissolées

YIELD: 10 SERVINGS

Potatoes	3 lb 5 oz	1.5 kg
Salt	2/3 oz	20 g
Peanut oil	1 pt 11 oz	800 ml
Seasoning (salt and pepper)	1x	1x
Butter	1 oz	30 g

MISE EN PLACE
Choose large potatoes.

Wash and peel potatoes and cut into 1/2-in. (12 mm) cubes.

Blanch potatoes in salted water, drain, and spread out to cool quickly and to prevent further cooking.

METHOD
Heat peanut oil in roasting pan, add cubed potatoes, and season with salt and pepper.

Start roasting on top of stove and continue in a hot oven until potatoes are golden brown and cooked. Turn potatoes frequently to achieve even browning.

Pour off oil and replace with butter. Continue roasting potatoes briefly in butter, turning them to coat them evenly.

NOTE: Small potatoes, especially early potatoes, can be roasted whole, with or without skin.

580

Oven-Roasted Potatoes with Parsley and Bread Crumbs

Bröselkartoffeln
Pommes sablées

YIELD: 10 SERVINGS

Potatoes	3 lb 5 oz	1.5 kg
Salt	2/3 oz	20 g
Parsley	1 oz	30 g
Peanut oil	1 pt 11 oz	800 ml
Seasoning (salt and pepper)	1x	1x
Butter	1 oz	30 g
Fresh bread crumbs (mie de pain)[a]	1 2/3 oz	50 g

MISE EN PLACE
Choose large potatoes.

Wash and peel potatoes and cut into 1/2-in. (12 mm) cubes.

Blanch potatoes in salted water, drain, and spread out to cool quickly and to prevent further cooking.

Wash parsley and chop leaves.

METHOD
Heat peanut oil in roasting pan, add potatoes, and season with salt and pepper.

Start roasting on top of stove and continue in a hot oven until potatoes are golden brown and cooked. Turn potatoes frequently to achieve even browning.

Pour off oil and replace with butter. Add bread crumbs. Continue roasting potatoes briefly with butter and bread crumbs, turning potatoes to coat and cook evenly.

Sprinkle with parsley.

581

*P*otato Chips

Chips-Kartoffeln
Pommes chips

YIELD: 10 SERVINGS

Potatoes	3 lb 5 oz	1.5 kg
Oil for frying (10% oil loss)	4 oz	120 ml
Salt	1/3 oz	10 g

MISE EN PLACE
Wash and peel potatoes.

Cut into very thin slices, using an electric slicer or a mandolin.

Wash in cold water to rinse out starch.

Drain and dry thoroughly.

METHOD
Deep-fry potatoes, in small amounts, at 350°F (175°C).

Use fryer basket, and shake while frying, until golden brown and crisp.

Drain on absorbent paper.

Sprinkle with salt.

NOTES: Potato chips can be served hot or cold.

The salt can be seasoned with paprika or curry if desired.

582

*F*ried Potato Puffs

Dauphine-Kartoffeln
Pommes dauphine

YIELD: 10 SERVINGS

Potatoes, russet type	3 lb	1.4 kg
Salt (optional)	1/3 oz	10 g
Parchment paper		
Peanut oil	1 2/3 oz	50 ml
Puff paste (Recipe 678)	14 oz	400 g
Seasoning (salt and nutmeg)	1x	1x
Oil for frying (10% oil loss)	5 oz	150 ml

MISE EN PLACE
Wash and peel potatoes and cut into even-sized chunks.

Steam potatoes or cook in lightly salted water and drain well.

When cooked, dry potatoes briefly in the oven.

Pass potatoes through a wire sieve or ricer.[a]

Cut parchment paper into 2-in (50 mm) wide strips and oil strips lightly.

Blend hot puréed potatoes with puff paste; season to taste with salt and nutmeg.

Shape into oval dumplings, using two tablespoons,[b] and line up dumplings along the parchment paper strips.

METHOD
At service time, heat oil in deep fryer to 350°F (175°C).

Dip paper strips in the hot oil; the potato dumplings will slide off.

Fry dumplings until golden brown and drain on absorbent paper.

Serve on paper doilies, as a side dish or garnish.

NOTE: The paper strips should be long enough for one or two portions. Fry portions to order.

---

[a] Potatoes should not be puréed in a food processor, or they will become gummy.

[b] This process requires practice. An oval shaped ice-cream scoop can be used when large quantities are needed.

583

*D*uchess Potatoes

Duchesse-Kartoffeln
Pommes duchesse

YIELD: 10 SERVINGS

Potatoes	3 lb 5 oz	1.5 kg
Salt (optional)	1/3 oz	10 g
Butter	3/4 oz	25 g
Egg yolks	3	3
Butter	1 oz	30 g
Seasoning (salt and nutmeg)	1x	1x
Egg yolks	2	2
Light cream	1 oz	30 ml

MISE EN PLACE

Wash and peel potatoes and cut into even-sized chunks.

Steam potatoes or cook in lightly salted water and drain well.

When cooked, dry potatoes briefly in the oven.

Pass potatoes through a wire sieve or ricer.[a]

Butter a sheet pan.

METHOD

Blend puréed potatoes with 3 egg yolks and 1 oz (30 g) butter. Season to taste.

Dress portion-size rosettes on sheet pan, using a pastry bag with a star tube.

Mix 2 egg yolks with light cream.

Brush potatoes with egg yolk/cream mixture and bake in hot oven until golden brown.

Serve immediately.

NOTE: The same potato mixture can be used for piped borders or to make potato nests, which can be filled.

584

*F*ried Potato Puffs with Cheese

Fritierte Kartoffelkrapfen mit Käse
Pommes Lorette

YIELD: 10 SERVINGS

Potatoes, russet type	3 lb	1.4 kg
Salt (optional)	1/3 oz	10 g
Peanut oil	1 2/3 oz	50 ml
Puff paste (Recipe 678)	14 oz	400 g
Sbrinz, grated[a]	3 oz	80 g
Seasoning (salt, nutmeg)	1x	1x
Parchment paper		
Oil for frying (10% oil loss)	5 oz	150 ml

MISE EN PLACE

Wash and peel potatoes and cut into even-sized chunks.

Steam potatoes or cook in lightly salted water and drain well.

When cooked, dry potatoes briefly in the oven.

Pass potatoes through a wire sieve or ricer.[b]

Blend hot puréed potatoes with puff paste and cheese and season to taste with salt and nutmeg.

Cut parchment paper into 2 in. (50 mm) wide strips and oil strips lightly.

Dress portion-size rosettes or rings onto paper strips, using a pastry bag with a star tube.

METHOD

At service time, heat oil in deep fryer to 350°F (175°C).

Dip paper strips in the hot oil; the potato rosettes will slide off.

Fry potatoes until golden brown and drain on absorbent paper.

Serve on paper doilies, as a garnish or a side dish.

NOTE: The paper strips should be long enough for one or two portions. Fry portions to order.

---

[a] Potatoes should not be puréed in a food processor or they will become gummy.

[a] Sbrinz is a hard grating cheese from Switzerland. Parmesan can be substituted.

[b] Potatoes should not be puréed in a food processor or they will become gummy.

585

$\mathscr{F}$ried Potato Balls with Ham

Fritierte Kartoffelkugeln mit Schinken
Pommes Saint-Florentin

YIELD: 10 SERVINGS

Potatoes	3 lb 5 oz	1.5 kg
Salt (optional)	1/3 oz	10 g
Ham, boiled	3 1/2 oz	100 g
Egg yolks	3	3
Seasoning (salt, nutmeg)	1x	1x
Vermicelli noodles, very thin	3 1/2 oz	100 g
Eggs	2	2
White wheat flour	1 2/3 oz	50 g
Oil for frying (10% oil loss)	4 oz	120 ml

MISE EN PLACE

Wash and peel potatoes and cut into even-sized chunks.

Steam potatoes or cook in lightly salted water and drain well.

When cooked, dry potatoes briefly in the oven.

Chop ham, or cut into very fine dice.

Pass potatoes through a wire sieve or ricer.[a]

Blend puréed potatoes, while still hot, with egg yolks and ham. Season to taste with salt and nutmeg.

Crush vermicelli into small pieces with a rolling pin.

METHOD

Shape potato mixture into small balls, about 1 1/4-in. (30 mm) in diameter.

Break eggs and mix with small amount of cold water.

Dredge balls in flour, then in egg mixture, then roll in vermicelli pieces. Press vermicelli into the balls, making sure balls are evenly covered.

Deep-fry at 350°F (175°C) until golden brown.

Drain on absorbent paper.

Serve on paper doilies, as a garnish or a side dish.

[a] Potatoes should not be puréed in a food processor or they will become gummy.

586

$\mathscr{T}$hin French Fries

Fritierte Kartoffelstäbchen
Pommes mignonnettes

YIELD: 10 SERVINGS

Potatoes, russet type	4 lb	1.8 kg
Oil for frying (10% oil loss)	5 oz	150 ml
Salt	1/3 oz	10 g

MISE EN PLACE

Wash and peel potatoes.

Cut into even-sized sticks, about 1/5 in. (5 mm) thick and 1 1/2 in. (40 mm) long.

Soak in cold water for 1 hour. Wash to rinse out starch. Drain well and dry.

METHOD

Fill deep-fryer basket about half full with potatoes and deep-fry potatoes at 265°F (130°C) until they are cooked, but not browned.

Spread out potatoes to cool quickly and to prevent further cooking.

Finish frying potatoes as needed at 350°F (175°C), until brown and crisp.

Drain on absorbent paper and salt lightly.

Serve on paper doilies, as a side dish or garnish.

587

$\mathscr{T}$hick French Fries

Fritierte Kartoffelstäbe
Pommes Pont-neuf

YIELD: 10 SERVINGS

Potatoes, russet type	4 lb	1.8 kg
Oil for frying (10% oil loss)	5 oz	150 ml
Salt	1/3 oz	10 g

MISE EN PLACE

Wash and peel potatoes.

Cut into even-sized sticks, about 3/4 in. (20 mm) thick and 2 1/2 in. (60 mm) long.

Soak in cold water for 1 hour. Wash to rinse out starch. Drain well and dry.

(continued on next page)

(continued from preceding page)

METHOD

Fill deep-fryer basket about half full with potatoes and deep-fry potatoes at 265°F (130°C) until they are cooked, but not browned.

Spread out potatoes to cool quickly and to prevent further cooking.

Finish frying potatoes as needed at 350°F (175°C), until brown and crisp.

Drain on absorbent paper and salt lightly.

Serve on paper doilies, as a side dish or garnish.

588

ꞙried Diced Potatoes

Fritierte Kartoffelwürfel
Pommes bataille

YIELD: 10 SERVINGS

Potatoes, russet type	4 lb	1.8 kg
Oil for frying (10% oil loss)	5 oz	150 ml
Salt	1/3 oz	10 g

MISE EN PLACE

Wash and peel potatoes.

Cut into even-sized cubes, about 1/4-in. (10 mm) square.

Soak in cold water for 1 hour. Wash and rinse out starch. Drain well and dry.

METHOD

Fill deep-fryer basket about half full with potatoes and deep-fry potatoes at 265°F (130°C) until they are cooked, but not browned. Continue until all potatoes are fried.

Spread out potatoes to cool quickly and to prevent further cooking.

Finish frying potatoes as needed at 350°F (175°C), until brown and crisp.

Drain on absorbent paper and salt lightly.

Serve on paper doilies, as a side dish or garnish.

589

ꞙried Potato Croquettes with Almonds and Truffles

Fritierte Mandelkartoffelkugeln
Pommes Berny

YIELD: 10 SERVINGS

Black truffles, canned, drained	1 oz	30 g
Potatoes	3 lb 5 oz	1.5 kg
Salt (optional)	1/3 oz	10 g
Egg yolks	3	3
Seasoning (salt, nutmeg)	1x	1x
Almonds, sliced	3 1/2 oz	100 g
Eggs	2	2
White wheat flour	1 2/3 oz	50 g
Oil for frying (10% oil loss)	5 oz	150 ml

MISE EN PLACE

Chop black truffles.

Wash and peel potatoes and cut into even-sized chunks.

Steam potatoes or cook in lightly salted water and drain well.

When cooked, dry briefly in the oven, and pass through a strainer[a] or ricer to purée.

Blend puréed potatoes with chopped black truffles and egg yolks. Season to taste with salt and nutmeg.

Shape into small balls, about 1 1/4 in. (30 mm) in diameter.

Crush sliced almonds.

METHOD

Break eggs and mix with small amount of cold water.

Dredge balls, first in flour, then in eggs, and then roll in almonds. Press almonds into the potato balls, making sure the balls are evenly coated.

Deep-fry at 350°F (175°C) until golden brown.

Drain on absorbent paper.

Serve on paper doilies, as a side dish or a garnish.

NOTE: Less expensive canned truffle peelings can be used instead of whole or sliced truffles. Also, black chanterelles can be substituted for the truffles.

---

[a] Potatoes should not be puréed in a food processor or they will become gummy.

590

*O*ven-Roasted Potato Balls

Gebratene Kartoffelkugeln
Pommes parisienne

YIELD: 10 SERVINGS

Potatoes	6 lb 10 oz	3.0 kg
Salt	2/3 oz	20 g
Oil	3 1/3 oz	100 ml
Butter	1 2/3 oz	50 g
Seasoning (salt and pepper)	1x	1x

MISE EN PLACE
Choose large potatoes.

Wash and peel potatoes. Scoop out balls[a] about 1 in. (25 mm) in diameter.

Blanch potato balls in salted water.

Drain and spread out on a sheet pan to cool quickly and to prevent further cooking.

METHOD
Heat oil in roasting pan and add drained potatoes.

Start roasting on top of stove and continue in a hot oven.

Turn potatoes frequently to brown evenly. Roast until potatoes are cooked and golden brown.

Pour off oil, replace with butter, and roast potatoes briefly, turning them to coat evenly.

Season to taste with salt and pepper.

591

*B*aked Potatoes

Gebackene Kartoffeln
Pommes au four

YIELD: 10 SERVINGS

Potatoes, russet type, medium-size[b]	20	20
Salt, coarse[c]	1 lb 2 oz	500 g

SAUCE

Sour cream	10 oz	300 ml
Chives, cut into slivers	1 2/3 oz	50 g
Seasoning (salt and pepper)	1x	1x

MISE EN PLACE
Wash potatoes thoroughly and dry.

METHOD
Spread salt on baking sheet and place potatoes on top.

Bake potatoes in oven at 350°F (175°C) until potatoes are cooked, and the skins are crisp. Test with a needle to be sure potatoes are cooked.

Blend sauce ingredients and serve on the side.

NOTES: Potatoes can be wrapped in aluminum foil, which helps to keep the potatoes hot, without drying out. (However, the foil wrap causes the potatoes to steam rather than bake.)

Baked potatoes can also be served with fresh, cold butter.

592

*T*omato-Flavored Duchess Potatoes

Gebackene Kartoffelrosetten mit Tomaten
Pommes marquise

YIELD: 10 SERVINGS

Potatoes	3 lb 5 oz	1.5 kg
Salt (optional)	1/3 oz	10 g
Egg yolks	3	3
Butter	1 oz	30 g
Tomato paste	1 2/3 oz	50 g
Seasoning (salt and nutmeg)	1x	1x
Butter	3/4 oz	25 g
Egg yolks	2	2
Light cream	1 oz	30 ml

MISE EN PLACE
Wash and peel potatoes and cut into even-sized chunks.

Steam potatoes or cook in lightly salted water and drain well.

When cooked, dry potatoes briefly in the oven.

Pass potatoes through a wire sieve or ricer.[a]

(continued on next page)

---

[a] Use the tool specially designed for this purpose, a "parisienne scoop," or a melon baller.

[b] One large potato per person can be served, instead of two medium-size potatoes.

[c] The salt should be "rock salt," the coarsest available. The salt can be reused over and over. The purpose of the salt is to distribute the heat evenly and to prevent the potatoes from cooking too much on the bottom.

[a] Potatoes should not be puréed in a food processor or they will become gummy.

(continued from preceding page)

Blend puréed potatoes with 3 egg yolks, 1 oz (30 g) butter, and tomato paste. Season to taste with salt and nutmeg.

Butter a sheet pan.

Dress portion-size, meringue-shaped, rosettes on sheet pan, using a pastry bag with a star tube.

METHOD

Mix 2 egg yolks with light cream. Brush onto potatoes and bake in hot oven until golden brown.

Serve immediately.

593

Roast Diced Potatoes

Gebratene Kartoffelwürfel
Pommes Parmentier

YIELD: 10 SERVINGS

Potatoes	3 lb 8 oz	1.6 kg
Salt	2/3 oz	20 g
Peanut oil	3 1/3 oz	100 ml
Seasoning (salt and pepper)	1x	1x
Butter	1 2/3 oz	50 g

MISE EN PLACE

Wash and peel potatoes.

Cut into small, even dice, about 1/5 in. (5 mm) thick.

Blanch potatoes in salted water.

Drain and spread out to cool quickly and to prevent further cooking.

METHOD

Heat peanut oil in roasting pan, add potatoes, and season with salt and pepper.

Start roasting on top of stove and continue in a hot oven.

Roast potatoes, turning frequently, until they are golden brown.

Pour off oil, replace with butter, and roast potatoes briefly, turning to coat evenly.

594

Baked Potatoes Stuffed with Spinach

Mit Spinat gefüllte Kartoffeln
Pommes florentine

YIELD: 10 SERVINGS

Potatoes, russet type, medium-size[a]	20	20
Salt, coarse[b]	1 lb 2 oz	500 g
Spinach, fresh	14 oz	400 g
Onions	3 1/2 oz	100 g
Garlic	1/6 oz	5 g
Butter	3/4 oz	25 g
Seasoning (salt and pepper)	1x	1x
Egg yolks	3	3
Sbrinz, grated[c]	2 oz	60 g
Mornay sauce (Recipe 75)	10 oz	300 ml
Butter, melted	2/3 oz	20 g

MISE EN PLACE

Wash and dry potatoes.

Spread salt on sheet pan and place potatoes on top.

Bake potatoes at 350°F (175°C) until cooked. Test with a thin skewer to be sure potatoes are cooked.

Remove from oven and let cool.

Trim and wash spinach. Blanch and drain. Chill and drain again.

Coarsely chop spinach.

Peel and chop onions and garlic.

METHOD

Cut off tops of potatoes.

Scoop out potato pulp, leaving shells. Coarsely chop the scooped out potato pulp.

Sauté onions and garlic in butter and add spinach. Season mixture with salt and pepper and heat. Add potato pulp.

Remove from heat, mix in egg yolks and half the grated cheese.

Stuff potato shells with spinach/potato mixture and place in an ovenproof serving dish (*gratin* platter).

Cover each potato with Mornay sauce and sprinkle with remaining cheese and melted butter.

Bake in hot oven until insides are hot and tops are brown.

---

[a] One large potato per person can be served, instead of two medium-size potatoes.

[b] The salt should be "rock salt," the coarsest available. The salt can be re-used over and over. The purpose of the salt is to distribute the heat evenly, and to prevent the potatoes from cooking too much on the bottom.

[c] Sbrinz is a hard grating cheese from Switzerland. Parmesan can be substituted.

595

Potatoes Anna

Gestürzte Kartoffeln
Pommes Anna

YIELD: 10 SERVINGS

Potatoes, small and oblong	3 lb 5 oz	1.5 kg
Seasoning (salt and pepper)	1x	1x
Clarified butter	5 1/3 oz	150 g

MISE EN PLACE

Wash and peel potatoes.

Cut into thin slices.

Do not wash slices, because the potato starch is needed to "glue" the slices together.

Dry the slices with a kitchen towel.

Season the potato slices with salt and pepper.

Butter a heavy timbale mold[a] with a little of the butter.

METHOD

Line mold attractively and evenly with potato slices.

Fill the center with remaining potato slices.

Press down, and pour remaining melted butter over potatoes.

Bake and brown in oven at 400°F (200°C) until potatoes are cooked. Test with a thin skewer to be sure potatoes are cooked.

Let potatoes rest a few minutes, press down again, and pour off excess butter.

Invert onto a heated service plate. Cut into wedges to serve.

NOTE: It is best to line the bottom of the timbale mold with a parchment paper circle to ensure that the potatoes will not stick to the mold.

[a] If no large timbale mold is available, a straight-sided cast iron pan can be used. Individual-portion timbale molds can also be used.

596

Mashed Potato Balls Baked with Cheese

Gratinierte Kartoffelkugeln
Pommes Byron

YIELD: 10 SERVINGS

Potatoes	3 lb 5 oz	1.5 kg
Onions	2 2/3 oz	75 g
Parsley, curly, fresh	3/4 oz	25 g
Salt	2/3 oz	20 g
Butter	3/4 oz	25 g
Seasoning (white pepper, nutmeg)	1x	1x
Butter	2/3 oz	20 g
Heavy cream (36%)	3 1/3 oz	100 ml
Sbrinz, grated[a]	1 2/3 oz	50 g

MISE EN PLACE

Wash and peel potatoes and cut into chunks.

Peel and chop onions.

Wash parsley and chop leaves.

METHOD

Put potatoes in hot water to cover, add salt, and bring to a boil.

Skim, cover, and simmer potatoes until cooked. (Potatoes can also be steamed.)

Drain off water, remove lid, and let steam escape.

Crush potatoes while still hot but do not purée.

Sauté onions in butter and add to potatoes.

Add parsley and season to taste with salt and nutmeg.

Butter an ovenproof dish (*gratin* dish).

Shape potato mixture into round mounds, using a large ice cream scoop or a small ladle.

Carefully pour heavy cream over potatoes and sprinkle with cheese.

Bake in oven until brown.

[a] Sbrinz is a hard grating cheese from Switzerland. Parmesan can be substituted.

597

Potato Slices Baked with Cheese

Gratinierte Kartoffelscheiben
Pommes savoyarde

YIELD: 10 SERVINGS

Potatoes, oblong	4 lb	1.8 kg
Butter	2/3 oz	20 g
Bouillon (Recipe 22)	1 qt 19 oz	1.5 L
Sbrinz,[a] grated	1 2/3 oz	50 g
Butter, melted	3/4 oz	25 g

MISE EN PLACE
Wash and peel potatoes. Trim into tube shapes if necessary.

Cut into thin slices.

Butter a deep baking pan.

METHOD
Shingle potatoes in the pan, in straight rows.

Pour hot bouillon around potatoes to reach two-thirds of the height of the potatoes.

Put in oven and bake at 360°F (180°C) until done.

Sprinkle with cheese and melted butter, brown under the salamander or under the broiler.

598

Mashed Potatoes Baked with Cheese

Gratiniertes Kartoffelpüree
Pommes Mont-d'Or

YIELD: 10 SERVINGS

Potatoes, russet type	3 lb 5 oz	1.5 kg
Salt	2/3 oz	20 g
Milk	10 oz	300 ml
Butter, cold	2 2/3 oz	75 g
Nutmeg	1x	1x
Seasoning (salt and pepper)	1x	1x
Sbrinz,[b] grated	2 2/3 oz	75 g
Butter, melted	3/4 oz	25 g

MISE EN PLACE
Wash and peel potatoes. Cut into large chunks.

METHOD
Put potatoes in hot water to cover, add salt, and bring to a boil.

Skim, cover, and simmer potatoes until cooked. (Potatoes can also be steamed.)

Bring milk to a boil.

Drain off water from potatoes, remove lid, and let steam escape.

While potatoes are still hot, pass them through a wire sieve or ricer.[a]

Add hot milk to potatoes. Add cold butter in small nuggets. Stir to make a smooth puree.

Season with nutmeg and salt and pepper to taste.

Mound puree in an ovenproof dish (*gratin* dish).

Sprinkle with cheese and melted butter.

Brown in hot oven.

NOTE: The amount of milk needed may vary depending on the moisture content of the potatoes.

599

Small Oven-Roasted Potatoes

Haselnuss Kartoffeln
Pommes noisettes

YIELD: 10 SERVINGS

Potatoes	6 lb 10 oz	3.0 kg
Salt	2/3 oz	20 g
Peanut oil	3 1/3 oz	100 ml
Seasoning (salt and pepper)	1x	1x
Butter	1 2/3 oz	50 g

MISE EN PLACE
Choose large potatoes.

Wash and peel potatoes. Scoop out balls[b] about the size of hazlenuts.

Blanch in salted water.

Drain and spread out on a sheet pan to cool quickly and to prevent further cooking.

---

[a] Sbrinz is a hard grating cheese from Switzerland. Parmesan can be substituted.

[b] Sbrinz is a hard grating cheese from Switzerland. Parmesan can be substituted.

[a] Potatoes should not be puréed in a food processor or they will become gummy.

[b] Use the tool specially designed for this purpose, a "parisienne scoop," or a melon baller.

METHOD

Heat peanut oil in roasting pan; add drained potatoes. Season with salt and pepper.

Start roasting on top of stove and continue in a hot oven.

Turn potatoes frequently. Roast until potatoes are cooked and golden brown.

Pour off oil, replace with butter, and roast potatoes briefly, turning to coat evenly.

600

*B*oiled Buttered Potatoes

Kartoffeln mit Butter
Pommes anglaise

YIELD: 10 SERVINGS

Potatoes	3 lb 5 oz	1.5 kg
Salt	2/3 oz	20 g
Butter	1 2/3 oz	50 g

MISE EN PLACE

Wash and peel potatoes.

Cut into even-sized large cubes, or "turn" into small egg shapes.

METHOD

Boil potatoes in salted water, skim, cover, and simmer until potatoes are cooked.

Drain off carefully. Melt butter and pour over the potatoes.

NOTE: Small new potatoes can also be used. They should be served whole.

601

*B*aked Potatoes Stuffed with Vegetables

Mit Gemüse gefüllte Kartoffeln
Pommes fermière

YIELD: 10 SERVINGS

Potatoes, russet type, medium-size[a]	20	20
Salt, coarse[b]	1 lb 2 oz	500 g
Parsley, curly, fresh	3/4 oz	25 g
Vegetables, cut into small dice (brunoise)[c]	5 1/3 oz	150 g
Butter	3/4 oz	25 g
Egg yolks	3	3
Butter	1 2/3 oz	50 g
Seasoning (salt and pepper)	1x	1x
Nutmeg	1x	1x
Sbrinz,[d] grated	1 oz	30 g
Butter, melted	2/3 oz	20 g

MISE EN PLACE

Wash and dry potatoes.

Spread salt on sheet pan and place potatoes on top.

Bake potatoes at 350°F (175°C) until cooked. Test with a needle to be sure potatoes are cooked.

Remove from oven and let cool.

Wash parsley and chop leaves.

METHOD

Cut off tops of potatoes.

Scoop out pulp, leaving shells. Coarsely chop scooped out potato pulp.

Sauté vegetables *brunoise* in butter, add small amount of water, cover, and braise until vegetables are tender.

Add potato pulp to vegetables.

Remove from heat, add egg yolks, chopped parsley, and 1 2/3 oz (50 g) butter. Season to taste with salt and pepper and nutmeg.

Stuff potatoes with vegetable/potato mixture and place in an ovenproof serving dish (*gratin* dish).

Sprinkle potatoes with cheese and melted butter.

Bake in hot oven until potatoes are heated through and tops are brown.

---

[a] One large potato per person can be served, instead of two medium-size potatoes.

[b] The salt should be "rock salt," the coarsest available. The salt can be re-used over and over. The purpose of the salt is to distribute the heat evenly, and to prevent the potatoes from cooking too much on the bottom.

[c] The vegetables *brunoise* should consist of equal amounts of carrots, celery, and leeks, cut into small dice.

[d] Sbrinz is a hard grating cheese from Switzerland. Parmesan can be substituted.

602

$\mathscr{P}$otato Cakes

Kartoffelgaletten
Galettes de pommes de terre

YIELD: 10 SERVINGS

Potatoes	3 lb 5 oz	1.5 kg
Salt (optional)	1/3 oz	10 g
Butter	3/4 oz	25 g
Egg yolks	3	3
Seasoning (salt and pepper)	1x	1x
Nutmeg	1x	1x
White wheat flour	3 1/2 oz	100 g
Clarified butter	3 1/2 oz	100 g

MISE EN PLACE
Wash and peel potatoes and cut into even-sized chunks.

Steam potatoes or cook in lightly salted water and drain well.

When cooked, dry potatoes briefly in the oven.

Pass potatoes through a wire sieve or ricer.[a]

Blend hot puréed potatoes with butter and egg yolks.

Put mixture on a floured work table; divide into two parts.

Shape into two tubular rolls about 1 1/2 in. (35 mm) in diameter.

Chill rolls.

METHOD
Cut rolls into 1/2-in. (12 mm) thick slices on a floured work table.

Decorate slices in a grate pattern with the back of a knife.

Flour slices and sauté in butter until golden brown on both sides.

---

[a] Potatoes should not be puréed in a food processor or they will become gummy.

603

$\mathscr{P}$otatoes au Gratin

Kartoffelgratin
Gratin dauphinois

YIELD: 10 SERVINGS

Potatoes	4 lb	1.8 kg
Gruyere cheese	3 1/2 oz	100 g
Sbrinz[a]	3 1/2 oz	100 g
Butter	2/3 oz	20 g
Garlic, chopped	1/3 oz	10 g
Milk	1 pt 4 oz	600 ml
Heavy cream (36%)[b]	3 1/3 oz	100 ml
Dry white wine	3 1/3 oz	100 ml
Seasoning (salt and pepper)	1x	1x
Nutmeg	1x	1x
Butter, melted	1 2/3 oz	50 g

MISE EN PLACE
Wash and peel potatoes and cut into 1/10-in. (2.5 mm) thick slices.

Grate both cheeses.

Butter a deep ovenproof dish (*gratin* dish) and sprinkle with garlic.

METHOD
Combine milk, heavy cream, and wine and bring to a boil. Season to taste with salt and pepper and nutmeg.

Add potatoes, return to a boil, remove from heat, and let cool slightly.[c]

Blend half the amount of cheeses into the potatoes and put mixture into the prepared *gratin* dish.

Sprinkle with remaining cheeses and with melted butter.

Bake in oven, first at 325°F (165°C) for 40 minutes and then at 425°F (220°C) to brown.

NOTE: Baking at a low temperature increases cooking time, but the potatoes remain moister. If desired, the raw potato slices can be arranged directly in the *gratin* dish, covered with the milk mixture, and baked as directed.

---

[a] Sbrinz is a hard grating cheese from Switzerland. Parmesan can be substituted.

[b] Heavy cream must be used, otherwise the mixture might curdle.

[c] It is best to cool the mixture before adding the cheese. If cheese is added to too hot a mixture, the cheese can become stringy and will not mix well.

604

$\mathcal{P}$otato Croquettes

Kartoffelkroketten
Pommes croquettes

YIELD: 10 SERVINGS

Potatoes, russet type	3 lb 5 oz	1.5 kg
Salt (optional)	1/3 oz	10 g
Egg yolks	3	3
Seasoning (salt, nutmeg)	1x	1x
White wheat flour	1 2/3 oz	50 g
Eggs	2	2
Bread crumbs, fine[a]	3 1/2 oz	100 g
Oil for frying(10% oil loss)	5 oz	150 ml

MISE EN PLACE

Wash and peel potatoes and cut into even-sized chunks.

Steam potatoes or cook in lightly salted water and drain well.

When cooked, dry potatoes briefly in the oven.

Pass potatoes through a wire sieve or ricer.[b]

Add egg yolks to potatoes and season to taste with salt and nutmeg.

METHOD

Sprinkle a work table with flour.

Using a pastry bag with a straight tube, dress tubular rolls about 1/2 in. (12 mm) thick, directly onto floured table.

Cut tubes into 1 1/2-in. (40 mm) long sections.

Roll croquettes in flour.

Beat eggs and mix with a small amount of water.

Dredge floured croquettes, first in egg mixture, and then in bread crumbs. Roll to shape evenly and to press crumbs to croquettes.

Deep-fry at 350°F (175°C) until golden brown.

Drain on absorbent paper and serve on a paper doily or as garnish next to meat.

605

$\mathcal{P}$otato Croquettes with Spinach

Kartoffelkroketten mit Spinat
Pommes croquettes florentine

YIELD: 10 SERVINGS

Spinach, frozen, chopped	5 1/3 oz	150 g
Potatoes, russet type	3 lb 5 oz	1.5 kg
Salt (optional)	1/3 oz	10 g
Egg yolks	3	3
Seasoning (salt, nutmeg)	1x	1x
White wheat flour	1 2/3 oz	50 g
Bread crumbs, fine[a]	3 1/2 oz	100 g
Oil for frying (10% oil loss)	5 oz	150 ml

MISE EN PLACE

Defrost spinach. Drain spinach and squeeze out liquid.

Wash and peel potatoes and cut into even-sized chunks.

Steam potatoes or cook in lightly salted water and drain well.

Add egg yolks and spinach to potatoes and season to taste with salt and nutmeg.

METHOD

Sprinkle a work table with flour.

Using a pastry bag with a straight tube, dress tubular rolls about 1/2-in. (12 mm) thick, directly onto floured table.

Cut tubes into 1 1/2-in. (40 mm) long sections.

Roll croquettes in flour.

Beat whole eggs and mix with a small amount of water.

Dredge floured croquettes, first in egg mixture, and then in bread crumbs. Roll to shape evenly and to press crumbs to croquettes.

Deep-fry at 350°F (175°C) until golden brown.

Drain on absorbent paper and serve on a paper doily or as garnish next to meat.

[a] Use more bread crumbs as needed. Bread crumbs can be dry or fresh, but must be finely grated.

[b] Potatoes should not be puréed in a food processor or they will become gummy.

[a] Use more bread crumbs as needed. Bread crumbs can be dry or fresh, but must be finely grated.

[b] Potatoes should not be puréed in a food processor or they will become gummy.

606

mall Potato Cakes

Kartoffelküchlein
Pommes Macaire

YIELD: 10 SERVINGS

Potatoes, russet type	4 lb	1.8 kg
Salt, coarse	1 lb 2 oz	500 g
Butter	3 1/2 oz	100 g
Seasoning (white pepper)	1x	1x
Nutmeg	1x	1x
Flour	1 2/3 oz	50 g
Clarified butter	1 2/3 oz	50 g

MISE EN PLACE
Wash and dry potatoes.

Spread salt on sheet pan and place potatoes on top.

Bake potatoes at 350°F (175°C) until cooked. Test with a needle to be sure potatoes are cooked. (Potatoes can be baked in aluminum foil, and the rock salt omitted.)

Remove from oven and let cool.

METHOD
Peel potatoes and crush.

Season to taste with white pepper and nutmeg.

Shape potatoes into small cakes on a floured work table.

Decorate potato cakes in a grate pattern with the back of a knife.

Flour the cakes and sauté in butter until golden brown on both sides.

NOTE: Leftover baked potatoes can also be used.

607

otato Gnocchi[a]

Kartoffelnocken
Gnocchi piémontaise

YIELD: 10 SERVINGS

Potatoes, russet type, boiled in their skins	2 lb 10 oz	1.2 kg
Eggs, broken	5 1/3 oz	150 g

Seasoning (salt and pepper)	1x	1x
Nutmeg	1x	1x
White wheat flour	7 oz	200 g
Salt	1 oz	30 g
Butter	2/3 oz	20 g
Fresh stewed tomatoes (Recipe 535)	1 pt 8 oz	700 ml
Sbrinz,[a] grated	3 1/2 oz	100 g
Butter, melted	3 oz	80 g

MISE EN PLACE
Peel boiled potatoes while still hot. Grate very fine, or press through a ricer.

Mix with eggs, season with salt and pepper and nutmeg, and let cool.

Place mixture on floured work table[b] and knead in flour. The dough should be rather stiff.

METHOD
Using pastry bag with a straight tube, dress tubular rolls about 1/2 in. (12 mm) thick, directly onto floured table.

Cut tubes with floured knife into 2/3-in. (20 mm) long pieces.

Roll pieces into oblong shape, and gently roll over the back of a dinner fork. This will give the gnocchis their traditional shape.

Bring ample amount of salted water to a boil.

Simmer gnocchis for about 5 minutes. They will float to the top when done.

Remove with skimmer and drain in a colander.

Butter a suitable ovenproof dish (*gratin* dish).

Heat stewed tomatoes and put into *gratin* dish.

Put gnocchis on top and sprinkle with grated cheese and melted butter.

Bake in hot oven until hot and brown on top.

NOTES: The amount of eggs and flour needed depends on the moisture content of the potatoes. The dough should be elastic, yet dry. If potatoes are very moist, use egg yolks only. (A small amount of dehydrated potato can be added to stiffen the dough.)

Potato gnocchis can also be served sautéed with butter.

---

[a] Also see Puff-Paste Gnocchi (Recipe 627) and Semolina Gnocchi (Recipe 630).

[a] Sbrinz is a hard grating cheese from Switzerland. Parmesan can be substituted.

[b] A marble table is recommended.

608

𝓜ashed Potatoes

Kartoffelpüree
Pommes purées

YIELD: 10 SERVINGS

Potatoes, russet type	3 lb 5 oz	1.5 kg
Salt	2/3 oz	20 g
Milk	10 oz	300 ml
Butter, cold	2 2/3 oz	75 g
Nutmeg	1x	1x
Seasoning (salt and pepper)	1x	1x

MISE EN PLACE
Wash and peel potatoes. Cut into large chunks.

METHOD
Put potatoes in hot water to cover, add salt, and bring to a boil.

Skim, cover, and simmer potatoes until cooked. (Potatoes can also be steamed.)

Drain off water, remove lid, and let steam escape.

While potatoes are still hot, pass them through a wire sieve or ricer.[a]

Bring milk to a boil. Add hot milk to potatoes.

Add cold butter in small nuggets. Stir to make a smooth puree. Season to taste with nutmeg and salt and pepper.

NOTE: The amount of milk varies, depending on the type of potatoes used and the moisture content.

609

𝓜ashed Potatoes with Cream

Kartoffelpüree mit Rahm
Pommes mousseline

YIELD: 10 SERVINGS

Potatoes, russet type	3 lb 5 oz	1.5 kg
Salt	2/3 oz	20 g
Milk	8 1/2 oz	250 ml
Heavy cream (36%)	3 1/3 oz	100 ml
Butter	2 2/3 oz	75 g
Nutmeg	1x	1x
Seasoning (salt and pepper)	1x	1x

---

[a] Potatoes should not be puréed in a food processor or they will become gummy.

MISE EN PLACE
Wash and peel potatoes. Cut into large chunks.

METHOD
Put potatoes in hot water to cover, add salt, and bring to a boil.

Skim, cover, and simmer potatoes until cooked. (Potatoes can also be steamed.)

Drain off water, remove lid, and let steam escape.

While potatoes are still hot, pass them through a wire sieve or ricer.[a]

Bring milk to a boil; heat heavy cream. Add hot milk and cream to potatoes.

Add cold butter in small nuggets. Stir to make a smooth puree. Season to taste with nutmeg and salt and pepper.

NOTE: The amount of milk varies, depending on the type of potatoes used and the moisture content.

610

𝓑aked Potatoes with Caraway Seeds

Kümmelkartoffeln
Pommes au cumin

YIELD: 10 SERVINGS

Potatoes, russet type, 10	2 lb 10 oz	1.2 kg
Salt, coarse[b]	1 lb 2 oz	500 g
Peanut oil	1 2/3 oz	50 ml
Caraway seeds, whole	3/4 oz	25 g

MISE EN PLACE
Wash potatoes well and cut in half lengthwise.

METHOD
Spread salt on sheet pan.

Brush potatoes with peanut oil and sprinkle with caraway seeds.

Place potatoes on salt, cut-side up, and bake at 350°F (175°C) until done. Test with a needle to be sure potatoes are cooked.

---

[a] Potatoes should not be puréed in a food processor or they will become gummy.

[b] The salt should be "rock salt," the coarsest available. The salt can be re-used over and over. The purpose of the salt is to distribute the heat evenly, and to prevent the potatoes from cooking too much on the bottom.

611

*P*otatoes with Leeks

Lauchkartoffeln
Pommes aux poireaux

YIELD: 10 SERVINGS

Potatoes	3 lb 5 oz	1.5 kg
Salt	2/3 oz	20 g
Leeks, green part only	9 oz	250 g
Butter	2/3 oz	20 g
Bouillon (Recipe 22)	1 qt 2 oz	1.0 L
Seasoning (salt and pepper)	1x	1x

MISE EN PLACE
Wash and peel potatoes. Cut into slices or cubes. Blanch potatoes in salted water.

Drain potatoes and spread out on sheet pan to cool quickly and to prevent further cooking.

Trim and wash leeks; be sure sand is removed from layers. Cut into wide strips or squares.

METHOD
Sauté leeks in butter.

Add potatoes and bouillon.

Bring to a boil, skim, cover, and simmer until potatoes are cooked.

Season to taste with salt and pepper.

NOTE: If desired, 7 oz (200 g) of blanched bacon strips can be added.

612

*P*otatoes Sautéed with Onions

Lyoner Kartoffeln
Pommes lyonnaise

YIELD: 10 SERVINGS

Potatoes, boiled or steamed in their skins	3 lb 5 oz	1.5 kg
Onions	5 1/3 oz	150 g
Parsley	2/3 oz	20 g
Clarified butter	3 1/2 oz	100 g
Seasoning (salt and pepper)	1x	1x
Butter	3 1/2 oz	100 g

MISE EN PLACE
Peel the cooked potatoes and cut into 1/12-in. (2 mm) slices.

Peel onions, cut in half lengthwise, and then into thin slices.

Wash parsley and chop leaves.

METHOD
Heat clarified butter in roasting pan.

Add potatoes and season with salt and pepper.

Start roasting on top of stove. Continue roasting in hot oven, turning potatoes frequently until golden brown.

Sauté onions in half the butter until light yellow and add to potatoes.

Add remaining butter, fold in, and continue roasting briefly.

Sprinkle potatoes with parsley.

NOTE: Cook potatoes one day ahead. They will stay firmer and the slices will not break easily.

613

*R*oasted Potato Cubes

Maxime-Kartoffeln
Pommes Maxime

YIELD: 10 SERVINGS

Potatoes, large	3 lb 5 oz	1.5 kg
Salt	2/3 oz	20 g
Peanut oil	3 1/3 oz	100 ml
Seasoning (salt and pepper)	1x	1x
Butter	1 2/3 oz	50 g

MISE EN PLACE
Wash and peel potatoes. Cut into 3/4-in. (16 mm) cubes.

Blanch potatoes in ample amount of salted water.

Drain and spread out on a sheet pan to cool quickly and to prevent further cooking.

METHOD
Heat peanut oil in roasting pan and add potatoes.

Start roasting on top of stove and continue roasting in hot oven, turning potatoes frequently until golden brown and cooked.

Pour off excess oil, replace with butter, and roast potatoes briefly, turning to coat evenly.

614

$\mathscr{P}$otatoes in Cream Sauce

Milchkartoffeln
Pommes maître d'hôtel

YIELD: 10 SERVINGS

Potatoes	3 lb 8 oz	1.6 kg
Parsley	1 2/3 oz	50 g
Cream sauce (Recipe 40)	13 1/2 oz	400 ml

MISE EN PLACE
Boil potatoes in their skins.[a]

Peel while still hot and cut into slices.

Wash parsley and chop leaves.

METHOD
Heat cream sauce.

Carefully blend potatoes with cream sauce, trying not to break slices. (Dilute cream sauce with hot cream if necessary.)

Sprinkle with chopped parsley at the moment of service.

615

$\mathscr{F}$rench Fries

Pommes frites
Pommes frites

YIELD: 10 SERVINGS

Potatoes	4 lb	1.8 kg
Oil for frying (10% oil loss)	5 oz	150 ml
Salt	1/3 oz	10 g

MISE EN PLACE
Wash and peel potatoes. Cut into even-sized sticks, about 1/3-in. (8 mm) thick and 2 1/2-in. (60 mm) long.

Soak potatoes in cold water for 1 hour. Wash to rinse out starch.

Drain well and pat dry with paper towels.

METHOD
Fill deep-fryer basket about half full with potatoes and fry potatoes at 265°F (130°C) until potatoes are cooked, but not browned. Continue until all potatoes are fried.

Spread out on a sheet pan to cool quickly and to prevent further cooking.

Finish frying potatoes as needed at 350°F (175°C) until brown and crisp.

Drain on absorbent paper and salt lightly.

Serve on paper doilies, as a garnish or side dish.

616

$\mathscr{R}$östi Potatoes (made with raw potatoes)[a]

Rösti aus rohen Kartoffeln
Pommes crues sautées

YIELD: 10 SERVINGS

Potatoes	3 lb 5 oz	1.5 kg
Seasoning (salt and pepper)	1x	1x
Clarified butter	5 1/3 oz	150 g

MISE EN PLACE
Wash and peel potatoes.

Coarsely grate[b] potatoes as close to serving time as possible to minimize discoloration.

METHOD
Heat clarified butter in large skillet.

Add potatoes, season with salt and pepper, and start roasting on top of stove.

Turn potatoes frequently and roast until potatoes start to brown.

Shape into a thin cake and put in a hot oven.

Roast until cooked and brown on both sides.

Invert potatoes onto a hot serving dish. The potatoes should be brown and crisp on both sides.

Cut into wedges to serve.

---

[a] These potatoes should *not* be boiled a day ahead. They should be fresh in order to absorb the cream.

[a] Also see Rösti Potatoes (Recipe 575).

[b] In Switzerland, a special grater is used to tear the potatoes into long shreds.

617

$\mathcal{B}$aked Potatoes with Rosemary

Rosmarinkartoffeln
Pommes au romarin

YIELD: 10 SERVINGS

Potatoes, russet type, 10	2 lb 10 oz	1.2 kg
Rosemary, fresh	1 2/3 oz	50 g
Salt, coarse[a]	1 lb 2 oz	500 g
Olive oil	1 2/3 oz	50 ml
Seasoning (salt and pepper)	1x	1x

MISE EN PLACE
Wash potatoes and cut in half lengthwise.

Wash rosemary and pluck off leaves (needles).

METHOD
Spread salt on sheet pan.

Brush potatoes with olive oil.

Season potatoes with salt and pepper and sprinkle with rosemary leaves.

Place potatoes on salt, cut-side up, and bake at 350°F (175°C) until done. Test with a thin skewer to be sure potatoes are cooked.

618

$\mathcal{H}$ome-Fried Potatoes

Röstkartoffeln
Pommes sautées

YIELD: 10 SERVINGS

Potatoes, boiled or steamed in their skins	3 lb 5 oz	1.5 kg
Parsley	2/3 oz	20 g
Clarified butter	3 1/2 oz	100 g
Seasoning (salt and pepper)	1x	1x
Butter	1 2/3 oz	50 g

MISE EN PLACE
Peel potatoes and cut into 1/2-in. (2 mm) slices.

Wash parsley and chop leaves.

[a] The salt should be "rock salt," the coarsest available. The salt can be reused over and over. The purpose of the salt is to distribute the heat evenly, and to prevent the potatoes from cooking too much on the bottom.

METHOD
Heat clarified butter in skillet.

Add potatoes and season with salt and pepper.

Sauté, turning frequently until golden brown on both sides.

Add butter and continue to sauté briefly.

Sprinkle with chopped parsley leaves.

NOTE: These potatoes should be boiled or steamed a day ahead, so they will keep their shape when sliced.

619

$\mathcal{B}$oiled Potatoes

Salzkartoffeln
Pommes nature

YIELD: 10 SERVINGS

Potatoes	3 lb 5 oz	1.5 kg
Salt	2/3 oz	20 g

MISE EN PLACE
Wash and peel potatoes. Cut into even-shaped, even-sized pieces.

METHOD
Start cooking potatoes in hot salted water.

Bring to a boil, and skim. Cover, and simmer until cooked.

Drain carefully.

620

$\mathcal{B}$oiled Potatoes with Herbs

Salzkartoffeln mit Kräutern
Pommes aux fines herbes

YIELD: 10 SERVINGS

Potatoes	3 lb 5 oz	1.5 kg
Salt	2/3 oz	20 g
Kitchen herbs, fresh	1 2/3 oz	50 g
Butter	1 2/3 oz	50 g

MISE EN PLACE
Wash and peel potatoes. Cut into even-shaped, even-sized pieces.

Wash herbs (parsley, chervil, dill, and chives). Chop leaves and cut chives into slivers.

METHOD

Start cooking potatoes in hot salted water.

Bring to a boil and skim. Cover and simmer until cooked.

Drain carefully; add herbs and butter.

Blend carefully without breaking potatoes.

NOTE: For this recipe, tiny new potatoes can be used. They do not need to be cut.

621

*O*val-Shaped Oven-Roasted Potatoes

Schlosskartoffeln
Pommes château

YIELD: 10 SERVINGS

Potatoes	5 lb 8 oz	2.5 kg
Salt	2/3 oz	20 g
Peanut oil	3 1/3 oz	100 ml
Seasoning (salt and pepper)	1x	1x
Butter	1 2/3 oz	50 g

MISE EN PLACE

Wash and peel potatoes.

Cut into crescent moon shapes with blunt ends (somewhat like a banana).[a]

Blanch in salted water, drain, and spread out to cool quickly and to prevent further cooking.

METHOD

Heat peanut oil in roasting pan.

Add potatoes, season with salt and pepper, and start roasting on top of stove.

Continue roasting in the oven, turning the potatoes until golden brown and cooked.

Be careful not to break potatoes.

Pour off excess oil, add butter, and continue roasting briefly, turning lightly in the butter to coat evenly.

622

*"M*elted" Potatoes

Schmelzkartoffeln
Pommes fondantes

YIELD: 10 SERVINGS

Potatoes	3 lb 5 oz	1.5 kg
Butter	2/3 oz	20 g
Bouillon (Recipe 22)	1 qt 19 oz	1.5 L
Butter	2/3 oz	20 g

MISE EN PLACE

Wash and peel potatoes. Cut into egg shapes (with flat bottom).

Butter a large baking pan.

METHOD

Place potatoes side by side in baking pan.

Add hot bouillon, to reach about two-thirds of the height of the potatoes.

Place pan in oven and bake at 360°F (180°C).

Brush potatoes occasionally with resulting pan gravy.

If the timing is correct, the potatoes will be shiny brown when cooked, and most liquid will be soaked up by the potatoes.

Brush potatoes with butter at the moment of service to give them a nice sheen.

NOTES: Some chefs brush the potatoes with melted *glace de viande* to give them additional sheen.

The potatoes should not have a crust; they should be velvety and "melted," as the name indicates.

---

[a] Many of the classic potato preparations distinguish themselves only by shape. This is one of those and it may require some practice to do well.

623

$\mathcal{P}$otato Snow

Schneekartoffeln
Pommes en neige

YIELD: 10 SERVINGS

Potatoes	3 lb 5 oz	1.5 kg
Salt	2/3 oz	20 g
Butter, cold	2 2/3 oz	75 g
Seasoning (nutmeg)	1x	1x

MISE EN PLACE
Wash and peel potatoes. Cut into cubes.

METHOD
Add potatoes to hot salted water. Bring to a boil and skim.

Simmer, covered, until potatoes are cooked.

Drain, remove cover, and allow steam to escape.

Purée[a] potatoes while still hot.

Serve with cold butter nuggets melting on top. Do not stir potatoes.

Sprinkle with nutmeg.

NOTES: The potatoes can also be steamed.

This recipe, without butter, is suitable for diet menus.

624

$\mathcal{F}$ried Straw Potatoes

Strohkartoffeln
Pommes paille

YIELD: 10 SERVINGS

Potatoes	4 lb	1.8 kg
Oil for frying (10% oil loss)	5 oz	150 ml
Salt	1/3 oz	10 g

MISE EN PLACE
Wash and peel potatoes. Cut potatoes into fine strips (*julienne*) using an appropriate tool, such as a mandolin.

Wash potatoes well to remove starch, drain thoroughly, and dry the potatoes.

METHOD
Deep-fry in small batches at 350°F (175°C) until crisp and golden brown, shaking fryer basket continuously. The potatoes must be crisp.

Drain potatoes over the fryer to recover all dripping oil.

Drain on absorbent paper. Salt to taste.

625

$\mathcal{F}$ried Waffle Potatoes

Waffelkartoffeln
Pommes gaufrettes

YIELD: 10 SERVINGS

Potatoes	4 lb	1.8 kg
Oil for frying (10% oil loss)	5 oz	150 ml
Salt	1/3 oz	10 g

MISE EN PLACE
Wash and peel potatoes. Cut into slices with a mandolin, using the *gaufrette* blade, turning the potato 90 degrees each time, so a waffle pattern results.

Wash out starch, drain thoroughly, and dry the potatoes.

METHOD
Deep-fry in small batches at 350°F (175°C) until crisp and golden brown, shaking fryer basket continuously. The potatoes must be crisp.

Drain potatoes over the fryer to recover all dripping oil.

Drain on absorbent paper. Salt to taste.

---

[a] The original recipe calls for a *passe-vit*, a type of ricer, to be used. A food mill can also be used, but not a food processor, which will make the potatoes gummy. These potatoes should be made to order.

626

*F*ried Matchstick Potatoes

Zündholzkartoffeln
Pommes allumettes

YIELD: 10 SERVINGS

Potatoes	4 lb	1.8 kg
Oil for frying (10% oil loss)	5 oz	150 ml
Salt	1/3 oz	10 g

MISE EN PLACE

Wash and peel potatoes. First cut into slices. Then cut into small sticks the size of matchsticks.

Wash out starch, drain thoroughly, and dry the potatoes.

METHOD

Deep-fry in small batches at 265°F (130°C) until potatoes are cooked, but have not browned.

Drain over a deep fat fryer to recover all drippings.

Spread out to cool quickly and to prevent further cooking.

Finish frying at 350°F (175°C) just before serving until crisp and golden brown. The potatoes must be crisp.

Drain on absorbent paper. Salt according to taste.

Serve on paper doilies, as a garnish or side dish.

Pasta Dishes

627

*P*uff-Paste Gnocchi[a]

Brandteignocken
Gnocchi parisienne

YIELD: 10 SERVINGS

Water	7 2/3 oz	225 ml
Butter	3 oz	80 g
Salt	1/6 oz	5 g
Nutmeg	1x	1x
White wheat flour	8 oz	225 g
Eggs, whole, shelled and broken up	8 3/4 oz	250 g
Butter	2/3 oz	20 g
Cream sauce (Recipe 40)	1 pt 11 oz	800 ml
Sbrinz,[b] grated	3 1/2 oz	100 g
Butter, melted	2 oz	60 g

MISE EN PLACE FOR PUFF PASTE

Combine water, butter, salt, and nutmeg and bring to a boil.

Remove from heat and add sifted flour all at once.

Return to heat and stir vigorously with a wooden spatula until the resulting stiff paste no longer clings to the bottom of the pot.

Cool mixture slightly; stir in eggs in small increments.

METHOD

Bring ample amount of water to simmer.

Put puff paste in pastry bag with a large, smooth tip. Pipe dumplings directly into the water. Cut extruding paste with a dressing needle or other suitable tool every inch (25 mm) to make dumplings.

Remove dumplings with skimmer as soon as they float to the top, and put them into cold water.

When all paste is used up, lift dumplings from cold water and let them drain off.

Butter a deep, ovenproof dish (*gratin* dish).

Bring cream sauce to a boil.

Spoon a small amount of cream sauce into the *gratin* dish and place dumplings on top. Do not crowd dumplings; they will expand during baking.

Cover with remaining cream sauce and sprinkle with cheese and melted butter.

Bake for 20 minutes, starting at 360°F (180°C), and finishing at 425°F (220°C).

NOTE: The dumplings should be golden brown, and should have risen like a soufflé. If not served at once, they will collapse.

---

[a] Also see Semolina Gnocchi (Recipe 630) and Potato Gnocchi (Recipe 607).

[b] Sbrinz is a grating cheese from Switzerland. Parmesan can be substituted.

628

$\mathcal{S}$almon Ravioli

Fischravioli
Ravioli de poisson

YIELD: 10 SERVINGS

Ravioli dough (Recipe 637)	1 lb 2 oz	500 g
Salt	1 oz	30 g
Oil	1/3 oz	10 ml

FILLING

Salmon fillets, skin off	10 1/2 oz	300 g
Heavy cream (36%)	8 1/2 oz	250 ml
Egg whites	1 1/3 oz	40 g
Seasoning (salt, cayenne pepper)	1x	1x
Dill, fresh, chopped	2/3 oz	20 g

SAUCE

| White wine sauce for fish (Recipe 103) | 1 pt 4 oz | 600 ml |
| Dill tops, fresh | 10 | 10 |

METHOD FOR FILLING

Using pliers, remove any tiny remaining bones from the salmon fillets.

Chill salmon. Chill heavy cream.

Grind or purée salmon with small amount of heavy cream in Buffalo chopper or food processor. Strain through wire sieve.[a]

Put puréed salmon in a bowl on ice and stir in remaining heavy cream in small increments.

Whip egg whites lightly and fold into salmon mixture.

Season to taste with salt and cayenne and add dill.

METHOD

Divide ravioli dough into two equal parts. Roll the parts into two very equal-size very thin rectangles, about 1/12 in. (2 mm) thick.

Place filling in equal mounds on one dough sheet. Mounds should be separated from each other by about 1 1/2 in. (35 mm).

Brush dough with water between mounds.

Place second dough sheet on top.

With a dowel, press down between fillings to seal.

Cut between mounds with a pastry wheel.

Add salt and oil to ample amount of water and bring to a boil.[a]

Drop in ravioli and simmer for 4 to 5 minutes.

Drain and serve with white wine sauce.

Garnish with dill tops.

NOTE: Fillings can be made using other fish or shellfish, or using a farce augmented with diced fish or shellfish.

629

$\mathcal{B}$aked Macaroni

Gratinierte Makkaroni
Gratin de macaroni

YIELD: 10 SERVINGS

Macaroni	1 lb 5 oz	600 g
Salt	1 2/3 oz	50 g
Butter	2/3 oz	20 g
Cream sauce (Recipe 40)	1 pt 1 oz	500 ml
Seasoning (salt, nutmeg)	1x	1x
Sbrinz,[b] grated	1 2/3 oz	50 g
Butter, melted	3/4 oz	25 g

MISE EN PLACE

Boil macaroni in salted water until cooked but still firm (*al dente*). Drain. (If not used right away rinse with cold water, drain again, and toss with small amount of oil to prevent macaroni from sticking together.)

Butter a deep, ovenproof dish (*gratin* dish).

METHOD

Bring cream sauce to a boil and blend into macaroni.

Season with salt and nutmeg and fill *gratin* dish with macaroni.

Sprinkle with cheese and melted butter.

Bake in hot oven until brown.

NOTES: If the macaroni is cold, the baking time must be increased to be sure dish is heated through.

This recipe is for 10 small appetizer or side dish servings. The recipe should be increased for main course servings.

---

[a] If a food processor is used, this step can be omitted.

---

[a] Fish stock can be used instead of water.

[b] Sbrinz is a hard grating cheese from Switzerland. Parmesan can be substituted.

630

Semolina Gnocchi[a]

Griessnocken
Gnocchi romaine

YIELD: 10 SERVINGS

Milk	1 qt 2 oz	1.0 L
Butter	1 2/3 oz	50 g
Salt	1/3 oz	10 g
Nutmeg	1x	1x
Semolina (made from durum wheat)	8 oz	225 g
Egg yolks	2 2/3 oz	75 g
Sbrinz,[b] grated	3 1/2 oz	100 g
Oil		
Parchment paper		
Butter	1 oz	30 g

MISE EN PLACE

Combine milk, butter, salt, and nutmeg and bring to a boil.

Add semolina, stirring with a roux whisk.

Cover and simmer 15 minutes over very low heat.

Remove from stove. Mix in egg yolks and half the grated cheese, using a wooden paddle.

Spread mixture about 3/4-in. (20 mm) thick on oiled sheet pan; cover with oiled parchment paper and let cool.

METHOD

Cut chilled semolina paste into attractive shapes. The traditional shapes are half-moons and circles.

Butter an ovenproof dish (*gratin* dish).

Place gnocchis slightly overlapping in dish.

Sprinkle with remaining cheese and bake in hot oven until brown.

NOTE: Semolina must cook the full time. The semolina must completely absorb all moisture, or the gnocchis will not hold together during baking.

[a] Also see Puff-Paste Gnocchi (Recipe 627) and Potato Gnocchi (Recipe 607).

[b] Sbrinz is a hard grating cheese from Switzerland. Parmesan can be substituted.

631

Home-Made Noodle Dough

Hausmachernudeln
Nouilles maison

YIELD: 10 SERVINGS

White wheat flour	14 oz	400 g
Semolina flour, fine[a]	3 1/2 oz	100 g
Eggs, whole, broken	8 3/4 oz	250 g
Egg yolks	1 2/3 oz	50 g
Olive oil, cold pressed	3/4 oz	25 g

METHOD BY HAND

Sift white and semolina flours together. Put flour on pastry board. Make a well in the center.

Into the well, add eggs, egg yolks, and olive oil, and a small amount of cold water if desired.

Knead mixture thoroughly, by hand, into a dense, smooth, elastic dough.

Let dough rest for at least 1 hour before use.

(Hand-made dough can also be made by kneading the mixture, letting it rest briefly, and then rolling the dough a number of times through a pasta rolling machine.)

METHOD BY MACHINE

Combine all ingredients in a mixer and work mixture with dough hook, at low speed, for at least 5 minutes or until thoroughly kneaded.

This dough can be used right away.

NOTES: The purpose of kneading the dough thoroughly is to develop the gluten in the flour, which makes the dough elastic.

Noodle and ravioli doughs are not salted, because salt would make the dough brittle.

NOODLE VARIATIONS

Basil noodles: Blend dough with chopped fresh basil.

Red beet noodles: Use beet juice in place of water.

Whole wheat noodles: Use sifted whole wheat flour in place of white wheat flour.

Black noodles: Use squid ink in place of water.

Saffron noodles: Steep saffron in small amount of hot water. Let the infused water cool, and use in place of water.

Tomato noodles: Use tomato paste in place of water.

Spinach noodles: Use spinach puree in place of water.

[a] The original recipe calls for *Dunst*, a fine, hard semolina wheat used in commercial pasta manufacturing.

632

Spinach Lasagna with Meat Sauce
Lasagne verdi
Lasagne verdi

YIELD: 10 SERVINGS

Salt	1 2/3 oz	50 g
Peanut oil	1 2/3 oz	50 ml
Green lasagna sheets, purchased	1 lb 2 oz	500 g
Butter	2/3 oz	20 g
Cream sauce (Recipe 40)	1 pt 1 oz	500 ml
Italian sauce[a] (Recipe 62)	1 pt 1 oz	500 ml
Parmesan, grated	1 2/3 oz	50 g
Butter, melted	3/4 oz	25 g

MISE EN PLACE
Add salt and peanut oil to water, bring to a boil, and cook lasagna sheets until *al dente*.

Butter an ovenproof dish (*gratin* dish).

METHOD
Heat sauces.[b]

Spread bottom of *gratin* dish with a layer of cream sauce, cover with half the lasagne sheets, spread with the Italian sauce, and top with remaining lasagne sheets. Cover with remaining cream sauce.

Sprinkle with cheese and melted butter.

Bake in oven until hot and brown on top.

NOTE: This recipe is for 10 small appetizer servings. The recipe should be increased for main course servings.

633

Home-Made Noodles with Vegetables
Nudeln mit Gemüsestreifen
Nouilles à la julienne de légumes

YIELD: 10 SERVINGS

Home-made noodle dough (Recipe 631)	1 lb 5 oz	600 g
Vegetables, assorted	7 oz	200 g
Salt	1 2/3 oz	50 g

Butter	3/4 oz	25 g
Seasoning (salt, nutmeg)	1x	1x

MISE EN PLACE
Make noodle dough according to Recipe 631. Roll out dough and cut into wide noodles, about 1-in. (25 mm) wide.

Wash, trim, and clean vegetables, such as carrots, celery, red and green peppers, and zucchini. Cut vegetables into fine strips (*julienne*).

Briefly blanch vegetables and drain.

METHOD
Boil noodles *al dente* in ample salted water and drain.

Heat butter and sauté vegetables.

Toss hot noodles with vegetables. Season to taste with salt and nutmeg.

NOTE: If boiled noodles are not used right away, rinse with cold water, drain again, and blend with small amount of oil to prevent noodles from sticking together.

634

Home-Made Noodles with Ham in Cream Sauce
Nudeln westfälische Art
Nouilles westphalienne

YIELD: 10 SERVINGS

Home-made noodle dough (Recipe 631)	1 lb 5 oz	600 g
Ham, Westphalian[a]	5 1/3 oz	150 g
Salt	1 2/3 oz	50 g
Butter	2/3 oz	20 g
Cream sauce (Recipe 40)	1 pt 1 oz	500 ml
Seasoning (salt, nutmeg)	1x	1x
Sbrinz,[b] grated	1 2/3 oz	50 g
Butter, melted	3/4 oz	25 g

MISE EN PLACE
Make noodle dough according to Recipe 631. Roll out dough and cut into wide noodles, about 1-in. (25 mm) wide.

Cut ham into fine strips (*julienne*).

METHOD
Boil noodles *al dente* in ample salted water and drain.

Butter an ovenproof dish (*gratin* dish).

---

[a] The ham in the Italian sauce should be replaced with ground beef. The original recipe calls for Bolognese sauce.

[b] If the dish is assembled ahead of time, sauces should not be heated.

[a] Westphalian ham is a heavily smoked ham. Prosciutto can be substituted.

[b] Sbrinz is a hard grating cheese from Switzerland. Parmesan can be substituted.

Bring cream sauce to a boil.

Sauté ham *julienne* in butter and blend with noodles and cream sauce.

Season to taste with salt and nutmeg.

Put noodles in *gratin* dish and sprinkle with cheese and melted butter.

Bake until golden brown.

NOTES: If boiled noodles are not used right away, rinse with cold water, drain again, and blend with small amount of oil to prevent noodles from sticking together.

This recipe is for 10 side dish or appetizer servings. The recipe should be increased for main course servings.

635

Buckwheat Noodles with Bacon and Vegetables, Polish-Style

Pizokel Puschlaver Art

YIELD: 10 SERVINGS

NOODLES

White wheat flour	8 3/4 oz	250 g
Buckwheat flour	8 3/4 oz	250 g
Eggs	2	2
Olive oil	1 1/3 oz	40 ml
Milk	6 oz	175 ml
Salt	1/3 oz	10 g

VEGETABLES

Potatoes	1 lb 2 oz	500 g
Spinach, fresh	10 1/2 oz	300 g
Green beans, fresh	7 oz	200 g
Cabbage	7 oz	200 g
Bacon, smoked, whole	8 3/4 oz	250 g
Butter	1 2/3 oz	50 g
Seasoning (salt and pepper)	1x	1x
Nutmeg	1x	1x
Sbrinz,[a] grated	3 1/2 oz	100 g

GARNISH

Onions	12 oz	350 g
Sage, fresh	2/3 oz	20 g
White wheat flour	2 oz	60 g
Paprika, Hungarian, sweet	1/3 oz	10 g
Seasoning (salt and pepper)	1x	1x
Oil for frying (10% oil loss)	1 1/3 oz	40 ml
Butter	1 1/3 oz	40 g

METHOD FOR NOODLES

Make dough as in Recipe 631, but using the ingredients in this recipe.

Let dough rest in refrigerator.

MISE EN PLACE FOR VEGETABLES

Wash and peel potatoes, cut into small dice, blanch, and drain.

Trim and wash spinach, blanch, drain, rinse in cold water, and drain again.

Trim green beans and break in half, blanch, and drain.

Cut cabbage into small dice, boil or steam until done, and drain.

Cut bacon into small dice, blanch, and drain.

MISE EN PLACE FOR GARNISH

Peel onions and cut into thin rings.

Wash sage and chop leaves.

METHOD FOR NOODLES

Roll out dough to about 1/12-in (2 mm) thick.

Cut dough into noodles about 1/2-in. (12 mm) wide.

Boil noodles *al dente* in ample salt water, drain, rinse in cold water, and drain again.

METHOD FOR VEGETABLES

Butter an ovenproof dish (*gratin* dish) with some of the butter.

Sauté bacon and all vegetables in remaining butter, toss with noodles, and season to taste with salt and pepper and nutmeg.

Place noodle mixture in *gratin* dish, sprinkle with cheese, and bake until hot and brown on top.

Blend flour, paprika, salt and pepper.

METHOD FOR GARNISH

Dredge onion rings in the flour mixture and shake off excess. Deep-fry onion rings at 360°F (180°C) until golden brown.

At the moment of service, place onion rings on top of baked noodles.

Heat butter in a deep cast iron pan, add sage, and pour foaming over the noodles and onions.

---

[a] Sbrinz is a hard grating cheese from Switzerland. Parmesan can be substituted.

636

Spinach and Cottage Cheese Ravioli

Quarkravioli
Ravioli au séré

YIELD: 10 SERVINGS

Ravioli dough (Recipe 637)	1 lb 2 oz	500 g

FILLING

Ricotta cheese	5 1/3 oz	150 g
Spinach, frozen, chopped	1 2/3 oz	50 g
Vegetables, diced (brunoise)	5 1/3 oz	150 g
Butter	2/3 oz	20 g
Cottage cheese, diet	3 1/2 oz	100 g
Parmesan, grated	1 2/3 oz	50 g
Egg yolks	3/4 oz	25 g
Seasoning (salt and pepper)	1x	1x

MISE EN PLACE

Strain ricotta cheese, if necessary, through a wire sieve or food mill.

Defrost chopped spinach and squeeze out liquid.

Smother vegetables in butter until tender and let cool.

METHOD

Blend ricotta, cottage cheese, and Parmesan with spinach and egg yolks. Add vegetables.

Season to taste with salt and pepper.

Make ravioli according to Recipe 628 but use above filling.

Serve ravioli with a sauce, such as Tomato Sauce (Recipe 99), Mushroom Cream Sauce (Recipe 37), or Provençal Sauce (Recipe 84).

637

Basic Ravioli Dough

Ravioli-Grundteig
Pâte pour Ravioli

YIELD: 10 SERVINGS

White wheat flour[a]	1 lb 5 oz	600 g
Whole eggs, shelled	8 3/4 oz	250 g
Sunflower oil	1 2/3 oz	50 ml
Water	3 1/3 oz	100 ml

[a] Use only a high-gluten flour, such as bread flour.

METHOD

Sift flour onto pastry table.

Make a well in the center and add all other ingredients.

Slowly start blending flour into the ingredients until all flour is used up.

Knead dough vigorously and thoroughly until smooth, elastic, and firm.

Let dough rest 1 to 1 1/2 hours before use.

NOTES: The water quantity varies, depending on the type of flour used.

Ravioli and noodle doughs should not be salted, because salt would make the dough brittle.

638

Meat Ravioli with Sage

Ravioli mit Salbei
Ravioli à la sauge

YIELD: 10 SERVINGS

Ravioli dough (Recipe 637)	1 lb 2 oz	500 g

FILLING

Veal shoulder meat, trimmed and boneless	8 3/4 oz	250 g
Pork shoulder meat, trimmed and boneless	7 oz	200 g
Shallots	1 2/3 oz	50 g
Garlic	1/3 oz	10 g
Spinach, fresh	14 oz	400 g
Kitchen herbs, fresh (oregano, thyme, and basil)	2/3 oz	20 g
Peanut oil	1 2/3 oz	50 ml
Dry white wine	3 1/3 oz	100 ml
Brown veal juice, thickened (Recipe 55)	10 oz	300 ml
Seasoning (salt and pepper)	1x	1x
Egg yolk	2 2/3 oz	75 g

GARNISH

Sage, fresh	1 2/3 oz	50 g
Shallots	2 2/3 oz	75 g
Butter	3 1/2 oz	100 g

MISE EN PLACE FOR MEAT FILLING

Cut veal and pork into small dice.

Peel and chop shallots and garlic.

Wash spinach, blanch, chill, and drain. Squeeze out most moisture.

Wash kitchen herbs and chop leaves.

METHOD FOR MEAT FILLING

Sauté diced veal and pork in peanut oil until golden brown; add shallots and garlic.

Add white wine and brown veal juice. Bring to a boil, cover, and simmer over low heat until meat is tender. Remove from heat and let cool.

Add spinach and herbs and season to taste with salt and pepper.

Grind mixture through fine plate of meat grinder, or purée in food processor.

Add egg yolk and chill filling thoroughly.

METHOD FOR RAVIOLI

Make and cook ravioli as in Recipe 628, but use this meat filling. Cook these ravioli for 5 to 8 minutes.

METHOD FOR GARNISH

Wash sage and cut leaves in fine strips (*julienne*).

Peel and chop shallots.

Sauté sage and shallots in butter and serve over hot ravioli.

639

$\mathcal{M}$eat Ravioli with Tomatoes and Cheese

Ravioli Nizza
Ravioli niçoise

YIELD: 10 SERVINGS

Ravioli dough (Recipe 637)	1 lb 2 oz	500 g
FILLING		
Beef chuck meat, trimmed and boneless	8 3/4 oz	250 g
Pork shoulder meat, trimmed and boneless	7 oz	200 g
Shallots	1 2/3 oz	50 g
Garlic	1/3 oz	10 g
Spinach, fresh	14 oz	400 g
Kitchen herbs, fresh (oregano, thyme, and basil)	2/3 oz	20 g
Peanut oil	1 2/3 oz	50 ml
Red wine	3 1/3 oz	100 ml
Brown veal juice, thickened (Recipe 55)	10 oz	300 ml
Seasoning (salt and pepper)	1x	1x
Egg yolks	2 2/3 oz	75 g
SAUCE		
Butter, melted	1 2/3 oz	50 g
Tomatoe concassé (Recipe 97)	1 pt 1 oz	500 ml
Sbrinz,[a] grated	2 2/3 oz	75 g

MISE EN PLACE FOR FILLING

Cut beef and pork into small dice.

Peel and chop shallots and garlic.

Wash spinach, blanch, chill, and drain. Squeeze out most moisture.

Wash kitchen herbs and chop leaves.

METHOD FOR FILLING

Sauté beef and pork in peanut oil until light brown, add shallots and garlic.

Add red wine and veal juice. Bring to a boil, cover, and simmer over low heat until meat is tender. Remove from heat and let cool.

Add spinach and herbs and season to taste with salt and pepper.

Grind mixture through fine plate of meat grinder, or purée in food processor.

Add egg yolk and chill filling thoroughly.

METHOD FOR RAVIOLI AND SAUCE

Make and cook ravioli as in Recipe 628, but use this filling. Cook these ravioli 5 to 8 minutes.

Butter an ovenproof dish (*gratin* dish) with some of the butter.

Toss ravioli with heated tomatoes *concassé*.

Put ravioli into the *gratin* dish and sprinkle with cheese and melted butter.

Bake in hot oven until heated through and brown on top.

---

[a] Sbrinz is a hard grating cheese from Switzerland. Parmesan can be substituted.

640

Spaghetti with Gorgonzola Sauce

Spaghetti mit Gorgonzola-Sauce
Spaghetti au gorgonzola

YIELD: 10 SERVINGS

Gorgonzola cheese[a]	7 oz	200 g
Spaghetti	1 lb 5 oz	600 g
Salt	1 2/3 oz	50 g
Butter	3/4 oz	25 g
Cream sauce (Recipe 40)	10 oz	300 ml
Light cream (15% fat content)	3 1/3 oz	100 ml
Nutmeg	1x	1x
Seasoning (salt and pepper)	1x	1x

MISE EN PLACE

Remove rind from cheese, and cut into small dice.

Boil spaghetti in ample salted water until cooked, but still firm (*al dente*).

Drain spaghetti. (If boiled spaghetti is not used right away, rinse in cold water, drain, and mix with small amount of oil to prevent spaghetti from sticking together.)

METHOD

If necessary, reheat spaghetti in boiling water and drain.

Melt butter and toss spaghetti in butter.

Combine cream sauce, light cream, and gorgonzola. Heat, stirring frequently, until sauce is very hot, but do not boil.

Purée sauce with hand-held mixer, if desired.

Season to taste with nutmeg, salt and pepper.

Serve spaghetti tossed with sauce.

NOTE: This recipe is for 10 small appetizer or side dish servings. The recipe should be increased for main course servings.

641

Spaghetti with Ham and Mushrooms

Spaghetti Mailänder Art
Spaghetti milanaise

YIELD: 10 SERVINGS

Spaghetti	1 lb 5 oz	600 g
Salt	1 2/3 oz	50 g
Ham, boiled	5 1/3 oz	150 g
Mushrooms, fresh	7 oz	200 g
Butter	1 2/3 oz	50 g
Nutmeg	1	1
Seasoning (salt, nutmeg)	1	1
Sbrinz,[a] grated	1 2/3 oz	50 g

MISE EN PLACE

Boil spaghetti in ample salted water until cooked, but still firm (*al dente*).

Drain spaghetti. (If boiled spaghetti is not used right away, rinse in cold water, drain, and mix with small amount of oil to prevent spaghetti from sticking together.)

Cut ham into strips (*julienne*).

Trim and wash mushrooms and cut into slices.

METHOD

If necessary, reheat spaghetti in boiling water, and drain.

Melt butter and toss spaghetti in half of it.

Sauté ham and mushrooms in remaining butter.

Season ham and mushrooms with salt and nutmeg and serve over spaghetti.

Sprinkle with grated cheese.

NOTE: This recipe is for 10 small appetizer or side dish servings. The recipe should be increased for main course servings.

---

[a] Gorgonzola is an Italian blue cheese. It is somewhat salty, and caution must be used to flavor the sauce properly. If Gorgonzola is not available, another blue cheese can be used, and the recipe name changed accordingly.

[a] Sbrinz is a hard grating cheese from Switzerland. Parmesan can be substituted.

642

Spaghetti with Tomatoes

Spaghetti mit Tomaten
Spaghetti napolitaine

YIELD: 10 SERVINGS

Spaghetti	1 lb 5 oz	600 g
Salt	1 2/3 oz	50 g
Butter	3/4 oz	25 g
Seasoning (salt, nutmeg)	1	1
Tomatoe concassé (Recipe 97)	1 pt 1 oz	500 ml
Butter, cold, shaved into flakes	1 2/3 oz	50 g
Basil tops, fresh	10	10

MISE EN PLACE

Boil spaghetti in ample salted water until cooked, but still firm in the center (*al dente*).

Drain spaghetti. (If boiled spaghetti is not used right away, rinse in cold water, drain, and mix with small amount of oil to prevent spaghetti from sticking together.)

Method

If necessary, reheat spaghetti in boiling water and drain.

Melt butter and toss with spaghetti. Season with salt and nutmeg.

Heat tomatoes concassé and serve over the spaghetti.

Place fresh butter flakes over spaghetti and garnish with basil tops.

NOTES: Serve grated cheese on the side.

This recipe is for 10 small appetizer or side dish servings. The recipe should be increased for main course servings.

643

Spaetzle (little dumplings)

Spätzli/Knöpfli
Spaetzli/frisettes

YIELD: 10 SERVINGS

White wheat flour	14 oz	400 g
Hard wheat semolina, very fine	3 1/2 oz	100 g
Whole eggs, shelled	8 3/4 oz	250 g
Milk	3 1/3 oz	100 ml
Water	3 1/3 oz	100 ml
Salt	1/3 oz	10 g
Nutmeg	1x	1x

METHOD

Sift white wheat flour and combine with semolina in a mixing bowl.

Add remaining ingredients and blend with a wooden paddle until the dough is smooth. It should have the consistency of a very thick batter. Work the dough with the paddle until it starts to form bubbles.

Drop spaetzle directly into boiling water by one of the following methods:

1. Use a china cap with very large holes and press the dough through with a wooden paddle; or

2. Use a food mill; or

3. Put the dough on a small cutting board and scrape little dumplings, with a wet spatula, into the water.

Remove the spaetzle with a skimmer as soon as they rise to the top, and put into cold water. Drain immediately.

Reheat spaetzle as needed by putting them into a basket, dipping them for a moment into boiling water, and then sautéing them in butter.

VARIATIONS

Spinach Spaetzli: Blend basic dough with 5 1/3 oz (150 g) cooked spinach, moisture squeezed out, and puréed. The amount of water in the recipe should be reduced by half to 1 2/3 oz (50 ml).

Saffron Spaetzle: Heat the 3 1/3 oz (100 ml) water and steep a small amount of saffron in it. Strain the water (optional), unless ground saffron is used. Let the water cool before it is used to make the dough.

Tomato Spaetzle: Blend basic dough with 1 2/3 oz (50 g) tomato paste.

Whole Wheat Spaetzle: Use whole wheat flour instead of white wheat flour.

Cottage Cheese Spaetzle: Replace the 3 1/3 oz (100 ml) water with 5 1/3 oz (150 g) low-fat cottage cheese.[a]

Glarner (Glarus)[b] Spaetzle: Serve spinach spaetzle mixed with soaked sultanas, and sprinkle with grated Schabzieger[c] cheese.

Tessiner[d] Spaetzle: Serve a mixture of spinach, saffron, and tomato spaetzle.

---

[a] It is best to purée the cottage cheese in order to obtain a smooth dough.

[b] Glarus is a canton (province) of Switzerland.

[c] Schabzieger is a small, cylindrical-shaped cheese, flavored with ground clover. It is sold in English-speaking countries as Sapsago cheese.

[d] Tessin, or Ticino, is an Italian-speaking canton of Switzerland.

644

Tortellini with Pesto

Tortellini mit Pesto
Tortellini al pesto

YIELD: 10 SERVINGS

Ravioli dough (Recipe 637)	1 lb 2 oz	500 g
FILLING		
Spinach, fresh	7 oz	200 g
Ricotta cheese	7 oz	200 g
Parmesan, grated	1 2/3 oz	50 g
Egg yolks	1 2/3 oz	50 g
Seasoning (salt and pepper)	1x	1x
Nutmeg	1x	1x
PESTO		
Basil, fresh	3 1/2 oz	100 g
Parsley, Italian	1 2/3 oz	50 g
Garlic	3/4 oz	25 g
Pine nuts, shelled	2 2/3 oz	75 g
Parmesan, grated	1 2/3 oz	50 g
Pecorino-romano cheese,[a] grated	2 2/3 oz	75 g
Olive oil, cold pressed	5 1/3 oz	150 g
Seasoning (salt and pepper)	1x	1x

METHOD FOR FILLING
Blanch spinach, drain in cold water, and drain again. Squeeze out most moisture and purée in food processor.

Purée or strain ricotta cheese to obtain a smooth paste.

Blend all filling ingredients.

METHOD FOR PESTO
Wash basil and parsley and chop leaves.

Peel garlic, and chop coarsely.

Grind basil, parsley, garlic, and pine nuts. The resulting puree should not be too fine.

Add the cheeses and olive oil and season with white pepper.

METHOD
Roll ravioli dough to about 1/10-in. (2 1/2 mm) thickness.

Cut circles with cookie cutter, about 1 1/2-in. (30 to 40 mm) in diameter.

Put small amount of filling in centers, using a pastry bag.

Moisten the circle edges with water and fold over dough to make half-moons. Be sure edges are well sealed.

---

[a] Pecorino-romano cheese is an Italian grating cheese made with sheep's milk. The taste is slightly sharper than Parmesan.

Pull together the pointed corners of the half-moons and press the two corners together, overlapping them slightly; press to seal. The result should be a closed circle, with filling on one side.

Put tortellini on a floured board until use.

Simmer tortellini for 5 to 6 minutes in salted water, with a little oil to prevent them from sticking together. Drain and save small amount of boiling water.

Dilute pesto, if necessary, with the small amount of the boiling water.

Serve pesto over tortellini.

645

Yorkshire Pudding

Yorkshire Pudding

YIELD: 10 SERVINGS

Veal kidney fat	7 oz	200 g
White wheat flour	11 1/4 oz	320 g
Milk	1 pt 3 oz	550 ml
Egg yolks	4	4
Nutmeg	1x	1x
Seasoning (salt and pepper)	1x	1x
Egg whites	5	5
Peanut oil	2/3 oz	20 ml

MISE EN PLACE
Remove membrane from kidney fat and break kidney fat into small pieces.

METHOD
Combine flour and kidney fat. Chop with a knife or briefly in a food processor, using the pulse feature. (Do not overmix.)

Add milk and egg yolks, season with nutmeg, salt and pepper, and mix well into a batter.

Whip egg whites and fold into batter.

Heat peanut oil in a deep baking sheet (2-in. deep pan).

Pour batter into hot oil and bake in 400°F (200°C) oven until golden brown.

Cut, while still hot, into 10 rectangles, slices, or lozenges; serve with roast beef. Drizzle some roasting *jus* onto pudding when plating.

NOTES: Traditionally, Yorkshire pudding was baked directly under roast beef, and the dripping juices added flavor. (Roast beef pan drippings can be used in this recipe instead of peanut oil, but saturated beef fat is not considered healthy.)

Yorkshire pudding can also be baked in timbale molds or muffin tins.

Rice and Grain Dishes

646

Rice Pilaf

Pilaw-Reis
Riz pilav

YIELD: 10 SERVINGS

Bouillon (Recipe 22)	1 qt 2 oz	1.0 L
Onions	5 1/3 oz	150 g
Butter	1 1/3 oz	40 g
Siam-Patna rice[a]	1 lb 5 oz	600 g
Bay leaf	1	1
Butter, cold	1 1/3 oz	40 g

MISE EN PLACE
Heat bouillon.

Peel and chop onions.

METHOD
Sauté onions lightly in butter, without getting color.

Add rice, and sauté briefly with onions.

Add bouillon and bay leaf and bring to a boil.

Cover and cook in the oven for about 15 minutes.

Remove from the oven and keep covered for about 5 minutes.

Remove bay leaf. Carefully stir rice with a fork to loosen the kernels.

Add the cold butter in small nuggets.

NOTES: The amount of liquid varies depending on rice variety.

Generally, larger amounts require less liquid.

---

[a] Any long-grain rice can be substituted.

647

Basic Risotto

Risotto

YIELD: 10 SERVINGS

Bouillon (Recipe 22)	61 oz	1.8 L
Onions	5 1/3 oz	150 g
Garlic cloves	2	2
Olive oil	1 2/3 oz	50 ml
Vialone rice[a]	1 lb 5 oz	600 g
Bay leaf	1	1
Sage leaves	2	2
Dry white wine	5 oz	150 ml
Butter, cold	1 oz	30 g
Sbrinz,[b] grated	3 1/2 oz	100 g
Seasoning (salt and pepper)	1x	1x

MISE EN PLACE
Heat bouillon.

Peel and chop onions and garlic.

METHOD
Sauté onions and garlic in olive oil, without getting color.

Add rice and sauté briefly with onions and garlic.

Add a small amount of bouillon and stir. Add bay leaf and sage.

Add bouillon in small amounts and bring to a boil each time, stirring with a wooden paddle.

Cook and stir the rice until all bouillon is used up, about 17 to 18 minutes.

Add white wine, cold butter, and grated cheese.

Season to taste with salt and pepper.

NOTES: The amount of liquid needed is approximately to 2 1/2 to 3 parts liquid to 1 part rice (by volume).

The wine is added at the end to stop the cooking process, and also to preserve the wine aroma. If the wine is added at the beginning, most aroma would boil away.

---

[a] The recipe specifies Vialone rice, which is a short-grain rice similar to Arborio; Arborio rice can be substituted.

[b] Sbrinz is a hard grating cheese from Switzerland. Parmesan can be substituted.

648

oiled Rice

Trockenreis
Riz créole

YIELD: 10 SERVINGS

Water	3 qt 22 oz	3.5 L
Salt	1 1/3 oz	40 g
Siam-Patna rice[a]	1 lb 2 oz	500 g
Butter, cold	1 2/3 oz	50 g
Buttered paper		

METHOD

Combine water and salt and bring to a boil.

Add rice and boil vigorously for 12 to 15 minutes.

Drain, rinse in cold water, and drain again.

Spread rice on a flat pan, season with additional salt if desired, and add cold butter in small nuggets.

Cover rice with buttered paper.

Warm rice in the oven, stirring occasionally with a fork.

NOTE: To heat rice to order, sauté with small amount of butter in a sauté pan (*sautéuse*); or season rice, add a small amount of butter, and heat in microwave oven or steamer.

649

Brown Rice Risotto (basic recipe)

Vollreisrisotto (Grundrezept)
Risotto de riz complet (recette de base)

YIELD: 10 SERVINGS

Brown rice, short grain	1 lb 2 oz	500 g
Onions	3 1/2 oz	100 g
Garlic	1/6 oz	5 g
Vegetable bouillon (Recipe 27)	1 qt 19 oz	1.5 L
Sage, fresh	1/6 oz	5 g
Olive oil, cold pressed	1 2/3 oz	50 ml
Dry white wine	3 1/3 oz	100 ml
Sbrinz,[b] grated	3 1/2 oz	100 g
Butter	1 oz	30 g
Seasoning (salt and pepper)	1x	1x

MISE EN PLACE
Wash rice and drain.

Peel and chop onions and garlic.

Heat vegetable bouillon.

Wash sage and chop leaves.

METHOD
Sauté onions and garlic in olive oil, without getting brown.

Add rice and sauté briefly with onions and garlic.

Add vegetable bouillon and sage. (Do not add salt yet, because it will prevent rice from getting soft.)

Bring to a boil and simmer for 30 to 35 minutes. (Do not stir, because rice will get mushy.)

Remove from heat, cover, and let rest for about 10 to 15 minutes.

Blend in white wine, grated cheese, and butter.

Season to taste with salt and pepper.

VARIATION
Barley Risotto: Soak raw barley for about 5 hours and prepare as directed for basic risotto. Add a small amount of tomato paste before adding the vegetable bouillon. Simmer for about 2 hours, and let rest, covered, for at least 30 minutes.

650

Green Wheat[a] (basic recipe)

Grünkern (Grundrezept)
Blé vert (recette de base)

YIELD: 10 SERVINGS

Green wheat (spelt, cracked)	14 oz	400 g
Vegetable bouillon (Recipe 27)	1 qt 2 oz	1.0 L
Bouquet garni (Recipe 8)	5 1/3 oz	150 g
Onion studded with 3 cloves	1	1
Thyme twig	1	1
Salt	1/3 oz	10 g

MISE EN PLACE
Wash the wheat.

Soak wheat in vegetable bouillon, in the refrigerator, for about 6 hours.

---

[a] Any long grain rice can be substituted.

[b] Sbrinz is a hard grating cheese from Switzerland. Parmesan can be substituted.

---

[a] The original recipe calls for *Grünkern*, which is spelt wheat that has not fully ripened. (Spelt is called *Dinkel* in German.)

METHOD

Bring rice and bouillon to a boil and skim.

Add *bouquet garni*, onion, and thyme twig.

Cover and simmer for 30 minutes.

Add salt and continue cooking for 30 minutes longer.

Let rest, covered, for about 10 minutes on side of stove.

651

Millet Risotto with Green Asparagus

Hirsotto mit grünen Spargeln
Risotto de millet aux asperges vertes

YIELD: 10 SERVINGS

Onions	5 1/3 oz	150 g
Parsley	1 oz	30 g
Chicken stock (Recipe 26)	2 qt 4 oz	2.0 L
Green asparagus	10 1/2 oz	300 g
Butter	1 2/3 oz	50 g
Millet, whole grain	1 lb 2 oz	500 g
Bay leaves	2	2
Herb butter (Recipe 444)[a]	1 1/3oz	40 g
Heavy cream (36%)	3 1/3 oz	100 ml
Seasoning (salt and pepper)	1x	1x
Sbrinz,[b] grated	3 1/2 oz	100 g

MISE EN PLACE

Peel onions and cut into fine strips.

Wash parsley and chop leaves.

Bring chicken stock to a boil.

Peel, trim, and wash asparagus, boil or steam, and cut into 3/4-in. (20 mm) long pieces.

METHOD

Sauté onions in butter, without getting color.

Add millet and sauté briefly.

Add chicken stock and bay leaves and bring to a boil.

Cover and simmer over very low heat for about 20 minutes. The kernels should be tender, but not mushy.

Remove bay leaves.

Add herb butter and heavy cream.

Carefully blend in asparagus tips, adjust seasoning, and heat briefly.

Serve grated cheese on the side.

---

[a] Use the herb butter from Recipe 444, but omit the *glace de viande*.

[b] Sbrinz is a hard grating cheese from Switzerland. Parmesan can be substituted.

652

Lentil, Whole Wheat, and Vegetable Curry

Linsen-Weizen-Gemüse-Curry
Curry de lentilles, de froment et de légumes

YIELD: 10 SERVINGS

Wheat kernels, whole	10 1/2 oz	300 g
Lentils	10 1/2 oz	300 g
Onions	5 1/3 oz	150 g
Garlic cloves, peeled	2	2
Bell peppers, assorted	10 1/2 oz	300 g
Eggplant	10 1/2 oz	300 g
Zucchini (vegetable marrow)	10 1/2 oz	300 g
Ginger, fresh	1/6 oz	5 g
Mushrooms, fresh	5 1/3 oz	150 g
Tomatoes, peeled and seeded	7 oz	200 g
Vegetable bouillon (Recipe 27)	1 qt 2 oz	1.0 L
Onion studded with 3 cloves	1	1
Sea salt	1/3 oz	10 g
Olive oil, cold pressed	3 1/3 oz	100 ml
Madras curry powder	1/3 oz	10 g
GARNISH		
Pineapple, fresh	1 lb 12 oz	800 g
Butter	1 1/3 oz	40 g
Yogurt[a]	5 oz	150 ml
Mint leaves, fresh, washed	10	10

MISE EN PLACE

Soak wheat for 5 to 8 hours in 1 qt 2 oz (1.0 L) cold water.

Wash lentils and soak for 2 hours in cold water.

Peel and chop onions and garlic.

Split peppers, remove seeds, wash, and cut into small dice.

Wash and trim eggplant and zucchini and cut into small dice.

Peel ginger and grate or chop.

Trim mushrooms, wash, and cut into fine slices.

Cut tomatoes into cubes.

METHOD FOR GARNISH

Peel pineapple, remove center core, and cut into 10 slices.

Sauté pineapple slices in butter and keep warm.

(continued on next page)

---

[a] The original recipe calls for Bifidus yogurt, a non-pasteurized yogurt.

(continued from preceding page)

METHOD

Bring wheat kernels and soaking water to a boil and simmer for 40 minutes, or until kernels are open.

Add drained lentils, vegetable bouillon, and onion studded with clove.

Simmer for 30 minutes and add sea salt.

Let rest, covered, for 30 minutes, at the side of the stove.

Sauté onions and garlic in olive oil, add peppers, and smother for 5 minutes.

Add eggplant and zucchini and dust with curry powder. Add ginger. Add mushrooms and cubed tomatoes; smother until vegetables are tender, but not too soft.

Drain wheat and lentils and save some stock.

Rinse wheat and lentils briefly in hot water and blend carefully with the vegetable mixture. Add a small amount of stock if mixture is too dry. It should have a risotto consistency.

Garnish with pineapple slices, mint leaves, and yogurt.

653

Polenta (basic recipe)

Polenta

YIELD: 10 SERVINGS

Onions	3 1/2 oz	100 g
Garlic	1/3 oz	10 g
Olive oil	1 2/3 oz	50 ml
Bouillon (Recipe 22)	1 qt 2 oz	1.0 L
Cornmeal, coarse[a]	8 3/4 oz	250 g
Bay leaf	1	1
Seasoning (salt and pepper)	1x	1x
Sbrinz,[b] grated	3 1/2 oz	100 g

MISE EN PLACE
Peel and chop onions and garlic.

METHOD
Sauté onions and garlic in olive oil, without getting color.

Add bouillon and bring to a boil.

Add cornmeal gradually, in a thin stream, stirring continuously with a strong wire whisk.

---

[a] The cornmeal should be coarse. The typical American cornmeal breakfast cereal is too fine.

[b] Sbrinz is a hard grating cheese from Switzerland. Parmesan can be substituted.

Simmer for 5 minutes, stirring with a wooden paddle.

Add bay leaf and salt and pepper, cover, and cook at 250°F (120°C) in oven, or over low heat on the stove, or side of the stove, for 1 1/2 hours. Do not stir during this time.

Remove bay leaf and blend in grated cheese.

NOTES: If a softer polenta is desired, the amount of bouillon can be increased to 1 qt 8 oz (1.2 L).

If a creamier texture is desired, half of the bouillon can be replaced with milk.

654

Whole Kernel Wheat and Rye (basic recipe)

Weizen/Roggen (Grundrezept)
Froment/seigle (recette de base)

YIELD: 10 SERVINGS

Wheat, whole kernel	7 oz	200 g
Rye, whole kernel	7 oz	200 g
Vegetable bouillon (Recipe 27)	1 qt 8 oz	1.2 L
Bouquet garni (Recipe 8)	5 1/3 oz	150 g
Onion studded with 3 cloves	1	1
Thyme, fresh	1	1
Salt	1/3 oz	10 g

MISE EN PLACE
Wash wheat and rye.

Soak wheat and rye in vegetable bouillon, for 8 hours, in the refrigerator.

METHOD
Bring kernels and soaking liquid to a boil.

Skim and add *bouquet garni*, onion, and thyme.

Simmer add salt after about 1 hour.

Continue simmering for 30 minutes longer, or until all liquid is absorbed.

Cover pot and let rest, over low heat, for 30 minutes longer.

Recipe 392, Glazed Veal Shank with Vegetables

Recipe 403, Grilled Club Steak with Tomatoes and Fried Onion Rings

Recipe 417, White Lamb Stew with Tomatoes and Herbs

Recipe 441, Pork Medallions Sautéed with Apples and Calvados

Recipe 463, Chicken in Red Wine

(clockwise from top): Recipe 561, Fried Knob Celery, Recipe 541, Braised Belgian Endive, Recipe 537, Stuffed Cucumbers

(clockwise from far left): Recipe 595, Anna Potatoes, Recipe 575, Rösti Potatoes,
Recipe 594, Baked Potatoes Stuffed with Spinach

Recipe 643, Spaetzle (clockwise from top left: spinach, plain, tomato, glarus, saffron)

Recipe 644, Tortellini with Pesto

Recipe 658, Hot Apple Charlotte

Recipe 674, Filled Doughnuts

Recipe 736, Butter Cookies, Recipe 688, Vanilla Custard

Recipe 698, Strawberry Mousse

Recipe 748, Pears Poached in Port

Desserts

655

Aargau[a] Carrot Cake

Aargauer Rüeblitorte
Tarte aux carottes argovienne

YIELD: 2 CAKES

Silicon paper[b] or bake-proof parchment paper	1 large sheet	
Carrots	1 lb 5 oz	600 g
Cake flour	12 oz	350 g
Baking powder	3/4 oz	25 g
Butter	10 1/2 oz	300 g
Crystal sugar	7 oz	200 g
Egg yolks	7 oz	200 g
Milk	3 1/3 oz	100 ml
Hazelnuts (filberts), ground	7 oz	200 g
Crystal sugar	3 1/2 oz	100 g
Egg whites	7 oz	200 g
Apricot glaze[b]	3 1/2 oz	100 g
White fondant icing[b]	7 oz	200 g
Lemon juice	2/3 oz	20 ml

MISE EN PLACE
Place two 9-in. (225 mm) cake rings[c] on a baking sheet lined with silicon paper or bake-proof parchment paper.

Peel, trim, and wash carrots and grate fine.

Sift together cake flour and baking powder.

METHOD
Cream softened butter with 7 oz (200 g) sugar.

Gradually add in egg yolks, creaming mixture continuously.

Fold in carrots, milk, and ground hazelnuts.

Add 3 1/2 oz (100 g) sugar to egg whites and whip into soft peaks.

Fold whipped egg whites and flour, alternately, into the carrot/nut mixture.

Pour batter into the prepared cake rings and bake at 375°F (190°C).

Check with a wooden skewer or cake tester to be sure the cake is baked all the way through.

Invert cakes onto glazing rack and let cool.

Melt apricot glaze. Combine fondant and lemon juice and melt in water bath.

Brush apricot glaze on cakes. Cover cakes with fondant icing.

NOTE: If desired, the cakes can be decorated with small marzipan carrots.

656

Apple Soufflé

Apfelauflauf
Soufflé de pommes

YIELD: 10 SERVINGS

Apple purée,[a] not too thin	7 oz	200 g
Butter	1/3 oz	10 g
Crystal sugar	1/3 oz	10 g
Egg yolks	3 1/2 oz	100 g
Crystal sugar	3 1/2 oz	100 g
Cinnamon, ground	1 pinch	1 g
Egg whites	13 oz	375 g
Crystal sugar	3 1/2 oz	100 g
Powdered sugar	1/3 oz	10 g

MISE EN PLACE
Warm apple purée slightly.

Butter a 1-qt (950 ml) soufflé dish and dust with 1/3 oz (10 g) sugar.

METHOD
Cream egg yolks with 3 1/2 oz (100 g) sugar and ground cinnamon. Blend with the apple purée.

Whip egg whites into soft peaks and whip in 3 1/2 oz (100 g) sugar.

Fold egg whites gently into the apple mixture.

Fill soufflé mold about three-fourths high.

Put soufflé mold in water bath on stove and let batter warm. Do not allow water bath to boil.

Bake on rack in oven at 400°F (200°C).

Dust with powdered sugar and serve at once.

---

[a] Aargau is a canton (province) in Switzerland.

[b] Silicon paper, apricot glaze, and fondant are commercially available from pastry supply houses.

[c] If cake rings are not available, buttered and floured cake molds can be used.

---

[a] The original recipe calls for apple mousse. Do not use Apple Sauce (Recipe 32) or Apple Mousse (Recipe 662), because they contain too much liquid. For this recipe, simply steam or bake peeled and cored apples without adding liquid, and then purée the apples.

CHAPTER

11

Desserts

657

*B*aked Apples Basel[a] Style

Äpfel Basler Art
Pommes bâloise

YIELD: 10 SERVINGS

Apples[b] (10)	3 lb 5 oz	1.5 kg
Butter	1 2/3 oz	50 g
Almonds, peeled and sliced	1 2/3 oz	50 g
Crystal sugar	3 1/2 oz	100 g
Dry white wine	5 oz	150 ml
Apple wine[c]	5 oz	150 ml
Red currant jelly	7 oz	200 g
Kirsch[d]	1 2/3 oz	50 ml
Powdered sugar	2/3 oz	20 g
Vanilla sauce (Recipe 780)	1 pt 1 oz	500 ml

MISE EN PLACE

Peel apples, cut in half horizontally, and remove core with melon baller.

Butter an ovenproof dish (*gratin* dish) with some of the butter.

Lightly toast almonds.

METHOD

Put apples in *gratin* dish, cut-side up.

Fill each cavity with sugar and remaining butter.

Pour wine and apple wine around apples.

Put apples in 325°F (165°C) oven and bake slowly until apples are soft.

Remove apples with slotted spatula and place on serving dish or individual plates.

Reduce baking liquid to a syrupy consistency and spoon syrup over apples.

Blend red currant jelly with kirsch and put a small dollop in each cavity.

Sprinkle apples with toasted almonds.

Dust with powdered sugar at the moment of service.

Serve vanilla sauce on the side.

---

[a] Basel is a Swiss city near the German and French borders.

[b] Use a cooking apple, such as Granny Smith. If no cooking apples are available, leave some peel on the apples. The peel will help to hold the apples together.

[c] Apple cider can be substituted.

[d] Kirsch is a clear cherry brandy. Swiss kirsch is renowned.

658

*H*ot Apple Charlotte

Apfelcharlotte
Charlotte aux pommes

YIELD: 10 SERVINGS

Apples, cooking[a]	3 lb 5 oz	1.5 kg
Butter	2/3 oz	20 g
Crystal sugar	5 1/3 oz	150 g
Raisins	1 2/3 oz	50 g
Lemon, zest[b]	1	1
Cinnamon, ground	1 pinch	2 g
Cloves, ground	1 pinch	1 g
Dry white wine	5 oz	150 ml
Butter	4 1/4 oz	120 g
White bread, Pullman loaf	1 lb 2 oz	500 g
Rum, dark	2/3 oz	20 ml
Suitable fruit sauce[c]	1 pt 1 oz	500 ml

MISE EN PLACE

Peel apples, remove core, and cut into fine slices.

Combine apples with 2/3 oz (20 g) butter, sugar, raisins, lemon zest, cinnamon, and cloves.

Add white wine and stew apples briefly.

Drain apples and save juice.

Remove crust from bread and cut into 1/5-in. (5 mm) slices. Chill mold.

METHOD

Melt 4 1/4 oz (120 g) butter.

Cut some bread slices in triangles, dip in some melted butter, and cover bottom of soufflé dish evenly.

Cut some slices in rectangles, dip in melted butter, and line sides of soufflé dish. The slices should overlap slightly. Save some bread and melted butter for the top.

Fill mold tightly with drained apples.

Reduce apple stewing liquid to a syrupy consistency.

Let cool slightly and add rum. Pour liquid over apples.

Cut remaining bread slices into triangles, dip in butter, and cover top of charlotte.

Bake at 425°F (220°C) until bread is browned on top. Sides should also be browned.

(continued on next page)

---

[a] Granny Smith apples are good for this recipe.

[b] Lemon zest is made by peeling the yellow rind with a vegetable peeler and cutting the rind into very fine shreds (*julienne*).

[c] Suitable fruit sauces are Apricot Sauce (Recipe 668), Strawberry Sauce (Recipe 699), Red Currant Sauce (Recipe 727), and Melba (Raspberry) Sauce (Recipe 719). Vanilla Sauce (Recipe 780) can also be used.

(*continued from preceding page*)

Let rest a few minutes; invert directly onto service platter.

Leave soufflé dish over the charlotte for a few minutes, but not too long.[a]

Remove dish and serve hot with a fruit sauce.

659

*A*pple Turnovers

Apfelkrapfen
Rissoles normande

YIELD: 10 SERVINGS

Puff pastry (Recipe 689)	1 lb 12 oz	800 g
Egg	1	1
Crystal sugar	2/3 oz	20 g
Vanilla sauce (Recipe 780)	1 pt 1 oz	500 ml

FILLING

Apples, cooking[b]	1 lb 5 oz	600 g
Butter	2/3 oz	20 g
Lemon, juice	1	1
Golden raisins	1 2/3 oz	50 g
Crystal sugar	1 2/3 oz	50 g
Dry white wine	3 1/3 oz	100 ml
Calvados[c]	3/4 oz	25 ml

MISE EN PLACE FOR FILLING
Peel apples, core, and cut into fine slices.

Combine with butter, lemon juice, raisins, sugar, and white wine.

Stew briefly, drain, and save juices.

Reduce juices to syrupy consistency.

Add the apples and add Calvados. Chill the mixture.

METHOD
Roll out puff pastry about 1/12-inch (2 mm) thick.

With cookie cutter, cut out circles about 5 in. (125 mm) across.

Break egg and mix with 1 tbsp cold water.

Brush circle rims with some of the egg wash.

Place apple filling on circles, somewhat off center.

Fold dough over filling; seal rim by pressing down with a fork or with the blunt end of a cookie cutter.

Brush turnovers with egg wash, sprinkle with sugar, and prick with a fork.

Bake at 400°F (200°C) for about 20 minutes.

Serve hot, with vanilla sauce on the side.

660

*O*pen-Face Apple Tart

Apfelkuchen
Tarte aux pommes

YIELD: 1 TART

Apple, cooking[a]	2 lb 3 oz	1.0 kg
Butter	1/3 oz	10 g
Short pastry (Recipe 710)	10 1/2 oz	300 g
Crystal sugar	3 oz	80 g
Apricot glaze[b]	3 1/2 oz	100 g

MISE EN PLACE
Peel apples, core, and cut into even wedges.

Butter an 10-in. (250 mm) tart mold.

METHOD
Roll dough about 1/8-in. (3 mm) thick and line bottom and sides of tart mold.

Poke a few holes in dough with a fork to let steam escape.

Arrange the apple wedges attractively in circles on top of dough.

Sprinkle apples with sugar.

Bake at 450°F (230°C).

Warm the apricot glaze and brush tart, while still hot, with glaze.

NOTE: Other fruits can be used. If the fruits are very juicy, the dough bottom should be sprinkled with ground hazelnuts or cake crumbs.

---

[a] If the soufflé dish stays too long over the charlotte, the resulting steam will make the bread soggy.

[b] Granny Smith apples are suitable for this recipe.

[c] Calvados is an apple brandy from the Normandy region of France. Applejack can be substituted.

---

[a] Granny Smith apples are suitable for this recipe.

[b] Apricot glaze is commercially available.

661

*A*pple Fritters

Apfelküchlein
Beignets de pommes

YIELD: 10 SERVINGS

Apples	2 lb 10 oz	1.2 kg
Lemon juice	1 2/3 oz	50 ml
Crystal sugar	1 2/3 oz	50 g
Kirsch[a]	3/4 oz	25 ml
Crystal sugar	3 1/2 oz	100 g
Cinnamon, ground	1 pinch	2 g
Vanilla sauce (Recipe 780)	1 pt 1 oz	500 ml
Frying batter (Recipe 672)	1 lb 5 oz	600 g
Oil for frying (10% oil loss)	5 oz	150 ml

MISE EN PLACE
Peel apples and remove core. Cut apples crosswise into slices about 1/4-in. (6 mm) thick. Marinate apples immediately with lemon juice, 1 2/3 oz (50 g) sugar, and kirsch.

Blend 3 1/2 oz (100 g) sugar and cinnamon and set aside.

Heat vanilla sauce.

METHOD
Dip apple slices, one by one, in frying batter, and deep-fry at 325°F (165°C) until golden brown.

Drain fritters on absorbent paper.

At moment of service, dredge fritters in the cinnamon-sugar and serve hot with warm vanilla sauce.

NOTE: Pineapple fritters can be prepared by the same method.

---

[a] Kirsch is a clear cherry brandy. Swiss kirsch is renowned.

662

*A*pple Mousse

Apfelmousse
Mousse aux pommes

YIELD: 10 SERVINGS

Gelatin, leaf[a]	1/4 oz	8 g
Heavy cream (36%)	13 1/2 oz	400 ml
Apple puree[b]	7 oz	200 g
Crystal sugar	5 1/3 oz	150 g
Egg whites	1 2/3 oz	50 g

MISE EN PLACE
Soak gelatin leaf in cold water.

Whip heavy cream.

METHOD
Combine apple puree, sugar, and egg whites.

Heat mixture to no more than 120°F (50°C) in water bath, stirring continuously.

Squeeze water from gelatin leaf and dissolve gelatin in small amount of hot water.

Add dissolved gelatin to apple mixture and stir until cool.

Fold whipped cream into apple mixture.

Fill crystal dishes or glasses with mousse and refrigerate.

NOTE: The mousse can be served with a fruit sauce, such as Melba (Raspberry) Sauce (Recipe 719).

---

[a] Powdered gelatin (unflavored) can be substituted. It does not need to be pre-soaked in cold water; it must simply be dissolved with a small amount of warm water.

[b] Do not use Apple Sauce (Recipe 32) for this recipe because it contains too much liquid. For this recipe, simply steam or bake peeled and cored apples without adding liquid, and then purée the apples.

663

*A*pple Dumplings

Äpfel im Schlafrock
Pommes en chemise

YIELD: 10 SERVINGS

Apples, 10	3 lb 5 oz	1.5 kg
Egg	1	1
Crystal sugar	3 oz	80 g
Golden raisins	1 2/3 oz	50 g
Puff pastry (Recipe 689)	1 lb 12 oz	800 g
Almond paste	5 1/3 oz	150 g
Vanilla sauce (Recipe 780)	1 pt 1 oz	500 ml

MISE EN PLACE
Peel apples and remove cores completely. Leave apples whole.

Break egg and mix with 1 tbsp. water.

Blend sugar and raisins.

METHOD
Roll puff pastry to about 1/12-in. (2 mm) thick.

Cut pastry into squares, about 6 in. x 6 in. (150 mm x 150 mm).

Place a dollop of almond paste in the center of each square and brush dough rims with egg wash.

Place apples on pastry square, on top of almond paste.

Fill apple cavities with sugar/raisin mixture.

Fold dough corners over apple tops to cover apples completely.

Decorate apple tops with dough trimmings and brush with egg wash.

Refrigerate for about 1 hour.

Bake at 360°F (180°C) until pastry is brown and the apples are cooked.[a]

Test apples with thin skewer to be sure they are cooked.

Serve apples, while still hot, with vanilla sauce.

---

[a] Be sure apples are not overcooked, or they will be like applesauce.

664

*A*pple Strudel

Apfelstrudel
Stroudel aux pommes

YIELD: 10 SERVINGS

Apples, cooking	2 lb 10 oz	1.2 kg
Lemon juice	1 2/3 oz	50 ml
Bread crumbs	4 1/4 oz	120 g
Butter	4 1/4 oz	120 g
Strudel dough[a] (Recipe 773)	10 1/2 oz	300 g
White wheat flour	1 oz	30 g
Hazelnuts (filberts), ground	2 oz	60 g
Crystal sugar	7 oz	200 g
Golden raisins	2 oz	60 g
Lemon, zest[b]	1	1
Cinnamon, ground	1 pinch	1 g
Butter	1/3 oz	10 g
Butter, melted	2/3 oz	20 g
Powdered sugar	2/3 oz	20 g
Vanilla sauce (Recipe 780)	1 pt 1 oz	500 ml

MISE EN PLACE
Peel apples, core, and cut in thin slices. Mix slices with lemon juice.

Sauté bread crumbs in butter until light golden. Let cool.

METHOD
Spread tablecloth over a kitchen table and dust with flour.

Roll out dough and eventually pull dough to a rectangle, until it is very thin and transparent.

Sprinkle dough with toasted bread crumbs.

Mix[c] apples with hazelnuts (filberts), crystal sugar, raisins, lemon zest, and a dash of cinnamon.

Lift wide end of tablecloth and roll strudel into a tight roll.

Butter a baking pan and slide strudel onto pan. Curve strudel to fit or cut into pan lengths.

Brush strudel with remaining butter.

Bake at 425°F (220°C) for about 20 minutes.

Dust strudel with powdered sugar.

Heat vanilla sauce and serve with the warm strudel.

NOTE: Pear strudel can be prepared by the same method.

---

[a] Strudel dough is commercially available under the name "filo" or "phyllo," from Greek or Middle Eastern purveyors. It is already rolled into paper-thin sheets.

[b] Lemon zest is made by peeling the yellow rind with a vegetable peeler and cutting the rind into very fine shreds (*julienne*). The lemon zest can also be grated.

[c] Mix apples with sugar mixture when ready to fill the strudel, not before, because the sugar will draw out the juices.

665

Apple and Cottage Cheese Mousse

Leichter Apfel-Zitronen-Quark
Mousseline de séré aux pommes et au citron

YIELD: 10 SERVINGS

Lemons	2	2
Apples	1 lb 2 oz	500 g
Cottage cheese, fine curd, low fat[a]	1 lb 12 oz	800 g
Heavy cream (36%)	6 3/4 oz	200 ml
Egg yolks	3 oz	80 g
Egg whites	3 1/2 oz	100 g
Crystal sugar	3 oz	80 g
Salt	1x	1x
Crystal sugar	3 oz	80 g

MISE EN PLACE
Make lemon zest.[b] Squeeze out lemon juice and strain.

Peel apples, core, and cut into small pieces.

Immediately purée apples with lemon juice and zest, and with half of the cottage cheese.

Whip the heavy cream.

METHOD
Cream the egg yolks[c] with 3 oz (80 g) sugar.

Add remaining cottage cheese and stir until smooth.

Add puréed apples and fold in whipped cream.

Whip egg whites into soft peak, add salt and 3 oz (80 g) sugar, and whip until sugar is dissolved.

Fold egg whites into apple mousse.

Fill crystal dishes or glasses with apple mousse.

NOTE: If desired, garnish with apple pieces and lemon balm leaves.

---

[a] Farmer's cheese or ricotta can be used.

[b] Lemon zest is made by peeling the yellow rind with a vegetable peeler and cutting the rind into very fine shreds (*julienne*). The lemon zest can also be grated.

[c] Pasteurized egg yolks are recommended, since the eggs won't be cooked.

666

Deep Dish Apple Pie

Apple Pie

YIELD: 10 SERVINGS

Golden raisins	1 2/3 oz	50 g
Puff pastry, lean (Recipe 715)	12 oz	350 g
Butter	1/2 oz	15 g
Lemons	2	2
Egg	1	1
Apples,[a] cooking	3 lb 5 oz	1.5 kg
Crystal sugar	8 3/4 oz	250 g
Cinnamon, ground	1 pinch	1 g
Ginger, ground	1 pinch	1 g
Apple cider, sweet	1 2/3 oz	50 ml
Butter	1 2/3 oz	50 g

MISE EN PLACE
Soak raisins in cold water.

Roll puff pastry into a circle slightly larger than the pie dish. Save dough trimmings for rim and decorations.

Butter a pie dish.

Squeeze lemons and strain juice.

Break egg and mix with 1 tbsp water.

METHOD
Peel apples, core, and cut into fairly thick wedges.

Blend apples with lemon juice, sugar, cinnamon, ginger, and cider.

Put mixture in pie dish and sprinkle cold butter in small nuggets over apples.

Brush rim of pie dish with egg wash.

Cut a dough strip about 1-in. (25 mm) wide, and as long as the circumference of the pie dish.

Put dough strip on pie dish rim; press down to adhere. Brush strip with egg wash.

Cover pie dish with dough circle.

Decorate pie with remaining dough trimmings and brush with egg wash.

Poke holes in crust to let steam escape.

Bake with low bottom heat for about 40 minutes.

NOTE: Pâte Dough (Recipe 245 or 246) can be used instead of puff pastry.

---

[a] Granny Smith apples are suitable for this recipe.

667

Apricot Custard Tart

Aprikosenkuchen mit Guss
Tarte aux apricots à la crème

YIELD: 1 TART

Butter	1/3 oz	10 g
Apricots, fresh, ripe	2 lb 3 oz	1.0 kg
Short dough (Recipe 710)	10 1/2 oz	300 g
Hazelnuts (filberts), ground	1 2/3 oz	50 g
Milk	6 3/4 oz	200 ml
Egg yolks	2 oz	60 g
Crystal sugar	3 oz	80 g
Heavy cream (36%)	1 2/3 oz	50 ml
Powdered sugar	1/3 oz	10 g
Heavy cream (36%) for topping	3 1/3 oz	100 ml

MISE EN PLACE

Butter a 10-in. (250 mm) tart mold.

Wash apricots, cut in half, and remove pits.

METHOD

Roll dough to about 1/8-in. (3 mm) thickness and line bottom and sides of tart mold.

Poke a few holes in the dough with a fork to let steam escape.

Sprinkle dough with ground hazelnuts.

Arrange apricots in circles attractively on top.

Start baking at 450°F (230°C) for 20 minutes.

Blend milk, egg yolks, crystal sugar, and 1 2/3 oz (50 ml) heavy cream. Strain and ladle over cake.

Continue baking at 350°F (175°C) until brown on top.

Let cool and dust with powdered sugar.

Whip 3 1/3 oz (100 ml) heavy cream for topping and decorate cake.

668

Apricot Sauce

Aprikosensauce
Sauce aux abricots

YIELD: 1 QT 2 OZ (1.0 L)

Apricots, fresh, ripe	1 lb 10 oz	750 g
Lemon	1	1
Water	8 1/2 oz	250 ml
Crystal sugar	7 oz	200 g

MISE EN PLACE

Dip apricots into boiling water, then into ice water. Peel off skin and remove pits.

Squeeze lemon and strain juice.

METHOD

Combine water, sugar, and lemon juice.

Bring to a boil and boil to light syrupy consistency.

Add apricots and stew in syrup until soft.

Purée the fruit with the syrup. Strain if desired.

NOTES: Use only fully ripe apricots.

The sauce can be flavored with apricot liqueur or Cognac (or another brandy), depending on use.

669

Omelette Soufflé

Auflaufomeletten
Omelettes soufflées

YIELD: 10 SERVINGS

Vanilla bean[a]	1	1
Butter	2/3 oz	20 g
Egg yolks	8 1/2 oz	240 g
Crystal sugar	7 oz	200 g
Lemon, zest[b]	1	1
Egg white	14 oz	400 g
Crystal sugar	3 1/2 oz	100 g
Powdered sugar	1 oz	30 g

[a] Vanilla-flavored sugar (adjust sugar quantity) or vanilla extract can be used.

[b] Lemon zest is made by peeling the yellow rind with a vegetable peeler and cutting the rind into very fine shreds (*julienne*). The lemon zest can also be grated.

MISE EN PLACE

Split vanilla bean and scrape out marrow.

Butter an ovenproof dish (*gratin* dish).

METHOD

Cream egg yolks and 7 oz (200 g) crystal sugar.

Add vanilla marrow and lemon zest.

Whip egg whites into soft peaks, add 3 1/2 oz (100 g) crystal sugar, and whip until sugar is incorporated.

Fold egg whites carefully into the egg yolk mixture.

Spread batter into *gratin* dish; keep some for decoration.

Using a pastry bag, decorate remaining batter on top.

Dust with powdered sugar; save some sugar.

Bake at 360°F (180°C), for about 10 minutes.

Dust with remaining powdered sugar and serve at once.

670

oufflé Pudding[a]

Auflaufpudding
Pouding saxon

YIELD: 10 SERVINGS

Golden raisins	1 2/3 oz	50 g
Butter	1/3 oz	10 g
White wheat flour	1/3 oz	10 g
Butter	3 oz	80 g
White wheat flour	3 1/2 oz	100 g
Vanilla bean[b]	1	1
Milk	13 1/2 oz	400 ml
Salt	1x	1x
Egg yolks	5 1/3 oz	150 g
Lemon, zest[c]	1/2	1/2
Egg whites	7 oz	200 g
Crystal sugar	3 1/2 oz	100 g

MISE EN PLACE

Soak raisins in cold water.

Butter a pudding mold[d] and dust with flour.

---

[a] The difference between a soufflé and a soufflé pudding is negligible. The batter for pudding is denser, because pudding is always served without the mold.

[b] Vanilla-flavored sugar (adjust sugar quantity) or vanilla extract can be used instead.

[c] Lemon zest is made by peeling the yellow rind with a vegetable peeler and cutting the rind into very fine shreds (*julienne*). The lemon zest can also be grated.

[d] Although there are specific pudding molds, a 1-qt (950 ml) china soufflé mold is commonly used. The pudding can also be made in individual soufflé cups.

Melt 3 oz (80 g) butter, add 3 1/2 oz (100 g) flour, stir well over low heat, and let mixture cool.

Split vanilla bean, scrap out marrow, and add to milk.

METHOD

Lightly salt vanilla-milk and bring to a boil.

Strain boiling milk over flour mixture, stir with wire whisk until smooth.

Return mixture to heat and stir with wooden paddle until batter is smooth and no longer clings to the sides of the pot.

Incorporate egg yolks in small increments. Add lemon zest and drained raisins.

Whip egg whites to soft peaks, add sugar, and whip until sugar is dissolved.

Carefully fold egg whites into batter.

Fill prepared mold about three-quarters full.

Warm pudding in water bath on top of stove, bake in water bath at 400°F (200°C) for 35 to 40 minutes.

Let pudding rest in a warm place for 5 minutes.

Invert mold; wait a few moments before removing mold.

NOTE: Serve hot, with a fruit sauce of your choice.

671

Soufflé Rothschild

Auflauf Rothschild
Soufflé Rothschild

YIELD: 10 SERVINGS

Candied fruits, diced	2 oz	60 g
Kirsch[a]	1 oz	30 ml
Butter	1/3 oz	10 g
White wheat flour	1/3 oz	10 g
Butter	3 oz	80 g
White wheat flour	3 oz	80 g
Vanilla bean[b]	1	1
Milk	13 1/2 oz	400 ml
Salt	1x	1x
Egg yolks	5 1/3 oz	150 g
Egg whites	7 oz	200 g
Crystal sugar	3 1/2 oz	100 g
Powdered sugar	1/3 oz	10 g

(continued on next page)

---

[a] Kirsch is a clear cherry brandy. Swiss kirsch is renowned.

[b] Vanilla-flavored sugar or vanilla extract can be substituted.

(continued from preceding page)

MISE EN PLACE
Marinate candied fruits in Kirsch.

Butter a 1qt (950 ml) souffle mold and dust with flour.

Melt 3 oz (80 g) butter, add 3 oz (80 g) flour, and stir over low heat.

Split vanilla bean, and scrape out marrow, and add marrow to milk.

METHOD
Lightly salt vanilla-milk and bring to a boil.

Strain boiling milk over butter/flour mixture and stir with wire whisk until smooth.

Return mixture to heat, and stir with wooden paddle until batter is smooth and no longer clings to the sides of the pot.

Incorporate egg yolks in small increments. Add candied fruits and Kirsch.

Whip egg whites to soft peak, add sugar, and whip until sugar is dissolved.

Stir small amount of whipped egg whites into batter, then carefully fold in the rest of the egg whites.

Fill soufflé mold about three-quarters high.

Warm in water bath on top of stove. Then bake on oven rack at 400°F (200°C) for about 20 minutes. Check doneness with a fine wooden skewer.

Dust with powdered sugar and serve at once.

NOTE: Individual molds take about 8 minutes to bake, providing the batter is prewarmed.

672

Frying Batter
Backteig
Pâte à frire

YIELD: 1 PT 11 OZ (800 ML)

White wheat flour	8 3/4 oz	250 g
Beer	8 1/2 oz	250 ml
Peanut oil	1 1/3 oz	40 ml
Egg whites	3 1/2 oz	100 g
Salt	1/3 oz	10 g

METHOD
Combine flour and beer and stir to a smooth batter. Strain batter to remove all lumps.

Cover top of batter with peanut oil to prevent drying out.

Let batter rest for 1 hour in a warm place.

Whip egg white with salt into stiff peaks and fold carefully into the batter.

Use at once.[a]

673

Bavarian Cream
Bayerische Creme
Créme bavaroise

YIELD: 1 QT 12 OZ (1.3 LITER)

Vanilla bean[b]	1	1
Milk	13 1/2 oz	400 ml
Gelatin leaf[c]	1/2 oz	12 g
Heavy cream (36%)	13 1/2 oz	400 ml
Salt	1x	1x
Egg yolks	3 oz	80 g
Crystal sugar	5 oz	140 g

MISE EN PLACE
Split vanilla bean, scrape out marrow, and add marrow to milk.

Soak gelatin leaf in cold water.

Whip heavy cream.

METHOD
Lightly salt vanilla-milk and bring to a boil.

Cream egg yolks and sugar. Add hot vanilla-milk, while stirring vigorously.

Return to stove and heat to 185°F (85°C), while stirring continuously with a wooden paddle.

Remove from heat and continue stirring.

Squeeze out water from gelatin leaf, add gelatin to hot cream, and stir to dissolve.

Strain through a fine wire china cap.

Pour cream into a stainless steel bowl and place over crushed ice.

Stir over ice until cream starts to thicken.

Fold whipped heavy cream into cream.

Portion immediately, or add flavorings, and then portion.

Chill until set.

---

[a] The beer and flour mixture can be made ahead of time. However, as soon as the egg whites are blended in, the batter should be used.

[b] Vanilla extract can be used.

[c] Powdered gelatin (unflavored) can be substituted. It must be dissolved with a small amount of warm water.

VARIATIONS

Bavarian Chocolate Cream: Dissolve 2 oz (60 g) dark chocolate *couverture*[a] in the still hot cream. Garnish cream with shaved chocolate and whipped cream.

Bavarian Coffee Cream: Replace vanilla bean with 1/3 oz (10 g) instant coffee. Garnish with whipped cream and chocolate coffee beans.

Bavarian Cream with Apples: Peel, core, and slice apples. Stew apples with small amount of white wine and lemon juice. Purée the apples, reserving a few wedges for garnish. Fold the apple puree into the cooling cream. Garnish with whipped cream and stewed apple wedges.

674

*F*illed Doughnuts
Berliner (Pfannkuchen)
Boules de Berlin

YIELD: 25 DOUGHNUTS

Milk	7 1/2 oz	225 ml
Yeast, fresh	2 oz	60 g
Crystal sugar	2 1/3 oz	65 g
White wheat flour	1 lb 3 oz	550 g
Salt	1/3 oz	10 g
Butter	2 2/3 oz	75 g
Egg yolks	3 1/2 oz	100 g
Lemon, rind, grated	1	1
White wheat flour for work surface	2x	2x
Oil for frying (10% oil loss)	3 1/3 oz	100 ml
Raspberry jam, bake-proof	8 3/4	250 g
Powdered sugar	3 1/2 oz	100 g

MISE EN PLACE
Warm milk to 86°F (30°C). Add yeast and sugar to dissolve.

Combine flour and salt in a mixing bowl.

Melt butter.

METHOD
Combine milk, butter, egg yolks, and grated lemon rind, and add to salted flour.

Blend ingredients thoroughly,[b] until dough is silky and smooth.

---

[a] *Couverture* is a coating chocolate with a high cocoa butter content. It is sold in solid blocks, and must be melted before use.

[b] The dough must be well worked. This is best done in a commercial electric mixer, using a dough hook and slow speed. The dough can also be kneaded on a pastry table.

Cover dough with a kitchen towel and proof in a warm place for about 1 hour.

Put dough on floured pastry table and roll out to about 1/2-in. (12 mm) thickness.

Cut circles with cookie cutter about 3 in. (75 mm) across. They should weigh about 1 1/3 oz (40 g).

Line a sheet pan with kitchen towels, dust with flour, and place the circles upside down on the towel.

Cover with kitchen towels and let proof in a warm place until the circles have almost doubled in size.

Deep-fry at 360°F (180°C). Put top side first in fat; when brown, turn and fry on the other side. Drain on absorbent paper.

With pastry bag, fill doughnuts from the side with raspberry jam.

Dust doughnuts with powdered sugar.

675

*B*irchermuesli
Birchermüesli
Birchermüesli

YIELD: 10 SERVINGS

Oat flakes, stone ground	4 1/4 oz	120 g
Milk	5 oz	150 ml
Apples	2 lb 10 oz	1.2 kg
Lemon juice	1 2/3 oz	50 ml
Heavy cream (36%)	6 3/4 oz	200 ml
Crystal sugar	4 1/4 oz	120 g
Yogurt, plain	7 oz	200 g
Fruits in season, trimmed, ready to eat	1 lb 2 oz	500 g
Hazelnuts (filberts), ground	5 1/3 oz	150 g

MISE EN PLACE
Soak oats in milk.

Peel apples, core, and grate apple coarsely. Blend immediately with lemon juice to avoid discoloration.

Whip heavy cream.

METHOD
Mix sugar and yogurt.

Carefully combine all ingredients.

NOTE: Garnish with nuts and seasonal fruits.

676

$\mathcal{P}$uff Pastry Pear Strip

Birnenjalousien
Jalousies aux poires

YIELD: 10 SERVINGS

Pears, ripe	3 lb 5 oz	1.5 kg
Butter	1 2/3 oz	50 g
Lemon, juice	1	1
Crystal sugar	2 2/3 oz	75 g
Cinnamon, ground	1 pinch	1 g
Golden raisins	3 1/2 oz	100 g
Dry white wine	1 2/3 oz	50 ml
Egg	1	1
Puff pastry (Recipe 689)	1 lb 12 oz	800 g
Powdered sugar	2/3 oz	20 g

MISE EN PLACE
Peel pears, quarter, remove core, and cut into thin slices.

Stew pears briefly with butter, lemon juice, sugar, cinnamon, raisins and white wine. Drain pears and save juice.

Reduce juice to a syrupy consistency and combine with pears again. Let mixture cool.

Break egg and mix with 1 tbsp water.

METHOD
Roll out puff pastry to a rectangle 10 in. (250 mm) wide and 1/10-in. (2.5 mm) thick.

Cut a 4-in. wide (100 mm) strip off the 10-in. width and place on baking sheet.

Place pear filling down the center of the strip. Brush dough edges with egg wash.

In remaining 6-in. strip, make incisions about 1/2-in. (12 mm) apart, but do not cut through the edges.

Place 6-in. strip on top of the filled 4-in. strip, and seal edges well.

Carefully brush with egg wash.

Refrigerate strip 1 hour before baking.

Bake at 375°F (190°C).

Dust with powdered sugar and return to a hot oven to let the sugar caramelize.

NOTES: The same recipe can be used with other fruits, such as apples, peaches, apricots, plums, and nectarines.

If fruit mixture is very wet, sprinkle cake crumbs on the bottom of the dough strip.

677

$\mathcal{P}$uff Paste (basic sweet recipe)

Brandteig
Pâte à choux

YIELD: 2 LB 3 OZ (1.0 KG)

Milk	13 1/2 oz	400 ml
Butter	5 1/3 oz	150 g
Crystal sugar	2/3 oz	20 g
Salt	1/6 oz	5 g
Bread flour	7 oz	200 g
Eggs, whole, shelled[a]	12 oz	350 g

METHOD
Combine milk, butter, sugar, and salt. Bring to a boil.

Add flour at once, stirring vigorously over heat with a wooden paddle until the mixture is smooth and no longer clings to the sides of the pot. This will take about 10 minutes.

Remove from heat, let cool briefly, and incorporate the eggs[b] in small increments.

NOTES: The paste should be smooth and silky, so it can be formed with a pastry bag.

If the items should have a rough surface, they should be baked with steam at the beginning.

If the items should be smooth, such as for eclairs or swan pastries, they should be baked without steam.

---

[a] Eggs can be purchased already shelled, mixed, and pasteurized.

[b] The eggs should be incorporated with a commercial electric mixer, using the paddle.

678

*P*uff Paste (basic nonsweet recipe)

Bradteig (gesalzen)
Pâte à choux (salé)

YIELD: 2 LB 3 OZ (1.0 KG)

Milk	6 3/4 oz	200 ml
Water	6 3/4 oz	200 ml
Butter	4 1/4 oz	120 g
Seasoning (salt and pepper)	1x	1x
Nutmeg	1 pinch	1 g
Bread flour	7 oz	200 g
Eggs, whole, shelled[a]	10 1/2 oz	300 g

METHOD

Combine milk, water, butter, and salt and pepper. Bring to a boil.

Add flour at once, stirring vigorously over heat with a wooden paddle until the mixture is smooth and no longer clings to the sides of the pot. This will take about 10 minutes.

Remove from heat, let cool briefly, and incorporate the eggs[b] in small increments.

679

*P*uff Paste Fritters

Brandteigkrapfen
Beignets soufflés

YIELD: 10 SERVINGS

Parchment paper or silicon paper		
Crystal sugar	3 1/2 oz	100 g
Cinnamon, ground	1 pinch	2 g
Vanilla sauce (Recipe 780)	1 pt 1 oz	500 ml
Puff paste (Recipe 677)	2 lb 3 oz	1.0 kg
Oil for frying (10% oil loss)	3 1/3 oz	100 ml

MISE EN PLACE

Cut strips of parchment paper or silicon paper about 2 in. (50 mm) wide.

Blend sugar and cinnamon.

Heat vanilla sauce.

---

[a] Eggs can be purchased already shelled, mixed, and pasteurized.

[b] The eggs should be incorporated using the paddle of a commercial electric mixer.

METHOD

With smooth tube of pastry bag, dress egg-shaped fritters onto the paper strips.

They should weigh about 1 oz (30 g).

Deep-fry[a] fritters at 325°F (165°C). Fry slowly until fritters are cooked through.[b]

Drain fritters on absorbent paper.

Roll fritters in cinnamon-sugar and serve with warm vanilla sauce.

680

*B*rioches

Brioches
Brioches

YIELD: 2 LB 3 OZ (1.0 KG)

Milk	2 oz	60 ml
Yeast, fresh[c]	1 1/3 oz	40 g
Crystal sugar	1 oz	30 g
Baker's malt, powdered	1/6 oz	5 g
Butter	5 2/3 oz	160 g
White wheat flour	1 lb 2 oz	500 g
Salt	1/6 oz	5 g
Butter	2/3 oz	20 g
White wheat flour	2/3 oz	20 g
Egg for glazing	1	1
Eggs, whole, shelled[d]	7 oz	200 g
White wheat flour for work table	1x	1x

MISE EN PLACE

In a large mixing bowl, combine milk, yeast, sugar, and malt. Warm to about 86°F (30°C).

Melt 5 2/3 oz (160 g) butter.

Sift together 1 lb 2 oz (500 g) flour and salt.

Butter brioche molds and dust with flour.

Break the egg and stir.

(continued on next page)

---

[a] Dip the paper strips into the hot fat; the fritters will slide off.

[b] They should burst before they are done as a sign that they are cooked through. If they haven't burst, they are not yet done.

[c] Dry yeast can be substituted.

[d] Eggs can be purchased already shelled, mixed, and pasteurized.

(continued from preceding page)

METHOD

Combine milk mixture, salted flour, and 7 oz (200 g) eggs. Work dough until smooth and silky.[a]

Cover bowl with a kitchen towel and let proof in a warm place until double in size.

Flour pastry table. Punch down dough and turn onto table.

Divide dough into small pieces[b], and roll with palm of hand until completely round.

Put pieces in the prepared molds, and top with small dough ball if desired.

Proof until double in size.

Bake at 360°F (180°C).

681

 read and Butter Pudding

Brot-und-Butter Pudding

YIELD: 10 SERVINGS

Golden raisins	1 2/3 oz	50 g
Butter	2/3 oz	20 g
Bread[c]	7 oz	200 g
Butter, melted	3 1/2 oz	100 g
Milk	1 qt 2 oz	1.0 L
Vanilla bean, split[d]	1	1
Eggs, whole, shelled[e]	9 3/4 oz	275 g
Crystal sugar	5 1/3 oz	150 g
Butter, cold	2/3 oz	20 g
Powdered sugar	1/3 oz	10 g

MISE EN PLACE

Soak raisins.

Butter ovenproof pudding dish or *gratin* dish.

Cut bread into slices.

Combine milk and vanilla bean, heat, cover, and let vanilla bean steep.

METHOD

Brush bread slices with melted butter and layer in the prepared dish.

Drain raisins and sprinkle over bread.

Mix eggs and sugar and strain hot milk into mixture.

Carefully ladle egg custard mixture over bread. The bread should be covered.

Place 2/3 oz (20 g) butter in small nuggets over the pudding.

Put dish in hot water bath to prewarm; then bake in water bath at 360°F (180°C) until top is brown and mixture has solidified.

Let stand 1 hour before serving (or serve chilled).

Dust with powdered sugar at the moment of service.

682

read Dough (basic)

Brotteig
Pâte à pain

YIELD: 2 LB 11 OZ (1.2 KG)

Water	1 pt 1 oz	500 ml
Yeast, fresh[a]	2/3 oz	20 g
Whole wheat bread flour[b]	1 lb 9 oz	700 g
Salt	1/2 oz	15 g

MISE EN PLACE

Warm the water to 86°F (30°C) and add yeast.

Sift together the flour and salt into mixing bowl.

METHOD

Add water/yeast to flour and mix with dough hook, first at slow, then at medium speed, for about 12 to 15 minutes.

Cover dough and proof in a warm place for 1 hour.

Punch down dough before use.

---

[a] This is best done with an electric mixer, using the dough hook and slow speed.

[b] The dough size must correspond with the mold size. The average breakfast brioche size is 1 oz (30 g) dough.

[c] The original recipe calls for *Einback*. Any porous bread can be used, such as leftover brioche, egg bread, or French bread.

[d] Vanilla extract can be substituted.

[e] Eggs can be purchased already shelled, mixed, and pasteurized.

[a] Dry yeast can be substituted.

[b] The original recipe calls for *Ruchmehl*.

683

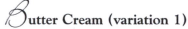

Butter Cream (variation 1)

Buttercreme (Variante 1)
Crème au beurre

YIELD: 2 LB 14 OZ (1.3 KG)

Crystal sugar	10 1/2 oz	300 g
Eggs, whole, shelled[a]	10 1/2 oz	300 g
Butter, sweet, room temperature	1 lb 2 oz	500 g
Powdered sugar	7 oz	200 g

METHOD

Combine crystal sugar and eggs in a mixing machine kettle, stir with whisk in water bath until mixture is warm and the sugar is dissolved.

Put kettle onto mixing machine and whip sugar/egg mixture until cold and foamy.

In separate bowl, cream butter and powdered sugar.

Fold sugar/egg mixture into the butter mixture.

NOTE: The cream can be flavored and colored as desired.

684

Butter Cream (variation 2)

Buttercreme (Variante 2)
Crème au beurre

YIELD: 2 LB 3 OZ (1.0 KG)

Egg whites	8 3/4 oz	250 g
Powdered sugar	8 3/4 oz	250 g
Butter, sweet, room temperature	1 lb 2 oz	500 g

METHOD

Combine egg whites and sugar in mixing machine kettle.

Whip mixture in water bath to 115°F (45°C).

Whip mixture at medium speed until cold and foamy.

Cream butter separately. Fold whipped egg whites into the butter.

NOTE: The cream can be flavored and colored as desired.

685

Neopolitan Ice Cream

Cassata napoletana

YIELD: 10 SERVINGS

Strawberry ice cream (Recipe 696)	1 pt 1 oz	500 ml
Candied fruits, diced	3 1/2 oz	100 g
Maraschino[a]	1 2/3 oz	50 ml
Vanilla ice cream (Recipe 778)	1 pt 1 oz	500 ml
Almonds, peeled and sliced	3 1/2 oz	100 g
Heavy cream (36%)	1 pt 1 oz	500 ml
Chocolate ice cream (Recipe 778 variation)	1 pt 1 oz	500 ml
Egg whites	2 2/3 oz	75 g
Powdered sugar	6 1/4 oz	175 g

MISE EN PLACE

Chill cassata mold.[b]

Spread layer of strawberry ice cream on bottom and freeze.

Marinate candied fruits in maraschino.

Spread layer of vanilla ice cream on top of strawberry ice cream and freeze.

Toast almonds. Whip heavy cream.

Spread layer of chocolate ice cream on top of vanilla ice cream and freeze.

METHOD

Combine egg whites and powdered sugar in mixing kettle.

Whip over warm water bath until mixture has reached no more than 120°F (50°C).

Place bowl into machine and whip egg white mixture until cool and foamy.

Fold in marinated fruits, almonds, and whipped cream.

Layer on top of chocolate ice cream. (This mixture should be the last layer.)

Freeze until solid.

To unmold, dip briefly in hot water.

Serve cassata in slices.

---

[a] Eggs can be purchased already shelled, mixed, and pasteurized. Only pasteurized eggs should be used.

[a] Maraschino is a clear cherry liqueur.

[b] The typical cassata mold is rectangular, in the shape of a box.

686

*C*old Charlotte Flavored with Kirsch

Charlotte Königliche Art
Charlotte royale

YIELD: 10 SERVINGS

Raspberry jam, bake-proof	5 1/3 oz	150 g
Sponge cake (Recipes 758, 759, or 760)	1/2	1/2
Bavarian cream (Recipe 673)	1 qt 2 oz	1.0 L
Kirsch[a]	3/4 oz	25 ml
Heavy cream (36%), whipped	6 3/4 oz	200 ml
Fruit sauce	1 pt 1 oz	500 ml

MISE EN PLACE
Line charlotte mold with plastic wrap.

Spread raspberry jam on sponge cake and roll tigthly to make a jelly roll. The roll should be about 1 1/2 in. (37 to 40 mm) in diameter.

Cut roll with wet knife into 1/5 in. (5 mm) thick slices.

Line charlotte mold completely with jelly roll slices.

METHOD
Flavor Bavarian cream with kirsch[b] and fill mold with the cream.

Refrigerate mold. Unmold when cold and set.

Garnish charlotte with whipped cream.[c]

Serve charlotte with a fruit sauce. Melba sauce is recommended.

NOTE: To facilitate portioning, the charlotte can also be made in a cake mold. (A charlotte mold is typically a tall cylinder.)

[a] Kirsch is a clear cherry brandy. Swiss kirsch is renowned.

[b] The Bavarian cream must be flavored during the preparation process, before it becomes solid.

[c] The whipped cream can be sweetened with powdered sugar if desired.

687

*C*harlotte Russe

Charlotte Russische Art
Charlotte russe

YIELD: 10 SERVINGS

Bavarian cream (Recipe 673)	1 qt 2 oz	1.0 L
Maraschino[a]	3/4 oz	25 ml
Heavy cream (36%)	6 3/4 oz	200 ml
Lady fingers (Recipe 733)	5 1/3 oz	150 g
Fruit sauce	1 pt 1 oz	500 ml

MISE EN PLACE
Flavor Bavarian cream[b] with maraschino.

Fill mold and refrigerate.

Whip heavy cream.[c]

METHOD
Unmold cream onto serving platter.

With pastry bag, dress a dollop of cream on the flat side of each lady finger and press against the sides of the charlotte. The charlotte should be evenly covered with lady fingers.

Garnish charlotte with remaining whipped cream.

Serve with a fruit sauce, such as Apricot Sauce (Recipe 668), Strawberry Sauce (Recipe 699), Red Currant Sauce (Recipe 727), or Melba (Raspberry) Sauce (Recipe 719).

NOTE: The charlotte can be garnished with fresh berries or stewed fruits.

[a] Maraschino is a clear cherry liqueur.

[b] The Bavarian cream must be flavored during the preparation process, before it becomes solid.

[c] The whipped cream can be sweetened with powdered sugar if desired.

688

$\mathcal{V}$anilla Custard

Creme Französische Art
Crème française

YIELD: 10 SERVINGS

Vanilla bean[a]	1	1
Milk	1 qt 2 oz	1.0 L
Crystal sugar	5 1/3 oz	150 g
Eggs, whole, shelled[b]	10 1/2 oz	300 g
Heavy cream (36%)	3 1/3 oz	100 ml

METHOD

Split vanilla bean, scrape out marrow, and add marrow and bean to milk. Bring milk to a boil.

Cream sugar and eggs. Add hot milk gradually to eggs and stir well.

Strain egg mixture through a fine wire china cap.

Fill china cocottes with egg mixture.

Put cocottes in a water bath of about 180°F (80°C).

Poach custard in the water bath, in a 300°F (150°C) oven, until light brown on top and set. The custard can also be cooked in a low-pressure steamer.

Let custard cool. Whip heavy cream and flavor with powdered sugar if desired.

Serve cold custard, without unmolding, garnished with whipped cream.

---

[a] Vanilla extract can be substituted.

[b] Eggs can be purchased already shelled, mixed, and pasteurized.

689

$\mathcal{P}$uff Pastry[a]

Deutscher Blätterteig
Feuilletage allemande

YIELD: 2 LB 3 OZ (1.0 KG)

Bread flour[b]	1 lb 2 oz	500 g
Salt	1/3 oz	12 g
Water	8 1/2 oz	250 ml
Butter, cold	2 2/3 oz	75 g
White wheat flour for pastry table	1x	1x
Margarine for puff pastry[c]	12 oz	350 g

MISE EN PLACE

Sift flour on a pastry table.[d]

Dissolve salt in water.

METHOD

Add butter to flour and rub together until crumbly. Make a depression in the center of flour mixture.

Put salted water in the center and combine the flour with water until all water is absorbed. Knead dough until smooth and elastic.

Cover dough and refrigerate for 30 minutes.

Flour the pastry table and place dough on top.

Roll out dough to rectangle about 1 in. (25 mm) thick.

Briefly knead the margarine. It should have the same consistency as the dough.

Shape margarine into a brick.

Place margarine in center of dough; fold dough corners over margarine.

Roll dough to a rectangle about 1 in. (25 mm) thick.

Fold sides toward the center. The dough edges should touch.

Fold over once more toward the center.

Repeat process, cover dough, and refrigerate.

Repeat the folding process twice more, refrigerating for at least 30 minutes between each folding process.[e]

NOTE: Puff pastry can also be made with butter instead of margarine. The butter and the dough should be cold, and the process should be done in a cool room.

---

[a] See also Puff Pastry (lean) (Recipe 715).

[b] The flour should have a high gluten content, so it will become elastic.

[c] Margarine for puff pastry is specially formulated, and is available from pastry supply purveyors.

[d] The room where the dough is processed should be cool.

[e] The dough is often refrigerated overnight between the second and third folding processes.

690

Vanilla Mousseline Cream

Diplomate-Creme
Crème mousseline

YIELD: 2 QT 4 OZ (2.0 L)

Gelatin, leaf[a]	1/6 oz	5 g
Milk	1 qt 2 oz	1.0 L
Crystal sugar	8 3/4 oz	250 g
Egg yolks	3 1/2 oz	100 g
Vanilla cream powder[b]	1 1/3 oz	40 g
Heavy cream (36%)	1 pt 9 oz	750 ml

MISE EN PLACE
Soak gelatin leaves in cold water.

METHOD
Combine 1 pt 14 oz (900 ml) of the milk with sugar, and bring to a boil.

Mix remaining cold milk with egg yolks and vanilla cream powder.

Pour hot milk on top, and bring to a boil, stirring continuously.

Squeeze water out of gelatin leaf, add gelatin to hot egg/milk mixture, and stir to dissolve.

Let cream cool, stirring occasionally.

Whip heavy cream and fold into cool, but not yet solid, egg cream.

691

Stewed Prunes

Dörrzwetschgenkompott
Compote de pruneaux

YIELD: 10 SERVINGS

Dried prunes	2 lb 3 oz	1.0 kg
Red wine	1 pt 1 oz	500 ml
Water	1 pt 1 oz	500 ml
Crystal sugar	3 1/2 oz	100 g
Honey	3 1/2 oz	100 g
Cinnamon stick	1	1
Lemon	1/2	1/2

---

[a] Powdered gelatin can be substituted. It should be dissolved in a small amount of warm water.

[b] Vanilla cream powder is a commercial product similar to pudding powder.

MISE EN PLACE
Soak prunes in cold water for a few hours.

METHOD
Combine all ingredients, except prunes, bring to a boil, and simmer for 10 minutes.

Strain through a fine wire china cap.

Add prunes, and poach for 10 minutes.

Let prunes cool in stewing liquid.

692

Hot Semolina Pudding

Englischer Griesspudding
Pouding de semoule anglaise

YIELD: 10 SERVINGS

Milk	1 qt 2 oz	1.0 L
Vanilla bean,[a] split	1	1
Salt	1x	1x
Semolina, hard wheat, coarse	5 oz	140 g
Lemon, zest[b]	1	1
Crystal sugar	4 1/4 oz	120 g
Eggs, whole, shelled[c]	3 1/2 oz	100 g
Butter	2/3 oz	20 g
Powdered sugar	1/3 oz	10 g

METHOD
Combine milk with vanilla bean and salt. Bring to a boil and simmer for 10 minutes. Strain through a fine wire china cap.

Bring milk to a boil again, add semolina, and stir with wire whisk. Cover and simmer for 10 minutes. Let mixture cool slightly.

Add lemon zest, sugar, and eggs and stir thoroughly.

Butter an ovenproof dish (*gratin* dish or pudding dish).

Pour mixture into dish.

Bake in hot oven until brown on top.

Dust with powdered sugar at the moment of service.

NOTE: Serve with fruit sauces, such as Apricot Sauce (Recipe 668), Strawberry Sauce (Recipe 699), Red Currant Sauce (Recipe 727), or Melba (Raspberry) Sauce (Recipe 719). Stewed fruits such as Stewed Peaches (Recipe 745) can also be served.

---

[a] Vanilla extract can be substituted. The extract should be added when the eggs are added and the milk does not have to be strained.

[b] Lemon zest is made by peeling the yellow rind with a vegetable peeler and cutting the rind into very fine shreds (*julienne*).

[c] Eggs can be purchased already shelled, mixed, and pasteurized.

Rice Pudding

Englischer Reispudding
Pouding de riz anglaise

YIELD: 10 SERVINGS

Arborio rice[a]	3 1/2 oz	100 g
Milk	1 qt 2 oz	1.0 L
Vanilla bean, split[b]	1	1
Salt	1x	1x
Lemon, zest[c]	1	1
Crystal sugar	4 1/4 oz	120 g
Eggs, whole, shelled[d]	3 1/2 oz	100 g
Butter	2/3 oz	20 g
Powdered sugar	1/3 oz	10 g

MISE EN PLACE
Blanch rice for 5 minutes and drain.

METHOD
Combine milk, vanilla bean, and salt. Bring to a boil.

Add blanched rice and simmer for 30 minutes.

Remove vanilla bean and let mixture cool slightly.

Add lemon zest, sugar, and eggs, and stir well.

Butter an ovenproof dish (*gratin* or pudding dish).

Pour rice mixture into dish.

Bake until brown on top.

Dust with powdered sugar before serving.

NOTE: Serve with fruit sauces, such as Apricot Sauce (Recipe 668), Strawberry Sauce (Recipe 699), Red Currant Sauce (Recipe 727), or Melba (Raspberry) Sauce (Recipe 719). Stewed fruits such as Stewed Peaches (Recipe 745) can also be served.

[a] Arborio rice is an Italian rice with a round kernel. Vialone rice can be substituted.

[b] Vanilla extract can be substituted. The extract should be added when the eggs are added and the milk does not have to be strained.

[c] Lemon zest is made by peeling the yellow rind with a vegetable peeler and cutting the rind into very fine shreds (*julienne*). Lemon zest can also be grated.

[d] Eggs can be purchased already shelled, mixed, and pasteurized.

Praline Ice Cream Cake

Eisbiskuit Jamaika
Biscuit glacé Jamaïque

YIELD: 10 SERVINGS

Praline ice cream (Recipe 778, variation)	1 pt 1 oz	500 ml
Hazelnut macaroons (Recipe 716)	3 1/2 oz	100 g
Dark rum	3 1/3 oz	100 ml
Heavy cream (36%)	13 1/2 oz	400 ml
Eggs, whole, shelled[a]	3 1/2 oz	100 g
Crystal sugar	3 1/2 oz	100 g
Heavy cream (36%)	3 1/3 oz	100 ml
Hazelnut macaroons for garnish (Recipe 716)	10	10

MISE EN PLACE
Line a 1 qt 19 oz (1.5 L) loaf cake mold with plastic wrap. Freeze mold.

Spread mold bottom and sides with praline ice cream. Freeze ice cream.

Cut 3 1/2 oz (100 g) macaroons into small dice and marinate with dark rum.

Whip 13 1/2 oz (400 ml) heavy cream.

METHOD
Combine eggs and sugar and whip in warm water bath to dissolve sugar, until mixture has reached no more than 120°F (50°C).

Whip mixture until cool and thick.

Blend marinated macaroons with whipped cream.

Fill molded praline ice cream with macaroon mixture and freeze until solid.

To unmold, dip mold one moment in hot water, and invert directly onto the serving platter.

Whip 3 1/3 oz (100 ml) heavy cream, and sweeten cream with powdered sugar if desired.

Cut ice cream mold into 10 slices.

Garnish each slice with whipped cream and one macaroon.

[a] Eggs can be purchased already shelled, mixed, and pasteurized. Only pasteurized eggs should be used.

695

Strawberry and Vanilla Ice Cream Bombe

Eisbombe Aïda
Bombe glacée Aïda

YIELD: 10 SERVINGS

Vanilla ice cream (Recipe 778)	1 qt 2 oz	1.0 L
Strawberries, fresh	1 lb 2 oz	500 g
Maraschino[a]	3 1/3 oz	100 ml
Heavy cream (36%)	10 oz	300 ml
Egg whites	2 2/3 oz	75 g
Powdered sugar	7 oz	200 g
Strawberry puree, unsweetened[b]	10 1/2 oz	300 g
Lemon juice	1/2 oz	15 ml

MISE EN PLACE
Freeze a 2 qt 4 oz (2.0 L) bombe mold.

Soften vanilla ice cream and spread on sides and bottom of mold. Mold should be lined evenly with ice cream. Freeze immediately.

Trim strawberries. Save 10 even-sized strawberries for garnish. Wash remaining strawberries, drain, and dice. Marinate diced strawberries in maraschino.

Whip heavy cream.

Freeze the serving platter.

METHOD
Combine egg whites and powdered sugar. Whip in warm water bath to dissolve sugar, until mixture has reached no more than 120°F (50°C).

Whip until mixture is cool and forms a stiff meringue.

Fold strawberry purée and lemon juice into meringue.

Carefully fold whipped cream into the mixture.

Fold marinated strawberries into the mixture.

Fill the ice cream-lined mold with the strawberry mixture and freeze until solid.

To unmold, dip mold one moment in hot water, then invert directly on frozen serving platter.

Wash strawberries reserved for garnish and decorate mold at the moment of service.

---

[a] Maraschino is a clear cherry liqueur.

[b] Strawberry purée is available ready-to-use from pastry supply houses. Very ripe fresh strawberries can be puréed, but they are often watery.

696

Strawberry Ice Cream

Erdbeerglace
Glace aux fraises

YIELD: 2 QT 4 OZ (2.0 L)

Crystal sugar	1 lb 2 oz	500 g
Glucose, liquid[a]	3 oz	80 g
Water	12 oz	350 ml
Strawberry puree, unsweetened[b]	2 lb 3 oz	1.0 kg
Heavy cream (36%)	10 oz	300 ml
Lemon	1	1

MISE EN PLACE
Combine sugar, glucose, and water. Bring to a boil, skim, and let cool.

METHOD
Combine sugar mixture with strawberry puree and heavy cream.

Freeze mixture in ice cream machine.

NOTES: To obtain a smooth, nongrainy ice cream, the sugar content of the mixture should measure 18 degrees on the Beaumé scale.

Other fruits, such as apricots, blackberries, peaches, and raspberries, can be used.

697

Open-Face Strawberry Tart

Erdbeerkuchen
Tarte aux fraises

YIELD: 10 SERVINGS

Strawberries, fresh	2 lb 3 oz	1.0 kg
Kirsch[c]	1 2/3 oz	50 ml
Egg	1	1
Strawberry jelly	3 1/2 oz	100 g
Heavy cream (36%)	3 1/3 oz	100 ml
Puff pastry, lean (Recipe 715)	14 oz	400 g

---

[a] Liquid glucose is available from pastry supply purveyors under various brand names.

[b] Strawberry purée is available ready-to-use from pastry supply houses. Very ripe fresh strawberries can be puréed, but they are often watery.

[c] Kirsch is a clear cherry brandy. Swiss kirsch is renowned.

METHOD

Trim and wash strawberries, cut in half, and marinate with kirsch.

Break egg and mix with 1 tbsp cold water.

Warm the strawberry jelly.

Whip the heavy cream.[a]

METHOD

Roll out pastry dough to about 1/6-in. (4 mm) thickness and cut out a 10-in. (250 mm) circle.

Place circle on baking sheet and poke some small holes. Brush circle rim with egg wash.

Shape remaining dough into a strip about 1 1/4 in. (30 mm) wide and 33 in. (825 mm) long. Place strip on rim of tart.

Make incisions in rim, from the outside, every 3/4 in. (20 mm). Cut all the way through.

Refrigerate tart for 1 hour.

Bake at 425°F (220°C) until brown and crisp. Let tart cool.

Fill tart with marinated strawberries.

Brush tart with melted strawberry jelly.

Garnish tart with whipped cream.

NOTE: The bottom of the tart can be spread with Vanilla Mousseline Cream (Recipe 690) if desired.

698

Strawberry Mousse

Erdbeermousse
Mousse aux fraises

YIELD: 10 SERVINGS

Strawberries, fresh	1 lb 10 oz	750 g
Lemon, juice	1	1
Kirsch[b]	1 2/3 oz	50 ml
Crystal sugar	1 2/3 oz	50 g
Gelatin, leaf[c]	1/2 oz	15 g
Heavy cream (36%)	10 oz	300 ml
Egg whites	2 2/3 oz	75 g
Salt	1x	1x

MISE EN PLACE

Trim and wash strawberries and cut into small dice.

Marinate strawberries for about 1 hour with lemon juice,

---

kirsch, and sugar.

Soak gelatin leaf in cold water.

Whip heavy cream.

METHOD

Purée strawberries and push through fine mesh strainer.

Squeeze water out of gelatin leaf. Melt gelatin in small amount of water in hot water bath.

Combine melted gelatin with strawberry puree.

Fold whipped cream into strawberry mixture.

Whip egg whites and salt into peaks and fold into strawberry mousse.

Pour mousse into a bowl and refrigerate until it is solidified.

To serve, scoop out small egg-shaped dumplings with 2 spoons[a] and place directly on plates. Serve 2 "dumplings" per person.

NOTE: The mousse can be served with stewed rhubarb, or with soft whipped cream.

699

Strawberry Sauce

Erdbeersauce
Sauce aux fraises

YIELD: 10 SERVINGS

Strawberries, fresh	1 lb 12 oz	800 g
Orange	1	1
Water	6 3/4 oz	200 ml
Crystal sugar	5 1/3 oz	150 g

MISE EN PLACE

Trim and wash strawberries.

Squeeze orange and save juice.

METHOD

Purée strawberries and strain.

Combine water, sugar, and orange juice. Bring to a boil and boil to syrupy consistency. Let syrup cool.

Add strawberry puree to syrup.

NOTES: Use only ripe strawberries.

The sauce can be flavored with Cointreau liqueur or kirsch,[b] depending on intended use.

---

[a] The whipped cream can be sweetened with powdered sugar if desired.

[b] Kirsch is a clear cherry brandy. Swiss kirsch is renowned.

[c] Powdered gelatin can be used. It should be dissolved with a small amount of water.

---

[a] This method requires a considerable amount of practice. An oval ice cream scoop can be used.

[b] Kirsch is a clear cherry brandy. Swiss kirsch is renowned.

700

Strawberry Toasts

Erdbeerschnitten
Croûtes aux fraises

YIELD: 10 SERVINGS

Strawberries, fresh	2 lb 3 oz	1.0 kg
Brioche bread[a]	14 oz	400 g
Butter	3 1/2 oz	100 g
Sugar syrup[b]	10 1/2 oz	300 g
Strawberry sauce (Recipe 699)[c]	1 pt 1 oz	500 ml

MISE EN PLACE
Trim and wash strawberries and cut into halves or quarters depending on size.

Cut bread into 20 slices.

METHOD
Sauté bread in butter until golden brown on both sides.

Combine strawberries with sugar syrup and stew briefly.

Put bread slices on plates and ladle warm strawberries over bread.

Pour fruit sauce around toasts.

NOTE: Other fruits can be used for this recipe.

701

Peach Cream Cake

Eugenia-Torte Melba
Gâteau Eugénie Melba

YIELD: 10 SERVINGS

Sponge cake, round (Recipe 709)	1	1
Heavy cream (36%)	6 3/4 oz	200 ml
Bavarian cream (Recipe 673)	1 qt 2 oz	1.0 L
Peaches, canned, yellow, drained	10 1/2 oz	300 g
Fruit sauce[d]	1 pt 1 oz	500 ml

MISE EN PLACE
Split sponge cake twice, to make 3 layers of equal thickness.

Whip heavy cream.

METHOD
Place an empty cake ring on a small sheet pan and place the bottom sponge cake layer inside. (The ring and the cake must be the same size).

Spread about one-third of the Bavarian cream on top.[a]

Place the second sponge layer on top of the cream and again spread one third of the Bavarian cream on top.

Place last layer of sponge cake on top. Press down lightly to make the layers level.

Top with remaining Bavarian cream, spread to make cake level, and refrigerate.

When the cake is cold and solid, remove the cake ring.

Garnish cake top with sliced peaches, and garnish sides with whipped cream.

Serve with fruit sauce.

VARIATIONS
Chocolate Cream Cake (Gâteau Eugénie au chocolate)—Use Chocolate Sponge Cake (Recipe 726), fill cake with Chocolate Bavarian Cream (Recipe 673 variation), and garnish top with whipped cream and shaved chocolate.

Pear Cream Cake (Gâteau Eugénie Williams)—Use Chocolate Sponge Cake (Recipe 726), fill cake with Bavarian cream flavored with pear brandy, and garnish cake with sliced pears, and whipped cream flavored with pear brandy.

702

Cold Semolina Pudding with Strawberries

Flammeri mit Erdbeeren
Flamri aux fraises

YIELD: 10 SERVINGS

Strawberries, fresh	8 3/4 oz	250 g
Crystal sugar	3/4 oz	25 g
Cognac (or any brandy)	1 2/3 oz	50 ml
Lemon, zest[b]	1	1
Gelatin, leaf[c]	1/2 oz	15 g

[a] The original recipe calls for *Einback*. Any sweet yeast bread can be used.

[b] To make sugar syrup, combine 3 parts sugar and 2 parts water (by volume), bring to a boil, and chill.

[c] Another fruit sauce, such as Melba (Raspberry) Sauce (Recipe 719), can be used.

[d] Raspberry Sauce (Recipe 719) or Strawberry Sauce (Recipe 699) can be used.

[a] This cake must be put together as soon as the Bavarian cream is made, because the layers must be filled before the cream solidifies.

[b] Lemon zest is made by peeling the yellow rind with a vegetable peeler and cutting the rind into very fine shreds (*julienne*). Lemon zest can also be grated.

[c] Powdered gelatin can be used, but it must first be dissolved in small amount of warm water.

Heavy cream (36%)	13 1/2 oz	400 ml
Vanilla bean[a]	1	1
Milk	1 pt 1 oz	500 ml
Semolina, hard wheat[b]	2 oz	60 g
Egg yolks[c]	4 1/4 oz	120 g
Crystal sugar	4 1/4 oz	120 g
Lemon balm, fresh	10	10

MISE EN PLACE

Clean and wash strawberries. Reserve 10 for garnish. Cut the rest into small pieces and marinate with 3/4 oz (25 g) sugar and Cognac.

Make lemon zest.

Soak gelatin leaf in cold water.

Whip heavy cream.

METHOD

Split vanilla bean, scrape out marrow, and add marrow and bean to milk.

Add lemon zest and bring milk to a boil. Steep for 5 minutes, and strain through a fine wire china cap.

Return milk to stove and add semolina, stirring vigorously with a strong wire whisk.

As soon as semolina starts to thicken, stir with wooden paddle, over heat, for about 10 minutes. Remove from heat.

Squeeze water out of gelatin leaf and incorporate gelatin into hot semolina.

Cream egg yolks and sugar, blend with semolina mixture, and stir mixture over ice until cold.

Fold in marinated strawberries and whipped cream.

Immediately fill 10 small molds (or one large mold) and refrigerate.

To unmold, dip molds briefly in hot water and invert.

Garnish with 10 remaining strawberries and lemon balm.

703

Hot Baked Almond Pudding
Frankfurter Pudding
Pouding Francfort

YIELD: 10 SERVINGS

Golden raisins	3 oz	80 g
Butter	1/3 oz	10 g
White wheat flour	1/3 oz	10 g
Butter	5 1/3 oz	150 g
Crystal sugar	5 1/3 oz	150 g
Egg yolks	10 1/2 oz	300 g
Almonds, ground	5 1/3 oz	150 g
Sponge cake crumbs, dry	5 1/3 oz	150 g
Cinnamon, ground	1 pinch	1 g
Cornstarch	1 1/3 oz	40 g
Egg whites	14 oz	400 g
Crystal sugar	5 1/3 oz	150 g
Red wine sauce with almonds and currants (Recipe 761)	13 1/2 oz	400 ml

MISE EN PLACE

Soak raisins.

Butter pudding mold[a] or soufflé dish and dust with flour.

METHOD

Cream 5 1/3 oz (150 g) butter with 5 1/3 oz (150 g) sugar.

Add egg yolks gradually and incorporate thoroughly.

Add soaked raisins, ground almonds, cake crumbs, and ground cinnamon.

Sift cornstarch into mixture.

Whip egg whites into soft peaks, add 5 1/3 oz (150 g) sugar, and whip until sugar is dissolved.

Fold egg whites into pudding batter and pour batter into mold. The mold should be about three-quarters full.

Prewarm pudding in water bath on top of stove; then bake in water bath at 425°F (220°C). Check with skewer to be sure pudding is baked through.

To unmold, invert pudding onto a warm serving platter. Keep the mold over the pudding for a few minutes until pudding settles.

Serve warm red wine sauce with pudding.

704

Stewed Fresh Figs with Cinnamon Sour Cream

Frische Feigen in Cassis-Likör
Figues à la crème de cassis

YIELD: 10 SERVINGS

Blue figs, fresh	2 lb 3 oz	1.0 kg
Dry white wine	1 pt 11 oz	800 ml
Creme de Cassis[a]	10 oz	300 ml
Lemon, juice	1	1
Crystal sugar	3 1/2 oz	100 g
Sour cream, diet	13 1/2 oz	400 ml
Cinnamon	1 pinch	2 g
Honey	1 oz	30 g

MISE EN PLACE
Wash figs, and split into halves.

METHOD
Combine white wine, cassis, lemon juice, and sugar and bring to a boil.

Add figs, remove from stove, and let figs steep in hot syrup.

Remove figs with skimmer.

Return fig juice to stove and reduce to about half.

Return figs to syrup and let figs cool in syrup.

Blend sour cream with cinnamon and honey and serve with figs.

705

Fruit Salad

Fruchtsalat
Macédoine de fruits

YIELD: 10 SERVINGS

Oranges, navel	14 oz	400 g
Pineapples, fresh	10 1/2 oz	300 g
Apples	8 3/4 oz	250 g
Pears	8 3/4 oz	250 g
Lemon juice	3 1/3 oz	100 ml
Peaches, fresh[b]	14 oz	400 g
Sugar syrup[a]	1 pt 1 oz	500 ml
Bananas	10 1/2 oz	300 g
Strawberries, fresh	8 3/4 oz	250 g

MISE EN PLACE
Peel oranges and seam out wedges.

Peel pineapple, remove core, and cut into dice.

Peel and core apples and pears and cut into dice.

Combine orange wedges and diced pineapple, apples, and pears with lemon juice.

Peel peaches, remove pits, and cut into dice. Add to fruits.

Pour sugar syrup over fruits and marinate, refrigerated, in sugar syrup for 2 hours.

METHOD
At the moment of service:

Peel bananas, slice, and add to fruit salad.

Trim and wash strawberries and add to fruit salad.

NOTES: Other fruits can be used according to season and availability.

If desired, the fruits can be flavored with kirsch (a clear cherry brandy), or with maraschino (a clear cherry liqueur).

Whipped cream can be served on the side.

706

Pastry Cream (without eggs)[b]

Füllcreme
Crème pâtissière

YIELD: 1 QT 8 OZ (1.2 L)

Vanilla bean[c]	1	1
Milk	1 qt 2 oz	1.0 L
Crystal sugar	7 oz	200 g
Vanilla cream powder[d]	3 1/2 oz	(100 g)

METHOD
Split vanilla bean, scrape out marrow, and add marrow and bean to 1 pt 11 oz (800 ml) milk. Add sugar, bring milk to a boil, and remove vanilla bean.

---

[a] Creme de Cassis is a liqueur made from black currants. A nonalcoholic Cassis syrup can also be used.

[b] When fresh peaches are not in season, use canned peaches, and reduce the amount to 8 3/4 oz (250 g).

[a] To make sugar syrup, combine 3 parts sugar and 2 parts water (by volume), bring to a boil, and chill.

[b] This recipe is made without eggs. Also see Pastry Cream made with eggs (Recipe 779).

[c] Vanilla extract can be substituted.

[d] Vanilla cream powder is a commercial product similar to pudding powder.

Mix vanilla cream powder with remaining milk and add to hot milk.

Bring to a boil, while stirring.

Chill cream in ice water, or pour into a shallow pan to cool.[a]

707

t. Honoré Cake

St-Honoré-Torte
Gâteau Saint-Honoré

YIELD: 2 CAKES

Puff pastry, lean (Recipe 715)	10 1/2 oz	300 g
Puff paste (Recipe 677)	1 lb 2 oz	500 g
Vanilla mousseline cream (Recipe 690)	6 3/4 oz	200 ml
Kirsch[b]	2/3 oz	20 ml
Crystal sugar	7 oz	200 g
Pastry cream (Recipe 706)	1 pt 4 oz	600 ml
Kirsch	2/3 oz	20 ml
Egg whites	3 1/2 oz	100 g
Crystal sugar	1 2/3 oz	50 g

MISE EN PLACE

Roll out puff pastry and cut out two circles 10 in. (250 mm) across.

Place circles on baking sheet and poke some holes to ensure even baking.

With a pastry bag, dress a border of puff paste on dough circles. The border should be 1/3 in. (9 mm) inside the rim.

Dress small cream puffs on the baking sheet with remaining paste.

Bake both at 425°F (220°C) and let cool.

Flavor the vanilla mousseline cream with kirsch and set aside.

Using pastry bag with small tube, fill cream puffs when cold, from the bottom, with vanilla mousseline cream.

METHOD

Caramelize (melt until brown) 7 oz (200 g) sugar. Carefully dip cream puffs into hot caramel, and place immediately on top of the borders of the dough circles. Keep caramel warm, to make the cream puffs stick.

Make pastry cream (half of Recipe 706). Keep cream hot.

Add kirsch to cream.

Whip egg whites into soft peaks, add 1 2/3 oz (50 g) sugar, and whip until sugar is dissolved.

Fold egg whites into pastry cream. Let cream cool and fill into centers of cakes.

NOTE: The cakes can be decorated with whipped cream and stewed fruits.

708

*C*rème Brullée

Gebrannte Creme
Crème brûlée

YIELD: 1 QT 2 OZ (1.0 L)

Crystal sugar	3 oz	80 g
Water	3 1/3 oz	100 ml
Milk	1 pt 1 oz	500 ml
Crystal sugar	2 oz	60 g
Vanilla cream powder[a]	2/3 oz	20 g
Egg yolks	2 oz	60 g
Heavy cream (36%)	13 1/2 oz	400 ml

MISE EN PLACE

Caramelize 3 oz (80 g) sugar (melt sugar until brown). Remove from heat and carefully add water. Bring to a boil to dissolve sugar and set aside.

METHOD

Add 13 1/2 oz (400 ml) of the milk to caramel and bring to a boil.

Mix 2 oz (60 g) sugar, vanilla cream powder, and egg yolks with remaining milk.

Pour hot milk into mixture while stirring. Return mixture to stove and bring to a boil. Chill the caramel cream.

Whip heavy cream and fold into cold caramel cream.

NOTE: Creme brulée is often served in individual ceramic soufflé cups. They are kept cold until service. At the moment of service, a thin layer of brown sugar is put on top and quickly browned under the salamander.

---

[a] If the cream is chilled over ice water, it should be poured into a stainless steel bowl and stirred frequently. If the cream is chilled in a shallow pan, it should be sprinkled with a little sugar to prevent the formation of a skin.

[b] Kirsch is a clear cherry brandy. Swiss kirsch is renowned.

[a] Vanilla cream powder is a commercial product similar to vanilla pudding powder.

709

Sponge Cake

Genueser Biskuit
Génoise

YIELD: 2 CAKES

Parchment or silicon paper		
Cake flour	7 oz	200 g
Cornstarch	3 1/2 oz	100 g
Butter	3 1/2 oz	100 g
Parchment paper or silicon paper		
Eggs, whole, shelled[a]	1 lb 2 oz	500 g
Crystal sugar	10 1/2 oz	300 g
Lemon, peel, grated	1	1

MISE EN PLACE
Line baking sheet with a sheet of parchment or silicon paper, cut in half, and place 2 cake rings on top, one on each sheet.[b]

Sift together cake flour and cornstarch.

Melt butter.

METHOD
Combine eggs and sugar in mixing machine kettle and whip in water bath until mixture has reached no more than 120°F (50°C).

Add grated lemon peel.

Whip at medium speed until mixture is cold and has increased considerably in volume.

Carefully fold in flour mixture.

Carefully fold in melted but cool butter.

Pour batter into the prepared cake rings.

Bake at 375°F (190°C), with open vent (no steam).

Test cake with fine wooden skewer to be sure it is baked.

Remove cakes and invert onto wire rack to cool. Leave the paper on cakes until they are cool.

710

Short Pastry (sugarless)

Geriebener Teig
Pâte brisée

YIELD: 2 LB 3 OZ (1.0 KG)

Cake flour	1 lb 2 oz	500 g
Salt	8 1/2 oz	12 g
Water	8 1/2 oz	250 ml
Butter, cold	8 3/4 oz	250 g

MISE EN PLACE
Sift cake flour.

Dissolve salt in water.

METHOD
Add cold butter to flour in small nuggets. Rub butter and sifted flour together into small granules.

Add salted water and work rapidly into a smooth dough. Do not knead the dough too long so as not to develop the gluten, which makes the dough tough.

Refrigerate dough for at least 1 hour before use.

NOTES: The dough can also be made with margarine or shortening. If shortening is used, reduce the amount by 10% and increase the water by 10%.

To make whole wheat dough, replace half of the cake flour with whole wheat flour.

---

[a] Eggs can be purchased already shelled, mixed, and pasteurized.

[b] The sponge can also be baked in buttered and floured cake pans.

711

$\mathcal{C}$ustard Creme Caramel

Gestürtzte Karamelcreme
Crème renversée au caramel

YIELD: 10 SERVINGS

Crystal sugar	7 oz	200 g
Water	1 2/3 oz	50 ml
Vanilla bean[a]	1	1
Milk	1 qt 2 oz	1.0 L
Eggs, whole, shelled[b]	10 1/2 oz	300 g
Egg yolks	3 oz	80 g
Crystal sugar	5 1/3 oz	150 g

MISE EN PLACE

Caramelize (melt and brown) 7 oz (200 g) sugar. Carefully add water, bring to a boil, and boil to a syrupy consistency.

Pour syrup on the bottom of 10 timbale molds.[c]

Split vanilla bean, and scrape out marrow, and add marrow to milk.

METHOD

Bring vanilla-milk to a boil and remove from stove.

Blend eggs and egg yolks and 5 1/3 oz (150 g) sugar. Do not whip; there should be no air bubbles.

Pour hot milk into egg mixture while stirring.

Strain through a fine wire china cap.

Top caramel in timbale molds with custard.

Place in water bath and poach in oven at 325°F (165°C) or until set.

The custard can also be cooked in a low-pressure steamer.

Check with a fine wooden skewer to be sure custard is cooked. Let custard cool.

Serve custard when cold.[d] Loosen custard from the sides with a sharp knife and turn upside down onto a deep dessert plate.

Garnish with whipped cream if desired.

NOTE: The custard can also be poached in a ring mold. To serve, the center of the ring should be filled with vanilla-flavored whipped cream and garnished with Almond Lace Cookies (Recipes 721 or 722).

---

[a] Vanilla extract can be used.

[b] Eggs can be purchased already shelled, mixed, and pasteurized.

[c] If timbale molds are not available, ceramic soufflé cups can be used.

[d] The custard should be refrigerated overnight before serving. This will allow the caramel on the bottom to melt, and provide a little syrup when the custard is served.

712

$\mathcal{P}$ound Cake

Gleichschwercake
Cake quatres quarts

YIELD: 4 CAKES, WEIGHING 1 LB 2 OZ (500 GRAMS) EACH

Butter	1/3 oz	10 g
Cake flour	1/3 oz	10 g
Cake flour	1 lb 2 oz	500 g
Butter	1 lb 2 oz	500 g
Crystal sugar	14 oz	400 g
Vanilla sugar[a]	1/3 oz	10 g
Egg yolks	5 2/3 oz	160 g
Eggs, whole, shelled[b]	3 1/2 oz	100 g
Egg whites	8 1/2 oz	240 g
Crystal sugar	3 1/2 oz	100 g
Apricot glaze[c]	3 1/2 oz	100 g
Fondant, white[d]	7 oz	200 g

MISE EN PLACE

Butter and flour 4 loaf pans.

Sift 1 lb 2 oz (500 g) flour.

METHOD

Cream butter, sugar and vanilla sugar.

Gradually add egg yolks and whole eggs.

Whip egg whites to soft peaks, add 3 1/2 oz (100 g) sugar, and whip until sugar is dissolved. Fold egg white/sugar mixture into butter/sugar mixture.

Pour batter into the prepared molds and bake at 400°F (200°C).

Check doneness with a fine wooden skewer or cake tester.

Unmold and let cool on a wire rack.

Melt apricot glaze and fondant in water bath.

Brush cakes, first with apricot glaze, and then top with fondant.

---

[a] Vanilla sugar is made by storing vanilla beans in sugar until the vanilla essence is absorbed. Vanilla sugar is also commercially available.

[b] Eggs can be purchased already shelled, mixed, and pasteurized.

[c] Apricot glaze is commercially available.

[d] Fondant is a boiled sugar icing, commercially available.

713

Soufflé Grand Marnier

Grand-Marnier-Auflauf
Soufflé au Grand Marnier

YIELD: 10 SERVINGS

Sponge cake (Recipe 709)	1 1/3 oz	40 g
Grand Marnier[a]	1 1/3 oz	40 ml
Butter	1/3 oz	10 g
Cake flour	1/3 oz	10 g
Butter	3 oz	80 g
Cake flour	3 oz	80 g
Milk	13 1/2 oz	400 ml
Orange, rind, grated	1	1
Salt	1x	1x
Egg yolks	5 1/3 oz	150 g
Egg whites	7 oz	200 g
Crystal sugar	3 1/2 oz	100 g
Powdered sugar	1/3 oz	10 g

MISE EN PLACE

Cut sponge cake into small cubes and soak with Grand Marnier.

Butter and flour a 1 qt (950 ml) soufflé mold.

Melt 3 oz (80 g) butter and add 3 oz (80 g) flour. Stir roux and let cool.

METHOD

Combine milk with orange rind and salt. Bring to a boil.

Pour over roux and stir with stiff wire whisk until smooth.

Stir with wooden paddle on stove until mixture has come to a boil and is a smooth paste.

Let cool slightly and gradually in egg yolks.

Whip egg whites, add sugar, and whip until sugar is dissolved and egg whites form stiff peaks.

Stir a small amount of whipped egg whites into batter, then carefully fold in the rest of the egg whites.

Pour a small amount of batter into soufflé mold and sprinkle with Grand Marnier–soaked sponge cake. Pour remaining batter over sponge cake. The mold should be about three-quarters full.

Warm soufflé in water bath on top of stove then bake at 400°F (200°C) on oven rack (without water bath). Check doneness with a fine wooden skewer.

Dust with powdered sugar and serve at once.

NOTE: If batter is prewarmed, the baking temperatures are 20 minutes for a large soufflé for 10 servings, or 8 minutes for individual soufflés.

[a] Grand Marnier is a Cognac-based, orange-flavored liqueur.

714

Cold Semolina Pudding

Griess Victoria
Semoule Victoria

YIELD: 10 SERVINGS

White wine jelly (Recipe 783)	6 3/4 oz	200 ml
Vanilla bean[a]	1	1
Milk	1 pt 1 oz	500 ml
Gelatin, leaf[b]	1/2 oz	15 g
Semolina, hard wheat	2 oz	60 g
Lemon, rind, grated	1	1
Egg yolks[c]	4 1/4 oz	120 g
Crystal sugar	4 1/4 oz	120 g
Heavy cream (36%)	13 1/2 oz	400 ml
Melba sauce[d] (Recipe 719)	1 pt 1 oz	500 ml

MISE EN PLACE

Melt wine gelatin and pour into 10 timbale molds.

Split vanilla bean, scrape out marrow, and add marrow to milk.

Soak leaf gelatin in cold water.

METHOD

Bring vanilla-milk to a boil. Strain[e] sauce through a fine wire china cap.

Return milk to stove and add semolina. Stir, first with a strong wire whisk, and then for about 10 minutes with a wooden paddle. Remove from stove.

Squeeze water out of gelatin and add to semolina. Add grated lemon rind.

Cream egg yolks and sugar and fold into the semolina mixture while the mixture is still hot.

Whip heavy cream.

Stir semolina pudding over ice until almost cold, and fold in whipped cream.

Fill timbale molds and refrigerate.

Unmold pudding by dipping molds very briefly into hot water. Unmold directly onto serving plates.

Surround cold pudding with Melba sauce.

[a] Vanilla extract can be substituted.

[b] Powdered gelatin can be substituted. It must be dissolved with a small amount of warm water.

[c] The egg yolks should be pasteurized, since they are not cooked.

[d] Melba sauce is the most suitable sauce because of flavor and color, but other fruit sauces can be substituted.

[e] If vanilla extract is used, this step can be omitted.

715

$\mathscr{P}$uff Pastry (lean)[a]

Halbblätterteig
Feuilletage maigre

YIELD: 2 LB 3 OZ (1.0 KG)

Bread flour[b]	1 lb 2 oz	500 g
Salt	1/3 oz	12 g
Water	8 1/2 oz	250 ml
Butter, cold	2 2/3 oz	75 g
Margarine for puff pastry[c]	5 1/3 oz	150 g

MISE EN PLACE
Sift flour onto pastry table.

Dissolve salt in water.

METHOD
Rub cold butter with flour to form fine granules. Make a well in the center of the flour.

Add the salted water and work into a smooth, elastic dough.

Briefly knead the margarine. It should have the same consistency as the dough.

Shape margarine into a brick.

Place margarine in center of dough; fold dough corners over the margarine.

Roll dough and fold sides toward the center. The dough edges should touch.

Fold over once more toward the center.

Repeat process, cover dough, and refrigerate for at least 20 minutes.

Repeat the folding process twice more, refrigerating for at least 20 minutes between each folding process.[d]

Store dough in plastic wrap.

716

$\mathscr{H}$azelnut Macaroons

Haselnussmakronen
Macarons aux noisettes

YIELD: 80 MACAROONS

Silicon paper[a]	as needed	
Hazelnuts (filberts), whole, peeled	3 1/2 oz	100 g
Hazelnuts (filberts), ground	8 3/4 oz	250 g
Crystal sugar	1 lb 2 oz	500 g
Egg whites	6 1/2 oz	180 g

MISE EN PLACE
Line pastry sheet pans with silicon paper.

Split whole hazelnuts for garnish. There should be 80 pieces.

METHOD
Blend ground hazelnuts, half the sugar, and half the egg whites into a fine purée. This is done with a special rolling machine. If this machine is not available, the hazelnuts can be ground very fine in a food processor. Be sure they do not overheat in the process.

Add remaining sugar and egg whites. Stir mixture in mixing machine with a paddle until very smooth and the sugar is dissolved.

With pastry bag, shape 80 little mounds on the silicon paper.

Place one half hazelnut on each mound, and bake at 375°F (190°C).

NOTE: The same recipe can be used for almond macaroons.

---

[a] Also see regular Puff Pastry (Recipe 689).

[b] The flour should have a high gluten content, to make it elastic.

[c] Margarine for puff pastry is specially formulated, and is available from pastry supply purveyors.

[d] It is recommended to refrigerate dough overnight.

[a] If silicon or Teflon paper is not available, line the sheet pan with brown kraft paper. Macaroons will stick to the paper. To remove, turn the sheet upside down and moisten slightly. The moisture will penetrate and the macaroons will come right off. (Do not use parchment paper because it isn't porous.)

$\mathcal{B}$undt Cake (with yeast)

Hefegugelhopf
Kouglof de pâte levée

YIELD: 2 CAKES

Milk	1 pt 1 oz	500 ml
Yeast, fresh[a]	3 oz	80 g
Crystal sugar	7 oz	200 g
White wheat flour	2 lb 7 oz	1.1 kg
Salt	1/2 oz	15 g
Butter	8 3/4 oz	250 g
Egg yolks	5 1/3 oz	150 g
Lemon, rind, grated	1	1
Raisins, golden	13 oz	375 g
Rum, dark	1 2/3 oz	50 ml
White wheat flour	2/3 oz	20 g
Butter	2/3 oz	20 g
White wheat flour	2/3 oz	20 g
Powdered sugar	1 2/3 oz	50 g

MISE EN PLACE

Warm the milk to 86°F (30°C).

Add yeast and sugar to dissolve.

Sift flour with salt into mixing bowl.

Melt 8 3/4 oz (250 g) butter.

METHOD

Combine milk mixture with sifted flour, egg yolks, lemon rind, and melted butter.

Mix at medium speed[b] with dough hook, until the dough is silky and smooth.

Blend raisins with 2/3 oz (20 g) flour. (The flour prevents the raisins from sinking to the bottom of the mold during baking.)

Add floured raisins to the dough. Add rum.

Butter two *gugelhopf* (bundt cake) molds and dust with flour.

Divide dough in half and place in molds. They should be about three-quarters full.

Cover molds with a dry towel and let proof. Let dough rise until molds are filled. (The cakes will rise even more during the baking process.)

Bake without steam at 400°F (200°C). Before removing cakes, insert thin wooden skewer to be sure cakes are baked all the way through.

Invert onto rack to let cool.

Sprinkle with powdered sugar.

$\mathcal{R}$aspberry Mousse

Himbeermousse
Mousse aux framboises

YIELD: 10 SERVINGS

Heavy cream (36%)	10 oz	300 ml
Egg whites, pasteurized	2 2/3 oz	75 g
Powdered sugar	7 oz	200 g
Raspberry purée,[a] nonsweetened	10 1/2 oz	300 g
Lemon juice	1/2 oz	15 ml

MISE EN PLACE

Whip heavy cream.

METHOD

Combine egg whites and powdered sugar; mix with whisk in water bath until the sugar is dissolved. The mixture should not be warmer than 120°F (50°C).

Whip with mixing machine until the mixture forms a cool, stiff foam (meringue).

Fold in fruit puree and lemon juice.

Fold in whipped cream and serve mousse in attractive glasses.

NOTE: The same recipe can be used to make mousse with other unsweetened fruit purees.

---

[a] Dry yeast can be substituted.

[b] Note that friction creates heat, and if dough is mixed too rapidly, it could overheat and kill the yeast.

---

[a] Fruit purees are commercially available.

719

$\mathcal{M}$elba (raspberry) Sauce

Himbeersauce
Sauce Melba

YIELD: 1 QT 2 OZ (1.0 L)

Raspberries, fresh	2 lb	900 g
Powdered sugar	8 3/4 oz	250 g
Lemon, juice	1	1

METHOD

Combine raspberries with powdered sugar, purée, and strain.

Add lemon juice according to taste.

720

$\mathcal{Q}$uick (Dutch) Puff Pastry

Holländischer oder Blitzblätterteig
Feuilletage rapide

YIELD: 2 LB 3 OZ (1.0 KG)

Margarine for puff pastry[a]	14 oz	400 g
Water	8 1/2 oz	250 ml
Salt	1/3 oz	12 g
White wheat flour	1 lb 2 oz	500 g

MISE EN PLACE

Cut margarine into 3/4-in. (20 mm) cubes and refrigerate.

Combine water and salt.

METHOD

Make dough with margarine cubes, salted water, and flour. The margarine cubes should remain somewhat intact.

Refrigerate dough; then roll out and fold 4 times as described in Recipe 689.

Refrigerate dough before use.

721

$\mathcal{A}$lmond Lace Cookies (variation 1)

Hüppenmasse
Appareil à cornets

YIELD: 2 LB 3 OZ (1.0 KG)

Butter	1/3 oz	10 g
White wheat flour	1/3 oz	10 g
Cake flour	4 1/3 oz	125 g
Almonds, peeled	7 oz	200 g
Crystal sugar	10 1/2 oz	300 g
Egg whites	7 oz	200 g
Milk	5 oz	150 ml

MISE EN PLACE

Butter and flour baking sheet pans.

Sift the cake flour.

Grind almonds very fine.

METHOD

Combine almonds, sugar, egg whites and two-thirds of the milk.

Add sifted flour and stir until smooth.

Add remaining milk to make a spreadable batter.

Use template[a] to spread batter on prepared baking sheets.

Prebake briefly, remove from oven for 20 minutes, and finish baking.

Bake until golden brown.

Remove from baking sheet with spatula while still hot and shape or twist to desired shape.

---

[a] Margarine for puff pastry is specially formulated, and is available from pastry supply purveyors.

[a] The batter is used to make cones (cornets), leaves, or other decorative items for desserts. The cookies will be brittle when cool, but will soften in humid conditions.

722

Almond Lace Cookies (variation 2)

Hüppenmasse
Appareil à cornets

YIELD: 1 LB 10 OZ (750 G)

Butter	1/3 oz	10g
White wheat flour	1/3 oz	10 g
Cake flour	4 1/3 oz	125 g
Almond paste[a]	7 oz	200 g
Crystal sugar	3 1/2 oz	100 g
Egg whites	7 oz	200 g
Milk	5 oz	150 ml

MISE EN PLACE
Butter and flour baking sheet pans, or line with silicon paper.

Sift the cake flour.

METHOD
Mix almond paste, sugar, and egg whites into a smooth batter.

Add two-thirds of the milk and the sifted flour and stir until combined.

Add remaining milk to thin out batter until it is spreadable.

Use template[a] to spread batter on prepared baking sheets.

Prebake briefly, remove from oven for 20 minutes, then finish baking.

Bake until golden brown.

Remove from baking sheet with spatula while still hot and shape or twist to desired shape.

723

Hazelnut Meringue

Japonais
Japonais

YIELD: 6 MERINGUES

Butter	1/3 oz	10 g
White wheat flour	1/3 oz	10 g
Cake flour	2 oz	60 g
Hazelnuts (filberts), peeled and ground	8 oz	225 g

---

[a] The batter is used to make cones (cornets), leaves, or other decorative items for desserts. The cookies will be brittle when cool, but will soften in humid conditions.

Butter	3/4 oz	25 g
Egg whites	8 3/4 oz	250 g
Crystal sugar	1 lb 2 oz	500 g

MISE EN PLACE
Butter and flour three sheet pans.

Sift the cake flour and mix in ground hazelnuts.

Melt 3/4 oz (25 g) butter.

METHOD
Whip egg whites and one-third of sugar into soft peaks.

Blend remaining sugar with sifted flour/hazelnut mix and fold this into egg whites.

Carefully fold melted butter into batter.

With template spread 6 circles on baking sheets,[a] two on each sheet.

Bake at 325°F (165°C) with open vent.

NOTE: *Japonais* are basic meringue cake bottoms, which are used in a number of classic cakes and desserts. They should be stored in a dry location, because moisture will soften the meringue.

724

Yogurt Cream

Joghurtcreme
Crème de yogourt

YIELD: 1 QT 12 OZ (1.3 L)

Gelatin, leaf[b]	1/2 oz	12 g
Heavy cream (36%)	1 pt 4 oz	600 ml
Egg yolks[c]	3 1/2 oz	100 g
Crystal sugar	3 1/2 oz	100 g
Yogurt, plain	1 lb 2 oz	500 g

MISE EN PLACE
Soak gelatin in cold water.

Whip heavy cream and keep chilled.

METHOD
Squeeze water from gelatin and melt in water bath.

Cream egg yolks and sugar.

---

[a] The meringue mixture can be dressed on baking paper.

[b] Gelatin powder can be used. It should be dissolved in the water bath with a small amount of water.

[c] The egg yolks should be pasteurized, because they will not be cooked.

Add yogurt and blend thoroughly.

Blend melted gelatin rapidly with yogurt cream and fold in whipped cream.

NOTE: Seasonal fruits and berries can be blended into the cream. The amount of sugar needed depends on the acidity of the fruits.

725

Yogurt Ice Cream with Cassis

Joghurtglace mit Cassis
Glace yogourt au cassis

YIELD: 1 QT 22 OZ (1.6 L)

Sugar syrup[a]	1 pt 1 oz	500 ml
Yogurt, plain	1 lb 5 oz	600 g
Cassis[b] purée, not sweetened	1 lb 2 oz	500 g
Egg whites	1 2/3 oz	50 g
Powdered sugar[c]	1 1/3 oz	40 g

METHOD

Thoroughly mix sugar syrup, yogurt, and cassis puree.

Combine egg whites and sugar and whip in water bath until temperature is no higher than 120°F (50°C). Whip mixture into soft peaks and let cool.

Blend meringue into yogurt mixture and process in ice cream freezer.

NOTE: The same recipe can be used with other unsweetened fruit purees.

726

Chocolate Sponge Cake with Yogurt Pear Cream

Joghurtschnitten mit Birnen
Tranches au yogourt et aux poires

YIELD: 10 SERVINGS

Plastic wrap

Chocolate sponge cake roll, not rolled (Recipe 759)	1/2	1/2
Pears, canned, drained	1 lb 2 oz	500 g
Pear brandy[a]	1 2/3 oz	50 ml
Gelatin, leaf[b]	3 oz	80 g
Yogurt cream (Recipe 724)	1 qt 12 oz	1.3 L
Heavy cream (36%)	6 3/4 oz	200 ml
Cocoa powder	1/3 oz	10 g

MISE EN PLACE

Line suitable cake mold, round or rectangular, with plastic wrap.

Cut sponge cake into pieces and line mold evenly. Save some cake for the top layer.

Cut pears into small dice, but save 20 nice wedges for garnish.

Marinate diced pears with 2/3 oz (20 ml) pear brandy.

Soak gelatin in cold water. Squeeze out water and melt gelatin in water bath.

Make yogurt cream according to recipe, but add the additional gelatin for extra stiffness.

Flavor yogurt cream with remaining 3/4 oz (25 ml) pear brandy.

Whip heavy cream and add cocoa powder.

METHOD

Fill mold with about half amount of yogurt cream.

Sprinkle marinated diced pears on top.

Fill mold with remaining yogurt cream and cover with remaining strips of sponge cake.

Refrigerate mold. When solid, invert, and cut into 10 slices.

Decorate each slice with whipped cream and 2 pear wedges.

---

[a] To make sugar syrup, combine 3 parts sugar and 2 parts water (by volume), bring to a boil, and chill.

[b] Cassis is black currant. The puree is available commercially.

[c] In the United States, powdered sugar is normally blended with a small amount of cornstarch. Very fine sugar may be substituted.

[a] The original recipe calls for the Swiss pear brandy, Williamine. Any pear brandy can be used.

[b] Gelatin powder can be used. It should be melted in the water bath with a small amount of water.

727

Red Currant Sauce

Johannisbeersauce
Sauce aux groseilles

YIELD: 1 QT 2 OZ (1.0 L)

Red currants,[a] fresh	1 lb 10 oz	750 g
Powdered sugar	1 lb 2 oz	500 g

METHOD

Wash the currants and remove stems.

Purée the currants and strain out seeds.

Mix pulp and juice with sugar.

728

Cold Meringue

Kalte Schneemasse/Meringuemasse
Meringage

YIELD: 1 LB 12 OZ (800 G)

Egg whites	10 1/2 oz	300 g
Crystal sugar	1 lb 2 oz	500 g
Cornstarch	1 oz	30 g

METHOD

Whip egg whites into soft peaks with one-third of the sugar.

Continue whipping, gradually adding another third of the sugar.

Blend remaining sugar with cornstarch and fold into mixture.

APPLICATIONS

Meringues with Whipped Cream: With pastry bag, dress egg-shaped mounds (like a half egg) on silicon[b] baking paper or parchment paper. Start baking at 285°F (140 °C), reduce heat, and continue cooking until meringues are dry. To serve, dress whipped cream onto flat side, put two mounds together, place on serving plates, and garnish with additional cream and fruits. Dust with cocoa powder if desired.

Vacherin with Whipped Cream: With pastry bag, using a smooth tube, dress meringue in a spiral. Start in the middle, and work your way outwards, until you have a cake-size disc. Make two discs. Start baking at 285°F (140 °C), reduce heat, and continue cooking until meringues are dry. To serve, spread whipped cream generously on one disc, place the second disc on top, upside down, and garnish the vacherin with additional cream and fruits.[a]

Vacherin with Strawberries: Follow the recipe for Vacherin with Whipped Cream, but add a generous layer of strawberries that have been marinated in maraschino and sugar.

729

Cat's Tongues

Katzenzüngli
Langues de chat

YIELD: 60 PIECES

Butter	1/3 oz	10 g
White wheat flour	1/3 oz	10 g
Cake flour	1 lb 2 oz	500 g
Heavy cream (36%)	10 oz	300 ml
Powdered sugar	14 oz	400 g
Vanilla sugar[b]	1/3 oz	10 g
Egg whites	12 1/2 oz	360 g

MISE EN PLACE

Butter a sheet pan and dust with flour.

Sift the cake flour.

METHOD

Stir together heavy cream, powdered sugar, and vanilla sugar.

Whip egg whites into soft peaks.

Fold the whipped egg whites and the sifted flour, alternately, into the heavy cream mixture.

With pastry bag, using a smooth tube, dress strips about 2 1/2 in. (60 mm) long, directly onto sheet pan.

Bake at 425°F (220°C) and remove from pan while still hot.

---

[a] These currants are known as *Rote Johannisbeeren* in German.

[b] Meringues must be dried thoroughly, and stored in a dry place. In many professional kitchens, meringues are stored overnight in a baking oven that is turned off.

---

[a] The vacherin can also be filled with ice cream, but must be served at once, because meringue will become too moist and limp in the freezer.

[b] A dash of vanilla extract can be substituted.

Crystal sugar	12 oz	350 g
Salt	1x	1x
Rum, dark	1/6 oz	5 ml

MISE EN PLACE

Cut cold butter into 1/2-in. (12 mm) cubes. Leave butter outside the refrigerator to reach room temperature.

Toast hazelnuts in oven and let cool.

Sift cake flour with baking powder and a dash of cinnamon.

METHOD

Cream eggs and sugar. Add butter cubes, hazelnuts, salt, and rum. Blend ingredients, but do not cream.

Put sifted flour on pastry table and make a well in the center.

Add egg/sugar/butter mixture and knead dough until all ingredients are combined.

Refrigerate dough before use.

730

*C*oconut Macaroons

Kokosmakronen
Macarons au coco

YIELD: 100 MACAROONS

Silicon paper[a]	as needed	
Cake flour	1 2/3 oz	50 g
Coconut flakes, dry, short-shred	8 3/4 oz	250 g
Crystal sugar	1 lb 2 oz	500 g
Egg whites	7 oz	200 g

MISE EN PLACE

Line baking sheet pan with silicon paper.

Sift the cake flour.

METHOD

Combine coconut flakes, sugar, and egg whites in a copper kettle.

Stir mixture over low heat until it reaches 170°F (75°C) to 180°F (80°C).

Keep stirring until mixture is cool. Fold in flour.

With pastry bag, using the star tube, dress small rosettes.

Bake at 425°F (220°C).

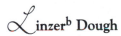

731

*L*inzer[b] Dough

Linzer Teig
Pâte de Linz

YIELD: 3 LB 5 OZ (1.5 KG)

Butter, cold	10 1/2 oz	300 g
Hazelnuts (filberts), ground[c]	8 3/4 oz	250 g
Cake flour	1 lb 2 oz	500 g
Baking powder	1/2 oz	15 g
Cinnamon, ground	1/3 oz	10 g
Eggs, whole, shelled[d]	5 1/3 oz	150 g

732

*L*inzer Tart

Linzer Torte
Tarte de Linz

YIELD: 2 TARTS

Egg	1	1
Raspberry jam, bake-proof	14 oz	400 g
Linzer dough (Recipe 731)	2 lb 3 oz	1.0 kg

MISE EN PLACE

Break egg and mix with 1 tbsp water.

Warm jam slightly and stir to make it spreadable.

METHOD

Divide Linzer dough into two parts.

Roll out one part to about 1/5-in. (5 mm) thickness. Cut out two circles, using two tart rings. Save the trimmings.

Place the same tart rings on a baking sheet and place the dough circles inside.

Brush the dough with raspberry jam, but leave a 3/4-in. (20 mm) rim.

Brush rim with some of the egg wash.

Roll out remaining dough to about 1/8-in. (3 mm) thickness.

Cut dough with pastry wheel or knife into 1/3-in. (10 mm) bands.

Place bands on tarts, making a lattice design.

(continued on next page)

---

[a] If silicon paper is not available, line the sheet pan with brown kraft paper. Macaroons will stick to the paper. To remove, turn the sheet upside down, and moisten slightly. The moisture will penetrate and the macaroons will come right off. (Do not use parchment paper because it isn't porous.)

[b] Linz is a city in Austria.

[c] Peeled hazelnuts are preferred.

[d] Eggs can be purchased already shelled, mixed, and pasteurized.

(continued from preceding page)

Knead together all dough trimmings, and divide in half.

Form each half into a long roll, the length of the circumference of the tart.

Place dough rolls on rim, press down, and decorate with small grooves using a table fork.

Brush tarts with egg wash and bake at 425°F (220°C).

Let tarts cool on wire rack.

733

ℒady Fingers

Löffelbiskuits
Pèlerines

YIELD: 2 LB 3 OZ (1.0 KG)

Silicon paper or parchment paper as needed		
Cake flour	5 1/3 oz	150 g
Cornstarch	5 1/3 oz	150 g
Egg yolks	8 3/4 oz	250 g
Crystal sugar	4 1/3 oz	125 g
Egg whites	7 oz	200 g
Crystal sugar	4 1/3 oz	125 g
Crystal sugar	2/3 oz	20 g

MISE EN PLACE

Line baking sheet pans with silicon paper or parchment paper.

Sift together the cake flour and cornstarch.

METHOD

Cream egg yolks with 4 1/3 oz (125 g) sugar.

Whip egg whites with 4 1/3 oz (125 g) sugar and fold into the egg yolk mixture.

Carefully fold flour mixture into the batter.

With pastry bag, using large smooth tube, immediately dress tubes about 5 in. (125 mm) long, onto baking paper.

Sprinkle with sugar and bake at 400°F (200°C), without steam.

734

𝒲hite Almond Cream

Mandelcreme
Blanc-mange

YIELD: 10 SERVINGS

Vanilla bean[a]	1	1
Milk	1 pt 1 oz	500 ml
Gelatin, leaf[b]	1/2 oz	12 g
Heavy cream (36%)	10 oz	300 ml
Salt	1x	1x
Almond paste[c]	8 3/4 oz	250 g

MISE EN PLACE

Split vanilla bean, scrape out marrow, and add marrow and bean to milk.

Soak gelatin in cold water.

Whip heavy cream.

METHOD

Add salt to vanilla-milk and bring to a boil. Let cool slightly.

Squeeze water from gelatin and add to milk to dissolve.

Remove vanilla bean.

Add almond paste and stir until dissolved.

With a commercial hand-held mixer, blend mixture thoroughly until smooth.

Let mixture cool over ice, stirring continuously.

When mixture starts to solidify, blend in whipped cream.

Immediately fill individual molds with the mixture, or use one large mold.

Refrigerate until solid. Unmold to serve.

NOTE: Serve with fresh red berries, such as strawberries or raspberries, and a sweet red sauce, such as Melba (Raspberry) Sauce (Recipe 719), Strawberry Sauce (Recipe 699), or Red Currant Sauce (Recipe 727).

---

[a] Vanilla extract can be substituted.

[b] Powdered gelatin can be substituted. It must be dissolved with small amount of water before it is added to the milk.

[c] The almond paste should contain 50% sugar, and should be made with white (blanched) almonds.

735

Frozen Mousse (basic recipe)

Schaumgefrorenes (Grundmasse)
Mousse glacée

YIELD: 1 QT 2 OZ (1.0 LI)

Heavy cream (36%)	1 pt 9 oz	750 ml
Egg whites	4 1/3 oz	125 g
Powdered sugar	7 oz	200 g

METHOD

Whip heavy cream.

Combine egg whites and sugar and stir with whisk over water bath until mixture has reached no more than 120°F (50°C).

Whip mixture into meringue and continue mixing until cold.

Fold in whipped cream.

Fill molds and freeze.

NOTE: Frozen mousse can be flavored with liqueurs, fruit flavors, or other flavors.

736

Butter Cookies[a]

Ochsenaugen
Oeils de boeuf

YIELD: 50 COOKIES

Butter	1/3 oz	10 g
Cake flour	1 lb 2 oz	500 g
Apricot jam	3 1/2 oz	100 g
Butter, cold	14 oz	400 g
Powdered sugar	7 oz	200 g
Egg yolks	1 2/3 oz	50 g
Lemon, peel, grated	1	1
Powdered sugar	2/3 oz	20 g

MISE EN PLACE

Butter a sheet pan.

Sift the cake flour.

Warm apricot jam.

---

[a] The original recipe calls these cookies "Ox Eyes."

METHOD

Cut cold butter into large cubes and put on pastry table.

Add 7 oz (200 g) powdered sugar and rapidly knead together.

Add sifted flour, egg yolks, and grated lemon peel.

Kneed all together into a cookie dough. Be sure to work rapidly.

Refrigerate dough until use.

Roll out dough about 1/8 in. (3 mm) thick.

Cut a hundred 1 1/4-in. (30 mm) circles with a cookie cutter and place on the buttered baking sheet.

Cut a small hole with a small cookie cutter in the center of 50 of the cookies.

Bake at 415°F (210°C).

Let cookies cool and spread apricot jam on the whole circles.

Put the circles with the center holes on top, so the jam shows through.

Dust with powdered sugar.

737

Strawberry Omelette

Omeletten Stephanie
Omelettes Stéphanie

YIELD: 10 SERVINGS

Cake flour	1 1/3 oz	40 g
Butter	2/3 oz	20 g
Strawberry jam	1 2/3 oz	50 g
Orange liqueur	1 2/3 oz	50 ml
Vanilla bean[a]	1/2	1/2
Egg yolks	3 oz	80 g
Crystal sugar	3 oz	80 g
Egg whites	5 1/3 oz	150 g
Heavy cream (36%)	1/3 oz	10 ml
Lemon, peel, grated	1/2	1/2
Butter	1/3 oz	10 g
Powdered sugar	1/3 oz	10 g

(continued on next page)

---

[a] Vanilla extract can be substituted.

(continued from preceding page)

MISE EN PLACE

Sift the cake flour.

Melt 2/3 oz (20 g) butter.

Blend strawberry jam with orange liqueur.

METHOD

Scrape out marrow from vanilla bean and add to egg yolks. (Save bean pod for other uses.)

Cream egg yolks with sugar.

Whip egg whites and fold into creamed yolks.

Fold in flour, melted butter, heavy cream, and grated lemon peel.

Melt remaining butter in a Teflon-coated omelette pan.[a]

Add batter, spread evenly, and bake until brown.

Put strawberry jam in center and fold over.

Slide omelette on to a hot serving platter.

Sprinkle with powdered sugar and serve at once.

738

lazed Oranges

Orangengratin
Gratin d'oranges

YIELD: 10 SERVINGS

Oranges	4 lb	1.8 kg
Orange liqueur	1 2/3 oz	50 ml
Powdered sugar	2/3 oz	20 g
Heavy cream (36%)	13 1/2 oz	400 ml
Egg yolks	4 1/4 oz	120 g
Orange juice	2 3/4 oz	80 ml
Powdered sugar	3 1/2 oz	100 g
Butter	2/3 oz	20 g

MISE EN PLACE

Peel oranges and seam out (cut out) wedges.

Marinate orange wedges with orange liqueur and 2/3 oz (20 g) powdered sugar.

Whip heavy cream.

METHOD

Combine egg yolks, orange juice, and 3 1/2 oz (100 g) powdered sugar.

Whip in water bath until mixture has reached 170°F (75°C).

Whip until cool and foamy.

Fold whipped cream into mixture.

Butter an ovenproof dish (*gratin* dish) and spread orange wedges on the dish.

Pour batter over oranges, spreading to cover oranges evenly.

Brown quickly in a very hot oven, or under the salamander.

NOTE: The same recipe can be used with berries.

739

Orange Mousse

Orangenmousse
Mousse à l'orange

YIELD: 10 SERVINGS

Gelatin, leaf[a]	1/2 oz	15 g
Oranges	5	5
Orange juice	1 pt 1 oz	500 ml
Crystal sugar	1 1/3 oz	40 g
Heavy cream (36%)	12 oz	350 ml
Crystal sugar	4 1/4 oz	120 g
Egg whites	2 2/3 oz	75 g
Salt	1x	1x
Peppermint leaves, fresh	20	20

MISE EN PLACE

Soak gelatin in cold water.

Make orange zest[b] from 3 oranges and add to orange juice.

Peel all 5 oranges and seam out (remove) sections.

Marinate sections with 1 1/3 oz (40 g) sugar.

Whip heavy cream.

METHOD

Combine 4 1/4 oz (120 g) sugar with orange zest small amount of orange juice and bring to a boil.

Squeeze water from gelatin, and add to hot orange juice.

When gelatin has dissolved, add remaining orange juice.

---

[a] It is advisable to use two omelette pans, and make two omelettes for 5 servings each. These omelettes collapse (deflate) rapidly outside the oven. Omelettes can also be made in individual pans.

[a] Powdered gelatin can be used. It must be dissolved in a small amount of warm water before use.

[b] Orange zest is made by peeling the rind with a vegetable peeler and cutting the rind into very fine shreds (*julienne*).

Strain orange liquid through a fine wire mesh china cap.

Whip egg whites with salt into soft peaks.

Stir liquid over ice until it starts to thicken.

Fold whipped cream and egg whites into orange mixture.

Pour mousse into a stainless steel bowl[a] and refrigerate.

To serve, make egg-shaped dumplings, using two spoons dipped in hot water.[b]

Serve two or three dumplings per person.

Garnish with orange sections and mint leaves.

740

$\mathcal{P}$arfait (basic recipe)

Rahmgefrorenes (Grundmasse)
Parfait glacé

YIELD: 1 QT 2 OZ (1.0 L)

Heavy cream (36%)	1 pt 9 oz	750 ml
Eggs, whole, shelled[c]	7 oz	200 g
Crystal sugar	7 oz	200 g

METHOD
Whip heavy cream.

Combine eggs and sugar and whip in water bath until sugar is dissolved, but not warmer than 120°F (50°C).

Using a mixing machine, whip until mixture is foamy and cool.

Fold whipped cream into the egg mixture and add desired flavor.

Pour parfait into molds or tall glasses and freeze.

NOTE: Parfait mixture can be flavored with liqueurs, fruit flavors, nuts, or chocolate.

741

$\mathcal{P}$ancake (crepe) Batter

Pfannkuchenteig
Pâte à crêpes

YIELD: 1 PT 1 OZ (500 ML)

Cake flour	3 1/2 oz	100 g
Butter	3/4 oz	25 g
Milk	8 1/2 oz	250 ml
Heavy cream (36%)	2 3/4 oz	80 ml
Eggs, whole, shelled[a]	3 1/2 oz	100 g
Salt	1x	1x
Crystal sugar	2/3 oz	20 g
Lemon, peel, grated	1/4	1/4
Orange, peel, grated	1/4	1/4

MISE EN PLACE
Sift the cake flour into a mixing bowl.

Melt butter.

METHOD
Mix remaining ingredients.

Add this mixture and melted butter to the sifted flour. Stir to make a smooth batter.[b]

Let batter rest for 1/2 hour before use.

742

$\mathcal{A}$pple Pancakes

Pfannkuchen mit Äpfeln
Crêpes normande

YIELD: 10 SERVINGS

Apples, cooking variety	1 lb 2 oz	500 g
Pancake batter (Recipe 741)	1 pt 1 oz	500 ml
Butter	1 oz	30 g
Raisins, golden	1 2/3 oz	50 g
Crystal sugar	1 2/3 oz	50 g
Cinnamon, ground	1/6 oz	5 g
White wine	1 2/3 oz	50 ml
Butter	1 2/3 oz	50 g
Powdered sugar	2/3 oz	20 g

(continued on next page)

---

[a] The mousse can also be poured into individual serving dishes or glasses.

[b] This requires some practice. An oval ice cream scoop can also be used.

[c] Eggs can be purchased already shelled, mixed, and pasteurized. Only pasteurized eggs should be used since this recipe doesn't get cooked.

[a] Eggs can be purchased already shelled, mixed, and pasteurized.

[b] It is advisable to strain batter through a china cap to remove all lumps.

(continued from preceding page)

MISE EN PLACE
Peel apples, cut into quarters, and slice thin.

Make 20 thin crepes using the pancake batter and 1 oz (30 g) butter.

METHOD
Stew apples with raisins, sugar, cinnamon, white wine, and 1 2/3 oz (50 g) butter until soft. Do not overcook. Keep warm.

Fill crepes and roll up.

To serve, dust crepes with powdered sugar and heat in hot oven until sugar browns.

NOTE: Crepes can be served with Apricot Sauce (Recipe 668).

743

*C*repes Suzette

Pfannkuchen Suzette
Crêpes Suzette

YIELD: 10 SERVINGS

Orange	1	1
Sugar cubes	3 1/2 oz	100 g
Butter	4 1/2 oz	130 g
Orange juice	13 1/2 oz	400 ml
Lemon juice	2 3/4 oz	80 ml
Crepes (Recipe 741)	20	20
Grand Marnier[a]	2 3/4 oz	80 ml
Cognac (brandy)	1 2/3 oz	50 ml
Vanilla ice cream (Recipe 778)	1 pt 1 oz	500 ml

MISE EN PLACE
Wash orange well. Rub sugar cubes on the orange to pick up the aromatic oils.

METHOD
Melt butter in flambé pan.[b]

Add sugar cubes to melt, and eventually to caramelize.

As soon as sugar is browned, carefully add orange juice and lemon juice.

Bring to a boil and simmer until sugar is dissolved. Lower the flame.

Dip crepes, one by one, into hot mixture, turn over, and fold. Place crepes to one side of pan.

Add Grand Marnier, and then Cognac. Ignite.[a]

Serve hot crepes at once with a scoop of ice cream.

744

*O*pen-Faced Apple Almond Tart

Pfarrhaustorte
Tarte aux pommes

YIELD: 2 CAKES

Silicon paper or parchment paper		
Apples	2 lb 3 oz	1.0 kg
Cake flour	7 oz	200 g
Baking powder	1/3 oz	10 g
Apricot glaze[b]	1 2/3 oz	50 g
Butter	10 1/2 oz	300 g
Crystal sugar	7 oz	200 g
Lemon, peel, grated	1	1
Egg yolks	5 2/3 oz	160 g
Egg whites	8 1/2 oz	240 g
Crystal sugar	3 1/2 oz	100 g
Almonds, blanches, grated fine	8 3/4 oz	250 g
Crystal sugar	2/3 oz	20 g
Powdered sugar	2/3 oz	20 g

MISE EN PLACE
Place two cake rings on a baking sheet lined with silicon paper or parchment paper.

Peel apples, cut in half, and remove core.

Make incisions on round side of apples, but do not cut all the way through.

Sift together cake flour and baking powder.

Warm apricot glaze.

METHOD
Cream butter, 7 oz (200 g) sugar, and grated lemon peel.

Add egg yolks gradually.

Whip egg whites and 3 1/2 oz (100 g) sugar into stiff peaks.

Alternately fold egg whites, flour, and almonds into the creamed butter.

---

[a] Grand Marnier is a Cognac-based, orange-flavored liqueur. Another orange-flavored liqueur can be used.

[b] Be sure the pan is large enough to hold the amount of liquid and crepes.

---

[a] Flaming in the dining room requires a considerable amount of skill, and is avoided in many restaurants. Since flaming can be dangerous, some insurance companies do not allow it any more.

[b] Apricot glaze is available commercially.

Pour batter into cake rings and spread to even out the surface.

Dip apples, round side down, into 2/3 oz (20 g) sugar and place apples, sugared side up, on top of batter. Press in lightly.

Bake at 400°F (200°C). Probe with needle to be sure cake is baked all the way through.

Remove from oven and brush, while still hot, with apricot glaze.

Let cakes cool on wire rack.

Dust with powdered sugar before serving.

745

Stewed Peaches

Pfirsichkompott
Compote de pêches

YIELD: 10 SERVINGS

Peaches[a]	3 lb 5 oz	1.5 kg
Water	1 qt 2 oz	1.0 L
Crystal sugar	1 lb 2 oz	500 g
Lemon juice	3 1/3 oz	100 ml

MISE EN PLACE
Dip peaches in boiling water, remove after a few moments, and plunge into ice water. Peel off skin, remove pits, and cut peaches into quarters.

METHOD
Combine water, sugar, and lemon juice and bring to a boil.

Add peaches and poach until peaches are tender.

Let peaches cool in cooking syrup.

NOTES: If desired, the stewed peaches can be flavored with peach liqueur.

The same method can be used to make other kinds of stewed fruits, but some fruits should not be peeled using boiling water.

---

[a] The peaches mentioned in the original recipe are "yellow peaches." There are many peach varieties. Choose a freestone variety if the pits are to be removed. Some cling peach varieties have more flavor than freestones, but the pits are hard to remove.

746

Pizza Dough

Pizzateig
Pâte à pizza

YIELD: 2 LB 10 OZ (1.2 KG)

Water	15 oz	450 ml
Yeast, fresh[a]	1 oz	30 g
White wheat flour[b]	1 lb 10 oz	750 g
Salt	1/2 oz	15 g
Olive oil, cold pressed	5 oz	150 ml

MISE EN PLACE
Warm water to 86°F (30°C) and add yeast to dissolve.

Sift together flour and salt.

METHOD
Combine all ingredients and knead[c] to smooth, elastic dough.

Cover and proof[d] until double in size.

---

[a] Dry yeast can be substituted. Prepare according to package directions.

[b] Hard wheat, high-gluten flour should be used to give the dough the necessary elasticity. Special pizza flour is sometimes available.

[c] The dough must be worked well to develop the gluten. This is best done in a mixing machine, at slow speed, using a dough hook. When a machine is used, the water should be ice cold, to counteract the heat caused by friction.

[d] The dough is best proofed in the refrigerator overnight, and then shaped/rolled into the desired size.

747

Plum Cake

Plum-Cake

YIELD: 5 CAKES

Butter	1/3 oz	10 g
Silicon paper or parchment paper as needed		
Candied fruits, diced	1 lb 5 oz	600 g
Raisins, golden	10 1/2 oz	300 g
Currants[a]	10 1/2 oz	300 g
Rum, dark	3 1/3 oz	100 ml
Cake flour	1 lb 10 oz	750 g
Baking powder	3/4 oz	25 g
Butter	1 lb 10 oz	750 g
Crystal sugar	1 lb 10 oz	750 g
Salt	1/6 oz	5 g
Lemon, peel, grated	1	1
Eggs, whole, shelled[b]	1 lb 14 oz	850 g

MISE EN PLACE

Butter five 1 qt 2 oz (1.0 L) cake molds and line with silicon paper or parchment paper.

Marinate candied fruits, raisins, and currants with rum.

Sift together cake flour and baking powder.

METHOD

Cream together butter, sugar, salt, and grated lemon peel.

Add eggs and flour alternately.

Fold marinated fruits into the batter.

Fill cake molds and bake at 375°F (190°C).

After 15 minutes, slash cakes with a wet knife so they will bake evenly.

Probe with needle to be sure cakes are baked all the way through.

Remove from molds and let cool on a wire rack.

---

[a] The currants in this recipe are actually small, dried, dark, seedless raisins (called *Korinthen* in German). They are different from fresh currants (called *Johannisbeeren* in German). Other small, dark raisins can be substituted.

[b] Eggs can be purchased already shelled, mixed, and pasteurized.

748

Pears Poached in Port

Portweinbirnen
Poires au porto

YIELD: 10 SERVINGS

Pears[a] (10)	3 lb 5 oz	1.5 kg
Red Port wine	10 oz	300 ml
Dry red wine	1 pt 11 oz	800 ml
Crystal sugar	5 1/3 oz	150 g
Cinnamon stick (rind)	1	1
Cloves	6	6

MISE EN PLACE

Peel pears, but leave whole. If possible, leave stems on fruits.

Remove cores from the bottom of the pears, using a melon baller.

METHOD

Combine all ingredients, except pears, and bring to a boil.

Add pears and poach until tender.

Carefully remove pears with a skimmer.

Reduce cooking liquid to syrupy consistency, add the pears, and let cool.

749

Palmiers (Pig's Ears)

Preussen
Prussiens

YIELD: 50 PIECES

Crystal sugar	3 1/2 oz	100 g
Puff pastry, lean (Recipe 715)	14 oz	400 g
Butter	1/3 oz	10 g

MISE EN PLACE

Sprinkle sugar on pastry table; place cold puff pastry on top.

Sprinkle some of the sugar on top also.

Roll out and fold over once. Refrigerate dough.

Butter baking sheet pan.

---

[a] The pears should be ripe, but not soft. There are many pear varieties on the market. In the United States, Bartlett, Bosc, and Nelis varieties are recommended.

METHOD

Roll out dough to a rectangle about 8 in. x 16 in. (200 mm x 400 mm).

Roll dough from both long sides toward the center. Roll very tightly. When the rolls have met, put one roll on top of the other, press together, and flatten lightly.

Refrigerate dough.

Cut roll into 1/5-in. (5 mm) slices. Put slices on baking sheet and refrigerate.

Bake at 410°F (210°C).

As soon as the pastry starts to brown, remove from oven, turn over, and continue baking. (The objective is to have the sugar caramelize on both sides.)

750

Pudding with Candied Fruits

Pudding Diplomatenart
Pouding diplomate

YIELD: 10 SERVINGS

Orange and lemon peel, candied, diced	1 2/3 oz	50 g
Raisins, golden	1 2/3 oz	50 g
Rum, dark	2/3 oz	20 ml
Sponge cake (Recipe 709)	5 1/3 oz	150 g
Butter	1/3 oz	10 g
White wheat flour	1/3 oz	10 g
Milk	1 pt 4 oz	600 ml
Vanilla bean,[a] split	1	1
Crystal sugar	3 1/2 oz	100 g
Eggs, whole, shelled[b]	8 3/4 oz	250 g

MISE EN PLACE

Marinate candied peels and raisins with rum.

Dice sponge cake.

Butter a pudding mold[c] and dust with flour.

METHOD

Combine milk, vanilla bean, and sugar and bring to a boil. Remove vanilla bean.

Stir eggs until well blended and add hot milk into eggs gradually, while stirring.

Strain milk mixture.

[a] Vanilla extract can be substituted.

[b] Eggs can be purchased already shelled, mixed and pasteurized.

[c] There are special pudding molds, but they are seldom available. China soufflé molds are a good substitute.

Add marinated fruits and diced sponge cake.

Pour mixture into prepared mold.

Poach in water bath in oven at 360°F (180°C). Probe with needle to be sure custard is cooked.

Let rest a few minutes before serving.

To serve, invert mold directly onto warmed serving platter (or onto individual plates if individual molds were used).

NOTE: A warm sauce such as Vanilla Sauce (Recipe 780), Red Currant Sauce (Recipe 727) or Red Wine Sauce (Recipe 761) should be served with the pudding.

751

Cottage Cheese Soufflé

Quarkauflauf
Soufflé au séré

YIELD: 10 SERVINGS

Butter	1/3 oz	10 g
Crystal sugar	1/3 oz	10 g
Cottage cheese, low fat[a]	1 lb 2 oz	500 g
Cornstarch	2 2/3 oz	75 g
Egg yolks	4 1/4 oz	120 g
Crystal sugar	3 1/4 oz	90
Lemon, peel, grated	1	1
Egg whites	2 2/3 oz	75 g
Crystal sugar	1 oz	30 g
Powdered sugar	1/3 oz	10 g

MISE EN PLACE

Butter a soufflé dish[b] and dust with sugar.

Purée cottage cheese.

METHOD

Thoroughly blend cottage cheese with cornstarch.

Cream egg yolks, 3 1/4 oz (90 g) sugar, and grated lemon peel.

Add cottage cheese and mix well.

Whip egg whites and 1 oz (30 g) sugar into soft peaks.

Fold egg whites into cheese batter.

Fill soufflé dish with batter about three-fourths high.

Warm soufflé first in water bath on top of stove and then bake on rack in oven at 375°F (190°C) for about 45 minutes.

Dust with powdered sugar and serve at once.

[a] Baker's cheese or ricotta can be substituted. These do not need to be puréed.

[b] Individual molds can also be used. They will bake in a much shorter time.

752

Hot Cottage Cheese Pudding

Quarkauflaufpudding
Pouding soufflé au séré

YIELD: 10 SERVINGS

Cottage cheese, low fat[a]	7 oz	200 g
Raisins, golden	1 2/3 oz	50 g
Butter	1/3 oz	10 g
Powdered sugar	2/3 oz	20 g
Butter	3 1/2 oz	100 g
White wheat flour	5 1/3 oz	150 g
Vanilla bean	1	1
Milk	10 oz	300 ml
Salt	1x	1x
Egg yolks	5 2/3 oz	160 g
Egg whites	7 oz	200 g
Crystal sugar	4 1/3 oz	125 g

METHOD

Purée cottage cheese and add raisins.

Butter a pudding mold[b] and dust with powdered sugar.[c]

Melt 3 1/2 oz (100 g) butter and add flour. Do not brown the roux.

Split vanilla bean, scrape out marrow, and add marrow and bean to milk.

METHOD

Add salt to vanilla-milk and bring to a boil.

Strain hot milk over roux and stir with wire whisk.

Return pot to stove and stir with wooden paddle until mixture is thick, smooth, and no longer clings to the sides of the pot.

Remove from stove and gradually blend in egg yolks.

Add cottage cheese.

Whip egg whites with sugar into soft peaks. Carefully fold egg whites into batter.

Fill prepared mold.

Warm soufflé first in water bath on top of stove. Then bake, still in water bath, in oven, at 425°F (200°C), for about 45 minutes.

Let pudding rest for a few minutes before serving.

To serve, invert mold onto hot serving platter. Leave mold over pudding a few minutes to let pudding settle.

Serve while hot.

NOTE: Pudding can be served with a warm sauce such as Vanilla Sauce (Recipe 780), Red Currant Sauce (Recipe 727), or Red Wine Sauce with Almonds and Currants (Recipe 761).

753

Cottage Cheese Cream

Quarkcreme
Crème de séré

YIELD: 1 QT 12 OZ (1.3 L)

Cottage cheese, low fat[a]	1 lb 2 oz	500 g
Gelatin, leaf[b]	1/2 oz	12 g
Heavy cream (36%)	1 pt 4 oz	600 ml
Egg yolks[c]	3 1/2 oz	100 g
Crystal sugar	3 1/2 oz	100 g
Lemon, peel, grated	1	1

MISE EN PLACE

Purée or strain cottage cheese.

Soak gelatin in cold water.

Whip heavy cream.

METHOD

Cream together egg yolks, sugar, and grated lemon peel.

Add cottage cheese.

Squeeze water from gelatin leaf and melt in water bath. Add to cheeze mixture.

Blend thoroughly and immediately fold in whipped cream.

NOTE: This basic cream can be blended with fresh fruits and berries.

---

[a] Baker's cheese or ricotta can be substituted. These do not need to be puréed.

[b] A china soufflé mold is advisable, but other molds can be used.

[c] The mold can be dusted with crystal sugar.

---

[a] Baker's cheese or ricotta can be substituted. These do not need to be puréed.

[b] Powdered gelatin can be used. It must be dissolved in warm water.

[c] The egg yolks should be pasteurized because they don't get cooked.

754

Cottage Cheese Turnovers

Quarkkrapfen
Rissoles au séré

YIELD: 10 SERVINGS

Cottage cheese, low fat[a]	14 oz	400 g
Crystal sugar	1 2/3 oz	50 g
Semolina, hard wheat	1 oz	30 g
Egg yolks	1 1/3 oz	40 g
Lemon, peel, grated	1	1
Raisins, golden	1 2/3 oz	50 g
Cinnamon, ground	1x	1g
Egg	1	1
Puff pastry (Recipe 689)	1 lb 12 oz	800 g
Crystal sugar	2/3 oz	20 g
Fruit sauce	1 pt 1 oz	500 ml

MISE EN PLACE

Purée cottage cheese. Combine cheese with 1 2/3 oz (50 g) sugar, semolina, egg yolks, grated lemon peel, raisins, and a dash of cinnamon.

Mix well and refrigerate for 1 hour to allow the semolina to swell.

Break egg and mix with 1 tbsp of water.

METHOD

Roll out pastry to about 1/12-in. (2 mm) thickness.

Cut out circles about 5 1/2 in. (130 mm) across.

Brush dough edges with egg wash.

Put spoonful of filling on each circle, somewhat off center.

Fold over dough, to make half moon-shaped turnovers.

Press down rims with the blunt edge of a cookie cutter, or press edges down with a dinner fork.

Place turnovers on baking sheet and brush with egg wash.

Sprinkle with 2/3 oz (20 g) sugar and poke some holes in turnovers to let the steam escape.

Bake at 400°F (200°C) for about 20 minutes.

Serve warm with a fruit sauce, such as Apricot Sauce (Recipe 668), Red Currant Sauce (Recipe 727), Melba (Raspberry) Sauce (Recipe 719), or Strawberry Sauce (Recipe 699).

NOTE: The turnovers can also be filled with bake-proof jams or fruit butter.

[a] Baker's cheese or ricotta can be substituted. These do not neeed to be puréed.

755

Hot Rice Soufflé Pudding

Reisauflaufpudding
Pouding soufflé au riz

YIELD: 10 SERVINGS

Arborio[a] rice	3 oz	80 g
Butter	1/3 oz	10 g
White wheat flour	1/3 oz	10 g
Raisins, golden	1 2/3 oz	50 g
Milk	13 1/2 oz	400 ml
Vanilla bean,[b] split	1	1
Salt	1x	1x
Lemon, rind, grated	1	1
Butter	1 oz	30 g
Egg yolks	4 1/4 oz	120 g
Egg whites	7 oz	200 g
Crystal sugar	3 oz	80 g

MISE EN PLACE

Blanch rice for about 10 minutes, drain, and discard water.

Butter a pudding mold[c] and dust with flour.

Soak raisins in water.

METHOD

Combine milk, vanilla bean, and salt and bring to a boil.

Add blanched rice and simmer over low heat for about 30 minutes.

Remove vanilla bean. Add lemon rind and butter.

Let mixture cool slightly, then gradually incorporate egg yolks.

Drain raisins and add to mixture.

Whip egg whites and sugar into soft peaks. Carefully fold egg whites into pudding.

Fill mold about three-fourths high.

Warm pudding first in water bath on top of stove. Then bake, still in water bath, in oven, at 425°F (220°C). Probe with needle to be sure pudding is baked through.

To serve, invert mold onto hot serving platter. Leave mold over pudding a few minutes to let pudding settle.

Serve while hot.

NOTE: Serve warm with a fruit sauce, such as Apricot Sauce (Recipe 668), Red Currant Sauce (Recipe 727), Melba (Raspberry) Sauce (Recipe 719), or Strawberry Sauce (Recipe 699).

[a] Arborio rice is an Italian rice with a round kernel. Other rice varieties can be substituted.

[b] Vanilla extract can be substituted.

[c] A china soufflé mold is advisable, but other molds can be used.

756

*C*old Rice Dessert

Reis Kaiserinart
Riz impératrice

YIELD: 10 SERVINGS

Arborio rice[a]	3 1/2 oz	100 g
Gelatin, leaf	1/2 oz	12 g
Candied fruits, diced	3 1/2 oz	100 g
Kirsch[b]	1 1/3 oz	40 ml
White wine jelly (Recipe 783)	6 3/4 oz	200 ml
Vanilla bean,[c] split	1	1
Milk	1 pt 1 oz	500 ml
Heavy cream (36%)	10 oz	300 ml
Salt	1x	1x
Crystal sugar	4 1/4 oz	120 g
Fruit sauce	13 1/2 oz	400 ml

MISE EN PLACE
Blanch rice for 5 minutes, drain, rinse with cold water, and drain again.

Soak gelatin leaf in cold water.

Marinate candied fruits in kirsch.

Melt wine gelatin. Line the bottoms and sides of chilled molds[d] with the gelatin. Refrigerate molds.

Split vanilla bean, scrape out marrow, and add marrow and bean to milk.

Whip heavy cream.

METHOD
Combine vanilla-milk with salt and bring to a boil.

Remove vanilla bean and add rice.

Bring to a boil again and simmer for 30 minutes.

Squeeze water from gelatin leaf and add to hot milk. Add sugar to hot milk.

Stir over ice until rice pudding starts to thicken.

Add marinated candied fruits and fold in whipped cream.

Fill prepared molds and refrigerate.

To serve, dip molds a moment into hot water, and unmold directly on to chilled serving platter.

Serve with a fruit sauce, such as Apricot Sauce (Recipe 668), Strawberry Sauce (Recipe 699), Red Currant Sauce (Recipe 727), or Melba (Raspberry) Sauce (Recipe 719).

757

*F*resh Berry Dessert

Rote Grütze
Entremets aux baies

YIELD: 10 SERVINGS

Red currants,[a] fresh	10 1/2 oz	300 g
Raspberries, fresh	10 1/2 oz	300 g
Strawberries, fresh	10 1/2 oz	300 g
Water	1 pt 8 oz	700 ml
Crystal sugar	5 1/3 oz	150 g
Cornstarch[b]	3 oz	80 g
Red currants,[a] fresh	7 oz	200 g
Raspberries, fresh	7 oz	200 g
Heavy cream (36%)	6 3/4 oz	200 ml

MISE EN PLACE
Remove stems from the 10 1/2 oz (300 g) of each berry variety; clean and wash the berries.

METHOD
Combine water and sugar and bring to a boil.

Add cleaned berries and boil for 10 minutes. Remove from stove.

Purée berries with hand-held mixer; then strain the puree through a fine mesh china cap.

Bring the strained puree to a boil again.

Blend cornstarch with 3 1/3 oz (100 ml) cold water and add to boiling fruit juice. Stir well and bring to a boil.

Let the mixture cool, stirring frequently.

Remove stems from remaining berries; clean and wash the berries. Drain well.

Fold berries into the cool fruit sauce.

Fill mixture into glasses and refrigerate.

Whip heavy cream into soft peaks and serve with the berries.

---

[a] Arborio rice is an Italian rice with a round kernel. Other rice varieties can be substituted.

[b] Kirsch is a clear cherry brandy. Swiss kirsch is renowned.

[c] Vanilla extract can be substituted.

[d] Suitable molds are timbale molds or soufflé cups. The molds should be made of metal. One large mold can also be used.

---

[a] The currants called for in this recipe are known as *Rote Johannisbeeren* in German.

[b] In Europe, potato starch is often used for this dessert.

758

Sponge Cake Roll (basic recipe, cold method)

Rouladenbiskuit (kalte Zubereitung)
Biscuit à rouler

YIELD: 2 CAKE ROLLS

Silicon or parchment paper	4	4
Cake flour	7 oz	200 g
Butter	3 1/2 oz	100 g
Egg yolks	8 3/4 oz	250 g
Crystal sugar	5 1/3 oz	150 g
Lemon, rind, grated	1/2	1/2
Egg whites	8 3/4 oz	250 g
Crystal sugar	3 1/2 oz	100 g
Crystal sugar	1 oz	30 g

MISE EN PLACE

Line two baking sheet pans with silicon or parchment paper.

Sift cake flour.

Melt butter.

METHOD

Cream egg yolks with 8 3/4 oz (250 g) sugar and grated lemon rind.

Whip egg whites into soft peaks with half of the 3 1/2 oz (100 g) of sugar; then stir in the other half of the sugar.

Fold egg yolks and flour into beaten egg whites.

Fold melted butter into the sponge batter.

Spread sponge batter about 1/2-in. (12 mm) thick on the two lined baking sheets.

Bake at 400°F (200°C), without steam.

As soon as batter is baked, sprinkle with remaining 1 oz (30 g) sugar and turn upside down on new sheets of parchment paper.

Peel off the paper the sponge was baked on. Let cake cool.

Spread sponge with a filling and roll into a tight roll if desired.

759

Sponge Cake Roll (with sponge mix)

Rouladenbiskuit (mit Aufschlagmittel)
Biscuit à rouler rapide

YIELD: 2 CAKE ROLLS

Silicon or parchment paper	4	4
Cake flour	11 1/4 oz	320 g
Baking powder	1/3 oz	10 g
Eggs, whole, shelled[a]	14 oz	400 g
Crystal sugar	10 1/2 oz	300 g
Water	1/2 oz	15 ml
Sponge mix[b]	1 1/3 oz	40 g
Lemon, peel, grated	1	1
Crystal sugar	1 oz	30 g

MISE EN PLACE

Line two baking sheet pans with silicon or parchment paper.

Sift together cake flour and baking powder.

METHOD

Combine eggs, 10 1/2 oz (300 g) sugar, water, cake mix, and grated lemon peel.

Mix at medium speed for 5 minutes.

Lower speed and add flour.

Increase speed to fast and mix for 5 minutes.

Spread sponge batter about 1/2-in. (12 mm) thick on the two lined baking sheets.

Bake at 400°F (200°C), without steam.

As soon as batter is baked, sprinkle with 1 oz (30 g) sugar and turn upside down on new sheets of parchment paper.

Peel off the paper the sponge was baked on. Let cake cool.

Spread sponge with a filling and roll into a tight roll if desired.

NOTE: To make chocolate sponge, add 1 2/3 oz (50 g) cocoa powder to flour.

[a] Eggs can be purchased already shelled, mixed, and pasteurized.

[b] The German name for the sponge mix is *Aufschlagmittel*. It is a volume enhancer.

760

Sponge Cake Roll (basic, warm method)

Rouladenbiskuit (warme Zubereitung)
Biscuit à rouler

YIELD: 2 CAKE ROLLS

Silicon or parchment paper	4	4
Cake flour	8 3/4 oz	250 g
Butter	1 2/3 oz	50 g
Eggs, whole, shelled[a]	1 lb 2 oz	500 g
Crystal sugar	12 oz	350 g
Crystal sugar	1 oz	30 g

MISE EN PLACE

Line two baking sheet pans with silicon or parchment paper.

Sift cake flour. Melt butter.

METHOD

Whip eggs and 12 oz (350 g) sugar in water bath until mixture reaches no higher than 120°F (50°C).

Mix at medium speed until egg batter is cool, has increased in volume, and has a creamy consistency.

Fold in flour, and then butter.

Spread sponge batter about 1/2-in. (12 mm) thick on the two lined baking sheets.

Bake at 425°F (220°C), without steam.

As soon as batter is baked, sprinkle with 1 oz (30 g) sugar and turn upside down on new sheets of parchment paper.

Peel off the paper the sponge was baked on. Let cake cool.

Spread sponge with a filling and roll into a tight roll if desired.

---

[a] Eggs can be purchased already shelled, mixed, and pasteurized.

761

Red Wine Sauce with Almonds and Currants

Rotweinsauce
Sauce bichof

YIELD: 1 QT 2 OZ (1.0 L)

Red wine	1 pt 1 oz	500 ml
Water	10 oz	300 ml
Crystal sugar	7 oz	200 g
Cinnamon stick	1	1
Clove	1	1
Cornstarch	1/3 oz	10 g
Currants, dried[a]	1 2/3 oz	50 g
Almonds, shredded[b]	1 2/3 oz	50 g
Kirsch[c]	1 2/3 oz	50 ml

METHOD

Combine red wine, water, sugar, cinnamon stick, and clove. Bring to a boil.

Simmer for 20 minutes and strain through a fine wire china cap.

Mix cornstarch with 1 oz (30 ml) water.

Bring strained wine mixture to a boil and add cornstarch, while stirring.

Return mixture to a boil and let cool, stirring occasionally.

Blanch currants, drain, and add to sauce.

Add almonds and kirsch to sauce.

NOTE: Sauce can be served hot or cold.

---

[a] The currants in this recipe are actually small, dried, dark, seedless raisins (called *Korinthen* in German). They are different from fresh currants (called *Johannisbeeren* in German). Other small, dark raisins can be substituted.

[b] Almonds should be blanched, and coarsely shredded, not sliced.

[c] Kirsch is a clear cherry brandy. Swiss kirsch is renowned.

762

$\mathcal{F}$ruits Marinated in Rum

Rumtopf
Fruits au rhum

YIELD: 20 SERVINGS

Apples	7 oz	200 g
Pears	7 oz	200 g
Apricots	7 oz	200 g
Plums, fresh	7 oz	200 g
Sour cherries, fresh	7 oz	200 g
Peaches, freestone	7 oz	200 g
Raspberries, fresh	3 1/2 oz	100 g
Blackberries	3 1/2 oz	100 g
Melon,[a] peeled, diced	3 1/2 oz	100 g
Kumquats	3 1/2 oz	100 g
Crystal sugar	1 lb 2 oz	500 g
Rum, dark[b]	1 qt 2 oz	1.0 L

METHOD

Wash and peel fruits, depending on variety. Cut into pieces and remove pits.

Dissolve sugar in rum.

Use a large ceramic jar. Pour in rum and add fruits as they become available.

Keep jar in a cool place.

Stir carefully each time more fruits are added. Place a clean plate on top of fruits in jar to keep them submerged. Keep jar covered at all times.

If needed, more sugar and rum should be added to keep fruits submerged.

The fruits need time to marinate, and can be used 2 to 3 months after the last fruits have been added.

Serve marinated fruits with Ice Cream (Recipe 778), Savarin (Recipe 766), or chantilly (lightly whipped cream).

NOTE: "Rumtopf" is a way of preserving fruits in alcohol. The cleaned fruits are added to the rum as they come in season, not necessarily at the same time.

---

[a] The original recipe calls for Cavaillon melon. Any melon, except watermelon, can be used.

[b] The rum needs to be high in proof to prevent fermentation. In the United States, 151 proof rum is available.

763

"$\mathcal{S}$andy" Cookie Dough[a]

Sabléteig
Pâte sablée

YIELD: 2 LB 3 OZ (1.0 KG)

Powdered sugar	5 2/3 oz	160 g
Egg whites	2 oz	60 g
Vanilla bean[b]	1	1
Cake flour	1 lb 2 oz	500 g
Butter, cold	11 1/4 oz	320 g

MISE EN PLACE

Combine powdered sugar and egg whites in a mixing bowl. Stir until sugar is dissolved.

Split vanilla bean and scrape out marrow. Add marrow to egg white mixture and stir until blended in.

METHOD

Place cake flour on pastry table, add cold butter, and rub together until all butter is absorbed by the flour. Make a well in the center.

Add egg white mixture to flour and butter and knead into a smooth cookie dough.

Refrigerate dough before use.

764

$\mathcal{S}$andy Cookies

Sablés
Sablés

YIELD: 80 COOKIES

"Sandy" cookie dough (Recipe 763)	2 lb 3 oz	1.0 kg
Crystal sugar	3 oz	80 g

METHOD

Shape the chilled dough into rolls about 1 1/4-in. (30 mm) in diameter.

Roll the dough in sugar and refrigerate again.

(continued on next page)

---

[a] This dough is called "sandy" because products made with it will be crumbly or "sandy" in texture.

[b] Vanilla extract can be substituted.

(continued from preceding page)

Slice dough into 1/5-in. (5 mm) circles.

Place circles on pastry sheet pan and bake at 415°F (210°C).

VARIATIONS

Almond Sablés: Add 6 oz (170 g) shredded almonds to dough.

Sablés with Candied Fruits: Add 6 oz (170 g) candied fruits, cut into small dice, to dough. Shape dough into rectangular blocks.

Marble Sablés: Flavor half of the dough with 1 2/3 oz (50 g) cocoa powder. When shaping dough into rolls, combine the two doughs to make an attractive swirl pattern.

765

Sacher Torte

Sachertorte
Gâteau Sacher

YIELD: 2 TORTES

Parchment paper	1	1
Dark couverture[a]	8 3/4 oz	250 g
Water	3 1/3 oz	100 ml
Cake flour	8 3/4 oz	250 g
Butter	8 3/4 oz	250 g
Crystal sugar	4 1/3 oz	125 g
Egg yolks	8 3/4 oz	250 g
Egg whites	8 3/4 oz	250 g
Crystal sugar	4 1/3 oz	125 g
Apricot jam	10 1/2 oz	300 g
Apricot glaze[b]	3 1/2 oz	100 g
Chocolate coating[c]	10 1/2 oz	300 g

MISE EN PLACE

Place 2 cake rings on a parchment paper-lined sheet pan.

Melt *couverture* in water bath and incorporate warmed water.

Sift cake flour.

METHOD

Cream butter and 4 1/3 oz (125 g) sugar.

Add egg yolks gradually.

Add melted *couverture* and continue stirring until batter is smooth and creamy.

Whip egg whites with 4 1/3 oz (125 g) sugar into soft peaks.

Fold whipped egg whites and sifted flour into batter, alternately.

Fill rings, spreading evenly, and bake at 400°F (200°C). Probe with needle to be sure cakes are baked.

Turn cakes upside down on wire racks; remove rings and paper. Let cakes cool.

Split cakes in half to make two layers, and fill with apricot jam.

Warm apricot glaze and brush cakes with apricot glaze.

Warm the chocolate coating and pour over cakes. Chill to let coating set, but do not store refrigerated.

766

Savarin Yeast Cake

Savarin
Savarin

YIELD: 1 LB 5 OZ (600 GRAMS) DOUGH,
OR 10 SERVINGS

FIRST DOUGH

Milk	2 1/2 oz	75 ml
Crystal sugar	2/3 oz	20 g
Yeast, fresh[a]	1/2 oz	15 g
White wheat flour	3 1/2 oz	100 g

MOLDS

Butter	2/3 oz	20 g
White wheat flour	2/3 oz	20 g

SECOND DOUGH

Milk	3/4 oz	25 ml
Yeast, fresh[a]	1/2 oz	15 g
White wheat flour	6 oz	175 g
Butter	3 1/4 oz	90 g
Eggs, whole, shelled[b]	7 oz	200 g
Salt	1/6 oz	5 g

---

[a] *Couverture* is a coating chocolate with a high cocoa butter content. It is sold in solid blocks, and must be melted before use.

[b] Apricot glaze is commercially available.

[c] The original recipe calls for *Überzugsmasse*, a commercial chocolate coating, made with vegetable fat, and easy to use. The sacher torte can also be covered with a boiled chocolate icing.

[a] Dry yeast can be substituted. Prepare according to package directions.

[b] Eggs can be purchased already shelled, mixed, and pasteurized.

SYRUP AND GLAZE

Tea, black, strong	6 3/4 oz	200 ml
Water	3 1/3 oz	100 ml
Crystal sugar	8 3/4 oz	250 g
Lemon, juice and grated peel	1	1
Orange, juice and grated peel	1	1
Clove	1	1
Cinnamon stick	1	1
Rum, dark	3 1/3 oz	100 ml
Apricot glaze	3 1/2 oz	100 g

CONCEPT

Savarin is made with a starter dough, which is proofed and blended with remaining ingredients to make a second dough.

MISE EN PLACE TO MAKE FIRST DOUGH

Warm the milk to 86°F (30°C), add sugar and yeast, and let sugar and yeast dissolve.

Add flour and knead to a smooth dough.

Cover dough and let proof in a warm place for about 2 hours.

MISE EN PLACE TO PREPARE MOLDS.

Butter savarin molds[a] and dust with flour.

METHOD TO MAKE SECOND DOUGH

Warm the milk, add yeast, and let yeast dissolve.

Put flour in mixing bowl and add dissolved yeast and prepared first dough. Mix at slow speed with dough hook until thoroughly blended.

Melt butter and incorporate into dough. Proof dough for 30 minutes.

Add eggs and salt gradually and blend until dough is smooth and silky. The dough will be rather soft.

Dress dough with pastry bag into prepared molds, using a smooth tube.

Proof dough once again.

Bake second dough at 415°F (210°C).

METHOD FOR SYRUP

Combine all syrup ingredients except rum (and apricot glaze) and bring to a boil.

Simmer for 15 minutes and strain through a fine wire china cap.

Add rum and use syrup while still warm.

METHOD TO FINISH

Unmold savarins and soak[a] with syrup while savarins are still warm.

Brush with melted apricot glaze.

Serve either warm or cold.

VARIATIONS

Savarin with Fruits: Fill the center cavity with Fresh Fruit Salad (Recipe 705), berries in season, or Fruits Marinated in Rum (Recipe 762). Fruit savarin is traditionally served with Vanilla Sauce (Recipe 780), or other fruit sauces, such as Apricot Sauce (Recipe 668), Strawberry Sauce (Recipe 699), Red Currant Sauce (Recipe 727), or Melba (Raspberry) Sauce (Recipe 719).

Savarin with Sabayon: Fill the center cavity with Sabayon Sauce (Recipe 782). This savarin is usually served warm.

Baba with Rum: Baba are traditionally baked in timbale molds. Raisins are blended into the savarin dough. The raisins should be dusted with flour, so they will not sink to the bottom during the baking process. Additional rum is added to the syrup.

767

Chocolate Sponge Cake (basic recipe)

Schokoladenbiskuit
Génoise au chocolate

YIELD: 2 CAKES

Silicon or parchment paper	1	1
Cake flour	7 oz	200 g
Cornstarch	3 1/2 oz	100 g
Cocoa powder	2 oz	60 g
Butter	3 1/2 oz	100 g
Eggs, whole, shelled[b]	1 lb 2 oz	500 g
Crystal sugar	10 1/2 oz	300 g

MISE EN PLACE

Line pastry sheet pan with silicon or parchment paper. Place two cake rings on top.

Sift together cake flour, cornstarch, and cocoa powder.

Melt butter.

(continued on next page)

---

[a] Savarins are baked in ring molds, either individual molds or one large mold. The center cavity is then filled with a garnish, and the savarin named accordingly.

---

[a] The savarin must be thoroughly soaked. A large amount of syrup is needed, and it is poured into a shallow pan. The savarin is put into the syrup top down, and turned over when soaked. It may be necessary to double the syrup amount.

[b] Eggs can be purchased already mixed, and pasteurized.

(continued from preceding page)

METHOD

Combine eggs with sugar and whip in water bath to 120°F (50°C), or until sugar is dissolved.

Whip at medium speed, until mixture is cool and creamy, and has considerably increased in volume.

Fold in flour mixture. Fold in melted butter.

Fill molds, spreading evenly, and bake at 375°F (190°C), without steam. Probe with needle to be sure cakes are baked all the way through.

Place sponge cakes upside down on wire racks to cool. Remove paper when cold.

768

Chocolate Mousse

Schokoladenmousse
Mousse au chocolat

YIELD: 10 SERVINGS

Dark chocolate couverture[a] with vanilla flavor	7 oz	200 g
Milk	1 2/3 oz	50 ml
Egg yolks[b]	3 oz	80 g
Vanilla sugar[c]	1/3 oz	10 g
Crystal sugar	1 oz	30 g
Heavy cream (36%)	13 1/2 oz	400 ml
Salt	1x	1x
Egg whites	3 1/2 oz	100 g
Heavy cream (36%)	13 1/2 oz	400 ml

METHOD

Combine chocolate *couverture* with milk and melt in water bath.

Cream together egg yolks, vanilla sugar, and crystal sugar until the sugar is dissolved.

Add melted chocolate and blend thoroughly.

Whip the heavy cream and fold into mousse.

Add salt to egg whites and whip into soft peaks. Fold egg whites into mousse.

---

[a] *Couverture* is a coating chocolate with a high cocoa butter content. It is sold in solid blocks, and must be melted before use.

[b] Pasteurized egg yolks should be used because this mousse doesn't get cooked.

[c] Vanilla sugar is made by storing vanilla beans in sugar until the vanilla essence is absorbed. Vanilla sugar is also commercially available. Vanilla extract can be used instead.

Pour mousse into a bowl or individual serving dishes or glasses, and refrigerate for at least 8 hours.

To serve, make egg-shaped dumplings, using two spoons dipped in hot water.[a]

Serve two dumplings per person and serve with double cream.

NOTES: If the mousse is chilled in individual glasses, it can be served after 3 hours.

White chocolate mousse is made by substituting 8 3/4 oz (250 g) white *couverture* for the 7 oz (200 g) dark *couverture*.

769

Chocolate Almond Cookies

Schokoladenrosetten
Rosettes au chocolate

YIELD: 50 COOKIES

Silicon or parchment paper		
Cake flour	9 oz	260 g
Cocoa powder[b]	1 1/3 oz	40 g
Cornstarch	3 1/2 oz	100 g
Marzipan[c]	5 1/3 oz	150 g
Kirsch[d]	1 oz	30 ml
Butter	10 1/2 oz	300 g
Powdered sugar	5 1/3 oz	150 g
Almond paste (50%)[c]	3 1/2 oz	100 g
Eggs, whole, shelled[e]	3 1/2 oz	100 g
Chocolate coating[f]	3 1/2 oz	100 g

MISE EN PLACE

Line baking sheets with silicon or parchment paper.

Sift together cake flour, cocoa powder, and cornstarch.

Blend marzipan with kirsch, dye any color if desired, and set aside for cookie filling.

METHOD

Cream together butter, powdered sugar, and almond paste.

---

[a] This requires some practice. An oval ice cream scoop can also be used.

[b] The original recipe calls for chocolate powder.

[c] The difference between almond paste and marzipan is that almond paste is a raw product. Marzipan is a ready-to-eat product, because it is made with boiled sugar syrup; it also is made with a small percentage of bitter almonds for flavor.

[d] Kirsch is a clear cherry brandy. Swiss kirsch is renowned.

[e] Eggs can be purchased already shelled, mixed, and pasteurized.

[f] The original recipe calls for *Überzugsmasse*. It is a commercial chocolate coating, manufactured with vegetable fat, and easy to use.

Add eggs gradually.

Mix in the flour/cocoa mixture. Blend until smooth.

Using a pastry bag with a star tube, dress 100 small rosettes on paper-lined baking sheets.

Bake at 425°F (220°C).

Spread rosettes with a dab of kirsch-flavored marzipan and sandwich two rosettes together.

Warm the chocolate coating. Dip sandwich cookies, sideways, halfway into warm coating. Place on wire rack to dry and harden.

770

Chocolate Sauce

Schokoladensauce
Sauce au chocolate

YIELD: 1 PT 8 OZ (700 ML)

Chocolate couverture, dark, vanilla flavored[a]	1 lb 2 oz	500 g
Crystal sugar	10 1/2 oz	300 g
Water	6 3/4 oz	200 ml

METHOD

Chop *couverture* into small pieces.

Bring sugar and water to a boil and remove from stove.

Add *couverture* and stir until mixture is melted and sauce is smooth.

---

[a] *Couverture* is a coating chocolate with a high cocoa butter content. It is sold in solid blocks, and must be melted before use.

771

Black Forest Cake

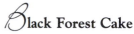

Schwarzwäldertorte
Tarte Forêt-Noire

YIELD: 1 CAKE

Chocolate sponge cake (Recipe 767, 1/2 recipe)	1 cake	1
Kirsch[a]	3 1/3 oz	100 ml
Sugar syrup[b]	3 1/3 oz	100 ml
Heavy cream (36%)	1 pt 4 oz	600 ml
Crystal sugar	1 2/3 oz	50 g
Gelatin, leaf[c]	1/8 oz	3 g
Sour cherries, pitted, canned, drained	7 oz	200 g
Chocolate shavings	3 1/2 oz	100 g
Powdered sugar	1/3 oz	10 g

MISE EN PLACE

Split sponge cake twice, to get three layers.

Combine 2 oz (60 ml) kirsch with sugar syrup.

Whip heavy cream with sugar.

Soak gelatin leaf.

METHOD

Squeeze water from gelatin leaf. Add gelatin to remaining 1 1/3 oz (40 ml) kirsch and melt in water bath.

Whisk melted gelatin into whipped cream.

Sprinkle sponge cake layers with kirsch-flavored sugar syrup.

Spread whipped cream on one layer, leaving about two-thirds for the next layer, the top, and the sides.

Sprinkle half the drained cherries on top of cream on first layer.

Place next layer on top and repeat with one-third of the whipped cream and the remainder of the cherries.

Place last layer on top. Spread top and sides with remaining whipped cream.

Set chocolate shavings on top and dust with powdered sugar.

---

[a] Kirsch is a clear cherry brandy. Swiss kirsch is renowned.

[b] Sugar syrup, called *Läuterzucker* in German, is made by combining 3 parts sugar and 2 parts water (by volume), bringing to a boil, and chilling.

[c] Powdered gelatin can be used. About 1 oz (30 ml) water must be added with the kirsch to dissolve gelatin properly.

772

Frozen Soufflé with Grand Marnier

Eisauflauf Grand Marnier
Soufflé glacé Grand Marnier

YIELD: 10 SERVINGS

Crystal sugar	8 3/4 oz	250 g
Glucose syrup[a]	1 1/3 oz	40 g
Water	5 oz	150 ml
Egg yolks[b]	8 3/4 oz	250 g
Grand Marnier[c]	3 1/3 oz	100 ml
Heavy cream (36%)	1 pt 9 oz	750 ml
Cocoa powder[d]	2/3 oz	20 g

CONCEPT
This frozen dessert should look like a hot soufflé, whereby the dessert is higher than the mold it is served in, imitating a baked soufflé that has risen.

MISE EN PLACE
Put a ring of strong paper, about 2 in. (50 mm) high, around each soufflé mold, and secure with a rubber band. The paper edge should be about 1 in. (25 mm) higher than the soufflé dish.

METHOD
Combine sugar, glucose, and water. Bring to a boil and let cool.

Add egg yolks and whip in water bath until very thick and creamy. Do not overheat.

Whip at medium speed until cool and thick. Add Grand Marnier.

Whip heavy cream and fold into mousse.

Fill molds and freeze.

Remove paper ring and dust with cocoa powder, so the soufflé looks "baked."

---

[a] Glucose syrup is commercially available.

[b] The egg yolks should be pasteurized because this recipe isn't cooked.

[c] Grand Marnier is a Cognac-based orange-flavored liqueur. Another orange-flavored liqueur can be used, but the recipe name should be changed accordingly.

[d] The original recipe calls for chocolate powder.

773

Strudel Dough[a]

Strudelteig
Pâte à stroudel

YIELD: 1 LB 2 OZ (500 G)

Bread flour	12 oz	350 g
Salt	1/3 oz	10 g
Water	3 1/3 oz	100 ml
Eggs, whole, shelled[b]	1 2/3 oz	50 g
Peanut oil	1 oz	30 ml
White wine vinegar	1/3 oz	10 ml

METHOD
Sift flour onto a pastry table and make a well in the center.

Combine salt and water.

Pour salted water and remaining ingredients into the well and knead to a smooth, elastic dough. The dough must be kneaded very hard to develop the gluten in the flour.

Cover dough and let rest for at least 1 hour, at room temperature, before use.

774

Almond Chocolate Cake

Tiroler Cake
Cake tyrolienne

YIELD: 4 CAKES, 1 LB 2 OZ (500 G) EACH

Butter	2/3 oz	20 g
Flour	2/3 oz	20 g
Almonds, blanched, sliced	1 oz	30 g
Couverture, dark[c]	7 oz	200 g
Cake flour	14 oz	400 g
Baking powder	1/3 oz	10 g
Butter	7 oz	200 g
Almond paste[d]	7 oz	200 g
Water	1 2/3 oz	50 ml
Crystal sugar	14 oz	400 g

---

[a] Strudel dough is commercially available under the name "filo" or "phyllo," from Greek or Middle Eastern suppliers. It is already rolled into paper thin sheets.

[b] Eggs can be purchased already shelled, mixed, and pasteurized

[c] *Couverture* is a coating chocolate with a high cocoa butter content. It is sold in solid blocks, and must be melted before use.

[d] Almond paste consisting of 50% almonds and 50% sugar.

Eggs, whole, shelled[a]	1 lb 2 oz	500 g
Hazelnuts (filberts), ground	5 1/3 oz	150 g
Powdered sugar	1/3 oz	10 g

MISE EN PLACE
Butter 4 cake molds, dust with flour, and sprinkle with sliced almonds.

Chop *couverture* into small, even pieces.

Sift together cake flour and baking powder.

Melt butter.

METHOD
Thoroughly blend almond paste with water.

Add sugar and eggs and cream the mixture until smooth.

Add *couverture* pieces, sifted flour, melted butter, and hazelnuts. Blend thoroughly.

Pour into prepared molds and bake at 375°F (190°C).

Probe with needle to be sure cakes are baked all the way through.

Unmold and let cool on wire rack.

Dust with powdered sugar.

775

Danish Pastry Dough
Tournierter Hefeteig
Pâte levée tournée

YIELD: 2 LB 3 OZ (1.0 KG)

Milk	8 1/2 oz	250 ml
Yeast, fresh[a]	1 1/4 oz	35 g
Malt powder	1/6 oz	5 g
Crystal sugar	1 2/3 oz	50 g
Butter	3/4 oz	25 g
White wheat flour	1 lb 2 oz	500 g
Salt	1/3 oz	10 g
Lemon, peel, grated	1/4	1/4
Eggs, whole, shelled[b]	3/4 oz	25 g
Butter	5 1/3 oz	150 g
White wheat flour	1 2/3 oz	50 g

MISE EN PLACE
Warm the milk to 86°F (30°C). Add yeast, malt, and sugar, and stir until dissolved.

Melt 3/4 oz (25 g) butter.

Sift 1 lb 2 oz (500 g) flour into a mixing bowl and add salt and grated lemon peel.

METHOD
Add milk mixture, melted butter, and eggs to sifted flour.

Blend at low speed, using dough hook, until a smooth dough is formed. Refrigerate dough.

Knead 5 1/3 oz (150 g) butter with 1 2/3 oz (50 g) flour, shape into a brick, and refrigerate.[c]

Roll out dough to a rectangle and place butter brick in center.

Fold dough edges over butter and roll out to a rectangle.

Fold dough edges toward the center until they meet, and fold over.

Refrigerate dough and repeat process two more times.

---

[a] Dry yeast can be substituted. Prepare according to package directions.

[b] Eggs can be purchased already shelled, mixed, and pasteurized.

[c] Dough should be worked cool, but must be proofed before baking.

776

Baked Alaska

Überraschungsomeletten
Omelettes surprise

YIELD: 10 SERVINGS

Sponge cake, baked	7 oz	200 g
(Recipe 709, 1/2 recipe)		
Maraschino[a]	1 2/3 oz	50 ml
Fruit salad, fresh	10 1/2 oz	300 g
(Recipe 705)		
Vanilla ice cream	8 1/2 oz	250 ml
(Recipe 778)		
Fruit ice cream	8 1/2 oz	250 ml
(Recipe 696)		
Vanilla bean[b]	1/2	1/2
Egg yolks[c]	4 1/4 oz	120 g
Crystal sugar	3 1/2 oz	100 g
Egg whites	7 oz	200 g
Crystal sugar	1 2/3 oz	50 g
Lemon, peel, grated	1/2	1/2
Candied fruits	2 2/3 oz	75 g
Powdered sugar	2/3 oz	20 g

MISE EN PLACE

Split sponge cake into layers about 1/3 in. (8 mm) thick.

Cut out an oval bottom piece, about 5 in. (125 mm) wide and 6 in. (150 mm) long. The bottom piece should correspond to the size of the serving platter used.

Add maraschino to fruit salad and let marinate, refrigerated.

METHOD

Place sponge cake oval on bake-proof serving dish.

Layer the two ice creams on top. Make an opening in the center for the fruit salad.

Put fruit salad into the cavity. Cover ice cream and fruit salad with sponge cake pieces.

Place dish in freezer while preparing the soufflé batter. Do not freeze too long, because the fruit salad should not freeze.

Split vanilla bean, scrape out marrow, and add marrow to egg yolks.

Cream egg yolks and 3 1/2 oz (100 g) sugar.

Whip egg whites and 1 2/3 oz (50 g) sugar into soft peaks.

Carefully fold egg whites and grated lemon peel into egg yolk mixture.

Spread mousse on the frozen ice cream mold and use a pastry bag to decorate mold with remaining mousse.

Decorate with candied fruits,[a] dust with powdered sugar, and bake in very hot oven until light brown. Serve at once.

777

Vanilla Soufflé

Vanilleauflauf
Soufflé à la vanille

YIELD: 10 SERVINGS

Butter	1/3 oz	10 g
Cake flour	1/3 oz	10 g
Butter	3 oz	80 g
White wheat flour	3 1/2 oz	100 g
Vanilla bean[b]	1	1
Milk	13 1/2 oz	400 ml
Salt	1x	1x
Egg yolks	4 1/4 oz	120 g
Egg whites	7 oz	200 g
Crystal sugar	3 1/2 oz	100 g
Powdered sugar	1/3 oz	10 g

MISE EN PLACE

Butter soufflé dish and dust with flour.

Melt 3 oz (80 g) butter and add 3 1/2 oz (100 g) flour. Stir roux until smooth and remove from stove. Do not brown the roux.

METHOD

Split vanilla bean, scrape out marrow, and add marrow and bean to milk.

Lightly salt vanilla-milk, bring to a boil, and steep for a few minutes.

Strain milk through a fine wire china cap over roux.

Stir mixture over heat, first with strong wire whisk, and then with wooden paddle, until mixture is smooth and no longer clings to the sides of the pot.

Cool mixture slightly and incorporate egg yolks gradually.

Whip egg whites and sugar into soft peaks.

---

[a] Maraschino is a clear cherry liqueur.

[b] Vanilla extract can be substituted.

[c] Egg yolks should be pasteurized, because they don't get fully cooked in this recipe.

[a] Candied fruits might burn if the oven is too hot. The baked Alaska can be decorated with candied fruits after baking.

[b] Vanilla extract can be substituted.

Add small amount of beaten egg whites to batter, stir to loosen batter, and fold in remaining egg whites.

Pour batter into prepared soufflé dish. The dish should be about three-fourths full.

Warm soufflé in water bath on top of stove.

Bake at 400°F (200°C) on oven rack. Probe with needle to be sure the soufflé is baked all the way through.

Dust with powdered sugar and serve at once.

NOTE: Baking time for large soufflés is 20 minutes, and for individual portions 8 minutes, providing mixture is thoroughly warmed first.

VARIATIONS

Mocha Soufflé: Add 1/3 oz (10 g) instant coffee to hot milk.

Chocolate Soufflé: Add 1 oz (30 g) unsweetened cocoa powder to egg yolks.

778

Vanilla Ice Cream

Vanilleglace
Glace à la vanille

YIELD: 1 QT 19 OZ (1.5 L)

Vanilla bean[a]	1	1
Milk	1 pt 11 oz	800 ml
Crystal sugar	8 3/4 oz	250 g
Egg yolks	7 oz	200 g
Heavy cream (36%)	6 3/4 oz	200 ml

METHOD

Split vanilla bean, scrape out marrow, and add marrow to milk.

Add half the sugar to milk and bring to a boil.

Mix egg yolks with remaining sugar.

Strain hot milk through a fine wire china cap over egg yolks, while stirring continuously.

Return mixture to pot and heat carefully to 185°F (85°C), while stirring with a wooden spatula.

Add cold heavy cream and chill mixture in ice water.

Freeze according to ice cream freezer machine directions.

---

[a] The actual vanilla bean is important to this recipe, although vanilla extract can be substituted.

VARIATIONS

Hazelnut (filbert) Ice Cream: Add 4 1/4 oz (120 g) hazelnut paste to hot milk.

Mocha (coffee) Ice Cream: Add 1/2 oz (15 g) instant coffee to cream while still hot.

Chocolate Ice Cream: Add 7 oz (200 g) chopped *couverture*[a] to hot milk.

Pistachio Ice Cream: Add 5 1/3 oz (150 g) finely ground pistachio nuts and 5 1/3 oz (150 g) almond paste to hot milk.

Stracciatella (vanilla fudge) Ice Cream: Add 5 1/3 oz (150 g) melted *couverture* in a thin stream during the freezing process.

Nougat Ice Cream: Add 10 1/2 oz (300 g) nougat,[b] chopped very fine, during the freezing process.

Praline Ice Cream: Add 5 1/3 oz (150 g) praline paste[c] to cream while still hot.

779

Pastry Cream (with eggs)[d]

Vanillecreme
Crème à la vanille

YIELD: 1 QT 8 OZ (1.2 L)

Milk	1 qt 2 oz	1.0 L
Crystal sugar	5 1/3 oz	150 g
Egg yolks	3 oz	80 g
Vanilla cream powder[e]	2 oz	60 g

METHOD

Bring 1 pt 14 oz (900 ml) of the milk to a boil.

Mix sugar, egg yolks, and vanilla cream powder with remaining milk.

Add in the hot milk, stirring to blend.

Pour mixture back into the pot and bring to a boil, stirring.

Chill cream immediately in ice water.[f]

---

[a] *Couverture* is a coating chocolate with a high cocoa butter content. It is sold in solid blocks, and must be melted before use.

[b] Nougat is a mixture of roasted hazelnuts or almonds, honey, and sugar (and sometimes cocoa powder). It is commercially available.

[c] Praline paste is made of equal amounts of roasted hazelnuts and almonds, cooked with sugar until the sugar caramelizes. The mixture is poured into metal pans (or onto a marble table) to cool and harden. When cold, it is broken or ground.

[d] Also see Recipe 706, Pastry Cream (without eggs).

[e] Vanilla cream powder is a commercial product similar to pudding powder.

[f] The cream can also be chilled by pouring it into a sterilized shallow pan and refrigerating it. The top should be sprinkled with sugar to prevent the formation of a skin.

780

$\mathcal{V}$anilla Sauce[a]

Vanillesauce
Sauce à la vanille

YIELD: 1 QT 12 OZ (1.3 L)

Vanilla bean[b]	1	1
Milk	1 qt 2 oz	1.0 L
Egg yolks	8 3/4 oz	250 g
Crystal sugar	5 1/3 oz	150 g

METHOD

Split vanilla bean, scrape out marrow, and add marrow and bean to milk.

Cream egg yolks and sugar.

Bring milk to a boil and strain through a fine wire china cap over egg mixture, stirring to blend.

Return mixture to pot and heat to 185°F (85°C), stirring with a wooden spatula.

Strain sauce through a small hole china cap.

Serve hot or cold.

781

$\mathcal{M}$eringue (hot method)

Warme Schneemasse
Meringage italienne

YIELD: 1 LB 4 OZ (600 G)

Egg whites	7 oz	200 g
Powdered sugar	14 oz	400 g

METHOD

Combine egg whites and sugar. Whisk in water bath until mixture has reached no more than 120°F (50°C).

Whip mixture at high speed until cool and thick.

782

$\mathcal{S}$abayon

Weinschaumsauce
Sabayon

YIELD: 1 QT 2 OZ (1.0 L)

Dry white wine	13 1/2 oz	400 ml
Crystal sugar	8 3/4 oz	250 g
Lemon juice	1 oz	30 ml
Egg yolks[a]	8 1/2 oz	240 g
Curaçao[b]	2 3/4 oz	80 ml

METHOD

Combine all ingredients, except Curaçao.

Whip in water bath until thick and foamy.

Add Curaçao, and fill warm glasses with sabayon.[c]

NOTE: Sabayon can be made with various sweet wines, such as Marsala, Port, sweet sherry, and others. The proportions should be 75% sweet wine and 25% dry white wine. (If the wine is excessively sweet, the amount of sugar may need to be adjusted.)

783

$\mathcal{W}$hite Wine Jelly

Weissweingelee
Gelée au vin blanc

YIELD: 1 QT 2 OZ (1.0 L)

Gelatin, leaf[d]	1 1/3 oz	40 g
Dry white wine	1 qt 2 oz	1.0 L
Crystal sugar	14 oz	400 g
Lemon, juice and grated peel	1	1

METHOD

Soak gelatin leaf in cold water.

Combine white wine, sugar, lemon juice and grated peel. Bring to a boil.

Squeeze water from gelatin leaf and add gelatin to hot liquid, stirring to melt it.

---

[a] This sauce is also known as *Sauce à l'Anglaise*.

[b] Vanilla extract can be substituted.

---

[a] The egg yolks should be pasteurized because they are not cooked.

[b] Curaçao is a bitter orange-flavored liqueur. Many different liqueurs can be used to flavor sabayon.

[c] Sabayon can be served as a sauce with fruits and berries, or alone as dessert, accompanied by Lady Fingers (Recipe 733), or other cookies.

[d] Powdered gelatin can be substituted.

Strain through a fine wire china cap.

Chill until serving.

VARIATIONS

Port Wine Jelly: Replace 50% of the white wine with Port wine.

Orange Jelly: Replace 50% of the white wine with orange juice, and flavor the jelly with Curaçao.

784

Cream Puffs
Windbeutel
Choux à la crème

YIELD: 10 SERVINGS

Butter	1/3 oz	10 g
White wheat flour	1/3 oz	10 g
Heavy cream (36%)	8 1/2 oz	250 ml
Puff paste (Recipe 677)	14 oz	400 g
Vanilla mousseline cream (Recipe 690)	8 1/2 oz	250 ml
Powdered sugar	2/3 oz	20 g

MISE EN PLACE
Butter a baking sheet pan and dust with flour.

Whip heavy cream.

METHOD
With pastry bag, dress 2/3 oz (20 g) rosettes, using medium-size star tube.

Bake at 400°F (200°C), with steam at the beginning, and finish baking without steam.

Cool, and split pastry puffs in half horizontally.

Fill bottom halves with vanilla mousseline cream.

With a pastry bag, dress whipped cream on top of the mousseline.

Replace top layer and dust with powdered sugar.

VARIATIONS
Eclairs with Chocolate Cream: Dress puff paste into 4-in. (100 mm) long tubes. Flavor vanilla mousseline cream with *couverture*.[a] Brush puffs with apricot glaze[b] and cover with chocolate fondant.[c]

Eclairs with Kirsch Cream: Dress puff paste into 4-in. (100 mm) long tubes. Flavor vanilla mousseline cream with kirsch.[a] Cover puffs with pink fondant.[b]

Small Cream Puffs (Profiteroles) with Chocolate Sauce: Make small cream puffs. Instead of cutting them in half, make a small opening in the bottom and fill them with whipped cream, using a pastry bag. Serve on top of chocolate sauce (Recipe 770).

785

Lemon Cream
Zitronencreme
Crème au citron

YIELD: 1 QT 12 OZ (1.3 L)

Gelatin, leaf[c]	1/2 oz	15 g
Milk	13 1/2 oz	400 ml
Crystal sugar	7 oz	200 g
Vanilla cream powder[d]	1 1/3 oz	40 g
Egg yolks	7 oz	200 g
Lemon juice	3 1/3 oz	100 ml
Lemon, rind, grated	1	1
Egg whites	7 oz	200 g
Crystal sugar	7 oz	200 g

MISE EN PLACE
Soak gelatin leaf in cold water.

METHOD
Combine milk, sugar, and vanilla cream powder. Bring to a boil, while stirring.

Blend egg yolks with lemon juice and grated lemon rind.

Pour the hot cream into the egg yolk mixture, stir thoroughly, return cream mixture to pot, and boil once more.

Squeeze water from gelatin leaf and add gelatin to hot cream mixture.

Whip egg whites and sugar into soft peaks.

Fold into cream mixture while still warm.

Use at once, or fill into serving dishes.

NOTES: The same recipe can be made with oranges instead of lemons.

If the cream is served in glasses, the gelatin can be reduced to 1/3 oz (10 g).

---

[a] *Couverture* is a coating chocolate with a high cocoa butter content. It is sold in solid blocks, and must be melted before use.

[b] Apricot glaze is commercially available.

[c] Fondant is a boiled sugar icing, and is commercially available.

[a] Kirsch is a clear cherry brandy. Swiss kirsch is renowned.

[b] Fondant is a boiled sugar icing and is commercially available.

[c] Powdered gelatin can be substituted.

[d] Vanilla cream powder is a commercial product similar to vanilla pudding powder.

786

$\mathcal{L}$emon Sorbet (water ice)

Zitronensorbet
Sorbet au citron

YIELD: 1 QT 29 OZ (1.8 L)

Water	1 qt 2 oz	1.0 L
Crystal sugar	1 lb 10 oz	750 g
Lemon juice	6 3/4 oz	200 ml
Lemon, rind, grated	2	2
Egg whites	1 2/3 oz	50 g
Powdered sugar	1 1/3 oz	40 g

METHOD

Combine water and crystal sugar, bring to a boil, and let cool.

Add lemon juice and grated rind to sugar syrup.

Combine egg whites with powdered sugar. Stir in water bath until sugar is dissolved and mixture has reached no more than 120°F (50°C). Whip egg whites until cool and foamy.

Fold egg whites into lemon syrup and freeze.

NOTES: All sorbets should have a sugar content of 15 degrees Beaumé.

Orange, lime, and grapefruit sorbets can be made by the same method.

787

$\mathcal{B}$raided Yeast Bread (challah)

Zopf
Tresse

YIELD: 4 LB 7 OZ (2.0 KG)

Milk	1 pt 1 oz	500 ml
Yeast, fresh[a]	1 2/3 oz	50 g
Crystal sugar	1/2 oz	15 g
Butter	5 1/3 oz	150 g
White wheat flour	2 lb 7 oz	1.1 kg
Salt	2/3 oz	20 g
Eggs, whole, shelled[b]	3 1/2 oz	100 g
Egg yolk	1	1
Light cream	1/3 oz	10 ml

MISE EN PLACE

Warm the milk to 86°F (30°C). Add yeast and sugar to dissolve.

Melt butter.

Sift flour into a mixing bowl and add salt.

METHOD

Combine milk, butter, flour, and eggs. Mix at slow speed, with dough hook, until dough is smooth and silky.

Cover and let proof until double in size.

Put dough on floured pastry table. Punch down.

Roll dough into strips and braid.

Cover bread and proof until double in size.

Refrigerate bread for 2 hours.

Break egg yolk and mix with light cream.

Brush bread with egg/cream mixture after 1 hour.

Brush bread with egg/cream mixture again before baking.

Bake at 425°F (220°C).

---

[a] Dry yeast can be substituted. Prepare according to package directions.

[b] Eggs can be purchased already shelled, mixed, and pasteurized.

788

$\mathcal{S}$ugar Dough

Zuckerteig
Pâte sucrée

YIELD: 2 LB 3 OZ (1.0 KG)

Cake flour	14 oz	400 g
Baking powder	1/6 oz	5 g
Vanilla bean	1/2	1/2
Butter	5 2/3 oz	160 g
Crystal sugar	8 1/2 oz	240 g
Eggs, whole, shelled[a]	3 1/2 oz	100 g
Lemon, rind, grated	1/2	1/2

MISE EN PLACE
Sift together cake flour and baking powder onto pastry table. Make a well in the center.

Split vanilla bean and scrape out marrow.

Cut cold butter into cubes.

METHOD
Cream together the sugar, eggs, vanilla bean marrow, and grated lemon rind.

Put creamed sugar/egg mixture and cubed butter into the well in the sifted flour. Break butter cubes and blend with egg mixture.

Combine with flour and knead dough until all ingredients are blended. Do not heat dough by kneading too long.

Refrigerate dough until use.

789

$\mathcal{Z}$uger[b] Kirschtorte

Zuger Kirschtorte
Tarte au kirsch de Zoug

YIELD: 2 TORTES

Hazelnut meringues (Recipe 723)	4	4
Butter cream (Recipe 683)	10 1/2 oz	300 g
Kirsch	1 2/3 oz	50 ml
Food color, red (optional)	5 drops	5 drops

Sugar syrup[a]	6 3/4 oz	200 ml
Kirsch	6 3/4 oz	200 ml
Almonds, shredded	7 oz	200 g
Powdered sugar	1 2/3 oz	50 g

CAKE CENTERS
Cake flour	5 1/3 oz	150 g
Butter	3 oz	80 g
Almonds, blanched	3 oz	80 g
Eggs, whole, shelled[b]	10 1/2 oz	300 g
Crystal sugar	6 1/2 oz	180 g

MISE EN PLACE
Have meringue circles ready.

Flavor butter cream with 1 2/3 oz (50 ml) kirsch and dye butter cream with red food color (optional).

Combine sugar syrup with 6 3/4 oz (200 ml) kirsch.

Toast shredded almonds.

METHOD FOR CAKE CENTERS
Sift cake flour. Melt butter. Grind blanched almonds fine.

Combine eggs with sugar. Whip in water bath until thick and creamy, but not warmer than 120°F (50°C). Whip eggs until cool.

Fold in flour, melted butter, and ground almonds.

Fill batter into two cake molds the same size as the meringue circles. Spread top evenly.

Bake at 400°F (200°C). Probe with needle to be sure the cakes are baked all the way through. Let cakes cool.

METHOD FOR ASSEMBLY
Spread one-third of the butter cream on two hazelnut meringue circles.

Place cakes on top. Soak cakes with kirsch-flavored sugar syrup.

Spread a thin layer of butter cream on cakes.

Place the other meringue circles on top, upside down, so the smooth side faces up.

Spread tops and sides of tortes with remaining butter cream.

Cover sides with shredded almonds.

Dust tops with powdered sugar and decorate in a criss-cross pattern, made with the back of a knife.

Index

406   I N D E X